143

THE LETTERS
OF
T. E. LAWRENCE

LAWRENCE, HOGARTH AND ALAN DAWNAY AT CAIRO

THE LETTERS
of
T. E. LAWRENCE

Edited by

DAVID GARNETT

LONDON
JONATHAN CAPE 30 BEDFORD SQUARE
& AT TORONTO

FIRST PUBLISHED, NOVEMBER 1938
SECOND IMPRESSION, NOVEMBER 1938
THIRD IMPRESSION, DECEMBER 1938

JONATHAN CAPE LTD.   30 BEDFORD SQUARE, LONDON
AND 91 WELLINGTON STREET WEST, TORONTO

PRINTED IN GREAT BRITAIN IN THE CITY OF OXFORD
AT THE ALDEN PRESS
PAPER MADE BY JOHN DICKINSON & CO. LTD.
BOUND BY A. W. BAIN & CO. LTD.

CONTENTS

Note: The symbols T or G following the date indicate that the transcript of the letter has been checked with the original, either by or for one of the Trustees, or by the Editor

PART ONE

ARCHAEOLOGY

PART TWO

THE WAR

PART THREE

DOG FIGHT IN DOWNING STREET

CONTENTS

PART FOUR

THE YEARS OF HIDE AND SEEK

B

PART V

FLYING BOATS

NAMES OF RECIPIENTS OF LETTERS
WITH REFERENCE NUMBERS
OF LETTERS ADDRESSED TO THEM

ACRES, J. B., 281
ADAMS, W. B., 61
AKLE, Fareedeh el, 70
ALTOUNYAN, Ernest, 479, 514, 545
AMHERST, Florence, 58, 64
Arab Bulletin, 91, 98, 102, 105
ASTOR, Lady, 391, 403, 434, 443, 455, 493, 508, 510, 582

BAILEY, H. W., 542
BAKER, Herbert, 186, 336
BANBURY, H. H., 302, 348, 380
BEAUFORTE-GREENWOOD, W. E. G., 447, 449
BEESON, C. F. C., 11, 12
BELL, Gertrude, 215
BERE, R. de la, 502
BLACK, Miss L. P., 476, 512
BLUMENFELD, R. D., 126, 339, 372
BRADBURY, W., 525, 561, 562
BRIDGES, Robert, 260
BROOK, W. H., 398, 400
BROUGH, George, 288, 289, 458, 574
BUCHAN, John, 265, 268, 273, 291, 367, 410, 454, 548, 565, 571
BUXTON, R. V., 185, 219, 223, 232, 253, 256, 259, 261, 267, 313, 358, 412, 430, 481

CAPE, Jonathan, 188, 198, 202, 227, 230, 264, 308, 361, 483, 487, 488
CARLOW, Lord, 536, 558

CARRUTHERS, Douglas, 520
CHAMBERS, A. E., 196, 197, 224, 383, 511, 552
CHURCHILL, Winston, 503
CLAYTON, General, 97
COCKERELL, Sydney, 152, 225, 226, 238, 244, 257, 278, 309, 340, 395,
COOPER, Archibald, 515
COWARD, Noel, 419, 422, 444
CRACE, W. J., 76
CUMBERLEGE, G. F. J., 463
CURTIS, Lionel, 205, 206, 207, 208, 209, 252, 277, 317, 331, 399, 513, 527
CURTIS, Mrs. Lionel, 494
CURZON, Lord, 116

DAVIES, Peter, 567
DAY LEWIS, C., 538, 550
DEHEER, Ian, 576
DIXON, Alec, 279
DOUBLEDAY, F. N., 122, 125, 388, 418, 420, 421, 475
DOUGHTY, C. M., 18, 108, 117, 118, 124, 128, 129, 135, 138, 140, 142, 144, 145, 151, 174, 216, 221, 245
DUNN, G. W. M., 436, 446, 473, 474, 477

EDE, H. S., 335, 350, 362, 375, 394, 573
ELGAR, Edward, 465, 506
ELLINGTON, Edward, 566

25

ILLUSTRATIONS

MAPS

PREFACE

'SINCERITY is the only written thing which time improves,'
wrote Lawrence in a letter of May 1st, 1928. I have kept this
dictum always in mind while selecting the following letters. Yet
sincerity is often impossible to the letter-writer, particularly if he
be addressing, not his most intimate friend, but a number of
persons who have been attracted by his achievements, or his fame.
This was Lawrence's fate. Hundreds of people wrote to him and
he replied to scores. From the mass of material put at my disposal,
my object has been to make a book in which Lawrence's career, his
intellectual development and the details of his life should be
recorded, traced and documented almost entirely in his own
words. To that end I have included not only private letters but
anything from his official reports, letters or articles in the press,
diaries, unpublished notes and memoranda which would serve
my purpose.

My dilemma has been to avoid repetition, which becomes
wearisome, without mutilating too many letters — which becomes
exasperating. The letter which is printed entire has a value which
is absent from the chosen paragraph. I have omitted many
passages where Lawrence simply was repeating what he had
already written elsewhere — but a large number of omitted
passages have been forced on me for other reasons. One class of
letter is inadequately represented: that in which Lawrence was
helping his friends with money. The scruples which prevented
him from earning money for himself disappeared when a friend,
or even an acquaintance, was in need.

I was asked to take over the work of editor after Mr. E. M.
Forster had decided that he could not go on with it. I have had
his friendly interest and, even more important, the use of all the
notes he had made on the letters he had read. These have been of
great moral assistance to me, fortifying my judgment and finger-
posting the way. Yet it would be unfair to him for me to suggest,
under the guise of gratitude, that this book is in any way his.
I have completely changed the plan which he sketched out for

dividing the letters into sections according to their subjects, in favour of chronological treatment. The greater quantity of material from Lawrence's earlier years which has become available has made this advisable.

I have had the continual help of Mr. A. W. Lawrence with whom I have worried out many difficulties.

In the third place I wish to thank Viscountess Astor who has been of immense service to me and without whom this book would be far more incomplete than it is. She has been the djinn in the bottle whom I have called upon again and again to do the impossible, and who has never failed me.

In the fourth place I must thank Mr. Rupert Hart-Davis who has helped me prepare the book for press.

I will not thank here the persons who have allowed their letters to be copied for publication as it is obvious that without their co-operation the material for this book would still be scattered over the world.

But the following persons have assisted me in noteworthy ways and I owe them my deepest thanks and acknowledgments: Sir Donald Banks, Permanent Secretary to the Air Ministry; Professor Ernest Barker; Flight Lieutenant Beauforte-Greenwood; Mr. Isaiah Bowman, President of Johns Hopkins University; Viscount Carlow; Mr. A. E. Chambers; Mr. Lionel Curtis; Sir Stephen Gaselee; Viscount Halifax; Sir Maurice Hankey; Lord Harlech; Mr. Thomas Jones; Mr. Eric Kennington; Mr. J. M. Keynes; Mr. Patrick Knowles; Captain B. H. Liddell Hart; Mr. B. E. Leeson; Sir Edward Marsh; 'A Pilot'; Mr. Charles Seymour, President of Yale University; Mr. and Mrs. Bernard Shaw; Sir John Shuckburgh; Mr. R. G. Sims; Air Commodore Sydney Smith; Mr. Charles Stonehill; Air Vice-Marshal Sir Oliver Swann; Sir Kingsley Wood, Secretary of State for Air; Professor William Yale, of the University of New Hampshire; and very many others.

DAVID GARNETT

NOTE ON THE TEXT

After Lawrence's death Mr. A. W. Lawrence published a request asking those who had preserved letters from his brother to allow the Trustees of the Lawrence Trust to make copies of them. In some cases the original letters were sent: in others only copies were forthcoming. Where the original letters were sent Mr. A. W. Lawrence or Mr. E. M. Forster checked the copies with the originals before returning them. In many cases it would have been impossible for me to do this work over again, and usually I have taken the texts checked by Mr. A. W. Lawrence or by Mr. E. M. Forster to be accurate. In the list of Contents (page 7 *et seq.*) I indicate such letters by the initial T, meaning 'letters checked by or for one of the Trustees', those I have checked myself by a G. Any text not seen and checked by Mr. E. M. Forster, Mr. A. W. Lawrence or myself must be taken as unchecked however great the presumption that it is accurate. The letters to his mother, and to members of his family other than Mr. A. W. Lawrence, are printed from transcripts made by his elder brother, Dr. M. R. Lawrence. Many of the originals of these were immersed for some considerable time in a tributary of the Yangtse Kiang, and great patience has been required in handling and deciphering them. The length of any portions omitted is indicated, though where the original letters have not been available the number of lines obviously refers to the typescript. I have followed Lawrence's spelling, capitalization and punctuation but have silently corrected obvious slips of the pen, and have added commas in places where the sense would otherwise be obscure. We know from *Seven Pillars of Wisdom* that Lawrence spelled Arab names in various ways. As a general principle I regard the accuracy of a text as more important than accuracy of spelling, and believe that it is not an editor's function to interfere where the sense is plain. Where I have inserted missing words I have enclosed them in square brackets. At the same time certain helpful conventions have been adopted. Titles of books, names of periodicals, etc., have been italicized,

c

and postscripts have been uniformly printed after the main body of the letter. In cases where they were meant to be read as qualifying particular sentences, they have been introduced into the text, unless Lawrence plainly intended them to be footnotes. All the numbered footnotes printed in small type are mine; those indicated by asterisks, etc., in large type are Lawrence's own.

D. G.

PART ONE

ARCHAEOLOGY

INTRODUCTION TO PART ONE

Lawrence's father was of the Anglo-Irish landed gentry; his mother partly Highland Scottish. They had five sons, of whom the second, Thomas Edward (always called Ned by his family) was born at Tremadoc in Wales on August 16th, 1888. During his first years, the Lawrences moved about: they lived in Scotland, at Dinard in Brittany, in Jersey, in the Isle of Wight and the New Forest. From early childhood, Ned was bold and strong and fond of climbing trees or rocks. Before he was nine he used to tell his brothers a story night after night, without any end. Long pieces of it were composed in rhyme. It was the tale of the successful defence of a castle against numerous foes: its heroes the fur animals, Fizzy-fuzz, Pompey, and Pete, belonging to his younger brothers. Castles were henceforward a lifelong interest and were to take him on his first visit to the East. It is possible that he had heard tales of the clang of the bullets on the steel shutters in the days of the Land League in Ireland, which his father once described to Ernest Barker.

In 1896 the family settled in Oxford and Ned and his brothers were sent to Oxford High School for Boys. A schoolfellow has described the Lawrence boys arriving in single file on bicycles, wearing dark blue and white jerseys which harmonized with their fairness of complexion and gentleness of speech.

A girl playmate of those days, now Mrs. Ryman, recalls: 'Many were the bicycle rides I engaged in with him to explore the old village churches round Oxfordshire [to make brass rubbings]. He would revel in old pieces of glass or pottery.'

Her brother, C. H. Hutchins, writes:

'I knew him intimately during his early school days. The gardens of our respective homes abutted upon each other and we were at school together. He was an unusual kind of boy, very shy and reserved but full of an impish sense of fun. He never played games and took no interest in sport with the exception of swimming. I do not think he took more than an ordinary interest in natural history but was always keenly interested in archaeology. He read widely far beyond the scope of the average schoolboy and at an early age was an authority on medieval armour and weapons. He was a collector of old copper coins and we spent many a half-holiday together exploring the Oxford antique shops in search of a find within the scope of our limited pocket money.

'Adjacent to my home was an old overgrown orchard where we boys used to wage mimic warfare; our side usually won owing to Lawrence's vastly superior generalship. In one corner of this orchard was a disused gravel pit, this under Lawrence's direction we converted into a fortress. He also invented a form of hand grenade composed of moist clay and flour; and these proved so very effective that their use was discontinued as not giving the enemy a sporting chance. School work he found easy and I think boring. I was still floundering about in the lower IV, long after he had learnt all the VI form could teach him.'

Neither Bob, Ned, nor Will took any interest in any organized games, and when Frank, the fourth brother, excelled at them, Ned felt that the family tradition was being broken.

Ned himself took delight in climbing trees, rocks, and buildings, in swimming, canoeing, wrestling, bicycling long distances, and all feats requiring great endurance and strength. He described his father, in a letter to Edward Garnett, as 'the best snipe-shooter in Ireland', and he himself practised continually until he became a remarkably fine shot with rifle and revolver. Ned enjoyed accompanying his father on his bicycling tours. In a note supplied by Lawrence to Captain Liddell Hart he spoke of learning to handle boats from his father who was a keen yachts-man, and in a letter to Air Vice-Marshal Sir Oliver Swann, he said that he was taught photography by his father.

L. C. Jane, who coached Lawrence in his last year at school, and while he was an undergraduate, pointed out Lawrence's non-physical resemblance to his father in a letter to Robert Graves: 'In many ways he resembled his father very much — quite one of the most charming men that I have known — very shy — very kind.'

A letter, part of which is printed in *Crusader Castles*, vol. II, describes a bicycling tour with his father to Colchester, Norwich and King's Lynn in the summer of 1905.

'Norwich Museum he [Will Lawrence] would have enjoyed.

NED, BOB, FRANK, WILL

There was the largest collection of raptorial birds in existence, 409 out of 470 species: I wonder if he'll shriek with horror when he hears that I did not look at them but went off and examined the Norman w.c.'s.'

Often the boy who avoids games does so because he wants to watch birds, collect plants, or study pond life. Lawrence had no taste for biology or science. 'Trees and cliffs interested him only as things to be climbed and not for the nests or fossils, or strata that might be found in them' (C. F. C. Beeson in *T. E. Lawrence by his Friends*). Instead of such interests he had a passionate absorption in the past: in heraldry, arms and armour, monumental brasses, castles, ruins, church architecture, old coins, and every fragment of brick or pottery which might throw light on the social history and ways of living of mankind. This was not a boyish hobby but a lifelong interest. In 1903 he was revealing the treasures of Oxford architecture to a school friend; thirty-one years later he switched from talking about flying to showing me relics of the ancient defences of Southampton.

While he was still a schoolboy he became known to a number of archaeologists including Leonard Woolley and D. G. Hogarth. Many other officials at the Ashmolean Museum became his close personal friends. His interest in medieval castles and military architecture led him to go for bicycling tours of French castles in the summer holidays of 1906, 1907 and 1908. On these tours he wrote long letters home packed with the detailed architectural notes he had taken, which he would wish to refer to later when writing a thesis he had planned.

This survey of English and French castles was the first step to a comparison of the castles built by the Crusaders in Syria and Palestine with those of Western Europe, which suggested that the Crusaders' castles had been copied from those of the West. This thesis, which was part of the material Lawrence submitted for his degree in 1910, has been printed in a limited edition.[1] The letters containing the records of his tours and the notes made on the spot in Wales, France and Syria are printed in a second volume. I have only used a few of these letters with such passages as reveal his character and mode of travel, here.

[1] *Crusader Castles*, Golden Cockerel Press.

The Lawrence boys had a religious Christian upbringing and attended church regularly. In the latter part of his time at school Lawrence was an officer in the Church Lads' Brigade and taught in Sunday school. His elder brother, Dr. M. R. Lawrence (Bob) who served with the R.A.M.C. in France throughout the war, and later became a member of the China Inland Mission, joined the Oxford University O.T.C. medical unit when he went to St. John's College, and Lawrence joined the cyclists when he went to Jesus College. Lawrence went to camp for the years 1908 and 1909, but perhaps not in 1910, the year he took his degree.

The house in Polstead Road was not large enough; as the boys grew up more space was needed and a little two-roomed bungalow was built for Lawrence at the bottom of the garden. He hung the walls of his study with green Bolton sheeting which made it very quiet, and he did most of his work there while he was an undergraduate. It was in this bungalow that he lodged his Arab friends, Sheikhs Hamoudi and Dahoum, when he brought them from the Carchemish diggings to visit England in the summer of 1913.

Lawrence found it easier to reveal himself to older men than to his contemporaries. The most important of his early friendships — perhaps the most important in his life — was with D. G. Hogarth, with whom he remained in close touch from when he attracted his attention as a schoolboy in the Ashmolean, until his death in 1927. 'He was the only person to whom I had never to explain the "why" of what I was doing', Lawrence wrote to Lionel Curtis.

Hogarth was, I think, the first to recognize the extent of Lawrence's genius: he encouraged him to learn Arabic and got him a demyship at Magdalen College which enabled him to work for three years at the Carchemish dig of which Hogarth was the first head. Hogarth's appreciation was expressed in a character of Lawrence written for *Twenty-Four Portraits* by William Rothenstein, published in 1920. It is anonymous.

In the three and a half years between December 1910 and August 1914 Lawrence did not spend more than seven months in England. When each season's work stopped he travelled about, often wearing Arab clothes and living with Arabs and Kurds and buying Hittite seals and visiting antiquities.

After his death in 1935, the following memory of Lawrence appeared in *The Times*. Published anonymously, it is by Ernest Barker.

'The years gave me, between 1900 and 1920, the chance of knowing Mr. and Mrs. Lawrence and their five sons. Three of them, whom I remember best, seemed to me young eagles — wilfully independent, far flying, eager in discovery. But they were always true to their home; and it was a wonderful home.

'One of them — unforgettable — was the younger brother of Colonel Lawrence, "Will" . . . he had a passion for Provençal poetry and for Greek . . . when the war came he took quickly to flying and was shot down in an aeroplane near St. Quentin in October 1915.

'Colonel Lawrence — "Ned" — was the eagle of eagles, already in his Oxford days and afterwards. He, too, was a student of history; and he, too, loved poetry and Greek. But he had a sheer speed and a consuming eagerness of discovery which were almost terrifying. It was his passion to find out, and to find out for himself, on the spot — whether, as a boy, he haunted some excavation in Oxford to discover bits of medieval pottery, or whether, as a young man, he climbed barefoot among the ruins of the castles in Palestine in order to discover the facts for his theses in his final school. A wilful independence was deep in him: it always carved its own way; sometimes, perhaps, it twisted into impishness, and left arabesques to mark its course . . . Speed and the sudden swoop — in life and in death.'

Dear Mother, I have arrived here quite right after an excellent crossing. The [*name omitted*] almost missed the train at Oxford of course, and came to the boat just with a minute to spare. The journey down to Southampton was uneventful, except for scares about the luggage going wrong. I rode straight to Netley, and caused a spirit of eager enquiry to be manifested by the youth of Southampton. Netley is as fine as if not finer than I had imagined. It is certainly the finest ruin I have seen, and much the most picturesque. I do not think that the Chapter House and guest room can be equalled. Coming back from Netley I went to Bakers and got my hat and then got notepaper and Post Card Album. In the Hartley Institute they have some excellent Encaustic Tiles, well worth going to see: the collection of local objects is also good. On going to the boat I passed the *Deutschland*, having her bows repaired as a sequel to the Dover collision. On board the boat I found my berth, and deposited all my spare goods and then put on the extra thick coat (this information is for Mother). The Moon was full and glorious: Mr. [*name omitted*] and I stayed up till about 11.30 looking at it; I cannot say whether the cloud effects or the reflection on the water were the best but the 'ensemble' was perfect and left nothing to be desired. I never before understood properly Tennyson's 'Long glories of the Autumn Moon' but I see his reasons now for mentioning it so often, it was so different from the pale moon of the land. The moon was out from about seven to four, and there were heavy clouds with continuous lightning in the East. We only had about $\frac{1}{2}$ hour's rain. The sunrise was on the whole a failure, there was nothing so good as the sunset before. About 2 we passed between Sark and Jersey. Tell Chimp[1] I was not much impressed with the latter. It was all too dark and gloomy, for a residence; the only bright spot was the Corbière Light-house. St. Malo was reached before six, but we had to wait till seven before landing. The sea was very choppy

[1] His brother Frank.

43

and irregular with a strong swell around the Channel Islands. Everyone in the boat appears to have been sick with the exception of four or five, among whom Mr. [*name omitted*] and myself were prominent. [*25 lines omitted*]

2: TO HIS MOTHER

Monday, 6th August, 1906[1]   *Dinard*

[*46 lines omitted*] I am rather surprised about the Morris; it should not have broken like that.[2] Tell Arnie[3] I am not coming back for a long time; not for weeks: there are wolves quite close to a part which we will visit on our tour (close means forty miles). It appears that there are a number of mountains about, and the country is quite wild; the wolves did a lot of damage last winter. I cannot promise to kill one for Will . . . all this morning I have been wrestling with the tyres of Will's old bicycle here, I removed three outer covers (without the one minute removers) took out and exchanged 3 inner tubes; changed two valves, tightened a chain, and adjusted the bearings of a wheel, all in two hours. Please give my kindest regards to Father and the rest and *don't work too hard*: do nothing rather than too much; you are worth more than the house; love to all: hope you are all well: I have not been bilious yet; don't expect to be. A flock of sheep disappeared in the sands round the Mont[4] this spring and so I will not try to find them. Ta Ta. Love. love. love. love. love. love.   NED

[In a letter to his father also written on August 6th, Lawrence said that he had been given a bad five franc piece at the bank 'but they will have to take it back to-day'.

A few days later he was joined by his schoolfellow 'Scroggs' — C. F. C. Beeson — who was to accompany him on his bicycling tour. They met at St. Malo.]

[1] August 6th 1906 was a Tuesday.
[2] The Lawrences had Morris bicycles. Lawrence's own machine was a racer with a specially high gear, on which he could do 180 miles a day. Lord Nuffield informs me, however, that he gave up making bicycles before 1900!
[3] His youngest brother, A. W. Lawrence.
[4] Mont St. Michel.

3: TO HIS BROTHER, WILL LAWRENCE[1]

August 16 1906   [*His eighteenth birthday.*]

My dear Will,   Your letter has put me in a fever heat of expectation: but: — what is it you are going to dig up? Your letter bristles with inconsistencies. You think it is a Roman or Celtic camp (the two things are absolutely opposed to each other) and then you proceed to say that it is a mound on some rising ground. If it includes a mound, say 40 feet high, it is a Saxon or Danish fortification, with probably an interment or two on the top; if the mound is 10 feet high or less, and is about 30 feet in diameter, then it is a barrow, as you said in the former part of your description, which has a lamentable lack of exact figures. You next say that you cannot see traces of vallum or fossa, which are both terms to be applied to a Roman camp, and not to a Celtic, Saxon, British, or Danish erection. These last three or four possibly might have *mounds* and *dykes*, but you see no traces of them. If the mound is British it will be closely encircled by its fortifications, (if it ever had any). If the mound is Saxon, the encircling lines of fortification may be half a mile away. The bayonets Florence describes are bronze spear-heads, of a very early pattern: they might point either to an encampment or a burial, probably the latter, if no great quantity was found. So far all that you have told me which stands is that the mound is round. If I had further details I could advise you where and how to dig: a camp would not be worth excavating: — you might dig over half a mile of ground and only find a spear head: a burial, if a low mound, should have a trench cut through it, from S.W. to N.E., on the level of the ground. Keep all flints, except the whole mound is flint and gravel, and by all means keep all bones; if you find human bones, do not disturb them, but dig round them, to find if they are male or female, and to recover the whole skeleton if possible: the skull is the most important part to determine the date. Any bronze implements found should not be disturbed at first, but try to trace the haft, which will have shrunk to the thinness of a pencil. You will find this very difficult but the result will repay it. If the mound is small sift the earth you throw out — Frank and

---

[1] Aged 16.

Arnie can help in this while you and Bob dig. Work very carefully, so as not to break any tender article: if the mound is large, you should begin in the same way from the top, and work down until you are sure the strata have not been disturbed: i.e. if you find pure clay with no admixture of earth, you may be certain that it has not been moved. You may discover the whole mound to be natural (you say it is 'unnatural', most archaeologists use 'artificial') in which case only the upper three feet need be dug supposing it is a large mound. You see I am trying to advise something for every case. In a small barrow 4–8 feet high, the articles would probably not be more than two feet from the body on each side: to search further out is an energetic course which occasionally repays itself, but not as a rule. It might be worth while trying to obtain some of those 'bayonets'. I think they are preserved in the village, unless those preserved are real bayonets, dating from 60-70 years back. They will probably not be so old as the civil war, although it is possible that they might be. I should advise you to find out where they were discovered, and why they dug there, and at what depth they lay. You should be able to draw conclusions from the answers to these questions. Let me know how the matter progresses, and unless it is very light soil, use small spades. Keep an accurate account of your progress, and mark on a plan where each important article is found. You have my best wishes for success. Don't give up at once if you don't find anything. Digging is an excellent exercise.

[In a second letter, on the same subject, to his brother Bob he enjoins him to write down everything on the spot 'and I will refer to Woolley'. Lawrence had got to know Leonard Woolley through his interest in ancient pottery, at which he had been working in the Ashmolean Museum.]

4: TO HIS MOTHER

Friday August 24. 1906   *Dinard*

[11 *lines omitted*] My ride to Fougères was very pleasant: part of it lay through woods where it was deliciously cool; (it was the hottest day of the year, I never felt such heat before). There is great difficulty in getting a decent drink in France: milk is not obtainable anywhere and eau de Seltz only occasionally. The result is that one gets very thirsty and the only fruits are plums and pears, their apples are uneatable: I have not had a good one yet. I upset myself with too many plums on Wednesday, effects visible today. Fougères Castle is splendid, outside. [21 *lines omitted*] No finer exterior exists I am certain. There are fields, orchards, etc. inside. I ate a glorious feast of blackberries; they were enormous, as large as mulberries and in great profusion since the Bretons will not eat them. They say that the Crown of Thorns was made from bramble. One is supposed to have a guide to go round the castle, but by coming at the dinner hour I escaped that appendage. [8 *lines omitted*]

5: TO HIS MOTHER

Sunday 26th August 1906   *Dinard*

[80 *lines, including* 47 *lines of quotations from Tennyson's 'Idylls of the King' etc., omitted*]

As I was returning I lingered about admiring

> Till the moon
> Rising in clouded majesty at length
> Apparent queen unveiled her peerless light
> And o'er the dark her silver mantle threw. [1]

You really must excuse this battery of quotations, but I have got into the habit of quoting any appropriate lines to myself, and this time I thought I would put them on record. The scene really was perfectly lovely; each of these lines might have been written to suit it; as well as many other phrases I remember, but I will be merciful and let you off with

> The beams of sunset hung their rainbow hues
> High 'mid the shifting domes of sheeted spray.

[1] Milton, *Paradise Lost*, Book IV.

The sea was of the wondrous blue met with sometimes here, and all was perfect; *there was no one else there.* This last makes such an addition to one's enjoyment of nature and her prodigal loveliness; all this scene was reserved for me alone: it is a wonderful surpassing thought on which to reflect. I can only wish my mind was more receptive and my emotions more deeply affected. Nature contains that spirit and power which we can witness but not weigh, inwardly conceive but not comprehend, love but not limit, imagine, but neither define nor describe. Nature is incomprehensible, fleeting, and yet immortal, and a love for it and its impressions are both ineradicable.   Next morning. My Ruskin[1] is better than ever. I will have him bound in Oxford, or will bind him myself. It gives a most masterly exposition of the meaning and method of Gothic, and he simply smashes the Renaissance styles. No wonder they are going out of fashion after this book. Father will devour it with avidity, and start for Venice next week. I wish I could go with him. By the way how did the last two elections at Cockermouth and Exeter go? Did the Unionist or the Liberal get in?[2] I have found another envelope, so I will write two more letters after these; one perhaps on Wednesday and one on Friday. After Friday expect no more till you see me. I hope you are still feeling well in Oxford, it is a glorious place, but its climate does not agree with you. By the way I believe I am as strong as M. Chaignon; I will try him some day. People here say that I am much thinner than Bob, but stronger, and have a better accent. Still Bob's fatness is much better than my muscle in their eyes, except for Mme. Chaignon who got a shock when she saw my 'biceps' while bathing. She thinks I am Hercules. Good-bye for the present; love to Arnie and others.   NED

[In February 1907 Lawrence won an exhibition enabling him to enter Jesus College, Oxford, the following October.

During the Easter holidays he made a tour of Welsh castles. The letters he wrote home have been printed in *Crusader Castles*, vol. II. Only one of those written on this trip is included here.]

---

[1] *Stones of Venice,* by John Ruskin.
[2] Like his father, Lawrence was a Conservative in politics at this period.

6: TO HIS MOTHER

Sunday, [*? April*, 1907]　　　　　　　　　*Caerphilly*

Dear Mother, Here I am at my last Welsh Castle and I think, in most respects, my best. Before going on with it however, I had better tell you what I have done since I wrote from Tenby. I left that place about 12 noon next day, rain and other things delaying me. I had a miserably wet uneventful ride to Kidwelly where I slept. (Carmarthen castle is not worth looking at). Kidwelly on the other hand is splendid. The state of it is good (just ruined enough to be interesting), and although quite plain, it is very large, and strong. I did not draw a plan because it was wet and late, but on my next visit I will have much photography and planning to do. Specially remarkable features were the ovens and the dungeons. The ovens were circular in shape, about 8 feet in diameter, and with low vaults (some 3 feet high). In front of the door was a fire-place and chimney: this seemed the only apparatus for heating. There had been two such ovens in the castle: one is perfect the other much damaged. The dungeons were under the gate tower. Two were of the ordinary kind, the third was conical, like the Treasury of Atreus, or one of the old fashioned straw bee-hives, with a way in only from the top. The depth must have been about 10 feet and the place always pitch-dark and very damp. There are records of many deaths in it . . . Caerphilly, to return to more important subjects, is magnificent. The Horn-work is most interesting, and the outworks could not be excelled, either for preservation or attractiveness. There are no good photos. to be obtained . . . the conviction has been continually growing stronger upon me, that I must tour round this part again with a camera. Details which interest me such as the moulding of a chimney piece, or the shape of the flue, even the vaulting of a room, are always neglected by the professional p.p.c. maker . . . I have come to the conclusion that two meals a day with a glass of milk at one o'clock, suit me better than three. At any rate I have always felt fresh on this trip in spite of very hard journeys, and the number of castles has not palled on me. I am fresh for any amount more, and could continue for months.

D

I also feel stronger as the day goes on: with my luggage left at home I could do 180 miles a day with ease.

[In July Lawrence left the City of Oxford High School for Boys and in August went on a bicycling tour of French castles with his father, taking photographs as he had planned.[1] It is perhaps worth mentioning that his father was a keen amateur photographer and that Lawrence learned a great deal from him.

The following letter describes a visit to Château Gaillard and records Lawrence's admiration for Richard I. It was probably about this time that Lawrence began to speculate on the influence of the crusades on medieval architecture. His interest in this subject was to send him to the East.]

7: TO HIS MOTHER

Sunday 11 August 1907   *Evreux*

Dear Mother, Father is out, and so I am at last writing to you. I would have written before, but was so busy taking photos. etc. at Château Gaillard. Beauvais was a wonderful place, and I left it with great regret for Gisors which was disappointing, (a large castle, but all the towers locked up), from Gisors we came to Petit Andelys. The Château Gaillard was so magnificent, and the postcards so abominable, that I stopped there an extra day, and did nothing but photograph, from 6.0 A.M. to 7.0 P.M. I took ten altogether, and if all are successful, I will have a wonderful series. I will certainly have to start a book. Some of them were very difficult to take, and the whole day was very hard. I think Pt. Andelys would be a good place to stop at. The hotel is cheap, and very pleasant. The Seine runs near the back door, and the bathing is excellent, from a little wooded island in the centre of the river. There are plenty of hills within sight, and many interesting places. Also the scenery all along the river is exceedingly fine. Long strings of barges pulled by a steam-tug pass the hotel occasionally, and the whole place is over-shadowed by the hills with the ruins of the Château. I have talked so much about this to you that you must know it all by heart, so I had

---

[1] Some of these are reproduced in *Crusader Castles.*

better content myself with saying that its plan is marvellous, the execution wonderful, and the situation perfect. The whole construction bears the unmistakeable stamp of genius. Richard I must have been a far greater man than we usually consider him: he must have been a great strategist and a great engineer, as well as a great man-at-arms. I hope Mr. Jane[1] will emphasise this in his book. It is time Richard had justice done to his talents. From Pt. Andelys we came on here, where there is a fair cathedral, with the most exquisite stained glass, all old, and of a glorious scheme of gold and red. The effect is magnificent, and makes a poor building look splendid. Our further movements are doubtful. [30 *lines omitted*]

8 : TO HIS MOTHER

26 *August* 1907 *Mont St. Michel*

Dear Mother, Here I am at last about to spend a night at the Mont. The dream of years is fulfilled. It is a perfect evening; the tide is high and comes some 20 feet up the street. In addition the stars are out most beautifully, and the moon is, they say, just about to rise. The phosphorescence in the water interests me specially: I have only seen it once or twice before, and never so well as tonight. The whole sea, when oars are dipped into it, seems to blaze, for several feet around. I rode here from Dinan getting Frank's p.p.c. in St. Malo on my way ... With Dinan and the Rance I am entirely in love. The Rue de Jersual from the old bridge to the 'place' is perfect: the river is most lovely. Above the town it becomes very quiet and peaceful like the Thames: lined with aspens and Lombardy poplars. When you add water-lillies, willows, and an occasional high bank, crowned with a quaint farmhouse or château, you have a fair idea of the characteristics of the stream. ...

Since I left Father I have had a very wonderful time. It began at Fougères, which I saw by moonlight and a more exquisite

---

[1] Lawrence coached with L. C. Jane in his last year at the City of Oxford School and as an undergraduate. Mr. Jane has given a short account of Lawrence in Robert Graves's *Lawrence and the Arabs*, p. 16.

sight I have seldom seen. That castle is quite above and beyond words. It pollutes it to mention any but Château Gaillard, Pembroke, and Caerphilly in the same breath, and I am not sure but that Fougères is the finest of them all. The Tour des Gobelins is six stories in height, and circular. It stands on a granite cliff 80 feet high, and in the moonlight had a marvellous effect. It set off the strength of the Mélusine, a tower near, with an enormous expanded base. The talus shoots right out like the Keep of Ch. Gaillard. Beyond the Mélusine, after a hundred yards of machicolated curtain come Raoul and Yrienne, two wonderful chefs-d'œuvre of the military architect. They are semicircular bastions, projecting some 70 feet from the wall, are over 80 feet in diameter, and more than that in height; neither has a window or projection in the face and over against them leans the spire of St. Sulpice the most crooked and the thinnest in Bretagne. I would have given anything to have been able to sketch or paint these things as I saw them. I really must return to Fougères soon and do justice to the whole. The neglect in which it has been left by the Guide-books is abominable.

From Fougères I glided S.E. to Le Mans, to photograph the effigy of Mrs. Richard I, Berengaria, in the cathedral there. The apse and nave of the building were splendid: the former especially. From Le Mans I rode to Saumur via Le Lude a most splendid Renaissance château, unhappily private. Saumur itself is still in parts as Balzac painted it in *Eugénie Grandet*, though the main streets have been rebuilt. The Castle is a military storehouse. I slept that night at Angers. The Cathedral roofed as it was in domes was a new style for me in architecture. From Angers I rode the next day through Lion d'Angers to Rennes and so on to St. Malo and Dinard. The vineyards were quaint but monotonous. At Dinard I tried 5 hotels but all were full. As it was then 8.0 P.M. I went to the Chaignons. When I spoke and revealed myself there was a most enthusiastic scene. All yelled Welcome at once ... M. Corbel was with them and collapsed when he heard where I had come from. I have given them a topic of conversation for a week — Deux cent cinquante kilomètres, Ah la-la, qu'il est merveilleux. Deux cent cinquante kilomètres.

Next day I went on to Lamballe meaning to go as far as

Guingamp. It however began to rain heavily so I stopped and made a careful study of the Rood screen in the church there. Next day I photoed it, and the time taken (3 hours to focus) should ensure a presentable result, better than the vile p.c. I sent you. Next day (by the way the Chaignons and the Lamballe people complimented me on my wonderful French: I have been asked twice since what part of France I came from) I went on to La Hunaudaye, and took 4 photos. In the evening at Dinan I wrote to M. de la Brière asking him to take steps for the preservation of the Château. Nothing like making his society of use. Tomorrow I am going to ride into Granville. [*omission*]

[About July 19th, 1908, Lawrence crossed to France again, for a bicycling tour. This time he was alone.]

9: TO HIS MOTHER

23 *July* 1908   *Cussy-Les-Forges* [*Yonne*]

[*58 lines omitted*] For myself I am riding very strongly, & feel very fit, on my diet of bread, milk & fruit (peaches (best) 3 a 1d.: apricots 5 or 6 a 1d. if very special: cherries don't count) — I wish you were here. I begin on 2 pints of milk and bread & supplement with fruit to taste till evening, when more solid stuff is consumed: one eats a lot when riding for a week on end at my pace. My day begins early (it's fearfully hot at mid-day) there is usually a château to work at from 12.0 to 2.0 and then hotel at 7.0 or 8.0. I have no time for sight-seeing: indeed sometimes I wonder if my thesis is to be written this November or next, I find myself composing pages and phrases as I ride.

10: TO HIS MOTHER

Sunday August 2 1908   *Aigues-Mortes*

Dear Mother, I had better begin from my last letter before Vézelay. This I found superb but rather in sculpture than in proportions. The carvings were the finest early work I had met till then: since ? you'll hear.[1] From Vézélay I rode to Nevers, arriving on Friday. It is a quaint rather than beautiful town, with a good renaissance ducal palace and a fine cathedral. I telephoned from here to Dunlop in Paris for a new tyre, which after anxious waiting arrived all right on Monday: since then all has gone like a marriage bell in the way of punctures, and I am generally happy. The cost was however immense with telephoning, carriage, fitting, etc. it cost nearly 20s. . . . . (I have changed a note quite successfully by the way: pocket proved admirable). From Nevers I went by Moulins to Le Puy. Tell Father I had a 20 mile hill up into Le Puy. Part of my ride was up a superb gorge, with river foaming in the bottom, and rock and hill on each side: it was the finest scenery I have ever come across: truly the Auvergne is a wondrous district, but *not* one for a cycle: I'll take a walking tour there some day I hope. The volcanoes (all extinct of course) are queer, being plumped down all over the country, without any order or connection. They are very diverse in material (sand, rock, etc.) and look ugly. At the same time the needle of which I sent you a p.c. is an impressive peak. It rises from the town of Le Puy where I was delighted to get 3 p.c.'s from Will and you and one from Scroggs; at the same time I am disgusted at what I fear was my mistake in antedating your departure for Jersey: but a trip like this upsets one's ideas of time. In the Auvergne by the way there are few if any trees and in parts to make a garden they have piled the stones from the ground in a wall around it. A garden our size would have a wall 5 feet thick, and 4 feet high so made. From Le Puy I rode up for 10 miles more, (oh dear 'twas hot!) consoling myself with the idea that my sufferings were beyond the conception of antiquity, since they were a combina-tion (in a similar climate) of those of Sisyphus who pushed a great weight up hill, of Tantalus who could not get anything to drink, or any fruit, and of Theseus who was doomed ever to remain sitting: — I got to the top at last, had 15 miles of up and down to St. Somebody-I-don't-want-to meet-again, and then a rush down 4000 feet to the Rhône. 'Twas down a valley, the road carved out of the side of the precipice, and most gloriously exciting: in fact so much so that with that and the heat I felt quite sick when

[1] i.e. the work in Provence is still finer.

I got to the bottom. I slept that night at Crussol, a fine xii century castle on a 500 feet precipice over the Rhône. Next day via Valence to Avignon, glorious with its town walls and papal palace, (Popes lived there 90 years, and built an enormous pile), and passed thence through Tarascon to Beaucaire, which I saluted for the sake of Nicolette, into Arles. *The* thing in Arles is the cloister of St. Trophimus: it is absolutely unimaginably fine with its sculptures and its proportion: all other architecture is very nearly dirt beside this Provençal Romanesque, when the scale is small (Provence has never done anything big in anything at all). I have seen the three best (almost the only 3) examples at Arles, Montmajour, and St. Gilles, and am absolutely bewildered. The amphitheatre (Roman) at Arles is magnificently and gigantically ugly, as everything of that sort must be: Nîmes is I believe better (that is for tomorrow). From Arles I rode to Les Baux a queer little ruined and dying town upon a lonely 'olive sandalled' mountain. Here I had a most delightful surprise. I was looking from the edge of the precipice down the valley far over the plain, watching the green changing into brown, and the brown into a grey line far away on the horizon, when suddenly the sun leaped from behind a cloud, and a sort of silver shiver passed over the grey: then I understood and instinctively burst out with a cry of 'Θαλασσα Θαλασσα' that echoed down the valley, and startled an eagle from the opposite hill: it also startled two French tourists who came rushing up hoping to find another of the disgusting murders their papers make such a fuss about I suppose. They were disappointed when they heard it was 'only the Mediterranean'!

From Les Baux I descended to Arles and thence to St. Gilles — Aigues-Mortes. I reached here late last night, and sent you a pencilled p.c. It is a lovely little place, an old, old town huddled along its old streets, with hardly a house outside its old walls, still absolutely unbroken, and hardly at all restored or in need of it. From it St. Louis started for his crusades, and it has seen innumerable events since. Today it is deserted by the world, it is decaying fast: its drawbacks are mosquitoes, (a new experience for me, curtains on all the beds). It is however almost on the sea, and exceedingly pleasant, (above all, if one could get acclimatised quickly to these brutes, I'm all one huge bite).[1] I bathed today in the sea, the great sea, the greatest in the world; you can imagine my feelings: the day was lovely, warm, a light wind, and sunny; the sea had not our long rolling breakers, but short dancing ripples, the true

ἀνηριθμον γελασμα

And from the waves sounds like delight broke forth.

The beach was hard sand as far as the eye could reach, and sand rippled like the waves themselves: 'twas shallow, and all most lovely, most delightful

> I love all waste
> And solitary places: where we taste
> The pleasure of believing all we see
> Is boundless, as we wish our souls to be.[2]

You are all wrong, Mother dear, a mountain may be a great thing, a grand thing, but it is better to be peaceful, and quiet, and pure, omnia pacata posse mente tueri, if that is the best state, then a plain is the best country: the purifying influence is the paramount one in a plain, there one can sit down quietly and think of anything, or nothing which Wordsworth says is best, one feels the littleness of things, of details, and the great and unbroken level of peacefulness of the whole: no, give me a level plain, extending as far as the eye can reach, and there I have enough of beauty to satisfy me, and tranquility as well! *that* one could never have in mountains: there is always the feeling that one is going up or down: that one will be better, will see clearer from the top than from the valleys, stick to the plains Mother and all ye little worms, you will be happiest there.

But for my bathe — that was a lovely time. I hope I'll 'hear the sea breathe o'er my dying brain its last monotony' on such a day as this, and also at the time of the setting sun. It was as warm as may be pleasant and the water refreshingly delicious: I felt that

---

[1] Lawrence contracted malaria from these mosquitoes and for the rest of his life was liable to sudden attacks of it.
[2] Shelley: *Julian and Maddalo.*

at last I had reached the way to the South and all the glorious East; Greece, Carthage, Egypt, Tyre, Syria, Italy, Spain, Sicily, Crete . . . they were all there, and all within reach . . . of me. I fancy I know now better than Keats what Cortes felt like, silent upon a peak in Darien. Oh I must get down here — further out — again! Really this getting to the sea has almost overturned my mental balance: I would accept a passage for Greece tomorrow: — and there I am, going to Nîmes: — I suppose it cannot be helped: well I am glad to have got so far. The heat is great, I was almost going to say excessive, especially between 11 & 3. Everybody wears tinted glasses (even the children) and stay within closed blinds till within 3 hours of sunset. Now (9.0 P.M.) all the world is awake and in the streets killing mosquitoes: fruit I find almost a necessity, but only pears and peaches procurable, & dear: however I am a disciple of Blake

> Abstinence sows sand all over
> The ruddy limbs and flaming hair
> But desire gratified
> Sows seeds of joy and beauty there.

So I take plenty and keep cool and well, albeit copper-coloured, & I think thinner: I will write again next Sunday at any rate if not before: till when, expect a couple of p.c.'s only. Shall get to Carcassonne on Wednesday I hope and may all be well there just as here: love to all: NED

11: TO C. F. C. BEESON

Dimanche, le 9 Août [1908]   *Hôtel du Nord, Cordes, Tarn*

Dear Scroggs, Oh Murder I've got in this letter to get from Avignon to Cordes, across about half France: expect a 'digest' only. Avignon — Tarascon (Beaucaire across the river glowing in the sunset, looked worthy of Nicolette). The Tarasconnaises are hideous, exactly like grey horses whereas the women of Arles are glorious: the matrons look superb with their Greek profiles, and tiny Phrygian caps of black cloth. Tarascon—Arles where *the* thing to see is not the Amphitheatre (most magnificently hideous: — , very Roman) but the cloister of St. Trophimus: in-describably grand: see photos, on return. Arles–Montmajour (noble Romanesque church, cloister second to Arles)–Les Baux, not as good as 'twas painted: houses as a rule either in-habited or too ruined: still 'twas most interesting and not to be missed for the world. don't expect too much tho'. Les Baux–St. Gilles, with the finest carved portal in the world (see photo)–Aigues-Mortes. This place is not at all dead: oh no; as alive as ever it was, no ruined houses, all occupied and flourishing. The walls look splendid, but no good photos. Tried to take one which will be bad: oh the mosquitoes! Have a matter of 20 p.c.'s to show you here. Aigues-Mortes to Nîmes (Maison Carrée a gem: amphitheatre fair: p.c.'s)–Agde, (superb fortified church a stumbling block to thesis)–Beziers, Narbonne (nothing here but memories)–Carcassonne. I'm not going to describe that: 'tis impossible, impious to attempt such a thing: go and see it, expecting to find the greatest thing of your life, and you'll find one many times finer. How on earth has it remained un-known with its memories and its remains, when people flock to a St. Michel or the Tower of London? It is ten thousand times finer than these, or a hundred like them, rolled into one. I have 40 odd photos. which do it sad injustice, but nothing could do it anything else: and there are no guides, no fees, no tips, no beggars, hardly any trippers: 'tis a paradise of a place, unhappily there's no hotel. Carcassonne–Toulouse (a dirty industrial dung-heap of factories and plate glass)–Albi: the cathedral looks like a blanc-mange mould: hideous but enormous and most imposing. –Cordes, which is another of the indescribable, never to be paralleled places. Imagine such a town to exist in our 20th cent. Europe. Perhaps however as you've never heard of it, and my précis has been so very much so I may enlarge a bit upon it, and try and construct a Cordes.

First of all, it is in Tarn, in dialect, geographically, ethno-graphically and climatically distinct from the rest of France. (I cannot understand a word of the patois: no more can the French.) One's hotel dinners in Tarn (I'm degenerating into a commis-voyageur, and ça criticisera a 'plat' with the best) are weird: I don't in the least know what I ate last night: — I fancy a plough-ox or two (is it nightmare?) some potatoes were they? stewed infant or monkey: things like paving stones but not quite so hard, haven't the faintest idea what; and to finish something indescribable, described apparently in patois as clargh-bult: they were quite possible, but anything from snail to ortolan. The bread—can you 'degust' in fancy (blessing your stars 'tis only so), leather, steeped in brine and bitter aloes, boiled till soft, with a crust like iron, and an aroma like a brandy snap? Milk they say is to be imported from Europe next year: butter was brought in the year before last, and is now turned into cream-cheese. I should be dead by now only for the Roquefort: 'tis as common as possible, and with enough of it anything is disguised, even the bread tastes not unlike charcoal. If you're bored or overworn, come to a Tarnais hotel for a week. For 3 francs a night (being the only guest one must maintain the place) one can have as many galvanic shocks following on gasping nerve-strained expectation as one can support. I'm coming back on a walking tour: (oh yes you've heard that before!)

Cordes is a paradise for a painter, albeit the man with the muck-rake[1] would find his hands full. Take a hill, too steep for a horse to pull a cart up: add houses, all of xiv century, except a few quite modern comparatively, say renaissance: streets — mostly stairs, irregular and broken, running under archways and tunnels, round corners and into courtyards, expanding sometimes into a 'place', sometimes into a cesspool. Cover these ruelles with grass, heap them with refuse, with vines and with flowers: fill them with a picturesque tho' squalid population, throw about plenty of ruins, a church or two, town walls, 8 or ten xv cent. fortified gates, exquisitely carved doors luxuriating in iron — wrought Renaissance locks and hinges that would be worth a fortune in England: make your houses of stone, or brick, of tiles, of plaster and wood, but not of one only: patch a stone house with brick or wood and vice-versa — make the plaster fall off where most artistically effective, let the dirtiest and most winding streets have the most flowers and creepers, the finest flamboyant

---

[1] A steel engraving of *The Man with the Muck Rake,* by Noel Paton, R.A., hung in the drawing-room at Polstead Road and provided Lawrence with a model for a brass lantern which he made.

windows and the best arcades: in fact put in whatever is quaint
or lovely and tumble-down just where it is most needed pictorially,
and most unlikely in reality: deluge it with a blaze of colour, and
of dirt, and you are in a fair way to construct a Cordes, though you
can never get the real thing with its hand looms and its threshing
floors, its pottery and its fruit. An artist might (barring fevers)
paint here for a year without a repeat, and all his pictures would
be lovely: it is a dream-city, with a little nightmare added as well:
and here endeth the paper.   E.L.

I hope you haven't to pay excess on these effusions. My people
never said anything about it.

Castillon I hope on Friday: Saintes 8 days later; after that
goodness only knows. 38 punctures: 1400 miles and finding it
very hard, but very interesting.

DOE YE NEXTE THYNGE ⎫
TIME FLIES   ⎬ *Mottoes for August*
                                        ⎭

12: TO C. F. C. BEESON

16 *August* 1908   *Grand Hotel du Midi, à Chalus (Haute-Vienne)*

Dear Scroggs, 1 week has passed since I began your letter:
I'm 'awfully' sorry; and as I've 4 letters written today you'll
excuse me the shortcomings of this one. From Cordes I rode
over ghastly hills to Najac. This little place proved to be as
picturesque as Cordes (I really can't say anything greater) with
the addition of plenty of water (a great boon here) and a splendid
xiii cent. castle, absolutely unrestored. The donjon was as fine
as Rouen, and there was a splendid cistern with about 10 feet of
water: why do they persist in calling them dungeons? or
oubliettes: nothing but a water rat could have lived in this one.
From Najac 'twas down hill nearly to Cahors (40 miles, and that
meant good-bye to the Tarn) where the Pont Valentré proved
curious rather than beautiful. It has been all scraped and
repaired —, and a white thing does not look well in this flood of
sunlight. At Cahors I was devoured by mosquitoes all night:
They simply whirled round my head. I understood Aeschylus[1]

[1] *Prometheus Bound*, line 126.

αἰθηρ δ᾽ἐλαφραις πτερυγων ῥιπαις ὑποσυριζει. That word ὑποσυριζει is superb.

Cahors to Fumel for Bonaguil which was glorious. 'tis hardly ruined at all: most picturesque (covered with plants and flowers) and architecturally most wonderful: mark it with a double asterisk, and visit it ὡς ταχιστα. Bonaguil–Montpazier, the most perfect of the bastide-towns (those chess-board planned towns of the xiii and xiv cents. in Aquitaine.) The market place was fine, with arcades all round. There were more cicalas there in the trees than I found anywhere else: it was really charming out there in the evening: since the best time of the day is after 10 at night (my Father is Irish you know, so I'm allowed these little things).

Montpazier–Castillon, with nothing to see, then Pujols, fine of xii cent. and interesting: an improved Gisors: then Montaigne, the estate and castle of the greatest one: this of course it was a great privilege for me to see. His library tower is unaltered, though the château is rebuilt.

Montaigne–Perigueux (St-Front more curious than beautiful, and quite spoilt by restoration)–Hautefort, the castle of Bertrand de Born, burnt, so the butler assured me, by the English under Chas. I. and only rebuilt in the xvii cent: quite so: the gateway is supposed to be B. de Bornish, but that's all rot: at least if so he was an astonishing anachronism. It may be xiv cent.

Hautefort — St. Yrieix (xii. tower good): St. Yrieix–Chalusset, a *most wonderful* thing of the xiii cent. [A] fine castle, with donjon of xii cent. *and a large beak on the front of it.* 'Eureka' I've got it at last for the thesis: the transition from the square keep form: really it is too great for words: it was impossible to photo: but I can plan, and have a SKETCH which it shall be your duty to render presentible. It is really indispensible (how *do* you spell that disgusting Americanism?) Chalusset–Chalus which is where Rich. I. got his final wound. At the same time 'twas his lunacy in beanfeasting and steeple-chasing before it had healed that killed him: he died near Poitiers, but the p.c.'s here have photo's of the stone beneath which he was buried, and show two towers about $\frac{1}{4}$ of a mile apart as *the* one from which the arrow came. 'Twas probably neither: the local antiquarian (a quaint spec. by the way) swears there was a third tower between the two: certainly those now existing are too far for a shot to the stone, on which he probably stood, since all else is swamp, and an Angevin couldn't get his feet wet. Well now, I hope to be in Saintes by Tuesday, Loches 10 days later (unless you're coming) and Dinard in another 6. This would be apparently about 100 miles a day: but I've ridden nearly 2000 to date, am as brown as a Jap, and thin as paper. Paper not long enough again: still all the polite messages and inquiries after health and happiness you'll take as read. I expect you'll be happier when the fair[1] is off your chest. I'll miss it in any case: Tootle'oo.   E.L.

[Having visited, planned and photographed the most important early castles in England and France (unfortunately, unlike his brother Will, he never visited Spain) Lawrence determined to study the castles built by the Crusaders in Syria and Palestine. He announced his intention of travelling on foot, though C. M. Doughty, to whom he had written at the suggestion of D. G. Hogarth, whom he had recently got to know at the Ashmolean Museum, advised him strongly against such an attempt in the following letter.

3. 2. [09]

Dear Sir, I have not been further North in Syria than lat. 34. In July and August the heat is very severe and day and night, even at the altitude of Damascus (over 2000 feet), it is a land of squalor where a European can find evil refreshment. Long daily marches on foot a prudent man who knows the country would I think consider out of the question. The populations only know their own wretched life and look upon any European wandering in their country with at best a veiled ill will.

The distances to be traversed are very great. You would have nothing to draw upon but the slight margin of strength which you bring with you from Europe. Insufficient food, rest and sleep, would soon begin to tell.

A distinguished general told me at the time of the English expedition against Arabia that no young soldier under 23 years old, who went through the campaign, had not been in hospital.

---

[1] St. Giles's Fair, Oxford.

I should dissuade a friend from such a voyage, which is too likely to be most wearisome, hazardous to health and even disappointing.

A mule or a horse, with its owner, should, at least in my opinion, be hired to accompany you.

Some Arabic is of course necessary. If you should wish to ask any further questions I shall be happy to reply so far as I can do so. Yours sincerely, CHARLES DOUGHTY

Lawrence, however, pursued his own plans, undeterred. He left England in June 1909 on the P. & O. steamship *Mongolia*. His first letter was written after passing Gibraltar and there was a second mentioning that Messina 'looks in a poor way' after the earthquake which had totally destroyed it the previous December. A third letter from Port Said gave his first impression of the East, but much of it is repeated in the following letter which gives a picture of Syrian life.]

13: TO HIS MOTHER

2 *August* 1909   *Hotel Victoria, Beyrout*

Dear Mother, I have now got back to Beyrout, in my former quarters, and therefore the first part of my work out here is finished. I think after all it will be best if I simply send you a very long account of everything that has happened in the last month, just as it occurs to me now. Of course there will be a tremendous lot missed out, to be remembered later on in scraps as occasion arrives: but on the whole it will give you an idea of Northern Palestine in summer. At the same time, Will, no purple patches for me: I never relished them myself, except done by a man like Ruskin: and also after a month's walking I am not quite inclined for any gambolling. Likewise, as I don't know whether you may not like to lend this production, strictly personal stuff will be banished to the last sheet.

First of all it is hot out here — not unbearable, and at times under the shade of a tree, near running water, the climate is almost pleasant: but generally it is too warm. The temperature is not very high; of course I have not much means of finding out, but in Beyrout itself it is settled at just under 90° day and night: that is what makes it trying: with a cool evening one could enjoy the heat of the day: but there is hardly any variation to be discovered. Inland, up the mountains, it is cooler, though when one gets among large rocks one is stifled: they seem almost to give off a vapour, or heat-breath, that is horrible; add to that a sirocco, a wind that shrivels every green thing it meets, that blisters one's face and hands, and makes one feel that one is walking towards some gigantic oven; and you get an idea of vast possibilities. Round about Galilee and along the Jordan valley is the hottest part of the country, and at Tiberias, where I stayed a couple of nights, it was 106° and 105° at mid-day, in the back of the hall of the hotel: — and that felt cool as an icehouse in comparison with the outer air! (there was a block of ice melting there all day). After that Will will not be disgusted to learn that the Lake of Galilee, and the lower Jordan are lukewarm at all times, and that near Tiberias are hot springs, rising at 180 degrees. However this should be enough for the climate: it has not prevented my walking about and sightseeing as I chose nor have I had to take a siesta at midday, though it is a habit that residents in the country soon fall into. I left Beyrout not long after the beginning of July, and walked straight to Sidon (30 miles or so). It was very pleasant, along the sea-shore the whole way; beginning with sand-hills and mulberry plantations; (for all N. Syria battens on silk-worms): it gradually improved to olive yards, and finally arrived at sterility and empty sarcophagi, at Heldua,[1] a famous place once, and now so freshly, for there I first tasted native bread and leben.[2] Native bread is of two kinds, one, with small loaves, about 6-10 inches across, circular, and of double thickness of material: it is lumpy outside, but not thinner than cardboard of some stoutness, and when fresh very good. Everybody likes to eat it hot, and when I get to a house in its district and ask for a loaf (proffering a half-penny) the woman goes out at once with her tray, made of straw closely woven, so as to be quite stiff, about 2 feet in diameter, slightly concave, on which are loaves already mixed up but not cooked, and in about 6 minutes she is

[1] The ancient name for the site of the present inn, Khan el Khalde.
[2] Sour milk, yoghurt.

back with the whole thing ready, sprinkled with grains of sesame and cummin, is it? I forget. At any rate bread No. 1 is good, when not dry. I think you saw a loaf some years ago at the Exhibition in Oxford. Bread No. 2 is more doubtful. It is light grey in colour, deepening to brown, very large, sometimes up to 3 feet across, and of course circular. It is very thin, quite as thin as ordinary brown paper, tough, and pliable, almost leathery when fresh, but when dry becoming brittle like a cheese biscuit or oatcake (it really does rather resemble oatcake, though not one-third as thick). To bake it they plaster it against the side of the oven, so that on the surface it is lightly dusted with clay. To eat leben, or burghul (boiled wheat) with it (the regular thing) one tears off a small part of one's loaf, and doubles it up into a spoon or poke-bonnet-shape: — this then makes a splendid dipper. Leben is when fresh rather thin and lumpy: when old it gets like cheese (cream-cheese that is) and has a distinctly acid taste. In colour it is pure white, with a sourish smell. Everybody tells me that it is quite distinct from buttermilk, not nearly so good, and some of these informants were Irish and Scotch women, who may be trusted. Leben certainly is not worth much, though it is nastily-refreshing if one is hot, and makes the bread go down. So far I have not found a European who approves of it, except some Americans of Sidon, who were accustomed to eat it with equal bulk of sugar, almost like crême goutée: I tried it so, and it was palatable. Now I am on the food question I had better go through with it. On the march one begins with breakfast; (by the way this diet is only my lunacy, and the native habit: no other European would think of it): if I have slept the night in a native house then it will be 'Haleeb' ordered overnight. The people do not usually take this, since it is fresh milk, (boiled, or heated rather, they fight shy of it cold), with quantities of sugar in it. They prefer their milk soured as a rule: though some take haleeb. With this will be eaten a sheet of bread no. ii (the more common variety). If I feel thirsty after it they bring me a bowl of prickly pears, and cut them open for me till I am satisfied. Prickly pears are the cheapest, most plentiful fruit, very refreshing, above all in the cool of the morning, and, with the rind cut away, the prickles are never happened on. Then at midday I eat another sheet of

E

bread (usually brought with me from stopping place; No. ii is not bad dry) next a spring, if there is one: if not it is consumed on the march, moistened with an occasional drop from my water-bottle. Sometimes, but only in exceptional country, I can get figs, or even grapes or watermelons: when I can there is great feasting: nothing is more refreshing than to march for an hour up a dusty road, eating the melon in one's arms: it is as pleasant as loitering in a country lane in England: here we have water-melons football size, streaming with juice, for 2d. I wish there were more places where one could find them. Grapes are very sickly things mostly: though not the best sort, long banana shaped, green ones. These are rare. Figs are very small and poor: pomegranates hardly ripe: tomatoes one can often get, and they are refreshing, when they are cool: cucumbers very plentiful and pleasant. Apricots of course are finished, and apples only cultivated and very badly near Beyrout. Still one can get along in Palestine for fruit. In the evening I get, either bread or leben, or more rarely haleeb. Sometimes I have to join in the native burghul, which is wheat, boiled in some way I fancy, but very greasy. One could not eat much of it, without a river near at hand to help it down. There are I believe other native dishes, but not among the peasant class at this time of year. I at least have found none, though the priests (native Arabs) give me stews and meat-messes of divers sorts. Nobody drinks anything but water, except coffee, for visitors. When I go into a native house the owner salutes me, and I return it and then he says something to one of his women, and they bring out a thick quilt, which doubled, is laid on the rush mat over the floor as a chair: on that I squat down, and then the host asks me four or five times how my health is, and each time I tell him it is good. Then comes sometimes coffee, and after that a variety of questions, as to whether my tripod is a revolver, and what I am, and where I come from, and where I'm going, and why I'm on foot, and am I alone, and every other thing conceiv-able: and when I set up my tripod (sometimes, as a great treat) there are cries of astonishment and 'Mashallah's', 'by the life of the Prophet', 'Heavens', 'Give God the glory' etc. etc. Such a curiosity has never been seen and all the village is summoned to look at it. Then I am asked about my wife and children, how many I have etc. I really feel a little ashamed of my youth out here. The Syrian of 16 is full grown, with moustache and beard, married, with children, and has perhaps spent two or three years in New York, getting together enough capital to start him in business at home. They mostly put my age as 15, and are amazed at my travelling on foot and alone. Riding is the only honourable way of going, and everyone is dreadfully afraid of thieves: they travel very little. However meanwhile the women have been getting my evening meal, served up on one of those large straw dishes I mentioned: (the 'charger' for John the Baptist's head is translated by this in the Arabic version) then they pour water on my hands from a pitcher (they have spouts like Breton cider jugs — I'll bring one home) and if very polite, will offer to wash my feet. The next thing is bed, which is the same quilt as that on which I am sitting, laid either in the house, or outside on the roof of an outbuilding or verandah. Another quilt on top acts as blanket and also there are pillows. These quilts are of course far too hot for a European to stand, since they are stuffed with wool, and feathers and fleas (in about equal quantities I fancy), so usually I lie on both mine, and hope for the best. One goes to bed soon after 9, and gets up at sunrise (about 4.30). Dressing consists of smoothing one's hair, and moistening one's hands and face in the stream from the pitcher: then on the road after bread and leben. Sometimes the people of the house will take money for one's lodging, sometimes not.

The houses are usually of one storey, built of mud, with door and unglazed window, shuttered in the daytime. The floor is of clay, very often of two levels, the upper for the humans, the lower for animals, with mangers in between (The animals are usually goats: sometimes cows; or even a horse). Over the floor are laid rush-mats, of long reeds 5 feet long and an inch across. There is no furniture except a few little stools, of wood and rush (about 8 inches high) a large chest, often inlaid, with bone or mother-of-pearl, and the straw dishes hanging on the walls. There will also be a large bedlike recess, for holding the quilts: in better class houses the room will be situated above the stables, and so at the end will be a kind of veranda, or terrace: the roofs of the dwelling rooms are not usually used. When they are pieces of mud drop all night through the brush and poplar poles that hold them up. The people are pleasant: very childish and simple of course, and startlingly ignorant, but so far quite honest. Very many of the men in all the mountain villages have visited America, and they love to display their English before their fellow-villagers. Once or twice they have tried to overcharge me excessively, but to their minds every Englishman is a Croesus: so one can hardly blame them. They usually wear baggy trousers, and short coats, or shirts, with a sash round their waist, but further from the coast they approximate nearly to the Bedouin dress: for head-gear, sometimes the fez, sometimes the keffiyeh, the black coiled rope of the desert Arab. They all carry revolvers, some of them guns, and you see them ploughing in the fields, or eating at home in a belt of 150 cartridges: enough for a campaign: however I had better get back to Sidon. All along the coast of course I skirted the Lebanon; from underneath a hill in Palestine looks entirely barren: from on top one finds that it is all terraces and has been cultivated: now all the corn is cut so that all day one walks over varying greys, and browns, and whites, and reds, never a touch of green, except small thorny oaks or at times a fig tree where there is water under the surface: one does so rejoice in a spring! There was nothing interesting on my road, except the place where according to the Arabs Jonah was cast ashore. Sidon was interesting, its streets are so narrow, and all built over above with houses: some were so narrow that 2 men could only with difficulty pass, and in others I had to bend even my head to pass: no wheeled vehicle can enter the gates. There are two castles, one standing on a mound of purple shells: neither very interesting: it is astonishing to see the number of antiquities dug up continually in Sidon: the neighbourhood is a perfect treasure ground. I was offered a small, perfect, Anadyomene (2nd Cent. B.C. probably) for £60; the lucky man bought it from the finder for £5! There are other nice pieces of carving, and terracottas, much glass, and dozens of seal-stones (many forged) however those do not appeal to you. From Sidon (this letter is getting too long) I had a long hot walk over waterless hills to Nabatiyeh, the Metawileh (Xtian[1]) Headquarters in the hills. It

---

[1] Actually a Moslem sect.

is near the elbow that the lower course of the Litani makes: as
the town was in fête I had the usual things to look at, the people
in the shops chaffering over infinitesimal sums, sweetmeat sellers,
the icedrink man who sells syrups, crying out 'Take care of thy
teeth' or 'Refresh thy heart', 'This for a metallik' ($\frac{1}{2}$d), or the man
with plain water in a goatskin with brass spout, then the fruit-
sellers, 'if an old woman eats my cress she is young tomorrow';
and funniest of all men with women's ornaments crying 'appease
your mother-in-law', and then as you are looking on at this comes
a hoarse gasp of 'dahrak' (your back) and a porter crashes into
you with a fresh-killed sheep on his back, or a load of charcoal,
or perhaps a camel loafs through the crowd with its bell round
its neck giving notice. If anyone neglects this warning they are
knocked down like ninepins: camels seem irresistible. They are
extraordinarily common at this season for all the corn of Bashan
and the Hauran and Esdraelon is coming down to the coast, and
all the nomads, who draw to the Jordan in summer for its water,
hire out their stock to the farmers. It is very sweet listening to
the ringing of the varied bells of a caravan of half a hundred
camels in a valley: all the roughness of the tone, and the growling
and grunting and cursing of the animals themselves is lost at a
little distance. They have horrible faces, and keep up a running
flow of apparently the most fearful language as they walk: a
camel always looks discontented, and apparently never misbehaves. However I can't discuss the town life this letter, or nobody
will ever get to bed (from a strict sense of duty to an absent
brother of course). At Nabatiyeh I got a guide or chaperon or
whatever you like to call it (male!) to go to Banias whose people
have the finest castle, and the worst reputation in S. Lebanon.
First of all though we went to a splendid castle Kalaát el S'ch'k'if
(perhaps you had better call it Beaufort) a fine fortress (early xiii)
well situated above the Litani about 1600 above sea level. The
view was very good up and down the said sea coast, and along
the Litani gorge for 20 miles. A stone I threw from the chapel
windows fell spattering after two rebounds into the river 1600
feet below. Across the low foothills and plain of the Jordan
springs to the E. we could see Hermon, still with snow in its
valleys, and the mountains of Bashan and to the North half the

Lebanon. Southward hills near Safed and Nazareth rather blocked the view. Still even so it was [*word illegible*] fine and very refreshing to catch a breeze, and find a spring of water on the top. We had then to get down to the river, which meant dancing down a goat path for an hour: the worst of it was my man proved to be a wonderful singer, the best of his district, and there was an echo in the gorge. He yelled all the time like a Syren (of the modern sort). Still just before we got to the bottom the sun managed to join (it only shines there at midday) so I had a delightful bathe. The river was shallow (up to 5 feet deep) with a raging current and full of rocks. No swimming was possible; one just hung on a rock and waved about in its eddy like a fish's tail. Still it served to wash the dust off. The banks of course were all oleanders so that generally the colouring was satisfactory. Unfortunately the water was very cold. We then climbed the other bank, fortunately only about a thousand feet high, and slept for the night in a village near the top and next day reached Banias, (Caesarea Philippi), on a hill above the plain of Huleh, the swampy lake North of Galilee. There is level ground intersected by numerous feeders of the Jordan which really rises from the lake, for some 5 miles to the N. of the water. Tell Arnie that pelicans are common, and ugly, and that jackals are too numerous to trouble much about. The Arabs call them 'ibn Wawi, sons of owls, from the noise they please themselves in making at night when one wants to go to sleep. Every stone has got its lizard on top or underneath, but scorpions and centipedes are rare, and snakes not very common. Of the other animals I have seen several herds of gazelles in the hills, and a few badgers and wolves. But Palestine is not a very inviting country for anything living. There is an ever-present plague of flies and everything in the world that bites. However we went across the plains with great joy for it meant soft roads and green fields until we reached Banias a small enough village now, but with a wonderful spring (you will find admirable descriptions in *The Crescent and the Cross* by Warburton or in *The Land and the Book* by Thompson, 'purple patches' both of them). Over the spring which rises in a hidden cave is a niche with Greek inscription mentioning Pan, who certainly might have had a hand in such a lovely water supply. Of course with that and the heat the vegetation is entirely tropical, and most delightful, after four days complete barrenness. The town was formerly fortified, but mostly Roman and Arab work I fancy: on top of a hill about 700 feet high however above the town is a much finer fortress. The view is extraordinary, one of the finest in Syria according to Baedeker. [5 *words omitted*] Still it is a castle 500 yards long, on a spur of Hermon, and has got in one place rudimentary machicoulis like those of Château Gaillard, so I was very satisfied with it. I got all over the place, and at last set fire to the brushwood in the inner court which burnt all the morning. Still in the evening I profited, by seeing the building as a whole, as no other person can have done for 20 years; it was simply choked with rubbish. The owner was a little surprised but did not expostulate, as it was a courtyard inaccessible to anything but a mountaineer or a spider. He had never got to it (entrance on the 1st floor of course, and the walls elsewhere still intact). It must have made a jolly bonfire from a distance, for there was a space of 30 yards square of old thorn trees. Banias Mother will remember from Matthew xvi or Mark viii and other places. To read such extracts on the spot is certainly much the best way: it may be that the Transfiguration took place on one of the neighbouring spurs of Mt. Hermon: of course though that is not known, but it would be a very pleasantly appropriate place.

We went downhill again through the olive groves into the village after tipping the owner of the castle, and then found the villagers very anxious to murder my man, as he was a Christian and they were going to make a foray in that direction soon. However we cleared (they would not have ventured to touch him as long as he was with me for fear of the consequences) (international), to Tell-el-Kadi a mound about 3 miles off. It is about 30 feet high and crater-shaped inside and now quite deserted, but with plenty of real trees, and such a spring! cold as ice, (my water-melon cracked when he got in) and splendid in scale: it makes at once a pool about 4 feet deep and 60 feet across (and very pretty it is too) from which rush forth two wide streams, uniting almost at once to make a river the width of the Cherwell but infinitely faster, and about 3 feet deep. It is glorious, a river springing full grown from a pine grove. It is absolutely deserted without even an Arab tent upon it, and historically, well it is the Laish of Judges xviii, and subsequently Dan, which should be enough for most people. What a weird story that of those Danites is: I can understand them being confident to surprise the Sidonians: anyone would live carelessly in Tel-el-Kadi except for the malaria. Indeed Dan must have been used to surprises for Abraham came up with his kings there, and later on it was again captured. It is a lovely place. From Dan we passed to the site of Abel-Beth-Maachah, where Sheba was finally run to earth by Joab, and then over a rocky spur into a delightful valley with gardens, running streams, etc. There I enjoyed myself greatly for that was one of the hottest days of all. Then in the evening up 2000 feet to Hunin, where we slept. The castle there was trifling in strength but as for fleas! I wanted to plan a loophole in one tower, so stayed in it for about 10 minutes, and then found myself fairly black with them to the knees. The Arabs say that the king of the fleas lives in Tiberias, but I can guarantee that he has summer residences elsewhere as well! Next day I went on alone to Tibnin (borrow *The Land and the Book* if you want a purple (very purple) account of the defiles) where the castle might have been worse, and then struck South intending for Safed. On the way I had refreshment at the springs of Kades, Barak's native place, and then a terrific climb up from a valley and over undulating country into Safed, itself on a hill 2700 feet high. In the day's march I went up and down the height of Mt. Blanc — and Palestine is all like that: a collection of small irritating hills crushed together pell-mell, and the roads either go up and down all the time, or wind in and about the rocks of the valleys, and never reach anywhere at all. Nobody ever built a house except on a hill-top or half-way up, the path is only a piece of land from which the smaller stones have been pushed; all day one steps from one sharp rock to another, which is not only tiring to the feet but to the brain also for one has to be continually on the alert, to find the best place for the next step, and to guard against slips. As a result one is soon satisfied with that sort of road. The alternative is a field path which is much better; these paths are very easily made and have an odd trick of dying away in the middle of a square mile of thistles from one to

three feet high of a blue grey colour and very hard. To walk
through them for any length of time is rather painful: one acts
as a pincushion. I got in the evening to Safed, a large town but
without a hotel: still I tried the English doctor (of the Hospital
of the Jews Mission) and he gave me a most admirable reception.
I stayed 4 nights and thoroughly refreshed myself. Mrs. Anderson (their name) comes from Abingdon and has 4 children out
here. They were exceedingly kind to me. I wanted plenty of
water for washing of all kinds! He is very anxious to get a young
medical colleague for he is *slightly* overworked (with about 250
out-patients a day and a big hospital full of better specimens and
half a hundred other things besides). From the castle (good)
⅔rds of the Holy Land is visible. I had great sport in an underground passage that is being excavated: xiii century work I think.
From Safed I visited Chastellet, now called the bridge of the
daughters of Jacob for some unknown reason: it is the main link
with the beyond-Jordan Arabs and crosses the river just below
Lake Huleh. I then walked down the Jordan valley to the lake of
Galilee and home past the site of Chorazin — all thistles for miles.
Next day I got going again and descended from Safed to Tell-
Hum (Capernaum) from which there was a beautiful view across
the Lake. The place itself has ruins, possibly those of a synagogue,
but those have been walled in by the Franciscans so it is pleasanter
to sit under the oleanders on the actual shore. The view is not
grand, the hills on either side of the lake are not high, and to the
S. is a level part of the Jordan Valley, but they are very pleasantly
broken up, with plenty of light and shade, in a brown purple tint.
The lake itself is very blue and always moving: never quite calm,
as seen from Capernaum there is not one dominating feature in
the whole — it is just a pretty little inland sea, without sign of
human occupation. The water is lukewarm, but quite fresh and
wholesome swarms of fish. There are of course no woods or trees
only oleanders everywhere. From there I walked along the plain
of Gennesaret to Tiberias. The plain is very fertile and very
highly cultivated, and the lake gives abundance of water: it is
the best place I have found yet in Palestine. Imagine walking on
a grass path (real grass green) by the water's edge through
oleander shrubs, which sometimes meet above one's head, and

were all in bloom: the actual beach, where the grass does not grow
in the water, is of a beautiful white sand — altogether charming.
This lasted for about 3 miles, then I reached Magdala, and had to
stumble along a rocky path for an hour into Tiberias. Tiberias is
a hot, dirty, not unpicturesque old town, with a lovely port, where
the fishermen loaf about all day: the circuit of the walls is interesting. Then I walked down the lake-side to its Southern end where
the Jordan leaves it, and down the river valley for miles. It was a
fair road, but it is such a comfort to *know* that the country was not
a bit like this in the time of Our Lord. The Renaissance painters
were right, who drew him and his disciples feasting in a pillared
hall, or sunning themselves on marble staircases: everywhere one
finds remains of splendid Roman roads and houses and public
buildings, and Galilee was the most Romanized province of
Palestine. Also the country was well-peopled, and well watered
artificially: There were not 20 miles of thistles behind Capernaum!
and on the way round the lake they did not come upon dirty,
dilapidated Bedouin tents, with the people calling to them to
come in and talk, while miserable curs came snapping at their
heels: Palestine was a decent country then, and could so easily
be made so again. The sooner the Jews farm it all the better:
their colonies are bright spots in a desert. From the Jordan
valley I climbed about 2000 feet to Belvoir, a castle, and then in
a straight line went through Endor to Nazareth seeing Nain on
my left. There is nothing outstanding in any of these except the
village spring at Nazareth, a most uniquely interesting spot. I
think I sent home a couple of postcards of it. From Nazareth I
went past the plain of Esdraelon to Harosheth where Sisera's
mother looked out of the lattice, and pictured her son dividing up
the spoil; what a glorious poem that is![1] The plain was very good;
so fertile, and all the people of the villages engaged in harvesting
and threshing: they take tents out and live in the fields, while
strings of camels and asses carry the corn to the threshing floors.
When the straw has been broken up and separated from the
wheat by the flint-studded sledge they fling it into the air and
winnow it, and then each man stamps his heap of grain with a
large sign so that no one can take away from his pile undetected:

[1] *Judges*, v.

and there are a thousand other things they do — I could write hours longer than you could read, if I haven't done so already! From Harosheth I crossed the back of Carmel, over the place of sacrifice, (one of the loveliest views in the world perhaps in spring), where the Druses still celebrate Elijah's [sacrifice], to Athlit, and so to Haifa. Then to Acre, so quaint and unspoiled a town, to Kala'at Ka'arn,[1] to Scandalium, to Tyre, to Sarepta, to Sidon, and so back to Beyrout. Tomorrow I hope to start N. up the coast to Latakieh, then inland to Antioch, next to Aleppo, and then across the Euphrates to Edessa and back again by train from Aleppo to Beyrout and home. I will try to send a line from Aleppo, in about 3 or 4 weeks, and perhaps a wire before starting back. NED

14: TO HIS BROTHER, A. W. LAWRENCE[2]

5.8.[09]

TO BE READ ALL BY HIMSELF. *Specially Well Written*

Dear Worm,[3] I'm going to stay one more day in Beyrout, and then going N. Tell Mother I have sent a long letter to her, which will reach you soon: it went yesterday, but by a longer road than this one I expect. It will tell you everything I mean to do. Father told me you had been top of the Form; that is *very* proper! Did you get any prizes? These stamps cost a lot, so take care of them: they are the Turkish set. The other 3 (10 paras, 20 paras, and 1 piastre) are of the Austrian Post Office: there are also English, French, German and Russian post-offices here, all with stamps. As they are going to do away with them soon, I will buy sets, while I can. The post-offices used to be necessary, for till a year ago the Turkish Post-Office was very bad. Remember that 40 paras make 1 piastre and that a piastre is worth from $1\frac{3}{4}$d. to $2\frac{1}{2}$d; in the shops they only count them as $1\frac{3}{4}$ d. In the Government things, (railways and post-offices) they are worth $2\frac{1}{2}$d. You

---

[1] The Crusader Castle of Montfort or Starkenberg.

[2] Aged nine.

[3] His joke of addressing his brother as 'Worm' and of offering 'loud worms', also 'loud snores', by way of greeting was repeated. See letters Nos. 283 and 322. The old meaning of dragon was in his mind. In one letter he wrote of 'embattled worms' outside the residence of Lord Lloyd when Governor of Bombay.

would be amused at the Turkish money: gold is never used, only a thing about as big as a 5/- piece worth 3/6 of silver, and then a copper cart-wheel worth 6d., and 10 little things like bronze 3d. pieces which go to make this cartwheel. So if you carry much Turkish money with you, you must have a porter to carry it. Once I had 25 bishlik's (the 6d. cart-wheels) in my pocket at once, and I felt quite off my balance.

I must stop now: offer my worms to Mother, Father, Bob, Will and Frank, when you see them, and take great care of Mother: I want her to get quite strong, so as to be able to come out here for a trip with me in a couple of years.

I hope you are happy in Jersey: try 'Prosit' to drink if the water is still bad, but the newspaper says that you have been having a lot of wet weather: it sounds so funny to me out here, because it is never wet or dull. Still then I expect Madame Pierre's well will be full. Loud worms to yourself,   NED

15: TO HIS MOTHER

29,8,09   *Latakia*

Dear Mother, Another chance for a note, this time hurried. I wrote last from Tripoli. I went thence to Aarka, and then to Kala'at el Hosn, passing one night on a house roof, and the second in the house of an Arab noble, reputed, as I was told next day, of the highest blood; a young man very lively, and rather wild, living in a house like a fortress on the top of a mountain: only approachable on one side, and there a difficult staircase. If you keep this note I can tell you all sorts of amusing things about him later: name Abdul Kerim. He had just bought a Mauser, and blazed at everything with it. His bullets must have caused terror to every villager within a mile around. I think he was a little cracked. Then I got to Hōsn which is I think the finest castle in the world: certainly the most picturesque I have seen — quite marvellous: I stayed 3 days there with the Kaimmakam, the governor: a most-civilised-French-speaking-disciple-of Herbert-Spencer-Free-Masonic-Mahommedan-Young Turk: very comfortable. — He sent an escort with me next day to Safita, a *Norman keep, with original battlements*: The like is not in Europe: *such a find*. Again I slept with Kaimakam & Co. (Co. here means fleas) and next day I went on again with a huge march, to two more castles, & a bed for the night in a threshing floor, on a pile of tibn, chopped straw, listening to the Arabs beating out their dhurra in the moonlight: they kept it up all night in relays, till about 2 a.m. when they woke me up, & said they were all exhausted, would I keep watch because there were thieves, & I was an Inglezi and had a pistol: I obliged, thinking it was humbug of the usual sort, (every village distrusts its neighbour) but they told me in Tartus next day that there really were not thieves, but *landlords* about! Isn't that charming? These dear people wanted to hide the extent of their harvest. Next day as above I went to Tartus, by another good castle: then struck far inland, (through a country of flint and steel and handmills, to Masyad, the chief city of the Assassins country: and then to Kadmus another of that gentry's strongholds, where the 'Old Man of the mountains' himself lived: (I slept in his château[1]) and so to Aleika, to Margat, a castle about as big as Jersey I fancy: one wanted a bicycle to ride round it: to another Banias, to Jebeleh, and here to Latakia, all well.

Monday I want to get off to Sahyun, and then in 4 or 5 days to Antioch, and then to Aleppo in 5. I hope there to hear from you because Bob's going to Germany is in the nature of an experiment: he will have better food than I have — last week only bread, & that bad: this is a considerable town however, with native restaurants. I have got to like leben. No smoking yet, though every man woman and child does. The peasants dry and smoke their own. I will have such difficulty in becoming English again: here I am Arab in habits, and slip in talking from English to French and Arabic unnoticing, yesterday I was 3 hours with an Orleannais, talking French, and he thought at the end I was a compatriot. You may be happy, now all my rough work is finished successfully, and my thesis is *I think assured*. *Iradé[2] invaluable*.

---

[1] Demolished by Ibrahim Pasha in 1838!

[2] Lawrence carried *Iradés* or letters of protection from the Sultan obtained for him by Lord Curzon, then Chancellor of Oxford University.

16: TO HIS MOTHER

Dear Mother, I arrived here all right yesterday, but found no letters from you: I have wired to Beyrout in case you mistook my directions: I hope nothing has happened. I wrote to you from Latakia: on the Monday I went from there to Sahyun, perhaps the finest castle I have seen in Syria: a splendid keep, of Semi-Norman style, perfect in all respects: towers galore: chapels; a bath (Arabian) and a Mosque: gates most original: and a rock-moat 50 feet across in one part, 90 feet in another, varying from 60-130 feet deep: there's a cutting for you! And in the centre had been left a slender needle of rock, to carry the middle of a drawbridge: it was I think the most sensational thing in castle-building I have seen: the hugely solid keep upstanding on the edge of the gigantic fosse. I wish I was a real artist. There were hundreds of other points of interest in the buildings. I stayed there two days, with the Governor, who was most obliging and then came on here by forced marches, 120 miles in 5 days, which no doubt Bob or Will will laugh at, but not if they had to do it stumbling and staggering over these ghastly roads: it took me 13 hrs. of marching per day, & I had an escort with me (mounted) so I lost no time. By the way it is rather amusing to contemplate a pedestrian guarded carefully by a troop of light horse: of course everybody thinks I am mad to walk, and the escort offered me a mount on the average once a half-hour: they couldn't understand my prejudice against everything with four legs. My trip was part of the time through very lovely country, almost English in parts: and also up rocky defiles, *packed with ruins*, Xian, of the vth and vith cent. mostly: massive basilicas and pandocheions and lauras: private houses a few: tombs in abundance: inscriptions were all in Greek: in parts of my journey I seem to have been the first European visitor.

At Harim I found a Crusading castle, too ruined & rebuilt to be valuable, with underground passages that would have rejoiced the rest of the world: I explored them with candles, followed by a very reluctant escort, swearing it smelt 'jinns': ask Arnie what a jinn is; I certainly smelt a lot of things: but didn't see anything. The passages went to water-springs etc. From Harim I paid a flying visit to Antioch, to see the walls; miles long: the modern town is not one-tenth the size of the old one. I didn't enter it, but broke away E. in a hurry here: over about the worst road on the face of the globe (or anywhere else on its body). Aleppo is European, with a decent hotel: much washing, for I hadn't had a bathe for 10 days (or any other kind of wash!). I am afraid I have to drive from here to Urfa (Edessa) which is going to cost me about £7: so bang go my proposed purchases in Damascus: I'm very sorry — but must make haste: wish the letters had arrived. Telegraphing is such slow work out here, & there is no telephone. Why can't somebody invent an occupation for flies? They have too much leisure: all this district is plagued with them & mosquitoes. My noble stockings have succumbed at last; 3 holes lately: but I have only the one pair with me (economy!) and they have now done 450 miles: not bad, because they are thin wool. Boots are worn out, but will perhaps last me through. I don't want to have them soled. By the way, I took the escort abused above because I was shot at near Masyad: an ass with an old gun: I suppose he was trying it. At any rate he put in a shot at about 200 yards, which I was able to return rather successfully: for his horse promptly bolted about half a mile: I think it must have been grazed somewhere: at any rate he stopped about 800 yards away to contemplate the scenery, & wonder how on earth a person with nothing but a pistol could shoot so far: & when I put up my sights as high as they would go & plumped a bullet somewhere over his nut he made off like a steeple-chaser: such a distance was far beyond his old muzzle-loader. I'm rather glad that my perseverance in carrying the Mauser has been rewarded, it is rather a load but practically unknown out here. I complained of course to the governor of the district: who was furious, and sent out all his police at once: he agreed with me however that the man simply wanted to frighten me into money-payment: no success for him. I am now of course far beyond any disturbed country, and there is no chance of a repetition of the joke: which is why I tell you: it is not very sensational I fear. I hope to reach Damascus in about a fortnight, but of course that depends on Urfa: I hope all is well at home: and that Jersey came up to expectation but I can't say more, being in ignorance: my last letter was dated July 16th, and no newspaper here.

NED

[On September 22nd Lawrence wrote to his mother to say he was coming home at once for lack of money, in a letter which is full of suppressions of alarming facts. Thus he said that his stomach had never been upset 'I suppose my exercise, etc. (I have walked 1100 miles) is responsible for my health'. He admitted, however, that his feet were in a bad state — and further long walks would be imprudent — besides which he would need a new camera for his had been stolen from a carriage while the coachman was asleep. 'I find an absurd canard in the Aleppo paper of a week ago: my murder near Aintab (where I didn't go) . . . The hotel people received me like a ghost. Mr. Edvard Lovance sounds like me.'

The following letter to Sir John Rhys puts a very different complexion on the matter. For the camera had not been stolen from a carriage but taken when he was 'robbed and rather smashed up'.

Fuller accounts of this incident, which are not quite reconcilable, are to be found in Graves's *Lawrence and the Arabs*, p. 19, and in Pirie-Gordon's memoir in *T. E. Lawrence by his Friends*, p. 74. According to the latter he was attacked by Kurds who beat him and left him for dead. They took most of his clothes and his money, but left his collection of Hittite seals and a map, which, stained with blood, is now in Mr. Pirie-Gordon's possession. I believe that in this passage of the Oxford text of *Seven Pillars of Wisdom*, after describing the ghastly flogging he endured at Deraa, Lawrence refers to this incident.

> I struggled to my feet and rocked unsteadily for a moment wondering that it was not all a dream, and myself back five years ago in hospital at Khalfati, where something of the sort had happened to me.

In the Subscribers' edition he altered the wording to 'five years ago, a timid recruit at Khalfati, where something less staining of the sort, had happened'.

Khalfati [Halifeti] is between Aintab and Urfa. If I am correct in my interpretation, it was eight years. Five years would make it 1912. It is quite possible there was such an incident then, but I have found no record of it.

It was typical of Lawrence's consideration for his mother to write about his good digestion and to say 'I suppose my exercise is responsible for my health', after having had four attacks of malaria, and having been so badly smashed up by Kurds that he was not fit to travel.]

17: TO SIR JOHN RHYS[1]

Sept. 24 [1909]   *Hotel Baron Aleppo*

Dear Sir John Rhys, I had asked my father to call on the College and explain to whoever was in residence that circumstances prevented my return in time for the beginning of term, but afterwards I thought that your kindness in the matter of obtaining those letters through Lord Curzon demanded a letter from me to yourself.

I have had a most delightful tour (the details naturally won't interest you) on foot and alone all the time, so that I have perhaps, living as an Arab with the Arabs, got a better insight into the daily life of the people than those who travel with caravan and dragomen. Some 37 out of the 50 odd castles were on my proposed route and I have seen all but one of them: many are quite unpublished, so of course I have had to make many plans, drawings and photographs. As a sideline I have bought about 30 Hittite seals. Mr. Hogarth asked me before I started to bring him back any I came across. Worthy ones will go into the collection in the Ashmolean.

My excuse for outstaying my leave must be that I have had the delay of four attacks of malaria when I had only reckoned on two: even now I am exceedingly sorry to leave the two Castles in the Moabite deserts unvisited.[2] I would go to them certainly, only that last week I was robbed & rather smashed up. Before I could be fit for walking again (and it is very hard physically in this country) the season of rains would have begun. It is most unfortunate, for the getting here is expensive: the actual travelling, my beggar-fashion, costs practically nothing of course.

[1] Sir John Rhys, archaeologist and first Professor of Celtic at Oxford, was Principal of Jesus College.
[2] Kerak and Shobek, east and south-east of the Dead Sea.

F

I expect therefore to return to college on the 15th. The loss of a week will not I hope be considered an unpardonable offence. Believe me, yrs. sincerely   EDWARD LAWRENCE

P.S. If my father should be happy enough to meet you personally please don't mention the matter of the robbery: I want to be returned reasonably whole before it comes out. Lord Curzon's *Iradés* were invaluable in the matter: they stirred up the local authorities to a semblance of energy, so that the man was caught in 48 hours. Before this I had employed them innumerable times: in fact without them there would have been several times unpleasantnesses.   E.L.

[On his return Lawrence naturally wrote to Doughty.]

18: TO C. M. DOUGHTY

Nov. 30,09   *Jesus College, Oxford*

Dear Sir, You may remember my writing to you in the beginning of the year, to ask your opinion on a walking tour in Northern Syria. That has ended happily (I reached Urfa Edessa my goal) and the Crusading Fortresses I found are so intensely interesting that I hope to return to the East for some little time. It struck me that I ought to see you first (having been scorned by an Arab near Lake Huleh, for not knowing you), and so I asked Mr. Hogarth if it were possible. He gave me the enclosed, but I confess that I am more interested in the author of *Dawn In Britain* and *Arabia Deserta* than in the traveller. I hope though that you will not put me out of court therefore, since there are really some points on which I wanted your advice. If you are willing — then I am due in Eastbourne about the 15th or 16th of next month (December). Of course that would not prevent my coming down earlier or later, if you wished.

This whole letter sounds rather offensively inane, but your books are at any rate the begetters of it.

I would be most delighted if you could fix a day.

Believe me, Yours sincerely,   EDWARD LAWRENCE

[When Lawrence was still a schoolboy in 1904, he had got to know Leonard Green, then an undergraduate at St. John's College, Oxford. The two friends took a fearful pleasure in breaking the regulation which forbids a schoolboy to visit an undergraduate in his rooms. After Lawrence's return from Syria they had a project of buying a windmill on a headland above the sea, where they would set up a press to print rather precious books which should be bound in vellum stained with Tyrian dye. Lawrence had brought jars of crushed murex back from Syria. The following letter is about Green's writings.]

19: TO LEONARD GREEN

Feb. 16. [1910]

This is *fine* the best of them all: some of the other people were rather too shadowy: like abstractions dissecting themselves (what would an abstraction find if it dissected itself?): but this is genuine flesh & blood: and uncommonly good at that. It is one of the best things of its class I have ever read: so please don't go & develop a sense of sin or anything prurient.

Don't polish it overmuch: there is perhaps the 'wind in the trees' too many times — but I can't criticise what is so obviously right. Wherefore go ahead & conquer (though I bet you will have a hunt for a publisher, until I set up).

Please continue pouring: if the rain is to be of this quality. It is something entirely new to me in style & substance: no Pater no Wilde (to speak of . . .) no anybody:

I know you will appreciate the sense of form in *this* letter. Yr.   E.L.

[Very similar plans for setting up a hand-press and retiring from the world were made with another friend, V. W. Richards, and these came near realization after the war, when Lawrence bought Pole Hill, near Chingford.

The friendship was lasting and important and Mr. Richards has given his own account of it in *Portrait of T. E. Lawrence*. Early in their friendship Lawrence began buying medieval oak beams to be used in building a hall. For many years Richards took charge of Lawrence's books, and they shared many things in common.

During 1910, Lawrence paid three visits to France: in June, in August with his brother Frank, and for a day or two in November to examine the collection of medieval pottery at Rouen Museum, making use of letters of introduction from M. Salamon Reinach. He intended submitting a thesis on pottery, at which he had worked at the Ashmolean Museum from the time he was a schoolboy. Indeed he knew far more about the collection of pots than any of the Museum staff at that time. Naturally some of his datings of pottery have since been proved wrong.]

20: TO V. W. RICHARDS

[Postmark, 19.6.1910]   *[Post Card of Beauvais Cathedral]*

Of course the nave was never built, only choir & transepts — It is better than ever this place; inside the most glorious choir ever dreamed of, & outside ... the houses of the town look ridiculous clinging round its feet — mere doll's houses inhabited by ants. Do come over & have a look at it; it is the sort of place that can never be forgotten — or imagined.   L.

21: TO HIS MOTHER

August 1910   *Le Petit Andelys*

[31 *lines omitted*] The book I had was *Petit Jehan de Saintré*, a xv Cent. novel of knightly manners — very good: — I have wanted to read it for a long time, but the Union copy was so badly printed that I had not the heart for it. Now I have found (for 1 f. 25) a series quite nicely typed on fairly good paper. So far I have only got 4 volumes, because they are rather much to carry: it is altogether glorious to have found good French books at last. I can read Molière and Racine and Corneille and Voltaire now: — a whole new world. You know, I think, the joy of getting into a strange country in a book: at home when I have shut my door and the town is in bed — and I know that nothing, not even the dawn

— can disturb me in my curtains: only the slow crumbling of the coals in the fire: they get so red and throw such splendid glimmerings on the Hypnos and the brasswork. And it is lovely too, after you have been wandering for hours in the forest with Percivale or Sagramors le desirous, to open the door, and from over the Cherwell to look at the sun glowering through the valley-mists. Why does one not like things if there are other people about? Why cannot one make one's books live except in the night, after hours of straining? and you know they have to be your own books too, and you have to read them more than once. I think they take in something of your personality, and your environment also — you know a second hand book sometimes is so much more flesh and blood than a new one — and it is almost terrible to think that your ideas, yourself in your books, may be giving life to generations of readers after you are forgotten. It is that specially which makes one need good books: books that will be worthy of what you are going to put into them. What would you think of a great sculptor who flung away his gifts on modelling clay or sand? Imagination should be put into the most precious caskets, and that is why one can only live in the future or the past, in Utopia or the Wood beyond the World. Father won't know all this — but if you can get the right book at the right time you taste joys — not only bodily, physical, but spiritual also, which pass one out above and beyond one's miserable self, as it were through a huge air, following the light of another man's thought. And you can never be quite the old self again. You have forgotten a little bit: or rather pushed it out with a little of the inspiration of what is immortal in someone who has gone before you.   NED

[5 line postscript omitted]

22: TO V. W. RICHARDS

le 29 Août [1910]   *Carentan*

The spirit is moving me to write to you tonight, & I suppose it will furnish me with words, for otherwise I have nothing to tell you. It should properly be your turn, to tell me about Salcombe in August, & your intentions, & the state of the Exchequer, and many other things.

For the rest when are you going to get into Northern France?
Take someone with you, or go alone to Rheims,[1] and sit down at
the base of the sixth pilaster from the West on the South side of
the nave aisle, and look up between the fourth and fifth pillars at
the third window of the clerestory on the North side of the nave.
Take all the direction in at a gulp, and find yourself looking at an
altogether adorable mist of orange and red, such a ruby, and
such a gold as I have seen nowhere else in glass. And here it is
all in a maze of colours, blended to despair, without a suspicion
of pattern or form in it. One can imagine saints & angels &
medallions and canopies, but without the smallest reason or
foundation. It is pure colour, perfect — . I don't suppose there
was a piece of glass in it of one colour more than 3 inches square
(in a window of 30 feet) and it stained the floor of the nave (there
being no chairs) an indescribable blend. The sun only came
through it about five o'clock, and the 'purple patch' climbed
from the floor up one of the pillars, and faded into grey, but while
it lasted I came to myself & abjured presumption & Rossetti
saints. We can't do it! or at any rate I can't and you are little
more ancient (i.e. mediaeval). Go also to Lisieux, the most perfect
town (all superlatives tonight) of wooden houses in Normandy.
Every other house at least is old, & I think two out of three, and
they have wooden pillars and brackets, & crochets & corbels,
and dormers, and gables, and barge-boards, & ravishing little
pillarettes alongside the windows, and gargoyles on the gutters,
with carved lintels & side posts, and many-beamed ceilings, and
an inn staircase with a roughly squared oak-trunk across its
midst, so that all people going up or down had to bow their heads
& do obeisance to sir beam, and the irreverent suffered. You
know Montaigne used to write up his best-liked saws & instances
on his rafters;[2] what do you think of something piquant and to the
point, on the business part of the log with which you are going to
block your staircase? I can't for the life of me think of anything
else to tell you: except that thin tile-like bricks look lovely and

---

[1] I have not been able to include Lawrence's description of Chartres which moved him
more deeply than any building and any sculpture he had seen. The letter from Chartres
is the most beautiful and emotional of his early letters.

[2] These are still to be seen. Lawrence had visited Montaigne the year before; see
letter 12.

that I like tall, narrow, much splayed & round-headed windows.
As you don't, accept this as the swan-song of one other part of
my independence & conceit.

Would it bore you (somewhat before Oct 2) to inquire of
Hollings what would be the cost of the first edition of Doughty,
the *Arabia Deserta*, published by the Cambs. Univ. Press about
20 years back? Also of a copy (now out of print) of the *Wandering Scholar in the Levant* by D. G. Hogarth, one of the best travel
books ever written. If this latter is reasonable in price (under
10/- c'est à dire) get it, and read it, sending the bill to 2 Polstead
Rd. which has strict orders to forward to me all things delicious,
or from you.

Now I am going to sleep, & tomorrow I am going on to Cher-
bourg, and on Wednesday I am going back into Normandy to
lose myself in the reading of some well-printed French books I
have found at last. A very cheap series, of which at the present
moment I am carrying 7. (Ye shades of light weights, & the
devotee of running shorts for comfort): but they really are jolly
books. Montaigne (2 vols), *Tristan and Iseult*, *Jehan de Saintré*,
xiiith cent. fabliaux, de Nerval & a French anthology.

[Lawrence took first class honours in history, partly on the
strength of his thesis *The Military Architecture of the Crusades*
(since published as *Crusader Castles*). D. G. Hogarth recommended him for a demyship at Magdalen College, Oxford,
and Lawrence set off for the Carchemish dig, then being begun
under Hogarth's leadership, for the British Museum, on the
Messageries Maritimes boat *Saghalien*. 'By extraordinary good
fortune' the boat kept breaking down. He thus had a day ashore
at Naples and another at Athens.]

23: TO HIS MOTHER

December 1910   *Messageries Maritimes*

[96 *lines omitted*] Before you reach Athens you pass through
green fields and over small streams, that effectually wash away

the taste and smell of the sea. The rail lands you in the midst of a very modern looking town of squares and gardens, with a character partly French but not wholly European or Asiatic; too bright for the one and too clean for the other. It was above all things quiet, the quietest town imaginable, with few trams, and those slow ones, no motors or bicycles and very few carts. The streets are usually asphalt-paved, and there seemed hardly any dogs to bark and fight. Even the vegetable-hawkers shouted like men, not like jackals or fog horns. Everywhere were palm trees and mimosa, with green lawns. I had to go back through the town to reach the Acropolis, and chose therefore to wander into by-streets, that I might come out at the Theseion; and the further I went the stronger became a curious sense of unreality, almost of nightmare. Here was a town full of people speaking the same tongue and writing the same character as the old inhabitants of 3000 years before. Some of them looked like what we know and hope the old Greeks were, others of them are visibly of the class of metics or βαναυσοι or freedmen, whom Aristotle so loudly scorned. The Athenians to whom he appealed were never more than a handful, a little party who held by themselves walking in the gardens, and looking out dispassionately upon the world around them: they had heard (as I did) tousled black-haired women calling loudly for their children Gorgo or Aristomenes, and they had seen (as I saw) the two women up the street hurrying breathlessly along, tiring their hair, to meet the procession of priests in vestments this time, but still the same undercurrent of back-biting and slander, and ill-natured comment of the neighbours. A cabbage-seller past me, before just such a sausage-stall as one had looked for in the street of Victory that leads to the Temple of Theseus, driving his ass, and chaffering with Demosthenes, a fisherman. It was all out of Aristophanes or Juvenal, all in keeping, so that it seemed quite natural when I walked up a little hill, and passed under the pillars of the temple. It stands today as perfect as ever it was, with the added beauty of the stains and hollows with which Time has endowed its stones. When you have passed around one of the angles of its cellar wall, you see framed between two pillars the sunlight on the steps of the Propylea and the pediment of the Erectheum. The rock of the

Acropolis is very large and high and steep. The quiet was really almost uncanny, as I walked up the shallow valley below Mars Hill, and along the processional way to the gateway of the citadel. There were no boys to bother one, no loud bellows'd leather sellers, only a misty sunlight in which all Attica, Phaleron, Salamis, Eleusis, and the distant Peloponnese lay motionless, 'drowned in deep peace', below the rock platform of the Wingless Victory. To get there I had to climb up the white marble staircase of the Propylea within the entrance gate. There were no porters, no guides, no visitors, and I walked through the doorway of the Parthenon, and on into the inner part of it, without really remembering who or where I was. A heaviness in the air made my eyes swim, and wrapped up my senses: I only knew that I, a stranger, was walking on the floor of the place I had most desired to see, the greatest temple of Athene, the palace of art, and that I was counting her columns, and finding them what I already knew. The building was familiar, not cold as in the drawings, but complex, irregular, alive with curve and subtlety, and perfectly preserved. Every line of the mouldings, every minutest refinement in the sculptures were evident in that light, and inevitable in their place. The Parthenon is the proto-cathedral of the Hellenes. I believe I saw the Erectheum, and I remember coming back to look again at the Propylea, and to stand again beside the Niké Apteros: but then I came down again into the town, and found it modern and a little different. It was as though one had turned from the shades of the ancestors, to mix in the daily vocations of their sons: and so only this about Athens, that there is an intoxication, a power of possession in its ruins, and the memories that inhabit them, which entirely prevents anyone attempting to describe or to estimate them. There will never be a great book on Athens unless it is one by an enemy: no one who knew it could resist its spell, except by a violent attack upon its spirit, and who can attack it now of artists, when Tolstoy is dead? He, and he alone, could have uprooted Greek culture in the world. I am coming back by Athens I think next year to stay a little time. For the present I am only confused with it: I do not know how much was Athens, and how much the colouring of my imagination upon it. **N.**

[The boat continued to break down. They were twenty-four hours in Smyrna and when they reached Constantinople 'the whole thing collapsed' and Lawrence was able to live on board the boat for a week, spending his days exploring the city.]

24: TO V. W. RICHARDS

Dec. 15, [1910]   *Constantinople*

You must not expect any tidings from me after this for some little time. I hope to reach Jebail in a week, & will settle there for six weeks or so, learning Arabic and Assyrian. As you will imagine I will not have leisure to do more than write perfunctory letters to my people. Concerning progress up to the present that is summed up in the words 'Athens' and 'Constantinople'. The first is glorious, the old town that is. Do you know that one can see the Acropolis framed in the pillars of the Theseion? and that the Acropolis is perfect, the Propylea, the Niké Apteros and the view from its platform, the Erectheum, the Parthenon. In books and drawings they look cold and mathematical, but in the flesh they are really alive with a most delightful variety of line and colouring. The curves and subtleties of modelling are as intricate as those of a Gothic cathedral, and the stains and colours in the marble more perfect than anything I have ever imagined. The marble when fresh is very greenish coloured, but it quickly turns gold, and not a smug, furniture-polish gold, but a modulation over all the tones and possibilities of gold, red, and yellow, and brown, in broad splashes, and the finest confusion of fine lines. It is altogether perfect, and if I go on any further I will only repeat myself, and annoy you out of imagining such an inspiration as is almost impossible.

The Propylea with their grand marble staircase are a very perfect prelude, almost too perfect, for the inside only just manages to be better: and you see the place in perfect quiet; there were no guides or tourists, or guards or refreshment stalls, or notices asking you not to spit: you can go anywhere you like without speaking a word. The day I went there was absolutely calm, and from Niké Apteros I could look over all Attica, Phaleron, Piraeus, Eleusis, Salamis, and the Peloponnese across the bay drowned in mist, and all in absolute peace: Athens (modern Athens) is the quietest of towns, without trams almost, no motors, no train whistles, no dogs even: so that there is never a sound from the outside to disturb the peace of the rock. I am going back.

Constantinople is as much life as Athens stood for sleep. It is a huge town, crammed with people, who all live and eat, and sleep in the streets apparently. All day the huge Galata bridge, on boats over the Golden Horn is pressed with a multitude of people, all foot-passengers, jostling each other, going all ways apparently. One cannot stand an instant without being hustled all over the road by passers by, or walk forward a yard without dodging to one side or other to avoid a carriage, or a pack of mules, or only a porter, with two asses' burden on his shoulders. The colour and movement in the streets are insurpassable: — Damascus is not within a call of it: — and besides there are glorious-coloured mosques, in blue and gold and cream and green tiles, and yellow glazed pottery of *exactly the shapes in England in the xivth cent.*, and a street, a whole street, of the most divine copper-ware. The modern stuff is sometimes good, more often polished after making till the hammer marks are ground away, or even machine pressed but in all the shops are the old out of date shapes exchanged for new, the wares of two or three generations back, perfect in shape and workmanship (before the French invasion), some bronze, some copper so heavy & thick, that they are not resold, but melted down, for the mere value of their metal. And I can't buy them, for I don't know Turkish: but I have bought a grammar, and started it: It won't be my fault if the hut is not full of old Turkish & Arab metal ware.

If you could only have seen the bronze water-cistern I saw yesterday.

25 : TO HIS MOTHER

Friday night, December 16 1910   *Messageries Maritimes Steamer*

[*56 lines omitted*] After the walls you have to jump to Turkish xvi century mosques for features of interest. I do not like them much. There seems to me to be a crudeness, a smallness of

conception and design about all their art. The Turks, when they
get a glorious broad wall-space and a deep porch, which should
rightly be bold sunshine and shadow, will insist on fretting the
wall into little confectionery-arcades, and on fitting up the porch
with bright coloured tiles. The result is you get a façade all of a
neutral strength, looking generally flat. To their eyes these petty
mouldings are delicacy sublime; but they certainly do not suit
my taste. There is a lack of sense of form, combined with a
perfection of detail, of ornament which I think runs through
most things oriental. The early Arab work is as fine as the
Mediaeval . . . but Turkish art in Constantinople is of a period of
decadence. These are of course only private opinions and a little
hasty. It may well be that in a little one's eyes get trained to seize
detail in the mass, and retain it. If so these mosques and palaces
are great, because their detail is unquestionably perfect. The
colours of the tiles are splendid, and the arabesques and the
intricacies of the inscriptions. I wish they had not had their
prejudice against the human form and the animal. Their inspiration is often dried up for lack of root. [118 *lines omitted*]

[On December 18th, Will Lawrence wrote to Leonard Green
to explain that as Ned was away he had opened Green's letter
before forwarding it, and was sending negatives of photographs of
Syrian castles for which Green had asked. He also sent the news
that Lawrence had been elected to the senior demyship at
Magdalen which would give him £100 a year for four years to
study his special subject, 'just now that is a mixture of Military
Architecture, Mediaeval Pottery, Cuneiform and Hittite Archaeology: not to mention History'.
Lawrence reached Syria in January 1911. In Aleppo he sought
out the last working maker of chain-mail in order to buy his tools
and study his methods on behalf of his friend Mr. C. J. ffoulkes.
The following letter is in answer to Leonard Green's asking
advice about lectures which he was giving on the Crusades. It is
in marked contrast to the youthful plans for living in a windmill.
Lawrence in his answer is concerned with the physical geography
of Syria from the point of view of a general conducting a military
campaign in it. It shows what an extremely clear grasp he already
had of the problems that he and Allenby would have to face
seven years later.]

26: TO LEONARD GREEN

[*Received January 14th*, 1911] *Jebail, Syria*

Dear Green, I am on a divan (anglicé — an American bentwood chair) inhaling haschich (a tannery next door but five) and dreaming of odalisques (who were upper-housemaids) and bulbuls. Your letter is a breath of Europe and things spiritual and sensual: most comfortable. You seem to be well placed in your particular post: to be your own master as much as you are, and to be able to put into practice (on such subjects!) some of your more attractive novelties must be fairly satisfactory. Only, I wish I could help the 'master of method' — that is if your assistance is not limited to providing materials for him to set straight.

Politics are quite shocking; I would like to have been in your audience tho', and to be one of your out-of-works: cannot a little writing be made out of that? There are opportunities there for one who does not attack it in a G. R. Sims[1] style?

Evidently your health is not yet quite on its sea-legs (those are things that prevent sickness). Your youths are the people most to be comforted.

Re your request: that I am afraid will be rather out of time, and I am most sorry for I have heaps of stuff I would have poured out on you: photographs are mostly labelled in ink on the films, and as they are entirely technical, to illustrate a discussion of military architecture, they will not avail you much. My camera was stolen before I could take anything interesting — I really meant to. I am writing to Will (long brother) to ask him to send you my thesis if it reappears in time for next term: you may find some ideas in it.

As for books, he is going on that to one of the best historians in Oxford. Von Sybel[2] says a few words, and Stevenson[3] in a book published a year or two back gives a sort of commentary: very dull but correct. 'E. Barker' (St. John's) in the new *Encyclopedia Brit.* would be most useful: if not out yet he might (through Will who

---

[1] Author-Journalist, and inventor of Tatcho for the Hair.
[2] *Geschichte des ersten Kreuzzuges.*
[3] *The Crusaders in the East,* by W. B. Stevenson.

has been useful to him) send you proofs. I fancy the book most suggestive to you would be Smith's *Historical Geography of Palestine*. It concerns S. Syria which I don't know, and biblical history, but the land and the strategical situation stayed much alike. It's a book worth reading anyway. Besides these there is only 'Archer and Kingsford' (*Story of Nations* series) and the map in Poole's Historical Atlas. The man more of all others in England who could help you would be C. H. C. Pirie-Gordon, 43 Kensington Mansions, Trebovir Road, Earl's Court, London: he is a 'young' Magd. graduate (24 or so) and is writing a book on the military organisation (specially geographical) of the Holy Land. If you wrote to him (say I told you to: — he is most original too —) he might expand upon you: or go & see him if you are in town.

What I felt most myself in Syria, put shortly, was the extreme difficulty of the country. Esdraelon, & the plain in which Baalbek lies are the only flat places in it. The coast road is often only 50 yards wide between hills and sea, and these hills you cannot walk or ride over, because they are strewn over with large & small boulders, without an inch of cultivated soil: also numberless small 'wadies' (torrent-beds) deep and precipitous: not to be crossed without a huge scramble. In one day's march, from Lake Huleh to Safed, one ascends & descends 16,000 feet in hills & valleys, often 1,500 feet deep & only 200 yards or so across, and in all the way only a single track path on which one can ride without fear of smashing horses' legs. Make a point that for heavy-armed horse operations in such country are impossible: they can march in single file, but cannot scout, or prepare against surprise: the battlefield of Hattin (near Tiberias) is like a dried lava-flow, or the photograph (only in rock) of the pack-ice of the Arctic seas. Blame the pen and ink not me for this letter's illegibility. Even when there are no mountains or rivers there will be hills & valleys enough, with rock-stretches, to make an impassable tract. You will never, without seeing it, conceive of the difficulty of the country. On the main road from Antioch to Aleppo my escort walked with their horses (after Harim) for nearly four hours: and for a Syrian to fare afoot is much against the grain.

The next point is the rivers: the Jordan is hardly passable

except at three points: just below Lake Huleh (Gisr Benat
Yakub, to-day: Castle Jacob or le Chastellet in the Crusade
authorities) a bridge & ford. Another ford just below lake
Tiberias, (near Semakh) and one more (very difficult) near
Jericho. The first two were available for or against the
Damascenes. From Lake Huleh northwards is a swamp & the
river Litani, until the hills get steep enough & high enough to be
impassable: and then (very quickly) comes the Orontes, which is
nearly always impassable (from Riblah downwards) to Esh
Shogr, on the road from Latakia (Laodicea) to Aleppo. There is a
ford there, and after a bridge near Antioch (the Iron Bridge).
Above Antioch came a large lake, and then very hilly ground
from the Kara Su to Alexandretta. So you see W. Syria is pretty
well defended. In the early days of the Latin kingdom they held
all this, and as well pushed across the Euphrates (via Harim, Tell
Bashar, and Biredjik) to Urfa (Edessa). This was a sort of outpost,
which kept apart the Arabs of Mesopotamia and the hills to the
north (Kurdistan) from the Arabs of E. Syria (Aleppo, Homs,
Damascus) and the Arabians. While the Crusaders held Edessa,
which is a tremendous fortress (of Justinian's) they were unassailable except through the Damascus gap, and one opposite Homs
(Emesa) extending to Tripoli. This last gap (which I forgot to
mention before) is a nearly sea-level pass between Lebanon & the
Nozairiyeh hills. It was defended by three tremendous Crusader
castles (Crac des chevaliers, in Arabic Kalaat el Hosn; Safita,
Chastel blanc in the French authorities; and Aarka, just above
Tripoli). These three places made this gap tolerably harmless,
except from Arab raids: these were continuous: but only did
temporary harm: still they neutralised the force of the county of
Tripoli[1] from 1140 onwards. The Damascus gaps were also
blocked: the northern one by Banias beyond Huleh, by Hunin,
above the lake, by Safed, and by Chastel Jacob, just beside the
ford, which last castle only existed a few months. Stevenson in his
book points out its importance rather more cheerfully than usual
with him. The Southern ford, below Lake Tiberias, was defended by the town of Tiberias by Kaukab el Hawa (one of the
Belvoirs, just above Beisan) and by an outpost, el Husn, occasion-

---

[1] The Count of Tripoli was one of the great princes of Crusader Syria.

ally held beyond Jordan: it is not marked on any map. The
Jericho ford was never very important. There were some little
Crusader castles on its Syrian side.

The whole history of the Crusades was a struggle for the
possession of these castles: the Arabs were never dispossessed of
Aleppo, or of Hamah, or of Homs, or of Damascus, and so they
had all possible routes open to them: they had unlimited resources
to draw upon, as soon as the Mesopotamians had recovered Urfa
(Edessa), which the Crusaders could not hold on account of its
isolated position (Euphrates 10 feet deep, 150 yards wide, very
rapid, & often flooded, much difficult hill thence to Seruj, &
even nearer Edessa) and the shiftiness of the Greek Armenian
population, who were allies, at times, but fighting men not at all:
more harm than good usually. The native population of Syria
very much sympathised with the Arabs, except the Maronite
Christians & the Armenians; and news travels amazingly in
the East: so that the Latins were more often surprised than not.
Any counter stroke in the nature of ambush against the Arabs
was impossible, since half their people were spies. Then in the
hills above Safita lived the Assassins (Haschishın) sometimes at
war with the Arabs, more often confederate, and linked with them
by an Orontes-bridge at Shaizar (Kalaat Seidjar). They could not
attack Tripoli because of the 'Gap' castles (see before) and
Markab (Margat) a huge fortress north of Tartus (another strong-
hold): but they could and did hold Antioch in check from the
South, while the Aleppines pressed on the Iron Bridge, and the
Greeks and Arabs attacked by Alexandretta & Beilan & Bagras
(the two last big castles). So Antioch could only just hold its
own, and the Tripoli castles, and when Damascus (Noureddin)
joined with the north, and added Egypt, Syria was ringed round.
The battle of Hattin was lost in an attempt to relieve Tiberias,
the second of the great 'gap' fortresses. Banias (the first) was lost
about 1150. For most of the occupation the Latin sphere of
influence was limited to their castles: the peasantry paid them
taxes, & wished for the Mohammedans to come: and come they
very often did, to plunder such Christian villages as were left.
So far as one can see they spared the Mohammedans. Latin
Syria lived on its fleets.

This is horribly condensed, & much platitudinous: if only I could tell you what you wanted to know: and there is no book written by a man who has been out, except Baedeker! Do emphasise the importance of the fortresses, which are all marked in a map in my 'thesis'. Salaams,   E.L.

[A letter of January 24th, 1911, shows that the project of starting a private printing press had been discussed with his parents but that he never had contemplated letting it take up all his time.

> You will see I think, that printing is not a business but a craft. We cannot sit down to it for so many hours a day, any more than one could paint a picture on that system. And besides such a scheme would be almost sure to interrupt *The Seven Pillars of Wisdom* or my monumental book on the Crusades.

This original *Seven Pillars of Wisdom* was described by him (letter No. 219) as:

> a youthful indiscretion book . . . . It recounted adventures in seven type-cities of the East (Cairo, Baghdad, Damascus, etc.) and arranged their characters into a descending cadence: a moral symphony. It was a queer book, upon whose difficulties I look back with a not ungrateful wryness: and in memory of it I so named the new book.

He burned the manuscript in August 1914.

Towards the end of February, Lawrence accompanied Hogarth and Gregori, Hogarth's Cypriote head-man, by sea to Haifa, where they visited the monastery on Mount Carmel before going on to Damascus by train. On the journey they saw Nazareth, 'no uglier than Basingstoke, or very little', the Yarmuk valley, and the pilgrims' route: 'the great Hajj road. Doughty is the only man who has been down it, and written what he saw'. The mountains were snow-covered, but Deraa was sunny; Hogarth talked Turkish and Greek and French, German and Italian. They reached Damascus late and went on next day to Aleppo.

In March they started work on the great mound at Carchemish, where Lawrence was to spend the greater part of the next three years.]

27: TO HIS MOTHER

March 31, 1911   *Jerablus*

Excuse this paper, and general appearance of letter. It is being
written on the mound, in a dull day of digging, with an empty
pen. The pen, by the way is a very distinct comfort out here.
Today we are moving great stones: the remains of walls and
houses are buried about $\frac{2}{3}$ of their height in fairly clean earth,
but the upper few feet are filled up with rubble, and small rocks,
with the ashlar masonry and concrete of the late Roman town.
Whenever we break fresh ground dozens of these huge blocks
have to be moved. Some of them weigh tons, and we have no
blasting powder or stone-hammers with us. As a result they have
to be hauled, prehistoric fashion, by brute force of men on ropes,
helped to a small extent by crowbars. At this moment something
over 60 men are tugging away above, each man yelling Yallah[1]
as he pulls: the row is tremendous, but the stones usually come
away. Two men out of three presume to direct operations, and no
one listens to any of them, they just obey Gregori's orders, and
their shouting is only to employ their spare breath. Now they
are raising the 'talul', the curiously vibrant, resonant wail of the
Bedawi. It is a very penetrating, and very distinct cry; you feel
in it some kinship with desert life, with ghrazzus[2] and camel-
stampedes. (Meanwhile the stone has slipped and fallen back
into the trench, and Gregori's Turkish is deserting him. Whenever he is excited he slips back into Greek in a high falsetto voice,
that convulses our hoarse-throated men.) To-day is a lovely day,
in the shade of the diggings as I am at present: outside it is a
little warm, with the usual streaming sunshine everywhere. We
have had no rain since we came to Carchemish, but generally
sun, with often after midday a gale from the North that drives
the workmen off the top of the mound, and tosses up the dust of
our diggings and dump-heaps in thick blinding and choking
clouds all across the site. If one can struggle up to the top of the
mound and hold on one can look over all the plain of the river
valley (a very narrow one to the N. wide to the S.) up to Biredjik
and down to Tell Ahmar, and over it all the only things to show

1 O God! = Hurry up!   2 Raids.

out of the dust clouds are the hills and the tops of the tells. There might be no river except when a side-shift of the wind splits the clouds, and shows it running brown underneath. It still is not in flood, but is very swift, and cold with the melting snows of the Taurus. We look out for the hill tops above Andiamar every morning and see them each time with more and more lines and black spaces on their white. Before very long I expect the $\frac{3}{4}$ of a mile of river-bed will be one unbroken race of water. That will be the time when our mound looks best, but at all times it is very impressive rising about 100 ft. direct out of the river very steeply as all those North Syrian mounds are. I have taken a photograph or two, and will try a drawing, when I have leisure enough, if ever that will be. It is not that there is much to do, of course: for most of the day we are not in the least necessary, and in those times I play with the pottery, which Mr. Hogarth has handed over to me as my particular preserve. Our house is half a mile away, and so we cannot all go back there and amuse ourselves, or work as the case may be during digging hours. Somebody must be within call of the diggers and so I am usually down here, with just sufficient interruptions to make writing or sketching not worth while. As soon as these Northern hurricanes stop, however, we intend to give up our house, and camp out on the mound. Then we will have time to do things. At present our evenings are filled up with the odd jobs that might have been done in the day, squeezing and copying inscriptions, writing up pottery and object lists, journals etc. Also it gets cold after sunset, and we go to bed early (about 10 or 11 as a rule), to avoid it. In the matter of food all goes quite easily, except for Haj's quite inadvertently emptying a curry tin into a pilaff! It was like eating peppered flames, and the other two are now crying aloud about their livers! That has so far been our only little hardship. I learnt a little about Syrian food from Miss Holmes'[1] servants, and this has come in usefully, for the Haj is not original, except in the matter of cakes that are half custard and half rubber sponge. Of course he has no oven which makes matters a little complicated. I am now building him one, out of a water jar. My power of sleeping through anything, which I acquired in my little house by aid of late hours and a

---

[1] Principal of the American Mission School at Jebail.

telephone bell is standing me in excellent stead. I am the only one out of the three who gets any sleep at all at night. Mr. Hogarth is always getting up, to chase cats or rats or birds or mice or dogs. Everything comes in and out of the window holes, and the light sleepers suffer. The only time I woke up was when a cat scratched my face, entirely without provocation so far as I am aware. We are tired of the village bread (the thin cloth-like galettes) and still more of the bread so made out of English flour. The villagers all live on barley-bread, but the Haj tried to use our home flour, and the result was a sheet, not of paper or cloth, but of wash leather or thin indiarubber sheeting. It is very tough and holds water, and most elastic. Mr. Hogarth's teeth refuse to eat it, and so he is brought very low. Thompson[1] can just get through it: I flourish, but the others got tired of seeing that, and have made arrangements with the Commandant of Biredjik to supply us with mule-loads of the soldiers' bread. This is thick, brown, whole-meal stuff, rather like the ideal bread of the Limousin, but darker in colour, and without the very slight sourness of the French stuff. By the way 'whole-meal' does not mean that it is like Veda bread, or the English 'whole-meal'. Sometimes we have Euphrates fish: the small ones taste of mud, and are more bony than herrings: and thick bones that choke a cat. The larger ones are much better. Another year we will have a sailing canoe, or something of the sort: it will be splendid to go down the river to Bassorah. This much is being written on the great mound, with the main branch of the river some 200 yards wide at my feet. The men behind, digging in the top of the tell have got down about 10 feet, through an Arab stratum, into a Roman one. This means cement and big stones, and slow work: but they have found a very nice little cup of early Arab ware, probably xith century. At present they are pulling up stones from the bottom of their pit, in a mist of 'Yallah's' and 'Issa's'[2]. The last is curious for they are all nominally Mohammedans. They can do nothing without noise. A man has just put off from the island across the near branch of the river, to swim across to us. Their antics on the inflated skins are more curious than beautiful. The skin itself is goat or sheep: (though a man came across the

---

[1] R. Campbell Thompson.   [2] Jesus Christ, who is a Moslem prophet.

other day between two wild-boar hides): very perfect vellum in appearance. I hope to buy enough to bind a Xenophon and another book or two, if I can find a new skin, for they have the bad habit of rolling them up tightly when dry, which lines them with cracks. The method of preparation must be most interesting. I cannot pretend to understand it yet, but in some way the skin is taken off whole, but for the head and lower legs, and the hair is stripped from it, and it is cured, without lime, or vegetable stupes and fomentations. I hope to get to know about it: and to get a few of the skins, at 6d each! Worth 5/- in England, you know, if such natural-coloured vellum could be got out of Italy. The legs are tied up with sinew, and the man inflates the skin through the neck, until it is as tight as he can blow it (42 blows, to be very precise in a biggish skin): then they lie down on it, face down, in the water, and paddle across with hands and feet. Being light, the current catches them little. They take their clothes across as well, on their backs. My faculty of making and repairing things has recently demonstrated how to make paint (black and red) for marking antiques, how to render light-tight a dark slide, how to make a camera-obscura, how to re-worm a screw (difficult this without a die), how to refit a plane-table, and replace winding mechanism on a paraffin lamp. Also I have devised a derrick, and a complicated system of human-power jacks (out of poplar poles, and rope, and Arabs) which have succeeded in setting an Ishtar on her legs again. The Romans or Assyrians had broken her off at the knees, and the men could not shift the slabs back again, with any delicacy: so Mr. Hogarth and myself set to, and with our brains, and the aid of 90 men, put all right again. Before this there had been 120 men playing about with the ropes quite ineffectually. Digging results will appear in *The Times* as soon as Mr. Hogarth gets back. They have been meagre, and not very satisfactory to date: but it is like Pandora's box with Hope always at the bottom: and we are not nearly at that yet. I will send drawings when I have a quiet Sunday. The women here weave very beautiful cloth: and sell it at about 1½d a yard: it is thick and coarse, like grey sacking: the probabilities are that I will bring home a bale: also enough camel-hide to bind my Doughty, when I get him. The book will be necessary, for I must know it by more than library use, if ever I am to do something of the sort. Mr. Hogarth thinks my idea of patronising the Soleyb,[1] instead of the Arab, promising, both in security, and novelty. They are an interesting people: however no hurry about that, with Carchemish and military architecture and above all the necessary Arabic first. There is one thing I think I will get you to do: this piece of country is all rock, and very hard on one's boots. Will you get down to Gillman, and order another pair of boots, as before, only with slightly thicker soles: nails as before, leather bootlaces. When these are made will you send them to Miss Holmes, and a letter asking her to be good enough to pay the Customs charges, and forward them to the Consul at Aleppo? They cannot be sent direct: as the adventures of my films, still held up somewhere in the country, go to prove. There is no hurry about them: it is only in case I am able to do some walking out here, if we knock off here before the rains. It would be appreciated if Will asked Blackwell's to write to Jean Gillequin, publisher Bould. St. Michel Paris, ordering the 3 volumes of the Rabelais in his 1f.25 collection (*La Renaissance du Livre*) to be sent to me C/o Consul, Aleppo. But not if you think books unnecessary! This letter is only an interim scrawl, to be strengthened by a heavy letter in a week: I hope by then to have heard of Mods.[2] We get weekly post from Biredjik. All very well.   N.

28: TO HIS MOTHER

[3.5.11.]

I did this this afternoon (Wed. May 3) and so I will send it off with the letter & map I wrote last week. You will excuse the badness of the drawing for the sake of the information it brings.

The thing in the middle distance is the great mound. You are looking right at the end of it, and so get no idea of its length: but it shows you how it stands from the little valley. Behind the mound (on the top of which is one of our dump-heaps and a workman with his basket) is the Euphrates, with an island in the middle, and hills on the far bank. These are about a mile away

---

[1] Metal-working nomads as opposed to the pastoral Arab or Beduin.
[2] His brother Will was in for this examination.

THE MOUND OF CARCHEMISH
from the drawing by T.E.L.

so you see they are fairly high. The smudge before the mound is a poplar-grove, irrigated by the little canal built up alongside it: it hides the low stone building of the mill: but you can see, like a shadow along the mound 20 feet above the water the little irrigation canal of the plan. It is cut into and built against the rock.

Below the trees is the little side stream (nameless) which runs into the Euphrates at this point. It comes from a large spring about a mile up, and its lower part (as you see) is now fairly full of water, due to the flooding of the great river. Below the copse is a grass field, running up to the mill-stream, and thence to the wall of the city. Just at this point is the N. gap mentioned on the plan. This side of the little stream is a bamboo-patch, an outcrop of bare rock, and then a field of young corn, cut up by two water-channels. Then a little space of stony ground, and a path (to Biredjik) through it rising to the hill-side on which I sat. The very dark object in the foreground is the far bank of another water-course. A square stone, with holes in it in the foreground is a Hittite tomb-monument. There may have been a statue, or a stela, in the socket. All this near hillside is covered with such stones, & pieces of carving, with two inscriptions. They point to a Hittite cemetery having preceeded the Arab one now on the site.

[There were always a number of visitors at the Carchemish dig; some of the first being Professor Sayce and Miss Gertrude Bell with whom Lawrence struck up a warm friendship. There were also the missionaries from the American college of whom Lawrence had become critical. Lawrence was very soon to try his hand at education himself. Among the workmen employed on the dig were two particularly outstanding characters: Sheikh Hamoudi, usually called 'the Hoja', the chief foreman, then a man about thirty, with a fighting record among the Arabs, whose memories of Lawrence form one of the most interesting chapters in *T. E. Lawrence by his Friends*, and Sheikh Ahmed, usually called Dahoum,[1] a charming boy of remarkable and individual character who had, on his own account, taught himself to read a few words and intended to go to school with the money he earned

[1] A nickname meaning Darkness, because he was very pale.

as house boy. Lawrence found in Dahoum not only an apt pupil whom he taught to read and to take photographs, but a kindred spirit who was happy to share every danger and hardship with him and who became his most intimate friend among the Arabs.

Hogarth left in the middle of April to return to Oxford, and was succeeded as head of the dig by Mr. Campbell Thompson.]

29: TO D. G. HOGARTH

May 21 [1911]   *Carchemish*

Thompson [13 *words omitted*] has dressed tonight, & something of the sadness of the last shirt & collar is overtaking him, for Gerty[1] has gone back to her tents to sleep. She has been a success: and a brave one. She called him prehistoric! (apropos of your digging methods, till she saw their result — an enthusiast ... young I think.) Your films came up bravely: they will be of great use: — and comfort. I have been photographing this last week — and will more next. Developing too inshallah.[2]

The Muktar carried off his cousin on his saddle-bow from amid the shrieking women at the spring last week. So perish all our enemies! Thompson has a high opinion of him now.

A new 'com'.[3] We are expensive in those things: our third. But no troubles of late: peace perfect peace in this dark world. . . .

Your Athens letter is an effort. Thompson is too judicial upon it. You say a second season unless

1. There is no more palace
2. Or public building
3. Or libu[4] wall on the mound.

The third is past praying for, Libu is dusted over as from a pepper pot on all the side of our big N.E. cut: at all levels & at all periods, but nowhere a platform, or a wall more than a few inches high. I will do my best to ensure one of the other conditions being left untried, so that there may be another year!

[1] Gertrude Bell.   [2] Please God.
[3] The Commissaire was an official representing the interests of the Turkish Government at the dig.
[4] Packed mud, like the English cob.

At present the second has not turned up to much: in 4 or 5 10 × 3 m. pits no great finds: a cylinder seal (worn, not inscribed, except with a sort of Fowler) some wall foundations: perhaps in one the last few courses of a wall (to clear). But we have not yet got properly into the W. end of the site, or touched on the most likely part: — in my unofficial hope and opinion. (I don't think there ever are official hopes).

On the first condition. The great wall certainly turns at rt. angles (we have found 5 feet of the other side already) and in the pit we were on a road, or court for carriages: (as arguable from a large egg-shaped block, upturned, which guarded the edge of the corner slabs from chipping): this you saw — or guessed — . That great wall is rough, unsquared, inside. So if that was the palace! You will note we find the sculptured slabs on the wrong side: there may have been others inside: or it is a quite earlier building, to which some later 'true-blue' has tacked a record of the number of his chariots.

Then at the end of the pit we have struck two nice little reliefs (about 5 ft. high) in basalt, and not *quite* the style of the chariots: more the style of the sacred palm relief: good work (one of them shows that the object on the rump of one of the figures with palm-tree that I tried to draw was the beginning of the tail of his bull-legs): these slabs Thompson proves prophylactic: which means that they reproduce (or one reproduces) the amulet designs to scare away demons from one's door: useful things: no well appointed household etc. ... If they do mark a door and I am as certain as nuts that they stood on a wall next which they were found, and built into it (we have only the core) as appears from the rough base of the stones, without rope pattern: then the long wall and stairs are no part of them: and there should be a biggish place under the tents, or towards the river: or even to the W.

This is all pure moonshine, & to be smiled over. But Thompson lacks flesh & blood in these reports: theories are what you (impersonal) want: and plenty of them.

Pots flourish: don't let Young hear that I am sticking them up with glue! Love to Leeds: if he had not had jaundice I would have tried his strength with a letter.　　　　　　　　　　L.

Thompson refuses to send this in his letter: he fears the competition of my style.   L.

By the way, you will have to alter your tentative dating of the site: we have got a large church (probably) with a relief, possibly of an iconastasis, of a man on a horse (? St. George). Byzant. in style ixth–xith cents. perhaps as apply to Gertie, who saw & admired: 6 ins. under grass all this. . . .

30: TO HIS MOTHER

23 May 1911   *Carchemish*

[40 *lines omitted*] Miss Gertrude Bell called last Sunday, and we showed her all our finds, and she told us all hers. We parted with mutual expressions of esteem: but she told Thompson his ideas of digging were prehistoric: and so we had to squash her with a display of erudition. She was taken (in 5 minutes) over Byzantine, Crusader, Roman, Hittite, and French architecture . . . and over Greek folk-lore, Assyrian architecture, and Mesopotamian Ethnology (by Thompson); prehistoric pottery and telephoto lenses, bronze age metal technique, Meredith, Anatole France and the Octobrists . . . : the Young Turk movement, the construct state in Arabic, the price of riding camels, Assyrian burial-customs, and German methods of excavation with the Baghdad railway (Thompson). This was a kind of hors d'œuvre: and when it was over (she was getting more respectful) we settled down each to seven or eight subjects and questioned her upon them. She was quite glad to have tea after an hour and a half, and on going told Thompson that he had done wonders in his digging in the time, and that she thought *we* had got everything out of the place that could possibly have been got: she particularly admired the completeness of our note-books. So we did for her. She was really too captious at first, coming straight from the German diggings at Kalaát Shirgat.[1] [3 *lines omitted*] Our digs are I hope more accurate, if less perfect. They involve no 'reconstruction', which ruins all these Teutons. So we showed her that, and left her limp, but impressed. She is pleasant: about 36, not beautiful, (except with a veil on, perhaps). It would have

[1] Compare letter No. 325.

been most annoying if she had denounced our methods in print.
I don't think she will. That is the finish of our news. Euphrates
has fallen, nearly to normal: the weather is hot, with thunder, and
showers occasionally. The harvest is now going on: all barley, no
wheat in this district: just alternate crops of barley, liquorice, and
fallow. They reap it green, and let it dry cut. No more trouble
from the men: since the high dispute of Monday fortnight the
days have gone as smooth as oil. Of course we got rid of some
30 of the ring-leaders, which 'pacifies' the rest. I forgot to say
that Miss Bell left us two Meredith's, the Sandra Belloni series:
great joy to one half the expedition at least. She is going back as
quick as she can (from Baghdad and Diarbekir), and so had done
with them. [*omission*] They prepare their inflated skins for swimming by rubbing into them salt and flour (barley-flour): it is
interesting. The hair is scraped off with a knife. I have had the goatskin that wrapped up the men's feast-meat so treated, and propose
to bind a book or two in it. It is really very good stuff, and to have
a book in the skin that one used to cross the Euphrates on would
be a pleasure. If I had thought of it I would have got a tolerable
looking Xenophon before I left Oxford, for the purpose. But if
we have a second season it will be the same thing. Crossing the
river is a matter of 20 minutes, and about a mile. Thompson,
using crawling and trudgeon strokes in swimming cannot advance
a single inch against stream, or even hold his own: he goes down
steadily at about 1 m.p.h.: and at a fast trot when he swims with
the current. It is such a pity to think of a huge iron girder bridge
across this river below us. They expect to be four years building
it, and that will mean a town of navvies, and all these beautiful
villages spoilt: not to mention that they will sack the ruins for
stone. I am going to take a few photos now.

Have taken them. My camera is proving a good one: and the
telephoto has been used several times of late: It acts (at a couple of
miles) rather better than the naked eye. Last week we dismissed
the son of Sheikh Ibrahim, a village worthy; the old man came
into our kitchen next day, and told Haj Wahid (who sends his
salaams to Father) that he was going to ensorcel Thompson and
myself and Haj Wahid, and our overseers, if his son was not put
back. The Haj came to us a little perturbed. He thought it might

be best to use force on the old man to dissuade him, and it really was serious, for a case of illness in the expedition would have put us under his thumb. So we told Haj not to mind: that you made a wax image of the man, with one of his hairs in it, that you said certain words, and stuck a pin through the heart at midnight: or warmed it over a charcoal fire, and as each drop spluttered and fell, a day would go from his life. Haj rushed out, and pulled one of his last hairs from the old man's head: and then triumphantly told him what was in store. The old man begged his peace of us, swearing good conduct for all our lives, and offered us a hen: (refused), but the request for peace was granted, and a hair, (not *the* hair I suspect) was returned. Our renown advances in the Arab-speaking world. In case former letter does not get through: I have books and films of last parcel: all very good.

We have a large beast like an 18 inch chameleon on the mound. I am trying to photo him for Arnie: such a quaint insect to look at, a small crocodile, almost.   N.

31 : TO HIS BROTHER, WILL LAWRENCE

June 8, 1911   *Carchemish*

[*5 lines omitted*] I will reply to Will's of the 18th since it is the only letter I have had lately: rather a gap just now! If he studies European history from the French point of view it will be fresh and valuable. Place-names are against the Teutonic element in E. Britain and also the little stories we have from Gildas etc. of the methods of the actual conquest. There was not overmuch welcoming. Had Britain accepted the Celtic church it would still be Catholic: do you really expect a history don who is abstract and constitutional-political to understand the mysteries of tattooing and the origin of the impi? I have recently read an attack on Chaka as only the reorganiser of the Zulu system.

The literature clause has been put in operation two or three times (I had leanings therewhither myself). Of course the ordinary history man thinks it a joke: but you would be safe with Mr. Hutton and Baskerville among your examiners: they are above the common scientific stock. In case I forget later, Baskerville is a quite exceptional man, rich, not a student, passionately fond of wandering in Italy and France. The more of such geography (especially physical) and mild architecture you could work in the better. Political poems are the only things not dry in history: do you call *Piers Plowman* dull? or *Renard*? and if you can read history and Bertrand together you would not dream of following Ezra Pound. If you touch Renaissance France read a little Rabelais (especially *L'ile Somnante* in book 5): between Villon, Rabelais, and Ronsard (with Clement Marot) you get the flesh and blood side of the Renaissance. The Scaligers don't touch.

What is a nympholept?[1] It sounds like a sort of newt: don't use these words: your letter on the whole needs a chastening of Bunyan, and perhaps Addison. Don't reply and say they are not alike.

I left my special subject (the Crusades) till the last two weeks of the last term. It was mostly done while the examination was actually in progress in three all-night sittings: special subjects, if you know all but the facts are a matter of simple cram. I should certainly not recommend doing it (except to know your ground, if it is territorial) before the last term: or the term before the last, leaving the last for revision. If it is a matter like the Crusades two or three weeks are more than enough. Other subjects have more to read: but always read something that throws a side-light on the set authorities (i.e. I didn't touch them till I had read the Armenian Chroniclers, William of Tyre, and the gestes.) You are going to too many lectures. The English Constitution did *not* develop out of domesday book. If you imbibe all Mr. Barker's lectures thereon, you will not be able to see it didn't. But it takes three terms to do so: give him up after the first term: you get nothing new from him, because it mostly comes from Pollock and Maitland (which don't read) and besides everybody goes there, so it is no use repeating anything he says: everybody else does. A. L. Smith is an institution: he delivered those lectures on Aristotle the year before his eldest daughter was born, and since

---

[1] Nympholept = one carried off by nymphs or inspired by the nymphs with an enthusiasm for the unattainable. Compare Lawrence's own use of unusual words such as vegetable stupe (Letter No. 27, p. 101).

then he has polished their style, while new interpretations and texts have passed over his head. He is an excellent joke, but you will get more out of Mr. Barker's book in ten minutes: Mr. Jane is very good on Aristotle. Don't make the mistake of over-much political science. I went astray on Utopia and Campanella and Harrington on S. Augustine: — and forgot Maine, whose errors I had to evolve out of Mill's *Political Economy* when the paper appeared. There is only one paper on Polit. Science, though classical dons forget that in their joy at finding a common ground between Greats and History ... do treat Aristotle historically; and Hobbes as a joke. Wakeling of B.N.C. is very useful (schools point of view) on Hobbes: and amusing too. Oman is a monument: and one doesn't need to look at such things over long. Hewlett[1] certainly has the courage of his convictions: but he is not a Greek, but an Italian of the early Renaissance: the time when they believed in Pan. I want to see *Brazenhead*. It may be another early work: one felt (in *New Canterburys*) that one had not all the story there. I can't imagine a man writing on Ch. Gaillard without reading le Breton: and to the Stubbs! It was a gross insult to the Society. I fancy there are echoes of the siege in *Reynard the Fox*. Atkinson is to be admired: did he know you were there? No one knows how the outwork at Gaillard was breached: I fancy (against V. le Duc)[2] that the angle tower was mined over the filled up moat: or that the moat was later made larger. Mustn't argue over Chandos[3] at this distance: but the Prince[4] was not a [*word illegible*] (c.p. his conduct in home politics). Of course Chandos was a sort of general: he knew how to win a fight, but he dissipated the energies of the English, and was a good deal responsible for the collapse. The Prince fell away at the end with that illness of his. A friendly (or at least neutral) Pyrenees was essential to Gascony: which excused downfall of Trastamara.[5] What did Chandos do in Aquitania but make Bordeaux disaffected, and the seigneurs all out of hand? The

---

[1] Maurice Hewlett, author of *Pan and the young Shepherd, New Canterbury Tales,* and *Brazenhead the Great.*   [2] See note to letter No. 532.

[3] Sir John Chandos, fought at Crécy and was constable of Aquitaine.

[4] The Black Prince.

[5] Henry of Trastamara succeeded his brother Pedro the Cruel, who was for a short time restored to the throne of Castile by the Black Prince. Henry of Trastamara was however a strikingly successful King of Spain.

Prince found his hardest work crushing the independent lords.

Digging is not good: though we have a fair bag of photographs for our book. Professor Petrie[1] seems a most exciting individual: no regularity but disorder continual. Homer result curious: perhaps the dear old philologists regard a unitary theory as an exploded one: but there will always be the fight of art and science over it. What on earth personal news is to write? I shave three times a week, and yesterday darned a hole in a sock — nothing more: remember we are only existing, and digging. No more over Thesis: let it grow a little worthy dust. Richards thinks little of everything else: I fear a great reaction of disgust when our first book is out. He is not fully prepared for its badness. Rabelais here: Plough Inn[2] a scandal.

32: TO HIS MOTHER

June 13, 1911   *Carchemish*

[*50 lines omitted*] I slept up here the other night after developing till past midnight: we had a little sleep, both of us, and were then roused by a rustle, which grew to a roar as a great white thing leaped through the hole near the roof which does duty for a window, right out towards my bed. Thompson was up at once with a fearful yell; and all his spare hairs on end; and we both grabbed the same revolver at the same instant, and tried to fire. But it was only the newspapers which we had stuffed in to keep out the birds and bats, and which a sudden puff of wind had flung into the room. We were just in the full force of this discovery when Haj Wahid (who sends salaams to Father) bounded in with the kitchen hammer in one hand and a rifle in the other, while our two Zaptiehs came thundering at the garden door, to learn what was the matter. Thompson's yell was the cause of all that and of the wondering requests of the villagers next day. He is a restless being at night, always getting up to souse the stray cats that come and sing by his bedside in buckets of water. [16 *words omitted*] We now have (good fortune for me) got rid of meat eating. It kept on being bad, and any little thing upsets Thompson: so

---

[1] Flinders Petrie.   [2] i.e. the demolition of the old building.

now a chicken once or twice a week, a fish or two from the river: but there is rice, and bread and leben which are better. Mohammed Jasim (a great man this) slays fishes in the river with his sword: and brings down doves, and hoopoes, for his pot, with stones. The hoopoes are glorious birds, and now being full-fed of flesh meat their plumage shines, and the crests on their heads ruffle and perk to see their mates. They are pairing, and to attract the females sit on great rocks and blow their beaks: at least it makes a noise like a snuffle. Today I cured a man of compound scorpion-bite by a few drops of ammonia: for that I have fame above Thompson's as a hakim: and as a magician who can conjure devils into water, from my mixing a seidlitz-powder for the Haj, in the kitchen before visitors. Am now going to scribble a very short line to Florence, and then to bed: the walk down of 15 minutes, in the gale that *always* blows, is just enough to cool one off. Salaams.   N.

33: TO FLORENCE MESSHAM[1]

June 13 [1911]   *Carchemish*

Dear Florence, I feel guilty for not having sent a letter to you before, but we are only two on this dig, and are always terribly busy. Even tonight I have cut short a letter to Mother to write this to you: and I believe she sometimes sends on to you letters of mine that she thinks might interest you. If she doesn't, she should.

We are having a splendid time out here: not that we are finding very much, but the place is splendid, and the workmen, and the climate. At present it is nearly warm enough to be just right (about 80 all day & night) and the new fruit is just beginning to come in. So we are going to enjoy ourselves the next months. We will be here another six weeks or so.

You would be amused at our workmen, and the curious tricks they play, to deceive us or to please us. Of course Thompson & I have to be doctors and fathers, & god-fathers and best men to all of them, and last week one man asked us to be good enough to

[1] His nurse in childhood.

pay the price (£12) of the wife he wanted to buy. She was a girl of the town, and so of course was a fearful extravagance for him, for he was quite poor, and could have got a girl from the villages round about for two pounds quite easily. And for that two pounds the girl would be very fat (a sign of beauty here) with lots of tattoo-marks over her face, and able to make bread and knead dung-cakes for fuel. So we refused to do anything at all for this Suleiman Hissu, but gave him good advice instead. Often too we are bothered by having workmen in the same pit who have a blood feud together. One may have run away with other's wife, or killed his father, and if these two men come together they will try to kill each other. So then we have to run down and separate them, by sending one of them to another corner of the digs.

Our house (a big stone one, with mud floors and roof) is alive with cats and fleas: so much so that I have given it up for sleeping in but go out to the great mound on the river that we are digging up, to sleep. The air there is delicious, and there are no insects to bother one.

I won't go on any further now: not tonight at any rate. Go to Oxford, sometimes, & try & get Mother away for a change. I know you won't mind taking her place for a little, and if you want to hear from me again, ask her to send you one of my family letters. Salaams,   NED

34 : TO D. G. HOGARTH

[*About June 24th*, 1911]

[40 *lines about technique of photography omitted*] The sour Zap[1] went from us, and a horrible fool has come in his place. He is continually interfering, & malingering, with demands for brandy. We got rather tired of this, and so when he produced a preposterous fever, we promised him medicine, and invited him into the kitchen. Thompson put on a pulpit face, and recited the Hebrew Alphabet and 'the House that Jack built' in a solemn voice, waving a cabalistic scroll in one hand, the other on

---

[1] *Zaptieh*, or Turkish gendarme, attached to the dig.

H

the man's pulse: the whole village crowded round the door to see.

We had given the Zap a glass of one half a Seidlitz powder to hold in the hand, and as Thompson said Amen I poured in the other half. The Zap. dropped the glass & leapt back with a yell, and in a twinkling there was not a man but ourselves in the room: some of the onlookers did not feel themselves safe till they had put the corner of the house between themselves and the devil visibly striving to void himself from the glass in white smoke. 'Am I not your friend, your raffik?'[1] said the Zap: 'Why did you give me that from which I might have died? What have I done to you which was not good?' (Many things, but he did not know). We forced Ahmed Hassan & Dahum, the two water-boys, to drink each half a glass, under pain of beating and being laughed at. And since they have gone about delicately, feeling their limbs, & shaking themselves, lest they be 'transfigured'. 'I drank some of their sorcery', declared Dahum on the works next day, importantly, 'it is very dangerous, for by it men are changed suddenly into the form of mares and great apes'. All the village, and above all the Maggot are rejoiced that the bully Zap is quelled. He can hardly show his face in the place: never on the mound. There are rumours of his return to Biredjik.

This is the third miracle that we have wrought, and our fame as nigromancers is gone abroad to Aintab & Membidj. The powder now foams a tall man's height from the glass with the noise of a dust-filled wind. [11 *lines omitted*]

I may live in this district through the winter: it strikes me that the strongly-dialectical Arabic of the villagers would be as good as a disguise to me: and there is I suppose no chance of any digging in the near future which would make Petrie advisable? If there is please send a card Consul Aleppo, or let my people know: I am off to Harran, Urfa, Biredjik etc. from Tell Ahmar. Salaams to Leeds & Mr. Bell.[2]   L.

---

[1] An Arab bound to give the protection afforded by his tribal membership.
[2] Both of the Ashmolean Museum.

35: TO MRS. RIEDER[1]

July 4 [1911]   *Carchemish*

[*15 lines omitted*]

Only make them think: that horrible 'Wullah ma arif'[2] of this district is regarded as a satisfactory reply to a question, instead of being a disgrace. I always get wild, & if there is the least hope in the man I force him to think it out. It is a great thing to be an employer of labour. I have had quite a success with our donkey-boy,[3] who really is getting a glimmering of what a brain-storm **is**. He is beginning to use his reason as well as his instinct: He taught himself to read a little, so I had very exceptional material to work on but I made him read & write more than he ever did before. You know you cannot do much with a piece of stick & a scrap of dusty ground as materials. I am going to ask Miss Fareedah[4] for a few simple books, amusing, for him to begin on. Remember he is to be left a Moslem. If you meet a man worth anything you might be good enough to remember this? A boy of 15 . . . I would be vastly obliged.

Mother hates writing . . . and has the usual feminine (apologies . . !) difficulty in finishing a sentence. You are exempted from this implied criticism, but don't trouble her with deep-burdened correspondence. She reads nothing now, though once she enjoyed it immensely. A Sense gets atrophied by disuse or misuse.

We too have had a visitor! Miss Christie, otherwise indistinguished: don't fancy my mouth is going to water over fireworks & shoals of callers and promenades. *We* made a huge fire-balloon for the Coronation, & terrified every man woman & child in the village unintentionally. They shot the poor thing to death before it got out of range.

Salaams to Miss Holmes, or anyone within reach   E. L.

If you see any of the Petra party please thank them from me; Very kind indeed of them.

[1] Mrs. Rieder, whose husband was French, taught languages at the American Mission School at Jebail, where she first met Lawrence. After 1911, she taught languages at St. George's School, Harpenden. In 1914 she was in the U.S.A.

[2] 'By God I don't know'.   [3] Dahoum.

[4] Miss Fareedah el Akle taught in the American Mission School at Jebail.

[On July 12th he wrote home from Tell Ahmar, also known as Tell El-Hamra, where Campbell Thompson and he had been working for four or five days after the Carchemish dig had shut down for the season. In this letter Lawrence said that he was setting off that afternoon towards Urfa, on foot.

The story of the trip he was undertaking is recorded in a diary which he kept from about July 12th until he embarked for Europe on August 12th. It has been published as *The Diary of T. E. Lawrence* MCMXI in a limited edition of 150 copies by the Corvinus Press. It was not a prosperous journey. All was well until Harran on July 17th when he notes 'slept badly with tooth trouble'. An abscess was developing at the roots of a wisdom tooth. On July 22nd both his feet were festering. On the 26th he records:

> Feet to-day nearly right from the blister point of view, and fester on my hand also healed up. This shows there is plenty of reserve force to draw upon yet. On the other hand my right instep has again collapsed. I suppose it will never get over the smash after my leg was broken.[1] It is painful now in the morning, and after every rest, however short.

On the 29th, the day on which he wrote the following letter to his mother, he noted in his diary:

> Hoja[2] started with me, but my distemper of the past two days increased suddenly, so I went on alone. Then it developed unexpectedly in a sharp attack of dysentery. I got on to the Kala'at into a lonely place and lay down on my back from about 8 till 2.30, feeling most weak and ill. About 3 I sat up and tried to dress, but fainted promptly for about an hour, and again then when I made a second try. Under the circumstances I was afraid to go near the edge of the pit with the measuring tape, and so could not work. About 5 P.M. I got to the village after a very hard walk. Decided to get out a tin of arrowroot, and send a man with letters tonight to bring a carriage from Biredjik. Cannot possibly

---

[1] In 1904 Lawrence broke his leg near the ankle struggling with a schoolfellow in the 11 o'clock break. He went back into school and went on with his work in class till one o'clock when his brothers wheeled him home on a bicycle. He was absent for a term and never grew much after the accident.

[2] Sheikh Hamoudi, the *Hoja* or chief foreman of the Carchemish dig. An interview with him is included in *T. E. Lawrence by his Friends*.

continue tramp in this condition. Can hardly lift hand to write this. Dreamed when fainting of milk and soda! Sublime. Greeting from every man woman and child in the district I fancy, but I could not see half of them, so only did a poor best at politeness. Fed on arrowroot and milk about 6 P.M. To bed at 8 on the roof: slept well.

Not a hint of all this was allowed to appear in the following letter which was written because there was a messenger to take it.]

36: TO HIS MOTHER

July 29 1911   *Jerablus*

I am sending in a man from here to Biredjik tomorrow, so I will send a line to you. From Biredjik I went up to Rum Kalaat; from there to Nizib, and thence to Tell Bashar and Jerablus. You will find most of these places on the map in my Thesis, if that sore battered body is now in peace. I have found nothing very new, nothing very good: the castle of Rum Kalaat yielded some new points, mostly Arab: it had a most enormous moat, a perfectly appalling thing — it cut off a mountain from a mountain along a col like the coupé at Sark. I am very well, and en route now for Aleppo. I got a letter from you here which Thompson sent up three weeks ago from Tell el Hamra. I am probably going now to stop wandering in Ramadan. I dare hardly ask for food from a Mohammedan house, and Christians are not common enough. I have had the pleasant experience since a week of being the best Arabic scholar in all the villages I entered. In every single one, except Rum Kalaat, someone knew a little Arabic, but I knew more than all: the people were all Turks & Kurds; a few Armenians and Yezidis: Rum Kala'at was my northern point.

This is nearly all I can write: the man is waiting anxiously — his own business, and I cannot delay him. I have the luxury of clean clothes, and am overhauling my stores: Thompson gave me a free run of all the spare stores of the expedition, & as a result I am fitted out like the Swiss Family [Robinson]: only I have no embroidery, silk or sugar mill.   L.

37: TO D. G. HOGARTH

Sunday August 6 [1911]   *Aleppo*

I have reached civilisation at last, and am vastly content with its beds. Last night was paradise and a half. Have tramped nearly a month — Tell Ahmar, Seruj, Urfa, Harran, Seruj, Biridjik, Rum Kala'at, Tell Bashar, Jerablus, Tell Ahmar, Bab. Only I didn't tramp in from Jerablus, but rode & drove for I got dysentery, and felt like Leeds' proverbial boiled rag.

At Jerablus I found a letter of yours to Thompson which he had sent on for me to read. You emphasise the importance of the palace: — most certainly that is the place. Thompson will have told you we went down inside the right-angle of [the] great wall with disappointing result, until the day before the last. Then we found a cross-wall & good floor inside, proving that there never had been anything just in the angle except perhaps a garden! We had only been uncovering the foundations and the true floor level lay somewhere in the neighbourhood of the top course of the wall. The palace was thus much raised above the street.

The floor we found was a good one, of square cobble-stones. I should say a court or path, not a room.

Thus we have there a great palace, most likely of Sangara[1] for it is the last Hittite building in Carchemish (c.p. pottery) not extending over much ground (it does not go far beyond those two rooms of the 'house' you uncovered & left: they were really part of the palace) not at all deep (about a 3 m. max.) fairly well preserved, for there is a good height of wall in your two rooms, and the stone-paved floors are there, and with very interesting pottery. Try & get a look at the rough notes I made on the 'Palace' pottery, the two or three photographs of it, and the coloured drawings Thompson made of some pieces. These were not very accurate but will give a better idea than the photographs. [4 *lines omitted*] A second season would clear all the palace, and be a fairly satisfactory wind up to the digs. If they are left as at present it will only mean someone going on in a few years time: and now I know $\frac{3}{5}$ of the pottery, and the men know their job & the railway has not come. Surely the ground plan of the palace

[1] Sangara, prince of Carchemish, 9th cent. B.C.

of Sangara would be a tolerable result? Or do they all want cuneiform? If so tell them they might find some.

I have had dysentery (at Jerablus after my tramp) and it has put an end to ideas of more walking this season. I expect to be in England in a month & will come and see you. I fear I have no antiques: not the will lacked, for I asked all over Urfa district, & in 16 villages near Bashar: I saw nothing worth buying, but at Jerablus I have set several people to collect for me, and I hope after the winter to send you a box of terracottas, at any rate. I hear there is a good deal of stuff in the village, at present afraid to come out. Thompson cut down the bakshish after you went: I fear false economy! Still if I can recover the booty for English hands so much gained. If there is to be a second season (and there should be I am certain, if only to save the B.M.'s face) try & have Gregori sent to us. He would have, I am convinced, saved us a lot this year: the Hoja is no use as a digger, and we (pianissimo) weren't very brilliant either. Salaams: but am writing to Leeds.   L.

38: TO MRS. RIEDER

Am August 11, 1911   *Hotel Deutscher Hof, Beirut*

[23 *lines omitted*] What I wanted for the donkey boy[1] was a history book or a geography which should be readable and yet Arab. I cannot give him such productions as those Miss Holmes uses, since nothing with a taste of 'Frangi'[2] shall enter Jerablus by my means. I have no wish to do more for the boy than give him a chance to help himself: 'education' I have had so much of, & it is such rot: saving your presence! The only stuff worth having is what you work out yourself. With which last heresy please be content a while. I will (probably . . .) write from England. Yours sincerely, [3 *line P.S. omitted*]   T. E. LAWRENCE

---

[1] Dahoum.　　　　[2] European.

39: TO NOËL RIEDER

[*Postmark Beyrouth*, 12.8.11]   *Deutscher Hof, Beirut, Syrien*

[8 *lines omitted*] Mr. & Mrs. Flecker[1] are coming out to Jebail next week-end. They usually go cavassless.[2] Please tell Miss Holmes this. They are in very good form just now; I have been doing little but talk to them. I had to wait an extra day here, because of things for me in the P.O. which was shut when I got there.

I was very sorry not to have seen you when I was going off: but you were deaf to my cries and Mrs. Rieder's entreaties. So we both shed crocodile's tears. Ask your mother what they are. [6 *lines omitted*]

And keep on brushing your hair.   L.

40: TO V. W. RICHARDS

Sat. Aug 26 [1911]   *Oxford*

I hope this may reach you on Monday: you evidently do great things. I would dearly have loved to have got up, but your p.c. reached me in bed with a double extra special bout of malaria and I felt much more like getting down. However better now, though still shaky. I hope by quinine & co. to stave off any more attacks until I can manage the arsenic treatment that alone roots it out. This however they will not give me at present, because of the upset in me left by my go of dysentery. As the dysentery is the proximate cause of the malaria I am in a giddy round that seems to have no opening. But don't imagine I am ill: merely a hopeless weakness that sits me down after a hundred yards is done on foot, and also I cannot go upstairs save crab-wise. These are explanations & excuses why I have not dashed up to see you: you would only have had to put me to bed. Hogarth is pressing the B.M. for a second season at Carchemish as a result of the wonderful pottery discoveries of the last two months . . . my star is in the ascendant you may imagine. If he can overcome the reluctance of

---

[1] James Elroy Flecker, the poet, then Vice-Consul at Beyrout.
[2] i.e. travel without a *cavass*, or consular guard.

the officials it will mean four months more joy next spring. We will see: he vows to raise Hell if his wishes are not conceded: a very good man, Hogarth.

You say back about Sept. 16: I think possibly a time just after then should see me fit for the exercise of a talk with you. It would be very pleasant tho' if you could run down here and stay a few days. If desired you shall inhabit my house and no philistine shall approach.

Have had a delightful present — *Guinevere* in the Kelmscote: very nice 'golden':[1] no illustrations. Salaams.

My 'proof' went to my people for admiration, & comes back (I hope) with them this afternoon. Shall be sent on *at once*.

41: TO MRS. RIEDER

Sept. 26. [*Postmark*, 1911]   *Oxford Union Society*

Dear Mrs. Rieder, Your letter came last night: and I felt the need was desperate, but *all* the shops were shut. So this morning I rushed down, and sent off what I could: — a little Morris: a Doughty: and M. Audoux:[2] you have probably read the latter: if so send it to your Jesuit friend, or to some other person who is starving for print. The Doughty is *Adam Cast Forth*: — you don't know this: and I like it immensely, whether you will remains to be found out. At any rate if it is a failure, it is a big one, & not unworthy of the man. It is out of print, or they think so; till I find out, or for ever, be content with the not-new copy on the way. I can vouch for its general cleanliness, & entire freedom from infectious disease: — since no one but myself has ever read it. I carried it once with me cycling, which battered it: that's all. The Morris is *Sigurd* & the early pieces: probably you know them. I haven't got, & couldn't find, any prose to hand immediately. Its nearly all in print, but has to be ordered. I must clear up the mystery of *The Roots of the Mountains*. Mother sent it, very late, by *Parcel Post* to Aleppo. It either has dropped by the way or it reached Aleppo after we left. All our stock (this,

[1] The Kelmscott Golden type.
[2] Marguerite Audoux, author of *Marie-Claire*.

if it came, included) is locked up there, waiting next season, which is actually to come off thanks to D. G. Hogarth: good man that! However if the book is in Aleppo it's there. It was in a special type, which took 2 months to find. If I reorder it the chances are it gets to me at the end of November & by Xmas I am in Syria. It's not worth it, I think.

Now about Doughty's other books. *Adam Cast Forth* is on the way. I like it: — but I would never venture to maintain its cause too openly. *I* think it's the best thing he's done: — and no one will ever agree about that, I'm sure. Let's leave it; you will judge for yourself. It is short at all events.

The Cliffs. A patriotic drama: invasion of Britain by aeroplane, & eventual victory of ourselves, chastened into a national frame of mind. I haven't read it: and I don't think I want to: I should be too much afraid of bathos: and the author of *Adam* & *Arabia* can't afford to fail.

Dawn in Britain. I have read this. If you express a wish, I'll send it by return. It will fill up many blank evenings. Behold an epic in 6 volumes: — a stage from Greece to the North Pole: — a period of 500 years, from the sack of Rome by Brennus, to the siege of Jerusalem, and the departing this life of Joseph of Arimathea.

You'll see that the 'epic' has no unity: there is no hero; plenty of characters: heaps of incidents told all in 'great' style. There is very little in the book which is less than magnificent: but do you want so much magnificence? Just as you like of course. It could well be read in sections, for there is little coherence in the whole: you get Cassivelaunus, Caractacus, Boadicea: most Romans: a few Greeks, Tyrians, water nymphs: some *perfect* 'songs', semi-lyrical narratives in blank verse of twenty or thirty pages: these have nothing to do with the book and I mean to print them: they are perfect.

Do you want this book: I would like to send it you; immensely: but I am afraid it will only irritate you: remember Doughty goes his whole way along as he pleases: there is not the least concession to use or custom or authority: he *calls* it an 'epic' and presumably one has to do the same: but it is rather an imaginative history: of course it is meant to glorify things English, which with Doughty means not the Empire and *The Times* and the House of Lords but the language and 'Spenser & Chaucer traditions'. It contains about 33000 lines: all blank verse: — like *Adam*, but more regular.

Will you let me know what other books you or anyone else would like? Oxford is a good place for buying them: though the post is deadly slow. Those sent off today will be 3-4 weeks getting to Beyrout, and will stick there in the B.P.O.[1] till the Press sends them on. No duty fortunately according to the P.O. If you answer this letter at once, I can send you another lot before the end of next month, and a third before I come out.

It wasn't really your letter which awoke me to the needs of you: *Marie-Clare* was on order, and came in the nick o' time: I felt a strong impulse for the last 3 weeks desiring me to write to you: but I am so slack. Doctors dispute over my carcase: they seem to agree that I mustn't go to E. again for 3 months[2]: as a matter of fact I am very busy, for it is the *pottery* (O the despised pottery!) which is the reason of our second year's dig. I am in the seventh heaven or thereabouts as a result. You will be shortly going to Jebail: my salaams to Misses Aseen & Fareedah: the latter is going to have a letter 'The strange, marvellous and most wonderful adventures of an ancient book: written in the tongue of the Saracens, and purporting a discourse of a hermit in the Holy Land'. *Miss Holmes is going to have a letter*, please break it gently to her: I would not retard her recovery for the world. Her pottery is labelled 'early Phoenician': they ask for more. . . .

My regards to Noel: burst a paper bag under his nose — for auld lang syne   L.

Mother talks of writing to you: but not if I can help it! Isn't this polite? But really she probably will, only she is a werry bad correspondent outside ye *Family*.

42: TO MRS. RIEDER

Nov. 9 [1911]

Dear Mrs. Rieder, I walked up and down the Strand and Oxford St. yesterday thinking out a few suitable biographies for

---

[1] British Post Office.   [2] He was back in Syria in two months.

Noël's amusement, until the police grew suspicious, and the news-boys irreverent: the result is nothing: not even a mouse.

Don't give up hope: — there is always a brother or two to fall back upon. Tomorrow I will consult Arnie (who has read most things) and give Noël the result of his wisdom and experience. It is so hard to go back a quarter of a century, and put oneself in his place.[1]

Meanwhile I send *Puck*,[2] just so that it will not appear a total defeat. If you have it (as I suspect) pass it on to someone English, if there is anyone English near you. It is very wrong to give it to Americans[3] or to half-and-halves (here halve is the fem. of half . . .)

Now I must consider if there is anything else in your letter.

Miss Holmes' niece (I cannot decipher her name, possibly because your pen was a bad one) will wait: that is, I'll hope to have the pleasure of meeting her when I reach you. Assure her, if it's good manners, that this is what I look forward to most in this year's trip in Syria. Please assure Miss F. and Miss A. the same — and tell Miss Holmes she is on a different footing.

That's all I owe to conventional politeness this time.

A   To get on again: — I think you are wise to wait for *Dawn in Britain* till you reach a library. I do, so it must be the best way.

B   *Iliad*: Yes, Lang-Leaf-Myers: not good, but the best I know. Will get it in Oxford.

C   Biographies: as above; a very good way to learn history. But Noël's rather small: or he was when I saw him last.

D   *Metternich* shall come: it will be very suitable for all parties, being meant for the upper forms in public schools.

E   Those few books wouldn't last me a week: though I don't make a habit of getting up in the dark. A clock is an artificial contrivance, and to regulate oneself by it is to run after one's own tail.

F   I must remember to look at you reading: it sounds an interesting performance.

G   I certainly prefer poetry: though prose, in type, makes a neater, blacker page.

---

[1] Lawrence was 23, Arnie (A. W. Lawrence) 11, and Noël Rieder nearly 7.
[2] *Puck of Pook's Hill*, by Rudyard Kipling.
[3] Mrs. Rieder was American by birth.

H   I have just made a convert to Doughty by way of *Adam Cast Forth*. He is white hot, and I had to run from him. Seems to know it by heart. However I'll tell Doughty next week what you think of him.

J   There are many things to discuss: e.g. H.G.C.A. above.

K   Morris writes admirable prose — but better verse.

L   I was disappointed with *Gulliver* till I got to the Houhynyms (?). They were fun.

M   *Marie-Claire* I don't class with Doughty.

N   I never discuss business: it's not worth the time & trouble.

O   Have now another *Adam*.

P   The press doesn't: type not yet ready.

Q   This is the end: Spelling Reform query will answer later.

L.

There's a wonderful lot in this letter: the style is too compressed for elegance. Your letter will act as a key.

[A letter to Mrs. Rieder written on November 23rd, 1911, explains Lawrence's subsequent movements.

I am coming out next Wednesday: am due in Beyrout Dec. 10. . . .

My orders are to go as quick as possible to Carchemish: inspect it: return to Egypt: go to Mr. Flinders Petrie for a month, get back to Syria: go and build me a house on the mound: get back to Aleppo: bring out Woolley (new chief), and the stores and dig for three months. Mr. Hogarth comes out early May. If the Italians permit, this programme will be.

Italy and Turkey were at war, Italy having invaded Turkey's North African province of Tripoli the previous September, and Beyrout was shelled by Italian warships in January 1912. Lawrence's programme was not interfered with. Trouble had been growing between the German engineers of the Baghdad railway and the British archaeologists. Their interests clashed not only because they were the two great employers of labour, but because the engineers had designs on the site of Carchemish and the archaeologists were doing all they could to protect it and to prevent any of the excavated stone being used for building.

Incidentally I have been told that Hogarth prevented any injury to the great mound by enlisting the support of the Kaiser, who had an amateur interest in archaeology.

These rivalries might have been bridged had there been good will on both sides, but the whole attitude of the Germans was so repellant to Lawrence and Woolley that this was impossible. I have reason to believe that many of the stories about Lawrence's practical jokes at the expense of the Germans are apocryphal.]

43: TO D. G. HOGARTH

Dec. 12 [1911]   *Aleppo*

Dear Mr. Hogarth, I got here today, and found Wilkie Young going off: Mr. Fontana[1] came yesterday. It seems Wilkie Young went over to Jerablus some time back, found a dozen German engineers sounding for rock-bottom etc. and was told by them that they were going through the big mound.[2] He explained that it was English property and gave them to understand we owned the whole place. This was to leave us a chance of buying it: very sporting of him I think.

Tonight one of these engineers told me that the plans are being changed for the third time. They now propose a temporary bridge to the N. of the site, for materials etc., and the permanent one to the South: he thought it possible that a slice might eventually be taken off either end, or one end, but now there are to be built in the spring large store-sheds, repairing shops, and living houses. These with sidings, he expects to take up most of the site. The building of the approaches and temporary bridge will be begun as soon as the final plans are published: in any case by the spring. This looks like high wages and a shortage of men.

Meanwhile a party of surveyors is still there, and has been since August, so that the hopes of my picking up our leavings of antiquities are practically nil. Everywhere else they have bought things most freely, and no doubt here also. Still I will go across in the hope of seeing what they have.

Again, I don't suppose Hassan agha will want to sell over-much, or if he did he will have sold already: Wilkie Young's

---

[1] British Consul at Aleppo.   [2] Of Carchemish.

stratagem will hardly last indefinitely. In any case I don't suppose the B.M. wants to buy a parcel of railway sidings.

As for the building of the house, that should be un-noticed, if they are going to put up such plant for the bridge and railway staffs as my man tonight suggested. Hassan a't can't possibly object to one more in a row of a dozen engineers' cottages. Only it will be a much more expensive building than I was told. Wood will be exceedingly dear, and possibly labour also. However I hope to be back in a week, and then I will write properly. I will not do any wandering about the 10-mile limit this visit, for I am not yet fit; not so fit as I thought.

I picked up two seals in Damascus yesterday: they are both quite ordinary, and rather dear, but Hittite, and it seemed a pity to pass them over.

One is a gable, with the usual four-legged, and one-horned ibex, but under its nose is a bird, which in shape rather supports your idea that the fill-up ornament was a decomposing bird. The other is a button seal, also steatite, with a two-horned goat(?) dancing clumsily, in the style of some of the red steatite buttons, and the last little beast I got — the one from Spink. I paid my own expenses to Damascus, so there'll be no need to encumber the B.M. drawers with them.

Four consuls send their kind regards to you.

I am starting for Jerablus tomorrow, for about a week as I said: it doesn't look very cheerful for I believe the Germans there have a gramophone. Still dulce et decorum. . . .

(By the way everybody is frightfully annoyed at the change of plans — due to us they say . . . and they don't seem to grasp that they may also be putting us out.)   L.

With this railway working really seriously, the country will soon be opened up.

44: TO D. G. HOGARTH

Dec. 16. [1911]   *Jerablus*

I hope you got my letter from Aleppo. I set off just after that, taking Haj Wahid with me as an afterthought that there might be buying to be done.

The arrival was a great success. The German works broke up
with a yell, and rushed down the path to meet me. The poor
engineers looked as though the Jehad[1] had arrived. We put up
with the Hoja, and had a most glorious night. All the village
dropped in, and I heard all about the Germans; they put on airs —
they are ignorant of antikas — not recognising a Hittite inscription; they know no language — they say sacral mento,[2] and when
we ask what they want shut, they only say it again — they drink
raki[3] all night, to two mejidies[4] — we work seven days a week —
they do no work with their hands, but sit in the tents — we may
not smoke: there is no bakshish — we may not speak to them, they
say it is adibis — they cannot swim — they make a bargain and
break it — Oh God the pigs, they eat crabs — and tortoises.

After this the talk drifted naturally to demons & ginns. The
Hoja and the rest told tale after tale, each more ghastly than the
last: till all, glancing furtively into the darkness, refused with
one voice to go home. So we slept there happily, the Hoja, his
wives, his four children, the Haj, Dahum, myself, and fifteen
others, in a house about the size of your room. I had a most
royal heap of quilts, all wonderful to say, nearly deserted. It was
one of the best nights I've had, and yet the Hoja told Thompson
there were no local demons: why, one tore in half the brother of
Khallaf Khalifa, another stole some halawi from Hassan Agha,
another so bereft Hamman of his wits for a year and six months!
The great mound is full of them, and all begged me for a few of
my experiences.

It's a splendid place, but I suppose I must be serious. There
are four or five Germans here: about 20 tents, and mud houses
building: everything in between the Kalaat and the village.
Their chief told me that the latest (and last) change of plan takes
the railway outside the walls, right to the river: not a sod or a
stone of the site is to be touched. This is splendid: for unless
under direction of one of us I feel sure no stone could have been
removed with safety. The bridge is to be S. of the site. I'm sorry
though that some beast (or fanatic for the really inspired in art)
has bruised the eyes of the basalt charioteers. I have sworn for

---

[1] Holy War against non-Moslems.   [2] Sakrament – German oath.
[3] Levantine brandy distilled from grapes.   [4] Turkish silver dollar, worth about 3s. 6d.

the offender when discovered flaying alive, and rolling in salt, and then a grill before a slow fire of quotations from Dickens. The chief engineer supports the idea warmly: says he has never seen it done.

About buying the site: it will possibly be worth it, but not yet. Hassan Agha wants £100: in two months it will be worth £20. Old Salem is fairly going it, but everything is so confused that we should (and can) wait till after the expropriations.

About antikas: all gone: to a former band of Germs. their dragoman, and an antikaji from Birajik. I got a view of the highest priced: it was rotten — an amulet possibly Syrian — and the ass gave a mejidi for it. I bought a few poor things: Kenyon & yourself will not scramble for them: also I am sending such a mass of pottery chips: it took me two days to gather them. I must apologise for their plainness — but so is the pottery, and the box of fine pieces, the select ones of last year, which I left with the zaptiehs, is still* locked up: they put it in the storeroom for safety, and Sahib effendi with the key is in Birijik. It's rather good that the commissaire should be guarding my thefts[1] in all innocence. I needn't talk here of the seals & chips, since I will send a note with each.

About halawi — I hope you remember the particularly sticky sweetmeat of which Thompson & myself used to eat pounds last year. It has struck Haj Wahid as an excellent idea that he should send a mass of it as a present to Billy.[2] He says he is just the age for it. I am encouraging him as far as possible, so some day you may find it arrived, and for weeks you will find tangles of it on the chairs and tables, and door-handles and floors and walls and papers and books. Halawi is such affectionate stuff, and yet *so* wholesome.

Salaamat kethir[3] to you from Haj Wahid: he sends a seal; which shall be labelled. It's a family relic, and is not meant as a

* Everything is in store still, and no talk of Constantinople. Touma aîné wants rent for the store room: if not will I buy contents for half a lira, as he wants the space? I will if I have half a chance.

---

[1] Pottery duplicates required by the Museum had to be secreted and smuggled out owing to the Turkish law against the export of antiquities.

[2] Hogarth's young son.   [3] 'Great salutation.'

I

tip-drawer. He had no idea you liked them. The village, which is admiring the writing of this letter, and interrupting vilely, also sends salaams in a body. It is looking forward very much to Gregori.

I have found an incised inscription, short, at Yarymja; and a couple of fragments from Yunus.

There is a new oath in the village — b'is-sait el khowaja[1] — by the aid of myself: so I have thrust down the prophet from his place. I shall grow a beard.

The Germans are not after the Yusuf Beg stone, so I will leave it till the summer.

I hope while building the house that I may be able to wander about a bit and buy some seals and things. At present I am rather a crock: to the extent of being glad to have Haj Wahid with me. [38 *lines omitted*]

45: TO D. G. HOGARTH

Dec. 27, [1911]   *Aleppo*

[60 *lines omitted*] I got a seal at Tell Kar, twelve miles W. of Jerablus: It will go in the bottom row but one? of the case in the place where three were wanted to fill the line: I have all these three now: — one from Spink, one Damascus, one Tell Kar. This last is quite a nice seal, decent size, and cutting. I should describe it as a tervacyclic discoid:[2] the device may be two scorpions: I am most glad the luck gives it you and not the B.M. I bought it on Xmas morning. We (Tagir, Haj Wahid, and I) got to the Sajur that midday. Then the ass of a driver tipped the carriage over the edge of a bridge into a branch of the river, where it settled comfortably on its side, submerged to the upper window, with one horse completely out of sight, one with its leg pinned under the concern, the last dancing on the other two trying to get out. Tagir and I were walking at the time, which was as well: we were thus able to admire it all without concern — the driver frantically

---

[1] 'By the aid of the gentleman', i.e. Lawrence.
[2] A parody of the technical terms invented by archaeologists in Egypt.

heaving up the head of the drowning animal: Haj Wahid groping in the body of the carriage for coats and things, spluttering the while between his teeth about the wives and religions of the horses. The red blankets floating away down stream, gave just the right touch of colour.

We spent hours there, in a steady downpour wading after things, and dragging out the carriage. I don't know what we lost: — I miss a terracotta from Jerablus, and some clothes etc — but we got out more than we expected. The things looked like lumps of mud. Tagir stood it very well, only sighing mildly 'Adventures are to the adventurous' when I fished up what had been his pet umbrella. Haj Wahid took a header off a patch of mud, which was unwise with his spare things still under water: he lost his tobacco box then: and when it ended they had not a match or a cigarette between them. Altogether a very novel Christmas. The unkindest cut was when we dragged out our glorious lunch-bag, specially stuffed in honour of the day. We emptied it out on the banks of the river, a horrible brown soup, with muddy lumps of eatables in it. However we were not entirely destitute, with heaps of water to drink and a walnut apiece.

I told Tagir I would pay all his actual losses, but if possible the B.M. should give him a little more than this. We had an icy cold drive across, two days difficult work in Biredjik with the authorities, and then this splodge on the way back, with a most ghastly night to follow. We had no bedding of our own left, only a huge spongy lump, and what little we borrowed was alive with lice. I have been having baths all today, and probably Tagir also. I expected a lot of complaining, but he was quite cheerful all the time, and in Biredjik exceedingly diplomatic. It would have been quite hopeless for me to have gone across alone. [25 *lines omitted*]

[Early in January 1912, Lawrence joined Flinders Petrie's dig at Kafr Ammar in Egypt for a few weeks in order to learn something of the methods of other archaeologists, and two impudent letters show his appreciation of Professor Petrie. That Petrie appreciated Lawrence's qualities is indicated by his suggestion that he should do work at Bahrein.

Lawrence left Petrie's dig to return to Jerablus and start building the house in which he and Leonard Woolley were to live for the next two years. That is for the second and third seasons. Lawrence stayed out in Syria that summer.

Woolley, whom Lawrence had known since his schooldays, became the third head of the Carchemish dig that spring. He has published a highly coloured account of life there in *Dead Towns and Living Men*. Lawrence seems to have felt that it was a vulgarization of the years which he looked back to as the best in his life. For Sir Leonard Woolley's impressions of Lawrence at this time, see his contribution to *T. E. Lawrence by His Friends*. Lawrence's work at Carchemish was arranging and reconstructing pottery, the photography, and a good deal of the management of the labour.]

46: TO D. G. HOGARTH

Jan. 18. [1912]   [*Kafr Ammar*]

Excuse pencil — Petrie camp — It struck me yesterday that I should write to you and ask you about house-building: — you probably haven't got any of my other letters — inshallah you got some seals. I suggest going away from here in about 12 days — if not dead before — and running up to Aleppo: then I would take up a couple of tents and Haj Wahid, and camp on the site for a month and build the new palace. That would run me near March 10, when I expect Woolley in Aleppo: For this I would want about £50: for I would take across with me to Carchemish a carriage load of stuff: — as much as it would hold: then the final caravan will be smaller. Also if it be possible give me £30 or £20 [and] liberty to buy the site[1]: if my letters have miscarried (as those to my people have done) you will not have heard the mess about it: only it's certain that the railway wants none of it. About this place, Mrs. P. is here, which is a novelty in camp. He is enormous fun, with systems of opening tins and cleaning his teeth and all else. [25 *words omitted*] Wainwright [is] a good man who loves

[1] The discovery of sculptures at Jerablus led to excavations at Carchemish being undertaken in 1878 by George Smith for the British Museum. Owing to his death their conduct devolved on Mr. Henderson, British Consul at Aleppo, and was unsatisfactorily carried out.

the Hittite nation and is writing a book upon them apparently —
or proving that they are not the Cypriotes. He is painfully anxious
to get you to talk and can't: digs better than anyone else here. It
seems to me very carelessly done compared with Carchemish:
however there are lots of little things with wax and such-like
tools to be picked up; only it seems to me that Wainwright is
better than the Professor just now. Why hasn't he died of
ptomaine poisoning? It's really rather amusing that they are all
in terror of instant death because three people in the village died
yesterday and yet cheerfully eat out of week-opened tins after
scraping off the green crust inside. I am going in for it all with
great relish and really enjoying it with the security of being
insured.

One good turn deserves another, and so I am persuading the
Prof. that a little skeleton I dug out and waxed yesterday is just
the thing for the Museum. It looks like a girl, and is crouched
up in a rotten wooden box, with rags of clothing over it. Besides,
it is really almost complete: when we lifted it up one of the feet
dropped off and a lot of toe-bones from the other, but you would
hardly notice that in a dark corner. There wasn't any pottery or
furniture with it, which will be an advantage, as reducing the cost
of carriage: Round the neck was a little bone button seal, which
Petrie will probably keep for his own collection. I have rather an
idea of persuading him to send you a few of the 24th. dynasty
wood and plaster coffins: they aren't very good, but you haven't
many like that in the Museum: and this is such a comfortable
existence that I feel I must do something. As a matter of fact the
stuff we are finding is very much alike, and most of it is already
in the Museum: if I can I'll get something you will want, but at
present it has not turned up: all late prehistoric stuff — cylinder
jars and little plain alabasters and at times a bronze or copper
tool — a very cheap lot. But what I want is that skeleton for
Leeds: he would enjoy it so.   L.

47: TO MRS. RIEDER

[*Postmark* 23.1.12.]   *Kafr Ammar (which is 40 miles S. of*
                                     Cairo, on the desert)

This letter is addressed to Mrs. Rieder, but quite impersonally —
only to keep in custom of spelling her name. It is really Miss
Holmes' just as well or Noël's (and to him I owe two): or to the
third adult of the party (away with 'female') whose name is yet
undeciphered: it is much after time but who can apologise to a
group so varied in taste? No one but I would have achieved a
letter at all from a Petrie dig. A Petrie dig is a thing with a
flavour of its own: tinned kidneys mingle with mummy-corpses
and amulets in the soup: my bed is all gritty with prehistoric
alabaster jars of unique types — and my feet at night keep the
bread-box from the rats. For ten mornings in succession I have
seen the sun rise as I breakfasted, and we come home at nightfall
after lunching at the bottom of a 50 foot shaft, to draw pottery
silhouettes or string bead-necklaces. In fact if I hadn't malaria
to-day I could make a pretty story of it all: — only then I wouldn't
have time. To begin with the Professor is the great man of the
camp — He's about 5′11″ high, white haired, grey bearded,
broad and active, with a voice that splits when excited, and a
constant feverish speed of speech: he is a man of ideas and
systems, from the right way to dig a temple to the only way to
clean one's teeth. Also he only is right in all things: all his subs.
have to take his number of sugar lumps in their tea, his species of
jam with potted tongue, or be dismissed as official bound un-
progressists. Further he is easy-tempered, full of humour, and
fickle to a degree that makes him delightfully quaint, and a constant source of joy and amusement in his camp. [7 *lines omitted*]

About the digging: 'we' have stumbled on what is probably
the richest and largest prehistoric cemetery in Egypt, and in our
first week have dug out about 100 graves: these contain wooden
coffins and bedsteads, boxes of alabaster jars, dozens of pots of
new and known types, some little ivory (spoons and gaming
pieces and scraps of caskets), a good many bronze implements,
axes, adzes, chisels, and other trifles. Also a good many baskets,
and the shrouds and cloths in which the bodies were wrapped.

We have found very few flints, and those not of the best, since the bronze was in general use. The graves are usually about 5 feet deep, and as all the soil is pure sand, digging is merely child's play. Owing to a hitch in his arrangements the Professor has all his workmen here, and so twice as many graves are found than we can record properly: with plenty of time it would be delightful, whereas now we are swamped with the multitude. We have about 900 pots (complete; — all broken ones are thrown away) about 120 alabasters, and a matter of twenty bedsteads. Also we have preserved a number of bodies and skeletons complete by soaking them with boiling parafin wax. These will go to Museums. About the next thing. I am leaving here in 8 or 9 days, and will stop at Jebail a night or two (with Miss Holmes' leave) on my way up to Aleppo. I cannot do better this time.

Salaams to Miss F. if she is returned: and to Miss A.　　　L.

48: TO D. G. HOGARTH

Feb. 10 [1912]　　　　　　　　　　　　　*Aleppo*

[32 *lines omitted*] Seriously, I hope the money will roll up soon, because it is now Feb. 10 and the house will not be built in a fortnight.

The claim of the Gov. to buy the site is odd. Halil must be cracked. However it may be on your behalf. It will be vile if (having got the money from K.[1] — promised that is to say —) I can't buy the land. Hassan Agha will grind his gums, if true. Woolley's idea of Kufti men I hope won't come off. Those Egyptians are such worms (though they can dig). As for Primus stoves, I'll write and tell him we don't want them. [10 *words omitted*]

Let Kenyon tell Henderson's heir[2] that his father paid a pair of yellow boots with blue tassels, and a red & yellow striped silk gown for Carchemish. The man will probably be content with this returned. Also tell him he is liable for 30 years arrears of taxes. I can send you facsimile boots.

About the Jerablus seals: — I can't give you those, only the

---

[1] Sir Frederic Kenyon of the British Museum.　　　[2] See note to letter No. 46.

five outsiders: the Jerablus ones were bought while living at Kenyon's expense (— promised that is to say —). If he gives them you all well and good. I valued them at about ¾ the lot. The foot seal must be worth a lira at the least: and if I give you that K. should fork over the rest of the bunch.

Didn't know you liked duck-weights: there are heaps here in town: or is it only Carchemish ducks?[1]

Very hard to make the 'railway' people love me. They think English people are spoiling their line: and by being turned out of the Kala'at they have lost that mid-stream rock to build their bridge on at Carchemish. However I'll do my best. Please salaam Billy from me.   L.

49: TO D. G. HOGARTH

Tues. Feb. 12 [1912]   *Aleppo*

[27 *lines omitted*] Prof. Petrie spoke to me two or three times in Egypt about the Persian gulf and S. Arabia. He told me Bent had dug ivories (early) in Bahrein: and when we found some very curious Mesopotamian-like bull's legs on prehistoric beds (one I hope goes to Oxford — really good things) he declared that he believed the early dynasties came round by sea from Elam or thereabout to Egypt: and that Bahrein was a stage of their going. Finally in my last week with him he suggested my going down there to dig, say next year, as a preliminary season, to be followed by a second on a larger scale, if it seemed promising. He said he could provide the funds.

I told him I'd ask you about it: and that I'd rather you got what profits were going: he didn't seem to think the ideas were incompatible: that he always liked to send you all he possibly could. I meant to wait till you came out, but after all I think you might like warning. Of course it could only be if Hittites were not going: — and on account of the railway works I think you will certainly interrupt the Jerablus digs for a little: they must go on some day though. At the same time I would like to dig in the Persian gulf, and as Bahrein is nominally British, I suppose we

[1] Weights in duck form dating from the 1st millennium B.C.

might carry off the stuff. It all depends on what Bent found, and of course that you probably know better than Petrie. P. by the way is rather tired of Egypt, and wants to expand. He suggested £700: — 200 the first year and 500 later. However first of all is it worth digging? Petrie is such an extraordinary person, that I'm inclined to think it must be. It is quite amazing to see him on a dig; and it made me pretty wild to see the sort of person he had with him: all [*word omitted*] wanting to do independent digs, whereas what P. needs is a pedestrian intelligence to do the hack-work for him, while he does the fine things. Am awfully glad I went to him. But what a life!   L.

Don't of course reply to this: but I want to talk to you about it when you come out.

50: TO D. G. HOGARTH

Feb. 20 [1912]   *Aleppo*

[24 *lines omitted*] I wrote to Woolley and told him not to bother about Primus stoves, that he could get them in Aleppo. I expect he could: at any rate to order. He wrote to say he was bringing his two Kufti people with him: they will be rather a blot on the landscape, but I don't care, for the railway has brought a horrible crew — the sweepings of Aleppo — already. They are building the temporary, wooden bridge. I shouldn't be astonished if the Kuftis got nerves and went home. Those Petrie had were worms. W. talked of bringing a gang another year! I have left a note for Gregori with Tagir telling him what tools we have: there were a lot of shovels left over. I hope to start for Jerablus tomorrow. It is delightful being out again; and I'm quite fit now. P's camp nearly laid me out!

I got a letter from you yesterday — coming up from Egypt with nineteen post-marks. It asked me to buy a cylinder, which I did of my own prompting for 10 frs. I'm not yet sure of its Hittity. In fact I think it isn't.

I've sent off Thompson's boxes to Catoni[1] with request to forward: so he will have lots of our things.

---

[1] British Consul at Alexandretta and shipping agent.

Am writing to ffoulkes: his armourers are not satisfactory.

Sorry my people bothered you: they have got absurd ideas that people may disappear quietly in the E. I can't persuade them everybody knows thereof five minutes after the disappearing.

I got your note too late of course to look at Ramesside pottery in Cairo. However Petrie didn't suggest any likeness in Egypt. He said he had the best collection of Egyptian pottery, in the Edwards Library in London. It might be worth looking there. Will acknowledge receipt of Kenyon's draft shortly.   L.

51: TO MRS. RIEDER

May 20 [1912]   [*Carchemish*]

Dear Mrs. Rieder, Miss Holmes wrote to me a little while back (just after an Arabic postcard from Miss Fareedah-Noël) to say that Mr. Rieder had died and that her letter to me about it had miscarried — which of course it had — and last post I got a poem from Noel and a letter in phonetics telling me you were going back to Europe. Please let me know, if not too late, whether you are going to France for good, or where, and for how long: I would have come down to Jebail only of course the work here is at its hottest: Woolley is new to the place and not very vigorous after 5 months in the Sudan and I cannot get off at any rate till a month is past. However please let me know: of course I have no idea of your circumstances or how this will affect Noël: I gathered from Miss Holmes' letter not adversely.

I am very glad you got to Baalbek and Tiberias and Damascus. All very good: but if only you could have drunk rose sherbet with snow and eaten grapes in the bazaars of Aleppo in the heat! You know you have been a long time in Syria, but not with Arabs: those are people you have not met, and should. I want to know also about Miss Fareedah: she joined you, I see, at Damascus: I had hoped to come down this summer to Jebail, and [to have] seen her, but an unknown male has given us £5000 and the B.M. has added £2000 and the whole 7 is to be spent here:[1] so there are

---

[1] A large donation for Archaeological Research had been placed in the hands of the Trustees of the British Museum who utilized part of it in paying for the excavation at Carchemish.

lots and lots more digs to come — and immediately a second season in September.

For some reason Mr. Hogarth is very anxious to make me learn Arabic; and so I am going to stay here July & August alone. I hope to go home at Xmas, and to carry Miss Fareedah away with me for six weeks in England. There will be more digs in Feb. but all through Jan. Miss Holmes will be bereft (inshallah!).

I hope the Parfit[1] proposal got better, or died: remember I haven't heard a word of Jebail for months: Of Carchemish — no bilingual, but very striking historical discoveries. We have nearly a complete post-Hittite history of the site worked out from Greek pottery and inscriptions; the first Hittite clay cylinder, hieroglyphically inscribed, historic-inscribed gate lions, and a new staircase, 400 other fragments of inscriptions, and complete tomb-groups of late Hittite bronze and pottery and cylinders, the first of their kind discovered. About 400 pots are on their way to London, for they were all bought by me in villages and so are our private property — 'we' is the B.M.

Mr. Hogarth, who has just visited us, has carried off four packing cases of my stuff for the Ashmolean. We have one piece of Hittite sculpture more realistic and artistic than anything Egyptian: it suggests a flood of light on the development of early Greek art: the Hittite is really finer than most 6th cent. Greek: — and 3 or 4 centuries earlier.   L.

Very egotistical this letter, but what can I say about Mr. Rieder's death? I am exceedingly sorry if it has distressed you: but I didn't know him or about him. Regards to Miss Holmes.

52: TO D. G. HOGARTH

June 23, [1912]   *Baron's Hotel, Alep. Syrie*

I couldn't remember Leeds' address: — or at least I wasn't supposed to, but he had given it to me most carefully in Oxford, and I had noted it down, and written it up at home in a book that I use exclusively for addresses — and the matter ended there.

---

[1] Canon Parfitt of Jerusalem who was setting up as a lecturer in England.

This is incoherent, but you will understand the ghastly morning that nineteen or twenty packing cases of Hittite pottery and squeezes turn up addressed to E. T. Leeds, 20 St. Giles, Oxford,[1] and nineteen pounds four shillings and twopence half-penny to pay; I have a lurking fear that Mrs. Hogarth may not wish to pay for Leeds' extravaganzas, or may not think the pottery worth it, and so refuse them: in which case the finest modern or ancient collection of Hittite pottery and squeezes will be lost to the world: in fact it will be dispersed in the G.E.R.[2] quarterly sale: Aleppo is a stew-pot and I am sick of it in eight hours, with still all the world to buy and eight cases of pottery to pack: Today I got a Damascus tile — quite nice — for $12\frac{1}{2}$ P.T. It is probably less good than the Persian plate, but I am more than proud.

Kelekian's man has been carried off by the cholera which is really working very hotly in Aleppo just now: this makes the iced sherbet of rose leaves a forbidden fruit, and exquisitely delicious. It also removes, since Marcopoli left, the last serious buyer in Aleppo.

I'm going out to look at Tell Halaf this summer if all goes well. I hear that Opp.[3] has found very little after all: but it may have all gone Berlining.

Fontana has given me leave to do much as I like this summer, (live at Jerablus etc.), since he found out much of his information about the present state of Syria was rot. As a matter of fact Aleppo is one of the few possible rowdy places, and to flee to the shelter of a consulate protected by Tagir and the fat cavass would be ludicrously ineffective: he is always in Souglouk himself.

Catoni sends salaams unto you: please give Bell my *love*.   L.

118° in the writing room.

---

[1] Lawrence had addressed them to the Assistant Keeper of the Ashmolean by name so that they should not excite the attention of the Turkish Customs, as boxes addressed to a Museum would have done. He had addressed them to Hogarth's house.

[2] Oddly enough not: he G.W.R. since they were at Oxford, but the text is plain.

[3] Baron von Oppenheim, the German archaeologist.

53: TO DR. A. G. GIBSON[1]

June 26, [1912]   *Aleppo*

Dear Dr. Gibson, Excuse the apparent fluency of my hand-writing above, but the pen-nib was working crossly, and I flourished it to put an end to its folly.

This place is having a cholera epidemic, and matters will probably get pretty bad with the arrival of the very hot weather at the end of this month. There are now about 40 deaths a day, and nobody is doing anything. I fear that in time we may have cases in our village, since there is much coming and going just now over the 70 miles in between, owing to the making of the Bagdad Railway. There are about 200 people in the village, and it has a lovely spring used for all drinking and washing, but a spring with a flow of about 200 gallons a minute: a very small, but very strong flowing stream.

Can you tell me, very shortly, more or less what to do? I mean in the way of medicines: I have corrosive sublimate in bulk, but not much else. If there is anything very necessary besides, could you be good enough to send a little out? You are not trespassing on the domains of any other medical man: you see I am local doctor. I don't like writing and telling my people, because they will only (or Mother will only) go wild with alarm: but my elder brother (Bob) is quite sensible and will pay for what is wanted: they come parcel-post to Aleppo to the British Consul there, which is my address: my brother knows. If the trouble comes I will probably have about 100 cases I suppose: it isn't that so much, as the trying to isolate them that matters. The people here in Aleppo are losing about 90 to 95% of their cases, so one cannot be much worse than that. It seems, however, very little contagious: seldom attacks more than one person in a family.

The town of Biredjik is about 20 miles up the Euphrates, which flows at 5 miles an hour with a stream of 400 yards wide and 15 feet deep. Will this water-supply be tolerably safe?

If there is a case in the village, and one fears the spring is affected (sick people bathe in it always) how long will it take to become clear? it flows very hard as I told you.

[1] Of 27 Banbury Road, Oxford.

Does a cholera germ require much boiling to become dead?

I hope there is a vaccine treatment: I can get that done quite easily for the Arabs do as I want them most charmingly: if there is, please don't forget a squirt! And say how shortly before contagion it can be administered.

I have to write to you, for there isn't anybody worth a potato for advice in Aleppo: and don't say it's hopeless to write anything, for you probably (if you compress) can put it in a post-card. And don't suggest I build a hospital (I can't) or import doctors [6 *words omitted*] all the lot will run away: there will only be the very best left, and those only enough to do Aleppo. Sala'amat.

E.L.

This is a most awful address to send a body: but no matter: don't bother if you don't want to. Turn matters of fact over to my brother.

As for sending things out, they must come continental parcel-post, not by British P.O. Beyrout. The G.P.O. at Oxford knows the route and will send them: it only costs a little more, and it is quick, which is essential.

As before refer to brother: a quite invaluable person if the course is plain.

L.

54: TO HIS BROTHER, A. W. LAWRENCE[1]

July 21, 1912

Ancient beast, It is about a year since we wrote letters to one another: suppose we do it again? It doesn't cost anything but time, and of time, do you know, I have mints just now. This is the first time for years and years that I have been able to sit down and think, and it is so precious a discovery: and one that so many people want to take from you.

Just now I am in Jerablus, and feeling matronly. Also I am house-physician, for you never saw such an establishment as mine has been this week. There are seven of us here — six Wahids and myself. First of all I had malaria — a short spell of the usual two-day sort. Mrs. Haj Wahid got a new baby, and turned very ill.

[1] Aged 12.

Haj's boy fell down and broke his head to pieces and had to be tied up; Haj himself went drinking and collapsed with internal troubles of sorts. So I brought in Dahoum to help Haj's mother in the kitchen, and he ungratefully produced malignant malaria (autumno-aestival) and raved his head off for three days until he nearly died. I had to sit on his chest half one night to keep him in bed. The little Armenian doctor did the main part of the work (he's our consulting physician) and now Haj and Dahoum are convalescent, and more trouble than ever. This morning, when I woke up, Dahoum (who can just stand) was trying to sweep out the big room with the [help of keeping] hold-fasts of the tables and chairs, and Haj Wahid was feeding his donkey. I have to watch them all day to keep them in bed. Mrs. Wahid has to go to Aleppo for an operation, much to the disgust of Haj. I had a mighty battle with him to get consent, for operation is anathema in the eyes of the doctors of his religion, and he wanted to save the money for a new one. He is angry because he has two daughters now. Nice people these . . . they think Father the most miraculously fortunate man — in fact they suspect him of female infanticide. In a few days therefore I am to be alone in Jerablus, for all the others (but Dahoum) will be in Aleppo. Nice place Aleppo, Worm, though too hot just now, and there is scarcity of water, for the crocodiles. They line all the canals you know, and swallow the water as it comes down from the river: everything in Aleppo loves water. Even the hippopotami sit all day on the kerb with their feet cooling in the gutters, and when sunset comes they boom for very joy, till all the valley is giddy with the sound. We have nothing like that here in Jerablus, which is a country place without hippopotami: but we have frogs who croak in chorus old, old tunes that Aristophanes taught them, and iguanas who sup in kings' sepulchres. And talking of sepulchres I bought such a lovely one last week: a crematory urn, a glazed jug of Babylonian work, some Hittite terracotta horses, and bronze fibulae: one of our first finds.

I have turned school-master, O tumult, and taught up to 11 times table a class whose average age was about seventeen. Then the house became a hospital, and I put an end to the local education authority. It was sad for they did so want to learn twelve times: It was a very wonderful school: everybody who got a table right got a lump of sugar each time. We finished two large tins! I took a class of four (including our Commissaire) in local history (special subject) and had the mollah of the district to listen to my lecture on geography. They can't make out why, if the world is really round, the people on the other side don't fall off. All this is stopped now and the head-master is reduced to writing nonsense to a worm.

The Kaimmakam visited me yesterday, to consult me about the destruction of Biredjik castle. I made him squirm — but they will pull it down all the same: the French bridge-builders have offered them £12000 for its stones. I hope to have the pleasure of a little talk with them next week. Von Oppenheim [5 *words omitted*] who is making excavations out at Tell Halaf in Meso-potamia came and saw me one night last week. He came about 5 P.M. (sunset at 7.30) stayed till 11 P.M. then went off to eat and sleep: came back at 4.30 and stopped till 10 A.M. and left with a two-hours gallop to his train: a special so it would wait for him — We have a train only 16 miles away. [6 *words omitted*] — I hardly was polite — but was interesting instead. He said they were the most interesting and important discoveries he had ever seen barring his own — Invited me over to his place by his relay of post-horses — 6 days journey in 36 hours! Not for me thanks! Have just been interrupted by a spider as big as a whale's nebula: bottled him in whiskey for you: such hooked teeth and toes: I took him for a crab when he knocked at the door and said 'come in'. Such a fright: Salaams to the world.   N.

55: TO HIS BROTHER, A. W. LAWRENCE

28.7.[1912]   *Jerablus*

Today, worm, I must tell you of a battle that took place lately here. About two days ago I was on top of our big hill, watching some men on the island carting sand for the railway cement-works into two boats, when I saw about twenty men spread out into a long line, advancing through the scrub-grass towards them: and in a few minutes this new body opened fire with revolvers. The sand-diggers raced for the river, and tumbled into one of the boats, and were off, only they left two of their number behind: one of these swam for it: the other was captured, and his revolver and clothes taken away. Then the invaders, (who were Kurds) took possession of the other boat and set out to invade Syria.

However the first boat had by then arrived and the men from that, reinforced by many others, lined the banks, and opened a hot fire with revolvers at 400 yards: you could see the bullets splashing up the middle of the river, and the Kurds decided not to try to cross. So they went back, and the Arabs jumped again into their ferry boat, and set out for the island, followed by other Arabs both sides shooting vigorously: the retreat became very rapid, and went as far as Mesopotamia, where about 200 Kurds came rushing down from their village to prevent the attack. Then the Arabs retired to our side, with both boats. Wasn't that a lovely battle? Absolutely no one hurt.

What more, puffet? The railway is not going to do any more digging for a month or so, and not very much even then for a bit, so I am going into Aleppo, and there will move up to some hilltop, either at Beilan with Mr. Fontana, or in the Lebanon with Miss Holmes and the Beyrout Consul. I won't live with them, because neither is alone, but will take rooms or a house near them: and will go on with Arabic with Dahoum, who is cheaper than local labour, and who can cook and wait very well. He was six months table-boy with the Railway Engineers here. Go on writing to Aleppo. It is good exercise for you, though nothing has of late arrived this end!

I have got you such a glorious spider: he is about four inches long in the body, hairy to the point of ugliness, with teeth and horns like a rhinoceros. His legs are very angular, very thick and very hairy, with such claws: and his body is wasp-shaped: a beauty if ever there was one, and now he is drinking whiskey in a bottle that used to be Carlsbad salts: poor fellow! I hope to find you a scorpion, when one will oblige us near the house, for I have got quite good at picking them up by the tail unharmed. You have only got to grip them each side of the sting from behind. Our scorpions are very miserable little beasts. We have had

K

hardly any snakes this year: next year I don't suppose we will have any: and that is sad, for Sandan the snake used to be great god of Carchemish, before the days of Ishtar, lady of heaven.

We have reached the season of grapes, ancient one, and that means many delights washed down with the sauce of the terror of appendicitis. Tell Mother I will write before long from Aleppo or my hill-top.   NED

56: TO V. W. RICHARDS

Sept. 12, [1912]   *Carchemish*

If more months have gone by, don't blame me, because there was never clearer case for delay. You sent me a letter, as excellent as usual, detailing in the main a superb scheme for building a wooden house in Epping Forest on the summit of a mountain-peak, with no neighbours, a dry subsoil, open views to Kent, water-supply, and drains: — and the last words in the letter (barring the crossings and corner-pieces as afterthoughts) said 'In a week I will write again'.

Well, of course, here was an economy in reply indicated to me; and I am still waiting the return letter: It has never come: — and reluctantly I must write to you, with the *absolute conviction* that next post will demand a renewed script from me.

Now where were we? Why yes, the Epping scheme: — a superb idea. I was beginning to have a fear that we were putting the hut before the press, so to speak. This would answer all critiques. Is it possible in any way to use the roof-beams of the Hall near Jesus? I mean those now stored in Oxford for us. There is a fair amount, and the king-posts are lovely things.

Please do everything, and let me come home at Xmas to rapture over all. I have more hopes than ever before. Sail in, and carry out all to your content and I will be more than acquiescent. How is the type-cutting? If you are hewing logs in a forest your hands are probably ruined for a six-months. No matter in the world.

I take it the accident to the Dulwich Scouts was the troop to which Berry belonged? Give me details if so.

Carchemish ii is over by three months, and in a few weeks I hope Carchemish iii will be on the way. A great place, and a great dig, I think, & certainly most admirable people. Today is the end of Ramadan, and they are surging in and out of the court-yard firing revolvers, & bringing me portions from the feast going on in the village. I have twelve sheets of bread, wrapping up twelve packets of parched corn, with grapes and cucumbers in abundance. But I can't yet talk Arabic!

There is a splendid dress called 'of the seven kings': — long parallel stripes of the most fiery colours from neck to ankle: it looks glorious: and over that they wear a short blue coat, turned up at the cuffs to show a dull red lining, and they gird themselves with a belt of thirteen vari-coloured tassels, and put a black silk & silver weave of Hamath work over their heads under a black goat-hair head-rope. You have then only to add a vest of gold-embroidered silk, and white under-tunics to get the idea of one man's dress (I have forgotten the Kurd knitted socks in 9 primary colours, & red shoes), and there are ninety & nine all different eating a sheep before the door!

All is well here (after bad waves of cholera & smallpox)[1] and I expect to get back at Xmas: till when build wooden houses in the air, and accept my benediction and salaams.   L.

57: TO MRS. RIEDER

Sept. 12, [1912]   *Carchemish*

Dear Mrs. Rieder, '8 pages, crossed' and I gave a huge sigh of relief, because it was a proof that you were not entirely estranged: you know the Ottoman Post is responsible for all my delin-quencies in letter-sending: it usually is: — and even Miss Holmes only got about two hurried scribbles all the season: I wrote more: I remember doing it. However why weep? I am exceedingly sorry to hear that Noël's glands have proved themselves not gentlemen: (Not that this was at all to be comprehended from

---

[1] Robert Graves in *Lawrence and the Arabs*, p. 19, states that Lawrence had smallpox, typhoid, and blackwater fever, 'and other varieties', but I have found no other evidence of this.

your letter, which was written in a language foreign to me, and for which I lack interpreter and dictionary): however I have been in Jebail, and Miss Holmes told me all about it. You are very wise to look after them before bothering about schools: Get them entirely out of the way before you bother him with work: you know a year or two doesn't matter in the end. I was reading (chiefly police news) at four, and learning Latin at 5, and at 17 I was no more forward than the rest of the school, beginning Latin only at 8½. And the most brilliant people of the early forms (except one) all dropped out of sight before they reached the Sixth: and then, after that in the University, it doesn't make an atom of difference if one is 22 or 19: Also Noël is learning French, and will know it better when he is fit to enter school, than the others when they come out at 19, having spent 12 hours a week grinding at what is, after all, absolutely a necessary accomplishment, if one is to leave England.

Arabic of course it would be a pity to forget — but Arabic is a luxury: — by the way don't run the risk of denationalising Noël. It is a very good thing to have a country to grumble over or praise as one wishes: it doesn't matter much which country I fancy! I only wish I could speak French without wasting six months trying thereto.

And don't bother about Latin. I take it Noël is more likely to be Modern than Classical in his tastes, and if one doesn't want to write Latin verse, and knows French, one can read the Latin one needs in a six-month, and other than that he will only have to write Latin prose, which is a mechanical stupidity, ground out of a Grammar and Dictionary, and to be handled at will. If he reaches 10 (an extreme age, probably) without Latin, he will merely be set to occupy his French hours in the older language. And a school is such a slow business that a little special training will overtake its standard in no time. Latin is a very important thing: but there are lots of Latin languages, and if he knows one it will make his way very easy for the rest, (e.g. I can read Italian prose, & even poetry not incorrectly: never having learnt them).

It is good news you are not sending him to a public school. I don't like the type they produce. In fact any sort of type is a nuisance. One shouldn't be such a thing. However that is a crank.

Our key at Oxford is always in the door! I heard of your fortune in finding everybody out. But we are quaint people anyway, and bear transplanting. Frank with us stands for law, order, and the British Constitution. But for him the society would have taken fire long ago, or wings: sometimes one thinks it good to have a heavy pair of boots!

I wonder what photos. of Jerablus you saw. I hope (vanitas!) that I was invisible. In connection with which I may say I was three weeks walking about Jebail in Arab dress: Excuse was an illness, which found rest only so: but the village made the most of it!

Nothing has come from you for months: in fact nothing but this letter this year: so if you really were good enough to send books they fell by the roadside. But don't trust the Ottoman post; you only waste money. Salaam me to Noël from the knees to the eyes: and down again. L.

Expect another letter soon: the frost has broken.

[In September 1912, Miss Florence Amherst, who was much interested in Saluki dogs, addressed a letter to Mrs. D. G. Hogarth asking for information about the breed in Arabia. Hogarth replied referring her to Lawrence, who being on the spot could provide first-hand information. The first Balkan War had broken out at the end of September.]

58: TO THE HON. FLORENCE AMHERST

Dec. 22 [1912]   2 *Polstead Road, Oxford*

Dear Madam, You will have been astonished at my not replying to your letter of Sept. 28. The fact is that I received it in the first week of December (the war has given the coup de grâce to the tottering Ottoman post office) at Carchemish, and in the hurry of closing down excavations it was quite impossible for me to answer it. I am not particularly doggy — but some of our men own greyhounds, and no doubt can tell me *something* about them: — though they are villagers only, without nice ideas of breeding or pedigree.

We only have the feathery sort . . . and they call them Shami, because the great sporting centre is Damascus;[1] Silogi (g=k in Bedouin Arabic) is the proper name for the species of dog, but there are as many family and tribal names for the dogs as there are for the horses. Only a town sportsman or a rich Kurdish chief could tell one these; and I am not likely to see any of these till the end of February.

The only trifle I know about them is that Arabs eat the flesh of the hares the dogs kill, (though not lawfully blooded) on the pretence that the iron collar of the dog has touched the wound, thus making the ceremonial slaughtering. Most dogs though don't bite their captures, but press them down till relieved.

I am going out to Syria again early in January, would information coming in the end of February or early March be of any use to you? I can ask some sporting Sheikhs for you . . . With apologies for knowing nothing! Believe me, yours sincerely

T. E. LAWRENCE

[On January 3rd, 1913, Lawrence and his youngest brother went with Miss Amherst to see her Salukis, kept by Harris at George Yard, Grosvenor Square. There was a golden dog and a team of four cream-coloured Salukis which Lawrence thought very beautiful.

While he was at Oxford Lawrence bought a Canadian canoe which was sent out by Salters to Beyrout, arriving there at the end of January and reaching Carchemish before March 6th. In *T. E. Lawrence by His Friends* Sir Leonard Woolley describes it as fitted with an outboard motor attachment, the engine of which gave Lawrence great pleasure, but this was not bought at the same time. Mrs. Fontana and others describe his paddling it, and his going on long trips down the Euphrates and having the canoe sent back overland.

On Lawrence's return to Syria he remained for a short time at Beyrout actively occupied in smuggling rifles into the Consulate. Mrs. Fontana gives the following explanation of this affair:

T.E. and Woolley appeared to believe that Kurds were planning an attack to sack Aleppo (their crops had failed)

[1] The Arabic name for Damascus is El Sham.

and persuaded Raff — my husband — to report to the Consulate-General. He, knowing how the British-Protected crowded to their Consulate, clamouring for help, when any trouble or even rumours were afoot, also, how unlikely it was that the Turkish Authorities would tackle a raid with any skill, accepted T.E.'s offer to smuggle up some rifles from a British Gunboat then stationed in Beirut harbour, with the idea of arming the consular staff and such members of the British colony as would be likely to keep their heads, for the protection of the Consulate. T.E., aided by two naval officers — who enjoyed themselves! — worked the gun-running without getting caught.

The story got about of course (there were rifles under most of my divans) and the German Consul, whom I remember chiefly as a beard and proud refusal to read Anatole France, was in a great flap about it. He pumped me over afternoon tea and I assured him, with appeal to his middle-aged sympathy (I was thirtyish), that T.E. and Woolley were romantic boys whose legs had been pulled by their Kurdish friends. What I really feared was that T.E. and Woolley were pulling their consul's leg.

In another letter Mrs. Fontana writes:

T.E. was certainly in touch with the Kurds.

It is quite likely that he knew of a smouldering project on the part of the Kurds to sack Aleppo, and acted as he did so that a rumour of the British Consulate being fully armed and in readiness might spread through the tribe and decide its leaders to give us a wide berth in the event of the raid being carried out. Raff would back up such a sensible scheme.

Lawrence's own view of the matter is reflected in the letter written by his younger brother, Will Lawrence, when he visited his 'Bedawi brother' in the October following (quoted on p. 158).

In a letter from which I am not allowed to quote (written at the end of February), he mentions the gun-running and also rifle-practice in which he hit a petrol tin four times out of five shots at 400 yards. The disturbed state of affairs was due to the defeat of Turkey in the Balkan War.]

59: TO MRS. RIEDER

April 5 [1913]   *Carchemish*

Dear Mrs. Rieder, This is only a scratch, provoked by your second unanswered letter to me: the second arrived while I was still wrestling with the linguistic problems of the first. Your reproaches about duck-weights are vain: the little beast is in Oxford, where my Mother (of all people to become dishonest) has had a ring put in his eye, & him hung on a watchchain. I am writing sternly, to insist on reparation being made.

Only you see, it will be 3 days before I have another chance to write, and so you won't get your duck for a week more: I am sorry for the mistake: I had pictured you to myself as sunning yourself in the shadow of his quacking all this month at Berck: where it must be very hot when it is hot.

I'm sorry to hear of the collapse at Jebail: Miss Holmes hasn't corresponded with me since the stimulus of your example was withdrawn.

As for Turkey, down with the Turks![1] But I am afraid there is, not life, but stickiness in them yet. Their disappearance would mean a chance for the Arabs, who were at any rate once not incapable of good government. One must debit them with algebra though ... Anatole France I am without at present, all but *l'Étui de Nacre*, which is of course delightful, but too much in one vein: so if you have any cheap paper-covered copy of him (paper-covers are customs free) preferably with interleaved translation, vocabulary & notes, I would be exceedingly grateful.

Let me hear how Harpenden[2] goeth: it is so seldom one is pleased with an expected pleasure. However there is always the unforeseen turning up ... as I said yesterday when 18 Kurds, mostly sheikhs & tribal chiefs, turned up 5 minutes before lunch: and I am alone these days, with Woolley in Aleppo getting

[1] The first Balkan War had ended in April, but peace negotiations broke down. The second Balkan War began on June 30, the Turks recaptured Adrianople on July 20. Peace between the Balkan States was signed on August 10, and between Turkey and Bulgaria on September 29.

[2] Mrs. Rieder had returned permanently to Europe and was in England. At the beginning of 1913 she joined the staff of St. George's School, Harpenden, where she taught languages.

his hair cut. Go to Oxford, when you can, and look at Hittite seals ... and Mother. Salaams to Noel: I'll write him in Arabic some day.   L.

60: TO FLORENCE MESSHAM

April 18, [1913]   *Carchemish*

Dear Florence, This is Friday, and writing day: and I am actually going to write to you. It is a *very* great compliment, for we are particularly busy. We have 200 men this year, but soon we will lose the most of them for harvest. After that perhaps we will have peace again.

We are finding a great deal this year: — great slabs of stone, carved with pictures of rows of foot-soldiers, and men hunting lions, and lions hunting bulls, and all sorts of strange beasts. We have found more this year than we have ever found before. The weather just now is splendid: warm, and sunny, but with a fresh wind, and every now and then a little splash of rain. The Euphrates is in flood, and it is great sport waving about over it in a canoe. We have a railway now, running regularly every day between Jerablus and Aleppo, so that we do get posts sometimes. It is not at all like last year: we are quite overrun with visitors: they are worse than fleas!

There is really nothing else to say! Everything is going on so well that nothing else matters. Yr.   NED

61: TO DR. W. B. ADAMS

April 19*th*, [1913]   *Carchemish, c/o H.B.M. Consul, Aleppo*

Dear Dr. Adams, I enclose you in this *two* possible patients;[1] I got your letter (which as usual I omitted to acknowledge) some two weeks back, and the delay since has been due to the press of work that has come upon us here. We are finding everything, and indeed we wish we weren't. Every day a bas relief, and sometimes two, besides pottery and bronze and ivory and apes and

---

[1] This letter was sent to Beyrout with two Arabs, a man and a boy affected with the 'Aleppo button', a swelling which develops into an ulcer, lasting a year and leaving a permanent scar.

peacocks:[1] — at least the apes and peacocks will be found next week I suppose.

When I wrote to you before, we were peacefully and quietly finishing the remains of a late Hittite temple; putting everything decently and in order; and then just when we thought ourselves safe, and were folding our hands in sleep, we tumbled over the corner of a new sculptured wall about 20 feet deep in the soil: We ran up this right and left and all of it was carved, so that now we have lion hunts, and a ποτνιος θηρων[2] and ranks of foot-soldiers and demons and winged monsters and outlandish beasts: all in good style, and most of them in condition good as new. Won't this even tempt you to come up and pay us a call? Euphrates is in flood and to dance about on it in a canoe is a most thrilling dream: besides we have sand-flies and fleas enough to take off the chill of the night-wind and in a few days it will be warm enough to go bathing. So you see you can have a variety of joys! In the matter of spelling;[3] why follow Carnegie, whose ideas of literature seem to be free-libraries? If you want something simple, and beginning with a C, take Chaucer as your guide and spell as you please: in fact spell on each occasion in the manner most fitting to your emphasis and meaning: — for example, if you mean terrible, very terrible, make it terririribble, and everybody knows how it comes off your teeth ... And otherwise, if you find it too difficult to make a language for the Saxon world upon your own, speak and write in French, wherein spelling is neither simplified nor simple. Incidently, my own spelling is considered admirable by most judges. To come back to business please look at these buttons, and it may be cure them ... and we send you a primitive terracotta as a reward. Your account please send to us, at the Consulate in Aleppo, and we will exchange it against a cheque.   T. E. LAWRENCE

Avoid annoying the boy: he swears like his father: — an expert.   L.

---

[1] *With a cargo of ivory, and apes and peacocks*, Masefield, *Cargoes* (*Ballads and Poems*, 1910). See also 1 Kings x. 20 and 2 Chronicles ix. 21.

[2] The Greeks had a term ποτνια θηρων applied to a goddess 'mistress of beasts', and used archaeologically for a female figure holding wild animals one in either hand by the hind legs. The masculine form is apparently Lawrence's own invention.

[3] Dr. Adams was an advocate of simplified spelling. See letter No. 71.

[In the following letter to Mrs. Rieder, Lawrence explains his future movements. In a letter of the same date to Hogarth he adds: 'I expect to get back about mid-July, and may bring the Hoja and Dahum with me: which will shock you.']

62: TO MRS. RIEDER

June 14, [1913]   *Carchemish*

[33 *lines omitted*] As for my movements, at this moment they are controlled by sand-flies: next week I go down the Euphrates by canoe (have you heard of the Canadian canoe?) four days to look at Rakka where I may dig for the Ottoman government, if miracles continue. Thence back to England in mid-July, for ten days, during which I fear it will be very doubtful that I see you.

Noël wants to know what happened to the 18 Kurds[1] ... they were representatives of two great feudal chiefs, who had made war on one another for 40 years ... and in our house they met on neutral ground, and fell each on all the others' necks (like a Rugger scrum) and kissed. Since there has been peace in N. Mesopotamia such as has not been for generations. Must tell W.-S.[2] all this next time I see him.

Tell Noël next that a feud broke out between two great families among our workmen, and that the digs for six days were two armed camps, not eating together, or speaking, walking the same path, or labouring in the same gang. And then we got angry, and shut the protagonists into the photographic dark room: ... (atmospherically the nth of H.[3] of Calcutta) for a couple of hours. They came out limp, & white, very much flea-bitten, but good friends and fellows in misfortune ... and by payment of a blood-money durable peace was cemented next day. Salaamât.   TEL.

[The dig at Carchemish closed on June 16th, when Woolley left, but Lawrence after visiting Rakka continued to live at the site till July 14th.

[1] See letter No. 59. There is an account of this meeting in Woolley's *Dead Towns and Living Men*.
[2] Willoughby-Smith of the British Consular service at Beyrout. Lawrence liked to tell him tall stories.
[3] The Black Hole of Calcutta.

He returned to Oxford towards the end of July and took Sheikh Hamoudi (the Hoja or foreman of the excavation work at Carchemish) and Dahoum with him.

He lodged them in the bungalow at the bottom of the garden of Polstead Road, which contained all his treasured possessions, and in which he had done most of his work while he was at the University. During their stay there was a fracas between them and an Egyptian student who was a friend of Will Lawrence's.

Lawrence returned to Carchemish in the latter part of August, taking them with him. He was in Aleppo on August 26th, when he wrote a letter to Miss Amherst about Saluki dogs.]

63: TO D. G. HOGARTH

29 Sept. 1913   *Baron's Hotel, Alep.*

I ran in to Aleppo today, thinking that it was about the time for the arrival of Woolley: — but no news of him as yet. A letter from you turned up yesterday: You have obviously got Deve Huyuk very nicely managed ... good business, because after all, the odds are against another place of the period being so completely collected again: incidentally Dahoum wrote to me yesterday from the Sadjur that he had bought seven more seals from the cremated cemetery at D.H.: I told him we wanted all D.H. ... he says one of the seals is good. Quaint that Scythian analogies should turn up. You know a lot of those quaint little bronze horses, like this ⌒ which an *Archaeologia* paper called Scythian are found in N. Syria. I wonder what Reitlinger will be like.

As for trepanning tools: of course for the moment I haven't any in stock! But I have written to Shepard in Aintab, and will ask Altounian[1] their names and appearances ... otherwise I might be imposed upon by a reaping hook in my ignorance. Greyhounds, as I have explained to Miss Amherst sundry times, must wait till I can pass out of Syria by way of Damascus: and as long as we are exporting material we are doomed to Alexandretta. Since the Thompson year I have not passed normally through a Turkish custom house. There was a report of more digging in

[1] Dr. Altounyan, senior, of Aleppo.

Serrin, and I hurried the Hoja across, but it was only Roman stuff. We don't pay much for the things we buy perhaps, but a devil of a lot trying to find them! It is interesting Evans putting the figurine at 3000 B.C. and the Hammam place also. I wrote to Leeds about Hammam: the place is Chiftlik,[1] and the four co-tenants of the graves were deadly afraid. They half suggested a royalty of a pound a head a day, as leave-way to dig, and then drew back . . . I was going to close, and put 50 men on to the place, and finish it in one strenuous day. I don't suppose there are more than half a dozen tombs left . . . just one tiny end of a modern graveyard: and the ground all scored across with early wall-foundations. I really thought it would have been madness to have dug that day I went. I would have been known and reported in 24 hours . . . and I don't suppose either the Turks or the B.M. would approve of that. Five graves in all were found by the Arabs there . . . one grave had nothing but pottery in it: only 9 pots . . . the important three graves you have in the Museum . . . the fourth grave had the worn handled seal in the Hittite case, and a few pots. The village has still a lot of pottery from these tombs in it . . . but only the big pieces: rather stupid stuff to bring away I think. I'll go down to Hammam after this season, and if it is in the least possible, dig it. In mid-winter there will be nobody about. [40 *lines omitted*]

Gregori came a week ago, and is now in Jerablus, house-building. We are raising the roofs in expectation of sitting out the winter on the site. He is very flourishing, and deadly jealous of the two who went to England. They talk very fully of what they saw: but are too sophisticated to be ridiculous about it. At any rate they declare to all the world that Syria is a mere flea-bite in public worth . . . and the Arabs too few in number to matter much. Please salaam me to Billy . . . though I don't suppose you'll see him for months. L.

I'm really very sorry about Hammam: but I'll go back there; which is heroic, for last time was worse than before with insects!

[In October his younger brother Will Lawrence visited him while on his way to India, and gave a rather highly coloured

[1] A communal farm.

account of his visit in a letter. The statement in it that there were massacres four months before, and that Lawrence was present in disguise, is not true. The massacres occurred in the spring of 1909, some months before Lawrence first went to the East. It seems probable that Will Lawrence had confused the story of the massacre with an incident at which Lawrence had been present, recorded in letter No. 67. At the time stated, he and Woolley had been working extremely hard before the Carchemish dig closed down on June 16th.

It is possible that Lawrence had been promised a share in the loot if Aleppo was sacked. This was probably what led him to get a supply of rifles to defend the Consulate. In any case the letter seems to me worth quoting on its own account.

It was this winter that Woolley and Lawrence kept a snow leopard which on one occasion got loose; Lawrence was amused by the local Arabs being afraid of it.

The following is an extract from a letter of Will Lawrence to a friend:

October 14th, 1913.

I went north through a really hot daylong train journey, far hotter than the Red Sea, with a wind one shrank from, hotter than the air, to Aleppo, where my Bedawi brother met me. He shewed me Aleppo well, taking me on calls to houses in the Moslem quarter, so bigoted still that he's the only European who knows it owing to his habit of going in Arab clothes, and to one Christian house where there was a marble court 200 years old, and a wonderful lacquered roof. The bazaar of Aleppo is considered the best in the Near East, all stone-work, with fields on top, on the roof, where I saw the goats grazing as I looked over the city from the minaret of the citadel (where very few Europeans have been). Then I went over to the Euphrates, 90 miles east or so, and lived in my brother's village, and swam the great river three times in the day, and practised pistol-shooting and looked at his excavations. Greater things were to follow.

One of his chief friends is Busrawi Agha, the chief of the Melli Kurds, and the greatest man in Kurdistan since the Young Turks poisoned Ibrahim Pasha. Busrawi is the man who carried out the massacres at Urfa, 8,000 people, and Adana, and Nezib just four months ago. At the last my brother was actually on the spot in disguise. And during the late war he and [*name of Kurd omitted*] planned the sack of Aleppo, actually arranging which should have the loot of which house, and apportioning two bankers' houses, great collectors of objets d'art, to Ned. They gave him a bodyguard of 200 Kurds whom he put up for some weeks. The failure of the Bulgars before Stamboul checked their plans which still simmer. Well, the old boy sent a force of horsemen to Jerablus to escort me to his tent, a huge open-sided marquee with 49 poles, and I stopped with him some days. Khalil came there at the same time to do me honour, and hundreds of men (they have 34,000 horsemen under them) raced and played the jereed, and fought in mock combats for my amusement. And then there was feasting and music and dancing, and I rode the best Arab mare in Mesopotamia for days, riding by night in the moonlight with summer lightning playing all the time. The old man sat on my left in the centre of a great dais next the curtain of the hareem, and fed me with his own hands, literally, out of a selection of more than forty dishes. Incidentally, these were very good but too highly seasoned for me, and I'm ill now in consequence, in a mild way, and must steer clear of curries for months. No matter: it was worth it.]

64: TO THE HON. FLORENCE AMHERST

Dec. 10, 1913   *Carchemish*

Dear Miss Amherst, I got your two letters about a fortnight ago — and I am ashamed to say that I had forgotten all about the collars.[1] However please accept very profound apologies . . . and the assurance that I have written to a Syrian I know in Damascus to try and find me the thing required in the bazaar there, or among his friends. Aleppo has nothing of the sort, and I fear that I will not be able to go South to Damascus this year.

Digs ended three days ago, and I only got back today from a visit I paid to a Kurd chief about 30 miles across the Euphrates. He had four Salugis, all hairless ones, of a biscuit colour, very large to my eyes. I measured them and they were from $22\frac{1}{2}$–24 inches high, very ugly dogs, of the slinking type: not your sort

See letters Nos. 58 and 70.

at all. He knew nothing of pedigree dogs, and said they did not keep them carefully enough for that, or of names for special breeds or colours: as he only spoke Turkish his knowledge, if any, would not have been of any use to you.

I ought to hear from Damascus almost at once: — at least I should get a collar, for I do not suppose my friend will write before. I will let you know (immediately, this time) as soon as anything happens.

We have found masses of stuff this year in the digs: rows of sculptured priestesses, and men carrying gazelles: alas no dogs with them!

More apologies for my neglect and rudeness, Believe me, Yrs sincerely   T. E. LAWRENCE

[Almost from the beginning, I think Lawrence had felt that the plan he had made with V. W. Richards to build a retreat and print books on a hand-press would not fill his life, or satisfy his ambitions. All his life he liked to look forward to retiring from the world, but the ivory tower — whether Pole Hill, or a barrack-room, or the cottage at Clouds Hill — did not satisfy him when he actually was about to enter it. The following letter is important as showing that he had realized this and quite early on had made the position clear to his partner.]

65: TO V. W. RICHARDS

Dec. 10, 1913   *Carchemish*

Dear Richards, It's quaint, isn't it, to begin again a correspondence which has lapsed for about a twelve-month? but, you know, I'm about as sick of myself and my affairs as one can well be, and it would be a consolation, if not exactly a comfort, to hear something of the sort from you. The fault was in ever coming out to this place, I think, because really ever since knowing it I have felt that (at least for the near future) to talk of settling down to live in a small way anywhere else was beating the air: and so gradually I slipped down, until a few months ago when I found myself an ordinary archaeologist. I fought very hard, at

Oxford and after going down, to avoid being labelled: but the insurance people have nailed me down, now.

All this preface is leading up to the main issue — that I cannot print with you when you want me. I have felt it coming for a long time, and have funked it. You know I was in England for a fortnight this summer, and actually found myself one afternoon in Liverpool St. coming up to you . . . and then went back again. I have got to like this place very much: and the people here — five or six of them — and the whole manner of living pleases me. We have 200 men to play with, anyhow we like so long as the excavations go on, and they are splendid fellows many of them (I had two of them: — head-men — in England with me this summer) and it is great fun with them. Then there are the digs, with dozens of wonderful things to find — it is like a great sport with tangible results at the end of things — Do you know I am keen now on an inscription or a new type of pottery? and hosts of beautiful things in the villages and towns to fill one's house with. Not to mention seal-hunting in the country round about, and the Euphrates to rest in when one is over-hot. It is a place where one eats lotos nearly every day, and you know that feeling is bad for one's desires to do something worth looking at, oneself.

Which is the end, I think, of the apologia . . . do write and tell me if there is any hope of your pulling it off on your own? Carchemish will not be finished for another four or five years: and I'm afraid that after that I'll probably go after another and another nice thing: it is rather a miserable come down. I haven't any money; can I offer you a carpet? They are about the only things remaining out here that are any good: Arabs have no handicrafts.

Remember me to Berry, if you see him: do you know I haven't read a book for months. L.

66: TO FLORENCE MESSHAM

Dec. 20, 1913   *Carchemish*

Dear Florence, I have not written to you this year yet . . . I think it is about time now.

We have had a very good season's digging this autumn: began on October 1, and stopped early this month: with about 200 men working. We found a great gateway, with long walls leading up to it, all lined with great carved slabs of black and white stone . . . a king and his children: men with drums and trumpets, and men dancing: a goddess at the head of a long procession of priests and priestesses, carrying corn and mirrors and fruit, and gazelles . . . Then a great base of two lions, holding up on their backs a great statue of a god, sitting on a stone chair, and holding a club: behind him the gateway, with very long inscriptions in Hittite (which of course we cannot read), and inside the house more sculptures: we have not cleared inside the house yet: that will be done in the spring. It must be a great temple, or the palace of the king. It seems a good deal bigger than a college.

Tomorrow we are leaving here (it is too cold & wet for pleasure) and going South, below Jerusalem, to help some Royal Engineers who are making a map of part of the desert. It will be warm down there, and sunny: which will be pleasant after our snow & frost up here.   N.

67: TO MRS. RIEDER

Dec. 26. [1913]   *Carchemish*

Dear Mrs. Rieder, Many thanks for a book on the Balkan War which came this week. Well written & very interesting: by a man who is rather an ass. It shows up the state of Constantinople very well. Here in the provinces it was the same or worse, with more openly expressed hostility to the Turks. It amused me especially to come across the reference to the Kurds who shot their doctor on the march. He has not got the story quite exactly as I happen to know, since I met them about half an hour after it, when they were excitedly looking for something else to kill. Fortunately I was in Arab togs.[1]

By the way, I wonder if you could do me a little job? Flecker (writing from a sanatorium in Switzerland — Montana to be exact —) has recommended to me Paul Fort *Choix de Poèmes:*

[1] See Will Lawrence's letter and my comment on p. 158.

Figuière. 6 frs. also Henri de Régnier's *Aréthuse*, and Albert Samain (*Jardin de l'Infante* & *Flancs du Vase*) . . . Could you be so good if you are feeling alive and kicking, (far be it from me to be literal!), to ask some indulgent bookseller to hurl them towards me, in Aleppo? I would be very grateful: to the extent of repaying you some day; This is only a scribble, for we are off tomorrow to Jaffa, to help survey Arabia Petraea. On the way we touch Beyrout, and will pull W— Smith's leg with dark suggestions of horrible political complots.

Salaam Noël from me: show him I remembered the two dots on his e. It looks distinguished. Yr.   E.L.

[The sentence in the letter to Miss Messham about helping Royal Engineers to map and that in the letter to Mrs. Rieder about 'horrible political complots' had more truth in them than perhaps Lawrence realized, when he wrote the words. For the archaeological survey which he and Woolley were asked to carry out for the Palestine Exploration Fund had been designed by Lord Kitchener as a piece of camouflage for a survey by Captain Newcombe, R.E., completing the one he had made himself as a young man. And the territory involved had already given rise to a serious incident between England and Turkey.

The Akabah incident of 1906 is described by Wilfrid Scawen Blunt in *My Diaries*, vol. II, chap. 5, as 'the beginning of Grey's blunders'. The matter is of some interest as determining the relations of England and Turkey in the years leading up to the Great War. A young Englishman, Bramley, had been making camel journeys about the deserts and Lord Cromer gave him a commission to find out whether a branch line of the Hedjaz railway was to be constructed to Akabah — a strategical threat to Egypt. Bramley ran into a Turkish detachment a few miles outside Akabah, at Tabah, and had high words with them. Lord Cromer took the matter up violently with the Sultan and laid claim to the whole of the Sinai peninsula for Egypt. The British Government and British public opinion supported him, and the British Fleet assembled at the Piraeus. Wilfrid Blunt was the only Englishman to protest against the claim of Egypt to Sinai. The Sultan yielded and the result was hailed as a triumph for Sir Edward Grey's diplomacy. Blunt's view (as always, a long-sighted one) was: 'The triumph proved an unfortunate one for our Foreign Office, as it was the beginning of the long quarrel between Sir Edward Grey and Constantinople, which resulted eight years later in the Turkish alliance with the Central European Powers in the Great War, a combination which gave Germany its victory over Russia. Not a soul in England understood its importance or cared to understand.'

The dedication of *The Wilderness of Zin*,[1] the report on their survey by Woolley and Lawrence, is: To Captain S. F. Newcombe, R.E. who showed them 'the way wherein they must walk, and the work that they must do'. This was Lawrence's idea.

Newcombe met them on January 10th and was relieved to find that he had not been saddled with a pair of ancient professors and that 'his rather primitive ways of living and ideas of comfort were not too far below their standards'. In a letter which I cannot include Lawrence did as a matter of fact complain with bitter humour of being restricted at one time to a diet of bread and Turkish Delight and drew up a menu ending with a savoury: *Turkish Delight on Toast.*]

68: TO A FRIEND[2]

Feb 6 [1914]   *In the wilderness of Sin. An Oasis*

Haven't written to you for a week or more, and feel mentally starved. Also this address is not a thing to be idly left alone. Really, it is a lovely little spot. On the west is a howling wilderness, to the Canal: Southwards desert to Aden: Northwards to Hebron, Eastwards to Baghdad. This is a valley between bare hills of limestone and flint: and in it are great springs of water coming out of the rock, and several great trees (Shittim and acacia) long hedges of brush-wood and broom in flower: young corn three feet high, splendid stuff . . . and all the flowers one needs. Nothing to eat at all however, except the beans on which the Camels feed, lentils, rice, potatoes, onions, Turkish delight, figs, raisins, eggs and marmalade, with bread. We are actually starving, you see! Whereas we are now rolling luxurious bellies

---

[1] *The Wilderness of Zin*, first published by the Palestine Exploration Fund 1915, and reprinted by Jonathan Cape 1936.

[2] This friend, who prefers anonymity, was also the recipient of letters Nos. 69, 75, and 100.

between pot-legs over the green earth. An immodestly pleasant place. We have sprung a new cook, and other fellows have lent us stores: and all is rosy. [3 *lines omitted*]

Kadesh Barnea, which is near here, was the place where the Israelites grumbled. I hear Moses led 'em up here, and all once more was peace. In fact they stayed forty years, and we are so sad that we cannot do so too. As it is, in two or three days we leave each other and the valley: Woolley goes due east, for the Dead Sea, I go South for the Red Sea: and when we meet in Aleppo on March 1st we toast one another in our respective oceans. The Dead Sea is hot, the Red Sea is hot: this oasis is cool, and Carchemish is snowbound. Don't you envy us our alternate frizzle and freeze?

We are digging up well preserved Amorites who were buried naked and headless.   L.

69: TO A FRIEND

Feb. 28 [1914]   *Hotel D'Angleterre Damas, Syrie*

Months since I wrote to you, and oceans have passed over my head since then, though alas! all the rest of me yet requires washing. Where was I? Aha ... I got down to Akabah alone and on foot, since my idiot camels went astray. Alone in Arabia! However it was only a day and a night, but by Jove, I was glad to see a tent (not mine) at the end of it. 48 hrs later, up came my camels, not smiling in the least.

Kaimmakam of Akaba was a bad man. He had (or said he had) no news of us and our little games: and so he forbade Newcombe to map, and me to photograph or archaeologise. I photographed what I could, I archaeologised everywhere. In especial there was an island, said to be full of meat. The bay of Akaba is full of sharks, hungry sharks (shivers) and the island was half a mile off shore. So, of course I engaged a boat ... and it never came, for the boatman went to prison at once. That looked to me a chance of a cheap sail, so I carried off the manless boat ... but a squad of police cut me off and robbed me of my treasure. I was alone alas! Well, I sent word to the Kaimmakam that upon his head was the forbidding me to go, and he said yes ... and while his police were carrying on mutual recriminations I puffed a zinc tank full of air, tied to its tail another for Dahoum, and one for a camera and tape and things ... and splashed off for the island with a couple of planks as paddles. The police returning a little later found my fleet sailing slowly seawards, and they had no boat, and no zinc tanks, and so could only weep while we worked. I had tied Dahoum to my tail, since I felt that any intelligent shark would leave me in the cold, but the whole squadron sailed across safely, saw, judged and condemned the ruins as uninteresting, and splashed homewards, very cold and very tired: there was a most unkind breeze in our teeth, and the return took hours. Kaimmakam was informed of his fate, and cursed my religion: he attached to me in revenge a lieutenant and a half company of soldiers to keep me always in sight. I remembered [*name omitted*] 's dysenteric servant, and took about six photographs so, and then dropped all the police in the ravines around Mount Hor. It's a long story ... they had camels, and couldn't walk and couldn't climb as fast as self and Dahoum ... and we walked them out of water, and they were hungry, and we dodged up valleys and slipped their trails; until the desired happened, and the last one left us, and I spent a splendid morning all in peace on top of Aaron's tomb in Mount Hor. Perfect peace without ... rather a strained situation within, mitigated partly by a sweet rain-pool, partly by the finding of my tents next afternoon after a two-day absence. I shot a partridge on the hill at dawn, and we cooked it over brushwood, and ate half each. A very good partridge but a small one. The night just under the hill-top was bitterly cold, with a huge wind and blinding squalls of rain. We curled up in a knot under a not-sufficiently-overhanging-rock and packed our sheepskin cloaks under and over and round us, and still were as cold and cross as bears. Not thirsty though, at all.

We had luck, since we found the two great cross-roads through the hills of the Arabah, that serve modern raiding parties entering Sinai, and which served the Israelites a bit earlier. Nobody would show them us, of the Arabs, which accounts for our rather insane wanderings without a guide ... but we did it all well.
[2 *lines omitted*]

Petra, [*name omitted*], is the most wonderful place in the world, not for the sake of its ruins, which are quite a secondary affair, but for the colour of its rocks, all red and black and grey with streaks of green and blue, in little wriggly lines . . . and for the shape of its cliffs and crags and pinnacles, and for the wonderful gorge it has, always running deep in spring-water, full of oleanders, and ivy and ferns, and only just wide enough for a camel at a time, and a couple of miles long. But I have read hosts of most beautifully written accounts of it, and they give one no idea of it at all . . . and I am sure I cannot write nearly as nicely as they have . . . so you will never know what Petra is like, unless you come out here . . . Only be assured that till you have seen it you have not the glimmering of an idea how beautiful a place can be.

I came up here on the Hedjaz line, after arresting three police-men at Maan, and marching them disarmed through the streets to the Serail, while my camels, which they had arrested, escaped. But that labour requires a letter to itself. Au revoir.   L.

[*P.S. of 5 lines omitted*]

[After Lawrence had discovered the two great cross-roads through the hills used by raiding parties, he travelled through little known country to Wady Musa and Petra where he acci-dentally met two English ladies, Lady Evelyn Cobbold and a friend, who were visiting it. On their return to Damascus they described to Miss Fareedeh el Akle how they had found a young Englishman called T. E. Lawrence stranded in the desert in a half-starved condition, and had rescued him. Actually they lent Lawrence the money to return from Maan to Damascus on the Hedjaz railway. The local knowledge obtained on this trip was vitally important for the strategy of the whole Arab campaign and it should be borne in mind that, during it, every advance took Lawrence into country better known to him.]

70: TO MISS FAREEDEH EL AKLE

March 8 [1914]   *Carchemish*

Dear Miss Fareedeh, Yes, I'm very sorry, I was a day in Damascus, and then fled away by the midnight train for Aleppo: and now I'm squatting in our own little hut here, and answering

my letters properly. I thought of coming to see you . . . even I
sent Dahoum to find out where your school was . . . and then I
was called out in the afternoon to the Salahiyeh district, and in the
evening I had to go to the Consulate: in short I couldn't get round.
If it had not been Sunday I would have called in the morning: —
but I knew that you would be beautifully dressed and singing
Arabic hymns: and I was in very ancient clothes, and very dirty:
and I cannot sing a single note.

I wrote to you and said that I was going along the Egyptian
frontier: well, with Mr. Woolley, my chief up here, we explored
the Northern half (say from Gaza to Kossaima–Kadesh Barnea)
in about five weeks. Then we separated: I went South to Akaba,
Woolley N. towards the Dead Sea.

In Akaba the Government tried to stop our working . . . it
forbade me to photograph, and Captain Newcombe, the surveyor,
to survey. Well of course I managed to take nearly all the photographs I wanted, and when they sent soldiers with me gave
Dahoum the camera, and he did the work.

My time was then up, and so I started up the Wady Arabah
for Wady Musa. The poor government was so afraid of me that
it sent after me a Uzbashi[1] and a whole squad of soldiers, and of
course they were a horrible nuisance. They tried to stop me from
going up Mount Hor, where Aaron's tomb is: so I went off on
foot with Dahoum, and in two days climbing over the hills we
had lost or tired out all the soldiers and at length reached the hill
top at dawn on the third day, quite alone.

My camels were all tired after two months' marching: however
I had sent them straight to Wady Musa, and by the time I got
there, at midday, they had the tents up and a huge lunch ready:
because when I set out for Mount Hor I could only take light
food with me, (just bread and eggs) since we had to carry it
ourselves. The English ladies you met came up with their tents
as I was finishing lunch.

I wasn't nearly starved: of course I could have always killed
and eaten Dahoum if the worst came to the worst . . . but I had
about a dozen camels, with five camel men and three tents . . .
so I was able to carry a lot of stuff with me.

---

[1] A lieutenant; the correct form is Yüzbashi.

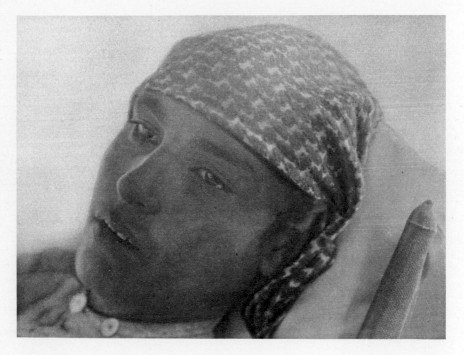

DAHOUM

Any luck about those dog-collars?[1] If you cannot find old ones please write to me, and I'll send you another letter asking you to have new ones made . . . and I want to know about Miss Holmes . . . My kind regards to Miss Hoel. Yours ever,

T. E. LAWRENCE

71: TO MRS. RIEDER

April 24, 1914   *Carchemish*

The thin end! your last letter begins with 66 words of English,[2] not counting the address. I will confine my reply to that part only, to encourage you.

You are in difficulties apparently with an agate seal. I wonder which it is, for I have sent home several, and I do not know which has escaped the pit and fallen into your hands. If it is a cylinder, it is very difficult to roll out beautifully: their intention was for sealing clay tablets: I find plasticine pressed out smooth & thin over card, and dusted with French chalk the easiest thing . . . but a superlative is misplaced. It can be done on sealing wax, but only with long practice.

The Odyssey of the books I explained in my last hurried note: they went over most of Arabia, seeking rest, and finally came to Aleppo, on the very day in which Fontana and his wife (both English, by the way) were hungering for Albert Samain. Who is very beautiful but hot air:— the latter literally and not of the radiator type common in the States. Paul Fort has lagged on the road . . . and *Le Horla* has fallen by the way-side. However Hogarth turned up a few weeks ago with a lot of Maupassant in his kit-bag, and a promise of the rest by post.

I don't think much of H. de Régnier.

A short story of Mérimée's, *La Vénus de l'Ile*, is most wonderful I think . . . and also several others I have read. I envy your pupils at St. George's the fun of reading all those trifles with you. You tell me that you are pleased with yourself there . . . and with the Grants[3] . . . some afternoon I will rush down and look at you

---

[1] See letters 54 and 68.

[2] Mrs. Rieder used to write to Lawrence in French, and once or twice he replied in it.

[3] Grant was headmaster of St. George's, Harpenden.

seated in the very midst of a Round Table singing a ballad of
Paul Fort.

Salaam me to Nöël . . . and tell him he must drop those plaguing
dots. Let him reform his spelling.

Did you hear that that horror Dr. Adams[1] sent me a letter
misspelt? . . . I returned it corrected in blue pencil: since then
peace: he only sends verbal messages now. I passed through
Damascus, but I didn't call on Miss Hoel or Miss Fareedah . . .
I had worn out all my clothes in Sinai, and turned up in Damascus
dressed à l'Arabe, and I don't know what Miss F. would have
said. I hear no news of Miss Holmes; Beyrout heard nothing
of her.

You reject the idea of Nöël's Gallicism: which has a good and a
bad sense: he is more Lamartine than Rabelais perhaps: but do
teach him to talk a decent French . . . the best I think is in the
South, where Provence has rounded it a little: it becomes more
meaty there. An old French general from Arles here yesterday
was too delicious in his accent: — Take Nöël there for his
holidays.

I regret that he is abandoning words of very many syllables. . . .

By the way we had two little Moores up here last week. They
went canoeing on the Euphrates, and got very wet and miserable.
So they won't come ever again. . . .

What more? Nothing: we have found nothing this year, and
don't expect to find anything . . . next year perhaps. It makes a
difference in one's working as to whether one has obtained a new
grant . . . or is in want of one. We are not, so no more advertisements in the manner of the *Illustrated London News*. Salaam me
unto your prickle.   E.L.

[As soon as Lawrence and Woolley had finished their respective
surveys, and before beginning to write up the results, they started
the new season's excavation work at Carchemish. The method of
paying workmen bonuses on all antiquities discovered had led
to a happy partnership of all engaged in the dig, a state of affairs
in marked contrast to that between their near neighbours the
German engineers building the Baghdad railway and their

---

[1] Dr. Adams was 'a horror' because he was an advocate of spelling reform. See letter
No. 61.

workmen, who were largely Kurds. The Germans offered high wages but had a system of fines, and of docking men for food and water, which led to continual friction. They maintained their authority with a guard of armed Circassians. The explosion came in March, the day after Lawrence and Woolley had returned, and the Englishmen were able to save their German neighbours from the consequences of their folly and inflict a moral punishment which must have been particularly galling. Lawrence wrote an amusing account of the affair at the time to a friend, but the fullest details are contained in a letter written two or three months later, after Lawrence had returned to England, to amuse his friend the poet James Elroy Flecker who was dying in a sanatorium in Switzerland. *An Essay on Flecker*, by T. E. Lawrence, was printed in a very limited edition (Corvinus Press, London and Doubleday Doran, New York, 1937), from a corrupt text. In it Lawrence wrote:

> 'Do write me a word. I'm sick and very miserable' was the last postcard, from his cruel mountain-side in Switzerland. With him there went out the sweetest singer of the war generation.]

72: TO JAMES ELROY FLECKER

Monday [*June* 1914]   [*From England*]

Seeing that you still show an unhealthy interest in the little fuss at Carchemish, despite my letter of explanation & derision from Aleppo, I have bought a large packet of thin paper, & with the help of the parcel post I will declare to you in order, most excellent Theophilus, all things that I have seen & heard.

Now for descriptions

The struggle was about the bridge-head, where the Company had built a little office & pay-house between two embankments. The bridge is only the temporary wooden thing, & at the moment they were making the permanent bank, thirty yards to the North of the temporary one. Each bank was about 8 feet high. North again of the new bank is the town-wall of Carchemish, *our wall*, a heap of earth grass-covered, perhaps forty feet high.

The Company was paying off some workmen on the completion of a subcontract, & as the contractor was bankrupt, they seized his books, & began to pay his workmen themselves. Unfortunately they omitted the very necessary inquiry (above all in Syria) as to whether the books were up to date, so naturally there was a little difficulty, when a certain Ali, a Kurd from Mesopotamia, found he was only to get 5 piastres for a full month's work. He protested, but the paymaster refused to listen to him. This paymaster was a German clerk, an awful rotter who

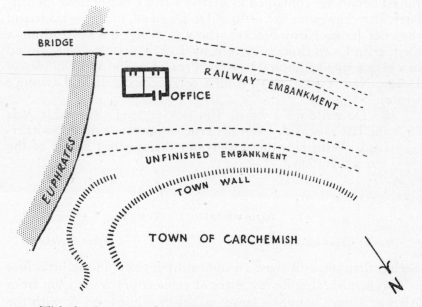

This is the map of the battlefield, & will be referred to constantly by me. Wherefore avoid losing it.

used to treat his men as beasts, & to swindle them in wages right & left; he used to charge for water and for bread, even though the men never ate the Company's bread. Of course they had to drink the water — but that was Euphrates, & the only cost of it was the wage of a water-boy to carry it. However, when Ali found his complaints unheeded, he threw his money back on the table. The German said to his Circassian 'Hit him', & the Circassian knocked the Kurd down. Getting up, he grabbed a stone & slung it at the Circassian who pulled out a revolver & shot at him.

Then the other hundred or hundred & fifty Kurds waiting their pay also picked up stones, & flung a volley, which broke the windows of the office in which three or four Germans were. They all grabbed rifles & revolvers, & through the windows blazed out at everyone they saw. These were mostly their own men at work on the Northern embankment thirty yards away, & they wounded five or six of them in the back.

After that of course everyone, Kurd or Arab, took cover behind the upper bank, & those who had revolvers let them off at the office. The Germans telephoned over the bridge & to their camp, & soldiers & Circassians rushed down with other engineers & foremen & mechanics, till they had about 30 wildly excited men with rifles about the bridge-head, shooting up & down stream, & across the bridge & at the embankment & in the air like lunatics.

Our house was only about 200 yards off, & we were down there immediately after the first shots were fired. We stood on the top of our town-wall & saw this happen. Then a Circassian stepped out from behind the office & took aim at Woolley & missed him badly. The bullet hit near his feet. The man was only about 60 yards off, & our men, about 7 or 8 of whom were with us, wanted to shoot the bounder. We said no, but ran down ourselves over the bank (now empty of men). I went to the office & told the chief Engineer that his men mustn't shoot at us. He at once gave orders thusly to his Circassians & subs, & we went back to our wall-top. When we got there we found to our astonishment that there were crowds of men coming up from the back. All the Kurd attackers, plus the men shot at by the Company from the Office, had slipped into the town ruins between the wall & the river, & were coming up to the hill top to take the bridge-builders in the rear. They had just to run down across the first bank & drive them into the river. When in cover behind the wall, they had all loaded their guns, & those unarmed had picked up iron bars or pick-axes or hatchets from a forge just below the wall. So they were feeling pretty fit, & very wild; about 300 of them.

We told our men — the seven or eight — to help us hold back these fellows. So we talked to them, & pushed them back, & took away their guns: even knocked down one or two, quite good-humouredly, & kept them on the wall-top. The Germans & the Circassians meanwhile were shooting at everything, & in particular at an unfortunate German on an island in the river. He had been working there, & was about 100 yards from the bank: but the bullets were fairly whizzing round him. He was dancing about & shaking his fist at them & talking in German, not softly, until finally some Kurds in a boat landed on the island & took him ashore with them. Our men laughed at this a bit, & things were getting easier, when for lack of other targets the German idiots began shooting again at us. They shot very badly, only hitting one boy next me, but it made the Kurds by us very wild, & we had an awful job to hold them in. However, our men who were with us helped us like anything, & we were able to prevent any rush or any shooting from our side. From beginning to end of the affair not a single shot was fired from the wall.

Finally about an hour later we managed to work the crowd back along the wall, & to get them up to the village. The Germans went to their camp & wired to Aleppo frantically about firing on the bridge. So the Railway Company sent out Aleppo's amateur fire-brigade by a special train about midnight. Next day the Government sent up 250 soldiers, & all the Consuls & Valis & Kaims. & Mutasarrifs & Commandants came out also & made independent inquiries. We got very sick of this, so we enrolled our men (the dispute happened on the day of our arrival only), & got to work. The Company thought it was going to make capital out of the row, so magnified it enormously, & said the whole country was thirsting for Christian blood. They said 200 soldiers were not enough to make safe their work. So the Vali trotted down to us and asked how many soldiers we had for our 250 men. We said of course that we didn't hold with soldiers, & the Germans were jeered at; but turned it off by saying that our side, the Syrian one, was quite safe, that it was in Mesopotamia that the danger lay. So to biff that, Woolley & I walked over next day to Mesopotamia alone & picked a lot of moon-daisies & came back, meeting the Government officials & the Consuls & engineers by accident at the bridge-head. So that was a further source of grief to them. The whole country was absolutely at peace, you know, all along.

The next day up came the German Consul, one Rössler, to our house at dusk alone. Fontana was holding forth upon Martial, but stopped. Old Rössler said that he had come to ask our help, that the Turkish Government was only fooling as usual & that as the German Consul he felt himself responsible for a peaceful settlement with the Kurds. We of course were inwardly chortling, but were quite polite, I hope. We pointed out how serious the matter was. First of all they had killed one Kurd, and wounded about twenty. We suggested £80 blood-money for the dead man, & about £40 in compensation for the rest. Rössler boggled a bit, but consented in the end. Then we pointed out that all the Circassians must go (each German had one as personal guard, & they were Membidj bullies, & not true Circassians, but awful bounders): this Rössler at once agreed to. Then we suggested that the paymaster & another engineer must go: this he promised: then we proposed about a dozen Kurds being put on the line to watch pay-days in the Kurdish interest, & in case of dispute to have appeal to him. This also was agreed to, so two days later we brought in the chief of that Kurdish tribe, a man called Busrawi, a very good fellow, whom we knew very well; & he went down with safe-conduct to Fontana, & thence to the German Consulate, & signed a treaty of peace on the above terms, with a very fat present to himself.

It's really very comic now — every engineer walks about with a huge frowning Kurd behind him, armed to the teeth, & very ready to shoot him down if he misbehaves. The improvement in German manners is incredible: only they don't seem to love us more than before.

There now, for your amusement I have detailed the wretched thing at full length. The only amusing part is the peace-making, which gave us great joy.

I don't think you can ever have got my Aleppo letter, written just after *Alsander*[1] & your letter came. I wrote to a pension Rheingold — perhaps it was too late, or did the Turkish post covet my letter. They often do, I'm afraid.

[1] *The King of Alsander*, a novel, by James Elroy Flecker.

However, I'm very sorry, for Woolley, Hogarth & I were all reading *Alsander* together with mutual jealousies. I have forgotten now Hogarth's remarks — they included a desire to know who *William Jordan Junior*[1] was ... Woolley was cut to the quick over the sad fate of Arnolfo ... He regarded it as apostasy on your part of the worst, & a deplorable tragedy, which blinded for him the book. I think myself that it is exceedingly annoying as a book: if it had been three it would have been streets more satisfactory ... all your characters seem so much more capable & interesting than they have room to show. It is more of a dream or a chapter of dreams than a novel. No doubt you meant it so, but I'm a pedestrian, & I don't like to see glorious things for a hundredth part of a second only. That's why I prefer *Samarcand*[2] as more satisfactory, though I quite agree that parts of *Alsander* are as good as anything going. By the way, you can write better prose than Snaith — the battle in *Alsander* & the descriptions of the disordered garden, & the crossing of the hills are very wonderful. As for the description of the girl with the pails — well you know it struck me as falling between the two pails: a little too exuberant to be solemn, & not as fat as a show fat-lady should be. You won't be able to make any sense of that as an 'art criticism'.

Two or three things of Ernest Dowson have pleased me lately. Alas I suppose you have read everything like that.

I have never read a book of yours called *The Grecians*. Do you approve of it?

Do you know that in January & February Woolley & I explored the desert of the exodus, looking for the foot-prints of the children of Israel. And now we have to write the next annual of the Palestine Exploration Fund to describe our non-success. The Fund inform us that the tone of the annual is usually slightly devotional, so prepare yourself for something hotter than *Alsander*.

I expect to be about another two or three weeks yet in England, & thereafter Eastward — I'm afraid it's not very easy to come out via Davos!

---

[1] *William Jordan Junior*, a novel by J. C. Snaith.
[2] *The Golden Journey to Samarkand*, a poem, by James Elroy Flecker.

Am exceedingly sorry to hear of your being so bad. To be in bed for six months must be a ghastly trial — unless you are really ill, when it would no doubt seem natural. Write to me here once more if it does not weary you. After writing you three sheets I deserve many things. However one doesn't get this usually. Yours, E.L.

PART TWO

THE WAR

INTRODUCTION TO PART TWO

Lawrence had, as is shown by his letter to Flecker, been in England for several weeks before the War broke out, engaged in writing his share of *The Wilderness of Zin* for the Palestine Exploration Fund. In a letter of September 18th, he complained of 'the horrible boredom of having nothing to do', but actually he seems to have been pretty busy. In a note on the typescript of Liddell Hart's '*T. E. Lawrence': in Arabia and After*, he wrote:

> Turkey was not in the war, but was sore about the Sinai survey, which it felt had been a military game. K.[1] (the only begetter of the survey) insisted on the Palestine Exploration Fund's bringing out its record of our archeological researching, p.d.q.[2] as whitewash. Woolley and I had instructions to get it done instanter.
>
> Woolley and I wrote to Newcombe, when the book was finished, and asked his advice about a war job. They were difficult to get. Newcombe told Cox, of the Intelligence, about us, and got our names on the waiting list. Woolley lost heart, waiting, and wangled a Commission in the Artillery. I asked Hogarth (prominent in the R.G.S.)[3] if he could expedite me something — and he asked Hinks, who got Hedley to take me. The interview with Hedley was by Hogarth's appointment. Of course Hedley was drawing the Sinai map, and knew about me. He had only one assistant left, Capt. (Walter) Nugent, who was within a week of departing to France. Nugent hurriedly instructed me in my G.S.G.S.[4] duties (we were M.O.4, O and I[5] being one!) and Hedley and I were left alone in the office.

The job in the map department was exchanged in December for that of map officer in the new department of Intelligence in Egypt, which contained a group of extraordinarily brilliant men.

---

[1] Lord Kitchener.
[2] Pretty damn quick.
[3] Royal Geographical Society.
[4] General Staff Geographical Section.
[5] Military Operations: Operations and Intelligence.

Lawrence, the youngest of them, was the most daring and original and profoundly influenced them all. A subaltern on the staff, with none of the regular officer's interest in the niceties of military appearance, scorching about between Cairo and Bulaq on a Triumph motor-cycle, he was an offence to the eyes of some senior officers.

But he was planning a strategy in the Middle East which was to liberate Syria from the Turks and involve England in violent friction with her chief ally, France. Indeed his letters putting forward his plan for seizing Alexandretta and making it an English naval base might lead one to think that England and France were on the brink of war! Within three months of his arrival in Cairo, Lawrence was explaining his plan 'to roll up Syria by way of the Hedjaz in the name of the Sherif . . . we can rush right up to Damascus, & biff the French out of all hope of Syria'.

There was a lack of sense of reality in his attitude to Anglo-French relations, since he seems to have refused to see that smaller interests must give way to those which are greater and more permanent, and that great and permanent interests, as well as cultural sympathy and similarity, would bind England and France together long after questions arising out of the war were over. This misconception of the future relations of England and France was at first because, like many Englishmen at the time, Lawrence conceived of Russia as France's closest ally. He was ignorant of the strength of the Russian revolutionary movement and did not know that Russia, like the peaceable dinosaurs of the Jurassic, becomes weaker as it grows larger, but regains its power as it loses provinces. He assumed that the war would end with an immensely strengthened Russian Empire, irrevocably in possession of Constantinople, dominating the Balkan States, and with the Mediterranean open to her.

With Russia holding the Dardanelles, and France Syria, the communications of the British Empire would have been at the mercy of its allies. By the time that the Russian generals, assisted by Lenin and Trotsky, had shown the emptiness of this dream, Lawrence was concerned with Arab freedom and with his conception of the British Empire as a voluntary association of Free

States of all sorts of different races. He was anti-French because he wanted a purely Arab Government in Damascus, just as he was anti-Government of India because he wanted a purely Arab Government in Baghdad.

The rest of the war years are the record of how he carried the campaign he had conceived in the spring of 1915 to a victorious conclusion. In Cairo Lawrence was constantly the scene of vast preparations for the most inefficient military operations: the procrastinating wasteful bungling of Gallipoli; the battles of Gaza, the defence of the canal zone, the campaign in Mesopotamia where thousands of British lives were flung away with less excuse on the score of necessity than on any allied front.

The generals responsible for these disasters had power and vast armies. Lawrence wanted only a free hand to preach: to convert leading Englishmen and Arabs to his ideas. He was able to do this, in the first place, by making himself obnoxious to the Staff and getting himself attached to the newly formed Arab Bureau. He found himself there among intelligent and brilliant men. An important stage was marked by the foundation and printing of a secret periodical, *The Arab Bulletin*, designed to keep the Foreign Office, the High Commands in India, Egypt, the Sudan and Mesopotamia fully informed of developments in Arabia. Lawrence was responsible for the earlier numbers and, when his work was taken over by Colonel Cornwallis, remained its most exciting contributor.

Thanks to the Arab Bureau, *The Arab Bulletin*, and to his own initiative, Lawrence got freedom to act himself, got his ideas accepted, and won for them a few shiploads of arms and bags of gold, and later on a few skilled men, to organize, drive cars, or demonstrate machine guns.

'All the subject provinces of the Empire to me were not worth one dead English boy', he wrote in the introduction to the Oxford edition of *Seven Pillars of Wisdom*, and the proud boast was almost true. He won his victories without endangering more than a handful of Englishmen — and they were won not to add subject provinces to our Empire but that the Arabs whom he had lived with and loved should be a free people, and that Arab civilization should be reborn.

In these years of desperate guerrilla warfare Lawrence was wrought up into a state of white-hot exaltation which alone enabled him to drive himself on, reckless of wounds and torture. Thus when he came to look back on those days he could write sincerely:

> It felt like morning, and the freshness of the world-to-be intoxicated us.

The record of the war years in Lawrence's private letters is a fragmentary one, and I have not been allowed to use all that I wished to publish. Detailed accounts like those with which he enabled his family to follow all his doings at Carchemish were impossible in wartime, yet he was writing very similar reports, for *The Arab Bulletin*. I have included a number of these as well as some other reports written for the eyes of one or two of his superiors. Through their matter-of-fact words one can see the figure of the man whom the Arabs nicknamed Prince Dynamite.

MAP 2.

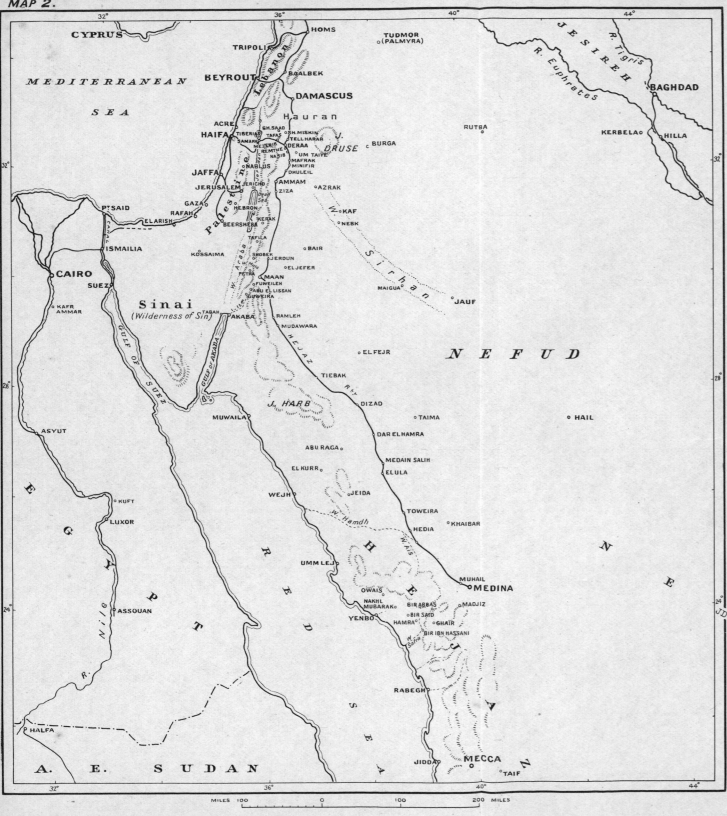

Sept. 18. [1914]   2 *Polstead Road, Oxford*

Dear Mrs. Rieder, 5 minutes ago your pistols came:[1] and very soon the post goes out: so I'll just dash you off a line, and let you know. They are exactly what I want: and your decency (an English expression not understood over there) in sending two is very great. Frank is Lieut. in the 3rd Gloucester Batt. and is near Woolwich training himself & his company: when he is trained, & there are vacancies in the regt. at the front, he'll be sent out. I am writing a learned work on Moses and his wanderings: for the Egyptian people say they want me but not yet, and the War Office won't accept me till the Egyptian W.O. has finished with me. I have a horrible fear that the Turks do not intend to go to war: for it would be an improvement to have them reduced to Asia Minor, and put into commission even there. It all depends on Enver's getting loose again. At present he has 'blood-poisoning' and is sulking in his palace. The abolition of the capitulations by Turkey is rather amusing. We are going (for the sake of a free hand in Egypt, where fiscal privileges are very inconvenient) to let her have fiscal & economic right over foreign property: that is she may tax lands & animals of foreigners in Turkey: but we maintain the personal inviolability and the sanctity of the foreign houses. The B.P.O.[2] will go: they have not made a profit during the last three years. The foreigners also have free right to travel without papers.

If Turkey refuses these suggestions, England will not go to war with her, but Greece & Roumania will look in, after having promised Bulgaria a slice for her benevolent aid. Then of course if Turkey attacked us in Egypt or in the Persian gulf, we would be justified in self-defence.

Don't come back to England. The horrible boredom of having nothing to do, & getting news about once a week, and hearing

[1] Mrs. Rieder, who was in the U.S.A., had sent two Colt automatics at Lawrence's request. For several weeks after war broke out there was a shortage of pistols in England. Lawrence had left his own pistol in charge of Dahoum.

[2] British Post Offices.

all the rumours and theories and anxieties of everybody all round
you gets on all our nerves. And you couldn't do anything. The
Govt. is very well prepared for our present needs, and is not
inviting volunteer aid. The first fortnight of war every 'female'
made 'Balaclava helmets', & when the W.O. received these
bundles they had to publish a statement that troops were not
allowed to wear such things on active service: (it deafens them,
like blinkers to the sight, and they would all be massacred in their
sleep). Then for six weeks all Oxford made nightshirts for the
hospital, until the patients became like Montezuma's daughter,
not needing to wear the same shirt twice: . . . : and so on. There
is nothing to do but wait, and waiting is very hard. You had much
better do it over there.   E.L.

I'm going to send you a letter of thanks very soon: tonight
perhaps: I'm also going to congratulate you on your quickness in
getting the things over. It will give Frank time to practise with
his.   E.L.

[In the War Office Lawrence was employed to produce a large
scale map of Sinai and a military guide to the country. In a letter
which I cannot include he remarks that a nemesis may be
awaiting him: he will be served out a copy of his own book and
told to find his way about the country with its help.]

74: TO MRS. FONTANA

Oct. 19, 1914   2 *Polstead Road, Oxford*

Dear Mrs. Fontana, Mr. Hogarth has been reading to me
something of the epic of the *Midlothian*.[1] I must congratulate you
warmly on your enterprise, and the recording talent you show in
the description of it. It is comforting no doubt, to know that you
have turned the incident to good account.

   Are the beast and the beaste with you? Offer them my salaams,
and explain that in England we don't come to dinner every
Thursday and Friday.

   [1] Mrs. Fontana had written an account to Hogarth of her flight with her two
children, Guido and Tacita, 'the beast and the beaste', from Alexandretta in the *Midlothian*, a small cattle-boat.

Mr. Hogarth no doubt has told you what Woolley & I are doing (— nothing — but we have good intentions) so I needn't bother you therefore.

Turkey seems at last to have made up its mind to lie down and be at peace with all the world.[1] I'm sorry, because I wanted to root them out of Syria, and now their blight will be more enduring than ever.

You have no news of Carchemish I suppose? I want to write to Mr. Fontana, and ask him to find out how things go. But sulphur and brimstone must be the atmosphere of the Consulate just now. Did you see that the Vali of Beyrout announced his power of arresting Mr. Cumberbatch?[2] An American guard-ship has opportunely turned up.

Read Cunninghame Graham.   T.E.L.

Woolley has made many anxious enquiries after you: and we couldn't find out in which continent you lay.

75: TO A FRIEND

Sunday [Autumn 1914]

This job is not going to be prolific in letters: — because there isn't much to say, and most of that shouldn't be said. No matter.

Today has been an awful scramble, for some unit (report says K's. private sec.) asked for a complete map of Sinai, showing all roads and wells, with capacity of latter, and a rough outline of hills. As Sinai is in manuscript in 68 sheets it meant a little trouble, for the sheets (because the surveyors were not like yourself) were not numbered or labelled, and so nobody could put them together. I came up like St. George in shining armour and delivered them (i.e. Col. Hedley said 'You go down and see what you can do with the damned thing') and by night behold there was a map of Sinai eighteen feet each way in three colours. Some of it was accurate, and the rest I invented. It took the three of us just eleven hours to get the thing traced.

It was proclaimed very good, and the request was made for an extension fifty miles to the E: that is Newcombe's part. However

---

[1] Turkey attacked Russia and the British Empire ten days later.
[2] British Consul.

by good hap the draughtsmen were gone to bed. So that remains for tomorrow.

Sinais are in much demand just at present ... if the P.E.F.[1] publish that thing of ours next month it will be confiscated probably: and I will have to do the confiscating. The position is an involved one, but no matter. I didn't get paid for it.

[23 *words omitted*] Though I'm not appointed to anything, yet they can't sack me now, as I know the most of their secrets. So I wait in a sure hope. The W.O. people are slow, except in the map department!   L.

Tell [*initials omitted*] the marble stairs are only for Field-Marshalls and charwomen.

76: TO W. J. CRACE[2]

Dec. 3 [1914]   M.O.4 [*War Office*]

Dear Mr. Crace, I only got the MSS[3] yesterday from Woolley — and it has been sent on today. I think it is in fairly complete condition ... though we would go tinkering on with it for months. Your $\frac{3}{8}$ map of Palestine is being prepared, on two sheets which suits the W.O. better than six! It is a very pretty map indeed.

I go off to Egypt on Tuesday, overland to Marseilles, with Captain Newcombe who is in the W.O. for a few days writing reports, and checking the maps. We are both almost uncomfortably busy, as you guessed.

Woolley goes off on Saturday from London by P. & O. I think these dates are certain: somebody got into a row for delaying our start so long.

The Newcombe map is nearly finished. I'm afraid it can't be sold by you for a few months yet! But it is going to be enormously useful. That survey was a very fortunate stroke.

Addresses of both Woolley and myself will be General Headquarters, British Army Occupation, Cairo. Don't send out

---

[1] The Palestine Exploration Fund.
[2] Hon. Sec. of the Palestine Exploration Fund.   [3] Of *The Wilderness of Zin.*

proofs, because the Censor would never pass them. Much better Egypt shouldn't know. Yours sincerely,   T. E. LAWRENCE

77: TO MRS. FONTANA

[*Postmarked 4. Dec. 14*]   *M.O.4, War Office, Whitehall, W.*

Dear Mrs. Fontana, I wonder if you have any news of Mr. Fontana? He got to Egypt, I heard, & I know nothing more. Will you send me news, if any. He carried away to Aleppo our silver, & rugs, and books, for which he deserves everlasting thanks. I wonder what has happened to the Consulate. It has been searched I know, but apparently the rifles[1] etc. were not found: should like to know about it.

Further, early in October Mr. Fontana was making efforts to have the military service of our head men carried out on the Dig, as guards. I wonder if he got this through, before he left. I hope the men will carry off everything from the house before any Turk can sack it. It would grieve me if any Turk shot me with my own revolver. However I asked Haj Wahid & Dahoum to see to them. Between them they can dispose of all things cunningly in the village.

Woolley goes E. with me: at least he leaves on Saturday P. & O.; and Newcombe (who salutes you) and I leave on Tuesday going overland. I have been up here for a couple of months overseeing Sinai maps being drawn, & writing Sinai reports. Now it's Cairo. All goes well, except among the Turks. Are there any commissions I can do for you in Aleppo next spring?

Salaam me to Beast: and report by wire if Beaste hateth me more, or Dandini.[2] What befell him, by the way?   E.L.

[Captain S. F. Newcombe, who had been sent to France, was eventually recalled and on December 9th he and Lawrence set off together to Cairo. George Lloyd, M.P. (now Lord Lloyd), Leonard Woolley, Aubrey Herbert, M.P. and Captain Hay were sent out at the same time but travelled independently. They were to reinforce Intelligence.]

[1] See pages 150, 151.
[2] The Austrian Consul at Aleppo. He was a friend of Lawrence's.

78 : TO D. G. HOGARTH

Monday, 20 Dec. [1914]   *Intelligence Dept., War Office, Cairo*

Newcombe and I got here last Tuesday, and Woolley with one Lloyd and Aubrey Herbert turned up on Friday. There wasn't an Intelligence department it seemed, and they thought all was well without it: — till it dawned on them that nobody in Egypt knew about Syria. This was the day we got there, so they changed their minds about sending us flying as a good riddance — and set us to collect intelligence instead. It isn't very easy, but we have rather a travelled lot of people at it! It promises to be good fun. It seems Woolley did want to stick to the Army permanently, & coming out here cuts that out: which is just as well.

I suspect that things may move quicker than I thought. Crace had better publish that book in Jan-Feb when he can: — or when you can. I hope it won't be too bad a job. It certainly was the filthiest manuscript made.

The interest may shift violently to the North almost any day: — so far as we are concerned it has shifted already. But our Intelligence has the capital 'I', and is a very superior sort of thing. I fancy there is a sort of censorship, which is a very annoying feeling. You might let me know if there is for this.

Turkey has gone one better than ourselves by forbidding ingress & egress for people, merchandise, & mails. The Syrian Protestant College is wailing by wireless to Washington. Precious useful place to appeal to! The only people whose news they won't cut off probably will be ourselves. I suppose censors are all rather like that.

There's one Thompson (I don't really know about his 'p'.) who is a son in law of Pears[1] from C.P. and speaks Turkish very well, in the office. Seems good.

Crace says he's going to pay us for the book: — My doubts on the matter: — but persuade him instead to put a colour on the map, or something. Please don't put my name on the thing — the book that is — Darbishire should sign the map. My advice very strongly is — rush it out.

---

[1] Sir Edwin Pears, president of the European Bar at Constantinople, and correspondent of *The Daily News.*

Those mysterious wireless telegrams early in the war were in Greek: — no such thing to make a loud fuss over.   L.

Pirie-Gordon is out here (R.N.R.) on the *Swiftsure*.

79: TO D. G. HOGARTH

Jan 15 [1915]   *Grand Continental Hotel, Cairo*

Blank! Am in an office all day & every day, adding together scraps of information, & writing geographies from memory of little details. It is the dullest job to hear of, but not so bad in action. The preparations of the Turks seem to be slacking off: I'm afraid there is nothing more cheerful I can tell you.

Our particular job goes well. We all pulled together hard for a month to twist 'them' from what we thought was a wrong line they were taking — and we seem to have succeeded completely: so that we today have got all we want for the moment, & therefore feel absolutely bored.

News has come through that the Germans have laid a light line through the S. Gate,[1] and are taking stone from the Kalaat at Jerablus. The bridge is being pushed ahead. I don't suppose that they will do serious harm merely to spite us: brutes they are. Syria is all turned upside down by the uncertainty of government measures. If last harvest had not been a record one things would not have lasted so long. As it is they will be quite happy till next spring. It seems to be a queer sort of happiness though. I'm afraid we'll never get our gang together again. This you will observe is the depression of complete success ... because we really have scored a very big thing.

Salaam me to Leeds. I can't write to him, because office work is not exciting, & I haven't had an off afternoon to go & see the pyramids, & write him a little letter all about them. I hope to get away for a day in the end of this month.

Musil[2] — the Austrian — is head guide to the General Staff in Damascus: queer things happen now a days! Moritz is also out there, and Meisner,[3] building railways.   L.

---

[1] At Carchemish.   [2] The distinguished traveller in Arab countries.
[3] Bruno Meissner, the Assyriologist.

You might address to me Continental Hotel, a print of any photos. of Beilan[1] you have.   L.

80: TO D. G. HOGARTH

2.2.1915   *Grand Continental Hotel, Cairo*

A long time since I wrote to you: — but office from 9 A.M. till 10 P.M. and all confidential work doesn't tend to letter writing: one has a pen in one's hand all day, and is sick of the thing by dark . . . We nearly wired for you the other day, to come & do civil governor of our conquests . . . but we decided it was too small a job to warrant it . . . How amused old Catoni would have been.

The P.E.F. are foolish in their generation, and so no doubt children of light. I hope Musil's knowledge among the Turks is more use than mine among the English. The Egyptian army officer is pathetically ignorant of across the border. Woolley sits all day doing précis, & writing windy concealers of truth for the press . . . Newcombe runs a gang of most offensive spies,[2] & talks to the General. I am map officer, & write geographical reports, trying to persuade 'em that Syria is not peopled entirely by Turks . . . Aubrey Herbert unearths futile conspiracies.

The ten principals of the last conspiracy were sold by their underlings, & then came each one independently & secretly by night to the General, & gave away his fellows. It was so hard to keep them from meeting on the doorstep . . . and when the plot matured it was like the man who was Friday.[3] None the less the Egyptian townsmen do hate us so. I thought it was only a coldness . . . but it is a most burning dislike. They are also very much afraid.   L.

[Lawrence was by no means limited to the job of map officer. The following letter shows his great political realism and an almost uncanny knowledge of how to get things done. It is indeed a remarkable letter for a subaltern to be writing. The last sentence predicts a renaissance of Turkey as a result of defeat in the war.]

[1] The Beilan Pass commands access to Alexandretta from the interior of Syria.

[2] Newcombe informs me that he had to interview would-be Intelligence agents, but found them all unsuitable.

[3] See *The Man Who was Thursday*, by G. K. Chesterton.

81 : TO D. G. HOGARTH

18 *March* [1915]   *Grand Continental Hotel, Cairo*

This letter is not going to be censored, so I'm going to let fly.

The Turks aren't coming back, they have only 50,000 disaffected troops in Syria, (200,000 Dardanelles, 200,000 Caucasus, 50,000 Mesopotamia) and the whole country is mad against them. Ibn Rashid has been heavily defeated by Ibn Saoud (Shakespear unfortunately killed in the battle): Idrisi is at open war with the Turks in Assyr: Sherif has almost declared himself, & the Vali & staff of Hedjaz have taken refuge in Damascus. We have sent troops from the Canal to Basra, to reinforce everybody there, (Indian troops there are shaky it seems), the Australians & New Zealanders, & some Indians are going to the Dardanelles, with the French, & Ian Hamilton's army. We will be left here in Egypt with 20,000 men or so. The French insist upon Syria — which we are conceding to them: there remains Alexandretta, which is the key of the whole place as you know. It's going to be the head of the Baghdad line, & ∴ the natural outlet for N. Syria & N. Mesopotamia: it's the only easy road from Cilicia & Asia Minor into Asia etc. etc. Also it's a wonderful harbour, & thanks to Ras Khanzir on the S. can be made impregnable. It is cut off from Syria, & is neither Syria nor Asia Minor. In the hands of France it will provide a sure base for naval attacks on Egypt — and remember with her in Syria, & compulsory service there, she will be able any time to fling 100,000 men against the canal in 12 days from declaration of war. The Sinai desert is not really any obstacle in the spring — or at any time when the railway (which is inevitable) is built. The only place from which a fleet can operate against Egypt is Alexandretta, because there is no English port from which one can blockade it. Smyrna & Constantinople are shut in by islands: whereas Alexandretta has only Cyprus in front of it, & the water round that is too deep for a large naval harbour to be built.

If Russia has Alexandretta it's all up with us in the Near East. And in any case in the next war the French will probably be under Russia's finger in Syria. Therefore I think it absolutely necessary that we hold Alexandretta ... and thanks to the Amanus we

N

needn't hold anything else, either in Syria or in Asia Minor. The High Commissioner is strongly of the same opinion, & General Maxwell also, [6 *words omitted*]. K. has pressed it on us: Winston seems uncertain, & Someone — not Grey — perhaps Parker in the F.O. is blocking it entirely. I think that perhaps you can get a move on.

K. is behind you in any case. Can you get someone to suggest to Winston that there is a petrol spring on the beach (very favourably advised on by many engineers, but concessions always refused by the Turks) huge iron deposits near Deurtyol 10 miles to the N. and coal also. Point out also that it is a splendid natural naval base (which *we* don't want but which no one else can have without detriment to us).

If Winston settles on a thing he gets it, I fancy: especially with K's help.

Then go to the F.O. if possible. Point out that in Baghdad Convention France gave up Alexandretta, to Germans, & agreed that it formed no part of Syria. Swear that it doesn't form part of Syria — and you know it speaks Turkish: & also tell F.O. (not Parker, whom I shall murder some day) that it is vitally important we hold it. One cannot go on betting that France will always be our friend. If F. has all Syria south of Alex, she ought to be content: — she is now trying to fob off Jerusalem on us. Don't touch it with a barge-pole.[1]

By occupying Alexandretta with 10,000 men we are impregnable and we cut

    i. Communication between Asia Minor & Syria.

    ii. Communication between Asia Minor & Baghdad, where the English are likely to be very hard pressed shortly.

    iii. We also relieve the Caucasus, especially after the centre of Turkey shifts to Konia. We must I think look for a renaissance of the Turk when he has lost Constantinople. They will be much more formidable militarily — and less so politically.   TEL.

[To a letter written on March 31st, 1929, to Liddell Hart on the latter's *Decisive Wars of History*, Lawrence appended the following note:

[1] Far-sighted!

'I am unrepentant about the Alexandretta scheme which was, from beginning to end, my invention, put forward necessarily through my chiefs (I was a 2nd Lieut. of 3 months seniority!). Actually K. accepted it, and ordered it, for the Australian and N.Z. forces: and then was met by a French ultimatum. A landing at Alexandretta in Feb. 1915 would have handed over Syria and Mespot. to their native (Arab) troops, then all in their home stations, and complete, and automatically established local governments there: and then attracted to Ayas (it was Ayas, not Alexandretta) the whole bulk of the *real* Turkish armies:* and that would have been the moment for the Dardanelles naval effort.'

* to fritter itself against the Arabs, not against us.

The following letter is probably the most remarkable document Lawrence ever wrote. It shows that he had already planned the campaign which he was to carry to a victorious conclusion three years later.]

82: TO D. G. HOGARTH

March 22 [1915]   *Port Said*

Another uncensored letter: at half an hour's notice last week I sent you a flood of stuff about Alex: please try & push it through for I think it is our only chance in face of a French Syria. I hope my letter was clear — because I dashed it off in such a sweat that I had no time to think of it at all.

This week is something else. You know India[1] used to be in control of Arabia — and used to do it pretty badly, for they hadn't a man who knew Syria or Turkey, & they used to consider only the Gulf, & the preservation of peace in the Aden Hinterland. So they got tied into horrid knots with the Imam,[2] who is a poisonous blighter at the best. Egypt (which is one Clayton, a very good man) got hold of the Idrisi family, who are the Senussi and Assyr together, as you know: and for some years we had a little agreement together. Then this war started, & India went on the old game of balancing the little powers there. I want to pull them all

---

[1] i.e. the Government of India.   [2] Ruler of Yemen.

together, & to roll up Syria by way of the Hedjaz in the name of
the Sherif. You know how big his repute is in Syria. This could
be done by Idrisi only, so we drew out a beautiful alliance, giving
him all he wanted: & India refused to sign. So we cursed them,
& I think that Newcombe & myself are going down to Kunfida
as his advisers. If Idrisi is anything like as good as we hope[1] we
can rush right up to Damascus, & biff the French out of all hope
of Syria. It's a big game, and at last one worth playing. Of course
India has no idea what we are playing at: if we can only get to
Assyr we can do the rest — or have a try at it. So if I write & tell
you that it's all right, & I'm off, you will know where for.
Wouldn't you like to be on it? Though I don't give much for
my insurance chances again. If only India will let us go. Won't
the French be mad if we win through? Don't talk of it yet. TEL.

83: TO D. G. HOGARTH

20.4.15   *Military Intelligence Office, War Office, Cairo*

There aren't going to be any nice schemes anytime, I believe, at
least everything boils up gloriously, & one is told to be ready to
start by the Thursday in next week — and then it never becomes
the Thursday of this week. Finally the Med-Ex.[2] came out,
beastly ill-prepared, with no knowledge of where it was going, or
what it would meet, or what it was going to do. So we took pity
on it, & said that we would be its Intelligence Base, and its map
base and so we'll be here till the end of it. Lloyd and Herbert
went off with it, to help it, & Newcombe & I are left. Woolley
is in Port Said, controlling the French Navy, & taking prize
ships. It's very dull: but of course I haven't any training as a
field officer, and I don't know that I want to go fighting up to
Constantinople. It would be bad form, I think. The only place
worth visiting is A.[3] and they are all afraid of going there, for
fear of hurting the feelings of our allies.

The Canal is still holding out, and we are forgetting all about
it. Turkey, if she is wise, will raid it from time to time, & annoy

---

[1] These hopes were disappointed: see letter No. 94, p. 219 and No. 107, p. 267.
[2] The Mediterranean Expeditionary Force, destined for Gallipoli and Salonika.
[3] Alexandretta.

the garrison there, which is huge, & lumbersome, & creaks so loudly in the joints that you hear them eight hours before they move. So it's quite easy to run down & chuck a bomb at it, & run away again without being caught.

Everything is going to sleep, & today is 90° in the room, and one feels rather limp and bored.

I bought you a seal the other day. It's probably the only one you'll get from us this year, which is almost its only virtue. One wouldn't have bought it anywhere else, but in Cairo it was refreshing.

For Leeds I am sending a mediaeval dagger pommel — or piece of horse-trapping — bought in Jerusalem lately.

Poor old Turkey is only hanging together. People always talk of the splendid show she has made lately, but it really is too pitiful for words. Everything about her is very very sick, & almost I think it will be good to make an end of her, though it will be very inconvenient to ourselves. I only hope that Aleppo and Damascus will escape a little the fate that has come upon Cairo. Anything fouler than the town buildings, or its beastly people, can't be: — and I shouldn't have believed in them six months back. Carchemish is a village inhabited by the cleanest & most intelligent angels.

I expected to find you on the staff of the Med Ex! however they hadn't anybody particular, except one Deedes (v. good at Turkish) and Colonel Hawker, who was deservedly in the Ottoman Gendarmerie: The expedition came out with two copies of some $\frac{1}{4}''$ maps of European-Turkey as their sole supply. I hope you get me some of Butler's N. Syrian maps.[1] Tell him the 1905 ones are ROTTEN. TEL.

84: TO D. G. HOGARTH

26.4.15 *Military Intelligence Office, War Office, Cairo*

By all means Cilicia: I was only afraid of asking too much. And Alex. as the naval base is the crux of the whole show.

By the way, in pushing the matter, if you can, it may help you

[1] Butler was the leader of the American Archaeological Expedition.

to know that opinion here and in India is very much in favour. It's only home that sticks us up.

Arabian affairs have gone all to pot. I've never seen a more despicable mess made of a show. It makes one howl with fury — for we had a ripping chance there.

Push on A therefore, if you can: it seems to me the only thing left for us.   TEL.

[The following letters to A. B. Watt show that Lawrence was pushing on with his plans for a landing at Alexandretta. Watt, a British resident of Alexandretta, had been of use to Lawrence before the war in smuggling archaeological specimens out of Syria.]

85: TO A. B. WATT

15.6.15   *Military Intelligence Office, War Office, Cairo*

Dear Watt, If you are alive, and in Cyprus, please tell me if you know the Amk? (you do —) if you have been in the Jebel Kosseir? if you have been to Jisr Shoghr? — if you know the Kurd Dagh? if Latakia is a familiar spot? You know Alexandretta I suppose? — how about Adana, and Ayas? in fact all of it?

My regards to Mrs. Watt: and tell her that there is nothing warlike doing in the above districts. Write me above address: Yours ever   T. E. LAWRENCE

86: TO A. B. WATT

[*undated*]   *Military Intelligence Office, War Office, Cairo*

Dear Watt, This is only a little scribble: of course I'd want your help if we were going to A: and I think the French would also; (mixed force, with enough of ours to justify an extra Intelligence Officer). You would get local and temporary rank — If my will was done, and be attached to the Intelligence Dept. No unit, but a Staff job. Your Company would recognise this. You would be able to look after their root interests in the province, meanwhile, or in your spare time.

No spying: Intelligence is mostly topography, (guiding, advising as to products, routes, people, etc.) and interpretation: interrogation of prisoners.

This is all in the air: nothing is proposed, settled or intended at present.

Pay would be about 15/- a day: and some £50 for outfit. Discharge when you wished, practically, at any rate as soon as local operations ended.

Don't say anything about it. Yours sincerely   T. E. LAWRENCE

87: TO WILL LAWRENCE

17.7.15   *Military Intelligence Office, War Office, Cairo*

[7 *lines omitted*] Your job — revolver practice sounds pleasant. We live in offices and in railway trains: also interviewing Turkish prisoners, & supplying information on any subject that crops up. No civil work however and much map-drawing & geography, both of which please me.

Frank's[1] death was as you say a shock, because it was so unexpected. I don't think one can regret it overmuch, because it is a very good way to take, after all. The hugeness of this war has made one change one's perspective, I think, and I for one can hardly see details at all. We are a sort of Levant Foreign Office, and can think of nothing else. I wonder when it will all end and peace follow?

All the relief I get [is] in *The Greek Anthology*, Heredia, Morris & a few others! Do you?

88: TO A. B. WATT

29.8.15   *Military Intelligence Office, War Office, Cairo*

Dear Watt, Many thanks for your letter in June last. I couldn't answer it, either then or now, as this Dardanelles show lags all the time. Of course you understand that you will be 'wanted' if ever we go your way: — and there's an off chance of it. Only the big

[1] Frank Lawrence was killed on May 9th, 1915.

show must go wrong or go right first. I never knew quite so leisurely a proceeding though!

For the enclosed business: — are you a map-reader? Because this thing is new, and very bad in places, and I want corrections where possible. Old Beard would be the man: — but he is missing!

Will you run over your routes in it, knock out what you see is wrong, and put it in right if you can: also where there is room, and you know other villages, can you fit them in? Corrections should be in red.

I'm not sending you hills: — only a proof of the black and blue: and despite my example of speed in reply to letters I'll ask for it back fairly soon. Remember me to Mrs. Watt, and Mr. Lorimer. Yours sincerely   T. E. LAWRENCE

P.S. The D.H.P.[1] Rly is right . . . and the Orontes course should be right also: they are proper surveys. The coast is Admiralty chart, for which not much can be said probably. Gebel Riha and Gebel Barisha are from American Expedition's maps.

                                                                TEL.

[Will Lawrence who had joined the Royal Flying Corps as an observer was shot down in September 1915. Lawrence took his death for granted, though proof of it did not come until the following May. The death of Will, his favourite brother, was a great shock to Lawrence, and in a letter I cannot quote, of November 16th, 1915, he expressed a feeling that it was not right for him to go on living safely in Cairo, and a dread of what returning to Oxford would be like. D. G. Hogarth (by that time a Lieutenant-Commander in the R.N.V.R.) had come out and Lawrence was grateful for his companionship.

In the spring of 1916 the Arab Bureau began to publish *The Arab Bulletin* — set up and printed by the Egyptian Government Press at Bulaq. Lawrence was responsible for the early numbers. It was perhaps this work which set his mind running on the old plan of starting a private press in England, and led to the following letter to V. W. Richards. As he speaks of 'banging about strange seas with a khaki crowd' it was almost certainly written while he was on his way out to Mesopotamia

---

[1] The Damascus-Aleppo railway.

on the *Royal George* transport. He was being sent with Aubrey Herbert, with secret instructions from the War Office to negotiate with the Turkish Commander, Khalil Pasha, besieging General Townshend's force in Kut.]

89: TO V. W. RICHARDS

End of March [1916]

This is a reply to a postcard about a year ago. I wonder how you are getting on ... I haven't much to show for myself ... except that now I have a little money, thanks to about a year and a half spent in Cairo doing nothing. I hope to have about £100 in hand when the war ends, if it does! This will be enough to cut a fount in the orthodox way, if the etching has failed. You were nearly at your last experiment, when I saw you.

If you can muster up the strength please write to me (via Oxford) and tell me how things look. I think we will have to do Apuleius, which is my present stand by. *Cupid and Psyche*, and the wonderful end of the book, after the sheer humour of some of the beginning, are worthy of anything we can do. I'm afraid my entanglements are going to keep me in the Near East a certain part of each year: however an apprentice, or a working partner, should more than fill that part of the work. I only want a niche which will not take up too much time in getting into every visit. You know Coleridge's description of the heavenly bodies in the *Mariner* 'Lords that are certainly expected'[1] etc. . . . I don't want to be a lord or a heavenly body, but I think one end of the orbit should be in a printing shed.

Now you will write and say that it is off altogether. If so, on with it again, sooner than later.

It's a bad life this, banging about strange seas with a khaki crowd very intent on banker and parades and lunch. I am a total abstainer from each, and so a snob. The Kelmscott *Coleridge* however relieves me at high moments, and Apuleius ordinary times.

I insist upon Heredia as another of the great men to be worthily dressed. We won't put many copies into vellum covers.

[1] See also p. 245.

Ordinary people must take them in a green-grey native cloth (dyed with pomegranate rinds) that I have. It is good for work: ... many times better than the Morris blue and grey linen.

Will you try to dye vellum in your spare moments? it wears so badly in dirty places when it is natural colour. Yr.   TEL.

[General Townshend had conceived the plan of buying off the Turks besieging him in Kut for a cash payment. Lord Kitchener had adopted it and General Lake, commanding in Mesopotamia, had accepted it. Most of the British officers in Mesopotamia were against it as they felt it was dishonourable. Sir Percy Cox opposed it as worse for British prestige than the surrender of the garrison. Lawrence believed it was impracticable as the Turks would certainly refuse. However Colonel Beach, Aubrey Herbert and Lawrence were sent to parley with Khalil, offering him first a million pounds, and on his refusal, two million pounds to let the besieged garrison go free. Khalil refused contemptuously, and of course published the facts of the offer which were most damaging to British prestige.

On his return to Egypt Lawrence submitted a report of Mesopotamian affairs in which, in the words of Colonel Stirling, 'he criticized the quality of the stones used for lithographing, the system of berthing barges alongside the quays, the inefficiency of the cranes for handling stores, the lack of system in shunting and entraining on the railways, the want of adequate medical stores, the blindness of the medical authorities and their want of imagination as to their probable requirements. And, horror of horrors, he criticized the Higher Command and the conduct of the campaign in general!'

His report was hurriedly bowdlerized by his staff officers before being shown to Sir Archibald Murray, the Commander-in-Chief in Egypt. The visit to Mesopotamia and Lawrence's sweeping criticism was the beginning of a hostility to him on the part of the Indian Army authorities and the Indian Government which lasted for the rest of his career. His own hopes for promoting a rebellion of Mesopotamian Arabs against the Turks and for co-operation between them and the British Army came to nothing. The last thing that the British Indian Army officers wanted was the Arabs as allies. And the Indian administration was looking forward to annexation. The only person in

Mesopotamia with whom Lawrence found himself in sympathy was Gertrude Bell.

In 1932 Liddell Hart submitted a long interrogatory to Lawrence in which are the following questions and answers.

33. How did you come to receive instructions for Mespot Mission?

I had put the Grand Duke Nicholas in touch with certain disaffected Arab officers in Erzerum. Did it through the War Office and our Military Attaché in Russia. So the War Office thought I could do the same thing over Mespot, and accordingly wired out to Clayton.

34. When did you become a captain?

I was Staff Captain. I lost it on going to Mespot, so Hedley arranged a local captaincy.

35. Were the General Staff going to get rid of you too?

While they were together on Maxwell's staff Holdich was my greatest ally. When appointed to Murray's staff his attitude changed — Holdich decent but a lunacy streak.[1]]

90: TO HIS MOTHER

May 18 [1916.]

We are at sea, somewhere off Aden, I suppose, so before it gets too late I am going to tell you something of what I saw in Mesopotamia. You must excuse the writing, because the ship is vibrating queerly. I went off, as I told you, about March 22: the transport I went on was the *Royal George*, a comfortable Canadian liner, and we got out to Kuweit without any happening of note. At Kuweit which is a wide inlet of the sea, with low sand-dunes round it, very desolate, but for the town which is neatly & regularly built — we transhipped on to a fast mail-steamer the *Elephanta*, of about 6000 tons. This took us across the bar at the mouth of the Shatt el-Arab, & up to Basra in the day. The joining of the river and the sea on the bar was very visible, as it

[1] Liddell Hart provides the following note: 'Newcombe says that he used to hear from Holdich, now dead, who was very bitter about L. – jealousy and resentment of what was regarded as L.'s cheek. The Murray crowd were trying to down Clayton as well as Lawrence. Further remark about this period: Philip Graves and L. got out Handbook of Turkish Army; may have been a dozen editions; L. supervised the printing of them. L. and Graves spent most of their time among the Turkish prisoners and came to know more about the Turkish Army than the Turks themselves.'

was a quiet day. The river came down in a grey-green flood, &
stopped abruptly in the sea, which was a heavy blue. You could
have straddled anywhere, one foot on each water, the line was not
straight though. It ran up and down irregularly as the tide pressed
it, and you could follow it for hundreds of yards each side of the
ship. The bar is about 18 feet under high tide, but it is really
only a cushion of liquid mud, and ships plough through it. It
looks odd to see the propeller churning in stuff like chocolate
cream. [49 *lines omitted*]

I don't really know what to say about Basra itself. You know
you have got there by the crowd of ships in the river, and by a
few houses along the shore;— the town lies some two or three
miles up a side-stream, deep enough only for small boats. However our headquarters are on the bank, and there are usually
dozens of row-boats and launches along the shore . . . no wharfs,
no piers, no signs of a port, no roads; — no one would ever dream
that we had been in occupation of the place for months & months.
When I landed it was pouring with rain & dark. The officer
who brought me off got a lamp, and we slid over the top of what
seemed to be a bank of soft soap and toffee for about three hundred yards. Then it got better for they had thrown some clinkers
on the mud: so we stood upright, (how my shoes resisted remaining in the tacky glue of the first part I don't know) and passed
down a garden into the headquarter house. It was watertight,
and I found Miss Bell and Campbell Thompson there, so that
was well. [43 *lines omitted*]

I only stayed three days in Basra, as the G.O.C. and all his
staff were up at the front. The people at the base gave me some
biscuits, ten loaves, ten tins of jam, ten tins of beef, and put me
on board a little paddle steamer that had been a ferry on the
Irrawaddy. Downstairs she was all engines, and the top was a
flat deck partly sheltered by an awning. The front $\frac{2}{3}$rds of the
deck was occupied by about 150 Territorials: behind the funnel
was a smaller space in which sat about ten of us, who all had ten
tins, etc. Each side of the steamer was tied a 100 feet steel barge
loaded deep with firewood and forage and stores. These were
intended partly to increase her carrying capacity, but more to act
as buffers and protect the paddles when we charged the banks.

We started in the afternoon, and shortly it began to rain . . . so we went to bed. [90 *lines omitted*]

The Arabs here are wonderfully hard, much rougher and poorer than our Jerablus men, but merry, and full of talk. They are in the water all their lives, and seem hardly to notice it. I shall not soon forget a flood perhaps twenty miles long and wide near Ezra's tomb, where the river had drowned both its banks for as far as one could see . . . and in the middle, walking up the hidden bank of the river to their necks in water, were three men pulling a laden mahaila up stream. They must have pulled her ten miles wading and swimming thus, and the nearest place they could hope to reach dry land would be another ten miles ahead.

[33 *lines omitted*] At the front I found Headquarters living in a steamer with good awnings and a saloon! I stayed with them for about three weeks, while Kut fell. We lost too many men at first in the relief and then tried too hard in the middle and before the end everybody was tired out. [3 *lines blotted out*] The weather cleared up and breeded myriads of flies. At sundown the awning over the deck used to change swiftly from grey to brown as the swarms alit on it to roost. The cavalry sometimes had to ride at foot pace, being blinded. Colonel Beach, one of the Mesopotamian staff, Aubrey Herbert (who was with us in Cairo) and myself were sent up to see the Turkish Commander in chief, and arrange the release, if possible, of Townshend's wounded. From our front trenches we waved a white flag vigorously: then we scrambled out, and walked about half-way across the five hundred yards of deep meadow grass between our lines and the Turkish trenches. Turkish officers came out to meet us, and we explained what we wanted. They were tired of shooting so kept us sitting there with our flag as a temporary truce, while they told Halil Pasha that we were coming — and eventually in the early afternoon we were taken blindfolded through their lines and about ten miles Westward (till within four miles of Kut) to his Headquarters. He is a nephew of Enver's and suffered a violent defeat in the Caucasus so they sent him to Mesopotamia as G.O.C. hoping he would make a reputation. He is about 32 or 33, very keen and energetic, but not clever or intelligent I think. He spoke French to us and was very polite, but of course the cards were all

in his hands, and we could not get much out of him. However he
let about 1000 wounded go without any condition but the release
of as many Turks — which was all we could hope for. We spent
the night in his camp, and they gave us a most excellent dinner in
Turkish style — which was a novelty to Colonel Beach but pleased
Aubrey and myself. Next morning we looked at Kut in the distance, and then came back blindfolded as before. We took with
us a couple of young Turkish officers, one the brother in law of
Enver, and they afterwards went up to Kut from our camp in the
hospital ship that removed the wounded. The ill-feeling between Arabs and Turks has grown to such a degree that Halil
cannot trust any of his Arabs in the firing line. [2½ *lines blotted out*]
After that there was nothing for us to do so the Headquarters
staff turned round again and came down to Basra. We got there
about the 8th and I spent four or five days settling up things and
then came away. This is an old Leyland liner now a transport.
There is only myself and a General Gillman on board. He is
from near Abingdon and is excellent company. We sit on the
deck and write reports and notes all day. The weather at Basra
began to get warmer before I left but 105° was our highest shade
temperature and there has not been any cold day or night on
the boat so far . . . indeed the thermometer has not gone below 80°
so that is pleasant for me. I expect the Red Sea will be warm also.
I wonder if in my former letter I told you of the wonderful
thunderstorm we had at Koweit? We were on the *Royal George*
and the lightning began about 3 P.M. After sunset it grew more
frequent until by 9 P.M. it was lightning almost continuously from
three sides at once. There was no thunder and only a few minutes
rain. The flashes were like a pattern in lace or an intricate net-
work stretched across the lower sky. Their colour was a very
intense green, and they made a long crackling noise that hardly
stopped. In their light you could see everything near by, up to a
mile or two very distinctly. The three-fold direction of the light
caused a most eerie impression of unreality, like lime-light rather,
because we are accustomed to see things lit up from one side
only. With these flashes one's rigging and the shape and position
of the ships in the harbour seemed all the time flickering and
moving. The storm ended in a sudden dry burst of wind which

swung our ship (very high built, about 80 feet above the water) right round like a pivot almost on top of a little sloop, the *Clio*, which had anchored too near us. They had to get up her anchor in a wild hurry (no winch, only a capstan) and dash away. We were within a few feet of over-laying her and as her masts were below our decks we would have rolled her over and sunk her.

(I wonder if I ever told you about a magnificent storm we had at Carchemish one night — Mr. Hogarth and the Fontanas were staying with us? It was a very cold week and after dinner we had all moved round the hearth, on which there was a big fire of olive logs burning. Busrawi had sent in his two musicians at our request. One was an old man, who had been a shepherd nearly all his life. He had a long white beard and a quiet weather-beaten face. He played on a pipe about 2 feet long that was of a kind of reed but looked like polished brass. Its tone was hoarse but flute like and had a wonderful range: he goes from high to very low notes which sound just like the wind dragging over rocky hill sides rustling in the dried grass of the valleys. The other man younger also plays a two stringed [*one word illegible*] and sings. He is darker and thin faced with very deep set [*one word illegible*] eyes. I think he is blind: at any rate he has wound a very massive turban and head-cloth over his forehead, so that his face is always in deep shade . . . and he generally keeps his eyes shut as he sings. They had been playing and singing Kurd war-songs, and love-songs and dirges for about half an hour when the storm suddenly broke. There was a torrential burst of rain which hissed down in sheets, and rattled over the shingle in our court-yard like the footsteps of a great crowd of men; then there would come a clap of thunder, and immediately after a blue flash of lightning which made our open door and window livid gaps in the pitch-black wall . . . through which we caught odd glimpses of the sculptures outside shining in the rain and dazzle of light. I remember particularly the seven foot figure of a helmeted god striding along an inscription towards the doorway: — and the dripping jaws of the two lions of the pedestal which seemed in the alternate glare and shadow of the flashes to be grinning at us through the window. The musicians did not stop, but changed their song for a wild improvisation which kept time with the storm. The pipe shrilled out whenever the thunder pealed and fell down again slow and heavy for the strained silences in between. One did not realise that they were men playing independently: the rhythm seemed so born of the bursts of wind and rain, so made to bind together the elements of the night into one great thunder-song. It all lasted about ten minutes, I suppose, but I think it was the most wonderful time I have had . . . and when it ended it ended suddenly: there was no quiet dragging away of the storm into distance and insignificance.)

There, I have written you a month of letters. I do not know how the Censor will find it in his heart to pass so Gargantuan a bale of manuscript . . . but I am afraid he will have to pass it for there is nothing in it to help our enemies — nor is that a fair description of you. Hereafter I will again be nailed within that office at Cairo — the most interesting place there is till the Near East settles down. I am very pleased though to have had this sight of Mesopotamia in war time. It will be a wonderful country some day, when they regulate the floods, and dig out the irrigation ditches. Yet it will never be a really pleasant country, or a country where Europeans can live a normal life. In these respects, and in the matter of inhabitants, it must yield to the upper river, where we are.

I expect to find letters and papers knee-deep in Cairo when I return. The accumulation of two months business and pleasure will be awful to see — so do not look for immediate news of me.

[The following unsigned passage in *The Arab Bulletin* is undoubtedly by Lawrence.]

91. MESOPOTAMIA

[Arab Bulletin. No. 23]

To the British Officers who were arranging the exchange of our wounded from Kut, Halil Pasha, Commander-in-Chief of the Turkish forces in Irak, spoke very freely on the question of the Arab attitude. At first he proposed the exchange of Indian sick for Arab prisoners of war; but later he went back on this, and refused to accept Arabs in exchange at all. He said that most of them were condemned to death, and would only be shot if they returned; and that in any case he did not want them.

He said that ninety per cent of Turks were good soldiers, and ninety per cent of Arabs were bad. He said their desire was only to get taken prisoner, and that the whole lot of them were unreliable. Under protest he excepted from his condemnation some of the Arabs of Mosul and Syria, who were, he said, sufficiently 'Turkised' to have some virtue. Kasim Bey, his Chief of Staff, agreed with what he said, and it seemed to be the view shared by the younger officers we met. I suggested to them the case of Sami Bey, and they said that the Russian War of '60 and the Defence of Kars fell on a different footing, when the Arabs were still loyal to the Ottoman Empire. Lieutenant Mehmed Riza classed the Kurd tribes with the Arabs in disloyalty and disinclination to fight. This may lend colour to previous reports of disaffection among some sub-tribes of the Mili confederation.

Representations were made to Halil Pasha concerning the fate of the Arabs of Kut. These had shown themselves, in the main, friendly to us, but had not been asked to take any active part in operations. Townshend's surrender having been unconditional, it was impossible to make any stipulation as to their treatment, but Halil was urged strongly to show moderation, and to treat them as compelled to side with us by force majeure.

He said that he had no intention of going to extremes, and seemed rather amused at our interest in them.

He broke the understanding, however, and has to date hanged nine individuals; they comprise a Turkish officer deserter, a Jew contractor, an Arab notable of Kut and his two sons, two Mukhtars and two prominent sheikhs. Halil's record of service, which includes some months Kurd-hunting in Van before the war, and a peculiarly ghastly Armenian massacre in the Melazgherd area compels one to look upon this performance as humane.

The executions are confirmed by British Officers engaged in removing General Townshend's wounded from Kut. It is reported that one prisoner, when being led to the gallows seized his Musbah (Mohammadan rosary) and flung it to a British officer over the heads of the Turks. The man may have been a

o

Shia, indeed probably was, but even so the incident is probably unprecedented in modern Islam.

NOTE. Halil's remarks about the Arabs, and the incident of the Musbah at Kut were reported by officers present under privilege from the Turks, and must not, therefore, be communicated in any way. They are given here as remarkable evidence of the relations existing in Irak between the Turks and their Arab subjects.

[On June 5th, 1916, Sherif Ali, the eldest son of the Sherif of Mecca, and Sherif Feisal, the third son, attacked Medina with several thousand Arabs but failed to take it by storm.

On June 9th the Sherif of Mecca revolted against the Turks and after three days smoked out and captured the small Turkish force in the Holy City. When Hogarth and other members of the Arab Bureau landed at Jidda on June 6th, they found to their surprise that the revolt had broken out. The situation which Lawrence had planned over a year before had come to pass, but it was many months before he could begin to exploit it.

In October Lawrence sailed with Storrs for Jidda (Chapters VIII and IX of *Seven Pillars of Wisdom*), meeting Sherif Abdulla, the Sherif of Mecca's second son; from there he took ship to Rabegh where he met the Sherif Ali, and his young half-brother Zeid, who dispatched him secretly to visit the camp of their brother Feisal (Chapters XII, XIII, XIV, XV, XVI, of *Seven Pillars of Wisdom*). From Feisal's camp he returned to Yenbo and, still wearing the Arab headcloth Sherif Ali had given him, returned in company with Admiral Sir Rosslyn Wemyss via Port Sudan to Khartoum where he reported to the Sirdar, Sir Reginald Wingate. At Port Sudan he met for the first time Joyce and Davenport who were to play important parts in the Arab Campaign. On his return to Cairo, Lawrence was ordered by General Clayton to go back to Arabia and thus paid a second visit to Feisal's camp, the account of which will be found in *Seven Pillars of Wisdom*, Chapters XIX and XX.]

92: TO COLONEL C. E. WILSON

6.12.16　　　　　　　　　　　　　　　　　　　[*From Yenbo*]

Dear Colonel Wilson, I got back yesterday and found your
wire saying that I was to wire urgently anything critical. As a
matter of fact the only thing urgent is for an air reconnaissance
of Bir Said and Bir Jabir and Wadi Safra — and that is not possible
till our landing ground here is finished (this afternoon) and I can
direct the planes where these places are.* Unless they get a better
map or local knowledge the planes simply are flying in the dark,
and their reports cannot be much use. As a matter of fact we
have never had any news from them at all to date. Perhaps they
have none, or else they don't know we are here!

About wiring urgently. It is not possible from the S.N.O.'s²
ship. Atmospherics are bad just now, and naval messages take
precedence, and the S.N.O. has a lot of wiring of his own, of
course. I don't suppose my wire of conditions in Feisul's camp
will get through for some days yet, as it is a long one of about
400 groups. This state of affairs will continue till we have a
station of our own. I am very sorry to hear that the despatch boat
is 'off'. It would have meant better touch with Rabegh, and less
wiring.

The *Minto* is coming today, and I am sending by it direct to
Cairo an expansion of my telegram No. 29, which I expect will
arrive quicker than the telegram itself via you.† The situation is
certainly not good — and in the maze of conflicting reports and
obvious exaggerations afloat here one can hardly see more. I am
afraid the morale of the Harb is badly shaken, and Feisul's
prestige and scope will suffer severely if he is confined to the
Juheina only. However as soon as the aeroplanes can find their
way about I will get up country again, and try and feel the inten-

* If they will take me up I will show them the roads.

† This is done to save the great delay of going to Jidda first:
and there is not enough news in it to make it worth while sending
a copy to you.

¹ C. E. Wilson was British representative at Yidda, the port of Mecca, and negotiator
with the Sherif. See Letter No. 200 and *Seven Pillars of Wisdom*, Chap. viii.
² Senior Naval Officer.

tions of Feisul and the Turks a little more closely.* Feisul treats me very well, and lets me ask hear and see everything, including his agents. Of course I still pass as a Syrian officer, which makes my style a little cramped. My three days nearly knocked me up. To begin with I only got an average of one hour's sleep per 24, then we did some very hard camel travelling, and the alarms and excitements of the camp were great.

As for when I will go up — that depends I'm afraid entirely on how things work out. General Clayton's orders to me were to go ashore and do what seemed best, and it would be hard to be more definite. I do not quite understand what the Sirdar can mean by my superintending the 'supply question'. All that comes is handed over to the Sherif's agent, Abd el Kadir, *in the steamer*, and discharged and stored by him. There is no possible road for us to butt into the matter, nor do I think it desirable. If each ship is given a full list of stores on board for Yenbo, in English or Arabic, then all necessary is the handing over that list to Abd el Kadir, and his receipt that he has had the contents.† Our interference in matters of internal organisation is not encouraged exactly!

I have asked you to let me hear occasionally about Sherif Abdulla and his movements. If he closes with the Turks he might be quite useful to the Wadi Safra operations, and fuller information would enable Feisul to coordinate. Of course it is quite probable that you have no news!

The 'old man of the sea' of those Q.F.[1] Mountain Batteries still weights us. If we could only get that responsibility off we would have done well and more than they asked.

One's isolation at Yenbo and lack of touch with everything will make one unable to see what news you need. So will you whenever a thing crops up send me a telegram asking for light on so and so? One gets so used to local things that one forgets they are unknown outside. Yours sincerely.   T. E. LAWRENCE

* Agents were not much good.

† If you think fit, please explain the local conditions to the Sirdar. Abd el Kadir is as efficient and reliable as any British officer.

[1] Quick-firing.

I have so much coding and decoding, and local work that I have been unable to write a word of a report which ought to be written on my visit to Feisul. If I can write one I will send it (or a copy, according to postal opportunity) to you.

Have just recd. a telegram from you, & one to Garland asking for news. I'm very sorry, but owing to atmospherics & press of naval work Capt. Boyle had to refuse my messages, and this meant two days' delay. I hope they most of them got off last night.　　　　　　　　　　　　　　　　　　　　　　　　　L.

93: TO COLONEL C. E. WILSON

22.12.16　　　　　　　　　　　　　　　　　　　　　　[*Yenbo*]

Dear Colonel Wilson, Many thanks for the supply note. I cannot suggest anything to add or subtract. I only hope they will accept it in Egypt and act on it. I am sure that the thing to avoid is multiplying the British Staff and activities in the Hejaz.

I got your wire last night, that you will be here probably on the 25th or 26th. I will arrange to meet you, but I hope, if there will be any profit in doing so, to run up first to Feisul and so put you au fait with his intentions.

The strategical centre of the Turk anti-Feisul operations is Bir Said. They threaten his rear and his base from it, and he cannot cut Wadi Safra or go for the Railway in any sort of security, until he has either contained or captured it. He has no troops capable of containing anything — so he must operate against it.

If he takes Bir Said the Turks at Hamra will, I think, have to draw back. On the other hand his troops are still quite unfit for work, and he estimates it will take him a week to get the Juheina and Northern Harb at work again. He is only going forward now because he is intensely nervous of a Turkish concentration against Ali.

I keep Capt. Boyle up in all my information, and he will probably be able to explain what is happening here. The situation is to my mind hopeful, if the Turks have not got a strong force in Wadi Safra. If they have we will have a cataclysm shortly. Feisul says he cannot get spies into the Wadi, but I hope he will take some informative prisoners, and we may find out that way.

The information from the deserter enclosed would be of value to Cairo, (Arbur)[1] if it can be got through to them soon. There is no ship in sight just yet, though. I have no copy but could reproduce the matter easily from my notes.

I am hoping great things from [8 *words omitted*][2] We sent him an elaborate list of points on which information is required.

As for money, I have £50 in gold, which I am using for my own expenses and for any intelligence needs. It will last me for months at the present rate!

I am glad you approve of the Egyptian volunteers. I was afraid I was rather exceeding my commission in countenancing it!

Will you please wire for

4 locks complete for

Gun Maxim Converted Mark 11

to be sent to Yenbo? The guns are out of order (two of them) and there are no spare locks in hand. The two British armourers are invaluable.

The *Hardinge* has got the feed-block of one of the E.A.[3] German Maxims which is going down to Rabegh today. They took it off for repair.

I have asked for telegrams after today to be sent up in ship's cipher, as I may be inland, and if the news is of importance Abd el Kader will send it after me. Yours sincerely   T. E. LAWRENCE

[The following report to Colonel C. E. Wilson, printed in *The Arab Bulletin*, gives a far more detailed account than the condensed version in *Seven Pillars of Wisdom*.]

94: TO COLONEL C. E. WILSON

January 8th, 1917

ROUTE NOTES[4]

On January 2, 1917, I left Yambo and rode across the plain to the mouth of Wadi Agida in five hours. From the mouth of Wadi Agida to the watershed into the Wadi Yambo basin was

[1] Telegraphic address of Arab Bureau.   [2] An Arab spy in the Turkish service.
[3] Egyptian Army.
[4] This letter was printed in *Arab Bulletin* No. 42, from which it is here reprinted, in part.

one hour, and thence to Nakhl Mubarak was one hour; all done at a four miles an hour walk. The lowest third of the ascent of Wadi Agida was over sand: soft, slow going. The upper parts were harder and better: the divide was low and easy, and it gave at once to the eastward, on to a broad open valley, coming from the left with only very low hills on each side (Jebel Agida?), down which the road curved gently into Nakhl Mubarak. The 'Sebil' stands about 400 yards east of the watershed.

The road down to Nakhl looked very beautiful today. The rains have brought up a thin growth of grass in all the hollows and flat places. The blades, of a very tender green, shoot up between all the stones, so that looked at from a little height and distance there is a lively mist of pale green here and there over the surfaces of the slate-blue and brown-red rocks. In places the growth was quite strong, and the camels of the army are grazing on it.

In Nakhl Mubarak I found Feisal encamped in tents: he himself was in his private tent, getting ready to go out to his reception. I stayed with him that day, while rumours came in that the Turkish force had evacuated Wadi Safra. One reported that from Bir Sheriufi to Bir Derwish was one great camp, and that its units were proceeding to Medina; another had seen a great force of camelmen and infantry ride East past Kheif yesterday. We decided to send out a feeler towards Hamra, to get news.

On January 3, I took thirty-five Mahamid and rode over a dull tamarisk- and thorn-grown plain past Bir Faqir (not seen) to Bir Wasit, which is the old Abu Khalaat of my first trip. We waited there till sunset, and then went to Bir Murra, left our camels with ten of the men, and the rest of us climbed up the hills north of the Haj road up to Jebel Dhifran, which was painful, for the hills are all of knife-like strata which are turned on edge, and often run in straight lines from crest to valley. It gives you abundance of broken surface but no sound grips, as the strata are so minutely cracked that almost any segment will come away from its socket in your hand.

The top of Dhifran was cold and misty. At dawn we disposed ourselves in crevices of the rocks, and at last saw three bell tents beneath us to the right, behind a spur at the head of the pass, 300 yards away. We could not get round to them to get a low view, so put a few bullets through their top. This turned out a crowd of Turks from all directions. They leaped into trenches and rifle pits each side of the road, and potting them was very difficult. I think they suffered some loss, but I could not be sure. They fired in every direction except towards us, and the row in the narrow valley was so awful that I expected to see the Hamra force turn out. As the Turks were already ten to our one this might have made our getting away difficult, so we crawled back and rushed down into a valley, almost on top of two very scared Turks, who may have been outposts or may have been at their private morning duty. They were the most ragged men I have ever seen, bar a British tramp, and surrendered at once. We took them with us, and bolted off down the valley for another 500 yards. From there we put a few shots into the Turks, which seemed to check them, and so got off gently to Bir Murra by 6.30 a.m. The prisoners could speak only Turkish, so we mounted them and raced up to Nakhl to find an interpreter. They said it was the 5th Coy. of the 2/55th Regiment which was posted on Dhifran, the rest of the battalion and two companies of the first battalion being at Hamra village. The other companies of the 1/55th were guarding the Derb el-Khayaa from Hamra to Bir Ibn Hassani; 3/55th in Bir Derwish; O.C. 55th Regiment, Tewfik Bey.

At Nakhl Mubarak I found letters from Captain Warren saying that Zeid was still in Yambo, and that the *Dufferin* would wait in Sherm Yambo till I came. As Feisal was just starting for Owais, I changed my camel and rode down with him and the army to the head of Wadi Messarid by 3 p.m. The order of march was rather splendid and barbaric. Feisal in front, in white: Sharaf on his right in red headcloth and henna dyed tunic and cloak; myself on his left in white and red; behind us three banners of purple silk, with gold spikes; behind them three drummers playing a march, and behind them again, a wild bouncing mass of 1,200 camels of the bodyguard, all packed as closely as they could move, the men in every variety of coloured clothes, and the camels nearly as brilliant in their trappings, and the whole crowd singing at the tops of their voices a warsong in honour of Feisal and his family. It looked like a river of camels, for we filled up the Wadi to the tops of its banks, and poured along in a quarter of a mile long stream.

At the mouth of Wadi Messarid I said goodbye to Feisal and raced down the open plain to Yambo by 6 p.m. I was riding Feisal's own splendid camel, and so managed to do the twenty-two miles fairly easily. To my great relief I found the *Dufferin* had already left for Rabugh with Zeid, and so I was saved a further ten miles' march to Sherm Yambo.

ARAB FORCES

The troops in Nakhl Mubarak were mostly camel corps. There were very many — according to Feisal's figures, over 6,000 — but their camps were spread over miles of the Wadi and its tributaries, and I could not manage to see all of them. Those I did see were quiet, and I thought in fair spirits. Some of them have now served six months or more, and these have lost their enthusiasm but gained experience in exchange. They still preserve their tribal instinct for independence of order, but they are curbing their habit of wasting ammunition, have achieved a sort of routine in matters of camping and marching, and when the Sherif approaches near they fall into line and make the low bow and sweep of the arm to the lips which is the official salute. They do not oil their guns — they say because they then clog with sand, and they have no oil handy — but the guns are most of them in fair order, and some of the men know how to shoot. They are becoming separate but coherent units under their sheikhs, and attendance is more regular than it was, as their distance from home increases. Further, they are becoming tempered to the idea of leaving their own diras,[1] and Feisal hopes to take nearly all to Wejh with him. As a mass they are not formidable, since they have no corporate spirit or discipline, or mutual confidence. Man by man they are good: I would suggest that the smaller the unit that is acting, the better will be its performance. A thousand of them in a mob would be ineffective

[1] Ranges of camping places.

against one fourth their number of trained troops: but three or four of them, in their own valleys and hills, would account for a dozen Turkish soldiers. When they sit still they get nervous, and anxious to return home. Feisal himself goes rather to pieces in the same conditions. When, however, they have plenty to do, and are riding about in small parties tapping the Turks here and there, retiring always when the Turks advance, to appear in another direction immediately after, then they are in their element, and must cause the enemy not only anxiety, but bewilderment. The mule mounted infantry company is very promising. They have got Mulud, an ex-cavalry officer, training them, and already make a creditable appearance. The machine-gun sections were disappointing. They say that the Egyptian volunteers are improving these and the artillery details.

[39 *lines on Camp life, here omitted, are virtually reproduced in* '*Seven Pillars of Wisdom*'.]

FEISAL'S TABLE TALK

Talking one day about the Yemen, as they call anything south of Mecca and Jiddah, Feisal remarked on the great docility and reasonableness of the Southern tribes, compared with the Harb, Juheinah and Ateibah of the North. He said that no Arabs of his acquaintance were so easily to hold and to rule. To imprison an officer, his sheikh had only to knot a thin string about his neck and state his sentence, and the man would henceforward follow him about with protestations of innocence and appeals to be set at liberty. Another good custom is that of naming boy or girl children after a favoured guest. They then belong literally to their name-father, who can dispose their actions as he pleases, to the exclusion of parental authority; they even incur their part-responsibility of the blood feuds of the name-parent. He was down south between Taif and Birk and inland up to Ebhah for months, and says that now whole tribes of boys are called Feisal, and that, over them and indirectly over their fathers, he has wide personal influence. Particularly he spent four months fortifying Muhail for the Turks, and made great friends of Suleiman ibn Ali and his family. He says that, given ten days leave, he would undertake to raise every fighting man in Asir against Muhieddin. Ebhah he says is not formidable to an attacking force with a battery of field-guns. The present bar on action is that Nasir is not weighty enough to counterpoise the Idrisi. The tribes all believe that Idrisi would egg on his friendly sheikhs to attack them in the rear, if they moved openly against the Turks.[1] The presence of Feisal or Abdullah would allay these fears.

Feisal says that Abdullah, though quick when he does move, is rather luxurious in taste and inclined to be lazy.

Stotzingen[2] told Feisal in Damascus that, from the Yemen, arms and ammunition were to be shipped across to Abyssinia, and an anti-foreign war begun in that country. He himself was going afterwards to German East Africa.

Frobenius[3] (calling himself Abd el-Kerim Pasha) turned up in Jiddah one morning by sea from Wejh soon after war had begun, Feisal was in Jiddah, and headed him off from Mecca. British naval activity dissuaded him from going on further south. Feisal, therefore, got him a boat, and gave him a letter of recommendation, and sent him back north again. When he got to Rabugh, however, Hussein Mubeirik took suspicion of him and locked him up in the fort. Frobenius had some difficulty in getting out, and made great complaints of his treatment when he got back to Syria.

In March, 1916, Jemal Pasha took Feisal to a cinema in Damascus. The star film showed the Pyramids, with the Union Jack on top, and beneath them, Australians beating the Egyptian men and raping the women, and, in the foreground, an Egyptian girl in an attitude of supplication. The second scene showed a desert, with camel-convoys and a Turkish infantry battalion marching on for ever and ever. The third scene returned to the Pyramids with a sudden appearance of the Ottoman Army in review order, the killing of the Australians and the surrender of General Maxwell, the joy of Egypt, the tearing down of the British flag from the Pyramids, and its replacement by the Turkish flag. Feisal said to Jemal: 'Why go on troubling my father and

[1] Compare letters No. 82 and No. 107, p. 267.

[2] The leader of the German military mission accompanying a Turkish force to the Yemen. See Liddell Hart, '*T. E. Lawrence*': in *Arabia and After*, p. 72.

[3] The German traveller, well known to archaeologists.

myself for recruits for your army if this film is true?' Jemal said:
'Well, you know it encourages the people. We do not expect or
try to conquer Egypt yet. Our policy is to hold the British forces
there with the least cost to ourselves; and Germany has promised
us that the last act of the war shall be the conquest of Egypt by
Germany and its restoration to the Ottoman Empire. On these
terms I agreed to join her in arms.'

Oppenheim came to see Feisal in Constantinople in early 1915.
He said he wanted to make rebellions. Feisal asked of what and
why? Oppenheim said there were to be rebellions of Moslems
against Christians. Feisal said the idea was sound. Where did
he propose to start them? Oppenheim said, 'everywhere' — in
India, Egypt, the Sudan, Java, Abyssinia, North Africa. Feisal
said they might consider India first. There was the technical
difficulty of lack of arms. Oppenheim said that would be put
right by a German-Turk expedition into Persia. He asked if the
Sherif would be prepared to co-operate with the Indian Moslem
societies. Feisal said his father would want to know whether,
afterwards, the Indian Moslems would be independent and
supreme, or would Hindus rule them, or India fall to another
European Power? Oppenheim said he had no idea: that it was
previous to think so far ahead. Feisal said he was afraid his father
would want to know all the same. Oppenheim said, 'Very well,
how about Egypt? We can arrange to give your family office
there, when it is conquered.' Feisal quoted the *Koran* to the
disparagement of Egyptians, and said that he had lately been in
Egypt, and had been offered the crown by the Nationalist party.
(*This took place in Piraeus.*) Egyptians were weather-cocks,
with no political principle except dissatisfaction, and intent only
on pleasure and money getting. Any Egyptian who talked of
raising a rebellion in Egypt was trying to touch you for something
on account. Oppenheim said, 'Well, then, the Sudan?' Feisal
said 'Yes, you are right. There is in the Sudan material to cause a
real rebellion: but do you know the Sudan?' Oppenheim said,
'Why?' Feisal said, 'They are ignorant negroes, armed with
broad-bladed spears, bows and shields. He, who would try to
stir them up against the English and their rifles and machine-
guns, is no good Moslem. The men, however, are sound material.

Give me arms, money and the command of the Red Sea for about
six weeks, and I shall be Governor-General of the Sudan.'
Oppenheim has hardly spoken to him since.

In January, 1915, Yasim, Ali Riza, Abd el-Ghani, and others
approached the Sherif of Mecca and suggested a military
rebellion in Syria. The Sherif sent Feisal up to report. He found
Divisions 25, 35 and 36 ready to revolt, but public opinion less
ready, and a general opinion in military circles that Germany
would win the war quite rapidly. He went to Constantinople,
and waited till the Dardanelles was in full blast. He then came
back to Damascus, judging it a possible moment: but he found the
well disposed divisions broken up, and his supporters scattered.
So he suggested to his father that they delay till England had
been properly approached, and Turkey had suffered crippling
losses, or until an Allied landing had been effected at Alexandretta.

[Lawrence had been responsible for printing the stamps for
the new Hejaz State from ancient Arab designs. This work had
been done with the help of Sir Ernest Dowson, Director-General
of the Survey of Egypt, to whom he had found time to write on
October 17th, 1916, on his first visit to Jiddah, saying that
they were well liked though 'some say that the design is rather
out of date and that a modern style (more like a cigarette picture)
would be fitter.']

95: TO HIS BROTHER, A. W. LAWRENCE[1]

28.2.17.

Dear Worm, Herewith a few $\frac{1}{8}$ piastre Hejaz stamps — a new
denomination just going to be issued. The perforation I think
better than the old style, and I like the design. What do you
think?

Inform me if there are any other values of which you want
more. Those published are 1 P.T. $\frac{1}{2}$, $\frac{1}{4}$, $\frac{1}{8}$ P.T. Blue Red Green
and Orange. Also tax stamps, but I don't suppose you care about
them. A 2 P.T. is under weigh [sic]. It has an arch and grill
design, and I like it.   N.

Just off again.

[1] Aged 16.

96: TO COLONEL C. E. WILSON

9.3.17   *Wejh*

Dear Colonel Wilson, Please excuse what is going to be a
hurried note. MacRury got here this morning, & his news is
rather sudden. I hoped to get it up to Newcombe, but cannot,
as he is coming in, without saying by what road. Fitzmaurice
very kindly offered me a sailor volunteer messenger to him —
but that's off.

In the circumstances, and as MacRury is not going to Yenbo
or Rabegh I got Feisul to take action. In spite of General
Clayton's orders I told him something of the situation. It would
have been impossible for me to have done anything myself on the
necessary scale. One must inform one's G.O.C.!

He has written to Sherif Ali to send the Eastern Juheina &
Harb direct to Bowat-Muheit as soon as possible. Letter leaves
by *River Fisher* this afternoon for Yenbo. F. says nothing in his
letter to give away our *knowledge* but the note is urgent enough to
impel Ali to action, I think.

A messenger has left for Abdulla telling him, at the risk of
losing $\frac{3}{4}$ of his force to smash and cut and attack everything
animate or material from Bowat up to Hedia.

Saad el Ghoneim has left for Fagair in W. Hamdh, to attack
the line temporarily till we reach him. I am off tomorrow with a
2.95 gun, a machine-gun company and perhaps Gillman with
his gunners, to try and hold up one of the water reservoirs &
smash it.

The Mule M-I[1] is being sent, probably to Abdulla, to make way
against the new Turkish Camel Corps. They are 160 strong, with
2 machine guns, & are good. They proceed first to Fagair, & if
in time, will join Abdulla. If not, they will go for the Turks
wherever they are.

Sherif Ali ibn Hussein has gone to Jeida, with 16 dynamite
experts, to interrupt the line from El Ula down to Toweira.

Abdulla ibn Muhanna has gone towards Medain Salih, to
capture 1400 camels sent there by Ibn Rashid. Feisul will send
the Rifaa and other troops to a point near El Ula, with a 2.95

[1] Mounted Infantry.

gun & some machine guns, to try and take action against the Turks there, & in any case to dynamite the line.

Sherif Nasir and Newcombe will be sent back North as soon as they get into touch with us. A squad of dynamiters is going N. there to occupy the Turks till they return.

Dynamite leaves tonight with experts for Dhaba, & Mohammed Ali el Beidawi will push them out to the Railway near Tebuk.

The plan (spur of the moment, I wish one had more notice) is to get something going at once against the water arrangements, to give time for concentration. For this purpose these light advance parties are going up, to risk anything to gain time. Then when the camels come, & Ali has moved, the main forces of the 3 brothers will be from Medina to El Ula along the line, & the Turks will find movement most difficult. That will, I think, take ten days, supposing the camels get here by the 15th. I think the weak part of the Turk plan lies in the trains of water & food. If we can cut the line on such a scale that they cannot repair it, or smash their locomotives the force will come to standstill. They must have little repair material in Medina — and will not be able to transport that much besides food & water. If only we can hold them up for ten days. I'm afraid it will be touch & go.

I am taking some Garland mines with me, if I can find instantaneous fuse, & if there is time, will set them, as near Medina as possible: it is partly for this reason that I am going up myself, & partly with a view to smashing Hedia, if it can anyhow be done.

Feisal will do everything he can. Only it's fearfully short notice. Yours sincerely, T. E. LAWRENCE

[Readers of *Seven Pillars of Wisdom* will remember that Feisal's army went up the coast from Yenbo and, after the British Navy had done most of the work, captured Wejh. While lying ill for eight days with dysentery, in Abdulla's camp, Lawrence's ideas of the war had clarified. He realized that the Arabs must avoid battle, that they must not try to take Medina, or tie themselves down to the Hedjaz. They needed a secure base — they needed Akaba — but from his visit in 1914 he knew it was hopeless to try to take it from the sea, and impossible to march an army across the desert to take it in the rear. But what an army could not do, a band of enthusiasts might attempt with some hope of success. Lawrence therefore decided to cross the desert with Auda Abu Tayi who had recently joined the Arab Revolt, with a small party, to raise the northern tribes and take Akaba in the rear. Auda separated from Lawrence and Nasir, to visit Nuri Shalaan, and rejoined them at Nebk.

It was also Lawrence's plan to visit Syria and to get in touch with Syrian members of the secret society of Arab Nationalists, many of them officers in the Turkish Army. An account of this trip through Syria was not included in *Seven Pillars of Wisdom*, though some particulars of it have been given by Graves and Liddell Hart. The latter ('*T. E. Lawrence': in Arabia and After*, p. 194) mentions the existence of a report to General Clayton written after the capture of Akaba, and says:

> When a friend asked to see this report a few weeks later, he [Lawrence] wrote back: 'I handed it to Clayton whose eyebrows went high (some of it was comic, some scurrilous, some betrayed horrible secrets) and who sat on it. I don't think anyone in the Savoy ever saw it whole. It certainly never went to H.C.[1] or W.O.[1] or F.O.,[1] and I am too tender-hearted to ask after it now. It was a MS. document of three pages, and compressed three months march into it: rather dull, except to one who knew Syrian politics . . . It is all ancient history now.'

I cannot understand the reference to *a few weeks later* since Lawrence could not have called the report ancient history within a few weeks of writing it. Most fortunately I have succeeded in having this report unearthed and have obtained permission to publish it, together with photographs of the maps which Lawrence appended to it. It covers not only the trip to Syria, but all the operations between his leaving Wejh and the capture of Akaba (Chapters XXXIX-LIV of *Seven Pillars of Wisdom*) and also an outline of his plans for a succession of Arab risings in various districts.]

---

[1] The High Commissioner of Egypt: the War Office: the Foreign Office.

97: TO GENERAL CLAYTON[1]

10th July, 1917   SECRET   *Cairo*

General Clayton, I left Wejh on May 9th, 1917 with Sherif*
Nasir Ibn Ali Ibn Radhi Beni Hussein of Medina as O.C.
Expedition, and Nessib Bey El Bekri as Political Officer to deal
with villagers and townspeople. Sherif Feisal's instructions were
to open Akaba for use as a base of supply for the Arab forces, and
to sound the possibilities of Sherifian action in East and South Syria.

We marched to Abu Raga where we increased our force to
36 men, and thence to the Railway at km. 810.5 which we
dynamited on May 19th. Our route then lay by Fejr to Maigua
in Wadi Soilan, for Jarf to see Nuri and Nawwaf. We heard
however that they were to the North of us, so marched to Nebk
(near Kaf) on June 2nd, where we met Auda Abu Tayi, and the
Huweitat. Sherif Nasir stayed in Kaf to enrol Rualla, Shererat
and Huweitat for the Akaba expedition.

I rode on June 4th with 2 men into Wald Ali† country, via
Burga and Seba Biar to Ain El Barida near Tudmor on June 8th.
Here I met Sheikh Dhami of the Kawakiba Aneza and heard that
Hachim was away N.E. and Ibn Murshid confined in Damascus.
I therefore went West with Dhami and his 35 men (whom I
enrolled) to Ras Baalbek on June 10th and dynamited a small
plate girder bridge there.‡ From Ras Baalbek we rode South to

* Nasir proved most capable, hard working and straightforward during the expedition. I took a personal liking to him,
and think him (after Faisal and Shakir) the best of the Ashraf I
have had to work with.

† My object was to meet the Bishr and compose their feud
with the Howeitat with a view to working between Homs and
Aleppo. The plan failed, but Dhami is in a position to act as
go-between, or to provide men to destroy the Orontes bridges
when required. He is now in Akaba — a good man.

‡ The effect on the traffic was of course very slight, but the
Metowila of Baalbek were most excited, and it was to arouse them
that I did it. The noise of dynamite explosions we find everywhere the most effective propagandist measure possible.

[1] Chief of Intelligence in Egypt and head of the Arab Bureau. See *Seven Pillars of Wisdom*, Chaps. VI and VII.

El Gabban, in the Ghuta 3 miles from Damascus where on June 13th I met Ali Riza Pasha Rehabi,* G.O.C. Damascus. Thence I rode to El Rudeine where I met Sheikh Saad Ed Din Ibn Ali of the Leja,† and passed on to Salkhad to see Hussein Bey El Atrash.‡ From Salkhad we went to Azrak and saw Nuri and Nawwaf,§ and returned to Nebk on June 18th.

I found the enrolment finished. Nessib Bey El Bekri went to Salkhad with Hussein El Atrash with the instructions attached,‖ and with Nasir I marched on June 19th to Bair where we re-opened the dynamited wells. From Bair I rode to Ziza and saw Fawaz Ibn Faiz,** and thence West of Amman to Um Keis on June 23rd where I looked at railway bridge Z in the Yarmuk valley and saw Shererat and Beni Hassan Sheikhs. From Um Keis I went to Ifdein (Mafrak on the map[1]) the first station below

* Ali Riza is the well known Turkish Engineer General, President of the Syrian branch of the Arab Secret Society. He informed me that he had only 500 Turkish gendarmes and three unarmed Labour battalions in Damascus, and was not in a position to demonstrate his real feelings unaided.

† With Saad Ed Din I discussed a provisional plan of action from the Leja when the need arises.

‡ Hussein told me the terms on which the Druses are prepared to rise. They seem to me to offer a basis for negotiation.

§ Their action depends on that of the Druses. I am sure that by himself Nuri would do nothing, but he recognizes the certainty of his being involved in the struggle, and is profoundly pro-Arab and pro-Sherif. He is now collecting his annual corn supply in the Nugra, and is playing double till we require him.

‖ Nessib El Bekri is volatile and short-sighted, as are most town-Syrians, and will not carry them out exactly — but no other agent was available.

** Who was fair spoken, but I am convinced pro-Turk at heart. The Beni Saklhad will mostly follow Trad and Ibn Zebbu, who are our men.

[1] Lawrence's own route map, attached to his report, is reproduced opposite.

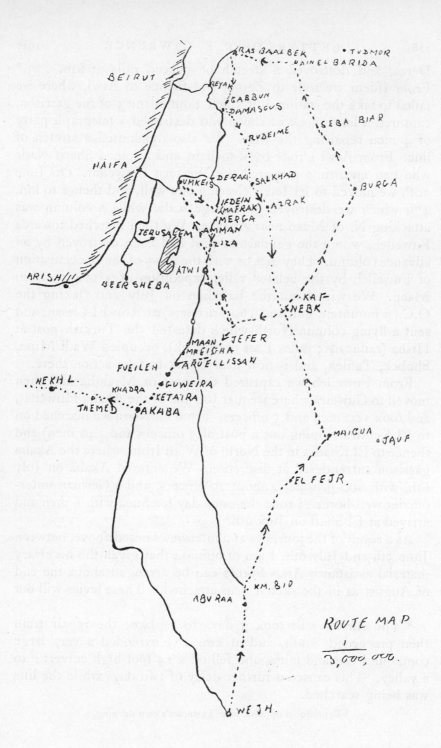

BEIRUT

RAS BAALBEK   TUDMOR
HAINEL BARIDA

REYAK
GABBUN
DAMASCUS
RUDEIME   SEBA BIAR

HAIFA

UMKEIS DERAA SALKHAD   BURGA
IFDEIN
(MAFRAK)   AZRAK
MERGA
JERUSALEM AMMAN
AZIZA
ATWI
ARISH
BEERSHEBA

KAT-
NEBK

JEFER
MAAN
MREIGHA
FUEILEH ARUELLISSAH
GUWEIRA
NEKHL KHADRA KETAIRA
THEMED AKABA
MAICUA   JAUF

EL FEJR

KM. 810
ABU RAA

ROUTE MAP
1
————
3,000,000

WE JH.

Deraa, and destroyed a stretch of curved rails at km. 173.*
From Ifdein we rode to Zerga, and thence to Atwi, where we
failed to take the station, but killed 3 out of the 5 of the garrison,
captured a large flock of sheep and destroyed a telegraph party
of 4 men repairing the wire. We also dynamited a stretch of
line. From Atwi I rode back to Bair, and rejoined Sherif Nasir
who had meantime prepared the Western Huweitat. On June
30th we moved to El Jefer, clearing one well, and thence to km.
479 which we destroyed on a large scale, while a column was
attacking N. of Maan near Aneyza. We then marched towards
Fuweileh, where the gendarmes post had been destroyed by an
advance column. They met us with the news of the re-occupation
of Fuweileh by the belated relief expedition of 4/174/59 from
Maan. We wiped out the battalion on July 2nd (taking the
O.C., a mountain gun and 160 prisoners) at Abu El Lissan, and
sent a flying column North which defeated the Turkish post at
Hisha (railhead 5 miles East of Shobek), occupied Wadi Musa,
Shobek, Tafileh, and is now near Kerak to take action there.

From Fuweileh we captured the post of Mreigha and then
moved to Guweira where we met Ibn Jad of the Akaba Huweitat,
and took 100 men and 5 officers. From Guweira we marched on
to El Kethira (wiping out a post of 3 officers and 140 men) and
thence to El Khadra in the North of Wadi Ithm, where the Akaba
garrison surrendered at discretion. We entered Akaba on July
6th, with 600 prisoners, about 20 officers, and a German unter-
offizier well-borer. I rode the same day for Suez with 8 men and
arrived at El Shatt on July 9th.

As a result of the journeys and interviews noted above, between
June 5th and July 6th, I am of opinion that given the necessary
material assistance Arab Forces can be arranged about the end
of August as in the sketch map attached.¹ These levies will not

---

* The curved rails took 3 days to replace: the repair train
then proceeded South, and at km. 174 exploded a very large
compound Garland mine, and fell off a 15 foot high culvert into
a valley. This caused a further delay of two days while the line
was being searched.

¹ Reproduced opposite from Lawrence's own drawing.

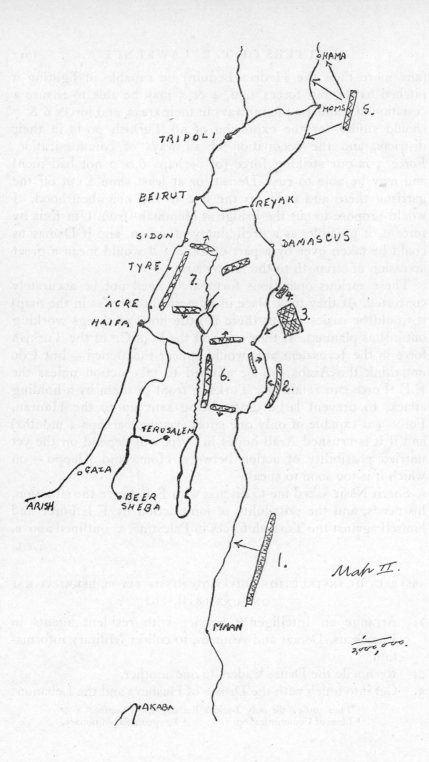

AMAMA

HOMS

5.

TRIPOLI

BEIRUT

REYAK

SIDON

DAMASCUS

TYRE

7.

ACRE

HAIFA

4.

3.

6.

2.

JERUSALEM

GAZA

BEER
SHEBA

ARISH

1.

Map II.

MAAN

1/2,000,000.

AKABA

(any more than the Hedjaz Beduin) be capable of fighting a pitched battle, but forces 1, 2, 4 & 5 may be able to ensure a cessation of traffic on the railways in their areas, and forces 6 & 7 should suffice for the expulsion of all Turkish posts in their districts, and the occupation of all ways of communication. Force 3 is our striking force (of perhaps 6,000 not bad men) and may be able to rush Deraat, or at least should cut off the garrison there and hold up the line in the neighbourhood. I would propose to cut the bridge at Hemmah[1] from Um Keis by force 2, if possible, as a preliminary of action, and if Damascus could be taken over by a part of force 3 it would mean a great accession of strength to the Arab cause.

These various operations fortunately need not be accurately concerted. If they took place in numerical order (as in the map) it would be easiest — but there is little hope of things working out just as planned. If they come off the L. of C.[2] of the Turkish force in the Jerusalem area would appear threatened — but I do not think the Arabs can be advised to take action unless the E.E.[3]Force can retain the Turks in front of them by a holding attack, to prevent large drafts being sent up to the Hauran. Force 3 is capable of only one effort (lasting perhaps 2 months) and if it is crushed Arab hopes in Syria will depend on the yet untried possibility of action between Homs and Aleppo — on which it is too soon to speak.

Sherif Nasir asked me to discuss with E.E.Force the situation, his needs, and the possibility of joint action by E.E.Force and himself against the Turkish forces in Palestine, as outlined above.

T.E.L.

ABSTRACT OF INSTRUCTIONS GIVEN TO NESSIB BEY EL BEKRI AT KAF
ON JUNE 18TH, 1917

1. Arrange an Intelligence Service with resident agents in Damascus, Deraat and Amman, to collect Military information.

2. Reconcile the Druse leaders to one another.

3. Get into touch with the Druses of Hasbeya and the Lebanon:

---

[1] Thus cutting the only Turkish Railway into Palestine.
[2] Lines of Communication.   [3] Egyptian Expeditionary.

also with the Metowala of the Jebel Amr and the Belad Bishara (using Sid Nasir's name), and re-assure the Maronites of the area on the nature of the Sherif's administration in the future.

4. Get in touch with the Ghawarineh of Lake Huleh and Merj Ayum.

5. Send Zeki Effendi to Leja, to examine the roads and water supply.

6. Send me an estimate of the needs of the Druses in warlike stores.

7. Discuss with Nuri the elimination of the Circassian colonies of the Nugra and Kuneitra.

8. Approach some of the chief Baalbek Metowila and find out what they are prepared to do.

9. Prepare the villagers of J. El Sheikh, J. El Shergi, and J. Kalamun.

10. Get on speedy terms with the Bishr.

[I have also included the much more detailed and picturesque accounts of the battle of Fuweilah and the occupation of Akaba printed in *The Arab Bulletin*, No. 59. All these extracts from *The Arab Bulletin* have a particular value owing to their being written within a very short time of the events they record.]

98: THE OCCUPATION OF AKABA

[Arab Bulletin No. 59]

By Monday, June 18, we had enrolled 535 Toweiha (of whom twenty-five were horsemen), about 150 Rualla (under Benaiah ibn Dughmi, Durzi's brother) and Shererat (under Geraitan el-Azmi), and thirty-five Kawachiba, under Dhami. Of these we chose nearly 200, and left them as guards for the tribal tents in Wadi Sirhan. With the rest we marched out of Kaf in the afternoon, and on June 20 entered Bair, after an easy but water-less march over the Suwan. At Bair we found one well filled in, two seriously damaged, and a fourth unhurt: the Turks had come there a little time before with Hamd el-Arar, and tried to blow them in with gelignite. They used an electric exploder clumsily, and we removed many tamped charges from the sides of the still open wells.

Circumstances forced us to stay in Bair till Thursday June 28. The time was spent in negotiations with Ibn Jazi and the smaller sub-sections of the Howeitat on the Akaba road. We also carried out demolitions against the railway at Atwi, Sultani, Minifir, and elsewhere. The Ageyl dynamitards were inefficient, and our supply of dynamite small, so that the demolitions were of a pin-prick character, meant only to distract the Turks, and advertise our coming to the Arabs. The staffs of two stations were killed, to the same intent.

From Bair we marched to El Jefer, where we stayed till July 1. The Turks had been more successful in their efforts against the wells here, and we had some difficulty in digging one out. The water proved sufficient for about 300 men and camels, when it was obtained. The station buildings of Maan and Hamra are visible from El Jefer, about twenty-four miles off, but the Turks did not realize that we had arrived in force, owing to the operations near Amman, undertaken at this time by a flying column of 100 men, under Sheikh Zaal. This led them to believe us still in Wadi Sirhan, and on the 30th they sent a force of 400 cavalry with four machine guns, and Nawaf ibn Shaalan as guide, from Deraa to go to Kaf and find us. The Turks seem unable to discriminate the true from the false, out of the flood of news unquestionably brought them by the local Arabs.

From El Jefer a flying column rode to Fuweilah, about seven-teen miles south-west of Maan, and in concert with the Dhumaniya Howeitat (Sheikh Gasim) attacked the gendarme post on the motor road to Akaba. In the fighting some mounted gendarmes got into a group of undefended Howeitat tents, and stabbed to death an old man, six women and seven children, the only occupants. Our Arabs in consequence wiped out the post, but not before some had escaped to Maan.

This news reached Maan at dawn on the 1st, and a battalion of the 178th Regiment which had arrived at Maan from Zunguldak on the day before, was immediately ordered out to Fuweilah to relieve the post. The same afternoon we descended on the line at kilometre 479, near Ghadir el Haj, and carried out

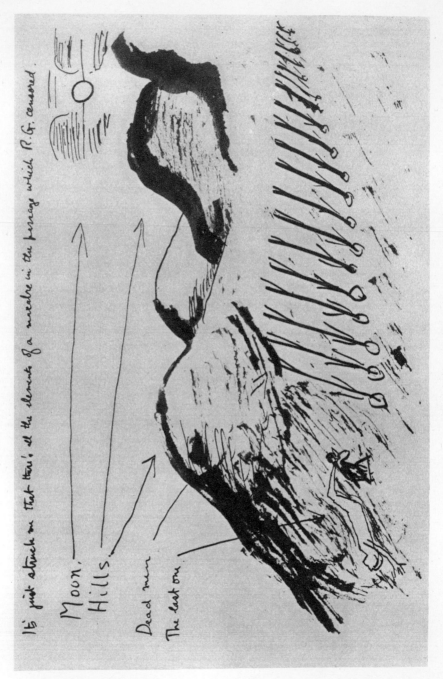

It's just struck on that thro', & the elements of a meerkat in the foreage which R.G. censored.

Moon.
Hills.
Dead men
The last on.

LAYING OUT DEAD TURKS from a sketch by T.E.L. sent to
Eric Kennington (*Seven Pillars of Wisdom*, Chap. LIV)

extensive demolitions till nearly sunset, when we marched westward, intending to sleep at Batra. On the way, however, we were
met by messengers from our Fuweilah column, reporting the
coming of new troops from Maan, and we swung northwards,
marching a great part of the night, till we were able at dawn to
occupy the crests of the low rolling grass-covered hills that
flank each side of the Akaba road near Ain Aba el-Lissan. The
Turks had reached Fuweilah, to find only vultures in possession,
and moved to Aba el-Lissan, fourteen miles from Maan, for the
night. The spring has been built round, and piped, and is much
smaller than it used to be before the war, but is still sufficient for
perhaps 2,000 men and animals. The battalion camped next the
water, and kept together in the bottom of the valley, so that we
were able to take the higher ground (at from 400 to 600 yards
range) without difficulty.

We sat here throughout July 2, sniping the Turks steadily all
day, and inflicted some loss. The Turks replied with shrapnel
from a mountain gun, firing twenty rounds, which were all they
had. The shells grazed our hill-tops, and burst far away over the
valleys behind. When sunset came, Auda Abu Tayi collected the
fifty horsemen now with us, in a hollow valley about 200 yards
from the Turks, but under cover, and suddenly charged at a wild
gallop into the brown of them, shooting furiously from the saddle
as he came. The unexpectedness of the move seemed to strike
panic into the Turks (about 550 strong), and after a burst of
rifle fire, they scattered in all directions. This was our signal, and
all the rest of our force (perhaps 350 men, for some were watching
the road on the east) dashed down the hillsides into the hollow,
as fast as the camels would go. The Turks were all infantry, and
the Arabs all mounted, and the mix-up round the spring in the
dusk, with 1,000 men shooting like mad, was considerable. As
the Turks scattered, their position at once became hopeless, and
in five minutes it was merely a massacre. In all I counted 300
enemy dead in the main position, and a few fugitives may have
been killed further away, though the majority of our men went
straight for the Turkish camp to plunder it, before the last shots
were fired. The prisoners came to 160 (three officers), mostly
taken by Sherif Nasir and myself, since the Arabs in the Maan

area are very bitter against the Turks, and are set on killing all they can. They have some reason for this attitude, in the slaughter of the women and children mentioned above, and in the previous execution of Sheikh Abd el-Rahman, a Belgawiya from Kerak. He was popular, and anti-Turk, but the Government caught him, and harnessing him between four wild mules tore him to death. This was the culmination of a series of executions by torture in Kerak, and the memory of them has embittered local opinion.

The Arab losses in the fight came to two killed (a Rualla and a Sherarat) and several wounded, including Sheikh Benaiah ibn Dughmi. Considering the amount of firing, the confusion, the close quarters at which we were, and the Turkish casualties, the Arabs must be held to have got off very luckily. Several horses were hit in the cavalry charge, and Auda himself (in front, of course) had a narrow escape, since two bullets smashed his field glasses, one pierced his revolver holster, three struck his sheathed sword, and his horse was killed under him. He was wildly pleased with the whole affair.

Unfortunately, many of our prisoners were wounded and we had very few spare camels with us. Those who could hold on were mounted behind Arabs on the spare camels; but we had to abandon the worst cases at Aba el-Lissan, and of those we took with us about fifty died of heat, hunger and thirst on the road down to Akaba. The heat in the Hesma and Wadi Itm was terrible, and the water between Fuweila and Akaba only sufficient for perhaps 200 men and animals. For the matter of food, Nasir and I had taken two months' supply with us from Wejh, and were now two months out; the Bedu had their own food with them in their saddle bags, but Arab rations are ill-adapted, in quality and quantity, for Turkish soldiers. We did what we could for the prisoners, but everybody went short.

From Aba el-Lissan we marched to Guweira (22 miles) after sending out a column which destroyed Mreiga, the nearest gendarme post to Maan, on the Akaba road. At Guweira we received the surrender of the garrison (of about 120 men), their intermediary being Hussein ibn Jad,[1] who joined us here on

---

[1] 'At Guweira lay Sheikh ibn Jad, balancing his policy to come down with the stronger: and today we were the stronger and the old fox was ours.' (*Seven Pillars of Wisdom*, Chap. LIV.)

July 4. The motor road is finished to the foot of Nagb el-Star, from Maan, but not metalled anywhere. As the soil is fairly hard loam, I think it should suffice for the passage of a series of light cars. The Nagb is very steep, with bad hairpin corners, and will require improvement. The Hesma is of fine red sand, soft along the track, but harder in the bed of the watercourse which runs down from the foot of the Nagb to Guweira. From Guweira we marched down Wadi Itm to Kethira (18 miles) where we overran a Turkish post of about seventy infantry and fifty mounted men, taking most of them prisoners,[1] and thence we went on to near Khadra, at the old stone dam in Wadi Itm (15 miles), where we came into contact with the garrison (300 men) of Akaba. They had retired here from the village itself (about six miles away) to be out of view of the sea, and on the line of retreat towards Maan. The news of our fight at Fuweilah had reached Akaba quickly, and all the Amran, Darausha, Heiwat and sub-tribes of the Howeitat near Akaba had risen, and collected round the Khadra post, which had held them at bay from their trenches with small casualties for two days. When Nasir and the banner turned up the Arab excitement became intense, and preparations were made for an immediate assault. This did not fall in with our ideas, since (pour encourager les autres) we wanted the news to get about that the Arabs accepted prisoners. All the Turks we met were most happy to surrender, holding up their arms and crying 'Muslim, Muslim' as soon as they saw us. They expressed themselves willing and anxious to go on fighting foreigners and Christians till they dropped, but with no intention of adding a Moslem enemy to the powers already against them. To save the Khadra garrison from massacre Sherif Nasir had to labour from afternoon till dawn, but he eventually carried his point (by our going ourselves between the Arab and Turkish lines, to break their field of fire), and with the prisoners (now about 600 in number) we marched into Akaba on the morning of July 6. The

---

[1] 'We assigned the honour, in irony, to ibn Jad and his unwearied men, advising him to try it after dark. He shrank, made difficulties, pleaded the full moon: but we cut hardly into this excuse, promising that to-night for a while there should be no moon. By my diary there was an eclipse. Duly it came, and the Arabs forced the post without loss, while the superstitious soldiers were firing rifles and clanging copper pots to rescue the threatened satellite.' (*Seven Pillars of Wisdom*, Chap. LIV.)

astonishment of a German N.C.O. (well-boring at Khadra) when the Sherif's force appeared was comic. He knew neither Arabic nor Turkish, and had not been aware of the Arab revolt.

The situation at Akaba was now rather serious, economically. We had no food, 600 prisoners and many visitors in prospect. Meat was plentiful, since we had been killing riding camels as required, and there were unripe dates in the palm groves. These saved the day, but involved a good deal of discomfort after the eating, and the force in Akaba was very unhappy till the arrival of H.M.S. *Dufferin* on the 13th with food from Suez. Before she arrived, Arab forces were sent northward to occupy the hills up to Wadi Musa (Petra), some sixty miles from Akaba, and south-ward to join up with the Beni Atiyeh, and reconnoitre the country with a view to an eventual offensive against the railway south of Maan.

[The passage in the following letter referring to a projected book shows that Lawrence was already contemplating *Seven Pillars of Wisdom*. It is interesting that at the time of enlistment in the Air Force he was also planning a book on his experiences. See letter No. 166.]

99: TO COLONEL C. E. WILSON

2.9.17   [*Akaba*]

Dear Colonel Wilson, I should have answered your very kind note before, but I was busy about stores and things when the Southward ships were sailing. The Hejaz show is a quaint one, the like of which has hardly been on earth before, and no one not of it can appreciate how difficult it is to run. However it has gone forward, and history will call it a success: but I hope that the difficulties it has had to contend with will be equally clear. All my memories of it are pleasant (largely due to you, of course, for on the face things should not be so), and if ever I can get my book on it out, I'll try to make other people see it. They do not seem always to appreciate that while we hop about the Railway and places smashing things up, and enjoying ourselves, someone else has to sit and stew in Jidda keeping the head of the affair on the rails. You would be glad to hear sometimes how Feisul and the rest speak of you.

However, here is a request. The Sherif never approved of Jaafar's[1] coming & has never been reconciled to it. Jaafar has done very good work, and has pulled the officers more or less together, & made himself recognised as the head of them. This is going to change the discipline & spirit of the whole force like magic, if he can get a few more officers. He's just gone to Egypt for this. Do you think you could get a letter from the Sherif to him, thanking him for his efforts, and saying something nice about their mutual hopes for the future? Jaafar is a little down in the mouth, & this letter would give him confidence.

I fancy it may not be as easy as it sounds to get the right letter from the Sherif — but if you could get a pleased moment or a tactful friend it might be done. A direct request would look a little odd.

I hope to go off towards Mudowwara in three days' time: have been held up for money. Yours sincerely,   T. E. LAWRENCE

100: TO A FRIEND

Sept 24. '17   *Akaba*

Dear [*name omitted*], I'm sorry, but I felt the usual abrupt beginning would be too much for your nerves, and that you would fall exhausted on to the floor [3 *words omitted*], without even a Turkish carpet to break the shock of my writing at last. What can have happened? I was pondering last night how for a year I had written no private letter (except to my people, and those don't count, for my mails are sunk or censored!) and today I go and break the habit. Perhaps it's because it was a habit, and I'm getting old and stiff (not to say tired, for every year out in Arabia counts ten) and habits must be nipped in their shells.

I'm in Akaba for two days — that for me spells civilisation, though it doesn't mean other than Arab togs and food, but it means you lunch where you dined, and not further on — and therefore happy. The last stunt has been a few days on the

---

[1] Jaafar Pasha El Askari, an Iraqi officer in the Turkish Army, had been captured by the Essex Yeomanry after the defeat of the Senussi, and volunteering to join the Arab Revolt, became Feisal's Chief of Staff, and afterwards (until his cowardly assassination) one of the most important ministers of Iraq.

Hejaz Railway, in which I potted a train with two engines (oh, the Gods were kind) and we killed superior numbers, and I got a good Baluch prayer-rug and lost all my kit, and nearly my little self.

I'm not going to last out this game much longer: nerves going and temper wearing thin, and one wants an unlimited account of both. However while it lasts it's a show between Gilbert and Carroll, and one can retire on it, with that feeling of repletion that comes after a hearty meal. By the way hearty meals are like the chopped snow that one scatters over one's bowl of grapes in Damascus at midsummer. Ripping, to write about —

This letter isn't going to do you much good, for the amount of information it contains would go on a pin's head and roll about. However it's not a correspondence, but a discourse held with the only person to whom I have ever written regularly, and one whom I have shamefully ill-used by not writing to more frequently. On a show so narrow and voracious as this one loses one's past and one's balance, and becomes hopelessly self-centred. I don't think I ever think except about shop, and I'm quite certain I never do anything else. That must be my excuse for dropping everyone, and I hope when the nightmare ends that I will wake up and become alive again. This killing and killing of Turks is horrible. When you charge in at the finish and find them all over the place in bits, and still alive many of them, and know that you have done hundreds in the same way before and must do hundreds more if you can. [*Two lines omitted*]

101: TO COLONEL P. C. JOYCE[1]

13.11.17   [*?Azrak*]

Dear Joyce, Please tell Feisul we rode to El Jefer, and found Zaal and the Abu Tayi afraid to come with us. Sherif Ali and Auda did their best to work them up, but they were not for it. The Abu Tayi have almost revolted against Auda, and I doubt whether we shall see much more good from them: they have seen too much good from us.[2]

Thence we went to Bair, where we found Mifleh ibn Zebn.

---

[1] Commanding at Akaba.   [2] *Seven Pillars of Wisdom*, Chap. LXXIII.

He with Fahad and Adhub ibn Zebn went with us, and did most splendidly. I think them three of the best Arab sheikhs I have met. Fahad was badly hit in the face in the train scrimmage, but will, I hope, recover.

From Bair we rode to Azrak where we met the Serahin. Sheikh Mifleh ibn Bali rode with us to the bridge, and did his best, but he and his tribe are not in it with the Beni Sakhr.

Emir Abd el Kader came with us to Azrak, where we made the plan of attack on the bridge at Tell el Shehab. He said he would come with us, and we had no idea anything was wrong, but the same day he rode off (without warning either Ali or myself or the Arabs with us) to Salkhad, where he is still sitting. Tell Feisul I think he was afraid: much talk, and little doing, in his way. Neither Ali nor myself gave him any offence.[1]

Tell el Shehab is a splendid bridge to destroy, but those Serahin threw away all my explosive when the firing began, & so I can do nothing — If the Turks have not increased their guard we can do it later: but I am very sick at losing it so stupidly. The Bedu cannot take the bridge, but can reach it: the Indians can take it, but cannot reach it![2]

From Tell el Shehab we turned back to the Railway south of Deraa, and destroyed two locomotives. We must have killed about 100 Turks too.[3] It was a most risky performance but came off all right. Little Ali is a very plucky youth, and came to my rescue on each occasion very dashingly. He will certainly get himself killed unless he continues to travel with a person as skilful and cautious as myself. Besides being in the thick of it when anything happens he keeps very good control of the Arabs on the march, and has been very decent to me — I think he is quite in the front rank of Sherifs — but he really must go easy with himself, or I will want a successor to travel with!

Please give Feisul (& Snagge) any extracts you like from the report to Clayton enclosed. Tell him the whole country of the Hauran fellahin is slipping towards him, and they only require arms, money and a shock to get all moving together. We can get no news of what happened at Gaza.

---

[1] *Seven Pillars of Wisdom*, Chap. LXXVI.　　　[2] Ibid, Chap. LXXVII.
[3] Ibid, Chap. LXXIX.

I think the attached might go to the Press. Ali deserves a
mention, for he is a very uncommon youth. My personal requests
in another paper. Yours,   T. E. LAWRENCE

[Enclosed with foregoing letter]

On November the eleventh a detachment of the Northern
Army of Sherif Feisul, under the command of Sherif Ali ibn
Hussein el Harith, attacked the Railway and troop trains between
Deraat and Amman. Two locomotives and some coaches were
completely destroyed, and a bridge blown up. The Turks lost
heavily in killed and wounded. The Arabs lost seven men.

[I also print here Lawrence's report in *The Arab Bulletin* No. 79
of the Battle of Tafila which Liddell Hart has described in
'*T. E. Lawrence*': *In Arabia and After* as 'a gem of a battle' and
a 'parody of military orthodoxy'. Lawrence's humour found
scope in his description in *Seven Pillars of Wisdom*.]

102: THE BATTLE OF SEIL EL-HASA

January 26 [1918], [*Arab Bulletin, No.* 79]   *Tafila*

A Turkish temporary regiment, commanded by Hamid Fakhri
Bey, acting G.O.C. 48th Division, and composed of 3/151,
1/152, a murettab battalion of 150, with a company of gendarmes,
a detachment of 100 cavalry, two Austrian quick-firing mountain
guns, and twenty-three machine guns, was railed to Kalaat el-
Hasa station on January 19, and left Kerak on January 23 to
retake Tafila. The troops had been hurriedly collected from the
Hauran and Amman commands, and came forward from Kerak
short of supplies, and leaving no food and few men there.

On January 24, they came in contact in the afternoon with our
patrols in Seil el-Hasa, and by night had driven them back into
Tafila. The Sherifian officers had laid out a defensive position on
the south bank of the great valley in which Tafila stands, and
Sherif Zeid left for this about midnight, taking with him the
sixty regulars and 400 irregulars (Ageyl, Bisha, Muteir) who had

come with him from Akaba. The Sherifian baggage marched away at the same time towards Buseira, and everybody thought that we were running away. I think we were.

Tafila of course panicked, and as Diab el-Auran (the busy-bodied sheikh) had given us ominous reports of the disaffection and treachery of the villagers, I went down from my house before dawn into the crowded streets, to listen to what was being said. There was much free criticism of the Sherif, distinctly disrespect-ful, but no disloyalty. Everyone was screaming with terror, goods were being bundled out of the houses into the streets, which were packed with women and men. Mounted Arabs were galloping up and down, firing wildly into the air, and the flashes of the Turkish rifles were outlining the further cliffs of the Tafila gorge. Just at dawn the enemy bullets began to fall in the olive gardens, and I went out to Sherif Zeid and persuaded him to send Abdullah Effendi (the machine gunner and the junior of our two officers) with two fusils mitrailleurs to support the peasants who were still holding the northern crest. His arrival stimulated them to a counter-attack in which they drove the Turkish cavalry back over the near ridge, across a small plain to the first of the low ridges falling into Wadi el-Hasa. He took this ridge also, and was there held up, as the Turkish main body was posted just behind it. The fighting became very hot, with huge bursts of Turkish machine-gun fire and a good deal of shelling.

Zeid hesitated to send forward reinforcements, so I went up to Abdullah's position (about seven miles north of Tafila) to report. On my way I met him returning, having had five men killed and one gun put out of action, and having finished his ammunition. We sent back urgent messages to Zeid to send forward a mountain gun, any available machine guns, and what men he could collect, to a reserve position, which was the southern end of the little plain between the Hasa valley and the Tafila valley. This plain is triangular, about two miles each way. The opening lay to the north, and was a low pass, through which the Kerak road ran, and up which the Turks were coming. The sides of the triangle were low ridges, and Abdullah's charge had taken all the western ridge.

After Abdullah had gone I went up to the front, and found

things rather difficult. It was being held by thirty Ibn Jazi Howeitat, mounted, and about thirty villagers. The Turks were working through the pass, and along the eastern boundary ridge of the plain, and concentrating the fire of about fifteen machine guns on the face and flank of the rather obvious little mound we were holding. They were meanwhile correcting the fusing of their shrapnel, which had been grazing the hill-top and bursting over the plain, and were beginning to sprinkle the sides and top of the hill quite freely. Our people were short of ammunition, and the loss of the position was obviously only a matter of minutes. A Turkish aeroplane came up and did not improve our chances.

The Motalga horsemen were given all the cartridges we could collect, and the footmen ran back over the plain. I was among them, since I had come straight up the cliffs from Tafila, and my animals had not caught me up. The mounted men held out for fifteen minutes more, and then galloped back to us unhurt. We collected in the reserve position, a ridge about sixty feet high, commanding an excellent view of the plain. It was now noon, we had lost about fifteen men and had about eighty left, but a few minutes later about 120 Ageyl came up, and my men with a Hotchkiss automatic, and Lutfi el-Aseli with two. We then held our own easily till 3 p.m. when Sherifs Zeid and Mastur came up with Rasim and Abdullah, one Egyptian army 2.95 mountain gun, two Vickers, two large Hotchkiss, and five fusils mitrailleurs, with twenty mule M.I.,[1] thirty Motalga horse, and about 200 villagers. The Turks were trying to shell and machine-gun our ridge, but found difficulty in ranging. They had occupied our old front line, and we had its range (3,100 yards) exactly, as I had paced it on my way back (this mountain country is very difficult to judge by eye). We mounted all our materials on our ridge, and Rasim took all the mounted men (now about eighty) to the right, to work up beyond the eastern boundary ridge. He was able to get forward unseen, till he had turned the Turkish flank at 2,000 yards. He there made a dismounted attack of ten men and five fusils mitrailleurs, keeping his horse in reserve. Meanwhile the Turks had just five Maxims and four automatics on the western ridge of the pass, and opened on our centre. We replied

[1] Mounted Infantry.

with Vickers and Hotchkiss, and put twenty-two rounds of shrapnel over the face of the mound. A reinforcement of 100 men from Aima now reached us (they had refused Sherifian service the day before over a question of wages, but sunk old scores in the crisis), and we sent them, with three Hotchkiss automatics, to our left flank. They crept down behind the western ridge of the plain till within 200 yards of the Turkish Maxims, without being seen, as we opened across the plain a frontal attack of eighteen men, two Vickers, and two large Hotchkiss. The ridge was a flint one, and the Turks could not entrench on it, as we had found in the morning; the ricochets were horrible. They lost many men, and our left flank were finally able by a sudden burst of fire to wipe out the Turkish machine-gunners and rush the guns. The mounted men then charged the retreating Turks from our right flank, while we sent forward the infantry and the banners in the centre. They occupied the Turkish line at sunset, and chased the enemy back past their guns into the bed of Wadi Hasa; where their cavalry in reserve put up a check that was not passed till dark. Our people mostly gave up the pursuit at this point (we had had no food since the day before, and the cold was pitiful) but the Bedouins of Kerak took it up and harried the flying mob all night.

Our losses were about twenty-five killed and forty wounded. The Ibn Jazi Howeitat, under Hamad el-Arar, did splendidly, and the villagers were very steady and good.

103: TO V. W. RICHARDS

15.7.18.

Well, it was wonderful to see your writing again, and very difficult to read it: also pleasant to have a letter which doesn't begin 'Reference your GS 102487b of the 45th'. Army prose is bad, and one has so much of it that one fears contamination in one's own. I cannot write to anyone just now. Your letter came to me in Aba Lissan, a little hill-fort on the plateau of Arabia S.E. of the Dead Sea, and I carried it with me down to Akaba, to Jidda, and then here to answer. Yet with all that I have had it only a month, and you wrote it three months ago. This letter will be submarined, and then it is all over for another three years.

It always seemed to me that your eyes would prevent all service for you, and that in consequence you might preserve your continuity. For myself, I have been so violently uprooted and plunged so deeply into a job too big for me, that everything feels unreal. I have dropped everything I ever did, and live only as a thief of opportunity, snatching chances of the moment when and where I see them. My people have probably told you that the job is to foment an Arab rebellion against Turkey, and for that I have to try and hide my frankish exterior, and be as little out of the Arab picture as I can. So it's a kind of foreign stage, on which one plays day and night, in fancy dress, in a strange language, with the price of failure on one's head if the part is not well filled.

You guessed rightly that the Arab appealed to my imagination. It is the old, old civilisation, which has refined itself clear of household gods, and half the trappings which ours hastens to assume. The gospel of bareness in materials is a good one, and it involves apparently a sort of moral bareness too. They think for the moment, and endeavour to slip through life without turning corners or climbing hills. In part it is a mental and moral fatigue, a race trained out, and to avoid difficulties they have to jettison so much that we think honourable and grave: and yet without in any way sharing their point of view, I think I can understand it enough to look at myself and other foreigners from their direction, and without condemning it. I know I'm a stranger to them, and always will be: but I cannot believe them worse, any more than I could change to their ways.

This is a very long porch to explain why I'm always trying to blow up railway trains and bridges instead of looking for the Well at the World's End. Anyway these years of detachment have cured me of any desire ever to do anything for myself. When they untie my bonds I will not find in me any spur to action. However actually one never thinks of afterwards: the time from the beginning is like one of those dreams which seems to last for aeons, and then you wake up with a start, and find that it has left nothing in your mind. Only the different thing about this dream is that so many people do not wake up in this life again.

ARABIAN CAMPAIGN

I cannot imagine what my people can have told you. Until now we have only been preparing the groundwork and basis of our revolt, and do not yet stand on the brink of action. Whether we are going to win or lose, when we do strike, I cannot ever persuade myself. The whole thing is such a play, and one cannot put conviction into one's day dreams. If we succeed I will have done well with the materials given me, and that disposes of your 'lime light'. If we fail, and they have patience, then I suppose we will go on digging foundations. Achievement, if it comes, will be a great disillusionment, but not great enough to wake one up.

Your mind has evidently moved far since 1914. That is a privilege you have won by being kept out of the mist for so long. You'll find the rest of us aged undergraduates, possibly still unconscious of our unfitting grey hair. For that reason I cannot follow or return your steps. A house with no action entailed upon one, quiet, and liberty to think and abstain as one wills — yes, I think abstention, the leaving everything alone and watching the others still going past, is what I would choose today, if they ceased driving one. This may be only the reaction from four years opportunism, and is not worth trying to resolve into terms of geography and employment.

Of course the ideal is that of the lords who are still certainly expected, but the certainty is not for us, I'm afraid. Also for very few would the joy be so perfect as to be silent. Those words, peace, silence, rest, and the others take on a vividness in the midst of noise and worry and weariness like a lighted window in the dark. Yet what on earth is the good of a lighted window? and perhaps it is only because one is overborne and tired. You know when one marches across an interminable plain a hill (which is still the worst hill on earth) is a banquet, and after searing heat cold water takes on a quality (what would they have said about this word before?) impossible in the eyes of a fen-farmer. Probably I'm only a sensitised film, turned black or white by the objects projected on me: and if so what hope is there that next week or year, or tomorrow, can be prepared for today?

This is an idiot letter, and amounts to nothing except cry for a further change which is idiocy, for I change my abode every day, and my job every two days, and my language every three days, and still remain always unsatisfied. I hate being in front, and I hate being back and I don't like responsibility, and I don't obey orders. Altogether no good just now. A long quiet like a purge and then a contemplation and decision of future roads, that is what [there] is to look forward to.

You want apparently some vivid colouring of an Arab costume, or of a flying Turk, and we have it all, for that is part of the mise en scène of the successful raider, and hitherto I am that. My bodyguard of fifty Arab tribesmen, picked riders from the young men of the deserts, are more splendid than a tulip garden, and we ride like lunatics and with our Beduins pounce on unsuspecting Turks and destroy them in heaps: and it is all very gory and nasty after we close grips. I love the preparation, and the journey, and loathe the physical fighting. Disguises, and prices on one's head, and fancy exploits are all part of the pose: how to reconcile it with the Oxford pose I know not. Were we flamboyant there?

If you reply — you will perceive I have matting of the brain — and your thoughts are in control, please tell me of Berry,[1] and if possible, Winkworth.[1] The latter was the man for all these things, because he would take a baresark beery pleasure in physical outputs. Very many thanks for writing. It has opened a very precious casement.   L.

104: TO MAJOR R. H. SCOTT[2]

27.8.18   [Aba el Lissan]

Dear Scott, I'm very sorry for bothering you, but I find my personal plans changed, and am without transport. So I rang you up today and asked you to get Sh. Yusuf to buy me (at N. O.[3] expense) four v.G. riding camels, complete with saddlery, to hire me two Ageyl servants, give them a month's flour and rice, £10 and send them up to Aba Lissan most urgent. Then I'll be off. My bodyguard is as usual spread out over about a thousand miles of Arabia. I hope old Yusuf will do it without bothering you at all. If they get off from Akaba on the 28th they will be here on the 29th and that will be top-hole.

Feisal wants £2000 in notes. Will you send them up, if you

---

[1] Friends of their undergraduate days.
[2] Commandant at Akaba.   [3] Hedjaz Northern Operations.

have them and debit it to Special Grant? If this is not easy, please debit it to September, pending Cairo approval (asked for) of a gift to Feisal of £12000 in paper.

About *blasting gelatine*. Last consignment sent up was gelignite which is different. Will you see if there is any of the former, and if so let Aba Lissan know? I'll send down two camels then for it. A small baggage column of mine will turn up about Aug. 30 in Akaba, asking for Lewis gun and things. All easy.

We are involved in rings and rolls of dates, meandering at least eight times with a mazy motion,[1] and I haven't the least idea if we are at last going to get anywhere and do anything or not. My head whirls. Salute the elect from me. Yours T. E. LAWRENCE

I just remembered that a lot of stuff for me, camel saddles and what-nots from Jidda, and tents from Egypt, are about due. If there are any such in Akaba will you send me up word?　　　　L.

105: THE DESTRUCTION OF THE FOURTH ARMY[2]

[*Arab Bulletin, No.* 106]

With the two thousand camels, given us in July by General Allenby, we calculated that we could afford to send up to Azrak, for operations about Deraa, an expedition of four hundred and fifty camel corps of the Arab regular army, four Arab Vickers, twenty Arab Hotchkiss, a French battery of four mountain Q.F. .65 guns, two British aeroplanes, three British armoured cars with necessary tenders, a demolition company of Egyptian Camel Corps and a section of camel-Ghurkas. Besides these, Sherif Nasir and myself had our private body-guards of Arab camel-men. This made our total force one thousand strong, and its prospects were so sure that we made no provision (and had no means) for getting it back again. The supply problem, especially in petrol and ammunition, was a very great one, and we lived from hand to mouth, without, however, ever being in serious need.

The force left Ab el-Lissan in detachments early in September, and concentrated, without accident, to time at Azrak on the

---

[1] Coleridge, *Kubla Khan.*

[2] This, Lawrence's last contribution to *The Arab Bulletin*, covers the period described in *Seven Pillars of Wisdom*, Chap. CVII to the end.

twelfth of the month. The distance from Akaba to Azrak was two hundred and ninety miles, and we used the wells of Jefer, Bair and Ammari on the way. At Azrak we had meant to collect the Rualla and descend in force on the Hauran, with direct assault on Deraa, which was only held by five hundred rifles — but this plan was spoiled by the unfortunate outburst of the King of Hejaz against Jaafar Pasha and the senior officers of the Northern Army, since the crisis he provoked upset the whole local temper, and delayed me in Ab el-Lissan till September 4. As a result, the Rualla never came together, and we had to modify our schemes. In the end, we decided to carry out a flying attack on the northern, western and southern railways at Deraa, with our regular troops, the Rualla horse under Khalid and Trad Shaalan, and such Hauran peasants as should be brave enough to declare for us.

As we sat at Azrak we put in a strong bluff towards Amman. Money was sent to Mithgal with very secret instructions to collect barley dumps for us and the British, in our combined surprise attack against Amman and Salt on the 18th. The Beni Sakhr were to mass at Ziza to help us. The rumour of this, and the rumour of our simultaneous intention on Deraa, confirmed by other factors supplied them from Palestine, kept the Turks' eyes fixed on the Jordan and east of it, where their lines were very long, expensive in men, and, despite their best efforts, inevitably vulnerable to a force of our mobility and range.

On the 13th we left Azrak and marched over the long Gian el-Khunna into the basalt screes of Jebel Druse. The Egyptian and Ghurka units were sent westward to cut the Amman line by Mafrak, but, owing to a misunderstanding with their guides, never got so far. However, our Bristol Fighter the same day brought down a German two-seater in flames near Um-el-Jimal: so all was well. We got to Umtaiye, thirteen miles southeast of Deraa, on the 15th. This (and its neighbour Um el-Surab) were our forward bases, as about them were many cisterns of water of last year's rain. We were at once joined by the male population of the nearest villages, and by Sheikh Talal el-Hareidhin of Tafas, the finest fighter of the Hauran, who had come to me in Azrak in 1917. He had agreed to be our guide, and marched with us till he died near Deraa, helping us day and night, our sponsor and backer in every village. But for his energy, courage and honesty, things would have gone hard with us many times.

It was still necessary for us to cut the railway between Deraa and Amman, not only to give colour to our supposed attack on the Fourth Army, but to prevent the reinforcement of Deraa from the south. It was our plan to put ourselves between Deraa and Palestine, to force the enemy to reinforce the former from the latter. Had we merely moved troops from Amman to Deraa we should be doing Palestine no good, and should probably have been rounded up and caught ourselves. The only unit now in hand to do this cutting — since the army must go forward at once — were the armoured cars, which are not ideal for the purpose, as you are almost as shut in to them as the enemy are shut out. However, we went down in all the cars we had to the railway and took a post of open-mouthed Turks too suddenly for them to realise that we were hostile. The post commanded a very pleasant four-arched bridge (kilo. 149) about twenty-five metres long and six metres high, with a flattering white marble inscription to Abd el-Hamid. We wrecked all this with one hundred and fifty pounds of guncotton, and did what we could to the station.

On the way back we had a mishap to one of the cars, and a vile road, so did not catch our army till after dawn on the 17th, going down to the line near Tell Arar, five miles north of Deraa. We suppressed a little post and some Kurdish cavalry, and put our demolition party on the line. The French blew up part of the bridge, and the Egyptians, working up the line towards Ghazale, did six hundred pairs of rails before dusk on our new 'tulip' system.* Meanwhile we climbed to the top of Tell Arar,

---

*After long experiment we found this the cheapest and most destructive demolition for a line with steel sleepers. Dig a hole midway between the tracks under a mid-rail sleeper, and work out the ballast from the hollow section of the sleeper. Put in two slabs of guncotton, return the ballast to the hole, and light. If the charge is properly laid, and not in contact with the sleeper, a 12-inch fuse is enough. The gas expansion arches the sleeper eighteen inches above the rail, draws the metals six inches towards

which commanded a complete view of Deraa, about four miles off, and we realised that there were nine enemy machines on the aerodrome. Our Bristol had been badly shot about, so they had no competition to fear, and for a time they did what they liked to us with bombs and machine-gunning. We had luck, and used our mountain guns and Hotchkiss for what they were worth, but were getting much the worst of it, till our only surviving machine, a B.E. 12 from Azrak turned up and sailed into the middle of the show. We watched with very mixed feelings, for the four Turkish two-seaters and their four scouts were all of them much more than its equal in the air: however, by good hap or skill the B.E. came through them and led the whole circus of them away westward, and after to Ghazale, in pursuit, while we took advantage of our respite to organise and send off a mixed column to Mezerib, to cut the Palestine line. Just after this was done, the B.E. came back again with its attendant swarm, and telling us that it had finished its petrol, landed near us and turned over on to its back in the rough, while a Halberstadt came down and scored a direct hit on it with a bomb. Our pilot was unhurt, and with his Lewis gun and tracer bullets was soon most usefully running about just outside Deraa in a Ford, cutting the railway to prevent any kind of sortie of rolling stock.

We reached the lake at Mezerib about one p.m., and by two, had taken and looted the French station. The main station on the Palestine line proved too difficult, and we waited till three for the Camel Corps and guns to arrive, and then attacked it formally, and carried it by assault a few minutes later. As our only demolition parties were on the Damascus line, still demolishing, we

---

one another, humps them three inches above the horizontal, and twists the web from the bottom inwards. It drives a trough a foot deep across the formation. This three-dimension distortion of the rails is impossible to straighten, and they have to be cut or scrapped. A gang of four men can lay twenty 'tulips' in an hour on easy ballast, and for each two slabs (and single fuse) you ruin a sleeper, a yard of bank and two rails. The effect of a long stretch of line planted with these 'tulips' is most beautiful, since no two look just alike.

could not do anything very extensive, but cleared the station, burnt a lot of rolling stock and two lorries, broke the points, and planted a fair assortment of 'tulips' down the line. The interruption of their main telegraph between Palestine and Syria, here and at Tell Arar, bothered the Turks a good deal. We spent the night at Mezerib, and were joined by hundreds and hundreds of the Hauran peasants: during the night some of us marched to within three hundred yards of Tell el-Shehab, intending to attack, but found that a German colonel with guns and reinforcements had just arrived. It was a consolation to know that on the critical 18th of the month we had moved the reserve regiment at Afuleh up to meet us, and we also pleased ourselves with blowing up the line west of Shehab, and, further west, at Zeizun.

Next morning we did some leisurely work on Mezerib station, and then moved past Remthe till mid-afternoon, when we were in position west of Nasib station. After considerable resistance and artillery work, we were able to carry the post on the big bridge north of the station, and to blow up the bridge. This was my seventy-ninth bridge. It had three seven-metre arches, was about twenty-five feet high, and had piers five feet thick — quite one of the finest we have destroyed.

We slept at Nasib and next morning marched gaily away to Umtaiye, speeded by a field gun which came to Nasib by train, and shelled our tail vigorously. At Umtaiye we rejoined the armoured cars, which had returned direct from Arar after covering the demolitions: and as we had that morning seen an enemy aeroplane land near the railway west of Umtaiye, we at once took two cars down to look at it. We found three two-seaters there, but for a deep gully could not rush their aerodrome. Two got up and troubled us, but we were able to put one thousand five hundred bullets into the third, and finished it. On our way back the other two machines returned from Deraa with bombs, and swooped at us four times; however, they placed them badly, and we escaped nearly unhurt. Armoured car work is fighting de luxe, but they give a sitting shot to a well-handled plane. All the rest of the day at Umtaiye we were much bothered by enemy aircraft.

That night (the 19th) an armoured car, with the Egyptian and

Ghurka units, went down to the railway about kilo. 154 and blew up some culverts and many rails. The object was to hinder the repair parties which (with escort of guns, machine guns, and infantry) were hard at work on our destroyed bridge of the 16th at kilo. 149. We were also able to engage the repair train (by armoured car and Ford) at eighty yards range, and persuade it back to Mafrak at top speed. Next day I went on to Azrak, thence by air to Ramleh, and returned on the 22nd to Um el-Surab, with three Bristol Fighters. Before these finished breakfast they had been up twice, bagged a Turkish two-seater, and driven down three scouts. After this the Turks troubled our air no more; and after breakfast I went again to Azrak, and returned to Um el-Surab in the evening with Feisal and Nuri Shaalan, to meet the Handley-Page. It turned the scale in our favour through all the Hauran.

Next day the regulars went down to bridge kilo. 149, as its repair was nearly finished, and after a sharp fight drove off its guards, including very persistent German machine-gunners, destroyed more of the line, and burned the timber framing which the Turks had erected in seven days' work. The armoured cars and French guns did specially well to-day, and the Rualla horse under Nuri Shaalan personally. Nuri is quiet, and retiring, but a man of few words and great deeds, intelligent, well-informed, decisive, full of quiet humour, and the best Arab sheikh I have ever met. His tribe are like wax in his hands, and he knows what should be done and does it. The British forces had now (September 24) advanced to such a point that the Turkish Fourth Army, whom we had arrogated to ourselves as our birds, were ordered back to cover Deraa and Damascus. As a result of their haste and our holding of the railway, they abandoned the idea of falling back from Amman by rail, and proceeded towards us by road with all their guns and transport. We sent our cavalry at them, and forced them to leave the guns and carts between Mafrak and Nasib. They also lost a lot of men, and what had been a formal column of route became a confused mass of fugitives, who never had time to reform again. It seemed to us, however, that we might now venture to put ourselves between Deraa and Damascus (at some such point as Sheikh Saad) so as to force the immediate evacuation of the former: we might then hope to be able to do business, not only with this mob of the Fourth Army as it emerged from Deraa, but with such remnants of the Palestine Army as escaped by Semakh and Irbid. Accordingly, the camelry, guns, and machine guns, marched northward on the 25th, till, on the afternoon of the 26th, they were able to descend on the railway and cross it between Ghazale and Ezra.

This move took the Turks (by now panic-stricken) completely by surprise. The railway had been opened for traffic (after our damage of the 17th) on the previous day, but we now cut it again — and it remained cut till the close of operations, and penned into Deraa six complete trains, which are now ours — took Ghazale with its two hundred men and two guns, took Ezra, held only by the Algerian, Abd el-Kader, a pro-Turk religious fanatic, and a good deal of stores. We then passed on and slept near Sheikh Miskin. The Turks received fantastic reports of our strength, and ordered the immediate evacuation of Deraa by road, while the Germans burnt their five remaining aeroplanes. This gave us a total of eleven enemy machines accounted by for our force since September 13.

At dawn on the 27th we reached Sheikh Saad, in time to take prisoner two Austro-Turk machine-gun companies on their way to Kuneitra to oppose the British advancing by that road. We then stood on the hill at Sheikh Saad, and watched the country-side. When we saw a small enemy column we went out and took it: when we saw a large column, we lay low. Our excuse must be physical exhaustion — also we were only nine hundred strong.

Aeroplanes now dropped us a message that there were two columns of Turks advancing on us. One from Deraa was six thousand strong, and one from Mezerib, two thousand strong. We determined that the second was about our size, and marched the regulars out to meet it just north of Tafas, while sending our Hauran horse out to hang on to the skirts of the large column, and some unmounted peasants to secure the Tel el-Shehab bridge, which the Turks were mining. We were too late (since on the way we had a profitable affair with an infantry battalion) to prevent the Mezerib column getting into Tafas. They strengthened themselves there, and as at Turaa, the last village they had entered allowed themselves to rape all the women they could catch. We attacked them with all arms as they marched out later, and bent the head of their column back towards Tell Arar. When Sherif Bey, the Turkish Commander of the Lancer rearguard in the village, saw this he ordered that the inhabitants be killed. These included some twenty small children (killed with lances and rifles), and about forty women. I noticed particularly one pregnant woman, who had been forced down on a saw-bayonet. Unfortunately, Talal, the Sheikh of Tafas, who, as mentioned, had been a tower of strength to us from the beginning, and who was one of the coolest and boldest horsemen I have ever met, was in front with Auda abu Tayi and myself when we saw these sights. He gave a horrible cry, wrapped his headcloth about his face, put spurs to his horse, and, rocking in the saddle, galloped at full speed into the midst of the retiring column, and fell, himself and his mare, riddled with machine-gun bullets, among their lance points.

With Auda's help we were able to cut the enemy column into three. The third section, with German machine-gunners resisted magnificently, and got off, not cheaply, with Jemal Pasha in his car in their midst. The second and leading portions after a bitter struggle, we wiped out completely. We ordered 'no prisoners' and the men obeyed, except that the reserve company took two hundred and fifty men (including many German A.S.C.[1]) alive. Later, however, they found one of our men with a fractured thigh who had been afterwards pinned to the ground by two mortal thrusts with German bayonets. Then we turned our Hotchkiss on the prisoners and made an end of them, they saying nothing. The common delusion that the Turk is a clean and merciful fighter led some of the British troops to criticise Arab methods a little later — but they had not entered Turaa or Tafas, or watched the Turks swing their wounded by the hands and feet into a burning railway truck, as had been the lot of the Arab army at Jerdun. As for the villagers, they and their ancestors have been for five hundred years ground down by the tyranny of these Turks.

Our Rualla horse were then sent on straight to Deraa, with orders to scatter any Turkish formations met with on the road,

[1] Army Service Corps.

and to occupy the place. They had two or three fights on their way down, and took Deraa station at a whirlwind gallop, riding over all the trenches, and blotting out the enemy elements that still tried to hold the place. Next morning they brought us three hundred mule-mounted infantry prisoners, and about two hundred infantrymen and two guns. The Turks and Germans had unfortunately burnt their stores before we took it.

The regular troops spent that night — a very uneasy night it was — at Sheikh Saad. We did not yet know that we had won, since there was always a risk of our being washed away by a great wave of the enemy in retreat. I went out to see our Haurani horse, near Sheikh Miskin, where they were tenaciously clinging on to the great Turkish column from Deraa, giving much more than they were getting. At midnight I was back in Sheikh Saad, and found Nasir and Nuri just off for Deraa: we had a race, in which my camel-corps beat the headquarters horses and joined Trad Shaalan in Deraa village at dawn. We had some little work to do then in making the necessary local arrangements.

Afterwards I rode out westwards till I met the outposts of the Fourth Division (British) and guided them into Deraa. They only stayed there one night and early on the 29th they left for Damascus, after assigning to us the duty of right-flank guard. Accordingly, we marched up the Hejaz line, which suited us very well, for first our three hundred Rualla and Abu Tayi horse, and then our nine hundred Rualla camels, caught up with our Hauran cavalry harassing the Turkish Deraa column near Mesmiye.

The aeroplanes had reported this column as six thousand strong. At Sheikh Miskin on the second day it looked about five thousand strong. At Mesmiye it was said to be three thousand strong, and at Kiswe, where our horse headed them into General Gregory's Brigade, there were about two thousand of them. The whole of this gradual attrition was the work of the irregulars, since the Arab Regular Army, not being skilled camel-men, marched little faster than the British cavalry, and never came into action after Deraa. The Kiswe fight was a satisfactory affair. The Turks came along the valley of the Hejaz line, in a long, straggling column, halting every few miles to bring their guns into action against the Arabs. Nasir knew that the leading brigade of the Fourth Division was nearing Khan Denun, so he galloped forward with his slaves, and Nuri Shaalan and his slaves, about thirty in all, headed the Turkish column off between Jebel Mania and the trees of Khiata, and threw himself into the trees to delay them till the British were ready. The British had not seen or heard of this enemy column, and were in order of march, but as soon as they had learned what was forward they got their cavalry to north, west, and south of them, and opened on them with their Horse Artillery. It was just sunset when the affair began, but before it was too dark to see, the Turks were a scattered mob, running up the steep slopes of Mania and over it, in their ignorance that the Wuld Ali and Abu Tayi were waiting for them there in force. This ended the history of the Fourth Army. Old Auda, tired of slaughter, took the last six hundred prisoners. In all we killed nearly five thousand of them, captured about eight thousand (as we took them we stripped them, and sent them to the nearest village, where they will be put to work on the land till further notice) and counted spoils of about one hundred and fifty machine guns and from twenty-five to thirty guns.

Our horse rode on that evening (September 30) into Damascus, where the burning ammunition dumps turned night into day. Away back at Kiswe the glare was painful, and the roar and reverberation of the explosions kept us all awake. In Damascus, Shukri el-Ayubi and the town council had proclaimed the King of the Arabs and hoisted the Arab flag as soon as Mustafa Kemal and Jemal had gone. The Turk and German morale was so low that they had marched out beneath the Arab flag without protest: and so good was the civil control that little or no looting took place.

Nasir, old Nuri, Major Stirling and myself, entered the morning of October 1, receiving a tremendous but impromptu greeting from the Moslems of the town.

I think I should put on record a word of what happened after we got it. I found at the Town Hall Mohammed Said and Abd el-Kadir, the Algerians, who had just assumed possession of the provisional civil government, since there was no one in Damascus who could fight their Moorish bodyguard. They are both insane,

and as well pro-Turkish and religious fanatics of the most unpleasant sort. In consequence I sent for them, and before the
belediyeh and the shiyukh el-harrat,[1] announced that, as Feisal's
representative, I declared Shukri el-Ayubi Arab Military
Governor (Ali Riza, the intended Governor, was missing), and
the provisional civil administration of the Algerians dissolved.
They took it rather hard, and had to be sent home. That evening
Abd el-Kadir called together his friends and some leading Druses,
and made them an impassioned speech, denouncing the Sherif as
a British puppet, and calling on them to strike a blow for the
Faith in Damascus. By morning this had degenerated into pure
looting, and we called out the Arab troops, put Hotchkiss round
the central square, and imposed peace in three hours, after inflict-
ing about twenty casualties.

The part played by the Druses was an ignoble one. We had
never expected them to join the Sherif, and had therefore excluded them from our calculations of war-wages. After the
British victory in Palestine they began to believe that perhaps they
were on the wrong side: so when we came forward the second time
to Deraa they all collected round Sultan el-Atrash and Husein
abu Naif, our two firm friends in Jebel Druse, clamouring
for military service. Sultan believed them, and marched to
Ghazale to join us with about one thousand five hundred of them
all mounted. They hung round behind our horse, never entering
the fight, and waited until Damascus was taken. They then
paraded before the Sherif, and began to loot the inhabitants.
After the Arabs checked them at this and drove them out of the
town to Jaraman, they came to me, and said that their real feelings
were pro-British. As they were the only people in all Syria to
volunteer for service against Egypt in 1914, this was hard to
credit, and I gave them little satisfaction. They are greedy
braggarts who soon knock under to a show of force.   T.E.L.

---

[1] The Municipality and Religious Leaders.

R

106: TO MAJOR R. H. SCOTT

14. 10. 1918   *Grand Continental Hotel, Cairo.*

Dear Scott, Many thanks for your wire. As we hoped we got to Damascus, and there I had to leave the Arabs — it is a pity to go, and it would have been unwise to stay. I feel like a man who has suddenly dropped a heavy load — one's back hurts when one tries to walk straight.

I'm off, out of Egypt. This old war is closing, and my use is gone. I'm afraid you will be delayed a long time, cleaning up all the messes and oddments we have left behind us.

I have only one thing in Akaba which I value — my engraved British rifle. Please see that it reaches Cairo safely. My regards to the Staff — and my very best thanks to you and them. We were an odd little set, and we have, I expect, changed history in the near East. I wonder how the Powers will let the Arabs get on. Yours sincerely   T. E. LAWRENCE

[Description and history of Lawrence's rifle written by himself and given with it to King George V. Now exhibited with the rifle in the Imperial War Museum.]

A short Lee Enfield rifle was captured by the Turks in Gallipoli, and sent to Constantinople as a trophy. The Turkish Government had it engraved near the lock in gold in Turkish 'Booty captured in the fighting at Chanak Kale'.

Enver Pasha then presented it to Emir Feisal (then a Turkish subject and the guest of Jemal Pasha in Damascus). It is inscribed near the bayonet clip 'Presented by Enver Pasha to Sherif Feisal' in Turkish.

Feisal sent the rifle to Mecca. The Arabs then joined the British and Feisal found that the ammunition supplied him fitted Enver's rifle. So he carried it with him from June 1916 to December 1916, when he gave the rifle to Colonel Lawrence near Medina. Colonel Lawrence carried the rifle till October 1918 when Damascus was captured.

The large notch near the magazine represents a Turkish officer.

A similar rifle (without the 'Enver' inscription) was given by the Turkish Government to Abdulla, Feisal's brother, and is now in the possession of Ronald Storrs.

PART THREE

THE DOG FIGHT IN DOWNING STREET

INTRODUCTION TO PART THREE

'I WONDER how the Powers will let the Arabs get on.'
The last line of his letter to Major Scott reveals what was to be Lawrence's preoccupation for the next three years. He was always a move ahead and returned to England on October 24th because he was already preparing for the Peace Conference.[1] During the three years which followed he was engaged in fighting for Arab independence at Versailles, Downing Street, and Cairo, finding the work more exhausting, physically, mentally and spiritually than any of the hardships and dangers he had undergone during the Arabian Campaign.

J. M. Keynes who observed him closely at the Peace Conference gives the following estimate:

> The first part of 1919 was the only time when I was really acquainted with T.E.L. I agree with you strongly that it was subsequent events which twisted him. I have always thought that the view which attributed his state of mind to the privations and experiences of the war years, was wrong. When I knew him in the spring of 1919, I should have said that he was a man fully in control of his nerves and quite as normal as most of us in his reactions to the world. He had, of course, his aloofness and his mingled like and dislike of publicity, but, reckoned nervously, he was a fit man.

A year later no one could have thought the same. There are two reasons which can be given for the change. One is a simple and physical one: he was in a bad aeroplane crash which resulted in broken ribs and an injury to one lung which troubled him for the rest of his life. The second and more important is the disillusion and the bitterness of defeat resulting from the Peace Conference. He had complete faith that President Wilson would secure self-determination for the Arab peoples when he went to the Peace Conference; he was completely disillusioned when he returned.

[1] In Sir Sam Fay's diary, *The War Office at War,* it is noted under the date October 30th, 1918: 'Colonel Lawrence of Arabia called at the War Office.' Many years later Lawrence told Liddell Hart that he had returned to England on Armistice day. This was no doubt an error of recollection, or a loose way of speaking.

What increased Lawrence's disgust, and strained and warped him far from the normal, was that during the years when he felt himself defeated and dishonoured, a popularized legend of his achievement was being broadcast in the newspapers, and in a series of lectures by Lowell Thomas.

His feelings are expressed, to some extent, in the introduction to *Seven Pillars of Wisdom*, part of which I quote here from the Oxford Text. It was omitted, on the advice of Bernard Shaw, from the Subscribers' edition. It is, in my opinion, one of the most moving things Lawrence ever wrote. It expresses the disgust and bitterness of the generation which had fought and won the war and which found all it had fought for was betrayed. It is because of that betrayal that the world is crumbling into war to-day, and I print it here as a fitting introduction to the fragmentary records of the Peace Conference.

We were fond together, and there are here memories of the sweep of the open places, the taste of wide winds, the sunlight, and the hopes in which we worked. It felt like morning, and the freshness of the world-to-be intoxicated us. We were wrought up with ideas inexpressible and vaporous, but to be fought for. We lived many lives in those whirling campaigns, never sparing ourselves any good or evil: yet when we achieved and the new world dawned, the old men came out again and took from us our victory, and re-made it in the likeness of the former world they knew. Youth could win, but had not learned to keep, and was pitiably weak against age. We stammered that we had worked for a new heaven and a new earth, and they thanked us kindly and made their peace. When we are their age no doubt we shall serve our children so.

This, therefore, is a faded dream of the time when I went down into the dust and noise of the Eastern market-places, and with my brain and muscles, with sweat and constant thinking, made others see my visions coming true. Those who dream by night in the dusty recesses of their minds wake in the day to find that all was vanity: but the dreamers of the day are dangerous men, for they may act their dream with open eyes, and make it possible. This I did. I meant to make a new nation, to restore to the world a lost influence, to give twenty millions of Semites the foundation on which to build an inspired dream-palace of their national thoughts. So high an aim called out the inherent nobility of their minds and made them play a generous part in events: but when we won it was charged against me that the British petrol royalties in Mesopotamia were become dubious, and French Colonial policy ruined in the Levant.

I am afraid that I hope so. We pay for these things too much in honour and in innocent lives. I went up the Tigris with one hundred Devon Territorials, young, clean, delightful fellows, full of the power of happiness, and of making women and children glad. By them one saw vividly how great it was to be their kin, and English. And we were casting them by thousands into the fire, to the worst of deaths, not to win the war, but that the corn and rice and oil of Mesopotamia might be ours. The only need was to defeat our enemies (Turkey among them), and this was at last done in the wisdom of Allenby with less than four hundred killed, by turning to our uses the hands of the oppressed in Turkey. I am proudest of my thirty fights in that I did not have any of our own blood shed. All the subject provinces of the Empire to me were not worth one dead English boy. If I have restored to the East some self-respect, a goal, ideals: if I have made the standard of rule of white over red more exigent, I have fitted those peoples in a degree for the new commonwealth in which the dominant races will forget their brute achievements, and white and red and yellow and brown and black will stand up together without sideglances in the service of the world.

Any hope of such an achievement appeared to have been for ever defeated by a Peace Treaty founded upon the principle of self-determination for all peoples. But Lawrence would not acknowledge defeat, and, after what he described as a 'dog fight in the corridors of Downing Street' lasting for three years, he brought two Arab Kingdoms into being and retired, feeling that he was quit of his Arabian adventure with clean hands. One further scruple troubled a conscience which had developed into an abnormal character sharply separating him from the vast majority of his fellows. He must not benefit in any way from what he had done in Arabia. The honours which he had won were refused. The jobs offered on account of his reputation had to be declined, nor would he allow himself to exploit his success by profiting from writing a single paid piece of journalism under the name of Lawrence. As the war receded, his scruples of conscience about profiting from the part he had played in it became greater. In February 1920 he referred to *Seven Pillars of Wisdom* as 'the-book-to-build-the-house'. In August 1923, an appreciation of the book by Mrs. Hardy made him wonder whether his decision not to profit from it might not be mistaken. 'So what you said cuts right across my belief ... the value of the book would give me an income which would keep me out of the army: and I'm wondering since Sunday whether perhaps I may be able to enjoy it.' The Subscribers' edition of the complete *Seven Pillars of Wisdom* resulted in a large overdraft at Lawrence's bank, but the profits of *Revolt in the Desert*, the abridged version, after wiping this debt off, were given by Lawrence to an Air Force charity.

The clue to what appears to many people to be Lawrence's abnormality, eccentricity, or whimsical refusal to behave like other people, is simply that his conscience forbade him to profit from the part he had played in the war. All conscientious scruples involve inconsistencies and absurdities: Lawrence was involved in many; though, as he wasn't married, not in as many as Tolstoy.

[The following report was written by Lawrence for the information of the British Cabinet on his return to England. Although a secret document, I have been allowed to copy it and to include it here. The reader who wishes to be reminded of the Agreements made with the Arabs and with France before the Peace Conference is advised to read, here, Lawrence's letter to *The Times* No. 113.]

4th November, 1918.

The wish of the last generation of British statesmen (expressed in many ways beside the Baghdad Railway Agreements and the Alexandretta negotiations of 1915) to withdraw from their Imperial position in the Middle East made it desirable to find indirect means of keeping intact our 'Monroe' area, the quadrangle of land between Egypt, Alexandretta, Persia and the Indian Ocean. When war broke out an urgent need to divide Islam was added, and we became reconciled to seek for allies rather than subjects. We therefore took advantage of the dissatisfaction felt by the Arabic-speaking peoples (formerly voiced by Abbas Hilmi) with their alien rulers, and of the tendency, each day more visible, of the subject Eastern peoples to demand a share in the dangers of government. We hoped by the creation of a ring of client states, themselves insisting on our patronage, to turn the present and future flank of any foreign power with designs on the three rivers. The greatest obstacle, from the war standpoint, to any Arab movement, was its greatest virtue in peace-time — the lack of solidarity between the various Arab movements. The local jealousies in Syria, in Mesopotamia, in Arabia and in Egypt made it hard to know where or with whom to begin. There were abortive attempts with Sayid Taleb and with Aziz el Masri before we made up our minds to concentrate upon the Sherif of Mecca. The Sherif was ultimately chosen because of the rift he would create in Islam, because his geographical position gave him a fair chance of surviving and because his preeminence amongst Arabs was based upon the arbitrary and empiric, but in the East unassailable, ground of family prestige.

The negotiations began between the Sherif and Sir Henry McMahon, who was given discretion by the British Government to conclude an agreement that would bring him in. Sir Henry was unfortunately not informed of the Sykes-Picot Agreement then in proof. The Sherif had no idea that we wanted him only as a figurehead; throughout the correspondence he spoke as the mandatory of the Arabs — meaning everyone under Turkish rule who spoke Arabic.

His first season as a rebel was not fortunate, and his chances were not improved by the dismissal of Sir Henry McMahon and the substitution of Sir Archibald Murray, Sir Reginald Wingate and Colonel Brémond as his advisers. Nevertheless he was able eventually to carry all Western Arabia with him from Mecca northwards, until the occupation of Akaba by Feisal in August, 1917, closed the Sherifian military movement.

Feisal now undertook for his father (who had aged very fast) the liberation of Syria. His status for so doing was as a sealed member of the Syrian Revolutionary Committee. He remained in constant touch with his fellow-members in Egypt, with [those with] him in the field, and in undelivered Syria, treating them as colleagues. For his instrument he formed a regular army of Syrians and Mesopotamians, and returned to the Hejaz all his Arabians. As a detail of interest I may mention that only 8 Hejazis shared in the entry into Damascus.

Feisal's military operations could not be independent: he made himself the handmaid of General Allenby, the allied Commander-in-Chief. I hope that in dividing the common spoils we will not descend to commercial arguments of the exact participating contingents of British, French, Indian, Arab, Jew, or Armenian troops. The Commander-in-Chief's Arab alliance enabled him to throw his cavalry, without lines of communications or the usual precautions, from Jaffa to Aleppo in pursuit of the Turks through country nominally hostile, but really our own. General Allenby reversed the old policy towards the Arabs, and helped them in every way he could in materials, advice and men. Their rapid success is due to him.

The war work of the ruling family of Mecca is now completed. We can hardly question the courage of King Hussein, who joined us, against Feisal's advice, soon after the fall of Kut, with the example of our other small friends before his eyes. It is also easy to see the moral ordeal it has been for the oldest, most holy, and most powerful family of the Arabs (a people who lay more stress on faith and pedigree than others), to cast off the friends and allegiance of a lifetime and to incur, on behalf of their national freedom, the unmeasured abuse of India, Turkey, Afghanistan and Egypt. The physical dangers and sufferings of the four princes in the very difficult campaigns of 1916, 1917, and 1918 must be reckoned to their credit. The loyalty to their word and allies of the old King and his sons, who have refused from the Turks successive offers of autonomy in Arabia, independence in Arabia with autonomy in Syria, and of the Khalifate, with independence in Arabia and autonomy in all the Arabic provinces, may be recommended as an example to the Power which persuaded him to revolt, but which was ready, without his knowledge, to hand him over, with the people for whom he stood guardian, to the Turks on much worse terms.[1]

THE PRESENT INTENTION OF THE ARAB GOVERNMENTS

(a) In Arabia, meaning the peninsula proper, the old man of Mecca intends to be the unquestioned head. If he has patience, he will become so by slow processes of time and pilgrimage. As, however, he is foolish, it would be well if one of his sons joined him soon at Mecca. In Yemen the Sherif has no concrete aims. Ibn Rashid and Kuweit are already in touch with him. In Nejd, the situation created by the indirect conflict of India and Egypt over Ibn Saud and the Idrisi presents no real difficulties. Both men are fortunately heretics in Islam, not much better than the Agha Khan in orthodox opinion. Idrisi tried to graft elements of African fetishism on the abstract creeds of Arabia, and is failing. His disappearance is only a question of years.[2] Ibn Saud is now striving to limit the puritan revival becoming too strong for him. If he is carried away by it, and attacks the Holy Places,

[1] The reference is to secret British negotiations with Talaat. See letter No. 397, to William Yale, and Yale's note.

[2] See letters Nos. 82 and 94, p. 219.

the orthodox Islam will deal with him, as with his ancestor. If he can control it he will remain Emir of Nejd after military failure has warned him to recognise the Sherif as his overlord. I think Ibn Saud is friendly to us and that he is the only person so minded in his dominions.

I would like to suggest that the experience of the last four years has shown the undesirability of allowing Arabia to be controlled by any or all of the present authorities in Cairo, Bagdad, Damascus or Simla. We have been provincial, if not parochial in view.

(*b*) In Syria the Arab movement becomes really important since its origin was to prevent the man-power and strategic advantages of that country falling into the hands of any continental power. For this purpose the Arabs require equal rights with any other power in the Gulf of Alexandretta, the coast line from there to Tripoli, the port of Tripoli and its railway to Homs, the Bukaa from Homs to Lake Huleh, access by treaty to Haifa, and all the country East of this line and the Jordan. Further, Feisal requires to be sovereign in his own dominions, with complete liberty to choose any foreign advisers he wants of any nationality he pleases. These advisers will be part of the Arab Government and will draw their executive authority from it and not from their own Government. It may be possible to secure Arab recognition of the Turkish Dette in return for an equitable share of the Beyrout and Haifa customs receipts. Feisal will, however, not consider himself bound by any agreement to which he is not a party.

His assets in Syria are not small. He controls most of the good corn land and the four industrial towns. He has 80% of the Moslems (including all the fighting men) on his side, all the Ansariya, all the Jews. He has inherited the old Turkish Civil Service, all of whose lower ranks, and many of whose upper ranks, are Arab. He himself is clear-sighted and well-educated, and is capable of satisfying the needs of Syria in local self-government. If he fails the responsibility will lie at the door of the European powers, in whose word he shows an undue simplicity of trust.

(*c*) In Palestine the Arabs hope that the British will keep what they have conquered. They will not approve Jewish Independence for Palestine but will support as far as they can Jewish infiltration, if it is behind a British, as opposed to an international façade. If any attempt is made to set up the international control proposed in the Sykes-Picot Agreement, Feisal will press for self-determination in Palestine, and give the moral support of the Arab Government to the peasantry of Palestine, to resist expropriation.

(d)   In Irak the Arabs expect the British to keep control. The Sherif, relying on his Agreement with us, hopes for a nominal Arab administration there.

(e)   In Jesireh there are very vivid Arab Nationalists, but they are in an unsatisfactory geographical position, until a proportion of the nomadic and settled Kurds can be persuaded to join hands with the local government required there.

I would suggest that areas (d) and (e) should be kept quite separate, at least administratively. The problems of Irak are those of great public works and of a highly developed agriculture. The problems of Jesireh are those of turbulent mountain villagers and semi-nomadic tribes.

The Kurdish question is likely to be much larger and more difficult than the Armenian one.

If representations of small nations are admitted to the Peace Conference the cry of self-determination is likely to be raised, and agreements made semi-secretly between the Powers previously may be regarded with some suspicion. For this reason I would suggest that no second edition of the Sykes-Picot Treaty be produced. The geographical absurdities of the present Agreement will laugh it out of Court, and it would be perhaps as well if we spared ourselves a second effort on the same lines. If we do not I hope that we will at least recognise our official inclusion of the Arabs among the belligerents, and make them a party to any decisions affecting Arab areas conquered by themselves.

T. E. LAWRENCE, *Lieut. Colonel*

[Lawrence followed this up with definite proposals which are outlined in the following telegram from the Secretary of State for India, the Hon. Edwin Montagu.]

TELEGRAM FROM SECRETARY OF STATE FOR INDIA TO FOREIGN,
DELHI, REPEATED BAGHDAD

[*Dated* 18*th and received* 19*th November*, 1918]

Foreign Secret. Colonel Lawrence, now home on leave from
Syria, has submitted proposal to H. M. G. for dealing compre-
hensively with Arab question. He advocates formation of three
Councils of Arab States outside Hedjaz and its dependencies,
viz.: (1) Lower Mesopotamia, (2) Upper Mesopotamia and (3)
Syria, to be placed respectively under Abdullah, Zeid and Feisal,
sons of King Hussein. Hussein himself would remain King of
Hedjaz and would ultimately be succeeded by his eldest son Ali.
He would have no temporal authority in three states above
mentioned, and, in fact, no position at all there beyond insertion
of his name in Friday prayers in all mosques as Emir-el-Momein.

Lawrence suggests boundaries between Upper and Lower
Mesopotamia should run from confluence of Tigris and Greater
Zab to Anah on Euphrates from which place to Birejik.
Euphrates would form western boundary Upper Mesopotamia.
Northern boundary would lie through Urfa and Diarbekir to
Tigris. Capital of it would be Mosul or Ras-el-Ain. It is of
course understood that both states would be in the British sphere
and Lower Mesopotamia under effective British control.

I recognise that these proposals as involving definite separation
of Mosul from Baghdad conflict with recommendations in
Baghdad telegram 8745, though interstatal boundary does not
appear inconsistent with that suggested in Baghdad telegram
8744; also that importation Abdullah into Mesopotamia would be
in direct opposition to [*word omitted*]. But I should be glad if you
would review whole question in the light of existing conditions,
and let me have your views on Lawrence's proposals with as
little delay as possible.

[I take the following facts partly from Liddell Hart's '*T. E.
Lawrence*': *In Arabia and After*:

Picot had landed at Beyrout on November 6th as French High
Commissioner in Syria and Armenia. On the 14th he telegraphed
to Paris: 'As long as the British army occupies the country there

will be a doubt in the spirit of the population, favouring those who are hostile to us. The only remedy is to send twenty thousand soldiers to Syria and ask England to hand it over to us.'

Feisal was invited to visit London by the British Government. He travelled on a British cruiser and was met by Lawrence at Marseilles. Their journey through France was interrupted by the appearance of Brémond, at Lyons on November 28th.

Lawrence discovered during dinner that some French representatives were going to London to discuss Syrian affairs during his absence, and left that night for London, crossing unrecognized by them, on the same boat as the Frenchmen. He met Feisal who had meanwhile been taken for a tour of the battlefields, in order to keep him out of the way, on the gangway of the boat which was to take him to England on December 9th.]

108: TO C. M. DOUGHTY

25.12.18   *[Carlton Hotel, Pall Mall, London, crossed out]*

Dear Mr. Doughty, It is exceedingly good of you to have written to me: and it happened just when I had made up my mind that I must write to you, and tell you that I had been over much of your country, (more securely and comfortably, but in somewhat the same fashion) meeting many of the people, and sons of the people who knew you out there. It has been a wonderful experience, and I have got quite a lot to tell.

I'm afraid it is not likely to be written for publication, since some of it would give offence to people alive, (including myself!) but I hope to get it put on paper soon.

When I can, I want to come down to Eastbourne and see you. That will not be till after the Peace Conference, I expect. Meanwhile I must tell you that I got a copy of *Arabia Deserta* the other day: the genuine edition!

I'm too late for Christmas: but my very best New Year wishes.
Yours sincerely,   T. E. LAWRENCE

P.S. I haven't any initials after my name — except B.A., which it is unusual to put!

109: TO EDWARD MARSH

7.1.18. [*really* 1919]   *Carlton Hotel, London*

Dear Marsh, This is owing, since I behaved like a lunatic yesterday.[1] But I have been trying for three years to think like an Arab, and when I come back with a bump to British conventions, it is rather painful, and I keep on deciding to put an end to it. However, nothing happens.

After I did come, I enjoyed things exceedingly. It's the process of coming that's awful.

With very many thanks, Yours ever   T E LAWRENCE

110: TO B. E. LEESON[2]

8.1.19   *London*

Dear Leeson, I'm just off to Paris, ('peace work', they call it) and if I don't reply to you before I go, nothing will happen.

As for jobs this time: it is too soon to say. In the Hejaz there is nothing for Jidda isn't a white man's country! In Syria everything depends on the conference. We may find ourselves shut out, or let in, or on the same ground as the rest of the earth. And till the end of the conference I cannot tell you.

At present everything is evenly balanced.

If anything is possible, I'll do what I can — easily, as I'm not a competitor myself.

If Goslett is still in your orbit, please salute him from me. Yours,   T. E. LAWRENCE

[The following are the first pages of a diary of the Peace Conference which unfortunately was not carried further. Almost all of Lawrence's work at this time was done in personal interviews and I have been able to find very little documentary material.]

---

[1] Sir Edward Marsh explains: 'Lawrence had accepted an invitation to dinner at Claridge's and a party afterwards at Mrs. Harry Lindsay's. He shirked the dinner, but came to the party in Arab dress.'

[2] An officer in the Royal Flying Corps at Rabegh and Wejh who explored Wady Hamdh with Lawrence.

III: DIARY OF THE PEACE CONFERENCE

Jan. 1919

The fun began when [*name omitted*] went off to Paris with seventy lady typists, & a doctor who was a Harley street obstetric specialist, as M.O.[1] to the Villa Majestic. Everybody was wondering how he knew that the Conference would last nine months. It says much for [*name omitted*] that the jests have been everywhere jests.

The allotment of delegates was a delicate business. Brazil got three, since there are many German interests there and they hope, by implicating her fully in the Conference, to cajole her into repressive measures there. It sounds almost unworthy of American principles.

The Portuguese were greatly sorrowful. The French went to their minister, and said how they regretted the inadequate representation, but that the English were quite firm. The Portuguese came to us more in anger than in sorrow, and protested. Sir Eyre Crowe had to cut out an extract from the official proceedings and send it them secretly, that they might see the protest against the extra delegate came from the French.

Mr. Balfour completely forgot the Hejaz representatives at the first sitting. I got Mallet, Tyrrell, and Cecil to go and protest. Then I went to see Eric Drummond, and explained myself vigorously. He tried first to persuade me that we had no standing, but later came round and promised to do his best. I dined with Mr. Balfour, and got his promise to the same effect, and loaded him full of ammunition. Philip Kerr did the same for Lloyd George on Lionel Curtis' advice. Meanwhile I told Feisal that his question was not prejudiced, only postponed a day for production of necessary papers. Next day Balfour proposed the Hejaz. Pichon protested. Clemenceau accepted one delegate, and Pichon said they could have no more since they were an embryo nationality, not an independent state. Balfour and Lloyd George countered sharply with the statement that they & France had recognised its independence, and the point — two delegates — was carried.

Feisal had meanwhile been visited by Gout,[2] who told him his

---

[1] Medical Officer.

[2] M. Jean Gout was a strong advocate for the French colonization of Syria.

omission was intentional, and the English were only playing with him. He said France was strong, & the sooner Feisal ceased to listen to the mischief-makers in Mesopotamia & Syria who were working against France, the better it would be for him. They recognised no Arab army in Syria, and Allenby lied if he said they did. So Feisal saw that his representation was contested, and spent a very miserable night in consequence. I found him wandering about the hotel at 2 A.M. When we won he took it as a good augury of all the future battles and was very joyful.

At the first sitting he was amused when Clemenceau, as temporary president, put the question of his own confirmation in the office to the delegates. He voted with the rest for him. Lloyd George in seconding the proposal said that while he was a boy at school Clemenceau was holding office.

The campaign in favour of America co-operating in the East, to secure the practice of her ideals, goes well. Kipling's enthusiasm had turned over Doubleday that night in England. Ellis is now in his sixth article, all tending that way, in the *Herald*.[1] Mrs. Egan has adhered, and of course old McClure. I want to frighten America with the size of the responsibility, and then that she should run us for it instead. The Americans are rather fed up with France. 'Reminiscences of the second Empire' are too common for their taste. Weizmann was asked by Wilson how he got on with the British — he said so well that he wanted them as his trustee. Then how he got on with the French. He said he knew French perfectly, but he could not understand, or make himself understood by, the French politicians. 'Exactly what I find,' said Wilson.

[On January 31st, 1919, Geoffrey Dawson wrote to Lawrence saying that he had hoped to see him, but that as Lawrence was still in Paris he was driven to write on a confidential matter. He then made the suggestion that Lawrence should be offered a fellowship at All Souls, which would provide him with a base at Oxford, and said that having secured the Warden's approval, he would put the proposal forward at the next College meeting if Lawrence wished. Lawrence accepted and was later on elected.

[1] *The New York Herald.*

I owe the following interesting memorandum, from the Edward
M. House collection, to Mr. Seymour, President of Yale University and the editor of Colonel House's papers.]

NOTES OF A CONVERSATION BETWEEN COLONEL HOUSE AND EMIR
FEISAL, HELD AT HOTEL DE CRILLON, ON MARCH 29TH, 6 P.M.,
COLONEL LAWRENCE BEING INTERPRETER.

Emir Feisal stated that he had come to take leave of Colonel
House, as he was going back to Syria in a few days.

Colonel House asked what Emir Feisal thought of the plan of
sending a Commission to Syria.[1]

Emir Feisal replied that it was the best thing he had ever
heard of in his life. He said he had been sent up by his people to
see the various European nations and select the one that they liked
best for a mandatory. He liked the English very well. Since then
he had come to know the Americans. He wished to know
whether the United States would undertake the idea of accepting
a mandate of Syria, as he found there was friction between Great
Britain and France on the subject.

Colonel House said he was very doubtful whether the United
States would accept the mandate.

Emir Feisal said he could assure Colonel House that the Arabs
would rather die than accept the French mandate.

Colonel Lawrence stated that, if the British accepted the
mandate, they would be accused by the French of being
hypocrites.

Emir Feisal asked Colonel House what the attitude of the
United States would be towards Armenia.

Colonel House replied that this again was a question he could
not answer.

Colonel Lawrence explained that the Arabs in Syria wanted
an English mandate and the Arabs in the United States an
American mandate. He hoped that the Chairman of the Commission being an American could be induced to report in favour
of an American mandate for Syria, after satisfying himself as to the
wishes of the inhabitants. He added that he found great opposition
in Paris in certain quarters to sending out a new Commission.

[1] The French refused to nominate a delegate to the international commission of inquiry
which eventually dwindled to two American delegates, King and Crane, who visited Syria
during the summer and reported that a French mandate would be wholly unacceptable
and recommended the U.S.A. as the mandatory power. The King-Crane report had no
influence.

[On April 7th, 1919, Lawrence received this telegram from his younger brother: 'Father has pneumonia come if possible.' A letter of the same day informed him that his father had died of pneumonia following on Spanish influenza. Lawrence came for a few hours and returned to Paris. He preserved both the letter and the telegram, which were found among his papers after his own death.

In the spring of 1919 Feisal's case had been heard, and the final decision postponed, and Lawrence decided to go to Cairo. General Groves, the British Air delegate at the Peace Conference, offered him a passage in one of the Handley-Page aeroplanes which were being sent at that moment to 'blaze the trail'. Since I regard this flight as a turning point in Lawrence's life, I have included an account of it written by one of the pilots.

The first machines started from Carnin near Lille in April 1919. Altogether fifty-one Handley-Page 0/400 twin-engined planes of 58 and 216 squadrons and detached flights were sent to Egypt in response to an urgent call. (See General Seely's statement of Oct. 28th, 1919)[1] Of these twenty-six had arrived by the end of October and fifteen had been written off. No one seems to know for certain what happened to the other ten.

One machine piloted by Lt. J. D. Vance after being delayed by bad weather crashed near Poursières (South of France). Lt. Vance, the second pilot, rigger and fitter were all killed. Another machine of 58 Squadron was forced to land at Givry-sur-Orbize in the district of Chalons due to trouble in the petrol system. The machine struck a tree and nose-dived into a field. The second pilot was injured and the machine wrecked. There were three other bad accidents involving four fatal and four non-fatal injuries.

Colonel Lawrence was in one of the first machines. Apart from nearly capsizing in the long grass at Pisa, he reached Rome safely and in fairly good time. But on attempting to land at Centocelle in semi-darkness the pilot, Lt. Prince, misjudged the length of the aerodrome and turned over. Lt. Prince was killed outright and his second pilot, Lt. Sprott, succumbed the next morning. Col. Lawrence, who was in the back of the

---

[1] General Seely stated in the House of Commons that 'the sending of these machines by sea would have meant that they could not have been ready for action until many months after they were required'. As it was the leading machines managed the trip in just under three months!

machine with two airmen, escaped with a broken collar-bone, broken ribs and mild concussion. The King of Italy and the British Ambassador, Sir E. Rennell Rodd, visited the injured. Lts. Prince and Sprott were buried with full military honours.

The second flight had been split up and delayed by bad weather. Col. L. was out of hospital by the time they arrived at Rome. Obviously still a sick man,[1] he scrambled into the nearest machine and continued writing. Looking back through the bomb-racks all that could be seen of him was his legs. They never moved.

Everything was supposed to be very hush-hush, but it had been given out that, with the Peace Conference over so far as Middle East matters were concerned, Col. L. was returning to Cairo merely to collect his kit. Knowing Lawrence and talking with him, it was fairly obvious that this was not the real reason. Anyway, not the whole story. For one thing, the only 'kit' Col. L. ever carried left enough room in a haversack for at least two books. Spare tooth-brush and all, it could have been sent to him by parcel post.

After a short halt at Foggia the squadron re-formed at Taranto. Most of the machines had been out of commission since the armistice and were badly in need of overhaul. Whilst this was being carried out it was debated whether to proceed via Malta or Athens. Weather conditions being unsettled and the range of the machines somewhat uncertain, it was finally decided to make the crossing in easy stages via Valona in Albania, Athens and Crete.

All the machines crossed the Strait of Otranto without trouble; but again at the landing ground near Valona, with the machines pegged out in the open, it was some days before the necessary repairs and adjustments could be done.

There were no quarters for the pilots or mechanics, and only iron rations were available. What little Italian currency the entire personnel possessed being at a decided discount in Albania, four-gallon petrol tins, which had been stowed in the machines to help keep them afloat in the event of coming down in the Adriatic, became the medium of exchange. The economic law of supply and demand, however, soon made itself felt. Immediately Albanian housewives within walking distance had all the tins they could use, the rate of exchange fell from a dozen eggs and a

---

[1] Lawrence was still encased in plaster of Paris. (Liddell Hart, 'T. E. Lawrence': In Arabia and After, p. 399).

string of dried figs to one can, to three or four eggs and perhaps a fig or two.

Finally, with Col. L's plane in the lead, the machines took off for Athens in two flights. Being unable to get over the hills, the squadron headed out to sea and flew around them. In sight of Corfu, one machine had to turn back with a broken cam-shaft and just managed to stagger over the hills and drop into a valley near the landing ground. Another came down near the Piraeus somewhere. The others after landing at the first aerodrome they saw, and finding it was the wrong one, took off again and came down at the right one. Meanwhile a reception committee which included the King of Greece had dashed off in cars to the first landing ground and had to dash back again. Needless to say Col. L. enjoyed the comic relief.

Whilst awaiting the stragglers and spares at Athens, what there was of the squadron took Greek flying-officers for joy rides and visited places of interest with Col. L. Strangely enough, although about half the entire flight was made over water, no machine came down in the sea.

After a week at Athens half a dozen machines, each with a number of Greek flying-officers in the back, crossed to Crete and landed at Suda Bay near Khania. Here it was discovered that one of the replacement machines had both propellers cracked and two of the eight cylinders of one of the engines were all but off. Lying peacefully at its moorings in the bay was a large *America* IV flying-boat.[1] The pilot being in hospital with sand-fly fever, the problem of spare propellers and exhaust valve springs was soon solved. Although for use with the same engines, Rolls Royce *Eagle* VIII, the props were metal tipped and of a much heavier pitch than those fitted to the Handley-Page machines. But with improvised cylinder holding-down-studs (lack of suitable tackle prevented lifting a complete engine), the land machine, with minimum load, just managed to stagger into the air.

No advance arrangements had been made to house and feed the crews, and no one apart from a few mildly interested olive growers came near the machines. But just as the flight was about

---

[1] Shortly after he had enlisted in the Royal Tank Corps, on April 18th, 1923, Private T. E. Shaw had to write an essay for the education officer. He began it: 'We were in Crete in Suda Bay, when there came a wireless message that a Handley-Page, with an urgent diplomat on board, would arrive in the afternoon.' The essay describes how the flying boat replaced the broken-down Handley-Page, and is written as though by one of the crew.

to leave, a sailor turned up on a bicycle bearing a 'signal' from the
S.N.O.[1] asking why the arrival of the machines had not been
reported. This was taken to Col. L. who finally agreed to frame a
reply. It was typical. A full foolscap page asking the S.N.O.
where he had been hiding. Within sight of what was left of the
Flying Boat, the senior officer of the R.A.F. personnel suggested
that perhaps an explanation and formal apology would be better
— but T.E. insisted upon all or nothing.

With no two compasses reading alike, it was perhaps fortunate
that the next stop, El Sollum on the edge of Libya, was hit
'right on the nose'. As the machines could not climb over the
hills, it was necessary to fly around the coast line on leaving Crete.
This, together with an attempt to get into some sort of formation,
added nearly an hour to the flight. With a cruising speed of
about eighty, this meant nearly four hours out of sight of land.

The night the machines landed at Sollum, a strong wind
sprang up and all hands were rushed out to the aerodrome in
tenders to prevent the machines being blown over. After
standing by until daylight the first flight took off for Amreh,
and late the same afternoon reached Heliopolis near Cairo.
Five machines landed at the aerodrome that day and for weeks
after others continued to arrive in ones and twos.

It took Col. L. the best part of three months to reach Cairo.
Within forty-eight hours he was on his way back to Paris. En
route the squadron had picked up St. John Philby. The last
seen of T.E. was with Philby and a staff officer leaving Shepheard's
Hotel. As cheerful as ever Col. L. insisted that he was by no
means fed-up with flying. In fact he was thinking of joining the
Air Force. 'They will always want people who can fly,' he
added, 'if they demobilize you too, you do the same. They may
make *you* a sergeant!'

In Paris Lawrence had begun to write his account of the
Arab Revolt, *Seven Pillars of Wisdom*, between February and
June. The introduction was written on the flight to Cairo,
which was indeed undertaken to collect his papers and reports
which had been left at the Arab Bureau. He returned from Egypt
to Paris and finished writing the first draft of *Seven Pillars
of Wisdom* in great bursts. Liddell Hart tells us that Lawrence
wrote as much as 30,000 words in twenty-four hours. Before

[1] Senior Naval Officer.

the end of August he returned to England and went home to Oxford.

The plan of retiring from public life, and of setting up a private press with his friend Richards, was revived, and Lawrence bought a field at Pole Hill, Chingford, where they intended to build.]

112: TO V. W. RICHARDS

1.Sept. [1919]   2 *Polstead Road*

Dear V.W.R., Your metaphysics are of the exact tone necessary to drive me to eat: so I went out and bought a sausage roll, that being in my mind the form of expression of eating least sensuous.

Seriously I want to talk over these things with you when we meet. I haven't the jargon required for putting them on paper. The final success — and the emptiness of it — in the Arab Front threatens to make me think, which would be a disaster.

I'm out of the army today: and today I have paid for 5 acres 2 roods 30 poles of Pole Hill: that is the whole upper field, down to the rudimentary hedge. I haven't yet got the conveyance, so am not yet the legal owner, but they cannot draw back from the bargain, and as far as I'm concerned it's finished. I feel years more settled in mind, and hope that we will acquire merit there together. When we meet next (or even before) we'll have to make up our serious minds how to tackle Gardiner. I have not yet been able to buy the hedge from the Chingford Estate, and am so short of funds temporarily that I am not pressing them vigorously.

I hope to have about £300 more in six weeks time, and we must then interview builders. The anti-aircraft station fate is still uncertain. The Air Ministry and the War Office cannot decide who is in charge of London air defence. I just thought I'd write and tell you of the Hill: and also that I've borrowed your Bradley. I'm not studying it, but find gobbets (e.g. the discussion of space) most stimulating and suggestive. How pleased Bradley would be if he knew I approved of it. a rivederci.   L.

[On September 8th, 1919, Lawrence sent a letter to *The Times*, part of which was suppressed by the Editor (see p. 284).

What follows appeared on Thursday, September 11th. It was accompanied by an editorial which reveals how far the public was being kept ignorant of our commitments in the Middle East.]

113: TO THE EDITOR OF 'THE TIMES'

Sir, Your Syrian Correspondent has just referred to British promises to the French and the Arabs. When on Prince Feisal's staff I had access to the documents in question, and as possibly the only informed free-lance European, I may help to clear them up. They are four in number.

DOCUMENT I. The British promise to King Hussein, dated October 24th, 1915. It undertakes, conditional on an Arab revolt, to recognize the 'independence of the Arabs' south of latitude 37deg., except in the provinces of Baghdad and Basra, where British interests require special measures of administrative control, and except where Great Britain is not 'free to act without detriment to the interests of France'.

(N.B. Hussein asked for no personal position, and for no particular government or governments.)

DOCUMENT II. The Sykes-Picot Agreement made between England and France in May, 1916. It divides the Arabic provinces of Turkey into five zones, roughly — (a) Palestine from the Jordan to the Mediterranean, to be 'international'; (b) Haifa and Mesopotamia from near Tekrit to the Gulf, to be 'British'; (c) the Syrian coast, from Tyre to Alexandretta, Cilicia, and most of Southern Armenia, from Sivas to Diarbekir, to be 'French'; (d) the interior (mainly the provinces of Aleppo, Damascus, Urfa, Deir, and Mosul) to be 'independent Arab' under two shades of influence: —

(i.) Between the lines Akaba-Kuweit and Haifa-Tekrit, the French to seek no 'political influence', and the British to have economic and political priority, and the right to supply 'such advisers as the Arabs desire'.

(ii.) Between the line Haifa-Tekrit and the southern edge of French Armenia or Kurdistan, Great Britain to seek no 'political influence', and the French to have economic and political priority and the right to supply 'such advisers as the Arabs desire'.

(N.B. The geography of the Agreement is the geography of the White Knight, and it makes a similar irruption into economics when it lays down that the Baghdad Railway may not be finished till a Euphrates Railway has been built!)

DOCUMENT III. The British statement to the seven Syrians of Cairo dated June 11, 1917. This assures them that pre-war Arab States, and Arab areas freed by military action of their inhabitants during the war, shall remain entirely independent.

> (N.B. This assurance was unqualified, and might have conflicted with Document I. or Document II., but was regulated locally by arrangement between Allenby and Feisal, by which the Arab Army operated almost entirely in the area given to the Arabs in Document II.)

DOCUMENT IV. The Anglo-French Declaration of November 9, 1918. In this Great Britain and France agree to encourage native governments in Syria and Mesopotamia, and without imposition to assure the normal working of such governments as the peoples shall themselves have adopted.

> (N.B. This was interpreted in the Orient as changing the 'direct' British and French areas 'b' and 'c' of Document II. to spheres of influence.)

(The author of Document I. was Sir Henry McMahon. Documents II. and III. were by Sir Mark Sykes. Lord Robert Cecil authorized IV. They were all produced under stress of military urgency to induce the Arabs to fight on our side.)

I can see no inconsistencies or incompatibilities in these four documents, and I know nobody who does.

It may then be asked what all the fuss between the British, the French, and the Arabs is about. It is mainly because the agreement of 1916 (Document II) is unworkable, and in particular no longer suits the British and French Governments.

As, however, it is in a sense the 'charter' of the Arabs, giving them Damascus, Homs, Hama, Aleppo, and Mosul for their own, with such advisers as they themselves judge they need, the necessary revision of this agreement is a delicate matter, and can hardly be done satisfactorily by England and France, without giving weight and expression also to the opinion of the third interest — the Arabs — which it created.

T. E. LAWRENCE

[I have been helped to an impartial view of the situation by papers put at my disposal by Professor William Yale, of the University of New Hampshire, a member of the American Commission to Negotiate Peace, who played an important part, unfortunately unauthorized by his Government, in trying to bring about a settlement.

Yale had expert knowledge of Syrian conditions, and had been in close contact with French opinion, and realized that a disastrous explosion of violence was likely to occur in Syria where a large and victorious Arab army was unlikely to submit passively to decisions taken at Versailles. Two considerations led him to decide to see what he could do to help. He realized, as he stated in his report, that 'the British, French and Arabs cannot come to a solution unaided. These three Powers are like three cats perched on three posts, spitting at one another. A common ground must be found on which they can meet. The United States alone can bring these three together.'

In the second place there was no time to waste, as Lloyd George and Clemenceau had concluded an agreement on September 13th, of which Yale reported:

The Agreement between Messieurs Clemenceau and Lloyd George, by which British troops will on Nov. 1st be withdrawn from Cilicia, Syria and Mount Lebanon, to be replaced by French troops in Cilicia and along the Syrian Littoral and by Arab troops in the four cities of Damascus, Homs, Hameh and Aleppo, is a most pernicious one.

Superficially this is not a political move, but simply a change in the status of the military situation in 'Occupied Enemy's Territory'. Actually it not only seriously compromises the political future of the Arab Provinces, but also seriously jeopardises the peace of the Near and Middle East.

The fulfilling of this Agreement means the establishment of French military and administrative control along the entire Syrian Littoral and throughout Syria and 'Little Armenia'. It means direct British military and administrative control throughout Mesopotamia. It means that the Arabs, without being recognised as a provisionally independent government, will be left in control of four great cities — Damascus, Homs, Hameh, and Aleppo.

All those who are intimately acquainted with the facts, be they British, French or American, are convinced that the carrying out of this Agreement, as it stands, and without a definite solution of the questions involved being arrived at in advance, will result in serious local disorders which, all agree, will spread to Kurdistan, Mesopotamia and Palestine, and perhaps to the entire Moslem world.

The Arabs will not accept this agreement, there will be conflict with the French along the coast and the shadowy border between the Syrian Hinterland and the Syrian Littoral. There will be a serious danger of a massacre of native Catholics of Damascus, Homs, Hameh and Aleppo. All competent observers are agreed that this conflict would spread to Mesopotamia; it is believed that the Arabs would then throw in their lot with the Turkish rebels and that in a short time the entire Near East would be engaged in a conflict with the Allies.

On September 27th Yale went to London to find out for himself the minimum demands of the British, the Arabs, and the Zionists. He had interviews with Ambassador Davis; Rustum Haidor, the Representative of the Hedjaz Government; Colonel Gribbon of the Intelligence Section of the British General Staff; Mr. Wickham Steed, editor of *The Times*; the Emir Feisal; Colonel Cornwallis; Colonel Stirling; Dr. Gaster, one of the extreme Zionists; D. G. Hogarth; Jules Cambon, the French Ambassador; Colonel Lawrence; Lord Robert Cecil; Sir Henry McMahon; Mr. Garvin; Field-Marshal Lord Allenby; General Nuri Said and Rustum Haidor; and Colonel Watson.

The following are the most significant points of the interviews. Colonel Gribbon of the Intelligence Section of the British General Staff said that 'every promise made by Colonel Lawrence to the Arabs will be brushed aside'.

Mr. Steed told me that the latter part of Col. Lawrence's recent letter to *The Times*, in regard to British-Arab Agreements, he had suppressed. Mr. Steed said that Lawrence had written that he had been led to believe that the British Government meant to live up to its promises to the Arabs, and that it was because of this belief he had encouraged the Arabs. He wished to inform the Arabs and the British public that he regretted what he had done because the Government evidently had no intention of living up to the promise it had authorised him to make to the Arabs.

Feisal said he could not accept a change in the military occupation of Syria, that should Great Britain withdraw her troops he would make a final appeal to the United States, and if America refused to take any action he would return to Syria to lead his people to armed resistance of foreign occupation. He would not state the minimum he would accept but declared that he would accept any solution the United States imposed.

Dr. Gaster said that Zionism was a dead letter: that the Arab movement had reached such large dimensions it was impossible to create a Jewish State, and that the Hauran and Trans-Jordania could no longer be included in Palestine; that the 'British and Zionists had made a bargain and the Zionists had gotten the worst of it'.

Hogarth discussed the oil situation and Yale pointed out that in his opinion the United States would not tolerate a British monopoly of the Mesopotamian oil field which would threaten good relations between Great Britain and the United States. The following is Yale's note of his interview with Lawrence.

Wednesday, October 8th — Colonel Lawrence

Colonel Lawrence called upon me and talked at length on the Arab question. He said that he had plainly told Lloyd George that the British Government would have to allow the Arabs to organise an Arab Government in Mesopotamia. Lawrence said that he made it quite clear to Lloyd George and Lord Curzon that the British without large forces could not remain in Mesopotamia if they did not live up to their promises and establish an Arab Government there.

He informed me that Lord Curzon had recently adopted a more liberal point of view in regard to British control in Mesopotamia, and was inclined to grant the Arabs their wishes. Lawrence said further that General Wilson[1] had been ordered back from Mesopotamia because he had carried out an Indian colonial policy there, and that General Wilson's successor had been instructed to carry out a policy of local self-government.

Lawrence went over my projected solution and approved of it heartily, saying that it gave the Arabs more than he

---

[1] Colonel A. T. Wilson (now Sir Arnold Wilson, M.P.) is meant. He remained Acting Civil Commissioner after the breakdown of the Yale Plan.

had dared to hope to secure for them. He urged me to see
Lord Allenby and Lloyd George.

I told Lawrence that I was acting entirely on my own
responsibility and, without the knowledge or permission of
my own government, I could not ask for interviews with
Lord Allenby and Lloyd George.

Lord Robert Cecil saw no reason why the Arabs of Upper
Mesopotamia should not be given a large measure of independence and asked why direct British control should be
necessary in Lower Mesopotamia. Sir Henry McMahon said
that Yale's proposals were in accordance with the agreements
he had made with King Hussein, and urged Yale to see Lord
Allenby. Garvin showed he had a considerable knowledge of
the oil question.

Lord Allenby sent for Yale, saying that he wanted to go
over the solution which he had heard from Colonel Lawrence
he had in mind. Yale said that the French would refuse to
be more liberal to the Arabs in Syria than were the British in
Mesopotamia. 'Allenby seemed to understand this and appeared
to favour a most liberal policy in Mesopotamia.' Lord Allenby
was very cordial indeed and anxious to find a solution that would
satisfy the French and content the Arabs.

Nuri Said and Rustum Haidor said they could accept such a
solution as Yale had proposed anonymously in *The Times* and
that Feisal would accept it when the time came. Yale's
solution of the question was as follows: PALESTINE to be under
the mandate of Great Britain and the Zionists permitted to carry
out their plan. MOUNT LEBANON to be a separate political unit
under the mandate of France, SYRIA from Maan and Akaba to
Aleppo with the ports of Tripoli and Latakia to be constituted
as a 'provisionally' independent state with an Arab government
representative of its inhabitants. This Arab state to be under the
mandate of France.

MESOPOTAMIA: to be divided into two areas, the northern one
embracing the former Ottoman vilayets of Mosul and Bagdad;
the southern one that of Bassorah and the Emirate of Moham-
merah. The Northern area to be a 'provisionally' independent
state with an Arab Government representative of the inhabitants.
This state to be under the mandate of Great Britain. The
Southern area to be given local self-government under the

mandate of Great Britain. A Federal Council of representatives from each of the four Arab areas should meet at stated intervals.

The flaw in this arrangement was of course that as Lawrence wrote in his letter to Yale of October 1929 (see letter No. 397) 'by the mandate swindle England and France got the lot'. But of course neither Yale nor anyone else at that time realized what an elastic term 'mandate' could be made.

Yale was suddenly informed by Colonel Watson that the British War Cabinet had adopted the Yale Plan. He at once returned to Paris intending to put his plan before the French statesmen with whom he had been in touch: M. Berthelot, M. Robert de Caix, M. Jean Gout, and M. Herbette, the editor of *Le Temps*.

The following draft of a letter to Lloyd George was found among Lawrence's papers after his death. I think it was written after the British Cabinet adopted the Yale Plan and that Lawrence wrote it in a moment of rejoicing: there is no evidence that it was sent. I have been informed by his secretary that Mr. Lloyd George has no memoranda or papers of Lawrence's.]

114: TO MR. LLOYD GEORGE

Thursday 9.19.

Dear Mr. Lloyd George, I must confess to you that in my heart I always believed that in the end you would let the Arabs down: — so that now I find it quite difficult to know how to thank you. It concerns me personally, because I assured them during the campaigns that our promises held their face value, and backed them with my word, for what it was worth. Now in your agreement over Syria you have kept all our promises to them, and given them more than perhaps they ever deserved, and my relief at getting out of the affair with clean hands is very great.

If ever there is anything I can do for you in return please let me know.

My first sign of grace is that I will obey the F.O. and the W.O. and not see Feisal again.[1]   L.

---

[1] The last sentence and the signature are added in pencil below a pencil line.

[Such rejoicings were premature.

When Yale returned to Paris and explained to his chiefs in the American Commission to Negotiate Peace what he had been doing, they refused him permission to put forward the Yale Plan to the French as President Wilson on his final return to the United States had left them without authority to make any decisions or to take any action. It was a remarkable position. All the parties to a deadlock were prepared to agree to a solution which had been formulated — provided it were imposed upon them from outside. But the Americans were not prepared to impose anything on any of them.

I have described the Yale Plan at some length because it throws a ray of light from the outside upon the tension prevailing at the time and the forces at work. The list of these would not be complete without mentioning that the United States was deeply concerned to prevent a British monopoly of Mesopotamian oil which would threaten to wreck the entire economy of the American oil industry if it cut off the market for American kerosene in India and China. On the other hand, in Yale's opinion:

> there are forces at work within the British Government which are most unwilling to give up direct control of Mesopotamia or to make any concessions to the Arabs there. It is supposed that such forces are exercised by the Anglo-Persian Oil Company, by the Admiralty and perhaps by the India Office.[1]

I have been allowed to copy the following secret documents by Lawrence, and to publish them here. They were actually being written or under discussion while Yale was thinking of starting on his visit to England.]

115:   MEMORANDUM TO THE FOREIGN OFFICE

15 *Sept.* 1919   129405

To satisfy French agitation, we should agree to evacuate Aleppo, Damascus, Deraa and Amman, and retire to the 'International' area of the Sykes-Picot Agreement. We may also be able to stop our subsidy to Feisal: but this is more difficult, since it involves

---

[1] For Lawrence's opinion on this point see letter No. 544.

the French accepting our back loans as liabilities, and probably the substitution of French military command on the Syrian coast for the present command by Marshal Allenby, and the delimitation of a Franco-Mesopotamian frontier, and the decision as to who shall be responsible for e.g. the Kurds.

Great Britain will in any case formally ask Feisal to accept a subsidy for area 'B' (Deraa-Akaba) and receive British advisers for that area.

Temporary arrangements will have to be made for imports and exports of the Arab zones, A. and B., through Haifa, Beyrout, Tripoli, and Alexandretta.

We should secure assurances from the French and the Arabs that they would mutually respect the boundary of the direct French zone of the Sykes-Picot Agreement (which Feisal had best initial for the Damascus Government). It should be understood that disorder in either sphere will be regarded by us as our concern, till peace is signed with Turkey.

In this concern it should be noted that hostilities between Arabs and French will cut off all the inland food supply of the coast. The French should be informed that we will provide neither transport nor food for either side in such contingency.

If the French are wise and neglect the Arabs for about twelve months, they will then be implored by them to help them. If they are impatient now they only unite the Arabs against them. An outbreak will be caused if French troops pass their 'direct' (S-P) boundary without Arab permission.

Above all things in our interest a conflict between French and Arabs is to be prevented. If the Arabs came off badly, first clash, the affair might fizzle out, but they hold the initiative, and a preliminary success would unite all Moslem Syria against the French in arms. Such action will probably force us back to the Baghdad and Jerusalem lines as a measure of security, and will probably make public a Mustafa Kemal-Feisal understanding against Cilicia. A.

Mustafa Kemal is alarmed at French activity there, he is just now pro-British since he trusts our Turcophils (Montagu, Amery, Aubrey Herbert): but in his connection I hope note is being taken of Bolshevist advance in Turkestan. B. C.

T

D.   A Wahabi-like Moslem edition of Bolshevism is possible, and would harm us almost as much in Mesopotamia as in Persia.

E.   We are preparing the way for this by allowing Noel to flirt with Kurds.

F.   I regard the situation in Mesopotamia as disquieting, and if we do not mend our ways, will expect revolt there about March next.

G.   To regulate our affairs in the old Turkish Empire and to have our weak forces there in condition to lend speedy aid to one another in the events that may happen shortly, it seems very desirable to have all our military commands continued into one. Marshal Allenby is qualified by seniority to control our generals in Asia Minor and in Mesopotamia, and would have leisure to do it, if he would devolve the direct administration of Egypt to the hands of a subordinate.

T. E. LAWRENCE

NOTES

A.   I should say that no Mustafa Kemal-Feisal agreement exists, but Arabs of the 'Young Arab' party are agreeable to it, and Feisal in a corner will be prepared to accept any help. There has been a revival of Frankfort Jewish concern in Turkey lately, and notes are passing in London on the point.

B.   The Armenians in the Caucasus are not in danger from Mustafa Kemal, unless they attack e.g. Erzeroum. The key to their question will probably be the political history of the Turkestan Moslems in the next six months.

C.   Mustafa Kemal cannot make up his mind between Cilicia and Smyrna for action, and will not act except in desperate or very favourable circumstances.

D.   I do not believe that the elements that concluded the Persian agreement with us have any deep root in Persia, and a Bolshevik success in the Meshed neighbourhood might change the attitude of the Persians radically.

E.   The Kurdish agitation is most mischievous. Kurds have no corporate feeling and no capacity for autonomy or nationality. Mustafa Kemal believes that we are doing it out of love for him.

F.   The dissatisfaction against us in Mesopotamia is mostly in

the towns: and will become active when the notables care enough
to go out and make agreement with the country people.

G.   I would like to know whether we have ever thought of using
Talaat to damage Enver. His memoirs would be useful to us:
and Mustafa Kemal is waving Enver like a banner in his movement. Of course Mustafa Kemal is much the more able of the
two, but lacks Enver's personal magnetism.

T. E. LAWRENCE

116: TO LORD CURZON

September 27th, 1919   *F.O. No.* 134231

Dear Lord Curzon, I am putting this note into the form of a
private letter, in order that you may feel free to deal with it as you
please.

If I am asked to make Feisal accept the Paris arrangement of
last week reasonably, I would point out to him that though it was
strictly provisional, yet its provisions might be so established by
him in Syria, that it would become the basis of the permanent
settlement.

A.   I would tell him that for it to be wholly satisfactory to him,
he required some interpretations and additions of special point,
and would suggest his asking H.M.G. for an assurance that our
pledges with regard to the Arab character of the Government of
Mesopotamia hold good, and that to relieve the local situation
now (pending the Peace Conference decision) Sir P. Z. Cox again
take charge there, and his present deputy be employed outside the
province.

Feisal would not expect Sir Percy Cox to make any particular
change. What is needed is not a change of fact but of spirit. At
the same time one consequence of the Milner commission will
probably be an altered relation of Egypt to the Home Government, and another will be a demand for a 'Milner commission'
to bring Mesopotamia into line with the new constitution of
Egypt.

My own ambition is that the Arabs should be our first brown
dominion, and not our last brown colony. Arabs react against

you if you try to drive them, and they are as tenacious as Jews: but you can lead them without force anywhere, if nominally arm in arm. The future of Mesopotamia is so immense that if it is cordially ours we can swing the whole Middle East with it.

B.   I would suggest to Feisal that he ask the officers of H.M.G. in persuading the French to accept, jointly with us as regards Syria: —

(i)   That on the evacuation the present Arab administration become civil, and that an elected assembly from areas A and B ratify this agreement, and Feisal's position.

(Of course this new agreement will be written down in Paris, and signed by us, by the French and by Feisal)

(ii)   That this new Local Government be then recognised: as promised in the Anglo-French declaration of November 1918.

(Poland and Slovakia are parallels for a war recognition)

(iii)   That H.M.G. concede the Arab administration a free port in Haifa, and the French concede a free port either at Tripoli or Alexandretta.

(By offering Haifa we force the French hand. Tripoli and Alexandretta are the future ports of Mesopotamia).

(iv)   The necessary railway convention be drawn up, to give proper effect to the free-ports concession.

(v)   That the evacuations of areas A and B be both complete.

(Neither British nor French wish this. We want to garrison Deraa, and the French want to keep their detachment in Damascus: but I think the French should pay for the privilege: see Section vi below).

(vi)   The half-subsidy be paid by the British, and Feisal accepts a British adviser on his staff to deal with area B. The other half-subsidy be paid by the French, and Feisal accepts a French adviser on his staff to deal with area A.

(The point is to keep Col. Cornwallis in Damascus, where his influence will probably ensure peace. The French may see a condominium in this. We might then concede their point of the 200 troops in Damascus (Sect. v) in return.

If they still refused to allow Cornwallis in Damascus, as adviser for Area B, I would go out to Syria, and transfer Feisal and the whole Syrian Government to Deraa in the British area,

and H.M.G. would of course forbid the residence of a Frenchman in area B. They will soon become reasonable.)

I think Feisal will accept these terms, if I explain them to
him. He has the Zionist proposals behind him, though I suggest
that H.M.G. remain ignorant of them!

C.   We might take the present conversations as an opportunity
of regulating the Hejaz subsidy. I would like to lift it off the
Imperial Exchequer and make it a first charge on the surplus of
the local Arab Governments of Syria and Mesopotamia, divided
according to taste, and estimated, for size, on the former Turkish
'Hejaz' budget.

As Syria and Mesopotamia are not yet solvent the Great
Powers overseeing them would guarantee the payment of the
Hejaz subsidy by them, for the present. In Syria this obligation
would be shared equally by the British and French Governments,
who would pay the amount annually to the Government of Syria
for transmission to the Hejaz.

The Government of Baghdad would remit direct to Mecca.

It seems to me inevitable that the next stage of the Arab
Movement will be the transfer of the Hejaz towns to Damascus
in the same relation as they formerly stood to Turkey (Just as
the third stage will be the transfer of both Mecca and Damascus
to Bagdad, when the density of population in Mesopotamia rises
to an Egyptian standard). This second stage risks great French
influence in Mecca: but if we pay half the Hejaz expenses direct
to Mecca, and another share direct to the Government of Syria,
we seem reasonably *à cheval* upon all possible contingencies.

D.   With regard to the French coastal area of Syria, they have
accepted the formula 'French in Syria as British in Mesopotamia'.
Therefore so long as we are the more liberal ('left' in the Parliamentary sense) we call the tune. The relation of French, Arab,
and British administration sandwiched across 'Arabia' will be a
very peculiar one: and I have no doubt that the middle-man
(Damascus) will always be urging on each of us the good features
of the other. Our remedy and safeguard will be to trend continually 'left'. I think the parallel of our constructive work in
Persia may help us materially in Mesopotamia.

                                          T. E. LAWRENCE

[It was no doubt this letter to Lord Curzon to which Lawrence referred in his interview a few days later with Yale.

The Yale Plan having broken down because there was nobody to impose what was acceptable, but disappointing to all, the British Government reverted to the Lloyd George — Clemenceau agreement. Feisal, finding himself deserted by the British and 'all Colonel Lawrence's promises brushed aside', made a separate agreement with Clemenceau, by which he retained Damascus, and the interior of the country. On April 25th, 1920, the Supreme Council of the Allies allotted the mandate for Syria to France; in the summer of 1920 M. Millerand tore up the agreement with Feisal, General Gouraud occupied the interior and Feisal had to leave. French misrule culminated with the bombardment of Damascus for forty-eight hours in October 1925. This was the act of the political soldier General Sarrail who had commanded the Allied armies at Salonika during the War, which was described by Ludendorff as our 'largest concentration camp'. England, which had been wobbling about Mesopotamia, reverted to the 'Indian Colonial policy' of Government.

At the very time when Lawrence was being defeated at the Peace Conference, he was being turned into a popular hero in London. In August 1919 Lowell Thomas, who had met Lawrence at Akaba in 1917, opened a series of lectures at Covent Garden entitled 'With Allenby in Palestine and the Conquest of Holy Arabia', which was afterwards altered to 'With Allenby in Palestine and Lawrence in Arabia'. The lectures were a tremendous success; they were attended by London society and members of the Cabinet and, transferred to the Albert Hall, ran to the following January, drawing, in all, audiences of over a million people. Lowell Thomas 'put Lawrence on the map'. He afterwards toured Australia and New Zealand, from where he wrote to Lawrence in October 1920: 'I suspect you are still hiding from Italian countesses with ankle watches in your retreat at Oxford.'

Lawrence had indeed returned to Oxford after his defeat, and lived partly at Polstead Road, sometimes at All Souls. His mother has described to me how at this period of extreme depression and nervous exhaustion Lawrence would sometimes sit the entire morning between breakfast and lunch in the same position, without moving, and with the same expression on his face.

Lawrence had found *Arabia Deserta* invaluable on account of its geographical information, during the Arab Campaign, for himself and other British officers working with the Arabs. The first edition, Cambridge University Press, 1888, is a rare book and had long been out of print. Lawrence now planned to get it reprinted and his first thought was to get it done by the Egyptian Survey Department, which had printed *The Arab Bulletin*. The following letter to Doughty also records the loss of all but the first nine chapters of the first draft of *Seven Pillars of Wisdom*, which was stolen from Reading Station.

This is perhaps the most fitting place to give a summary of the subsequent history of *Seven Pillars of Wisdom*. Urged by Hogarth, Lawrence began to rewrite Version No. 2 immediately after his loss, and stated that he completed a text in about three months. Actually he may have finished it by the end of September 1920. This is referred to in letters to Richards as 'the-book-to-build-the-house', and as 'my Boy-Scout book'. Lawrence's original plan was for F. N. Doubleday with whom he had formed a close friendship in Paris during the Peace Conference, to publish a cheap edition of this book in America and to keep it off the English market.

But Version No. 2 did not satisfy Lawrence and he is said to have burnt it at Chingford with a blow lamp in 1922.

Version No. 3 was written in 1921 in London and Jidda, and finished in London in 1922. The manuscript of this is in the Bodleian Library. It was set up and eight copies printed by the *Oxford Times* Press, between January and July 1922, at a cost of £175. I believe that five copies of this still exist. The text of the Oxford edition was extensively rewritten and revised at Clouds Hill and at Cranwell in 1923, 1924, 1925 and 1926. It is this version which was reprinted after Lawrence's death and which the public know. It was first printed by Manning Pike and C. J. Hodgson for T. E. Shaw. One hundred and twenty-eight complete copies were subscribed at 30 guineas each, 36 complete copies, and 26 incomplete copies were given away by the author. In addition 22 copies without plates, with two variant passages and no introductory matter or appendixes, were printed for George H. Doran in America to secure the copyright.]

117: TO C. M. DOUGHTY

November 25th, 1919   *Oxford*

Dear Mr. Doughty, Many thanks for your two letters, and for the enclosure from Mr. Duckworth. I went and saw him, afterwards, and found as I expected that the major part of his estimate was for cost of type-setting. This would be nearly £1500, today in England, I fancy.

As I told you I have hopes that the Government Press in Cairo would do it for little more than a quarter this amount. In that case the two volumes could be republished by Messrs. Duckworth for about £2 2. o, which is what I aim at. The text would be set in Cairo, and stereos made, for transport to England. The book would then always remain in print. I think there will be a constant, though small, demand for it, and that it should always be in a condition to be reprinted easily. This is the advantage of plates.

I am writing to the Director of the Arab Bureau in Cairo (the Intelligence office that deals with Arabian affairs) asking him to get an exact estimate from the Government Press for the resetting of the book. It is to be feared that the present disorders in Egypt may make the matter slower and more difficult. When I get his answer I will let you know, and we can then decide whether to go ahead or not. It seems to me that in any case Duckworth should be the publisher, since a cheap reprint of *Arabia Deserta* will kill his abridgement, and there is no good reason for causing him a loss. Can you tell me what happened to the blocks, for the illustrations of the original edition? Did Clay destroy them, or are they in store somewhere? If they still exist it would be a small economy.

Until Cairo replies to me matters must wait. They print quite well, and have the great advantage of cheap labour, and government subsidies. Yours sincerely   T E LAWRENCE

I have lost the MSS of my own adventures in Arabia: it was stolen from me in the train. So now I have the opportunity of thinking of doing it again!

118: TO C. M. DOUGHTY

5. 1. 20.

Dear Mr. Doughty, I fear you will have thought me remiss in not answering you before, but I have been away, and when I got back at last decided that it was so old now, that I had better read *Mansoul* before replying.

I finished it today, in London, and I think I like it better than *Adam* and next to *Arabia Deserta*, of your books. Of course nothing can replace *Arabia*, to me, but *Mansoul* is very nearly doing so, in parts, though not as a whole. The *Arabia* is a complete picture of the life of the best sort of Arabs in the desert, & in the markets about the desert, and no picture of one people, by a stranger, has ever been painted like it, in my experience of books.

Did I ever tell you of our lunch with Mr. Balfour when the table voted on the best books of travel . . . five for you, and two for Marco Polo?

There are some things about *Mansoul* which I want to ask you about, but I will keep them till I see you. I want to contest one point . . . perhaps because I'm 30 and you 70!

Did I tell you about Augustus John? He has to go to Paris at the moment, but will be free perhaps at the end of the month, and will then write to you and try to arrange a date to come down and have a sitting.[1] That is unless something unexpected happens: and it generally does, with John.

No news from Cairo yet, of course.

Please give my best wishes for the New Year to Mrs. Doughty.
Yours sincerely   T E LAWRENCE

119: TO LORD HARTINGTON

Wed. Jan. 10. [1920]   *All Souls College. Oxford.*

Dear Hartington, You'll have thought me remiss in answering: as usual: but I thought I'd see Feisal first & learn for sure that he was coming.

[1] Lawrence wanted a drawing of Doughty by John as a frontispiece to the new edition of *Arabia Deserta*.

It's very good of you to ask him; he's had a rotten time, & must wait yet some months in England, & the more he moves about the better.

I'll be delighted to come along and help talk to him: it's the most boring job in the world, to have great foreigners in your house to keep entertained.

We did it splendidly last week end. Feisal said he'd had a most profitable & amusing time. Inshallah,[1] for the next occasion too! Yours sincerely,   T. E. LAWRENCE

120: TO COLONEL S. F. NEWCOMBE

16. 2. 20

Dear S.F., I owe you five letters! At first it wasn't worth while for you were reported to me in one week as at Aleppo, Azrak, Bagdad & Cairo: and then it became a habit.

However the arrival of a smaller (I hope not cheaper) edition[2] is an occasion for a bookworm like myself. The editio princeps always has a special value: but in some cases (Shakespeare folios e.g.) new matter is embodied in the reprints, which give them a market reputation little, if any, less than original. At the same time collectors, and especially collectors of sentiment, always prefer the genuine article.

However Mrs. Newcombe will regard the graft as the first. These things, as Solomon quoted from Adam's table-talk, depend on the point of view. Please give her my heartiest congratulations.

Then about business. Of course Lawrence may have been the name of your absolutely favourite cousin or aunt, (observe my adroitness in *sex*), and if so I will be dropping an immodest brick by blushing — but if it isn't, aren't you handicapping 'it'? In the history of the world (cheap edition) I'm a sublimated Aladdin, the thousand and second Knight, a Strand-Magazine strummer. In the eyes of 'those who know'[3] I failed badly in attempting a piece of work which a little more resolution would

---

[1] Please God.
[2] Colonel Newcombe's son, Stewart Lawrence Newcombe, had just been born.
[3] Translation of Dante's *Color chi sanno*.

have pushed through, or left un-touched. So either case it is bad for the sprig, unless, as I said, there is a really decent aunt.

As for god-fathering him, I asked two or three people what it meant, & their words were ribald. Perhaps it is because people near me lose that sense of mystery which distance gives. Or else it was because they didn't know it was you — or at least yours. Anyhow I can't find out what it means, and so I shall be delighted to take it on. Everybody agrees it means a silver mug — but tell me first if his complexion is red or white: I wouldn't commit a colour-discord.

Give Rose my ~~love~~ you will know what to say . . . something neat, & not too Newcomian. As for the rugs, please take any that seem worthy to you. There were two Afghans in the Arab Bureau, & a big (and not bad but thin) Shiraz, in the Savoy.

I have abandoned Oxford, & wander about town from a bed-room in Pimlico, (temporary, for Bethnal Green is nicer to the nose) looking at the stars. It is nicer than looking at Lord Curzon.

Please give Mrs. Newcombe my very best regards. How odd it must be having married you. Tell her my letter wasn't fit for her to see.   L.

Hogarth sends his warmest congrats. to all three.

Seriously I am changing my own name, to be more quiet, and wish I could change my face, to be more lovely, & beloved!

121: TO V. W. RICHARDS

27.2.20

I've written a letter to Gardiner saying that if we can build in 1921, we'll let him know in good time, and ask him for his last twenty-nine days. I've told him that meanwhile you will set up a hedge, and asked him whether there are any improvements he can think of, since there seems to me no reason why they shouldn't be done.

It seems monstrous that you should put up the fence yourself, while I sit at peace and dream of having written a book. Why can't Rogers hire a man? I can afford that easily.

I'm glad the nurse was not too down on me: it's horrible to know that one is not so good-looking as one's portrait in the *Strand*. Hoots.

About the book-to-build-the-house. It is on paper in the first draft to the middle of Book vi: and there are seven books in all. But the first draft is a long way off the last one and I feel hopeless about ever finishing it. I work best utterly by myself: when I speak to no one for days. So that's a consoling prospect for you in the hut (or Hall: q.e.v.) days of garrulity divided by days of silence. Hoots again. Gardiner to return to business says 'Hut, Hawkes Head'. Stokes & Stokes say 'King's Head': you say 'Pole Hill'. Which? Pole Hill Press sounds nicest. I'm sorry to raise this again. Hawkes are poor eating, and Kings, if eaten, would taste like them. Also heads are the worst part of everything except asparagus.

I haven't read *Boon*: and I don't like Wells. He has written eighty books.

McDougall reproaches me on the shelf. He has not been taken down since I began Book vi. Do you ever come into London. Because if so, I'll return him, & Bradley,[1] it's a shame to keep them so long.   L.

122: TO F. N. DOUBLEDAY

March 20, 1920.

Effendim (this is more formal than Effendi,[2] and not servile like Effendina).

I expect Florida is now finished for you. I refrained from writing before, since your holiday ought not to be profaned. The Garden City book came to me correctly: what a beautiful place you have! It must be great fun trying to work there: do you go out and count the cedar trees instead, sometimes?

It gave me rather a shock to realise for the first time what a plutocrat you must be. However it doesn't matter, because I'm not a Bolshevik, merely a person who doesn't care sufficiently

---

[1] McDougall the psychologist and Bradley the logician and metaphysician.
[2] Doubleday was widely known by this pun on his initials.

about money to try hard to make any. My father was kind to me, and spent none of the capital he received from his father . . . and unless I marry non-self-supporting wives or have children, all will be well with me. My present burst of labour is only to find enough cash to build myself a house.

However I won't talk shop: the book is in hand, and likely to remain there.

There are two little bindings by me, which might interest you, or your French artists, and when I have another fit of paper and string I'll send them across. One is a rarity, a Ricketts binding in pigskin: he usually kept to vellum, and was not very good at it. This, in white pigskin, on the contrary seems to me charming. The other is a rather florid piece of de Santy. He's stopped work, so I presume it is acquiring unearned increment: but I don't much like de Santy.

As for hand-made paper: it ceased during the war, but they are now beginning again to manufacture. If you print my *Seven Pillars* I'll send a ream across, and then we can pull a large paper copy for you and one for me. Or do you regard such parerga as Mr. Henry Ford regards 'outside specifications'?

I don't like bothering Kipling with my problems, and so have not kept up correspondence: perhaps if the thing is ever finished to my taste I'll ask him for the kindness of an opinion on doubtful points: but he must be very busy, and I'm not a literary artist. It would be like asking Sargent to advise on the colour of one's street door.

No I didn't see Bott afterwards. You know a Mr. Lowell Thomas made me a kind of matinee idol: so I dropped my name so far as London is concerned and live peacefully in anonymity. Only my people in Oxford know of my address. It isn't that I hate being known — I'd love it — but I can't afford it: no one gets so victimised by well-meaning people as a poor celebrity. Also now I'm trying to write, which is a trouble to me, and there are the books produced since 1914 for me to read. So that I'm too busy to care about meeting people.

You know, publishing Conrad must be a rare pleasure. He's absolutely the most haunting thing in prose that ever was: I wish I knew how every paragraph he writes (do you notice they are all paragraphs: he seldom writes a single sentence?) goes on sounding in waves, like the note of a tenor bell, after it stops. It's not built on the rhythm of ordinary prose, but on something existing only in his head, and as he can never say what it is he wants to say, all his things end in a kind of hunger, a suggestion of something he can't say or do or think. So his books always look bigger than they are. He's as much a giant of the subjective as Kipling is of the objective. Do they hate one another? Yours ever   T.E.L.

P.S.   Please remind Mrs. Doubleday that her wishes last time were expressed in a margin: an afterthought of your pen: *therefore* I put my second sending of regard of the very kindest in the postscript. It is the most important part of the letter.

[The administration of Mesopotamia on the Indian model, and with administrators from India, was proving an expensive and unpopular business: unpopular that is to say with the inhabitants and with the British taxpayer.
Lawrence had an alternative plan which he was able to put in operation later on, and the following letter is the first hint of the plan of holding Mesopotamia by air control only, which proved a great economy and success after the establishment of the kingdom of Iraq.]

123: TO LORD WINTERTON

22. 4. 20   *All Souls College Oxford.*

Dear Winterton, I've hopped off here — more or less broke — for a month. They give one credit. . . .

Yes I saw Trenchard last night. He has, as you say, 'grown' beyond measure. Pre-1914 he'd have been downed for a little-Englander: now I think he is right in all points, and after quite a lot of talk I feel inclined to back his scheme. It means Salmond as H.C.[1] in Bagdad (a happy deliverance from the I.C.S.[2] tradition) with probably the Colonial Secretary nominally responsible, and with an Arab army under an Arab-British administration to defend the country.

---

[1] High Commissioner.   [2] Indian Civil Service.

Trenchard sounded to me clean & honest (for the Lord's sake don't repeat this!) and means to play fair by the local people. He thinks as little of the worth of bombing as we did!

I told him Joyce would make the Arab army for him[1] : it would be pleasant to see Nuri and Jaafar & the rest doing their job over again.

However more of this when we meet: but unless something provokes you beyond measure don't knock him on the head in the House, because I think he means rightly. So odd to find a man without entanglements in the city!

That talk will be great sport, and I'll look forward to it: but I doubt whether Aubrey[2] will come so soon. Albania seems to be revolting in several ways at once, and he will probably assume its crown for a few weeks. Yours ever,   T E L

This letter goes to the H. of C[3] : a bad address, I think, but I always forget the other.   L.

124: TO C. M. DOUGHTY

7. 5. 20.   *All Souls, Oxford.*

Dear Mr. Doughty, After a great deal of writing Egypt[4] have at last been able to make up their minds — of course wrongly. They say that the arrears due to the interference of the local troubles will take them two years to work off. After that they will be able to take on outside work again.

I do not believe it, for I am sure that their local troubles are not nearly over. It is most unsatisfactory.

There remain possibilities of America, and subscription. The younger poets are very anxious for the latter, since they all want *Arabia Deserta*, and cannot afford her (she now stands at £32. 10. 0) but it would mean getting a very long list (at least a thousand copies, I think) and I do not know if this is possible. As for America, the book is unfortunately not copyright there. However, if I may, I'll have another talk with Duckworth. There is so large and worthy a demand for the book that it seems shameful not to get it out again somehow.

---

[1] He did, with Jaafar.   [2] Aubrey Herbert.
[3] House of Commons.   [4] See letter No. 117.

Then about a tame artist. That also has been difficult. John had to finish a lot of things for a show, to raise himself money: then he went to hospital, for an operation, and now he's in France being made fit again.

He is of course the great man: but meanwhile, would you allow Mr. W. Rothenstein to draw you? He sounds German, but did very well in the war: and makes a special point of men of books. He knows *Arabia Deserta*, of course, and would very much like to make a drawing of you. It would take him about an hour and a half, and would not trouble you at all, and it would be a very pleasing and honest piece of work. Rothenstein is a quite safe draughtsman — not a genius, good and bad, like John. If you will allow him, it would give all of us a great deal of pleasure.

I'm sorry about Cairo: but it only means finding another way: a nuisance. Yours sincerely   T. E. LAWRENCE

125: TO F. N. DOUBLEDAY

14.5.20.

Effendim, A fine pen, for this will be an inordinately long letter. First of all, very many thanks for your luscious Kipling. It's very good to have the three volumes in one in such excellent type, and on good paper. Did you print it from plates, or was it re-set? It's beautifully done anyhow.

Then the binding. I'm very glad to see your Frenchmen's work. I took it to Bain who was much puzzled at it, and finally confessed he did not know them. He felt this as a personal loss, for it was his pride to recognise every binder. I think it's very pleasantly done, technically as good as anyone ever wants, and the style of tooling is so quiet and respectable. One is ashamed of a Cobden Sanderson on one's shelves: it shouts out its virtue so loudly. This is a self-respecting binding, which will mellow and improve every year it is handled. In fact, as I said once before, very many thanks indeed. It stands between two vellum books, and looks as good as they do, or better. You seem, despite your lament, to get good leather still in U.S.A.

I sent you a little Ricketts binding in white pigskin two days after Kipling came: and have a florid de Santy Xmas-present sort of thing still in hand. It is so hard to get corrugated packing-paper! I hope you will like the Ricketts. It's a feminine sort of thing, I'm afraid.

What I really wanted to write about was Doughty's *Arabia Deserta*. It's a long book in two volumes (some 500,000 words, I should think) published by the Cambridge Press thirty years ago: full of little cuts and very wise. They printed 240 copies, and broke up the type. A copy now costs £30 in England, and is very hard to find. Duckworth (a publisher in London) produced an abridgement about 10 years ago, and has reprinted it three or four times since: the abridgement was of about ⅔ of the original. The whole book is a necessity to any student of Arabia, but is more than that. It's one of the greatest prose works in the English language, and the best travel book in the world. Unfortunately it's solidly written (not dull at all, but in a queer style which demands care at first), and because of its rarity is far too little known.

Now I'd like to get it out again. I hoped to do it at the Cairo Press: but then Egypt became riotous, and they are vastly in arrears. To do it in England would cost £1,500 for type setting only, and Duckworth won't do it, because it would kill his abridgement. Doughty owns the copyright, and is willing to let it out again for nothing or thereabouts. Do you think any wise man in America would undertake it? I think I could get about 500 subscribers at 2 or 3 guineas a copy — perhaps more: but it would mean a lot of correspondence, and I'm a lazy person by nature. So I thought I'd ask your advice, as a publisher: it's a very great work, and it's a shame it should be so rare: and I like it better than almost any other book. It has of course an immense reputation amongst the elect. Please tell me what you think: and give my regards (as last time) wholly and entirely to Mrs. Doubleday. Yours sincerely,   T.E. LAWRENCE

A jest about my own screed. One [*name of publisher omitted*] and a dull fellow came to see me after some persistent correspondence. I told him I'd not publish in England at any price, but hope to do something for America. He said it was an

U

impossible idea, as it would be pirated, and hinted that I knew nothing of copyright law. I don't — but no one ever heard of a law which could not be avoided by either side, when necessary. So then I said you would probably publish for me in U.S.A., and that the Clarendon Press or someone would do it in England, only the American edition would cost a shilling or so, and the English one be published at £1000 a copy. This sent him off silent, but very angry. As I said, a dull man, and greedy.

I think my MSS may be ready for abridgement about 1921 autumn — or 1922: and I'm aiming to give you about 150,000 words of it: I hope it comes off.   L.

126: TO R. D. BLUMENFELD

11.7.20.

Dear Blumenfeld, This is altogether too kind of you,[1] and I feel rather uncomfortable about it. It looks almost as though you thought there was an obligation, which of course is very far from being the case. In those short pushes the *Daily Express* achieved some things which I wanted very much,[2] and I am still therefore deeply in your debt. Unfortunately I cannot pay my side of it with beautiful books — but please let me know any time I can be of use to you. You have my addresses, 14 Barton St. and All Souls, and I'm nearly always at one or other, and will be delighted to come and see you. Yours sincerely,   T. E. LAWRENCE

127: TO THE EDITOR OF 'THE TIMES'

July 22   *All Souls College*

Sir, In this week's debate in the Commons on the Middle East a veteran of the House expressed surprise that the Arabs

[1] Blumenfeld, then Editor of the *Daily Express,* had sent Lawrence a rare copy of *Arabian Nights* as a gift in lieu of pay for an article which he insisted on writing for nothing.

[2] Articles on the subject of the administration of Mesopotamia. The Arabs rose in rebellion this month and the British army had to be heavily reinforced from India. The rebellion was not suppressed until the end of the year.

of Mesopotamia were in arms against us despite our well-meant
mandate. His surprise has been echoed here and there in the
Press, and it seems to me based on such a misconception of the
new Asia and the history of the last five years, that I would like
to trespass at length on your space and give my interpretation of
the situation.

The Arabs rebelled against the Turks during the war not
because the Turk Government was notably bad, but because they
wanted independence. They did not risk their lives in battle to
change masters, to become British subjects or French citizens,
but to win a show of their own.

Whether they are fit for independence or not remains to be
tried. Merit is no qualification for freedom. Bulgars, Afghans,
and Tahitans have it. Freedom is enjoyed when you are so well
armed, or so turbulent, or inhabit a country so thorny that the
expense of your neighbour's occupying you is greater than the
profit. Feisal's Government in Syria has been completely independent for two years, and has maintained public security and
public services in its area.

Mesopotamia has had less opportunity to prove its armament.
It never fought the Turks, and only fought perfunctorily against
us. Accordingly, we had to set up a war-time administration
there. We had no choice; but that was two years ago, and we have
not yet changed to peace conditions. Indeed, there are yet no
signs of change. 'Large reinforcements', according to the official
statement, are now being sent there, and our garrison will run
into six figures next month. The expense curve will go up to
50 million pounds for this financial year, and yet greater efforts
will be called for from us as the Mesopotamian desire for independence grows.

It is not astonishing that their patience has broken down after
two years. The Government we have set up is English in fashion,
and is conducted in the English language. So it has 450 British
executive officers running it, and not a single responsible Mesopotamian. In Turkish days 70 per cent of the executive civil
service was local. Our 80,000 troops there are occupied in police
duties, not in guarding the frontiers. They are holding down the
people. In Turkish days the two army corps in Mesopotamia

were 60 per cent Arab in officers, 95 per cent in other ranks. This deprivation of the privilege of sharing the defence and administration of their country is galling to the educated Mesopotamians. It is true we have increased prosperity — but who cares for that when liberty is in the other scale? They waited and welcomed the news of our mandate, because they thought it meant Dominion self-government for themselves. They are now losing hope in our good intentions.

A remedy? I can see a cure only in immediate change of policy. The whole logic of the present thing looks wrong. Why should Englishmen (or Indians) have to be killed to make the Arab Government in Mesopotamia, which is the considered intention of his Majesty's Government? I agree with the intention, but I would make the Arabs do the work. They can. My little experience in helping to set up Feisal showed me that the art of government wants more character than brains.

I would make Arabic the Government language. This would impose a reduction of the British staff, and a return to employment of the qualified Arabs. I would raise two divisions of local volunteer troops, all Arabs, from the senior divisional general to the junior private. (Trained officers and trained N.C.O.'s exist in thousands.) I would entrust these new units with the maintenance of order, and I would cause to leave the country every single British soldier, every single Indian soldier. These changes would take 12 months, and we should then hold of Mesopotamia exactly as much (or as little) as we hold of South Africa or Canada. I believe the Arabs in these conditions would be as loyal as anyone in the Empire, and they would not cost us a cent.

I shall be told that the idea of brown Dominions in the British Empire is grotesque. Yet the Montagu scheme and the Milner scheme are approaches to it, and the only alternative seems to be conquest, which the ordinary Englishman does not want, and cannot afford.

Of course, there is oil in Mesopotamia, but we are no nearer that while the Middle East remains at war, and I think if it is so necessary for us, it could be made the subject of a bargain. The Arabs seem willing to shed their blood for freedom; how much more their oil!   T. E. LAWRENCE

128: TO C. M. DOUGHTY

30. 7. 20.   *All Souls Oxford.*

Dear Mr. Doughty, I have been very much at fault lately: but I wanted to get things settled a little before I wrote to you. I have no doubt that Duckworth will have written to you about the Medici edition of *Arabia Deserta*. I hope you will accept it, for it is very difficult to get any book out now-a-days. Your share is miserable: and the price is very high: but the original now stands at over £30, and this is at least an improvement on that. Also I feel that the great thing is to get it set up. This is only a first printing of 500 copies, but it has been designed to cover its expenses, and the book will always be in hand to reprint when the 500 are sold. I think that these later reprints can be sold cheaper, and so the book may at last reach a full public.

There are just two difficulties. To catch the collector of editions, this should be a little different from the old. Nothing can be changed in it as it stands, so I suggested that you might be persuaded to write an additional preface. My hopes were that perhaps you would just put down on paper, easily, the 'why' you went to Arabia. I don't mean Medain Salih, but to write something: and it should be exceedingly interesting if you would say how you wrote it — the relation between the notes you took and the finished book: and how you were able to take such notes without being stopped. These are only suggestions — but I hope you will do *something*, because it would help to clear the 500 off, and till then Mr. Lee Warner is risking a good deal of money.

The other difficulty is worse. They have asked me to write a note introducing it. I feel this as absurd as it would be to introduce Shakespeare. However they urged that I had an advertisement value, especially in America which has hitherto hardly known you, and which ought to buy nearly half the 500 — and so I said that I would do it, if you would allow it to be done. I'm afraid you will feel it rather an outrage on the book; and I shall be delighted if you do. The only risk is of Mr. Lee Warner then trying to avoid the contract: and I'd do almost anything to get *Arabia Deserta* on sale again.

I have left no room to thank you for the ostrich egg: it is a very splendid egg, to have such a pedigree, and I will see it properly bestowed.[1]

About the portrait: Rothenstein has been house-moving, and then a little ill. I hope to send Mrs. Doughty a collection of his drawings soon to reassure her on his sobriety (he is almost too sober I am afraid): John is greater: Do you think it could be put into the new edition? Yours sincerely   T E LAWRENCE

129: TO C. M. DOUGHTY

Aug. 7. 1920.   *All Souls College, Oxford.*

Dear Mr. Doughty, I'm afraid I wrote too quickly: no doubt the business men are still drawing up the precise clauses of their contracts. Still I'll be in London on Tuesday, and will then go to Duckworth's and find out.

The facts are roughly, that Mr. Lee Warner, of the Medici Society in Grafton St., who has published bibliophile editions of the classics, (Virgil, Horace, Caesar, Catullus) and a few English books (no new ones) has agreed to do an *Arabia Deserta*, subject to your approval. He proposes a limited edition of five hundred copies at £9. 9. 0. If these sell he will have made ten per cent: and in addition he will have the book set up, ready for further, & I hope cheaper, editions. He wanted a new preface, and the use of my name on an introduction, because America has an idea that I know more about Arabia than anyone: and so I may advertise you. It's a topsy-turvy world!

Your share was to be ten per cent. It is a poor return after so many years, but I hope you will agree to it, for this edition should raise the value of the book very much, and the subsequent editions ought to be profitable. The contract you sign ought to reserve your rights in all future editions, I think: but there is no one so little apt at business as myself, and I hope you will not take my advice.

I'd like a first-class portrait as a frontispiece.

About my own book. I'm going in the next two or three months to re-write it in short form, as a story of adventure, for

---

[1] I believe this egg was given to the Oxford Natural History Museum.

America. It will appeal to Boy Scouts, I hope. This will keep me in Oxford, I'm afraid for the next time: otherwise I would have liked to come down: perhaps in the autumn. Please give my regards to Mrs. Doughty. Yours sincerely   T E LAWRENCE

[The post-war boom had been followed by a slump and the need to economize was urgent. Mesopotamia was being held by an army which cost sixty million pounds in the years 1920 and 1921. Liddell Hart has pointed out that it thus cost about six times as much to hold down the Iraqis as to finance the whole Arab Revolt against Turkey for about equal periods of time. Yet some of the men who involved England in this prodigious waste of money and waste of life, have repeatedly attacked Lawrence on the ground that he could not have achieved what he did without paying subsidies to the Arabs![1] The letter to *The Times* of July 23rd, was followed up by two articles, more forcibly expressed. That in *The Observer* of August 8th was published without comment but the second one in *The Sunday Times* of August 22nd, 1920, was accompanied by an extremely forcible leading article:

> Why are we in Mesopotamia? Uninformative statements which have been issued by the Government convey the impression that officialdom is bewildered and anxious rather to conceal its blunders than to mend them. But they can be concealed no longer ... the men we have appointed to reconstruct the country have been neither supervised nor restricted. They have been as wildly extravagant in money and militarism as any Turkish Pasha]

130: FRANCE, BRITAIN, AND THE ARABS[2]

BY COL. T. E. LAWRENCE

There is a feeling in England that the French occupation of Damascus and their expulsion of Feisal from the throne to which

[1] They were paying subsidies themselves. Thus Colonel Leachman prevented some of the Arabs in his district from rising by distributing £21,000 in 1920.

[2] Printed in *The Observer* of August 8th, 1920.

the grateful Syrians had elected him is, after all, a poor return for
Feisal's gifts to us during the war: and the idea of falling short of
an oriental friend in generosity leaves an unpleasantness in our
mouths. Feisal's courage and statesmanship made the Mecca
revolt spread beyond the Holy cities, until it became a very active
help to the Allies in Palestine. The Arab army, created in the
field, grew from a mob of Bedouins into an organised and well-
equipped body of troops. They captured thirty-five thousand
Turks, disabled as many more, took a hundred and fifty guns, and
a hundred thousand square miles of Ottoman territory. This was
great service in our extreme need, and we felt we owed the Arabs
a reward: and to Feisal, their leader, we owed double, for the
loyal way in which he had arranged the main Arab activity when
and where Allenby directed.

Yet we have really no competence in this matter to criticise
the French. They have only followed in very humble fashion, in
their sphere of Syria, the example we set them in Mesopotamia.
England controls nine parts out of ten of the Arab world, and
inevitably calls the tune to which the French must dance. If we
follow an Arab policy, they must be Arab. If we fight the Arabs,
they must fight the Arabs. It would show a lack of humour if
we reproved them for a battle near Damascus, and the blotting out
of the Syrian essay in self-government, while we were fighting
battles near Baghdad, and trying to render the Mesopotamians
incapable of self-government, by smashing every head that
raised itself among them.

A few weeks ago the chief of our administration in Baghdad[1]
was asked to receive some Arab notables who wanted to urge
their case for partial autonomy. He packed the delegation with
some nominees of his own, and in replying, told them that it

---

[1] Colonel A. T. Wilson, the Acting Civil Commissioner. The following information
concerning this meeting is taken from 'Iraq: a Study in Political Development, by
Philip Willard Ireland. 'The group of fifteen Baghdad Nationalists, known locally as
the Mandubin or Delegates, had approached the Acting Civil Commissioner asking for
an opportunity to lay their proposals before him for transmission to H.M. Government.
He had tried to avoid giving the interview . . . he finally gave them an appointment of
June 2nd. He took the precaution, however, of inviting about forty other dignitaries . . .
special police arrangements were made, troops were held in readiness at the barracks and
R.I.M.S. Comet with steam up and trained guns was stationed on the Tigris opposite the
Sarai.'

would be long before they were fit for responsibility. Brave
words — but the burden of them has been heavy on the
Manchester men this week at Hillah.

These risings take a regular course. There is a preliminary
Arab success, then British reinforcements go out as a punitive
force. They fight their way (our losses are slight, the Arab losses
heavy) to their objective, which is meanwhile bombarded by
artillery, aeroplanes, or gunboats. Finally, perhaps, a village is
burnt and the district pacified. It is odd that we do not use poison
gas on these occasions. Bombing the houses is a patchy way
of getting the women and children, and our infantry always incur
losses in shooting down the Arab men. By gas attacks the whole
population of offending districts could be wiped out neatly; and as
a method of government it would be no more immoral than the
present system.

We realise the burden the army in Mesopotamia is to the
Imperial Exchequer, but we do not see as clearly the burden it is
to Mesopotamia. It has to be fed, and all its animals have to be
fed. The fighting forces are now eighty-three thousand strong,
but the ration strength is three hundred thousand. There are
three labourers to every soldier, to supply and serve him. One in
ten of the souls in Mesopotamia to-day belongs to our army. The
greenness of the country is being eaten up by them, and the
process is not yet at its height. To be safe they demand that we
double our existing garrison. As local resources are exhausted
this increase of troops will increase the cost by more than an
arithmetical progression.

These troops are just for police work to hold down the subjects
of whom the House of Lords was told two weeks ago that they
were longing for our continued presence in their country. No one
can imagine what will be our state there if one of Mesopotamia's
three envious neighbours (all nursing plans against us) attack us
from outside, while there is still disloyalty within. Our communications are very bad, our defence positions all have both
flanks in the air, and there seem to have been two incidents lately.
We do not trust our troops as we did during the war.

Then there are the military works. Great barracks and camps
have had to be constructed, and hundreds of miles of military

roads. Great bridges, to carry motor-lorries, exist in remote places, where the only local transport is by pack. The bridges are made of temporary materials, and their upkeep is enormous. They are useless to the civil Government, which yet has to take them over at a high valuation; and so the new State will begin its career with an enforced debt.

English statesmen, from the Premier downwards, weep tears over the burden thrust on us in Mesopotamia. 'If only we could raise a local army,' said Lord Curzon, 'but they will not serve' ('except against us,' his lordship no doubt added to himself). 'If only we could find Arabs qualified to fill executive posts.'

In this dearth of local talent the parallel of Syria is illuminating. Feisal had no difficulty in raising troops, though he had great difficulty in paying them. However, the conditions were not the same, for he was arbitrarily deprived of his Customs' revenue. Feisal had no difficulty in setting up an administration, in which the five leading spirits were all natives of Baghdad! It was not a very good administration, but in the East the people are less exigent than we are. Even in Athens Solon gave them not the best laws, but the best they would accept.

The British in Mesopotamia cannot find one competent person — but I maintain that the history of the last few months has shown their political bankruptcy, and their opinion should not weigh with us at all. I know ten British officials with tried and honourable reputations in the Sudan, Sinai, Arabia, Palestine, each and all of whom could set up an Arab Government comparable to Feisal's, in Baghdad, next month. It also would not be a perfect government, but it would be better than Feisal's, for he, poor man, to pull him down, was forbidden foreign advisers. The Mesopotamian effort would have the British Government behind it, and would be child's play for a decent man to run, so long as he ran it like Cromer's Egypt, not like the Egypt of the Protectorate. Cromer dominated Egypt, not because England gave him force, or because Egypt loved us, or for any outside reason, but because he was so good a man. England has stacks of first-class men. The last thing you need out there is a genius. What is required is a tearing up of what we have done, and beginning again on advisory lines. It is no good patching with the present system.

'Concessions to local feeling' and such like rubbish are only weakness-concessions, incentives to more violence. We are big enough to admit a fault, and turn a new page: and we ought to do it with a hoot of joy, because it will save us a million pounds a week.

131: MESOPOTAMIA[1]

BY EX.-LIEUT.-COL. T. E. LAWRENCE
(Fellow of All Souls College, Oxford)

(*Mr. Lawrence, whose organisation and direction of the Hedjaz against the Turks was one of the outstanding romances of the war, has written this article at our request in order that the public may be fully informed of our Mesopotamian commitments.*)

The people of England have been led in Mesopotamia into a trap from which it will be hard to escape with dignity and honour. They have been tricked into it by a steady withholding of information. The Bagdad communiqués are belated, insincere, incomplete. Things have been far worse than we have been told, our administration more bloody and inefficient than the public knows. It is a disgrace to our imperial record, and may soon be too inflamed for any ordinary cure. We are to-day not far from a disaster.

The sins of commission are those of the British civil authorities in Mesopotamia (especially of three 'colonels') who were given a free hand by London. They are controlled from no Department of State, but from the empty space which divides the Foreign Office from the India Office. They availed themselves of the necessary discretion of war-time to carry over their dangerous independence into times of peace. They contest every suggestion of real self-government sent them from home. A recent proclamation about autonomy circulated with unction from Bagdad was drafted and published out there in a hurry, to forestall a more liberal statement in preparation in London. 'Self-determination papers' favourable to England were extorted in Mesopotamia in

[1] Printed in *The Sunday Times*, August 22nd, 1920.

1919 by official pressure, by aeroplane demonstrations, by deportations to India.

The Cabinet cannot disclaim all responsibility. They receive little more news than the public: they should have insisted on more, and better. They have sent draft after draft of reinforcements, without enquiry. When conditions became too bad to endure longer, they decided to send out as High Commissioner the original author of the present system, with a conciliatory message to the Arabs that his heart and policy have completely changed.[1]

Yet our published policy has not changed, and does not need changing. It is that there has been a deplorable contrast between our profession and our practice. We said we went to Mesopotamia to defeat Turkey. We said we stayed to deliver the Arabs from the oppression of the Turkish Government, and to make available for the world its resources of corn and oil. We spent nearly a million men and nearly a thousand million of money to these ends. This year we are spending ninety-two thousand men and fifty millions of money on the same objects.

Our government is worse than the old Turkish system. They kept fourteen thousand local conscripts embodied, and killed a yearly average of two hundred Arabs in maintaining peace. We keep ninety thousand men, with aeroplanes, armoured cars, gunboats, and armoured trains. We have killed about ten thousand Arabs in this rising this summer. We cannot hope to maintain such an average: it is a poor country, sparsely peopled; but Abd el Hamid would applaud his masters, if he saw us working. We are told the object of the rising was political, we are not told what the local people want. It may be what the Cabinet has promised them. A Minister in the House of Lords said that we must have so many troops because the local people will not enlist. On Friday the Government announce the death of some local levies defending their British officers, and say that the services of these men have not yet been sufficiently recognised because they are too few (adding the characteristic Bagdad touch that they are men of bad character). There are seven thousand of them, just half

---

[1] It had been decided that Sir Percy Cox was to return as High Commissioner the following October to form a provisional Government of Arab notables.

the old Turkish force of occupation. Properly officered and distributed, they would relieve half our army there. Cromer controlled Egypt's six million people with five thousand British troops; Colonel Wilson[1] fails to control Mesopotamia's three million people with ninety thousand troops.

We have not reached the limit of our military commitments. Four weeks ago the staff in Mesopotamia drew up a memorandum asking for four more divisions. I believe it was forwarded to the War Office, which has now sent three brigades from India. If the North-West Frontier cannot be further denuded, where is the balance to come from? Meanwhile, our unfortunate troops, Indian and British, under hard conditions of climate and supply, are policing an immense area, paying dearly every day in lives for the wilfully wrong policy of the civil administration in Bagdad. General Dyer was relieved of his command in India for a much smaller error, but the responsibility in this case is not on the Army, which has acted only at the request of the civil authorities. The War Office has made every effort to reduce our forces, but the decisions of the Cabinet have been against them.

The Government in Bagdad have been hanging Arabs in that town for political offences, which they call rebellion. The Arabs are not rebels against us. They are still nominally Turkish subjects, nominally at war with us. Are these illegal executions to provoke the Arabs to reprisals on the three hundred British prisoners they hold? And, if so, is it that their punishment may be more severe, or is it to persuade our other troops to fight to the last?

We say we are in Mesopotamia to develop it for the benefit of the world. All experts say that the labour supply is the ruling factor in its development. How far will the killing of ten thousand villagers and townspeople this summer hinder the production of wheat, cotton, and oil? How long will we permit millions of pounds, thousands of Imperial troops, and tens of thousands of Arabs to be sacrificed on behalf of a form of colonial administration which can benefit nobody but its administrators?

---

[1] Not to be confused with Colonel C. E. Wilson.

132: TO V. W. RICHARDS

[*August*, 1920]

[22 *lines omitted*] (II) Re Oxford. To finish my 'Boy-Scout' book by Sept. 30 will mean my spending August & September in All Souls: solid: the more you can come down in that time the better I will work: so please don't limit yourself to Sept. 24 etc. Any date in those days will do perfectly: and the longer the better. Your critical faculty would be invaluable: because though it's only a cheap book written to buy Pole Hill & build its house, yet it's got to have my name on it — therefore I don't want it to be despicable.

(III) *Re prose.*[1] *The extract sent* is nearly perfect: but prose depends on a music in one's head which involuntarily chooses & balances the possible words to *keep tune* with the thought. The best passages in English prose all deal with death or the vanity of things, since that is a tune we all know, and the mind is set quite free to think while writing about it. Only it can't be kept up very long, because of mortal weakness and the wear & tear of things, & the function of criticism, revision, & correction (polishing) seems to me to be either

(i) *putting* a thing into thought
(ii) [putting] thought into rhythm
(iii) putting *expression* into meaning.

It seems to me that if you think too hard about the form, you forget the matter, & if your brain is wrestling with the matter, you may not have attention to spare for the manner. Only occasionally in things constantly dwelt upon, do you get an unconscious balance, & then you get a *spontaneous* and perfect arrangement of words to fit the idea, *as the tune.* Polishing is an attempt, by stages, to get to what should be a single combined stride.   L.

----

[1] This letter is in pencil and much worn. I have italicized certain words which have been copied over.

133: TO H. R. HADLEY

2 Sept. 1920   *All Souls College, Oxford.*

Dear Hadley, It's very pleasant hearing from you, and of course I'll send you a photo. I can't do it today, because I haven't got one in stock ... but I'll look for one tomorrow. They were mostly done by that wild American, Lowell Thomas, who came to Akaba and took us all, and he never gave me copies. However as I looked a perfect idiot in most of those he published, there probably isn't much lost.

I remember your name, because Marshall[1] used to talk of you. I can't fit it with a face at present, but then I'm very bad at faces; indeed I always was, and my family also. My father one day stepped on my toe in the street, and apologised & went on without knowing who it was!

It's Tell el Shahm ... you've lost an h in writing it down: and it means the hill of fat.

I'm glad you found Arabia interesting. It was of course most interesting for me, because I understood all the Arab side of it: I often used to wonder whether you were not having a very dull time of it. I used to be up country on stunts nearly always, and many of you had to live in the dust & heat and flies of Akaba.

You mention a diary ... did you keep a full one, or did any of the other fellows? I was too busy, or too lazy to write down what happened properly, and none of the other officers wrote anything much. I wish there was a proper account of it for publication.

Marshall is, I think, in Khartoum. He was at Jidda, the port of Mecca, in the Red Sea for some time after the armistice, and then he went to the Sudan. I haven't seen any of the others for some time.

I wonder if you were of the Mudowwarah party which at last took the place? We had four boss shots at it, and took it the fifth try, when the I.C.C.[2] came along and rushed it in the dark. Marshall was there, for the second, fourth & fifth tries.

I enclose a couple of prints of that time, copies of some which Colonel Buxton who commanded the camels sent me. I have

---

[1] Medical Officer at Akaba.   [2] Imperial Camel Corps.

quite a good set of photos of the war (that is of our little bit of it) which I have collected from various people.[1]

I wish we could meet some time: Goslett is keeping all the addresses of the people as far as he can, & some day if we can manage it we'll have a dinner together somewhere.

I'll get you that photo in the next week or so, as soon as it can be copied. Yours sincerely   T E LAWRENCE

By the way, I'm not a Colonel now: just Mr. like yourself: if you have time write again & tell me what you are at, and if you ever see any others of us.

134: TO H. R. HADLEY

25.9.20   *All Souls College, Oxford.*

Dear Hadley, Here's this — it isn't much of a thing, but the best I can lay my hands on. I think Goslett took it, outside his tent at Akaba one day when I hadn't got my cloak on.

About Mecca.[2] I send you three photographs of it, taken by an Arab doctor. It is a curious place, without trees or running water, a very hot town, in narrow valleys between limestone hills. About 120000 people. It's not really so difficult to go there, if they know you, because the people are not fanatical. They keep Christians out because the other Moslems of the world (India & elsewhere) would be annoyed if we were allowed in: and if they were annoyed they might stop coming on pilgrimage, & the pilgrim traffic is all the revenue of the place. So if anyone asks me if I've been there I have to say 'no' in public: but in private you can guess about it! It mustn't get into the papers, because it would do the old King's[3] reputation harm.

We'll get that dinner some day: but I'll have to make some money first. Perhaps I'll write a book and make it that way. At present I'm completely on the rocks, and as I like my leisure very much I don't want to have to go and do a job of work again! The Govt. wanted me to go back East! Yours sincerely   T E LAWRENCE

---

[1] Some are to be seen at the Imperial War Museum. Others in private possession.
[2] See also last paragraph of letter No. 210 and letter No. 309.
[3] King Hussein of the Hejaz, the Sherif of Mecca.

135: TO C. M. DOUGHTY

Nov. 7. 1920.   *All Souls College, Oxford.*

Dear Mr. Doughty, Here is the proof back again, inked as you suggested, except on p. xxxv, where I have not put in 'Ottoman'. I've taken out the past participle, which broadens the sense. In some other places I have not used your actual word, mainly for the printer's sake, to lessen the disturbance of type. It is very good of you to have changed so little.

I quite understand your saying about your neglect of *Arabia Deserta*: and I'm entirely of your opinion that it is less than *Dawn in Britain*, *Mansoul*, & *Adam*: but it is easier than these others, & so it's the best wedge to drive into the public. They will all read *Arabia Deserta*, & those who are seized with it will go on to the poems afterwards. I advise those who ask me, to read *Adam* second, *Mansoul* third, & then *Dawn* — because *Dawn* has to be read whole, and it takes courage to start so long a book. Those who have taken my advice have all become partisans of yours: and the clan is getting a large one. Still, it may be years yet before you sweep the board, and meanwhile the best weapon is *Arabia*. It's exceedingly good to have it out again, and as fifty copies have been sold already, it looks as though it might sell fairly quickly. I hope so very much, because then we'll have a third, and cheap edition. Yours sincerely   T. E. LAWRENCE

136: TO COLONEL S. F. NEWCOMBE

Nov. 16 [1920].   *All Souls College, Oxford.*

Dear S.F.N., I came down last night & found masses of over-due letters: amongst them several of yours. The last should have been fire & brimstone: instead they showed forth an over-angelic sweetness of reason, which has prostrated me. It's no good writing to me at all: neither fair treatment nor foul move me to answer soon enough.

Your article I took up to London very quickly: as soon as I could after I got it. *Morning Post* I don't touch: it seems to me not sane. So there remained the *Daily Telegraph*. I tried to get

x

Lord Burnham, but failed (He was away in country). So then I left it for him, with an explanation.

I don't read the paper,[1] so I don't know on what date it appeared: judging from the two enclosed, it must have been last month. I don't like writing to ask when, because it would show that I don't every day lap up the food he offers. I take it the cheque was sent me for their convenience: and because I forgot to give them your address. I wish I had got it sooner, & that I had noted the day on which the article appeared.

I've signed the effort (the cheque) to facilitate your cashing it. I believe that is how things are done.

A sentence in your 3rd-letter-from-the-last troubles me: it concerns those beastly carpets. Has Mrs. Newcombe understood that carpet No. i. is her commission for retrieving them from Arab Bureau?

Carpet No. ii. is my instalment of wedding present, pending the receipt of a new fortune from some unspecified but overdue quarter.   E.L.

Pour les Irish: only one horrid word
You can't make war upon rebellion.   L.

[It was the newspaper campaign against the scandal of our Mesopotamian administration, with its cry of 'Evacuate Mesopotamia' made popular by the slump and the call for economy, rather than any desire to do justice to the Arabs, or to redeem our broken promises to them, which led Lloyd George to reverse the British policy in Mesopotamia for which, as Prime Minister, he had been responsible.

As early as June 9th, Colonel A. T. Wilson had telegraphed:

> We must be prepared to furnish alike men and money and maintain continuity of control for years to come. We must be prepared, regardless of the League of Nations, to go very slowly with constitutional or democratic institutions ... If His Majesty's Government regard such a policy as impracticable or beyond our strength, they would do better to face the alternative ... and evacuate Mesopotamia.

---

[1] The *Daily Telegraph* article appeared on October 30th, 1920, under Lawrence's name by mistake; it was really by Newcombe.

The alternatives were not acceptable and the Cabinet replied that they were entrusting Sir Percy Cox with the task of forming a provisional Arab Government. But this first step was not enough to appease either the inhabitants of Iraq or the newspaper critics at home. Sweeping changes, bringing sweeping economies, were required and Lloyd George decided to take the Middle East out of the hands of Lord Curzon at the Foreign Office and entrust it to Winston Churchill who went to the Colonial Office. Lawrence who had previously discussed the situation with Lloyd George, was appointed political adviser by Churchill and took up his duties in the same room as Sir John Shuckburgh and Major Hubert Young. Lawrence had stipulated that the promises made to the Arabs should be redeemed as far as was consistent with a French Syria, and that the plan which he had discussed with Trenchard, of evacuating the Army and making the Air Force responsible for internal order in Iraq, should be adopted.

In 1933 Lawrence made the following note on the typescript of Liddell Hart's '*T. E. Lawrence*': *In Arabia and After*.

As for the effect of the bombing, the war showed me that a combination of armoured cars and aircraft could rule the desert: but that they must be under non-army control, and without infantry support. You rightly trace the origin of the R.A.F. control in Irak, Aden & Palestine to this experience. As soon as I was able to have my own way in the Middle East I approached Trenchard on the point, converted Winston easily, tricked the Cabinet into approving (against the wiles of Henry Wilson[1]) — and it has worked very well. The system is *not* capable of universal application.

It will be realized from the letter to Lord Winterton of April 22nd (Letter No. 123) that he had discussed the scheme of Air Control with Trenchard long before he was appointed political adviser, and it would appear from that letter that Air Control in Iraq was Trenchard's idea.]

---

[1] Field-Marshal Sir Henry Wilson.

137: TO ROBERT GRAVES

Saturday [Dec. 1920]

My Lord, I'd just got as keen as mustard on going out with Kennington[1] when Winston Churchill in his third effort to get me to join his new Middle Eastern Department used arguments which I could not resist.

So I'm a Government servant from yesterday: and Palestine goes fut (or phut?).

Kennington is going all the same: (that man is a great man) and as an official I'll be able to help him even more than ever: but what a beastly mess.

They let me fix my own terms: so I said a temporary billet, and £1000: out of evil comes good for ———.

I had meant to publish the enclosed muck[2] in U.S.A., to raise £1000: and now I've written to say that I've made other arrangements. Will you read them now they are born to blush unseen? They are literal extracts from a book I wrote: but all the personal (subjective) part is left out for dignity's sake. It's bloody cheek asking you to read such muck: but the intrinsic interest may atone for the lack of technique: and as an artist you should be glad to peep behind the scenes of another's affair. [*omission*]

138: TO C. M. DOUGHTY

28. 1. 21.   *2 Smith Square Westminster.*

Dear Mr. Doughty, I hope to come down to Eastbourne on Wednesday next, arriving about half-past three, and leaving in the evening. I have had a great deal to do lately, and am still very busy.

About *Arabia Deserta*. Feisal would not wait for his large-paper copy, but is having the ordinary edition read to him, and is enjoying it very much. He is most tolerant, & would not take

---

[1] Lawrence had got to know Robert Graves while he was at All Souls, and Graves had introduced him to Eric Kennington who became eager to go out to paint several of the Arab leaders, and members of Lawrence's bodyguard, to illustrate *Seven Pillars of Wisdom*.

[2] Four articles in *The World's Work*.

offence at what was said about Islam, in any case. And in *A.D.* there is nothing very bad about Islam. These forty years have changed the Moslems very much.

When the weather gets warmer Feisal is going to drive down to you some day, and call. I am sure you will like him.

The portrait is to be regretted. One is necessary, I think, but it should not have been the old one. I'll try and exclude it from my private copy. These large-paper copies are going, inshallah, to be very sumptuous.

However we can talk of this when we meet. Yours sincerely

T E LAWRENCE

I think you were wise to discourage the translation of *A.D.* into Arabic.

139: TO LADY SCOTT[1]

2. 2. 21   2 *Smith Square S.W.*1.

Dear Lady Scott, This is very sudden! Once I was 'portrayed in bronze' by Derwent Wood. I met it suddenly in the Academy, & felt like the man in Rossetti who met himself in a wood! But then perhaps he isn't very deep. Dobson seems to me better. Once I played with stone & clay myself & dreamed of doing something: and the war spoiled it. So you'd find me critical.

Seriously if you want an object, I'll agree with pleasure: only it won't be a good speculation: it won't sell afterwards: and my face isn't so-to-speak virgin. John did it, as you say (though I liked the larger, full-faced one: the clothes were beautifully painted, & the face can't be worse than the truth): also D.– Wood: and Orpen: and now Rothenstein: really the features are quite worn away with so much study of them.

If you do do it, please hold me as a model, & not as 'the most romantic figure of the war' (American film-artist). I'm tired of the lime light, & am really not stagy at all, & not ever going to be a public figure again. It was a war effort, imposed, involun-

---

[1] Lady Scott, now Lady Kennet, made a statuette of Lawrence. Terra-cotta squeezes, in different colours, have since been made from the mould.

tary. Don't do me as Colonel Lawrence (he died Nov. 11. 1918) but because my shaped head suits your whim.

All this sounds very vain & silly. To be earthy again: am off tomorrow (wherefore this sudden haste to reply) till Tuesday. Could come Wed. morn: Fri. morn: or the week after: but won't unless on reflection you write here again & tell me you do really want it. That gives you three days to think it over. Probably start for Palestine Feb. 28.

Apologies for this long stupid screed, yours sincerely

T E LAWRENCE

140: TO C. M. DOUGHTY

Monday Feb. 7. [1921]   2 *Smith Square S.W.*1.

Dear Mr. Doughty, I got back from Oxford today to find your letters and parcel waiting for me: and the gift of *Arabia Deserta* makes me feel very embarrased. You have written my name in it, so it is a thing finished, & there is nothing to be said but thanks: — but it's a disproportionate present (£30 worth), and I don't think that you ought to have done it. Of course I'll value it as much as it should be valued . . . but I feel myself too deeply in your debt for the moment. I begged so many things off you last Wednesday.

Marsh, who is Mr. Churchill's secretary, was delighted with the Ateyfa manuscript. He's a very good fellow, who has done great work in helping young poets, & the reward he likes for himself is knowing them. It is not possible for you to come to town, so the autograph was the next best thing: and you gave him a very splendid extract. I expect it comes about p. 74-75 of *Mansoul*: and it must make that desert section very much richer. A man at Oxford who writes, called Masefield, was speaking properly about *Adam* and *Mansoul*, to me yesterday. He's not very much of a poet, but is a popular one, and is valued as a critic, so that it is not entirely empty praise. People are talking much about *Arabia* just now. The reviews, and the challenge of the £9 9. 0 price, wake them up. Garvin seemed to me good in the *Observer* yesterday.

About the ordinary copies I bought. Two of the officers who served with me in Feisal's armies are just getting married. They are both good people, and fond of books, which are a handy present, as they can be carried about from garrison to garrison. So it was most fitting that I should give them *Arabia Deserta*, and especially copies with your autograph in them. At the same time the essence of wedding-presents is that they be something bought, and so it was at once necessary & pleasant to buy them. I only wish three or four more of my friends would get married before the edition is exhausted: but there is little chance of that. Please don't think of sending me anything more. I'm overpaid many times already in the pleasure of seeing *A.D.* in shop windows for sale. I hope you will help me never to let it out of print again. The third edition is now the thing to think about.

Will you please tell Mrs. Doughty that the drawing is being photographed in the best conditions by the South Kensington Museum people? If the results are passed by you, they will ask for permission to keep a copy for their library. I hope to hear of it tomorrow, and will write when I do.

There is another request, but not mine this time. I'm only a pillar-box. The War Office are drawing a new and very elaborate map of parts of Arabia. They include the Hejaz, Jebel Shammar, & the Kasim-Mecca routes. They have used all published maps, including yours: but the scale is 1/300,000, about 5 miles to an inch, in some places, and so to supplement the published material they have used the MSS sketches in the note-books of Huber, Shakespear, Philby, myself, and others. I was looking at the sheets of this map, still of course in pencil, only drawing sheets, & mentioned to the officer in charge that your notes are full of local sketches: (particularly I remembered one of the Medowwara kella, and the hills round it, which shows more than anyone else has shown.) He asked me at once if you would lend your notes. I said I'd write and ask. He would take the greatest care of them, and return them without marking or soiling them in any way: and would be very glad if he might keep them for some weeks at least, while his compiler went along the route and added what was to add. He knows of course that you will probably not care to risk them out of your hands: but if you are willing, will you send them, registered of course, to Captain D. A. Hutchison R.E. M.I.4. War Office S.W.1. He will acknowledge receipt, & express great gratitude! This has been a very long letter: my apologies, & please give my best regards to Mrs. Doughty & your daughters. Yours sincerely   T E LAWRENCE

141: TO EDWARD MARSH

24.2.21.

I don't know that you read prose, except on official subjects: this is unofficial. They are objective extracts* from a MSS story I wrote of Feisal's campaign.

I was short of cash, and wrote these for an American magazine, which was willing to blow £1000 on the speculation.

Now I'm going to get my £1000 by the sweat of my brain: so these retire into the darkness again.[1]

They may make you laugh: and after all it's not like a telephone call. You needn't unhook them: they can be minuted back to me saying 'have seen' or 'good': or 'most amusing': or 'I really think you ought to publish them'.

These are only suggestions.

I don't ever want to see them again: but they would be difficult to destroy: so perhaps you might return them next year or so.   E.L.

*35,000 words: 10°/₀ of the whole.

[The lines along which the new Arab state of Iraq should be organized were decided in London, before Churchill with Lawrence and Major Hubert Young went out in March to the Cairo Conference which was attended by all those responsible for British Government and military organization in the Middle East. It included Sir Herbert Samuel, Sir Percy Cox, Miss

---

[1] These extracts were published in 1921 in the July, August, September and October numbers of *The World's Work*, New York, under the titles: 'With Feisal at Court and Afield'; 'Arabian Nights and Days'; 'Adventures in Arabia's Deliverance'. Robert Graves has explained that Lawrence gave him the money he received for these contributions to save him from the bankruptcy court. (*Lawrence and the Arabs*, p. 153.)

Gertrude Bell, Jaafar Pasha, Sir Hugh Trenchard and General Geoffrey Salmond.

Feisal was put forward as a candidate for the throne who was persona grata with the British Government, and, largely owing to the influence of Gertrude Bell, was elected the following June by an overwhelming majority of the Iraqis. Trenchard, backed by Lawrence, put forward the plan for Air Control in Iraq at an estimated cost many millions below the lowest conceivable for an army of occupation. This, incidentally, was of a double benefit to the British taxpayer, since Iraq provided an ideal training ground for the R.A.F. and was its great opportunity. The settlement of Iraq naturally disappointed many ambitions and some British officers who left the service were unable to see any good in the regime and have consistently attacked Lawrence's reputation not only as a political adviser but as a soldier and a writer and a man, and indeed on every possible occasion.]

142: TO C. M. DOUGHTY

20. 5. 21.   *Colonial Office*

Dear Mr. Doughty, I'm back again in England, for a little bit (next move probably Jidda), after spending six weeks across Jordan, most of it in Amman, where conditions are strange, & rather exciting.[1]

I'd like to see you, but I hear you are away from Eastbourne.

Your third edition is just being made ready, so Cape tells me: it's very good to have sold out in three months, better than I ever hoped: for the really large sales will not be touched till the cheap edition appears, and for that we will probably have to wait some years.

I got a note from you when I got back, enclosing a cutting from the *Times* Correspondent at Maan! I'm afraid he got no

---

[1] Compare the following statement from Sir Arnold Wilson's *Thoughts and Talks*, 1938.

'Mr. Winston Churchill induced "T. E. Shaw" to immure himself for a year in Downing Street as an adviser on Arab policy. He was not happy looking at the East from a secluded corner. He never revisited Arabia or Syria and he gladly threw the mantle of office from his shoulders'. See also Lawrence's Report of Trans-Jordan (No. 147) *et seq*.

nearer than Jerusalem in the flesh, & not so near as that in his facts. My regards to Mrs. Doughty.

Yours sincerely   T E LAWRENCE

143: TO ERIC KENNINGTON

12 *June.* [1921]   *Colonial Office.*

Dear Kennington, I should have written a fortnight ago: but I was always hoping to have some news to tell you.

I saw your brother: but can't find Clark:[1] he is not in when I pass up Knightsbridge.

About myself: I nearly came straight out again: but then they stopped me: till Winston's speech: and that's not till Tuesday: and now in the postponement plans have changed, and instead of Jordan it's Jidda, the port of Mecca on the Red Sea, for me. I'm off there, for July, the most stinking month in the year: and then Aden for August. Enough said. I'm fixed and finished and very sorry. I hope your affairs are not going too dully.

There was a fight — but it won't be big this summer: no general rising yet.   yrs.   E.L.

144: TO C. M. DOUGHTY

13.6.21.   *Colonial Office*

Dear Mr. Doughty, I should have replied earlier, but I've been hoping to come down to see you, and have only just given up hope of it. There is too much to do here: Winston is going to make his speech in the house tomorrow, and when the trouble of that is over I will probably be sent to Jidda to see King Hussein. In that case I will try to steal a journey to Taif, and have a look at the country round about it.

Abdulla is in Trans-Jordan, carrying on a government there with our help, but without any formal appointment. Indeed he refused one, until his father had been consulted, and had approved. That was a polite way of saying never.

---

[1] An artist who drew for *Seven Pillars of Wisdom.*

No, I'm afraid there is no blue-book of the Hejaz war, & probably will never be. We sent some reports back to Egypt, but they were kept secret, and are now buried somewhere among the records.[1]

My friend Aubrey Herbert, a very splendid creature, has asked me to get your autograph to his copies of *Arabia Deserta*. One, that with Feisal's signature upon it, is for a wedding present to his brother. I'm sending them you by post, with two things of my own — the first sheet of the large-paper *A.Ds*. I'd be very much obliged if you would sign all four!

With apologies for troubling you, yours sincerely T E LAWRENCE

145: TO C. M. DOUGHTY

18. VI. 21.   *C. O.* [*Colonial Office*]

Dear Mr. Doughty, Many thanks for signing those books: Aubrey Herbert asks me to thank you specially for his copies. Autographed *A.D's*. by you are found rather thrilling things by people.

The Middle East is all upset: and Hussein is, as you suspect, not popular in Mecca! However, he is strong, & if I go up to Taif it will probably be in one of his cars: and they are too quick for the hand of the ordinary fanatic. We are going to give him some armoured cars, which will make the roads quite safe for the pilgrims. They are much better than camel-police.

About the 3rd edition of *Arabia*. I've withdrawn my note because it's in bad taste. Lee Warner faced the gamble of the reprint more readily because my name was on the title-page, with yours, and I've been much advertised, & so would help sell it — perhaps. Well, it sold excellently, & now *A.D.* will go on selling. Lee Warner and Cape have both done better than they ever hoped out of the 2nd edition: and they can stand on their own feet quite well for the 3rd, which will cost them very little, and pay them handsomely. I hope it will be profitable to you also.

The cheaper edition must come some time, but not just yet, in deference to those who have made it possible by paying for the dear edition. I think perhaps in 1925, or thereabouts.

[1] *The Arab Bulletin.*

If you write a new preface for this third edition (I see no real need for writing anything new at all), I think it should only be something formal. It isn't really possible for you to say why I withdraw my bit, ('he felt he had acted like a tourist, & scribbled his name on a monument' . . . but you are the monument, & it wouldn't be manners to call yourself that), and I don't see why the public should want to know at all.

If I were you I'd change the photograph for the reproduction of the French sketch of you in Damascus, & let it go out without new work at all!

Though of course if you feel inclined to say anything it's worth saying: only don't say it just because Cape wants it!

There'll be a fourth edition in 1922, I expect. Please get an increased royalty every time. *A.D.* should be a little gold mine, eventually. Yours sincerely   T E LAWRENCE

[On June 30th, 1921, 'Our most trusty and well-beloved Thomas Edward Lawrence Esquire, Lieutenant Colonel in Our Army, Companion of Our Most Honourable Order Of the Bath, Companion of Our Distinguished Service Order', had been appointed a plenipotentiary under the great seal of England to treat with the King of the Hejaz. Lawrence preserved this document and, strange to say, took it to Uxbridge R.A.F. depot with him the following year, when he enlisted under the name of J. H. Ross and was anxious to hide his identity!

Lawrence left for Arabia on July 8th, 1921, going to Jidda, to negotiate with King Hussein. It was during this summer that he had the two carved doors of teak, now at Clouds Hill but at one time at Pole Hill, Chingford, sent back to England.

From the Hejaz, Lawrence went down to Aden during the summer and returned to Trans-Jordan in the early autumn, meeting his mother and his brothers at Jerusalem, and driving with them to Es-Salt. The Lawrences' home in Oxford had been disposed of earlier in the year. His elder brother, Dr. M. R. Lawrence, was on his way out to join the China Inland Mission, where his mother followed him a year later.

The establishment of Abdulla in Trans-Jordan was due not to Lawrence, or to the decisions of the Cairo Conference, but chiefly to Abdulla's own initiative in going there. Lawrence explained the matter in a conversation which Liddell Hart summarised as follows.

'When and how did Abdulla receive Trans-Jordan?'

'Abdulla went up to Amman with idea of reprisal for his brother's expulsion from Damascus by the French. Trouble threatened. L. suggested solution to Churchill: "I know Abdulla: you won't have a shot fired". L. fetched Abdulla to Jersualem, avoiding taking him through city, and Churchill's personal decision was taken in half an hour's talk at Mount of Olives — it was exactly contrary to the decision reached at Cairo Conference.'

This statement is borne out by the undated 'Minutes of a meeting on Trans-Jordania' between Abdulla, Sir Herbert Samuel, Mr. Churchill and Lawrence, which I have read.]

146: TO ERIC KENNINGTON

1 *October.* [1921] *Grand Continental Hotel Cairo.*

Dear Kennington, Your letter today. It made me realise that I never wrote to you from Jidda to explain my wire stopping W. & G.[1] Peccavi: always I have. Why does a person who fails to write letters feel unfit to live? There's nothing wrong in it: and the feeling is sterile, because it does not make one write. Now I owe you two or three letters.

The reasons for stopping work are three. I do not know their order of magnitude. A lump of money I was expecting has not (probably will not) come. My house in Epping has been burnt down. In the leisure hours of this trip I have read half the manuscript of my book: and condemned it. Not good enough to publish, because it isn't as good as I can make it, (unless I deceive myself).

The stoppage is only to prevent too big a bill this year. Next year I will have more money, and will be able to carry on. Meanwhile I'll be barely solvent. Penury is as mean an ill as toothache. The job will go through none the less. I'm glad you find it good: am looking forward to seeing Ghalib[2] on my return.

---

[1] Whittingham and Griggs, The Chiswick Press, were preparing the collotype plates of Kennington's portraits of Arabs to be used in *Seven Pillars of Wisdom*. Their preparation went on for many, many years.

[2] Kennington's pastel portrait, reproduced in *Seven Pillars of Wisdom*.

The return is yet vague. Tomorrow I go to Trans-Jordan, to end that farce. It makes me feel like a baby-killer. The last two months I've been in the Red Sea, and things are not ended there. I'd like to come home before ending them: if I am to end them. So perhaps at the end of October? God knows.

The preface[1] I have now forgotten all the sense and shape of, except that it was too long. As it is forgotten it must have been light, and little-thought-on. Aden is not good for work: and I'd written a good one in London after seeing the collection, and left it buried somewhere. However I hope the show goes well. Prefaces are only excuses (by the salesman) for charging a shilling for the catalogue.

What more? Nothing. I'm bored stiff: and very tired, and a little ill, and sorry to see how mean some people I wanted to respect have grown. The war was good by drawing over our depths that hot surface wish to do or win something. So the cargo of the ship was unseen, and not thought of. This life goes on till February 28 next year. Au 'voir   TEL

[I have been allowed, by the Colonial Office, to make use of the first two paragraphs of the following confidential report. The remainder of the document, dealing largely with the financial affairs of Trans-Jordan, afforded less scope for Lawrence's humour, which was entirely at the expense of the British and not of the Arabs, who, as he reported, were doing very well with the means at their disposal.]

147: COLONEL LAWRENCE'S REPORT OF TRANS-JORDAN

24/10/21

I went over to Amman on October 12th to enquire into the present position there.

(1) BRITISH UNITS

The Armoured Cars were not fit for use. We obtained them

---

[1] Lawrence wrote a preface to the Catalogue of Kennington's show of Arab portraits at the Leicester Galleries.

with some difficulty from the War Office, in the expectation that
they would assist in maintaining order in Trans-Jordania. They
had not been out of Camp for weeks before my arrival. The cars
were in fair mechanical condition. They had no covers or tubes,
no mechanical spares, no lamps or batteries, no jacks or pumps,
no petrol. For the two cars there were two drivers and two
gunners — not enough to man the cars or fight the guns, though
in this case it was no matter since there were no gun belts, no
ammunition, no gun spares. Of the two drivers, one was a 'second
driver', intended to take over in an emergency. How good he is
I do not know. The first driver, who is supposed to be qualified,
can drive the car forward but is not good at reversing. He is
practising this on the path between the tents. I think the Air
Ministry should be informed of the condition of the section before
they are called upon to pay the War Office for its maintenance
charges.

Group Captain Gordon arrived to take over the command of
the Royal Air Force and attached cars a few days after my arrival.
I believe he will make the units under his charge efficient in a
few days time. We will then carry out a programme of operations.

(2) ARAB UNITS

The Reserve Force under Zaim Peake Bey now numbers 500
odd. The men are good, some of the Officers very good. The
tone and condition of the Unit is very promising. I think
internally it is as well as possible and it reflects great credit on
Zaim Peake Bey that it is so.

Externally things are less satisfactory. At first people in Trans-
Jordania said we were making an Army to smash them for our
own purposes. Then as time went on they said we were pur-
posely creating an inefficient force to give us an excuse for sending
British troops across. The reason for this has been the delay in
supplying equipment and materials. Uniforms, saddles, machine
guns, rifles, have all been held up. Peake cannot show his men in
public till they are reasonably smart and till they have rifles, for
in Trans-Jordania every man of military age carries a rifle as a
mark of self-respect, and Peake's, the so-called Military Force, is
the only unarmed body of men in the country. When this is set
right public suspicion will go to rest. [*remainder of the report omitted*]

148: TO COLONEL S. F. NEWCOMBE

8.XI.21   *Amman.*

Dear S.F.N., There's only one thing to tell the French: that
the catching of assassins is no doubt desirable, & one of the functions of government: but that we in Trans-Jordan have first to
make the government, and then to make public opinion disapprove of political assassination. After this the capture of assassins
becomes timely. Meanwhile it would be silly, & I'll have no part
in it. We cannot afford to chuck away our hopes of building
something to soothe our neighbour's feelings: and the French
have made our job here as difficult as possible — if it is possible
at all — by their wanton disregard of the common decencies
observed between nations.

Please remind them that they shot Arab prisoners after Meisa-
lun and plundered the houses & goods of Feisal & his friends.
The dirty-dog work has been fairly shared, & I thank what Gods
I have that I'm neither an Arab nor a Frenchman — only the poor
brute who has to clean up after them.

Last week we went to Maan by train & trolly: as soon as we
get a petrol depot in Maan we'll go to Tebuk. Have got an
excellent trolly thanks to Holmes who's a Prince.

If you can, drop over here friendly-fashion some time, & I'll
show you the French picture from underneath. Not lovely. à toi
                                                         TEL.

149: TO ERIC KENNINGTON

8. XI. 21.   *Amman.*

Dear Kennington, Scott has sent me a note from you, written
in the Euston Hotel. It crossed one from me which largely
answered it. Also three days back I got your volume of portraits,
with letter. It's very good of you to have sent me that, and they
came most timely. The household here is delighted with them.
Ghalib is in ecstasies, and all the other subjects are talking about
one another. I'm very glad the show was a success, and it's good
that it may tour the country. I've asked my bank to pay you £720,

which was, I think, our bargain. I want you to cancel it, if you are losing money by it. They say everything sold off, and I don't want to do you out of possibly better prices than the one I paid.

Many thanks for guaranteeing Whittingham & Griggs. I've mislaid their address, and so can't write to them: but when I get back will look them up in the Telephone book and pay them. I hope to have a little money in the new year, and will then carry on with the colour work. Ghalib is v.G.

Your personal news did not surprise me. Of course it makes a muddle, and to that extent is disagreeable. Our social state is at fault in making exceptions to its rules so difficult. It's not right that the individuals should have all these troubles in putting themselves straight. I hope in your case that it will go as well as possible.

You say you are going abroad. I wish I was keeping on here, because this place is getting fit for women now, and it would have been delightful and profitable (how Scotch one gets) to have had you wandering about the country. However I'm due to leave in about a fortnight, and should be in London about December 10. If plans change I'll let you know. Do let me know yours also, so that if possible we can meet somewhere.

Very best of luck in the new effort. Yours   E.L.

150: TO ERIC KENNINGTON

12. 3. 22.   14 *Barton St. S.W.*1.

Dear Kennington, Your drawings all came down to the Colonial Office, where they had a tremendous success. The Department did no work for three days while the Office came and looked at them: and now the wives of the Office are constantly here in the dinner hour. It's very proper, and very good.

When they came there were about 27 of them. Some obviously not mine (including the Storrs) I've sent to Brown Phillips.[1] [12 *lines omitted*]

I can't come anywhere now. Left the C.O. on Feb. 28 and have been there daily since: more happening than ever: and it's

---

[1] Proprietors of the Leicester Galleries.

hopeless. Will you make me your chauffeur when you come home. I suppose about May? Fed up: Yours,   T.E.L.

[Lawrence had learned that Doughty was in financial difficulties and set to thinking of devices to remedy this. One was to purchase the manuscript of *The Dawn in Britain* and present it to the British Museum. I have reason to think that Lawrence contributed the lion's share of this money himself.]

151: TO C. M. DOUGHTY

23. 3. 22   14 *Barton Street Westminster*

Dear Mr. Doughty, I did write to you too soon. The group last night sent me a final offer of only £400. There is precedent for this figure in the case of another living poet: and that has out-weighed my arguments for £500. If I could have used the argument that you really needed the money they would have given the five: it is the price paid for nice feeling. I'm very sorry for the false expectation. In your yesterday's letter you hope they are not your friends. I have seen five of them. One says he once met you, but he can advance no details, and I think flatters himself. The others know only your work. They are an informal group, like the Amis du Louvre, and acquired e.g. the MS. of *The Dynasts*, a long poem by Hardy, for the Museum. The principals each assume responsibility for a fraction of the price. Perhaps they pay it themselves, perhaps they ask friends to help them. Anyway they do not tell, & I'm not supposed to mention even their names. The objects are put in the Museum labelled 'from a body of subscribers'. I do not think you need fear their making appeals to anyone not very able to pay.

Of course the transaction is not possible to class commercially. The manuscript is unique, & made rarer by the destruction of most of your others. It is worth as little as you will sell it for: as much as anyone will give: only in this case you preferred the British Museum as the repository, and that limited competition. The offer made is an act of faith, or a gamble, as you look on it. They estimate that the eventual popular reputation of your poetry will be what their expert opinion now thinks it. Work merely good does not always prevail, and no one on earth can say what your manuscripts will be worth fifty years hence: possibly much more than £400 put out at compound interest: possibly less.

Will you let me have your reply, if possible this week? If you agree to sell (and in spite of that missed hundred I think it a fairly good offer) I'll tell the people. They say they will send me the money in a week after, and I could bring it down in one of my tea-time excursions to Eastbourne, & carry off the book when I go.

People I meet are delighted at the *Observer* article. Hogarth should take a leaf out of my bad book, and ask you to let him use it as a preface to the second edition of his history, which will probably be one of its results!

I hope Mrs. Doughty continues to improve. Yours sincerely

T E LAWRENCE

We can discuss other ways of making money when we meet. It is rather fun. If I had been appointed your press-agent about 1900 I'd have grown fat on my commission long ago!   TEL.

152: TO SYDNEY COCKERELL[1]

31.3.22   [14 *Barton Street*]

Dear Cockerell, I went down to Eastbourne yesterday, paid Doughty his £400: and carried off *The Dawn in Britain*. No difficulty arose at the last moment.

I'll give it to the B.M. this afternoon, & the fact will be published possibly next week. And on Thursday I may start for Bagdad!

Homer arrived: he's very handsome, & the inscription does you credit after my remarks on Saturday. I'm very grateful to you for the kindness: and will hope in turn to re-read the *Odyssey* duly when I get back from the East. The Air Mail restrictions of baggage will not allow me to carry it out across the desert.

John is finishing Mme. Suggia tomorrow & sending her to the Academy. She will make a splash.

[1] Director of the Fitzwilliam Museum, Cambridge.

When I get back from the East (d.c.) perhaps we will meet in Cambridge: but improbably. I fear you will have to come to London. Yours sincerely   T E LAWRENCE

153: TO ERIC KENNINGTON

10. 4. 22.

Dear Kennington, I'm afraid Lenin isn't coming: or Trotsky, only people like Litvinoff, Tchicherin & Co, who look like woodworms.[1] I don't know any of them, but if you want to try for them you'd better take this note in your own hand and get through with it to Sir Edward Grigg, who is secretary to Lloyd George, and one of the men of reason. If you tell him that you are a member of the Round Table (mine, not his) and show him this scrawl he'll do what he can: how much that is depends on the way the Conference goes. It's likely to be rather more than any other foreigner can do.

I've had my tenth resignation to Winston rejected, and am sitting in my attic, writing at the never-to-be-presentable-published-or-finished book. Your Arabs disturb the course of work in the Colonial Office as much as ever. Lady Cowdray has hopped the Kensingtons[2] out of Milbank, and Aitken wants two or three Arabs on loan to brighten up his modern room. About July I hope to get Whittingham & Griggs on to do a block of four. I discover that Ageyli is necessary for myself: he's v.g. I'll settle when you come back. I hope all's well. Aloes[3] are rather shock-headed friends.   E. L.

It's easier to do creative imaginative work under 30: though you can go on doing it after, if you have
<blockquote>
(i) a memory of what youth was like
or (ii) an incapacity for fixed ideas.
</blockquote>
Very often after 40 the hardness of the thirties breaks down, and

---

[1] Kennington, then in Italy, had hoped to draw Lenin, who he had heard was coming to attend the Economic Conference at Genoa.

[2] A picture on glass by Kennington of the Kensington Regiment at Laventie.

[3] Kennington had been drawing them.

men become artists again, till nearly 60. I personally at 33 notice very little change in myself since about 1914.   L

Can't find Dobson: but he is rumoured alive and fit.

154: TO D. G. HOGARTH

7.6.22.   *14, Barton Street,*

You know Carruthers'[1] address. He was very honourable about Doughty, and has edited Shakespear[2] honourably. Do you think he'd like the enclosed? Your copy of the whole will come later, but this lot covers the scrap of traverse which I once worked out and sent him. If he doesn't want it I'd like it back. I'm conscious of a horrible word about geographers in the middle of it: but perhaps he'll excuse it. There's been a bad habit lately among Arabians (Butler and Aylmer, Leachman, Shakespear, Philby) of dehumanising their journeys. This I'm in revolt against, though I'm afraid my own treks are rather barren of life: however I had the excuse of a main preoccupation with the war. In peace time a leisurely person could pick up a mass of good stuff.

These chapters run from Wejh to Nebk in Wadi Sirhan. My translation is rather individual. I try to keep some of the phonetic variety one meets.

If C. is interested I've got a mass of photographs of the section covered. They are all bad for we had to carry them for 3 months before they could be developed: and the heat blistered them all.

Tell him that of course I don't want this stuff circulated. I have no intention of publishing any part of it: but it may interest him. I don't think that there's much more than this and the compass readings in my notes. And here's a list (N. to S.) of the water-supplies I noted in Sirhan. It has only an academic interest. By the way Philby proposes (at Jauf) to go across to Bagdad! He's done all Sirhan from Azrak southwards now, and is establishing landing grounds and car tracks. Soon everybody will be running down for weekends — like Biskra.   T.E.L.

[37 *Arabic names of water holes omitted*]

¹ Douglas Carruthers, Arabian explorer and author, had contributed to the purchase of Doughty's *The Dawn in Britain*. He used the material sent him in *The Desert Route to India*.

² Captain Shakespear, see letter No. 81.

[While Lawrence was at the Colonial Office the Anglican Bishop in Jerusalem, Dr. McInnes, became much disturbed at the following passage in *Zionism and World Politics* by Horace M. Kallon:

> Animated perhaps by the vision of a continuous British protectorate, from the Mediterranean to India, the military administration, backed by the missionary interest, took advantage of the rules imposed by the Hague Convention regarding the government of occupied enemy territory, to sabotage the Balfour Declaration and to establish their own programme as a fait accompli. Anti-Semitism among high officials had not a little to do with the matter; ignorance, stupidity, and incompetence among their subordinates not a little. That they were not officially made aware of the Balfour Declaration helped. That, as Colonel Lawrence pointed out to Dr. Weizmann, Episcopal dioceses with missionary interests organized anti-Jewish propaganda, helped.

The Bishop on December 15th, 1921, wrote to Lawrence demanding a denial of the statement attributed to him, and suggesting that he might find it necessary to publish their correspondence in the Press. On February 2nd Lawrence seems to have replied, referring the Bishop to the High Commissioner for Palestine, Sir Herbert Samuel. The following 10th May Winston Churchill pointed out that 'the book in question was published before Colonel Lawrence became a member of the Colonial Office, and consequently, that expressions of opinion attributed to him by the writer are of no concern to this Department.'

The Bishop however stuck to his point and on June 23rd wrote once more demanding a reply, adding that he would shortly be arriving in London.

Two drafts of Lawrence's replies to the Bishop exist.]

155:

1ST DRAFT OF LETTER TO THE ANGLICAN BISHOP IN JERUSALEM

My dear Bishop, I will now answer your letter. You wish me to deny statements which a third person declares I made to Dr.

Weizmann. I will do nothing of the sort. I have never in my life denied any published statement attributed to me, and am not tempted to begin in your three-cornered case. Especially as I suspect you want my denials only to assure yourself and triumph over Dr. Weizmann, a great man whose boots neither you nor I, my dear Bishop, are fit to black. I beg you not to consider this letter in any way rude. When we next have the happiness to meet (it will be here in England) I will have the pleasure of showing you that its rudeness is only relative.

[Lawrence tried his hand again and the second draft, though less insulting, must have been exasperating since it gave the Bishop nothing to take hold of.]

156:
2ND DRAFT OF LETTER TO THE ANGLICAN BISHOP IN JERUSALEM

[1922].   [*Colonial Office*].

My dear Bishop, Really! I had hoped that in the long delay since you first wrote you would have realised what you were asking. In effect you say that Dr. Kallon says that Dr. Weizmann said that I said something three years ago in Paris: that this something might ingeniously be held to reflect on you — and will I deny it!

Many odd remarks have been attributed to me in the last four years: but I have never denied any of them, because I never saw one worth denial: and this seems to me two-penny half-penny. Frankly I do not understand such sensitiveness on your part.

And you wish to send the letters to the press! That's your taste, not mine. I'd like to advise you not to issue a blank denial — it's a futile, sterile, incredible thing: nor would it be good play for you to give Dr. Kallon the benefit of your enviable publicity. In your place I'd either allow it to be stated that personally and officially you have supported the policy of the British Government in Palestine: or else I'd have it pointed out that your situation as Bishop precludes you from expressing public views on political matters. I confess to being ignorant on just how you stand on Zionism: but am sure that it is correctly.

If you are coming to England, as I suspect by the address you give me, then do drop in and see me some day — prefacing yourself if possible by a note, as my habits are as irregular as my handwriting with this awful pen. Believe me, Yours very sincerely

T E LAWRENCE

[The following letter appeared in *The Morning Post* of July 20th, 1922, under the heading, 'Arabian Politics: Resignation of Colonel Lawrence as Adviser'.]

157: TO SIR JOHN SHUCKBURGH

4th July, 1922.

My dear Shuckburgh, It seems to me that the time has come when I can fairly offer my resignation from the Middle East Department. You will remember that I was an emergency appointment, made because Mr. Churchill meant to introduce changes in our policy, and because he thought that my help would be useful during the expected stormy period.

Well, that was eighteen months ago; but since we 'changed direction', we have not had, I think, a British casualty in Palestine or Arabia or the Arab provinces of Irak. Political questions there are still, of course, and wide open; there always will be, but their expression and conduct has been growing steadily more constitutional. For long there has not been an outbreak of any kind; and while it would be foolish to seem too hopeful, yet at the same time I think there is no present prospect of trouble.

As I said, I think of myself as an emergency appointment. There are many other things I want to do and I came in unwillingly in the first place. While things run along the present settled and routine lines I can see no justification for the Department's continuing my employment — and little for me to do if it is continued. So if Mr. Churchill permits, I shall be very glad to leave so prosperous a ship. I need hardly say that I'm always at his disposal if ever there is a crisis, or any job, small or big, for which he can convince me that I am necessary.

I have to thank you personally for the very pleasant conditions under which I have worked in the Department itself.
yours sincerely,   T. E. LAWRENCE

[Lawrence left the Colonial Office in the early summer of 1922, and it is perhaps appropriate to insert here his own view of the work done while he was Churchill's adviser on Arab affairs. The following extract is from the manuscript Preface, dated November 18th, 1922, to an abridgement of the Oxford Text of *Seven Pillars of Wisdom*, made by Edward Garnett but never published. It shows that Lawrence regarded his work as ended.]

158: DRAFT PREFACE

18. 11. 22

The book dates itself to 1919, when powerful elements in the British Government were seeking to evade their war-time obligations to the Arabs. That stage ended in March 1921, when Mr. Winston Churchill took charge of the Middle East. He set honesty before expediency in order to fulfil our promises in the letter and in the spirit. He executed the whole McMahon undertaking (called a treaty by some who have not seen it) for Palestine, for Trans-Jordania, and for Arabia. In Mesopotamia he went far beyond its provisions, giving to the Arabs more, and reserving for us much less, than Sir Henry McMahon had thought fit.

In the affairs of French Syria he was not able to interfere, and the Sherif of Mecca can fairly complain that the settlement there is not yet in accordance with the Anglo-French agreement of 1916, or with our word to him. I say 'not yet' advisedly, since the McMahon proposals (being based on racial and economic reasons) were likely to have imposed themselves eventually, even if Mr. Churchill's progressive British military withdrawal from Mesopotamia had not come to prejudge the future of all the Arab areas.

I do not wish to publish secret documents, nor to make long explanations: but must put on record my conviction that England is out of the Arab affair with clean hands. Some Arab advocates (the most vociferous joined our ranks after the Armistice) have rejected my judgment on this point. Like a tedious Pensioner I showed them my wounds (over sixty I have, each scar evidence of a pain incurred in Arab service) as proof I had worked sincerely on their side. They found me out-of-date: and I was happy to withdraw from a political milieu which had never been congenial.

PART FOUR

THE YEARS OF HIDE AND SEEK
1922 — 1929

INTRODUCTION TO PART FOUR

159: TO AN UNKNOWN CORRESPONDENT[1]

[*omission of uncertain length*]
On the whole I believe that not doing is better than doing, and I
believe mankind will reach its zenith when it determines to
propagate art no more . . . I have done with politics, I have done
with the Orient, and I have done with intellectuality. O Lord,
I am so tired! I want so much to lie down and sleep and die.
Die is best because there is no reveille. I want to forget my sins
and the world's weariness.   13 years after Paris.[2]

A SAINT is abnormal; a film star is abnormal; Lawrence was
subjected to the strains of the states of mind attaching to
each. He, and the figure he had created, 'Colonel Lawrence of
Arabia', were partly the one, partly the other. He was sick of
Colonel Lawrence and determined to escape him, in spite of
Bernard Shaw's pointing out that it was impossible for him to do
so, in these words.

'You didn't keep quiet; and now Lawrence you will be to the
end of your days and thereafter to the end of what we call modern
history. Lawrence may be as great a nuisance to you sometimes
as G.B.S. is to me, or as Frankenstein found the man he had
manufactured: but you created him and must now put up with
him as best you can.'

The Ivory Tower — the hut at Pole Hill — did not solve his
problem. He could not find a refuge in a sheltered life, or in
hand-work. He could not go back to archaeology — for the
East was closed to him, and he seems never to have been attracted
towards the buried cities of Mexico, or British Honduras. He

---

[1] This extract was copied by Colonel Isham from a letter of Lawrence's sold at the
Anderson Galleries, New York. The word 'art' in line 3 was copied as 'and', which
makes nonsense.

[2] Comparison of this with letter No. 386 inclines me to believe it was written about
June 1929, ten years after Paris.

knew also that every broken pot he might have turned up would have led to fresh paragraphs in the newspapers.

The project for enlisting in the ranks of the R.A.F. which he seems to have formed as early as 1919, and which was perhaps the recurrence of a very much earlier impulse, had been strengthened by contact with the highly placed officers of the R.A.F. at the Cairo Conference, who had urged him to take a commission. The conquest of the air seemed to Lawrence the job of the men of his time, and to enlist in the ranks as one of the humblest servants, helping towards that achievement, offered a way of escape from being the Lawrence he hated. It would provide him with a completely fresh experience. He would live with simple men who cared only for realities, not for reputations, and he would have the happiness of sharing work which he believed was worth doing, with them. It would also provide him with material for another book — for one of the motives which led him to enlist was to write about the experience. He was not, in the first instance, at all sure how long he meant to stay in the ranks.

With the help of those R.A.F. officers with whom he had worked at the Cairo Conference, he enlisted under the name of John Hume Ross. But Bernard Shaw was right: he could not escape from Lawrence, and his attempts to do so often have a childish air of make-believe about them. In a letter to Lawrence written on December 17th, 1922, Bernard Shaw puts the position with a delightful freshness which must have had a very wholesome effect. Lawrence needed teasing and Bernard Shaw was one of the few people who could do it well.

'Nelson slightly cracked after his whack on the head after the battle of the Nile, coming home and insisting on being placed at the tiller of a canal barge and on being treated as nobody in particular, would have embarrassed the Navy far less. A callow and terrified Marbot, placed in command of a sardonic Napoleon at Austerlitz and Jena, would have felt much as your superior officers must in command of Lawrence the great, the mysterious, save in whom there is no majesty and no might. . . .

'You talk about leave as if it were a difficulty. Ask for three months leave and they will exclaim, with a sob of relief, "For

God's sake take six, take twelve, take a life-time, take anything
rather than keep up this maddening masquerade that makes us
all ridiculous." I sympathise with them.'

The position was easy so long as Ross was unrecognized: but
he was identified by the newspapers after four months, and the
gossip and the suspicion among R.A.F. officers, caused by the
publicity, led to Ross being turned out of the Air Force.

Lawrence immediately exerted all his energies to get taken
back into it. Since the period at Uxbridge had been a time of
great suffering when he was continually on the verge of breakdown, one wonders whether his will had not become greater
than his intelligence. Such a predominance of the will was
Lawrence's chief danger. It shows itself frequently in his treatment of his body, on which all his life he was apt to impose quite
unfair strains, often of a stupid character. For example he
neglected a broken arm in 1926 and so made a less satisfactory
recovery, just as he had gone back to his work in class with a
broken leg in 1904. The courage of the boy too proud to make a
fuss is something we admire: in an educated man it is ridiculous
and a sign of abnormality. The desire to suffer, the readiness to
suffer, was in my opinion the most abnormal feature of Lawrence's
character: the revelation of this the only thing (apart from the
early training in the R.A.F. sixteen years ago) which could shock
anyone but a fool in *The Mint*. He realized himself that it was
almost madness: 'It's terrible to hold myself voluntarily here
until the burnt child no longer feels the fire' (Letter No. 416).
There are rational and logical explanations why Lawrence
enlisted, but the final and most compelling was an irrational urge
to submit and to subject himself to men most obviously his
inferiors.

Lawrence fully realized the absurdity of the position himself.
'It's like having a unicorn in a racing stable. Beast doesn't fit',
he wrote in a letter to an Air Marshal.

A letter from Hogarth to Bernard Shaw written when the latter
was trying to obtain a pension for Lawrence (see p. 446) contains
the following passages:

'The fact is that money weighs much less with him than his

mode of life.[1] I cannot conceive any Government post, such as the P.M. could offer, which L. would accept, or if accepted, retain. He begins at once to talk of "moral prostitution" and quits! . . . Lawrence is not normal in many ways and it is extraordinarily difficult to do anything for him! In some measure the life of letters is best suited to him. He will not work in any sort of harness unless this is padlocked on to him. He enlisted in order to have the padlocks rivetted on to him.'

One result of the 'maddening masquerade' was that Lawrence was peculiarly exposed to the persecution which attends famous people to-day, but had none of the defences provided by money and high position. He was hunted by pressmen, by free-lance journalists, and photographers. Foxhunters tell us that the fox enjoys giving the hounds a good run, and it is no doubt true that Lawrence would not have liked to have been forgotten. He had the vanity of so many Irishmen. But the frontier between what was satisfying to Lawrence's vanity and what increased his persecution mania fluctuated extremely, and cannot be drawn. For example at moments he genuinely disliked Robert Graves's book *Lawrence and the Arabs*, though a book ready to be published by Robert Graves shows that Lawrence had written some exaggerated bits of it himself. But one may say that, with the passage of years, his vanity became more fastidious, and his persecution mania greater. During the period after his enlistment, especially before he had become settled in his work on speed boats, J. H. Ross, T. E. Smith, Aircraft Hand Shaw, Colonel Lawrence and No. 338171 played a game of psychological hide and seek, and a physical Box and Cox performance, which is hard to understand. The clue to it is not vanity, but Lawrence's conscientious scruples against being the man he was.

Yet though all these motives were involved in leading him to enlist and to remain in the ranks, there was undoubtedly another reason too. Being in the ranks gave Lawrence unbounded opportunities for indulgence in his special brand of humour. Though he might be driven by his conscience, or by an abnormal

[1] Lawrence's attitude to money had not changed since he had written (on May 19th, 1911): 'I fear Father is right about us and our careers, but this idealist disregard for the good things of the world has its bright side. And to say that he had five sons, none making money, would be a glorious boast — from my point of view at least.'

readiness to make himself suffer, he never lost his sense of humour. Life in the ranks was for a large part of the time a secret joke, by which he kept himself in a state of rich amusement at the expense of officers and sergeants. Later on, when he began to make his influence felt throughout the R.A.F., the difficulty of getting things done from below added to his zest in doing them. His sufferings were at times great, his motives of conscience very deep-rooted, but these handicaps added humour and interest to the game.

When Lawrence had busied himself in getting *Arabia Deserta* reprinted, he found that Jonathan Cape, who was associated with the Medici Society, and was about to set up as a publisher on his own account, was contemplating an edition of the book, which Edward Garnett was urging on him. In this way Lawrence met both Cape and Garnett. Garnett was from 1902 onwards a great admirer of Doughty and by an abridgement of *Arabia Deserta* had helped to make the book known. He had also persuaded his employer, Gerald Duckworth, to publish Doughty's epic *The Dawn in Britain*, in six volumes, and *Adam Cast Forth*, as well as *The Cliffs* and *The Clouds*, poems prophetic of war with Germany. I think, throughout their friendship, Lawrence always thought of Edward Garnett as a man who for years had exerted himself to get Doughty's work known. It was therefore natural that Lawrence should ask Edward Garnett's opinion of the Oxford Text of *Seven Pillars of Wisdom*, the last eight chapters of which were delivered by the *Oxford Times* on July 21st, 1922. The entire cost of composition and printing was £175. Lawrence could not face the idea of publishing the whole book and asked Edward Garnett to make an abridgement of it.

z

17, VIII, 22.   [*postmarked London S.W.*]

[*3 lines omitted*] The binders have not yet delivered my three copies.[1]

Yours shall go to you as soon as I get it: but as I'm going off[2] in a few days, if the beasts don't hurry up there will be a delay.   E.L.

[Lawrence had met Bernard Shaw through Sydney Cockerell. Their meeting is described as follows by Bernard Shaw in a private memorial to Mr. Stanley Baldwin, then Prime Minister, on May 31st, 1923. The subject of this memorial is referred to on p. 446.

> About a year ago my wife presented a portrait to the Fitzwilliam Museum in Cambridge; and the curator, Mr. S. C. Cockerell, came to my house to receive it. He induced a man who was lunching with him to come and help in the porterage, assuring him that I should not be at home. To my astonishment, I recognised in this shy bird Luruns Bey. We hit it off together fairly well; and he presently sent me a history of the Arabian campaign which he had written.]

161: TO BERNARD SHAW

17.viii.22   14 *Barton Street Westminster*

Dear Mr. Shaw, You will be puzzled at my writing to you: but Cockerell some months ago took me round to you and introduced me, and you did not talk too formidably.

I want to ask you two questions: the first one, 'Do you still read books?', doesn't require an answer. If you still go on reading I'm going to put the second question: if you don't, then please skip the two inside pages of this note and carry over to my

---

[1] Of the Oxford *Seven Pillars*.

[2] This was to join the R.A.F. An authorization for him to do so under the alias of John Hume Ross A/C2 No. 352087 had been signed that day. The authorization expressly states that Lawrence was taking this step in order to learn what was the life of an airman, and gives orders that if any application to be released is received from Lawrence he is to be discharged immediately, without formality.

signature at the end, and burn it all without replying. I hate letter-writing as much as I can, and so, probably, do you.

My real wish is to ask if you will read, or try to read, a book which I have written. It's about the war, which will put you off, to start with, and there are technical unpleasantnesses about it. For instance it is very long: about 300,000 words I suspect, though I have not counted them. I have very little money and do not wish to publish it: however it had to be printed, so I got it done on a lino. press, in a newspaper office. That means it's beastly to look at, two columns on a quarto page, small newspaper type which hurts your eyes, and dozens of misprints, corrected roughly in ink: for only five copies exist, and I could not afford a proof. The punctuation is entirely the compositor's fancy: and he had an odd fancy, especially on Mondays.

That's the worst to be said on the material side. So far as concerns myself you must be told, before you commit yourself to saying 'yes', that I'm not a writer, and successfully passed the age of 30 without having wanted to write anything. I was brought up as a professional historian, which means the worship of original documents. To my astonishment, after peace came I found I was myself the sole person who knew what had happened in Arabia during the war: and the only literate person in the Arab Army. So it became a professional duty to record what happened. I started out to do it plainly and simply, much as a baby thinks it's easy to talk: and then I found myself bogged in a confusion of ways of saying the easiest things, and unable to describe the plainest places: and then problems of conduct came along, and the people with me had to be characterised: — in fact I got fairly into it, and the job became too much for me. *Your* first book was not perfect, though it was a subject you had chosen for yourself, and you had an itch to write!

In my case, I have, I believe, taken refuge in second-hand words: I mean, I think I've borrowed expressions and adjectives and ideas from everybody I have ever read, and cut them down to my own size, and stitched them together again. My tastes are daily mailish, so there's enough piffle and romance and wooliness to make a realist sick. There's a lot of half-baked thinking, some cheap disgust and complaint (the fighting fronts were mainly hysterical, you know, where they weren't professional, and I'm not the least a proper soldier): in fact all the sham stuff you have spent your life trying to prick. If you read my thing, it will show you that your prefaces have been written in vain, if I'm a fair sample of my generation. This might make you laugh, if the thing was amusingly written: but it's long-winded, and pretentious, and dull to the point where I can no longer bear to look at it myself. I chose that moment to have it printed!

You'll wonder, why if all this is true (and I think it is) I want any decent person still more a person like yourself* to read it. Well, it's because it is history, and I'm shamed for ever if I am the sole chronicler of an event, and fail to chronicle it: and yet unless what I've written can be made better I'll burn it. My own disgust with it is so great that I no longer believe it worth trying to improve (or possible to improve). If you read it or part of it and came to the same conclusion, you would give me courage to strike the match: whereas now I distrust my own judgement, and it seems cruel to destroy a thing on which I have worked my hardest for three years. While if you said that parts were rubbish, and other parts not so bad, and parts of it possible, (and distinguished those parts variously) then your standards might enable me to clear up mine, and give me energy enough to tackle the job again. (If you say it is all possible then I will reluctantly get rid of your own books from my shelves.)

All this is very unfair — or would be, if you knew me: but deleting that twenty minutes with Cockerell we are utter strangers, and likely to remain so, and therefore there is no pressure on you to answer this letter at all. I won't be in the least astonished (indeed I'll write another of the same sort to a man called Orage[1] whom I have never met, but whose criticism I enjoy): and my opinion of you will go up. Yours with many apologies   T E LAWRENCE

Incidentally: I don't want people to know that the book exists. So whether you reply or not, I hope you will not talk of it.

* ambiguous: but I wanted to avoid expressing my liking for your work.

[1] Editor of *The New Age*.

162: TO EDWARD GARNETT

22. VIII 22.   [*Postmarked London S.W.*1]

I should have warned you before I sent it (only it seemed so remote a contingency) that if your opinion was favourable it would be wasted on me. Perhaps as you haven't yet finished it, this is still not too rude to say. The thing is spotted in nearly every line with blemishes of style, and while my critical sense doesn't reach as far as subject matter and construction, I judge them equally bad, by analogy.

So please don't consider the point of publication. That never came into my mind when writing it: indeed I don't know for whom I wrote it, unless it was for myself. When it came to the point of printing it, several passages had to come out, for fear of the compositor, and I cannot imagine showing it except to a few minds (like yours) already prejudged to kindness.

If that Deraa incident whose treatment you call severe and serene (the second sounds like a quaint failure to get my impressions across, but I know what you feel) had happened to yourself you would not have recorded it. I have a face of brass perhaps, but I put it into print very reluctantly, last of all the pages I sent to the press. For weeks I wanted to burn it in the manuscript: because I could not tell the story face to face with anyone, and I think I'll feel sorry, when I next meet you, that you know it. The sort of man I have always mixed with doesn't so give himself away.

I shall hope for help from your pencilled notes, and am very grateful for your goodness in reading it, and for what praise you have given it: only please don't do more, because it only underlines what I know to be my failure. Hitherto I've always managed, usually without trying my hardest, to do anything I wanted in life: and it has bumped me down, rather, to have gone wrong in this thing, after three or four years top-effort. That shows the difference between mere brick-laying and creative work. It's what I told Nicholson[1] and yourself that day in Piccadilly: there's no absolute in the imaginative world, and so journeymen like myself are confused and miserable in it.

[1] William Nicholson, the painter.

I'm afraid this is a very affected note: but your letter has upset me. Sorry.   E.L.

That other passage you mention, where the tommies went wrong:[1] — I may be in order exhibiting myself: but how can I give them away? They were such decent fellows, and we treated them so poorly.

When you have had enough of it I'd like to come down and ask you some technical questions.

163: TO EDWARD GARNETT

23.8.22.   [*Postmarked London S.W.*1]

These things are matters of opinion, or of will, rather: — like your diagnosis of my obstinacy to ambition conceit or idealism, which are earthly devilish and divine points of the same view. It's no good writing them: because letter-writing is a vice: and I'll wait to talk till you report that the last pillar is fallen.

It's no remedy or consolation for my lack of style to point to Dostoevsky in the same dock: it's partly why people prefer to read him in the English version. *War and Peace* I thought decently written on the whole. Of course not a miracle of style like *Salammbo* or the *Moralités Légendaires*: or like Doughty and *Eothen* and *Idle Days in Patagonia*. If mine had been simple stuff it wouldn't have mattered. It could have gone into the Hakluyt category as a good yarn: but it's elaborate and self-conscious: ambitious if you like: and that makes failure a discredit. It doesn't matter missing if you don't aim: thereby Lane's *Arabian Nights* is better than Burton's.

Don't call me an artist. I said I'd like to be, and that book is my essay in the manner of an artist: as my war was a decent imitation of soldiering, and my politics chimed well with the notes of politicians. These are all good frauds, and I don't want you to decorate me, for art, over the book in which I explode my legend as man-of-war and statesman!

[1] A chapter of the Oxford Text omitted in the Subscribers' edition of *Seven Pillars of Wisdom*.

It's feminine to have the last word: which comes in well here, since it apologises for an unnecessary letter, and will influence you to let the matter drop! Once more, many thanks for the trouble you are taking. It's obviously going to make the book pages better than it was: and I'm very grateful for any help. I can argue for ever: but when it comes to writing something out of my head!   E.L.

164: TO EDWARD GARNETT

26. VIII. 22.   [*Postmarked London S.W.*1. *Aug.* 28. 1922]

Yes, I saw that you were shaken: and ascribed part-cause of it to my writing. So, it was a half-compliment, but only half, for great tragedy plays a Καθαρσις and leaves its readers calm at the end. I looked on *The Seven Pillars* as, in essence, tragedy — a victory in which no man could take delight.

In revenge you shook me for the moment. Confession is in the air. Do you remember my telling you once that I collected a shelf of 'Titanic' books (those distinguished by greatness of spirit, 'sublimity' as Longinus would call it): and that they were *The Karamazovs, Zarathustra,* and *Moby Dick.*[1] Well, my ambition was to make an English fourth. You will observe that modesty comes out more in the performance than in the aim!

I thought that the mind I had, (and I've matched it competitively often against other fellows, and have an opinion of it), if joined to a revival of the war-passion, would sweep over the ordinary rocks of technique. So I got into my garret, and in that month I told you of, excited myself with hunger and cold and sleeplessness more than did de Quincey with his opium. It gave me a foundation, and on that I worked for two years, biting the lines deeper. Nearly all the points you touched upon with praise were the things laboured over many times. I had hopes all the while that it was going to be a big thing, and wrote myself nearly blind in the effort. Then it was finished (pro tem) and I sent it to the printer, and when it came back in a fresh shape I saw that it was no good.

That of course was quite lately, and I enlisted in the R.A.F.

[1] Compare letter No. 255.

to find a fresh plane of activity : for it is very difficult for me to do nothing, and I've tried soldiering, and science, and politics, and writing : and manual labour seemed the obvious next. Only as often as I've a bit forgotten the look of my book the idea comes back that perhaps I'm playing the Roman father trick, and it's not as bad as I think : and when you said practically that, for the moment I dreamed again of publishing a little, and so getting cash in hand. Of course it won't do, and I mustn't : but very many thanks for being willing to help.

Please don't read this as a cri de cœur. I'm perfectly cheerful. If I'd aimed low I could have hit my target as squarely as Max Beerbohm or Belloc hits it : but their works are only a horrid example, and I'm much happier to have gone high and flopped than not to have tried, or to have tried half-measures. It's only that my weathercock of a judgment, which would like, in secret, to believe *The Seven Pillars* good, blows round that way whenever it finds a fair wind from someone else. I go on exercising the poor bird wantonly, by thinking to send the copy to more people for comment. You happen to be the first person to have read it : but there is Kennington half-way through and chuckling over it, and another man, whose work I admire, has got it on loan by his own request. So I'll go on veering about the point of publication, as with you, so often as any of them praise it : but at the end I'll say, No, once more — and it's the right decision. T.E.L.

An old friend of mine, to whom I sent the sculpture prints writes back agreeing that they are good, and suggesting that he may give him a commission, *to sculp me*! This is rather embarrassing, and will probably be impossible. However he knows my present circumstances, so that I've replied telling him the difficulty of times etc. I've always sat to people of decent repute, when they wanted to do me : but this is rather different and I feel not very inclined. Don't say anything to Miss Heath about it, till the old man answers me again. I'm under obligations to him, so if he accepts my conditions I'll have to agree, supposing he can fix it up with Donnithorne.[1] E.L.

---

[1] A sculptor whose work Garnett had shown Lawrence.

165: TO BERNARD SHAW

27.viii.22   14 *Barton St. Westminster*

Dear Mr. Shaw,* *First.* Very many thanks for your kindness I'll take advantage of it, though I'm sure you'd rather I didn't: and so the volume shall roll over to you at Welwyn in the middle of September. I told you how beastly it was to handle, so there's no fraud on that side of it: and as you say I'm privileged, I'll try it: though it's an unwholesome state to live in: and I don't think I won there by my own efforts.

Second. Publication. I'm sorry, but I don't want to publish it. It's good of you to think of Constable's. They would be willing to publish part of it. I don't think it's good enough to bother about doing that: and to publish it all would be impossible. As you are going to try to read it I'll leave that to your later judgement: — but you will be of my mind. If you aren't, I won't be of yours.

I'd like you to read it (so far one other person has seen it, besides myself,[1] but I mean to show it to six in all)† partly because you are you: partly because I may profit by your reading it, if I have a chance to talk to you soon after, before you have got over it. You see the war was, for us who were in it, an overwrought time, in which we lost our normal footing. I wrote this thing in the war atmosphere, and believe that it is stinking with it. Also there is a good deal of cruelty, and some excitement. All these things, in a beginner's hands, tend to force him over the edge, and I suspect there is much over-writing. You have the finest cure for flatulence, and I have great hopes that you will laugh at parts of what I meant to be solemn: and if I can get at you before you have forgotten which they are, then I'll have a chance to make it better.

You'll be amused at my amateur method of getting help: and at my having a standard of work: but it's the only book I'll write, and so I want it to be tolerable. You write a new one whenever you remember something not fully brought out in an old one!

* Ceremony: also A.D. [Anno Domini] and you are a great man!
† This reminds me of what Abraham didn't find in Sodom.

[1] Kennington and **Edward Garnett** had already given opinions and it had been lent to a third person.

So as it's not going to be published, and as you say it will not waste your September time, and as it may be very profitable to me: — yallah[1] as the Arabs say! And more thanks for lending yourself so kindly, Yours very sincerely   T E LAWRENCE

My illustrious name has no letters after it. They offered me some, but I knew that I was just going to behave badly according to their lights, and so said 'no'.[2] *Who's Who* next year will not have me in it, so I'd suggest your putting off its purchase six months. If you want to get my envelope just right the 'Colonel' should come off, since that's a sign that you know me. The Press use it.   E.L.

[Lawrence was enlisted at Henrietta Street on August 30th, 1922, under the name of John Hume Ross, A/C 2 No. 352087.
Air Vice-Marshal Sir Oliver Swann has kindly consented to my publishing the letters which Lawrence wrote to him at the Air Ministry. He has supplied the following information.

'One would think, from the letters, that I was a close correspondent of Lawrence's, possibly even a friend of his. But, as a matter of fact, I never met him until he was brought to me at the Air Ministry and I was *ordered* to get him into the R.A.F. I disliked the whole business, with its secrecy and subterfuge; I discouraged communication with or from him. I handled all the matters of his entry and movements entirely myself. I don't think a soul in my department knew who Aircraftsman No. ...... was, and his eventual discovery at Farnborough was solely due to carelessness at the Colonial Office and to Lawrence's unfortunate love of drawing a veil of mystery about himself.']

166: TO AIR VICE-MARSHAL SIR OLIVER SWANN

1.IX.22.   [*Uxbridge*]

Dear Swann, I can't ask the corporal how an aircraft hand addresses an air-vice-marshall: — so please take this letter as a work of my late existence! I hadn't meant to write, except when I changed station, but the mess I made of Henrietta St. demands

_____
[1] Go ahead.   [2] cf. p. 332.

an apology. I thought I was fitter: but when it came to the point, walked up and down the street in a blue funk, and finally went in with my nerves dithering, and my heart dancing. My teeth never were any good, so the doctors threw me straight downstairs again. There Dexter caught me, and lent me what was no doubt his right hand to steer me past the medical, and through other rocks of square roots and essays and decimals. However I was obviously incapable of getting through on my own, so he got another chit from you, and that did the trick satisfactorily. If I'd known I was such a wreck I'd have gone off and recovered before [join]ing up: now the cure and the experiment must proceed together. I'm not very certain of myself, for the crudities, which aren't as bad as I expected, worry me far more than I expected: and physically I can only just scrape through the days. However they are a cheerful crowd; and the N.C.O.s behave with extraordinary gentleness to us (there's no other word fits their tone — except on the square, from which good Lord deliver us!) and I enjoy usually one hour of the sixteen, and often laugh in bed after lights out. If I can get able to sleep, and to eat the food, and to go through the P.T.[1] I'll be all right. The present worry is 90% nerves.

Would you tell the C.A.S.[2] that he's given me the completest change any mortal has had since Nebuchadnezzar:[3] and that so far as I'm concerned it's to go on? Fortunately I told him I wasn't sure how long I could stick it, so that there is always a bridge — but it isn't required yet, and I hope won't be: only it's a comforting thought for the fifteen bad hours.

As for the special reason for which I came in — there's masses of gorgeous stuff lying about: but the scale of it is heart-rending. I found the Arab Revolt too big to write about, and chose this as a smaller subject to write about: but you'd have to be a man and a half to tackle it at all decently.

I must say you have an amazing good crowd in the ranks: as a new force it ought to be pretty alive: but its keenness and life is better than I dreamed of.

In case I'm wanted by the Colonial Office I'll send you a note as often as I change station: but not more unless I want something,

---

[1] Physical Training. [2] Chief of the Air Staff. [3] See letter No. 204.

which will be a sad event. Less than two years won't do what I planned, in my present opinion: and they all say that things are easier outside Uxbridge. Also I'll have got used to being a dog's body.

Please tell the C.A.S. that I'm delighted, and most grateful to him and to you for what you have done. Don't bother to keep an eye on what happens to me. Yours sincerely,

T E LAWRENCE.

I've re-read this letter: it gives too dismal an impression. It's only the sudden change from independence to dish-washing, and from mental to physical living which has been too much for my strength. And I'd harmed my health more than I thought by these three years trying to write a war book. It's hard to squeeze the last drop out of your memories of two years, and I sweated myself blind trying to make it as good as possible. Result that I leap into the air when spoken to unexpectedly, and can't reply a word: only stand there shivering! And it's hard not to give oneself away at such moments. The actual conditions are better than I thought. E.L.

167: TO EDWARD GARNETT

7.9.22. [*R.A.F. Depot, Uxbridge*]

Your letter came to me here (which is Uxbridge) after a long delay. I've been shut up in camp for a while, and will be for the next while.

It's very good of you to praise my book so, and makes me very proud. I lap it up with both hands — the praise that is — the more greedily that it's the first judgement I have had.

(Don't be shocked by the accidence of this letter. It's being written in the barrack room, and there are 27 lusty people doing jobs about me and muddling me up.)

And there's a depth of contrast here. Your letter was dished out at 11 A.M. I put it in my pocket while I went off to hump their swill to the camp pigs: and read it in an easy, as we sat on the stye roof. When I came to your suggestion about a magazine to be called *Belles-Lettres* I'm afraid I laughed. It seemed so far from my swill-stinking overalls! Seriously though, an editorship could hardly be given to a man who had never had any training: or written anything himself (published, that is, in my case!). However it was a pleasant relief to the pigs, and I'm grateful to you.

The criticism touches me exactly. The personal revelations should be the key of the thing: and the personal chapter actually is the key, I fancy: only it's written in cypher. Partly it's a constitutional inability to think plainly, an inability which I pass off as metaphysics, and partly it's funk — or at least a feeling that on no account is it possible for me to think of giving myself quite away. There would be only two ways out of this — one to do like Pepys, and write it in cypher, as I have done — one to write what is not true, or not complete truth — and the second I don't like.

I'm glad you feel the veracity of the story. It was written in dead earnest, and with as much feeling as a 'don possessed' can muster: and I think it's all spiritually true. Kennington tells me however that some of the incidents will strain people's credulity to snapping point. He finds them improbable.

One of your remarks alarms me: the feeling you admit that parts of it made you wish to do the heavy father. This would be all right if I were writing about a third person — but it seems to approach the indecent to give this impression of oneself. Are they incidents or reflections that cause this trouble? Will you do your best to excise all that seems sentimental when you re-read it?

It's very good of you to be willing to try and cut it down. I think that I may have to publish something after all: for I'm getting too old for this life of rough and tumble, and the crudeness of my company worries me a bit. I find myself longing for an empty room, or a solitary bed, or even a moment alone in the open air. However there is grand stuff here, and if I could write it . . . what mania is it that drives a man who has half-killed his brain for four years over one book, so soon as it is finished, to contemplate another? I've been thinking for the last week of writing a study of man in the ranks of the R.A.F. The worst is I'm dead tired, and the disappointment of *The Seven Pillars* (if you knew how rounded a pearl my conception of it was) has thinned my temper.

However I was thanking you for offering to edit the old thing. Isn't there a certain cowardice in publishing for money (the only motive: a means of escape from the crowd) less than the whole facts I found it needful to put on record? I can understand editing it for artistic reasons: but not for others: and I rather think that should be our standard.

I'll send you the sheets when they release me for long enough to get up to London and pick out the mass of them. They will have to go to you uncorrected, and you will find some of the omissions tiresome: however spots look smaller to a stranger: so perhaps they won't matter as much as I think.

It's very good of you, amongst all your work, to think of attempting it for me: and you will think me very ungrateful if after all I say 'No' . . . I hope I won't, but things are variable, and myself most of all: and I must have the deciding word over my own writing while I'm alive.

More gratitude for your praise, which came exactly at the right moment.   E.L.

My address is No. 352087 Aircraftsman J. H. Ross, No. 2 Hut, T Squadron, R.A.F. Depot, Uxbridge, if you need it: but 'ware letter writing. It's a bad habit.

168: TO EDWARD GARNETT

Saturday [A day or two after 7.9.22.]

Well, here it is, the whole mass of it,[1] absolutely uncorrected. I pity you, wading in it. I've numbered the chapters in pencil: the pages are still blank: so if you spill them, all you can do is to write me a p.c. for help!

It is very good of you to try and re-shape it.   E.L.

I should have thanked you more graciously for the offer of *Belles-Lettres*: but the hour was a short one: and I don't really know why I don't want to do it — and that puzzled me.   L.

[1] A copy of the Oxford Text of *Seven Pillars of Wisdom* in sheets.

I'm going to stick it in some post office on my way back. Camp has been awful the last 3 days: a solid grind of work.

169: TO EDWARD GARNETT

Monday 9.x.22.   [*Postmarked Uxbridge*]

Your Tuesday letter came, not to the pig-stye but to the barrack square. The Government's scare over Turkey (wind and vanity) has pushed forward our training and we wheel and turn and form fours and mark time and forward and wheel again from dawn till dark. I'm completely dead to decency: but your letter has been a sort of life-line, and I've read it about six times to cheer myself.

It's good of you to (or rather that you should) like my effort more on the re-reading. My test for a book is that one should finish it each time with a mind to read it again — some day. It's particularly interesting that the last fifty pages seem to you alive: I've never been able to see them at all: always by the time I have got so far my eyes have carried forward to the end, and I've gone through the last fighting like a dream. Those pages have been worked at very hard, but I've never got them in perspective: and I've always had a lurking fear that they were flatter than the vith and viith parts (the failure of the bridge and the winter war) and formed an anticlimax — a weak ending. It was impossible for me to last out so long a writing with my wits about me: and I've feared that there would be found no reader long-winded enough to get there either. Your judgment that the book is in excess, as regards lengths, is also, I judge, true as regards intensity and breadth. I've had no pity on myself writing it — nor on my readers reading it. There's a clamour of force in it which deafens. A better artist would have given the effect of a fortissimo with less instrumentality. It's unskilled craftsmen who are profuse.

What you say about the oddity of my brain doesn't surprise me — but it helps to explain the apartness of myself here in this noisy barrack room. I might be one dragon-fly in a world of wasps — or one wasp among the dragon-flies! It's not a comfortable place: but if the oddity of my standing produces a fresh-feeling book, I suppose I shouldn't grouse about my luck.

The personal chapter clearly bothers you. A man (a meta-physician by nature, who was at Oxford with me and knows me very well)[1] read it, and told me that it stood out as the finest chapter in the book. I tend more to your opinion: it's not meant for the ordinary intelligences, and *must* mislead them: but to set it out in plain English would be very painful. However six months away from it, and then a fresh approach may work a change in my feeling towards it: may even give me energy to re-write it. At present nothing sounds less probable. I don't even feel capable (though I'd love to) of writing a fresh book on this place. I've made some rather poor notes, which show me how hard it would be to bring off a picture of the R.A.F. Depot.

I wonder how the reduction seems to you now. If you get it to 150,000 and satisfy yourself, and then I take out 20,000 or so, that should do the trick. What an odd book it will be! It's over-good of you to attempt such a business. I decided yesterday in church (church-parade!) that I ought to publish nothing. Today I feel inclined to publish. Am I neurasthenic or just feeble-willed?

I'm afraid I can't come away, even for a day.   E.L.

(Glad you like Auda, I did!)

170: TO COLONEL S. F. NEWCOMBE

15. X. 22.

Dear S.F.N., I've behaved scummishly, I'm afraid: and in reparation had better tell you plainly that I've enlisted (under another name, of course) and so can no longer control my own times or movements. Otherwise I'd have liked very much to have come down to Devonport for a while.

It's a plan in my mind since 1919, but first my book on Arabia, & then Winston delayed me, till I was almost too old. However my health is bucking up, and I hope to come through the training period intact. The reasons why, & the purpose of it, may keep till it's all over. As you may imagine the contrast is keen enough to give me a very lively pleasure.

The world doesn't know of me now: & God forbid that the

---

[1] V. W. Richards.

Press should. Only three people have both my old & my new name, & I don't propose to enlarge that circle. So if you need me for anything, please write as before to Barton Street, & it will reach me in a seven-day course or so — while I am in England: & I don't suppose we will be sent abroad till next trooping season.

I want Boyle's portrait very much: but now it's not possible for me to put it through. Will you ask him whether he'd sit? If in London he'd spare one sitting (of two hours) to Kennington, then the job would be over. Roberts takes time, & I don't suppose Boyle in London could manage more than a day.

I'm writing to Kennington with this, & warning him that Boyle may fix a time, and that if he possibly can, he's to be free & draw him when & where fixed. Kennington is rather run after, so it's not certain. His address is, Eric Kennington Esq., 1 Riverside, Chiswick Mall, London.

I'd most like Boyle to write to him direct. Don't tell Boyle (or anyone) where I am (you don't know) but say that I can't arrange it, & that Kennington knows & will do his best to be satisfactory.

More apologies; & best regards to the family.   T.E.S.

171 : TO EDWARD GARNETT

23. X. 22.   [Postmarked Uxbridge]

Only red ink in hand: —

I'm afraid I seemed arrogant to you the last time: but it wasn't that. My mind on literature is not yet crisp. I have looked in poetry (the crown and head, the only essential branch of letters) everywhere for satisfaction: and haven't found it. Instead I have made that private collection of bonbons: chocolate éclairs of the spirit: whereas I wanted a meal. Failing poetry I chased my fancied meal through prose, and found everywhere good little stuff, and only a few men who had honestly tried to be greater than mankind: and only their strainings and wrestlings really fill my stomach.

I can't write poetry: so in prose I aimed at providing a meal for the fellow-seekers with myself. For this the whole experience, and emanations and surroundings (background and foreground) of a man are necessary. Whence the many facets of my book, its wild mop of side-scenes and side issues: the prodigality and profuseness: and the indigestibility of the dish. They were, when done, deliberate: and the book is a summary of what I have thought and done and made of myself in these first thirty years. Primarily it's that, and not a work of art: and when the book was finished and I read it, the fact that it wasn't a work of art rose up and hit me in the face, and I hated it, because artist is the proudest profession. I never hoped to be nearly one, and the chance allures me.

So far for the architecture of the book: — and now for the ornament: the style of it. As you, a critic, have seen, the thing is intensely sophisticated: built up of hints from other books, full of these echoes to enrich or side-track or repeat my motives. It's too elaborate and conscious a construction to admit simplicity — or rather, if I were limpid or direct anywhere people would (should) feel it a false stillness. Yet I felt that I could reach the static, by very exercise of this fault. Will can only be expressed by activity: thought exists for others only when it comes out in words: so I could transfuse my feelings, by putting them into a gesture, a conversation, and sunset or noon-day-heat, or even into the cadences of vowels and consonants which made up a phrase. By avoiding direct feeling I would keep the emotional expression on the plane of the rest of the construction. That's the reason of all that resolution of the personal, the indirectness of which offends you: and my temptation is to go more abstract, more complex, rather than more open.

I never tried (before last time) to say, or even to think concretely, upon my technique, and I was feeling after words all the debate. Whence the hesitation and the too abrupt statements, for which I apologise heartily.

I've been reading a little of your abridgement, and doing my last corrections: but the difficulty of working in this gust of life is heart-rending: and so it is going slowly. The necessary changes are less drastic than I expected: and the excisions so far are not enough to cause you any disappointment.   E.L.

172: TO ERIC KENNINGTON

27. x. 22.   [*R.A.F. Depot, Uxbridge*]

Dear Kennington, This should have been written when I got back: but my time here is so utterly at others' mercy that I hope you will excuse me.

Your drawings are wonderful. The dysentery, the nightmare, the snow-storm: I never imagined my chance of getting such pictures. The tangled thought is only less good than these.

I remember the dead-village-at-night as a horrible and powerful thing. I hope you will pass it finally.

The last dream is wonderful at top and bottom: but the middle is either too restless, or not right. I've been pondering since if I meant or thought of cities while I worked: the Arab East to me is always an empty place: and I don't know whether just open country: with perhaps a settlement in the distance: or hills: (*and* hills) I don't know.

There's a hypnotic suggestiveness about your work, which makes me give in to it, when I stare at it. So I like the dream very much in retrospect. Don't you think it might do if you just scratched out half the windows, or made them fewer houses — or blotted one half of the town out. There was a little bit of land behind the palm tree, leading to the sword, which felt peaceful.

The sword was odd. The Arab Movement was one: Feisal another (his name means a flashing sword): then there is the excluded notion, Garden of Eden touch: and the division meaning, like the sword in the bed of mixed sleeping, from the *Morte d'Arthur*. I don't know which was in your mind, but they all came to me — and the sword also means clean-ness, and death.

The comic drawings are what I hoped for: but in the light of the imaginative ones they go rather pale. Still, like the book itself, the pictures mustn't all be mountain peaks: it would be a better book if it had more soft and smooth places in it, where people could rest their minds before a new march: and the comic drawings will provide what I didn't.

I've written off in search of Jedda Wilson, since he may be in England now, and if so your drawing him would fill a big gap.

Roberts has sent me Buxton's head. That makes two I have to show you.

I hear (third hand) that Nicholson has done Clayton. Details later. I've written to Clayton to find out.

Will come up in a week or ten days and search for you.

E.L.

I'm sorry for bothering you so frequently and at such length with my doubts over publication. I hate the notion of it more than I can say: and there is no doubt that I will have to do it, some time: and the motive will be money, from which I have always hitherto steered clear.

173: TO D. G. HOGARTH

29.X.22

The delays of getting me here are so great that I asked A.J.B.[1] to write you direct: however it seems by today's note from you that Ll. G.[2] did it after all. That's decent of him as a last act. I'll write and say thanks: — for I suppose that's the answer to my request. I wish he had warned me & saved you the bother of getting up the memorial.[3]

Here's the Feisal paper back — with only a trivial change. I think it contains all there is to say in matters of fact.

I'm a private — or rather a photographic-aircraftsman-second-class:[4] and reasonably miserable at it. Kennington has done me ten comic pictures for *The Seven Pillars*, & six or seven wonderful imaginative things in colour — drawings, Blake-like, of states of mind. One, illustrating dysentery, is as powerful a thing as I have ever set eyes on: & there is a lightning-coloured picture of the night over Tafas which is almost painful, in spite of its beauty. He's also done a good head of Boyle. Roberts has done a gorgeous McMahon, and I hope to put him on to Wingate (in red chalk). Would you let yourself come in to the gallery? So

---

[1] Mr., afterwards Lord, Balfour.　　[2] Lloyd George, then Prime Minister.
[3] Of a Civil List pension for Doughty.
[4] Lawrence went to Farnborough School of Photography a week later.

far only Young has refused to sit, & I'm going to put in a white page saying so baldly.[1]

If you can sit I'd suggest Wyndham Lewis as your executioner. An artist of great power, & if he would, capable of making a splendid thing of it. He is very fast, so that one sitting (in London) would do the trick. I'm trying to get hold of him, but he is so often abroad.

With all the drawings (over 50 now) I feel less & less inclined to publish the whole work, & almost decided not to publish anything. My mind wobbles between the need of money & the desire to be withdrawn, & it's a pitiable exhibition on my part. I wish the beastly book had never been written. Garnett's reduction is in my hands, & is a good one: but it's a bowdlerising of the story & the motives of it, & would give the public a false impression. I don't like the notion of doing that. It's a favourably false impression, you see.   E.L.

[E. M. Forster, in a note on Lawrence's letters to Doughty, points out the consideration and gentleness in them all. Lawrence never bothered Doughty, for example, with his changes of name.]

174: TO C. M. DOUGHTY

6. XI. 22   14 *Barton Street S.W.*1.

Dear Mr. Doughty, Your letter reached me after a long delay: for I got so tired of politics during my year with Winston that so soon as it ended I leaped off on a new line, which makes itself master of my time & movements: consequently I have no real address, and go nowhere now.

I'm very glad the pension has been notified to you.[2] There were muddles in the giving of it. Normally a memorial is presented to the Prime Minister, signed by influential people, recommending the 'victim' to his attention. It seemed to me that in your case the procedure was unnecessary, since your work

---

[1] See note to letter No. 195.

[2] Doughty had received an official intimation that he had been granted a Civil List pension of £150 per annum on October 17th, 1922. Just over a year later he relinquished it on coming into an annuity of £2000 a year.

put you 'hors concours'. So I suggested to Ll.G. that the pension be awarded just like that: — and he agreed to it. Personally he didn't know your books: but everyone he asked said 'Of course' . . . and he confessed that it was obviously his duty to read *Arabia* at once, since everybody spoke so of it.

That was in June: and the pension might have been made public in July, only that Poincaré came across two critical days before — and the new lists were consequently unsigned. It didn't make any difference to the pensions (which are paid, as Sylvester wrote you, in arrear, as from March 31 of the preceeding financial year) but it meant that you were left uninformed. I was away & couldn't find out what had happened: indeed I feared that Ll.G. had let me down! However it was all well. Cockerell and Hogarth meanwhile were getting up a memorial, to supplement my apparent failure. It was decent of Ll. George to clear it up (by sending you news) as he was going out. It makes a good ending to a very momentous term of office.

I hope *Mansoul* is sailing through calm weather;[1] and that you and Mrs. Doughty are feeling well. You mention that you have been in bed lately. I often wish that I was: but out of laziness, not from need: and it is only voluntary bed which is delicious.

Though I have put myself out of action so far as politics and ordinary living are concerned, yet of course I am at your disposal, so far as possible for anything you need: and I can probably get leave for a night if ever you want to see me particularly, as I have not asked for any leaves for my own purposes. So if there is anything urgent please write or wire to 14 Barton Street, Westminster, & it will reach me within three days.*

Philby is in London, and has, I expect, been to see you. I

* Of the present ministry, three or four are Fellows of All Souls, & most of the others friends of mine. The Duke of Devonshire, & Lord Salisbury, & Amery, & Wood & three or four others would be glad to serve you in any way you wished. Please don't delay to let me know if, or when, anything comes to your mind. You are a public character, & can make any claim you like on the public. That's one of the privileges of greatness! EL

[1] Doughty was rewriting *Mansoul*, see letter No. 221.

have looked at his book, but not yet read it. I'm afraid it won't be an improvement on the last book of Arabian travel: but that is much your fault for giving us later men too high a standard. It's brave of Philby to have dared to publish: I can't bring myself to the point. I wonder if Abdulla will screw himself up to the point of visiting Eastbourne. He is comfort-loving and feeble in decision, but wishes always to be agreeable.

My regards to Mrs. Doughty and the family. Please tell them I will hope to come down in six weeks' time or so, unless something unusual happens meanwhile.

Yours sincerely   T E LAWRENCE.

[From the following letter it would appear that Lawrence had arrived at Farnborough School of Photography on November 6th, but his letter of November 19th, states: 'My coming here was on Tuesday', and November 8th, 1922, was a Tuesday.]

175: TO EDWARD GARNETT

6.XI. 22.   [*Postmarked* 8. Nov. 1922 *Farnborough*]

No, I couldn't come to you last Sunday. Have been having a hectic time of late, and didn't write because I was firmly of a mind not to publish anything of *The Seven Pillars*. I am still like that. Meanwhile my second self carries on correcting your abridgement, under the greatest difficulties. It's nearly hopeless to do it decently, in such distractions. I can't get enough time to read through any paragraph hard enough to catch its rhythm: and to feel that my corrections probably aren't any good discourages my doing them. Actually I'm at Chapter 35, and very little beyond your erasures has as yet come out.

Address now No. 352087, A.C. 2 Ross, B. 3 Block, S.O.P., R.A.F., South Farnborough, Hants.

S.O.P. means School of Photography. It sounds bad. *Lady into Fox*[1] is very remarkable. I sandwiched it between Flecker's *Hassan*, and the *Religio Medici*: and it kept its character. So there

---

[1] By David Garnett.

is more than skill to it. It's what I mean by style: but I'm sorry for the sophisticated simplicity. That's decadence. If a man is not simple by nature he cannot be simple by art, and if he tries he only achieves a falseness. You can only (if complex) get simplicity by my 'third degree': by distilling a scene into quintessential action.

I hope to come up shortly: but if possible after getting half-way in the abridgement, so that we'll have something to discuss. Am getting keen on the R.A.F. Was writing freely about Uxbridge when they snatched me away from it. This place is easier, but less intense and interesting — however after two months perhaps it too will shape itself to something in my wits.   E.L.

176: TO AIR VICE-MARSHAL SIR OLIVER SWANN

9.XI.22.   *Farnborough. School of Photography.*

Dear Swann, I expect my move here is your doing. When the order came to Uxbridge I nearly burned the camp down in joy: — for Uxbridge is pretty miserable in its way: miserable and splendid at once, since the fellows rise to it so well. I'm awfully glad I went there and stayed a couple of months: and awfully glad to have got away. It will amuse you to hear that this place seems almost disagreeably loose now to my depot-educated eyes! That's a great compliment to Uxbridge, for it never had a recruit less adaptable than myself. However I mustn't tell tales about my school.

My own work? Well, I made some notes of Uxbridge.[1] After the first few weeks they came thicker, and perhaps there is something in them which I will find fit to write up, when the time comes. I can't really say now, for I have not re-read them since they were written: and the writing was done under difficulties, for I'm awkward anyway at rifle-drill, and when my mind went off truant down the square after a phrase, what remained behind was even more awkward — and used to get jumped on! It's hard to detach oneself and make mind-pictures, while actually in a squad: and also I was always tired physically.

[1] There were later rewritten to form *The Mint*.

However the notes don't really matter, for I've got curiously bitten with the chance you have here of making a first-class show, and am now mainly working to help it on. The fellows are first-class (90 per cent of them) and a little push will keep them so: the contrast between new and old airmen is astonishing, and it is a little hard for the commissioned to see it, because there is a very sharp break in your organisation there. It's different, of course in squadrons: but in these depots you seem to me to run a risk, on that head.

Telling tales again! Apologies: and more thanks for shifting me to this easy comfort. I find I'm a better photographer than I thought! Please leave me to go through with the normal training, unless I squeal about it: though I said the same about Uxbridge, and nearly raised a monument to your glory when you drew me out of it, unasked. It was very good of you, but please don't make benevolence your habit.

Will you tell the C.A.S. all's well: and that I'm going on? also that in me he hasn't got a hard bargain, photographically speaking. It's a subject I always liked, and worked at, privately: and apparently I taught myself somewhat well. I have hopes of earning my pay: which up to date I haven't done, except by keeping a hut of rookies cheerful. I'd have liked to have introduced him to Hut IV of Uxbridge. They are devout worshippers: and it's rather enviable, I think, their worship. At any rate if I was the God I'd feel pleased at them and it. Yours sincerely   T.E.L.

Thanks also for the arrangements about meeting Winston. They would have worked beautifully — only that the gods didn't wish it.   E.L.

177: TO ROBERT GRAVES

12. XI. 22   [*Farnborough*]

I can't get up to London at present. It's out of bounds, because of a rumoured small-pox epidemic. What truth lies in that, I don't know. The streets of Farnborough are more full of election-posters than of newsboys: and it feels mean, somehow, to buy a paper, after one has run away in this obscurity, to escape politics

... if it was to escape politics. I wasn't like Coleridge: I haven't written any letters home (by the way, Comberback was a self-comment on his riding: odd creature he was!)[1] for anyone: and the routine would be beastly, if there was any: but each day brings its breathless order and each night its breathless cancellation: so that I live in a whirl. It's an animal whirl, though, and my nerves have quieted under it, in a healthy way. I nearly went off my head in London this spring, heaving at that beastly book of mine. My conscience always pricks me for not sending it you: and yet I'm proud of having had enough strength of mind to keep it to myself. It makes me miserable and angry, and I feel it a thing unfit to show to honourable or happy people.

Honestly I couldn't tell you exactly why I joined up: though the night before I did (a very wonderful night by the way: I felt like a criminal waiting for daylight) I sat up and wrote out all the reasons I could see or feel in myself for it. But they came to little more than that it was a necessary step, forced on me by an inclination towards ground-level: by a despairing hope that I'd find myself on common ground with men: by a little wish to make myself a little more human than I had become in Barton Street: by an itch to make myself ordinary in a mob of likes: also I'm broke, so far as money goes, by an unexpected event. All these are reasons: but unless they are cumulative they are miserably inadequate. I wanted to join up, that's all: and I am still glad, sometimes, that I did. It's going to be a brain-sleep, and I'll come out of it less odd than I went in: or at least less odd in other men's eyes.

I'm stuck in Farnborough nearly indefinitely: unless small-pox ends. If it does I'll come to London or to All Soul's, at Xmas for a week. Send me the Sybil poem, please.   E.L.

178: TO EDWARD GARNETT

12. XI. 22.   [*Postmarked Farnborough*]

I've got on to Akaba with the cutting-up process, for Farnborough gives me more leisure (and less leave) than Uxbridge did. There is a good deal coming out of the Akaba history: I feel a horrible satisfaction when I'm able to cut a piece out of

---

[1] Coleridge, like Lawrence, enlisted in the ranks. He took the name of Comberbatch.

myself, and draw the edges neatly together. By the way, I think all excisions will have to be marked by an asterisk.

The book comes fresher to me. There is an old-maidish neatness and fastidiousness about the style, and that pleases me, even where it passes over the edge into priggery: but it's a perverse work. I shy off all the 'popular' moments. For instance one night I went down to destroy a bridge, and found it occupied by a working party. We had the nearest shaves: I leave them to be inferred. Creeping back I stepped (bare-foot) on a snake. The fact is mentioned, in *one* line: and the next *four* lines give a precise and elaborate description (done with the finicky perfection of an armchair sitter) of the reflection of star-light on rocky ground. That's what I mean by perversity: the shying off the obvious and personal, and the stressing detached points, which a one-eyed man (or a man with his heart in the job) would not have seen. It makes the book unearthly in feel: but I like parts of it. The feast in the Howeitat tents, for a set-piece, is well done: and after all set-pieces are legitimate, though less breath-catching than sky-rockets. By the way there aren't any sky-rockets in *The Seven Pillars*.

Barracks forbid the leisurely consideration of style-niceties. So I'm not making those tiny improvements which would mean so much in the general flavour of the work. It all sounds, doesn't it, as if I meant to publish the abridgement: and I shall very much despise myself if I do. Only to face thirty-five years of poverty hurts even more than to smash my self-respect. Honestly I hate this dirty living: and yet by the decency of the other fellows, the full dirtiness of it has not met me fairly. Isn't it a sign of feebleness in me, to cry out so against barrack-life? It means that I'm afraid (physically afraid) of other men: their animal spirits seem to me the most terrible companions to haunt a man: and I hate their noise. Noise seems to me horrible. And yet I'm a man, not different from them; certainly not better. What is it that makes me so damnably sensitive and so ready to cry out, and yet so ready to incur more pain? I wouldn't leave the R.A.F. tomorrow, for any job I was offered.

The Uxbridge notes you have misunderstood. They aren't third degree: or like my lost Arabian notes: but photographs, snap-shots rather, of the places we lived in, and the people we were, and the things we did. I haven't dared to read them: they are about 15000 words, and were scribbled at night, between last post and lights out, in bed. In a sort of artistic shorthand. There was the makings of big book on Uxbridge: but an iron, rectangular, abhorrent book, one which no man would willingly read.

I withdraw my words about *Lady into Fox*: but it's the line of thought which couldn't ever cut my track — the fantastic. Everything of mine is dry.

Next time I come up (Saturdays will be possible from here when the authorities permit us London. At present they say that smallpox there makes it dangerous for us). I'll bring my box of moral éclairs with me, and we shall lick them together. You'll find enough sugar in that anthology to make six people sick: but my stomach is that of seven men. Boasting again.   E.L.

[From the following letter it is clear that Lawrence had written to Air Vice-Marshal Sir Oliver Swann since letter No. 176 asking to have his training expedited. The proof of this is that on November 18th an order was sent that No. 352087 Ross was rather urgently wanted in a unit and that as he had a good knowledge of photography already he should be put into any course then proceeding. This order was acknowledged on November 23rd.]

179: TO AIR VICE-MARSHAL SIR OLIVER SWANN

19.11.22.   *B3 Block S.o.P. R.A.F. S. Farnborough.*

Dear Swann, I wrote to you to the Air Ministry ten days ago: and have heard nothing, so perhaps you never got it. Anyway I'll repeat it in this to your house.

My coming here was on Tuesday, and the November class of photography began the day before. The C.O. has put me back therefore until the next class, which is said to begin on January 6.

This irks me a little, because it is a nine months' course anyhow, and it seems a pity to make it eleven. I'd have no difficulty in joining even a class earlier than the November one, for except in enlarging and mosaic work, (learned in two of the later months) I'm already as good as the men passing out. My father, one of the pioneer photographers, taught me before I was four years old, and I've done the photographic work of several British Museum Expeditions, and exhibited a good deal at the Camera Club, regularly.

I asked, accordingly, if you could put me straight into the School, for my technical training. Except for that, Farnborough doesn't offer me much scope. The camp isn't quite the sort of R.A.F. I want to write about! At the same time the technical work is A.1. and I'd like to watch the growth of a class. It was the coming-into-being of the squad which was so exciting at Uxbridge.

I'm exceedingly glad to have got away from Uxbridge. The physical side of that was knocking me up, and this place is a jolly rest cure by comparison. I'm reading German and Spanish to keep myself busy: for my nature doesn't second the demands of discipline very well, and unless I keep working at something I get Bolshie!

It's possible you have had my letter, and can't do anything. In that case would it help if I re-mustered as an aircraft hand? Could you then post me off to an active squadron, home or abroad? You will realise that I have the softest of fatigue-jobs here (in the orderly room): but want to escape the scrappiness of a training camp (which is an abnormal unit, and cannot have a character outside its classes) for the more normal show.

I'd prefer to go to the School: but failing that would remuster if you could then shift me. Apologies if this letter reopens a subject you have closed. I only write because possibly you haven't had my other letter. I don't want to bother you by urging what I have no right to ask. Yours sincerely   T E L

180: TO EDWARD GARNETT

20.XI.22.   [*Postmarked Farnborough*].

I have laboured greatly, in a week which confined me to camp,
fulfilling a fire-picket: for I am still an Ethiopian so far as my
conduct-sheet goes. The results are on their way to you, in a
bulky envelope, lent me by our gracious King.

I wonder what you will think of them. I haven't numbered or
dated the chapters, or indexed them, or divided them into books:
because — perhaps you will think my work on them too lenient
or too drastic, and scrap the pile. The total is about 160,000
words. I've taken out more than I expected, when I began it.
The camel-charge is mutilated, for reasons of self-respect. The
death of Farraj is taken out, because it looked awkward, hanging
in the air, where you had kept it. You kept it only because it was
a purple patch: but I think purple patches endurable only in the
midst of lumps of dough. Most of the rest stands. I feel the transition from the winter war to the expedition against Damascus to be
rather abrupt: but that's because of the strain we went through in
the intermediate period which seemed interminable to me, and
some of whose longueurs I successfully passed into print. But for
the public I'm sure the abridgement will be better than the full
text. Your cuts have the effect of speeding up the action in a
remarkable fashion.

I found myself utterly unable, in this environment, to make
those alterations which my calm moments tell me are necessary
to achieve style.

You will laugh at the vanity of an author, who read the whole
surviving text from end to end last night, and got up from the
reading with a sense that the barrack room was gone dead quiet.
It was half an hour before outside things came home to me once
more. I wonder what I would think of the work, if I read it
again in 1940? It is certainly uncommon, and there's power
sensible under its peculiarly frigid surface.

I recant my judgment of *Lady into Fox*. It's remarkable. By
the way isn't it unusual that literary power should carry on from
generation to generation like that. He's the third, isn't he? Yet,

to my scholar's taste, *The Twilight of the Gods*[1] is more attractive.

Farnborough is three quarters prison, so that I can't yet say when I can get up. I'm hoping to find a regular means of dodging up to London, as from Uxbridge. In a few days, insh'allah: and I shall hope to find you recovered.

By the way, enclosed with the text is a draft preface,[2] saying what I would have said. You will cut some of it, and add more: and then we will have to think which of us shall sign it: if you decide that this mutiliated trunk is fit to exhibit.

I'm rather proud of having achieved any sort of revision, in circumstances as distracting as ever encompassed a writer.

I fancy Uxbridge may work into a 30,000 work [*sic*] sketch, of the *Maggie*[3] sort.   E.L.

181: TO EDWARD GARNETT

[*November* 22, 1922]

Our letters crossed.

[10 *lines omitted*] I can't come this Saturday: and don't yet know about next. But we can leave that momently, till I hear how much you hate my cutting up of your cutting up of me. You are wrong to imagine that I disliked the abridgement. I like the complete book, of course, much better: but I fully realise that artistically it has no shape: and morally I detest its intimacy: and the abridgement is a good chance of screwing up my mind to lop it: it's now like one of those most genial trees of a bird-shape. Things I've always laughed at and longed to possess. Now I'm going to have one of my own: and it will be a delight. I'm most grateful to you for doing it: and when we meet we will have a talk about what to do with the stuff. Though I'm expecting abuse from you for some of my excisions.

There is another piece can come out — a long by-incident of perhaps 6,000 words. If you like the idea we'll amputate it together.

Do turn over in your mind who should write the preface: what

---

[1] By Richard Garnett 1888.   [2] See p. 345.
[3] *Maggie: a Girl of the Streets*, by Stephen Crane.

book-divisions, if any, we should sub-divide it into: if and how we should indicate where bits have been cut out.

I've bought a motor-bike, so can get up to London in my spare time: when I have any spare time.

Yes, I've read that poem in Waley's translation[1]: but all his translations are too subtle for my taste.

You said that my remark that I liked flowers in banks but not singly was illuminating, as regards my taste. Do tell me what my taste is —   E.L.

182: TO EDWARD GARNETT

Friday. [Postmarked 1.Dec.1922]

I liked *M. Grubbe*[2] so much that I've got her in Danish, and am reading her slowly: (v. slowly): with the help of your crib.

I didn't call Shakespeare 2nd rate: only his intellect. He's the most consummate master of vowels and consonants: and the greatest poet. As a philosopher and moralist I have no abnormal respect for him: but the Elizabethan age was tempered rather than forged steel.

The best sculptor of my generation is a man of 30, called Frank Dobson, who lives at 14 Trafalgar Studios, Manresa Road, Chelsea: but he is not cheap: and I don't know if he would do a posthumous head, you might try him. He's Cornish,[3] and so might do for Hudson what he would not for another.

Mention the book to Cape, by all means: but tell him that it will be a costly production, and that I am making Curtis Brown my agent in disposing of it. Of course I'd be very glad if he got it: but it seems to me a speculation unjustifiably large for his resources. The thing may be a complete frost, and will cost £3,000 to produce: and I reckon that would about bust him.

I liked one of R's[4] drawings of H. He had the just-about-to-thaw-frostiness perfectly hit off, so that it made an independent

---

[1] 170 *Chinese Poems* translated by Arthur Waley.
[2] *Marie Grubbe*, by J. P. Jacobsen.
[3] A double mistake. Dobson is a Londoner. W. H. Hudson, an Argentine by birth, stayed in Cornwall because of the winter climate there.
[4] William Rothenstein's drawings of W. H. Hudson.

BB

and likeable old head. Others, I agree, weren't up to the mark: but H. was a very restless sitter.   E.L.

183: TO EDWARD GARNETT

7. XII. 22   [*Postmarked Farnborough*]

Your concern flatters me — but is misplaced. Lack of sleep hurts when it is due to brain-weariness, or to a man's chumbling his miseries or regrets over and over till his mind is on fire and scorches him. I now stay awake out of sheer pleasure, and invested strength, my day having no worries and little physical activity. Such sheer pleasure never hurts: it ceases with its causes. For instance when I ride up to London and back I sleep soundly for six or seven hours.

For the R.A.F. —— no, it still interests me, and as long as it does I'll stick to it: though my hankering after flesh-pots is, I fear, too strong to be resisted when there shall be an alternative livelihood, of a workless character, within reach. So I won't ask for a loan, thanks: and my puritan self hopes that *The War in the Desert*[1] will be a failure, to compel me to dwell longer in barracks.

The private press has been a life-dream of mine — and has been twice (1909 and 1914) on the point of coming true. It will come, and will, I hope, be as good as my expectations.

No, the born writer is the real fact, and without such ichor in his veins a man only makes a journeyman's job of book-writing: and my critical sense makes me not covet the creation (even while I enjoy it) of those who do so, by pain, make literature.   E.L.

Lady into Fox is having a succès fou down here at Farnborough. Room after room has borrowed it, and handed it round from bed to bed; and the end isn't yet reached with them. The airmen say it's 'posh', and argue it fiercely among themselves.

[On December 1st Bernard Shaw wrote in reply to a letter from Lawrence:

'My dear Lawrence, Patience, patience: do not again shoot your willing camel through the head.[2] The truth is I haven't read

---

[1] An early title for the abridgement — *Revolt in the Desert*.
[2] See *Seven Pillars of Wisdom*, Chap. LIII.

it yet. I have sampled it: but I must read it all through. . . I am
curious as to how you will come out of it — out of the reading
I mean. Take the case of Gordon for example. He was a most
infernal scoundrel according to any workable standard of human
morality . . . Have you ever considered the question as affecting
yourself? . . . You have a conscience which would have prevented
you acting as Gordon did in China; so there will be a deep
difference; but I wonder what, after reading the book through, I
will decide to do with you if ever I become one of the lords of the
east. As I shan't perhaps I shall put you into a play, if my play-
writing days are not over.']

184: TO BERNARD SHAW

7.XII.22

Dear Mr. Shaw, The camel-shooting, first time, was a fluke:
and I have not inclination to repeat it. Suddenly it came to my
mind that you still had the book: and I remembered that it was
the longest book written: and that your time was rubies: and that
if you spent hours over it I might be preventing, and would
surely be delaying, another *Caesar* or *Heartbreak*: and in remorse
I wrote to you. Please don't, out of kindness, bore yourself. It's
more like the heaps of stone-chips left in the quarry after the
builders had finished, than like the great pyramid itself: though
I'll confess that I found the pyramid a sad sight: vulgar in size,
untidy in surface, singularly sedative in shape. (As many s's in
that as ever Swinburne used.)

It's amusing, though probably you meant it without significance, that you mention Caesar. Your picture of him is one of
the few of great men with any life in them: and to it and *Heartbreak* are due my sending you *The Seven Pillars*. Also the *Com-
mentaries* are one of my pet books. I carry them, and read them
regularly: in fact I'm reading them now. They are the antithesis
of mine: indeed I suspect that no successful general ever spilled
so much of himself on to paper as I did.

Why Gordon? There is only a superficial likeness I think:
though my mother was a Gordon. My father was Anglo Irish,

with Dutch strain. The death of Childers struck me as a very definite tragedy: Greek type.

I wonder what you will do with my 'dangerous potentialities' when you have finished the book: if you do finish it, and your letter sounds determined. It won't be so odd as what I've done with myself. I'm now an airman in the Air Force: one of those funny little objects in blue clothes who look forlorn when they walk about the Strand. It keeps me alive (just) and keeps me out of mischief. One of its consequences is that I'm afraid I can't come and see you: they give us very little leave, and rather too much work. At present I'm stationed by Aldershot. As the Press would talk rot about my eccentricity, please don't talk very much of it. It's not a secret, and not common knowledge: you see, people generally took for granted that I had enough money — or the determination to make some: whereas I have none at all, and have never worked for it: and won't.

The book is being abridged. Edward Garnett, a critic, has cut it to 150,000 words, and I'm going to see if a publisher will pay for these miserable orts. If so I'll become a civilian again. You have no idea how repulsive a barrack is as permanent home. It reconciles me to the meanness of the abridgement. Yours sincerely   T E LAWRENCE

185: TO R. V. BUXTON[1]

21. XII. 22   14 *Barton St.*

Dear Robin, Advise me out of your goodness. Doubtless you know that a while ago I changed my name & enlisted in the R.A.F. The old name bored me with its length & its associations: The new ones John — Hume — Ross were chosen by chance, but seem to me to fit my length & breadth: also I could drop the Ross & sign a book 'John Hume' without its seeming odd.

The difficulty is about cheques. As my balance is nil that may seem to you not pressing: but I've decided to sell an abridgement (rather less than one third) of my Arabian narrative, & this will bring in some thousands (perhaps £6000) next year. After that

[1] Buxton, who commanded the Imperial Camel Corps in Arabia, had become a director of Martins Bank.

I'm quite likely to chuck the R.A.F. but meanwhile I hang on to it with no more expenses than artists & a motor-bike. I'll pay in £200 or £300 shortly, so as to meet these cheques which I must occasionally draw.

Can I draw as J. H. Ross? and pay in cheques made out so to me? I believe that the change of christian names is not legal . . . but is it difficult? Other authors get paid in their pen-names — but I'd like to use the old 'Lawrence' as a pen-name, & live under the new one.

Very sorry for bothering you: but I haven't the power here to get hold of a solicitor, & the matter will come up for decision early in January. Yours   T.E.L.

186: TO HERBERT BAKER

25.XII.22.

Dear H.B., This is only a scrawl of reply to your Delhi[1] letter — as I'm no writer, and the hope of meeting you soon dries up what little flow of words I have.

It was good of you to write: and better of you to lend my mother No. 2 for so long. She enjoyed every minute of her stay there. She seemed to agree with Mrs. Donnett: my young brother stayed there for weeks, and I ran up several times a week, and that made Mother even happier, for she has the maternal instinct, and likes seeing such of her chickens as survive. It's odd, for we aren't a very satisfactory brood, motherly speaking: — but there's nothing accountable in our crew, Mother least of all. I'm at Farnborough, suffering many things just lately, and provoking my persecutors by laughing at them. It isn't quite so provoking as being meek — but I can't do the meek touch.[2]

I'll come in again when I get a free afternoon. My regards to Mrs. Baker and to Anne.   EL.

[The following letter is in reply to one from Bernard Shaw from which I have quoted passages on pages 350 and 351.]

---

[1] Herbert Baker was one of the chief architects of New Delhi. Mrs. Donnett was his housekeeper.

[2] Bernard Shaw should have remembered this. See letter No. 462.

187: TO BERNARD SHAW

27.XII.22

Dear Mr. Shaw, Your letter reached me on Christmas day, and has interested me immensely — especially one phrase. No doubt it was used to help me with Constable's (gratitude etc.) and it's immodest of me to refer to it — but you say that it's a great book. Physically, yes: in subject, yes: an outsider seeing the inside of a national movement is given an enormous subject: but is it good in treatment? I care very much for this, as it's been my ambition all my life to write something intrinsically good. I can't believe that I've done it, for it's the hardest thing in the world, and I've had such success in other lines that it's greedy to expect goodness in so technical a matter. However your phrase makes me hope a bit: will you let me know your honest opinion as to whether it is well done or not? When I was actually writing it I got worked up and wrote hardly: but in the between-spells the whole performance seemed miserable, and when I finished it I nearly burned the whole thing for the third time. The contrast between what I meant and felt I could do, and the truth of what my weakness had let me do was so pitiful. You see, there's that feeling at the back of my mind that if I really tried, sat down and wrung my mind out, the result would be on an altogether higher plane. I funk this extreme effort, for I half-killed myself as it was, doing the present draft: and I'd willingly dodge out of it. Isn't it treated wrongly? I mean, shouldn't it be objective, without the first-person-singular? And is there any style in my writing at all? Anything recognisably individual?

Apologies for bothering your eminence with 'prentice questions: but I'm mad-keen to know, even if it's to know the worst.

About business. Curtis Brown — or rather Savage, his manager, served with me in the war, and is doing my money-worries on the usual 10% terms. I hate business, and would be child's play for any publisher. I believe Cape, a new publisher of the respectable sort (he runs that divine book of extracts from yourself) is first in the running for my thing: but I've told Savage that I want £300 a year, to live on, and have left it at that, with only two conditions, a. that I have the last word as to type, paper and format. b. that it be a royalty, not an out and out sale. It's good of you to have worked up Meredith[1] to the point of offering, and I'll tell Savage about it: but Garnett reads for Cape, and liked parts of the book: so that Cape has a special wish for it. I fancy film and serial rights are worth more than royalties: and my only motive in publishing a scrap of the book is money: so that I'm as bad as [*name of publisher omitted*] in the matter.

So far from getting £20,000 from Parliament I had the utmost difficulty in getting a gratuity of £110 from the War Office when they demobilised me. I'm not such a figure as you think.

You ask for details of what I'm doing in the R.A.F. Today I scrubbed the kitchen out in the morning, and loafed all the afternoon, and spent the evening writing to G.B.S. Yesterday I washed up the dishes in the sergeants' mess in the morning (messy feeders, sergeants: plates were all butter and tomato sauce, and the washing water was cold) and rode to Oxford in the afternoon on my motor-bike, and called on Hogarth to discuss the abridgement of the Arabian book. It being Christmas we do fatigues in the morning, and holiday in the afternoon. Normally I'm an 'aerial photographer, under training': it doesn't mean flying, but developing the officers' negatives after they land: and the 'under-training' part means that I'm a recruit, and therefore liable to all sorts of mis-employment. For three weeks I was an errand-boy. I've also been dustman, and clerk, and pig-stye-cleaner, and housemaid, and scullion, and camp-cinema-attendant. Anything does for airmen recruits: but the life isn't so bad, when the first crudeness works off. We have a bed each, and suffer all sorts of penalties unless they are 25 inches apart: twelve of us in a room. Life is very common, besides being daily. Much good humour, very little wit, but a great friendliness. They treat my past as a joke, and forgive it me lightly. The officers fight shy of me: but I behave demurely, and give no trouble. Yours sincerely

T E LAWRENCE

[In a report of December 16th, 1922, the O.C. Farnborough sent information that two reporters — one from the *Daily Mail* and one from the *Daily Express* — had got wind of Ross's identity,

---

[1] A partner in Constable, the publishers.

had interviewed junior officers who could only tell them that Colonel Lawrence was not in the mess, had been refused permission to see the men, but had waited outside the gates, and had been seen talking to airmen. The C.O. was naturally anxious lest the gossip and conjecture which followed in the camp should be bad for discipline.

The matter was considered by the Secretary of State, who on December 19th decided that Ross's training should proceed normally. In *Lawrence and the Arabs* by Robert Graves it is stated that an officer recognized him and sold the information to a daily paper for £30. Lawrence himself says — Letter to No. 192. 'It was one of the beastly officers who gave me away'. On the other hand he was valiantly protected for many days at Farnborough by his friends in the ranks, including A. E. Chambers who has told me how they broke up the slides of a camera, with which Lawrence had been photographed.

But on December 27th, 1922, the *Daily Express* came out with the news on the front page.

'UNCROWNED KING' AS PRIVATE SOLDIER

LAWRENCE OF ARABIA

Famous War Hero becomes a Private

SEEKING PEACE

OPPORTUNITY TO WRITE A BOOK

The story was splashed over the centre pages as well and boomed the following day. The following extract is typical:

No one had any idea that Aircraftman Ross was the world famous man who united the wild Arab tribes, created two kingdoms in the East, and became the only white man ever made a Prince of Mecca. ... Sometimes in the evenings he would tell astonishing stories of the East, of wild tribes, and exciting fights, of tight corners, and marvellous marches over desert sands. ...

The subject was not however taken up in Parliament and there is no reference to Lawrence in *Hansard* at that period. The immediate consequence was to make him frightened of the publicity which would follow the publication of an abridgement of *Seven Pillars of Wisdom*, and this resulted in the following letter.]

188: TO JONATHAN CAPE

7.1.23.   *R.A.F. South Farnborough.*

Dear Cape, I've thought it over, up and down, and have decided that I can't publish anything, while I'm in the R.A.F. That rules out this year, at any rate.

I'm very sorry to behave in this way, and to do harm to your firm and its prospects. The initial fault was mine, in agreeing to publish the abridgement: and it's another fault to cancel it so late: — but I feel that the fault of letting the thing go to press would be far greater than any of the others, and is one to be avoided at all costs. I'm telling Savage[1] and Garvin.

Yours sincerely,   T. E. LAWRENCE

[The newspaper chatter was perhaps more than the Secretary of State had expected. My own opinion, unsupported by documentary evidence, is that the question of Lawrence's service was carefully reviewed by the Chief of the Air Staff and the Secretary of State, and that the decision to turn Lawrence out of the R.A.F. was taken not because of the newspapers, but after the newspaper sensation had begun to die down, because his presence was resented by officers of the R.A.F., some of whom were willing to entertain the idea that he had been irregularly enlisted as a spy on them, or that, at any rate, he would tell tales about them to their superiors. The existence of such a belief might do a great deal more harm among the officers than Lawrence's presence could do good among the men, and he was accordingly dismissed.

The explanation given to Lawrence was that owing to his being recognized the officers were put in a very difficult position. In another letter he was told, in a very friendly way, that one of

_____
[1] Raymond Savage, Lawrence's literary agent.

his drawbacks was his friendship with the writer — a highly placed officer in the R.A.F.

At the same time those responsible for turning him out tried their best to find him another job which he would be ready to accept.]

189: TO T. B. MARSON[1]

Sunday 28.1.23   *Frensham Pond Hotel near Frensham. Surrey.*

Dear Marson, This is for the C.A.S., when he is not momentarily burdened with big politics. I've been looking round, these last few days, and find an odd blank: — there is nothing I can think of, that I want to do, and in consequence, nothing that I will do! And the further I get from the R.A.F. the more I regret its loss.

So I'm writing, not hopefully, to ask whether he thought (and turned down the idea) of giving me another chance? The Newspaper chatter I don't take seriously, (and you won't still it much by throwing them the fresh tit-bit of my discharge!), so it seems the real difficulty must be the disturbance I caused, unwillingly and unwittingly, at Farnborough. I can't help thinking it must have been, in large part, because the finding me out happened there, [*tear*] don't see why there should be further discomfort over me if I were posted, openly, to a more remote place, (such as Leuchars, whose C.O. is a solid and masterful person), with a note to the C.O., saying whom I was, and why, and that I'd be sacked if he found me inconvenient to him.

The C.A.S. said the other day (when I was too [b]othered with the news) that I was an unusual person, and inevitably embarassing to a C.O. — but I don't agree. I've had a lurid past, which has now twice pulled me down, and of which I'm beginning to despair: but if my C.O. was a decent size he'd treat me as average, and I'd be average.

As I say, this isn't hopefully written. I fear it's too late and the business closed. If you know, please tear it up and tell me so in a note from yourself: but the contrary chance would be worth so

---

[1] Secretary to the Chief of the Air Staff.

much to me that I'm trying it. The last thing I wish to seem is importunate: but I'm so sure that I played up at Farnborough, and did good, rather than harm, to the fellows in camp there with me, that I venture to put in a last word for myself. Yours ever

T E LAWRENCE

190: TO EDWARD GARNETT

30.1.23.

I'm overdue in writing, but have been inordinately worried. The R.A.F. have sacked me, for the crime of possessing too wide a publicity for a ranker: and as I'm as broke as usual the sacking is immediately and physically inconvenient. Also it's annoying to have worked myself up to the point of seeing much good and some thrills in barrack life, and then to be kicked out of it suddenly.

One result is that I'm unlikely to write an epoch-making book about man — or Englishman — in the ranks.

I should have written about *The Breaking Point*.[1] I read it — and as you expected, the point of it missed me. I can't understand a fuss about such things. Marriage-contracts should have a clause terminating the engagement upon nine months notice by either party. I could admire its nervous writing, and the economy and power of the business: but its point lies so much in its content that it's nearly an impertinence to admire its other qualities.

Having been unequal to it myself, I tried it on the dog. In other words it went the round of B. block. There were debates about the four fires upon its subject, and these I found very interesting. On the whole opinion was liberal: though the dilemma of the book's close gives no scope for party feeling. The fellows treated it not as a work of art, but as a story of plain fact, and grew very keen following its track. Judged by their interest it should have drawn well as a play.

Lyeskov:[2] did I write about him? He was fair to good. I liked

---

[1] A censored play by Edward Garnett.

[2] *The Sentry and Other Stories*, by Nicolai Lyeskov, with an introduction by Edward Garnett.

the cruelty of the first story (*The Sentry*) more than the unnecessary harshness of some of the later ones.

Marie Grubbe is for return to you next time I come to London, if I do shortly. For the moment I'm rather at a loss for interest in anything. The motor-bike still runs like a dream, But I can't stay anywhere, for restlessness, and so haven't an address. I like *Marie Grubbe* immensely: *Nils Lyhne*[1] even more: both magnificent books.

Sidney Webb (on a sight of some pages) said that *The Seven Pillars* reminded him of Borrow (of whom he had read just as many pages). Any views?

Of course everything in connection with Cape and *The Seven Pillars* is over. I now feel that I was an ass ever to have dreamed of publishing anything.   E.L.

191: TO BERNARD SHAW

30.1.23.

I've now been sacked from the R.A.F., as a person with altogether too large a publicity factor for the ranks: — and feel miserable about it. As a last resort I've written to Trenchard asking for another chance in some remote station, where there are no papers, and no one will have heard of me. The reply to this is still not come. I've only a few days' money, so will do something decisive soon.

Those letters have come back.[2] Decent of the finder to notify you. I dropped them with my cheque book when the bank told me that I hadn't any more need of cheques. It wasn't rage or astonishment, but an agitation of mind which made me stuff them into a slit in my motoring overalls. The slit is a way to a pocket, not a pocket in itself. Also I haven't a motor, but a motor-bike. It goes 80 miles an hour, and is a perfect thing. I hope to eat it shortly . . . or rather, when regretfully I have to eat it, I hope it will last me for a very long while.

---

[1] Both by J. P. Jacobsen.

[2] A packet of Bernard Shaw's letters to Lawrence had been picked up in Lombard Street by Mr. Cope Hand, a clerk in a City merchant's, who returned them.

I've been wanting to tell you about the misfortunes of my proposed book: (if I remember rightly your first book also isn't yet
published: my only score over you is that I haven't written a
second): however: —

When the first foul shout about me came in the *Daily Express*
I cancelled (or rather I refused to complete and sign) the contract
with Cape for publishing an abridgement. Cape was furious.

My mind is like a lump of putty, so that a while later I was
sorry to have cancelled it, and I began to think of publishing,
not an abridgement, but the whole story, as you have advised.
So I sketched to Cape the possibility of a limited, privately-
printed, subscription edition of 2000 copies, illustrated with all
the drawings made for me by some twenty of the younger artists.
Cape was staggered for the first moment, but then rose to it —
suggesting half-profits, and a serial-issue of a quarter of it in the
Observer, and American copyrights, and all the necessary decora-
tions. It took the form of a beautiful contract, sent me to sign:
and that very day I got my dismissal from the Air Ministry: and
so I've cancelled it too.

The present position is that nothing is going to appear: and
this is the most comfortable state of affairs, so far as my mind is
concerned. Whether my body will cry out for more food after
it's eaten my quite perfect motor bike, I don't know. Sufficient
for the month, anyway: and it's been a bad month, for the R.A.F.
was the most interesting thing I ever did (after the squalid difficulty of getting used to it) and I'll regret its loss for good.

Please give Mrs. Shaw my regards. I tried to call last week
end.   T.E.L.

192: TO B. E. LEESON

4.2.23.   14 *Barton Street, Westminster*

Dear Leeson, One sentence near the beginning of your letter
made me shed tears: for it seems you have written vainly to me in
the past: but the next sentence made me shout with joy, for you
announced that now 'with the assistance of the Press' you had at
last definitely located me.

NO SUCH LUCK! When the Press let itself go in that hideous

fashion the Air Ministry said 'Quite impossible to permit an A.C.2 to have such publicity.' I was meek and said I didn't really want it: they might have it if they could get it. In reply they slung me out. Since then I've been in very low water (did you understand that I enlisted not to write books, but because I was broke?) and am not yet quite in the deep stuff, though three Govt. Departments exhaust themselves trying to find me a billet ... I turn down all their ideas, and ask for something poorer, and they think I mean richer. Soon they will burst themselves. You see I'm fed up with being called Colonel in this ridiculous year 1923: and am determined not any more to be respectable. Besides I liked being an A.C.2. and would like to be something of the sort in future: However, they won't have me back, so that hope is vain.

I never got any previous letter from you, or don't remember any, though I'm a bad letter-writer. This present effort of yours came to me via Trenchard, who seems to be my post-office. He's a very great man, and has never cursed me for bothering him so horribly. I gather that I nearly wrecked the Air Force. It was one of the beastly officers who gave me away. [10 *lines about officers in the Arab Revolt omitted*]

I go, when my dress clothes are out of pawn, to the G.H.Q. dinner, with Allenby and Staff. It's frightfully solemn.

No news of Williams!

I'm glad you are alive, and hope that it's more than just alive. There is nothing so repulsive as working merely for a living — only things are so bad just now that many people are doing that in despair. I refuse to do it, and have never actually died in consequence: but shall soon if something doesn't turn up.

You see news in the Press every six months or so (or I do) that my book on the Arab Revolt is either lost, or just about to be published. Actually I printed a few copies of it nearly three years ago, and there it rests. I wrote all my heart out, and so it's rather intimate and indiscreet. It contains only my adventures, so that a certain car adventure up W. Hamdh didn't figure.[1] I

---

[1] Leeson had been in the Royal Flying Corps in the Hejaz, in the early days of the Arab Revolt. Lawrence and he had taken a Crossley car through the very difficult country of Wadi Hamdh to search for a missing plane.

turned out my notes of those three days a while ago. How we
stuck! After you left us the Arab Adventure got rather too black
and heavy and the gaiety died out: while the end of it left a nasty
taste in my mouth. Hence partly my disgust for my war personality! So please pardon a change of name. Yours ever, J. H. ROSS

193: TO LADY SCOTT[1]

5. 2. 23.

How could I wish to see your statue of my brother[2], when I did
not know that you had embarked on it? It was bold and long of
you, and forms a sure reason why I must call again. Deplorable
that is, for probably I'll have to come on Monday, which is tomorrow, and two calls so close are perilously near a habit: and
there are no good habits (except riding habits): deplorable. If
you had told me towards the end of the third hour of my last call,
I would, by the news, have been levered gently out of your room
down stairs as far as the studio: and as the studio is very cold (I
know it, for I sat there blue-toed all one winter and estimated it)
my delay in it would have been short, and you would have got to
bed, not yawned stiff, at much your usual time. Kismet!

My most grateful thanks for your pumping of Shaw.[3] I'm sorry
that he was not critical. To me he would only say cryptic words,
all of commendation. Those are nice, like chocolate éclairs or
cream puffs, but not a meal. Mrs. Shaw praised even more than
he did. I hung on until nearly four o'clock, but not even boredom
would show through his courtesy, so that my curiosity came away
unfed. My private opinion is that she's read it, and he hasn't:
and can't: but is much afraid to shock her by letting on.

You want a copy! Unfortunately so do I. Of the six copies

---

[1] Now Lady Kennet.

[2] This bronze statue of A. W. Lawrence was one of the attractions of the British
Empire Exhibition at Wembley. Designed as a war memorial, it bore the inscription
'1914-1918. These had most to give'. It was later unveiled by Mr. Baldwin and stands
in the nude outside the Polar Research Institute in Cambridge, where its subject is
Reader in Classical Archaeology.

[3] For his opinion of *Seven Pillars of Wisdom*.

which exist[1] only one has ever been returned by a borrower: and that copy was foolishly lent a second time, and hasn't come back. So as a fact I want six copies. Do you think D.G.H. would trust you with a lóan of his? Shaw apparently won't: Kennington has lent his to Clutton Brock. Garvin has one. A colonel called Bartholomew in the War Office has one: and I forget where the sixth is. Horrible I call these people's morals. I'll have to send them bills.

No news from Amery[2] yet: I've had other suggestions, but none poor enough for me to consider.

Don't really expect me tomorrow. The bike is out of order, momentarily, and any way I never do what I mean.   E. L.

194: TO R. O'CONOR

8. 2. 23.   14 Barton St. S.W.1.

Dear Sir, Your letter went about the counties looking for me: it's the usual fate of people who write to other than the above address.

Probably your lecture[3] is well-delivered by now: the best source of information would have been Valentine Chirol's continuation of Lord Eversley's *History of the Ottoman Turks*.

I don't believe in any form of religious revival in the Western Islamic countries. Their present passion for nationality has driven out their former fanatical interest in creeds — and I do not believe that anything will make political a faith which has become, like our Christianity, a purely ethical concern. Ireland and Poland are the two Christian parallels to India, where Islam is still a power at the polls. In Turkey, Egypt, Persia and the Arab countries, orthodox Islam is no longer a fighting creed.

On the other hand, the depth and fire of this new nationality can hardly be questioned. In fourteen years it has re-shaped the political map of the Middle East and the zenith is still far off. Odd that Turkey should be getting national, just as the better

---

[1] Of the Oxford Text of *Seven Pillars of Wisdom*.   [2] See p. 425.
[3] Lieutenant O'Conor of H.M.S. *Excellent* was about to lecture on 'The Rise and Fall of the Ottoman Empire'.

classes of European thinkers are climbing slowly out of nationality, into an international atmosphere, in which the divisions are horizontal rather than vertical.

With apologies for being too late to help you Believe me Yours Sincerely   T. E. LAWRENCE

195: TO LADY SCOTT

16. 2. 23   14 *Barton St. S.W.*1.

If Your Serenity doesn't think it hitting below the belt (when I fight it's with everything anyhow & everywhere) will She carry out Her idea of doing something summary of H. W. Young.[1] (Major, Indian Army) ? It would greatly gratify my unworthy self.

This self lacked courage to tell you that it has changed its name, (without proceeding to the dreadful extremity of marriage) and now answers to Mr. J. H. Ross, at Barton Street and where else men do collect.

No luck with the work-hunt, except in the Free State, which is willing, but from which I shrink a little. In fact I've postponed it a week, in the hope that the British Army (to which I've made advances) may offer me a shilling. Light-houses seem to be all booked.   JR.

My mother sends her kind regards. She is called Mrs Lawrence.

[With the help of some friends in the War Office Lawrence joined the Royal Tank Corps early in March 1923 under the name of T. E. Shaw and was stationed at Bovington Camp, near Wool, Dorset. The last sentence of the following letter shows it was written after enlistment, as Lawrence was expecting to be sent on foreign service.]

---

[1] Major, now Sir Hubert, Young, had fought with Lawrence in the Arabian campaign. See his book, *The Independent Arab*. Lawrence wanted a portrait of him for *Seven Pillars of Wisdom*, and eventually secured a drawing by Lady Young.

196: TO A. E. CHAMBERS

Saturday 10 *March* [1923]

Dear Jock, You will have thought me slow in sending you this:[1]
but I am contented only to have remembered it. I go seldom to
Chingford, where my books lie idle: and when I go have many
things to look after.

I hope you will like it: had it not been meant to improve the
American Navy it would have been a better book: but at least
that is an honourable fault, & the particular aim was achieved.
I would willingly have done something in this manner upon
the R.A.F. — a much finer show than the States' Navy of 1820: —
but that's another of the undone things.

The book is part of a set, so I hope you'll be able to return it
eventually: (J. H. Ross, Pole Hill, Chingford, Essex): for it's
my ambition some day to live there & read again. Yours ever   R.

Above address will always find me — at long last: & don't
hesitate to write if you think I can ever be of use to you. Probably
I go abroad in October.

197: TO A. E. CHAMBERS

21.3.23

Dear Jock, It makes a good letter: but god help you if ever
you decide to write a book. Your bill for raw paper!

To start *Sartor* requires courage. To finish it is pretty near
folly, to my mind. I don't think Carlyle was quite the best
possible (as H.M.[2] was) and I don't think he has much to say to
the mind of 1923. Some day people will draw pleasure from him:
but not us.

You want to know about Lilith! I once read a mediaeval
German philosopher (in Latin) who made her a great figure in

---

[1] *White Jacket*, by Herman Melville. Lawrence had been reading Melville about this
time: the previous autumn he had given an inscribed copy of *Redburn* to Edward Garnett.
[2] Herman Melville.

the first world: but I forget his name & his book hadn't a name. Look up Lilith in the *Encyclopaedia Brit.* and see if they refer you to other authorities. The only thing I've ever seen in English about her is Rossetti's poem, & that is more beautiful than informing. I've written to a learned man who lives near a reference library, & he perhaps will reply to the point — but I haven't a book dealing with the lady, & she's so rare an interest that all her books will be even rarer. However patience & hope.

The British Museum allow no books to be taken outside their Reading Room. It's an Act of Parliament says so. For books to borrow & read at home you would have to go, for educational books to the Workers Educational Association, who have a very decent library, & are very decent to deal with ... and for more learned books to the London Library. The W.E.A. is run by Albert Mansbridge, a very earnest but excellent man. The L.L. by Dr. Hagbert Write [*sic*] a scholar with an international reputation. Let me know which you choose & I'll write the proper him a letter smoothing your path.

Yes, it was hard luck that my A.C.11ship should have come upon two such as [*name omitted*] and [*name omitted*] conjoined. I bear them a grudge, because I liked B.iii and the R.A.F. and this Army life feels very drab in comparison. Also you know we really were a decent crowd: and the present lot with me are the sort who'd always throw something at any cat they saw. It's a moral difference, I feel, and unless I can get over it I'll find myself solitary again.

The camp is beautifully put — a wide heath, of flint & sand, with pines & oak-trees, & much rhododendron coming slowly into bloom. When the heather flowers in a few weeks there will be enough to please me.

One of my sorrows is the recruits' course (new name, naturally, new age, no previous service) & a consequent imprisonment in the camp for a month, being damnably shouted at.

No there's no book coming out yet. You don't call it selfish of some women to refuse to any man what prostitutes give: and so why should I expose myself for money, or for others' edification? Besides, is it edification? Often I think the book is a pernicious one.

Regard me to B3.[1] My only present likeness to it is another corner bed! Yours   R.

The W.E.A. is in Eccleston Sq. near Victoria. The L.L. in S. James' Square. The L.L. would cost a little.

198: TO JONATHAN CAPE

23.3.23.   14, *Barton St. S.W.*1.

Dear Cape, Glad you are back — I hope with good fortune from the States.

I can't call now. Nothing else showed up, after I got the push from the R.A.F. so I've signed on with the Army for seven years, and am at a camp in Dorsetshire. There is a chance of their sending me to India in the Autumn, and if I get leave as a preliminary to that I'll drop in and see the firm.

Played you a dirty trick when you were away, by lending Garvin (at his request) one of the copies of the complete book. Consequence will be that the *Observer* won't deal again, if there is an again.

Would you give Garnett the cut-down copy of the thing?[2] It was his work, and very well done, and he spent much vain time upon it, and I feel guilty in his sight.

Since you went I've received three more pictures — portraits — for illustrations to *The Seven Pillars*. It will be a really good show, when it comes out: if it comes out.

Nothing doing now, of course. Yours ever,   T. E. LAWRENCE

199: TO A HIGH OFFICIAL AT THE AIR MINISTRY

28.3.23   *Wool*

Dear [*name omitted*], Sorry, your letter was too late. I've been here nearly three weeks, and am (as a recruit) too completely possessed

---

[1] See address to letter No. 179. Chambers was still an occupant of Hut B3, at Farnborough.
[2] The Oxford Text of *Seven Pillars of Wisdom*.

by the authorities to get leave or anything. It's like and unlike
Uxbridge — a camp on a great heath, little less beautiful than
the park round Hillingdon House, but unlike it in that the
country round is nearly desert. We can't run up to London every
evening — nor can we spend much money.

It's run like Uxbridge, but in small squads, of twenty each.
The training period is eighteen weeks, half as long again as yours.
It is less urgent too: the standard not less, but the approach to it
gentle: nor is there the same tightness of control over our walking
about, nor as many penalties or threats as in your place.

You will be glad to hear that the camp is more lavishly run
than yours. Fuel, food, bedding etc. all plentiful. Also baths and
libraries.

The education section is crudely run by N.C.Os, who at
Uxbridge would be taught themselves: but then that's accounted
for by the very different class of fellows.

It's astonishing that. The fellows at Uxbridge had joined the
R.A.F. as a profession — or to continue in it at their trades. They
talked of futures and jobs all day, and were excited about life.
These fellows have joined up as a last resort, because they had
failed, or were not qualified, for anything else, and they take no
interest in the Army, and hope no more from it than food, and
not too much work, and pocket money. There is no wish, as
there was at Uxbridge, to do better than the standard required.

There is one improvement I see. At Uxbridge when I joined
I went straight to fatigues, for five weeks (an average experience):
and they were real fatigues, all day, and often till 8 P.M. and heavy
work too. Here there is practically nothing of that. The duty
men, not the recruits, do the fatigues, and the camp is so arranged,
with civilian contracts, that the balance of military work is very
light. I do not think the average here is more than half the
working standard of Uxbridge.

The officers too are different. They speak and act with
complete assurance, believing themselves better than ourselves: —
and they are: whereas in the R.A.F. I had an uncomfortable
feeling that we were better than the officers: and this feeling was
strengthened, if not founded on the fact that the officers were
treated by the men, off parade, as rather humorous things to

have to show respect to. The officers played up to this impression by avoiding all contact with us.

The Army has the better of you, in this only.

Yours sincerely
                                                    T E LAWRENCE.

200 : TO ERIC KENNINGTON

30. 3. 23.   *Tank-town.*

Dear K., You're a hero — a . . . . . ero they'd say in this place: which is Hardy's Egdon Heath. The Heath is good . . . and I saw Hardy yesterday: paid for seeing him too, for it meant cutting a parade! However it was worth it, and I'm going again, if ever he asks me. His weakness in character-drawing is a reflection of himself. A very sensitive little man: faded now: with hope yet that mankind will give up warfare. He felt incredibly old to me.

It's very good that you got Wilson,[1] and got him well. He's the best type of colonial-governing-Englishman, would be broader if he wasn't so clean, too. I wish I could see it, but this place won't let us away till we finish our course (in August or September). Time is going very slow.

Will you look at Roberts' painting of me? it's heroic in size: and is in his hands. I'd like your opinion of it. It flatters me, I think.

John made some new drawings of me the other day, and one of Hogarth, for me. They may be in his new show at the Alpine. Hogarth was v.g.   y.e.   .l.

201 : TO D. G. HOGARTH

Easter-day [April 1] [1923]   *Tank-town*

Yesterday fatigues for us ran short at 10 A.M. (usually their ingenuity keeps us at it till near noon): so I leaped for my bike, & raced her madly up the London road:[2] Wimborne, Ringwood, Romsey, Winchester, Basingstoke, Bagshot, Staines, Hounslow

---

[1] Eric Kennington had done a portrait in pastels of Colonel C. E. Wilson which was afterwards used in *Seven Pillars of Wisdom*.

[2] See letter No. 203.

by 1.20 P.M. (three hours less five minutes). Good for 125 miles: return journey took 10 minutes *less*!

In London I went straight to the Alpine Gallery. John's thing of you is wonderful. Might have been drawn by a drunken giant, after eating a mammoth. I doubt whether he's ever done anything quite so strong before. Knewstub [1 *line omitted*] thinks it's the height of John: and the critics have all been hit by it. That's wonderful, for on the other three walls are such portraits in oils as very few artists have ever been able to show.

Yours isn't beautiful: it's savage: but the performance of it is so masterly that one forgives the rudeness & splash of the chalk-work. Was he drunk? Anyway for once John has worked with his brakes off, letting everything rip. It is (as it should be) the biggest thing in my portrait gallery. What shall happen to it? John sends it to Barton St. when the show ends. It remains mine till reproduced, of course; I don't know if you'd like it in your house. One's Self-portraits are rather hard to live up to, I fancy. Besides Mrs. Hogarth won't like it.

I hope you'll see the show. The other things are mixed, but the average is surpassing. The big composition is almost mad. I felt my eyes dancing with it, & preferred to look at Mme. Suggia, who is just a great portrait. It's good that John should boast such a middle age.

The wall with you in its middle is all spotted with drawings of me in various incarnations. One looks like a budding sergeant . . . it's a pity Trenchard didn't see it before he decided to sack me.

Don't like the Army. It's so unlike the R.A.F. No feeling for it in the ranks. Everyone is here because he is broke, & they want nothing & hope nothing from their service, except food, pay, & little work. In the R.A.F. people talked of their technical jobs, & of flying, & of the future of the air, half their time.   .L.

No leave from here till August, & uncertain then. So won't reappear yet, unless I buy out, which on one head I'd be glad to do.

I should have said that I bust the bike, just outside camp. Ran over a broken glass bottle at speed, burst front tyre, ran up a bank & turned over. Damage to self nil; to bike somewhat. There goes my power of breaking bounds!

202: TO JONATHAN CAPE

10.iv.23

Dear Cape, It's a relief to me that there won't be a serialization if or when we think about publication. My present mood is contra . . . and my present engagement is for seven years, so that I'm independent, financially. The team of artists continue to draw heads for me. John's Hogarth, (now in his Alpine Club Gallery show) is the last and most splendid yet: but the two Spencers are working on two others which may be very good.

Bevan is an educational officer: and I've not met him. There have been a number of Tank Corps books, and his will have to be very good to justify itself.

Yes, I've made wills and things, leaving my book — all I possess now — to my young brother, who has agreed not to publish it unless he's faced with starvation! This is an improbable contingency, for he has £300 a year of his own, and is sober. I suggested to him 1950 as a suitable date to publish!

In these very uncongenial airs I've rather lost interest in the book: indeed I often forget that I wrote it, or acted the affairs of which it treats! With luck and time I'll believe myself to be Pte —— and not an ex-fellow of All Souls!

Thanks for the word about translating. I'd like to make however-few pounds, and it would be nice to play with words again. Squad-drill is a little heavy on the mind. Yours ever,

T.E.LAWRENCE.

203: TO EDWARD GARNETT

12.iv.23.

Good news of Shaw and Doughty. What guts the man has: to read a great part of my book, and *at once* to go on to Doughty: magnificent!

Yes I'm at Wool — camped not by Lulworth, but on Bovington Heath — Hardy's Egdon. We go to Lulworth for gunnery later on, after the end of drills.

I've seen Hardy twice, but have had no other adventures:

More about illustrations

W. & Griggs have in hand the completed Ghalib, & 4 others half done.

I want them to reproduce John's oil painting of Feisal, now in my rooms at all Souls' College Oxford: the manciple will part with it to any agent of yours if I write to him. It is framed & not glazed: about 3 feet square.

I want a John drawing of myself reproduced: it is now in the hands of Colonel R.V. Buxton of Hans Rd. (59) Sloane St. He has also a drawing of D.G. Hogarth by John, also to be reproduced.

I want the Kennington portrait of Allenby reproduced. (now in hands of E.H.K)

I want the Sargent drawing of Storrs to be reproduced. Mrs Cust has it. It contrasts preciously with the much more exact Kennington portrait: & Storrs deserves two appearances.

I want the drawing of General Sir Gilbert Clayton by Nicholson (now with E.H.K)
"   "   "   Colonel Wilson by Kennington   "   "
"   "   "   Adm. Boyle

I want the drawing of Alan Dawnay, by Rothenstein: now in Colonel Dawnay's house (1 Brewer St. St. Aldates' Oxford)

I want the Guy Dawnay, by Henry Lamb. now in E.H.K.'s hands

I want the General Bartholomew, by Colin Gill: now in hands of
         Colonel W. H. Bartholomew
                  D.M.I.
                      War Office London. S.W.1.

I want the Colonel Newcombe
         Sir A.H. McMahon   } now in Wm. Roberts' show at the
         Colonel Buxton   Chenil Gallery.
         General Sir F. Wingate)

I want the Lord Winterton (unfinished) by W. Roberts now in hands of Wm. Roberts.

I want the Colonel Joyce, now with E. H. K.
I want the Jaafar Pasha, now with E. H. K.

These are all the portrait drawings, I think. 37 in all, unless the two Spencers get their heads of Air Marshal Sir G. Salmond, + Flight Lieut. Junor, done in time.

MEMORANDUM TO ERIC KENNINGTON

barring one race up to London (2 hrs. 55 mins.) to see John's show. I got back, perforce, in 2 hrs. 45 mins. (126 miles each way),[1] and was in place to answer my name for both noon and evening roll-calls. A good ride, or race, rather. Everyone thought it impossible for me to get up and down in the afternoon.

The Camp Authorities are very narrow towards us recruits — giving no leave till August, and few spare afternoons. Lulworth not allowed without a pass — but I risk it and run down occasionally for a smile at the sea. Too cold to bathe — except in the rain.

My number is 7875698: Name Pte. T. E. Shaw. Address is Mr. T. E. Shaw, c/o H. Smith, (Stationer), Bovington Camp, Wool, Dorset.

I've really struck bed-rock — or base material — this time. The army is unspeakable: more solidly animal than I believed Englishmen could be. I hate them, and the life here: and am sure that it's good medicine for me.

Revise the book? Do you know, I've now reached the happy point of being really sorry that ever I wrote it! Apologies: I must be exasperating to work with: but what can I do about it? Any idea of working over it again must wait. Projects of epochal writings flit — or flash, through my head. If I can take one on the wing I'll look at it carefully . . . but this atmosphere is hostile to everything.

Meanwhile pictures grow: the Spencers are drawing, and John has done me a glorious head of Hogarth — now hanging in his show. Do go and look at it.   L.

204: TO EDWARD GARNETT

24. IV. 23.

It wasn't *Nino Diabolo*: it was *The Piebald Horse*[2], in the first edn. of *The Purple Land*, transferred geographically to the Banda Oriental; whereas it was written of the pampas, and is

---

[1] An average of 44.5 miles an hour.

[2] *Niño Diabolo* and *The Piebald Horse* are two of the stories published in *El Ombú* by W. H. Hudson. *The Piebald Horse*, included in *The Purple Land that England Lost*, 1885, was omitted from *The Purple Land*, 1904.

so returned in the *El Ombu* volume, with its place-names corrected back to truth.

The book[1] filled a gap and gave me three evenings very great pleasure. There is something in Swedish stuff which gives me satisfaction. Sorry for the prose, but I'm writing, a single hod-carrier on Babel, and no one with ears could write straight. It's an odd penance to have set oneself, to live amongst animals for seven years. Nebuchadnezzar did it, I suppose: the feel of tanks is so utterly unlike the R.A.F. and everything here disgusts me. My motor-bike is called into use when I find myself on parade facing an unconscious sergeant with my fists hard clenched. A hundred fast miles seem to make camp feel less confined afterwards.

Do you think Neb. made himself animal, like his companions? I thought of trying to write about him: a psychological study of the Frederic Manning manner . . .

When if you write again will you send me the *London Mercury* Office address?

Must stop writing: head gone to pap. .L.

[The reader will observe that I have printed the following letters out of chronological position. They are the most revealing letters of Lawrence's I know, and since they were written as a series they should be read in sequence.]

205: TO LIONEL CURTIS

19.3.23. *[Bovington Camp]*

Lorde, My mind moves me this morning to write you a whole series of letters, to be more splendid than the *Lettres de Mon Moulin*. Nothing will come of it, but meanwhile this page grows blacker with the preliminaries.

What should the preliminaries be? A telling why I joined? As you know I don't know! Explaining it to Dawnay[2] I said

---

[1] I believe this may have been *Trail of the Elk*, by H. Fonhus, translated from the Norwegian, not the Swedish.

[2] Colonel Alan Dawnay had helped Lawrence to join the Tank Corps.

'Mind-suicide': but that's only because I'm an incorrigible phraser. Do you, in reading my complete works, notice that tendency to do up small packets of words foppishly?

At the same time there's the reason why I have twice enlisted, in those same complete works: on my last night in Barton Street I read chapters 113 to 118,[1] and saw implicit in them my late course. The months of politics with Winston were abnormal, and the R.A.F. and Army are natural. The Army (which I despise with all my mind) is more natural than the R.A.F.: for at Farnborough I grew suddenly on fire with the glory which the air should be, and set to work full steam to make the others vibrate to it like myself. I was winning too, when they chucked me out: indeed I rather suspect I was chucked out for that. It hurt the upper story that the ground-floor was grown too keen.

The Army seems safe against enthusiasm. It's a horrible life, and the other fellows fit it. I said to one 'They're the sort who instinctively fling stones at cats' . . . and he said 'Why what do you throw?' You perceive that I'm not yet in the picture: but I will be in time. Seven years of this will make me impossible for anyone to suggest for a responsible position, and that self-degradation is my aim. I haven't the impulse and the conviction to fit what I know to be my power of moulding men and things: and so I always regret what I've created, when the leisure after creation lets me look back and see that the idea was secondhand.

This is a pompous start, and it should be a portentous series of letters: but there is excuse for it, since time moves slower here than elsewhere: and a man has only himself to think about. At reveille I feel like Adam, after a night's pondering: and my mind has malice enough rather to enjoy putting Adam through it.

Don't take seriously what I wrote about the other men, above. It's only at first that certain sides of them strike a little crudely. In time I'll join, concerning them, in Blake's astonishing cry 'Everything that is, is holy!' It seems to me one of the best words ever said. Philip Kerr would agree with it (one of the engaging things about Philip is his agreement with my absence), but not many other reflective men come to the same conclusion without a web of mysticism to help them.

[1] Of the Oxford Text of *Seven Pillars of Wisdom*.

I'm not sure either that what I've said about my creations is quite true. I feel confident that Arabia and Trans-Jordan and Mesopotamia, *with what they will breed*, are nearly monumental enough for the seven years' labour of one head: because I knew what I was at, and the others only worked on instinct: and my other creation, that odd and interminable book. . . . do you know I'm absolutely hungry to know what people think of it — not when they are telling me, but what they tell to one another. Should I be in this secret case if I really thought it pernicious?

There again, perhaps there's a solution to be found in multiple personality. It's my reason which condemns the book and the revolt, and the new nationalities: because the only rational conclusion to human argument is pessimism such as Hardy's, a pessimism which is very much like the wintry heath, of bog and withered plants and stripped trees, about us. Our camp on its swelling in this desolation feels pustular, and we (all brown-bodied, with yellow spots down our front belly-line), must seem like the swarming germs of its fermentation. That's feeling, exterior-bred feeling, with reason harmonising it into a picture: but there's a deeper sense which remembers other landscapes, and the changes which summer will bring to this one: and to that sense nothing can be changeless: whereas the rational preference or advantage of pessimism is its finality, the eternity in which it ends: and if there isn't an eternity there cannot be a pessimism pure.

Lorde what a fog of words! What I would say is that reason proves there is no hope, and we therefore hope on, so to speak, on one leg of our minds: a dot and go one progress, which takes me Tuesday Thursday and Saturday and leaves me authentic on the other days. Quelle vie.   R.

206: TO LIONEL CURTIS

27.3.23.   [*Bovington Camp*]

It seems to continue itself today, because I've been wondering about the other fellows in the hut. A main feeling they give me is of difference from the R.A.F. men. There we were excited about our coming service. We talked and wondered of the future, almost exclusively. There was a constant recourse to imagination, and a constant rewarding of ourselves therefore. The fellows were decent, but so wrought up by hope that they were carried out of themselves, and I could not see them mattly. There was a sparkle round the squad.

Here every man has joined because he was down and out: and no one talks of the Army or of promotion, or of trades and accomplishments. We are all here unavoidably, in a last resort, and we assume this world's failure in one-another, so that pretence would be not merely laughed at, but as near an impossibility as anything human. We are social bed-rock, those unfit for life-by-competition: and each of us values the rest as cheap as he knows himself to be.

I suspect that this low estimation is very much the truth. There cannot be classes in England much more raw, more free of all that the upbringing of a lifetime has plastered over you and me. Can there be profit, or truth, in all these modes and sciences and arts of ours? The leisured world for hundreds, or perhaps thousands of years has been jealously working and recording the advance of each generation for the starting-point of the next — and here these masses are as animal, as carnal as were their ancestors before Plato and Christ and Shelley and Dostoevsky taught and thought. In this crowd it's made startlingly clear how short is the range of knowledge, and what poor conductors of it ordinary humans are. You and I know: you have tried (Round Tabling[1] and by mouth) to tell all whom you can reach: and the end is here, a cimmerian darkness with bog-lights flitting wrongly through its gas.

The pity of it is, that you've got to take this black core of things in camp, this animality, on trust. It's a feeling, a spirit which colours every word and action, and I believe every thought, passing in Hut 12. Your mind is like a many-storied building, and you, its sole tenant, flit from floor to floor, from room to room, at the whim of your spirit's moment. (Not that the spirit has moments, but let it pass for the metaphor's sake.) At will you

---

[1] Lionel Curtis was Editor of *The Round Table*, a quarterly Review of the Politics of the British Commonwealth.

can be gross, and enjoy coffee or a sardine, or rarefy yourself till the diaphancité [*sic*] of pure mathematics, or of a fluent design in line, is enough to feed you. Here —

I can't write it, because in literature such things haven't ever been, and can't be. To record the acts of Hut 12 would produce a moral-medical case-book, not a work of art but a document. It isn't the filth of it which hurts me, because you can't call filthy the pursuit of a bitch by a dog, or the mating of birds in springtime; and it's man's misfortune that he hasn't a mating season, but spreads his emotions and excitements through the year . . . but I lie in bed night after night with this cat-calling carnality seething up and down the hut, fed by streams of fresh matter from twenty lecherous mouths . . . and my mind aches with the rawness of it, knowing that it will cease only when the slow bugle calls for 'lights out' an hour or so hence . . . and the waiting is so slow. . . .

However the call comes always in the end, and suddenly at last, like God's providence, a dewfall of peace upon the camp . . . but surely the world would be more clean if we were dead or mindless? We are all guilty alike, you know. You wouldn't exist, I wouldn't exist, without this carnality. Everything with flesh in its mixture is the achievement of a moment when the lusty thought of Hut 12 has passed to action and conceived: and isn't it true that the fault of birth rests somewhat on the child? I believe it's we who led our parents on to bear us, and it's our unborn children who make our flesh itch.

A filthy business all of it, and yet Hut 12 shows me the truth behind Freud. Sex is an integer in all of us, and the nearer nature we are, the more constantly, the more completely a product of that integer. These fellows are the reality, and you and I, the selves who used to meet in London and talk of fleshless things, are only the outward wrappings of a core like these fellows. They let light and air play always upon their selves, and consequently have grown very lustily, but have at the same time achieved health and strength in their growing. Whereas our wrappings and bandages have stunted and deformed ourselves, and hardened them to an apparent insensitiveness . . . but it's a callousness, a crippling, only to be yea-said by aesthetes who prefer clothes to bodies, surfaces to intentions.

These fellows have roots, which in us are rudimentary, or long cut off. Before I came I never visualised England except as an organism, an entity ... but these fellows are local, territorial. They all use dialects, and could be placed by their dialects, if necessary. However it isn't necessary, because each talks of his district, praises it, boasts of it, lives in the memory of it. We call each other 'Brum' or 'Coventry' or 'Cambridge', and the man who hasn't a 'place' is an outsider. They wrangle and fight over the virtues of their homes. Of solidarity, of a nation, of something ideal comprehending their familiar streets in itself — they haven't a notion.

Well, the conclusion of the first letter was that man, being a civil war, could not be harmonised or made logically whole ... and the end of this is that man, or mankind, being organic, a natural growth, is unteachable: cannot depart from his first grain and colour, nor exceed flesh, nor put forth anything not mortal and fleshly.

I fear not even my absence would reconcile Ph.K.[1] to this.

E.L.

207 : TO LIONEL CURTIS

14.V.23.   *Tanktown*

I should have written before, but a split thumb, and the sudden discovery of the authorities that I belonged to a criminal class, have put me out of the mood for subjective writing: — and since politics passed out of me the only theme between us is myself.

There was one injustice in your letter. My crying-out here was not at the foul talk. To me it's meaningless, unobjectionable, on a par with heedless fair-talk. The R.A.F. was foul-mouthed, and the cleanest little mob of fellows. These are foul-mouthed, and behind their mouths is a pervading animality of spirit, whose unmixed bestiality frightens me and hurts me. There is no criticism, indeed it's taken for granted as natural, that you should job a woman's body, or hire out yourself, or abuse yourself in any way. I cried out against it, partly in self-pity because I've con-

[1] Philip Kerr, now Lord Lothian.

demned myself to grow like them, and partly in premonition of failure, for my masochism remains and will remain, only moral. Physically I can't do it: indeed I get in denial the gratification they get in indulgence. I react against their example into an abstention even more rigorous than of old. Everything bodily is now hateful to me (and in my case hateful is the same as impossible). In the sports lately (they vex us with set exercises) I was put down to jump, and refused because it was an activity of the flesh. Afterwards to myself I wondered if that was the reason, or was I afraid of failing ridiculously: so I went down alone and privily cleared over twenty feet, and was sick of mind at having tried because I was glad to find I still could jump. It's on a par with the music for which I'm hungry. Henry Lamb is in Poole, and will play wonderfully to me if I go over: and I won't go, though I'm so starved for rhythm that even a soldier's stumbling through a song on the piano makes my blood run smooth (I refuse to hear it with my head).

This sort of thing must be madness, and sometimes I wonder how far mad I am, and if a mad-house would not be my next (and merciful) stage. Merciful compared with this place, which hurts me, body and soul. It's terrible to hold myself voluntarily here: and yet I want to stay here till it no longer hurts me: till the burnt child no longer feels the fire. Do you think there have been many lay monks of my persuasion? One used to think that such frames of mind would have perished with the age of religion: and yet here they rise up, purely secular. It's a lurid flash into the Nitrian desert: seems almost to strip the sainthood from Anthony. How about Teresa?

I consume the day (and myself) brooding, and making phrases and reading and thinking again, galloping mentally down twenty divergent roads at once, as apart and alone as in Barton Street in my attic. I sleep less than ever, for the quietness of night imposes thinking on me: I eat breakfast only, and refuse every possible distraction and employment and exercise. When my mood gets too hot and I find myself wandering beyond control I pull out my motor-bike and hurl it top-speed through these unfit roads for hour after hour. My nerves are jaded and gone near dead, so that nothing less than hours of voluntary danger will prick them into life: and the 'life' they reach then is a melancholy joy at risking something worth exactly 2/9 a day.

It's odd, again, that craving for real risk: because in the gymnasium I funk jumping the horse, more than poison. That is physical, which is why it is: I'm ashamed of doing it and of not doing it, unwilling to do it: and most of all ashamed (afraid) of doing it well.

A nice, neurotic letter! What you've done to deserve its receipt God knows ... perhaps you have listened to me too friendly-like at earlier times. Sorry, and all that. You are a kind of safety-valve perhaps. I wish you were an alienist, and could tell me where or how this ferment will end. It makes me miserable on top of all the curiosity and determination: and sets me so much aside that I hardly blame the powers for jumping on me with their dull punishments.   L.

208: TO LIONEL CURTIS

30.V.23.

My Lord, Your letter was black and white: — white because of that Albright story. There seems a pitiful irony in my helping a mind diseased. A hair of the biter? or was it the picture of a sickness graver than his own? You know with neuroses the causeless ones are worst. If my success had not been so great, and so easy, I would despise it less: and when to my success in action there was added (according to those whose judgement I asked) success in book-writing, also at first venture — why then I broke down, and ran here to hide myself.

Isn't it just faintly possible that part of the virtue apparent in the book lies in its secrecy, its novelty, and its contestability? My hard verdict upon it commands your sympathy? The hope that it isn't as good as Shaw says sustains me ... And the blackness of your letter? Because it tempts me to run away from here, and so doing it marches with all my wishes against my will. Conscience in healthy men is a balanced sadism, the bitter sauce which makes more tasteful the ordinary sweets of life: and in sick stomachs the desire of condiment becomes a craving, till what is hateful feels therefore wholesome, and what is repugnant to the moral sense becomes (to the mind) therefore pure and righteous and to be pursued. So because my senses hate it, my will forces me to it . . . and a comfortable life would seem now to me sinful.

When I embarked on it, a year ago (it was June '22 that Trenchard accepted me for the R.A.F.) I thought it a mood, and curable: while today I feel that there is no change before me, and no hope of change. That's why your suggestions of one hurt me.

Your arguments, while they make me very grateful to yourself, are not heavy. I called you rich, once, in ideas and in furniture of mind: and you are rich, relative to these poor fellows here. You say my friends feel the absence of me — but personality (which it is my gift to you to exhibit) is of a short range, and in my experience has not touched more than ten or twelve friends at a time: and here I live with twenty very barren men, who feel my being with them. The hut is changed from what it used to be, and unlike what it would be (will be?) if I left. This isn't conceit, but a plain statement; for there would be a change if any one of us twenty was taken away: and I am richer and wider and more experienced than any of the others here. More of the world has passed over me in my 35 years than over all their twenties put together: and your gain, if you did gain by my return, would be their loss. It seems to me that the environment does not matter. Your circle does not draw from me (except superficially) more than theirs: indeed perhaps caenobite man influences as much as man social, for example is eternal, and the rings of its extending influence infinite.

For myself there are consolations. The perfect beauty of this place becomes tremendous, by its contrast with the life we lead, and the squalid huts we live in, and the noisy bullying authority of all our daily unloveliness. The nearly intolerable meanness of man is set in a circle of quiet heath, and budding trees, with the firm level bar of the Purbeck hills behind. The two worlds shout their difference in my ears. Then there is the irresponsibility: I have to answer here only for my cleanness of skin, cleanness of clothes, and a certain mechanical neatness of physical evolution upon the barrack-square. There has not been presented to me, since I have been here, a single choice: everything is ordained —

except that harrowing choice of going away from here the moment my will to stay breaks down. With this exception it would be determinism complete — and perhaps in determinism complete there lies the perfect peace I have so longed for. Free-will I've tried, and rejected: authority I've rejected (not obedience, for that is my present effort, to find equality only in subordination. It is dominion whose taste I have been cloyed with): action I've rejected: and the intellectual life: and the receptive senses: and the battle of wits. They were all failures, and my reason tells me therefore that obedience, nescience, will also fail, since the roots of common failure must lie in myself — and yet in spite of reason I am trying it.

Albright should have told his physician to heal himself ... but yet my best thanks for handing on the story. It cheered me a little bit, as Brutus must have been cheered when the Roman gossip praised his executed son.

This must be the end of egoistic writing: a safety valve may be good for a boiler, in saving it from bursting — but it's an abuse of it, to make it a pretext for habitually overloading the poor engine. Wherefore apologies, and it shall not happen any more.   L.

209: TO LIONEL CURTIS

27.VI.22 [*really* 23]

Old thing, This correspondence nearly died: might have died if you had not asked whether I did not join for the sake of the others here. Of course I didn't: things are done in answer to a private urge — not one of altruism.

You've been talking to Hogarth about my discomfort in the Tank Corps: but you know I joined partly to make myself unemployable, or rather impossible, in my old trade: and the burning out of freewill and self-respect and delicacy from a nature as violent as mine is bound to hurt a bit. If I was firmer I wouldn't cry about it.

It isn't all misery here either. There is the famous motor-bike as a temporary escape. Last Sunday was fine, and another day-slave and myself went off with it after church-parade. Wells we got to, and very beautiful it was: — a grey sober town, stiffly built of prim houses, but with nothing of the artificial in it. Everything is used and lived in; and to make the xvth century habitable today they have put in sash-windows everywhere.

One 'close', the Vicar's close, was nearly the best, it was so cloistered off (even from its quietest of streets): and so grey and green: for the local limestone has turned very sad with time, and has crannied, so that its angles are living with flowers of many sorts: and each of the 'cells' in this close has a little grass-plot between it and the common path down the centre: and on these plots poppies stood in groups like women at a garden party. There was sunshine over it, and a still air, so that all the essence of the place was drawn out and condensed about our heads. It was a college-like place, and looked good to live in: so for a while the camp waiting here for me became an ungrateful thought. Hogarth had written, hoping to get me back into the R.A.F. and the prospect of such happiness had made the Army nearly intolerable. However that's over, easily, for I was only hoping against the knowledge that it wouldn't be possible.

Afterwards I trailed into the cathedral precinct, and lay there on the grass, and watched its huge west front, covered over with bad sculpture, but very correct and proper still, in the manner of the town. There is a remoteness about cathedrals now-a-days — : they are things I could not contribute to, if they were still a-building: and in front of Wells today there was a white-frocked child playing with a ball; the child was quite unconscious of the cathedral (feeling only the pleasure of smooth grass) but from my distance she was so small that she looked no more than a tumbling daisy at the tower-foot: I knew of course that she was animal: and I began in my hatred of animals to balance her against the cathedral: and knew then that I'd destroy the building to save her. That's as irrational as what happened on our coming here, when I swerved Snowy Wallis and myself at 60 m.p.h. on to the grass by the roadside, trying vainly to save a bird which dashed out its life against my side-car. And yet had the world been mine I'd have left out animal life upon it.

An old thing (it pleased me to call him Canon) doddered over and sat by me on the grass, and gave me a penny for my thoughts:

and I told him (reading Huysmans lately) that I was pondering over the contrasts of English and French cathedrals. Ours set in closes so tree-bound and stately and primly-kept that they serve as a narthex to the shrine: a narthex at Wells grander and more religious than the building proper. Whereas French cathedrals have their feet in market places, and booths and chimneys and placards and noise hem them in: so that in France you step from your workshop into the aisle, and in England you cannot even enter till the lawns have swept the street-dust from your feet. The old clergyman gave me another penny to read him the riddle and I did it crab-wise, by a quote from du Bellay, and that Christchurch poem about Our Sovereign Lord the King. He was a book-worm too, and we talked Verhaeren and Melville and Lucretius together, with great pleasure on my part, and the vulgar relish that I was making a cockshy of his assurance that khaki covered nothing but primitive instincts.

He took me round the bishop's palace-garden, pumping me to learn how I endured camp life (living promiscuous seemed to his imagination horrible, and he by profession a shepherd of sheep!), and I hinted at the value of contrast which made all Wells crying-precious to me: and then we leaned over the wall and saw the fish in the moat, and it came upon me very hardly how excellent was their life. Fish are free of mankind you know, and are always perfectly suspended, without ache or activity of nerves, in their sheltering element.

We can get it, of course, when we earth-in our bodies, but it seems to me that we can only do that when they are worn out. It's a failure to kill them out of misery, for if there isn't any good or evil but only activity, and no pain or joy, only sensation: then we can't kill ourselves while we can yet feel. However I'd rather be the fish (did you ever read Rupert Brooke's 'And there shall be no earth in heaven', said fish')[1] or the little bird which had killed itself against me that morning.

There, my letters always end in tears!   E.

[The following letter to Colonel Wavell appears to me particularly important as an exposition of Lawrence's military

---

[1] 'And in that Heaven of all their wish, There shall be no more land, say fish'.

ideas. The last sentence records his visit to Mecca in 1918 to choose his gold dagger. A reference to this visit also occurs in Nos. 134 and 309]

210: TO COLONEL A. P. WAVELL

21. V. 23.

Dear Wavell, Many thanks for the book[1] (which has gone forward to its next) and for your long letter. It's exactly the sort of thing which I wanted to read.

No, I don't feel confident militarily. All the while we fought I felt like a conjuror trying an insufficiently-rehearsed trick — surprised when it came out right. A succession of such chances gave me the feeling I was apt at the business: that's all.

Chap. 35. The substance of this was boiled up for Guy Dawnay some years ago, when he started a thing called the *Army Quarterly*, & asked me for a contribution.[2] You will find it in the 1st number of the *Quarterly*. He liked it better than I did. Most people found it either recondite, or too smart.

I met your cousin once, at a push in London: had no proper talk of him.

As for the reply to raiding tactics. As you say, it's greater mobility than the attack. This needn't mean large drafts from the harrassed G.O.C. If the Turks had put machine guns on three or four of their touring cars, & driven them on weekly patrol over the admirable going of the desert E. of Amman & Maan they would have put an absolute stop to our camel-parties, & so to our rebellion. It wouldn't have cost them 20 men or £20,000 . . . *rightly applied*. They scraped up cavalry & armoured trains & camel corps & block-houses against us: because they didn't think hard enough.

I held the Rolls-Royce Armoured Cars in Akaba as a riposte if (or when) Turk cars came at us: for I couldn't imagine our being left free all the time: but we had only 5 R.R. and would

[1] A copy of the Oxford Text of *Seven Pillars of Wisdom*, which Wavell had returned.
[2] *The Evolution of a Revolt*, by T. E. Lawrence, *The Army Quarterly* No. 1, 1920.

have been on the defensive with them, quite unable to guard our raiding front. They would have sufficed only to cover Aba el Lissan–Tafileh, the Arab Regular Army front.

Well-destruction was possible only at Bair & Jefer, as our other waters were superficial: & we could have dispensed with B. & J. So that the Turks couldn't stop us with demolitions.

There is one other thing of which every rebellion is mortally afraid — treachery. If instead of counter-propaganda (never effective on the conservative side) the money had been put into buying the few venial men always to be found in a big movement, then they would have crippled us. We could only dare these intricate raids because we felt sure and safe. One well-informed traitor will spoil a national rising.

Bombing tribes is ineffective. I fancy that air-power may be effective against elaborate armies: but against irregulars it has no more than moral value. The Turks had plenty [of] machines, & used them freely against us — and never hurt us till the last phase, when we had brought 1000 of our regulars on the raid against Deraa. Guerrilla tactics are a complete muffing of air-force.

Jurgen I've read.[1] As you say v.G. Many thanks for offering me a copy: but in this atmosphere one reads very little.

As for writing more — to tell you the truth I'm sick of all manner of effort, & want never to do anything again. I've put my mind to sleep, coming here.

Yes, I've promised not to admit the Mecca jest. I did it because I wanted to choose my own gold dagger, & it was not serious for me. Hussein will never forgive it me.   .L.

211: TO MRS. THOMAS HARDY

21.v.23

Dear Mrs. Hardy, I'm afraid I'll come on Saturday next at tea-time! De la Mare is known to me only by his books — but he should be delightful, if he lives up to them: and most good people are better than their books.

---

[1] *Jurgen*, by James Branch Cabell.

It sounds greedy, always to come when you ask me: but your house is so wonderfully unlike this noisy room that it is difficult to resist, even for its own sake: and then there is Mr. Hardy, though you mustn't tell him so, for the thrill is too one-sided. He has seen so much of human-kind that he must be very tired of them: whereas for me he's Hardy, & I'd go a long way even to see the place where he had lived, let alone him living in it.

There, you will think me absurd: but still I'll arrive on Saturday! Yours sincerely   T E SHAW

212: TO D. G. HOGARTH

13.VI.23

It's a difficult question you ask me. The Tanks are interesting, the company hardly tolerable, even to my stomach. There is an animal reek here which keeps me awake at night with horror that mankind should be like it: because I feel that we are the unnatural, & that Hut F.12 is the truth about human-kindness.

Contrast this with the R.A.F. (not Uxbridge: the exercise there was too severe for me) in which I was as contented as ever I had been: even my mind stopped working there: whereas here I lie awake nights on end, thinking about everything germane.

And why I enlisted? The security of it first: seven years existence guaranteed. I haven't any longer the mind to fight for sustenance. As you realise I've finished with the 'Lawrence' episode. I don't like what rumour makes of him — not the sort of man I'd like to be! and the life of politics wearied me out, by worrying me over-much. I've not got a coarse-fibred enough nature for them: and have too many scruples and an uneasy conscience. It's not good to see two sides of questions, when you have (officially) to follow one.

Exit politics (Irak candidates had no share in my disgust. Indeed I don't think I did badly, in sum.). There went most of my money value. Exit Lawrence: and there is most of the residue of my earning power gone. I haven't a trade to follow: and won't do the two or three things for which I'm qualified: hence I'm reduced to soldiering. You see, I'm 35 nearly: and that's too old to make a fresh start in a skilled business.

When I joined the R.A.F. it was in the hope that some day I'd write a book about the very excellent subject that it was. At that time I thought my Arab Revolt book very bad. Since then Shaw has turned my mind slowly to consider it good: and there's another ambition gone, for it was always in my hope to write a decent book: and if I've done it there seems little reason to do another. A pity, for my Uxbridge notes were good, & there was the making of a very good thing out of the life of a squadron. It will be a puzzle for my biographer (if I have one of those unprofitable things) to reconcile my joy in the R.A.F. with my disgust with the Army. The R.A.F. is utterly unlike this place: the men are so different, & their hopes & minds & talk. They weren't happy: it used to be said at Farnborough that I was the only happy man there. . . . but they were essentially decent: and the going has been rather a jerk to me. I feel queerly homesick whenever I see a blue uniform in the street.

But for going back to the R.A.F. — there my hands are tied. Trenchard (in sacking me) offered me a commission. I said I couldn't take it: and begged to be left in: but he couldn't do it: asked me to take my discharge as final: and he's not a mind-changer, & I don't want to bother him with my personal whims. So I don't think there is any remedy.

You talk about Govt. money. I take it every week, so that I haven't any scruples: but I'm worth more than 3/- a day only in politics & Middle East, & there I don't play: and a temporary job at a high salary would only cart me worse than ever at the end. It's hard enough, now, to go poor again: and every year of money would make it far worse.

When I saw Amery he was thinking of coastguard or lighthouse for me: and the latter felt to me like so complete a withdrawal from the world as to enable me to publish that book & get the job over.

Now that notion has gone of course, & I propose to let the book blush unseen. After all, so long as I can keep alive in other ways, why bother with the unpleasant way?

I took the All Souls' money this year, & have spent it on

pictures. I felt nervous at the length of time my drawings were taking, & anxious to end them quickly; & I distrusted my power of earning enough in the Army or R.A.F. to pay for the six or seven yet required.

As a matter of fact I am earning a little — translating a French novel just now: and Cape, the publisher, has written suggesting I do Mardrus' *Arabian Nights* into English for him. I'm willing — if unsigned — and that would bring me in the price of some more drawings.

There, that's how I stand: and I see no way out of it. It's good that A. has got that thing at the end.[1] He has wanted it persistently: & therefore presumably deserves it. I agree with you about hellenistic sculpture.   T E.

213: TO D. G. HOGARTH

*Wed.*27.vi.23

I was rather expecting such an issue: so am not worrying. A commission is out of the question. My prejudice against exercising authority would prevent my becoming even an N.C.O.!

(By the way it was Hoare who first moved to get me out of the R.A.F.: Trenchard felt it not a big enough point to fight) As for the Navy, I asked Amery for it since I felt he might agree, & that the W.O. would not entertain the idea of admitting me. The contrary proved the case. I doubt whether there is a pin to choose between Navy & Tanks, & prefer the devil I know.

As for getting reconciled to Tanks. ... Well, I expected much of what I have received — and so discounted it in advance: and the reality of it is probably not worse than the reality of any other unit. It's only that the R.A.F. is so much better. However please leave things. Trenchard is not good to force — & has major worries. [*5 lines omitted*]   T.E.

I feel I've explained myself so badly to you. Would Faust's phrase 'von allem Wissensqualm entladen'[2] be any good? It's a like case.

---

[1] His younger brother, A. W. Lawrence, had got a scholarship for travel and research in Hellenistic sculpture.
[2] 'Relieved from all the steam of knowledge.'

214: TO MRS. THOMAS HARDY

15.VIII.23.

Dear Mrs. Hardy, Your remark about 'uplift' has been puzzling me. One of my reasons for suppressing the book was that I believed it to be perverse and disturbing: a book likely to harm rather than [do] good to the normal person who would read it. It is meant to be the true history of a political movement whose essence was a fraud — in the sense that its leaders did not believe the arguments with which they moved its rank and file: and also the true history of a campaign, to show how unlovely the back of a commander's mind must be.

So what you said cuts right across my belief, & has puzzled me. Will you tell me what you would do — publish or leave private — if yourself or Mr. Hardy had written such a book? Apologies for bothering you: but the value of the book would give me an income which would keep me out of the army: and I'm wondering since Sunday whether perhaps I may be able to enjoy it. Yours sincerely   T. E. SHAW.

Another matter. *If* Mr. Hardy does such things, would he inscribe me copies of his thin-paper *Poems* & *Dynasts*. I have them & could bring them across. I know it's a vulgar desire; but I live in vulgar company: and they would be very precious possessions.

215: TO GERTRUDE BELL

18.VIII.23

Dear Gertrude, The £300 was an old estimate for setting up 350,000 words. Chiswick Press. There is a slight smugness about the Clarendon Press, & I shrink from the task of educating them suddenly.

The difficulty of a subscription edition is how many to print, & what to do with the materials left over (plates etc.). For this reason I would rather be indebted to one than to many. I'm turning over in my mind the alternative — to publish Garnett's abridgement (approved by Hogarth) & do the subscription edition with its profits. On Monday I may go to Oxford (they may send me near there as escort to a lorry column) & if so will try to see D.G.H. Yours   T E L

216: TO C. M. DOUGHTY

18.VIII.23

Dear Mr. Doughty, I believe that tomorrow you become eighty years old. That's magnificent, for I hope that you are faced with leisure for the moment: *Mansoul* finished very honourably, *Arabia* famous (after forty years), Merriecroft[1] comfortable. It sounds to me like a satisfactory eighty years in retrospect: at least I'd be content to look back so. I hope your health is good: inland air isn't always easy after long use of sea air: I hope also that Mrs. Doughty is glad. Yours sincerely

                                                    T E LAWRENCE

217: TO D. G. HOGARTH

23.VIII.23

Gertrude wrote and asked for a copy of *The Seven Pillars*. I wrote back & said I had none, but if she had a tame millionaire who would put up say £300 for a reprint, then I was willing to reprint it.

She replied that she hadn't a millionaire handy, but that several people, anxious for copies, would contribute.

It puts me back at the 'subscription' edition, privately printed, the obstacle last raised by Cape, & from which I finally withdrew. Now I'm hesitating again. It's pitiful to have a mind so feeble in purpose.

What am I to do? Publish the Garnett abridgement after all, with such restrictions as seem fit to me, and use its profits to publish a limited illustrated complete edition . . . publish nothing . . . or print privately?

[1] Doughty's house at Sissinghurst in Kent.

Hardy read the thing lately, & made me very proud with what he said of it. Shaw (have you seen him?) praised it. Alan Dawnay compares it, not unfavourably, with the lost edition. I still feel that it's a pessimistic unworthy book, full of the neurosis of the war, & I hate the idea of selling it. If I won't make profit of my war-reputation, still less should I make profit of my war-story. Yet Lowell Thomas lurks still in the background, & if his book is the fulsome thing I expect, he will force the truth out of me. It might be better to get my blow in first.

You have read the original and the abridgement . . . will you tell me what, in my place, you would do?   T.E.

218: TO ROBERT GRAVES

8.ix.23

Peccavi: but always that happens. Look upon me as a habitual incorrigible sinner: and blame upon yourself part of this last silence: for in your letter to me (that which caused the silence) you said 'Tell me about Max Gate'[1] — and I can't!

The truth seems to be that Max Gate is very difficult to seize upon. I go there as often as I decently can, and hope to go on going there so long as it is within reach: (Sundry prices I've paid in Coy Office for these undefended absences) but description isn't possible. Hardy is so pale, so quiet, so refined into an essence: and camp is such a hurly-burly. When I come back I feel as if I'd woken up from a sleep: not an exciting sleep, but a restful one. There is an unbelievable dignity and ripeness about Hardy: he is waiting so tranquilly for death, without a desire or ambition left in his spirit, as far as I can feel it: and yet he entertains so many illusions, and hopes for the world, things which I, in my disillusioned middle-age, feel to be illusory. They used to call this man a pessimist. While really he is full of fancy expectations.

Then he is so far-away. Napoleon is a real man to him, and the country of Dorsetshire echoes that name everywhere in Hardy's ears. He lives in his period, and thinks of it as the great war:

[1] Thomas Hardy's house which he had built himself on the outskirts of Dorchester.

whereas to me that nightmare through the fringe of which I passed has dwarfed all memories of other wars, so that they seem trivial, half-amusing incidents.

Also he is so assured. I said something a little reflecting on Homer: and he took me up at once, saying that it was not to be despised: that it was very kin to *Marmion* ... saying this not with a grimace, as I would say it, a feeling smart and original and modern, but with the most tolerant kindness in the world. Conceive a man to whom Homer and Scott are companions: who feels easy in such presences.

And the standards of the man! He feels interest in everyone, and veneration for no-one. I've not found in him any bowing-down, moral or material or spiritual. [6 *lines omitted*] Yet any little man finds this detachment of Hardy's a vast compliment and comfort. He takes me as soberly as he would take John Milton (how sober that name is), considers me as carefully, is as interested in me: for to him every person starts scratch in the life-race, and Hardy has no preferences: and I think no dislikes, except for the people who betray his confidence and publish him to the world.

Perhaps that's partly the secret of that strange house hidden behind its thicket of trees. It's because there are no strangers there. Anyone who does pierce through is accepted by Hardy and Mrs. Hardy as one whom they have known always and from whom nothing need be hid.

For the ticket which gained me access to T.H. I'm grateful to you — probably will be grateful always. Max Gate is a place apart: and I feel it all the more poignantly for the contrast of life in this squalid camp. It is strange to pass from the noise and thoughtlessness of sergeants' company into a peace so secure that in it not even Mrs. Hardy's tea-cups rattle on the tray: and from a barrack of hollow senseless bustle to the cheerful calm of T.H. thinking aloud about life to two or three of us. If I were in his place I would never wish to die: or even to wish other men dead. The peace which passeth all understanding; — but it can be felt, and is nearly unbearable. How envious such an old age is.

However, here is enough of trying to write about something

which is so precious that I grudge writing about it. T.H. is an experience that a man must keep to himself.

I hope your writing goes: that your household goes: that your peace of mind grows. I'm afraid that last does not. Yet I have achieved it in the ranks at the price of stagnancy and beastliness: and I don't know, yet, if it is worth it.   E.L.

219: TO R. V. BUXTON

22. IX. 23.

Dear Robin, Glad you are reading the thing. Please don't inhibit yourself from scribbling comments of an insulting sort in the margins, made especially wide for the purpose. Your praise makes my stomach warm: but your criticisms are really helpful: whether in the field of morality, belles-lettres, tactics, or just manners. Down with them while you can!

The 'Seven Pillars of Wisdom' is a quotation from *Proverbs*: it is used as title out of sentiment: for I wrote a youthful indiscretion-book, so called, in 1913 and burned it (as immature) in '14 when I enlisted. It recounted adventures in seven type-cities of the East (Cairo, Bagdad, Damascus etc.) & arranged their characters into a descending cadence: a moral symphony. It was a queer book, upon whose difficulties I look back with a not ungrateful wryness: and in memory of it I so named the new book, which will probably be the only one I ever write, & which sums up & exhausts me to the date of 1919.

S.A. was a person, now dead, regard for whom lay beneath my labour for the Arabic peoples. I don't propose to go further into detail thereupon.[1]

Quelle vie qu'on mène ici!

About a private printing. A hundred copies could be plain-printed for £3 each: or 300 copies could be produced, with the fifty or sixty portraits I've bust myself upon, for £10 a copy. My hesitant mind slides between them uncertainly. The dear book would be a wonderful volume, in every sense except the writing. I wish my prose wasn't so academic. There is a literary-priggish-ness about it which sets an open-aired man's teeth on edge.

[1] See dedication to *Seven Pillars of Wisdom*.

Have you read my account of the I.C.C. march?[1] Please say honestly what parts of it, or of its tone, hurt your feelings. I was wrapped up in my burden in Arabia, & say things only through its distorting prism: & so did third parties wrong. It wasn't meant: just the inevitable distraction of a commander whose spirit was at civil war within himself.   E.

220: TO EDWARD GARNETT

26. IX. 23.

I'm hardly fit to write to — the replies come so late and are so slattern. The last chapter of *Gulliver* explains it,[2] for I'm becoming (at last . . . it's been a tough process) one of my company.

To such, books as refined as Hudson's are not proper: and yet I'd like one very much. Will you send me that which people least want? the one which has lingered on your shelf? There isn't anything else to say. I'm trained now, and tanks are behind me. [16 *lines omitted*]

221: TO C. M. DOUGHTY

27. IX. 23.

Dear Mr. Doughty, I'm reading *Mansoul*[3]: it's not ended yet, for my reading time is only snips and snippets of time: but I want to give you my opinion that the added parts work perfectly into the old, and fill it out to a much better roundness. There is a strange finality across the whole poem, which makes a queer impression on me as I read it. What to call it (the impression) I

---

[1] Colonel Buxton commanded the Imperial Camel Corps in Arabia during the campaign.

[2] The last chapter of *Gulliver* – the reference is to Captain Gulliver's slowly overcoming his intense disgust at the human species – Yahoos – on his return: 'I began last week to permit my wife to sit at dinner with me at the farthest end of a long table; and to answer (but with the utmost brevity) the few questions I asked her. Yet, the smell of a Yahoo continuing very offensive, I always keep my nose stopped with rue, lavender, or tobacco leaves. And although it will be hard for a man late in life to remove old habits, I am not altogether out of hopes in some time to suffer a neighbour Yahoo in my company.'

[3] The first edition of *Mansoul*, published by Selwyn & Blount, 1920, was considerably revised and added to in the second edition, Cape, 1923.

don't know. I feel less human as I read, as if I'd been taken out of the world of living things, and had been made part of the hills or woods.

Probably I won't feel like this when I end the book: which is why I'm sending you this interim note on the power with which you have written it.

I mentioned Lord Hartington to you, didn't I, once in Eastbourne? He has just written to me asking for an introduction to you. I've replied that you have moved, and that he needs no introduction. If he can still come (Kent is not, like Eastbourne, a place where he visits of necessity) you will find him very good. His brother-in-law, Harold Macmillan, would like to come with him.

My regards to Mrs. Doughty. I hope that Merriecroft succeeds well. Yours ever   T. E. LAWRENCE

222 : TO EDWARD GARNETT

4. x. 23.   [postmarked Bovington]

The Hudson's are sumptuous. How well the old man reads in them. The *Shepherd* has found two friendly readers already: yet I like better, much better, the memories of his childhood.[1]

Wonderful that one man should have written that, and *Patagonia*, and *The Purple Land*, and *Green Mansions*: and I go about thinking that into his first book anyone not a born writer can put all that his spirit holds.

Hudson is hardly a born writer, either. Not for him that frenzied aching delight in a pattern of words which happen to run true. Do you know that lately I have been finding my deepest satisfaction in the collocation of words so ordinary and plain that they cannot mean anything to a book-jaded mind: and out of some of such I can draw deep stuff. Is it perhaps that certain sequences of vowels or consonants imply more than others: that writing of this sort has music in it? I don't want to affirm it, and yet I would not deny it: for if writing can have sense (and it has: this letter has) and sound why shouldn't it have something of pattern too? My sequences seem to be independent

[1] *Far Away and Long Ago*, by W. H. Hudson.

EE

of ear . . . to impose themselves through the eye alone. I achieved a good many of them in *Le Gigantesque*[1] : but fortuitously for the most part.

Do you think that people ever write *consciously* well? or does that imply an inordinate love for the material, and so ruin the art? I don't see that it should. A sculptor who petted his marbles from sheer joy in their grain and fineness would (pari passu) be better than a mere block-butcher. In scathing me for wasting my talent in an unproductive way you miss that I do it perversely and on purpose: that I came here to wipe out my inconvenient power of doing things at other people's bidding. Here they only bid me scrub floors or dig holes or move things material like mountains: and such ruck-jobs (while they irk very deeply) give me a wholesome secure feeling that I am harmlessly employed.

Of course it would be better to be benefiting humanity: but I don't see how I can, when I disbelieve in my own products. And better do nothing than make *Gigantesques*. I said in *The Seven Pillars* that I'd botch another man's work and better it: but would create nothing more my own.

More thanks for the Hudsons.   T.E.

Robin Buxton (a humane banker) suggests 120 copies of *The Seven Pillars*, with all pictures, at perhaps £25 each, if that would cover charges. I feel tempted. . .

223: TO R. V. BUXTON

4. X. 23

Dear Robin, Your idea of 120 copies at £25: it sounds V.G.

Lionel Curtis (whom R. Holland-Martin knows) was thinking of something such. I've told him of your idea.

Also have written to the colour-printers to ask for a new estimate of costs.

Will you put the enclosed in to your manager? Yours   T.E.

If the idea comes off I want to wangle enough to fill up my overdraft. It worries me rather, & yet is magnificent: for it has

---

[1] Lawrence was translating *Le Gigantesque*, by Adrien le Corbeau, published under the title of *The Forest Giant*, by Cape.

enabled me to take a ruined cottage in a wood near camp, & this I'm fitting up with the hope of having a warm solitary place to hide in sometimes on winter evenings. This district is unusually desolate (of good company) & I covet the idea of being sometimes by myself near a fire.

[The cottage Lawrence had taken, Clouds Hill, is a mile and a half from Bovington Camp, across the heath over which the tanks career, in an oasis of privately owned land. The road rises a little before reaching it to a crest and dips sharply through a saucer-shaped bit of ground (the contour is that of a saucer tipped up on one side). There are some acres of wooded land, with oak trees rising among rhododendrons. Under the steepest edge of the hill is Lawrence's cottage: on the other side of the road a cottage formerly belonging to Sergeant Knowles and now inhabited by Pat Knowles. E. M. Forster has recently published a description (in *The Listener*, September 1st, 1938) of Clouds Hill as it was when he first visited it and of the part it played in Lawrence's life, from which I take the following passages.

In those days the two bottom rooms were full of firewood and lumber. We lived upstairs, and the sitting room there looks now much as did then, though the gramophone and the books have gone, and the fender with its bent ironwork has been remodelled. It was, and it is, a brownish room — wooden beams and ceiling, leather-covered settee. Here we talked, played Beethoven's symphonies, ate and drank. We drank water only or tea — no alcohol ever entered Clouds Hill . . . and we ate — this sounds less romantic — out of tins. T.E. always laid in a stock of tinned dainties for his guests. There were no fixed hours for meals and no one sat down. If you felt hungry you opened a tin and drifted about with it. . . . T.E. slept in camp, coming out when he could during the day, as did the rest of the troops. It was fine being alone in Clouds Hill at night: so silent. . . .

I don't know whether I'm at all conveying in these trivial remarks the atmosphere of the place — the happy casualness of it, and the feeling that no one particularly owned it. T. E. had the power of distributing the sense of possession among all the friends who came there.[1] When Thomas

[1] See letters Nos. 511, 523 and 552.

Hardy turned up, for instance, as he did one sunny after-noon, he seemed to come on a visit to us all, and not specially to see his host. Thomas Hardy and Mrs. Hardy came up the narrow stairway into the little brown room and there they were — the guests of us all. To think of Clouds Hill as T. E.'s home is to get the wrong idea of it. It wasn't his home, it was rather his *pied-à-terre*, the place where his feet touched the earth for a moment, and found rest.

I insert here, out of its place, a description of Clouds Hill which Lawrence sent the following summer to A. E. Chambers, whom he had got to know first at Farnborough, but who was at that time stationed at Duxford.]

224: TO A. E. CHAMBERS

3.VIII.24.   *Clouds Hill Moreton Dorset*

[34 *lines omitted*] Wool is the Station, the cottage is alone in a dip in the moor, very quiet, very lonely, very bare. A mile from camp. Furnished with a bed, a bicycle, three chairs, 100 books, a gramo-phone of parts, a table. Many windows, oak-trees, an ilex, birch, firs, rhododendron, laurels, heather. Dorsetshire to look at. No food, except what a grocer & the camp shops & canteens provide. Milk. Wood fuel for the picking up. I don't sleep here, but come out 4.30 p.m. till 9 p.m. nearly every evening, & dream, or write or read by the fire, or play Beethoven & Mozart to myself on the box. Sometimes one or two Tank-Corps-slaves arrive & listen with me ... but few of them care for abstract things. If you came you would be very much alone all day.

Nearly I came to look for you the over day. Wells (a novelist, H. G., nearly famous) asked me to his place at Dunmow for a week-end, & Duxford lay on my right as I returned by motor-bike. Only the poor beast wasn't running well, & I was in khaki & was ashamed. Ave   TES.

(ex J.H.R.
ex T.E.L.)

225: TO SYDNEY COCKERELL

22. X. 23   *[Bovington]*

Excellenz, It's a choice between Sassoon[1] & Squire? . . . Well,
let the poet win: I'd always put poets first, & men afterwards.
In sending it to S.S. will you ask him to return the copy to you
after reading? then you can send it on to Squire . . . If my memory
is straight yours is a black-leather copy, not ill-tooled, though a
little too assertive for the very squalid text of its contents. S.S.
will not hold it over-long if he knows that you intend it for
another after him. Your discretion is complete, and accordingly
you will know whether to tell each that the other is, or is about to,
read it.

'A tremendous masterpiece' . . . no, you are wrong there. It's
not a masterpiece, for it lacks form and continuity & colour:
αχρωματος ασχηματιστος . . .[2] & it is not tremendous, for it can be
no bigger than my petty self. Hysterical, curious, a human document: those are its proper adjectives.

My view of Doughty? But I like him too much (or his books,
rather) to start an analysis: you see the analysis proceeds always
on its own rails, beyond your control, except to set a bound to:
and my instinct forewarns me that in my sketch of Doughty
would be much criticism. His greatness is achieved by limiting
himself and his judgement, so that he is few-sided and confident
in himself. A fuller man would be more modest in attempted
performance. D's moral pride is betrayed by the scale of his
works' designs. It is the man less than great who dares to write
greatly. D. holds no multiplication of characters in him: he is a
man rather than a universe.

There is a prospect (Hogarth can tell you more) of a private
edition of my book next year. Three hundred copies, perhaps,
at a ten-guinea price, to cover the reproduction of pictures. A
subscribed edition of course, without publishers or book-sellers
or reviews.

In giving my MS to the Bodleian I acted perhaps unhumorously

---

[1] A copy of the Oxford Text of *Seven Pillars of Wisdom*. Both Siegfried Sassoon and
J. C. Squire, wanted to read it.

[2] Plato, *Phaedrus*, line 247 C. This passage is quoted in *Seven Pillars of Wisdom*,
Chap. III.

taking myself a little too seriously as a classic. Cowley was equal
to the occasion, & never smiled at all throughout the transaction.
Whether he has a treasure or not the next century can tell. It rids
me of a bulky weighty volume. A neat manuscript don't you
think? There is of course no need of restriction in its use: the
man who could read so much of my handwriting would deserve
what he found. It's the third edition (identical with the printed
copies) but the fourth, if it comes out, will be widely different —
and better, if my skill has not wholly gone.

I have not been to Max Gate lately: the army is dyeing me
khaki by degrees, & I don't know that I'm any longer much company for real people. At least I feel that way, so shall abstain till
I'm different.   T.E. ?

226: TO SYDNEY COCKERELL

27. X. 23.   [Bovington Camp]

[36 lines omitted] Tolstoy is a very great man (War & Peace,
above all else) & I'd like to see the Conversations. A while ago
(2 years perhaps) the Hogarth Press published some by Gorki.

Good news about Doughty.[1] Wish I had a relative.

Of course I admire him enormously, but I'd admire his simplicity more if it was artificial, a laborious surface covering thousands of facets & phases, than now, when it is natural to him. A
bigger man would not read the Morning Post.[2] Yours ever

                                                      T.E.L.

227 : TO JONATHAN CAPE[3]

[October, 1923]

Sturly, by Pierre Custot, is a picture of the ocean written
from beneath the waves. The author is learned in deep-sea
fish, a little of a poet, a skilled hand at prose. He has used
his beloved fish as a vehicle to convey to us his comments on the

---

[1] Doughty had unexpectedly come into an annuity of £2000 a year.

[2] See letter No. 136. 'Morning Post I don't touch: it seems to me not sane.' The simplicity
of Doughty's patriotism, which was without reservations, was not possible to Lawrence
after the Peace Conference.

[3] This was written as a 'blurb' for Sturly which Lawrence had undertaken to translate.
It is a parody of the advertisements on book wrappers. See Cape's contribution to
T. E. Lawrence by His Friends.

.T.E.L.

Instruct me when it is the proper
moment for me to journey out to
Chiswick.

When the staff is stitched up I'll
send you the mass for your amusement.

Bateman is a sound suggestion: though
your lighter efforts are not so far from
kin to his.

.E.L.

He's got a telephone! Help

.L.

Yours

The Army is muck, stink,
& a desolate abomination

your wife at my not seeing her yesterday: but that!

Meynell wouldn't ever come in. He could say
simply that Pike had hired of him a press:

world, and nature, and human kind; but with so much skill that the fish always keep the fore-front of the view, and tinge the whole story with a vivid strangeness. These hardly-known inhabitants of deep water have hitherto been the preserve of scientists, and their marvels have been guessed at rather than described. M. Custot is widely read and has digested what is to be studied of their lore ... while his interest in human life is strong enough everywhere to subordinate the scientist to the philosopher and man of letters. Consequently the instincts and accidents and reflexions of his fishes are lively for us; and they are embedded in such word-pictures of the sea and coasts that the complete work is memorable. There is no moralising, no rhetoric, no verbiage: just a sinewy tale, so swiftly told that the labour of its writing is unperceived.

228: TO ERIC KENNINGTON

5. XI. 23.

Dear Kennington, I sent you a day ago four Dobson's, numbered 1. 2. 3. 4. They are all of Colonel Joyce, and one of them (3) is his choice for himself.

I'm to buy one: have paid for it out of C's.[1] bounty. I like 2, the slighter chalk, and 4, the rather too smooth pencil profile. Will you judge for me, take the best drawing, and send the odd three back to Dobson.

It's a case which I can't judge. They seem to me all very good ... and very like. ... Yours ever [*a scrawl: see plate opposite*]

The Army is muck, stink, and a desolate abomination.

229: TO D. G. HOGARTH

14.XI.23

I'll send back your drafts when I next write from the hut: this is being scribbled standing up elsewhere.

Curtis & yourself are considering the idea of 10 guinea subscribers. Buxton is seeing the chance of one hundred at 30

---

[1] Lionel Curtis had bought Lawrence's gold-sheathed Meccan dagger which is now at All Souls College in the custody of the Manciple.

pounds. Cape is looking for a single millionaire at £3000. I'm waiting events.

One of the three alternatives may happen. In anticipation of it I've taken a cottage (at 2/6 a week) near camp, & fitted up a writing room in it. There I can revise my text, in about a twelve-month, allowing say 2 hrs average per day. More than this is too much. I've got into an 'employed job' here, which will keep me in camp a year or two. I can let you (or whoever edits) have the revised text a book at a time, gradually. The pictures will take about a year to do, I expect. So that the whole project may be complete within 18 months.

For the text I want your copy, the only one left in sheets. It can be replaced with a bound copy, if you wish it: though of course if the new text feels better I'll destroy all the six copies of the old one.

Saw Trenchard on Sunday. He said something about a month's leave for me. I said no, since returning here would be unpleasant after so long a holiday. The Army does not improve upon longer knowledge.

Clarendon Press might well print: I want Caslon eleven point or its nearest monotype equivalent.

The book's size is determined by the ready plates (10 × 8, I think it is, a large quarto, much that of the 1st Edition). If I can get it to 250,000 words it will go in one vol. of 450 words a page.

.L.

I should have written earlier, but things have been muddled.

230: TO JONATHAN CAPE

14.XI.23.

Dear Cape, I think this is a coming thing, though you won't think it, the man being a poet and his work verse.[1] Augustus John showed it me, and I think it very good. Man is 21, and a believer in Keats and Shelley and *Moby Dick*, with other influences visible: — but the thing is very good. He wants a publisher, so

[1] *The Flaming Terrapin,* by Roy Campbell.

John told me, and I think it might pay you (especially if you covet the Heinemann succession) to write to him. Keep Aug. John also in mind. A John drawing would help the book, and J. is keen on the man: has painted him rather well.

About my own work: Buxton, my banker, holds to his 100 copies at £30: and is sounding about to see what names he can find. Curtis and Hogarth are exploring the region of £10. 10. 0 subscribers. So these are variant plans. The millionaire solution is easiest.

If you get that copy out of Garvin please let me know. Yours,

T.E.

231: TO MRS. THOMAS HARDY

2. XII. 23

Dear Mrs. Hardy, I've been waiting since Wednesday for the moment fit to write in about that night: and it has not come. So here goes, in the cleaning-up hour, with a babble of songs & quips over my head, & the trumpets just blowing 'First Post', outside. Also it is raining, & I am tired. Please pardon the inefficiency therefore.

I asked Russell[1] his mind. He said, again, that the audience were unworthy: that they interrupted his notice of the play.[2] He much liked the Chorus: its slow speech, and the continuity it gave the action, & the brevity. The two songs were 'luvely': the words spoken in the balcony were superfluous. A look & gesture would have been enough. (I, too, felt that the Queen's 'I can't bear this' was dangerously near common speech.)

So far Russell. We tried to get over together once more: but facts (and the Orderly Sergeant) were not kind. We got no penalty for Wednesday's crime however: yet I would have liked the second hearing.

What took away my mind, so that I could only stammer to you in the hall, was the beauty & power of the verse. The phrases

---

[1] Private Russell, Royal Tank Corps.
[2] A performance of *The Famous Tragedy of the Queen of Cornwall*, by Thomas Hardy, given at Dorchester.

preserved their full force in that artless limpid speech of the actors: and I've never heard finer English spoken. That's the profit of the simple acting . . . Your people had no technique, no arts and graces, to put between their 'book' and us. It took my breath away . . . and then the two silly people behind you began to giggle. I suppose they have had no agony in their lives, & cannot see tragedy in others even when it is great & very greatly put. The 'O Jan' was like a benediction after a very stormy sermon: a blessed piece of foolery to give our poise back to us.

You must have felt very happy after all the nights were over.

I'm so glad that I enlisted, because daily troubles here make desperately sharp the pleasures — speed, the country-side, quietness — which I get in my leisure: and one of the best hours I've had in my life was that one in the Corn Exchange.

Russell asks me to send you his best thanks: and his hopes that Tristram will be done again where he can hear it. Yours sincerely   T.E.S.

232: TO R. V. BUXTON

13. XII. 23   *Clouds Hill Moreton Dorset*

Dear Robin, This is to report what we did the other Sunday: Hogarth, Curtis, Dawnay & me. Decided to begin straight away. To print 100 copies at 30 guineas, & a matter of twenty *incomplete* copies to be given away by myself free to protagonists of the campaign.

Myself, a man of straw, to be solely responsible for the printing, production, & distribution of the book. This because it must inevitably be libellous. Civil Libel Actions break down because I have no money: criminal, because prison wouldn't seem to me worse than the Tank Corps.

Procedure

Hogarth, Curtis (& I hope especially yourself) will tell their friends that the book is coming, in about a year's time, & that if they want a copy they must write to me.

I'll reply explaining the conditions of subscription:

They will (if so minded) pay in a cheque. Will you decide the technicalities of this payment? I mean, in what name it should be, (if, as I expect it should be a special account), and how & in what name I draw upon it.

I'm writing to a private printer, to ask him for a scheme & estimate. It is my intention that the production shall contravene the copyright act (in that no printers' name shall appear on the finished copies) & probably I'll take a £10 share in the firm to create the fiction that the printing is done by myself.

I propose to send the first block of four drawings to Whittingham & Griggs, the colour-printers, so soon as the paid subscriptions amount to £200, the necessary cover.

I think this is all that is necessary to say. The text will be revised, but the sole criterion of the revision will be literary fitness I propose no improvement in morals or decency: & it will be very little (not more than 10% probably) shorter.

Will you see if you can contribute towards the list of subscribers? and advise upon the banking account which must grow up (& down)?

I propose, in my letter of conditions to each subscriber, to explain that my proposed edition of 100 copies is based on the estimate of £3000 for the cost of production, with a 10% margin for eventualities: but that if the book costs less I'll distribute fewer than 100 copies: & if more as many more as are required to meet the bill: the price always remaining 30 guineas, & the total proceeds always equalling the total cost.

I hope you'll be satisfied with this decision. My determination to take the sole charge is that I may carry the sole responsibility. It's well to profit in *some* way by being a soldier!

Hogarth will literary-edit the proofs for me: & Kennington art-edit the blocks.　　　　　　　　　　　　　　　　　　　T. E.

New Address: to supersede all others. Any name: mine being the only house on the hill. Clouds Hill, Moreton, Dorset.

233: TO EDWARD GARNETT

16. XII. 23.

I enclose (for return) Sassoon's[1] letter. Such expressions of pleasure it's hardly decent to hand about.

[1] Siegfried Sassoon.

He likes the chapters in which I ramble round among the cobwebs of my own mind — those you wanted cut! Quaint, isn't it? He also likes others, which you praised.

That's one infuriation of letters, of all artistic effort . . . their lack of an absolute. It was my first grumble to you.

It's mad of Lane to pay for my profound introduction[1] . . . and I'll write it if I can, and confess to you if I can't. There's one good thing about cheques . . . they are delicate things, quick to disappear if you feel them unearned.

Thanks for the two books (not read yet, but what can you expect? I'm passing a particularly bad time just now: a sort of sentient tennis-ball . . .) can I have the reprinted pamphlets?

No please, no literary studies of anyone. I'm unfitted by my present for such.

Dead Souls[2] was very good. I read an edition of it some while ago.

This is a 'duty' letter, evoked by thankfulness for your books, and written with one eye on your letter. So no more of it. I'm not in the mood.   T.E.

Address now of everything: Clouds Hill, Moreton, Dorset. I've agreed to revise and print 100 copies of the complete *Seven Pillars*, with illustrations, if so many subscribers at 30 guineas can be found to meet the estimated bills of £3,100. Am I mad? Please tell Cape.   L.

[The following is the first draft in manuscript of the letter Lawrence circulated to would-be subscribers to *Seven Pillars of Wisdom*.]

234: TO SUBSCRIBERS TO 'SEVEN PILLARS'

[19.XII.23 *deleted*]   *Clouds Hill, Moreton*

Dear —

I asked Buxton to refer everyone to me that I might explain to each the details of my proposed private issue of *The Seven Pillars*.

---

[1] Lawrence had written an Introduction to a new edition of Richard Garnett's *The Twilight of the Gods*, illustrated by Henry Keen and published by John Lane.

[2] *Dead Souls*, by Nikolay Gogol, translated by Constance Garnett.

For copyright reasons, and because the book is somewhat outspoken regarding myself, I am not publishing it, but am trying to raise enough private subscribers to cover the cost of production.

Estimates (necessarily provisional) for block-making and printing total about £3000. Consequently I've suggested 100 subscribers at 30 guineas. If the bills come to more I'd print 105 or 110 copies (supposing extra subscribers are to be found). If it costs less I'd dock its tail of the list. Circumstances make me unable to profit by its job.

Type, paper, and illustrations will be decent of their kinds (I hope!) and the complete work, as sent to subscribers, will not be reissued in my lifetime.

At the same time the people who were partners with me in the Arab Revolt will want copies, and I propose to GIVE to them (at my expense) copies of the text, with such illustrations as immediately concern them. No such copy will be complete: and I will give them only to people mentioned in my text, and only to such of those as I think fit. At present I don't know how many of them will want copies: more than twenty, less than fifty, I fancy. The fact that the free copies will be incomplete prevents their affecting the rarity value of the subscribers' edition.

I'm bound to say that I think the book exceedingly dear, an unjustifiable purchase either as investment for resale, or as a thing for reading: and I hope no one will decide to get it unless he is in the position to (mis) spend thirty guineas without a regret.

The printers estimate that they will take ten months block-making (fifty illustrations): and I don't propose to put the work in hand except as subscriptions to cover each section of it are assured. You will be lucky to get the finished work in 1924 ... and it may drag till the summer of '25. I promise no date.

The text will be copyrighted, and publication of it, or of extracts from it, in U.S.A. and the European copyright union will be impossible. No copies are going to libraries (if I can prevent it) nor will it be reviewed.

I much regret the necessity I am under of multiplying the book at all: but I want my illustrations reproduced, and cannot pay the cost of them: and the least evil, in the circumstances, seems to be for my friends to find me a hundred discreet subscribers!

I'd be glad if all of them found the book too dull to read, and locked it, forgotten, in cupboards!

If after this explanation you still feel inclined to plunge. — then please pay in the £15.15.0 to Buxton as you suggest: and you will be subscriber no v. Yours sincerely   T. E. LAWRENCE

Apologies for the length of letter: but I can't put all I want to say in a word.

[On May 31st, 1923, Bernard Shaw wrote a private memorandum to Mr. Baldwin, then Prime Minister, expressing his great concern at Lawrence's poverty.

'Clearly this is a bad case of Belisarius begging obols in an ungrateful country ... the fact remains that he is serving as a private soldier for his daily bread: and however much his extraordinary character may be accountable for this, it strikes all who know about it as a scandal that should be put an end to by some means. They feel that the private soldier business is a shocking tomfoolery and are amazed to find that Lawrence is not in a position of a pensioned commanding officer in dignified private circumstances.'

Bernard Shaw sent the letter to Hogarth, who corrected some of his statements, before sending it to the Prime Minister. Shaw did not rest content with a refusal but continued to press Mr. Baldwin, and afterwards Mr. MacDonald, on the subject of a pension for Lawrence, but without success.

From several of Lawrence's letters it would appear that he would have accepted a pension, had one been offered him, but I cannot think he would have been pleased that the sentence 'the private soldier business is a shocking tomfoolery' should be read by Mr. Baldwin.]

235: TO BERNARD SHAW

20.xii.23   *Clouds Hill*

Your lordship errs, and libels me in assuming that I'm intractable and rebellious: ask any of my officers for witness! There is not a humbler little beast: but it would be a long worm without a turning, and so have at you for your letter! You've forgotten that I'm Irish, or that Irishmen persuade only the rest of the world.

It seems I'm to regret the fall of Mr. Baldwin: and to thank you very much for the attempt at a pension. It was exceedingly good of you. Hogarth gave me no idea of it. Why did you think I wouldn't take it? It's earned money which sticks in the throat:— that a man should come down to working for such stuff. . . .

The Government have been very decent to me. They would give me political employ (only I won't look upon the Middle East again) or a commission (only I won't again give an order): and at my asking have twice let me enlist, against their judgement.

People come into the army often, not because it is brutal and licentious, but because they haven't done very well in the fight of daily living, and want to be spared the responsibility of ordering for themselves their homes and food and clothes and work — or even the intensity of their work. Regard it as an asylum for the little-spirited.

You suggest that I'm not genuine in the ranks: but I am: just as good, now, as the others. Not very good, I'm afraid (I will be if I can) since I'm slow, having to learn to do all the daily trifles which others used to do for me. If it wasn't that I've been somebody or something else the authorities would have a fair opinion of what I am.

Your picture of my ending up to find that I am a soldier, by dint of much playing at it, comforts me: for it's the end I want, and am wanting with deadly seriousness. The peace of finding that my horizon was grown so near! If I could be happy drunk I'd drink: but so to take the control off myself might be to loose myself out again: and I want not to be big any more.

You *can* understand this, for in your phrase 'another magnificent play' isn't it the judgement of the word 'another' which makes you spend time over poor futile Poincaré and his Ruhr?

As for my book, I'll leave that (a trifle, now far behind me) till we meet, if we meet, in Bournemouth. You prompt my writing another: but the first one was compulsory, and soldiers don't do voluntary things. What is not enjoined upon us is forbidden.

While for subject I could only write about the army, and I hate it: and it would be a mean fugitive, wouldn't it, who grumbled at his cave, finding it evil-smelling, and draughty, and too dark?

You ask me what I do with my spare time. Well, the army uses me from 6 A.M. till 6 P.M. most days: and I'm tired and in bed just after nine. If you fit a meal in, between 6 and 9, there is not very much over. Half-days and Sundays I spend either riding abroad, or in my cottage, reading, writing such letters as this, or turning French books into English to provide the running expenses of the bicycle. I don't sleep much after midnight, so that I've time for thinking then.

I want to talk to you some day about *Methuselah*. We aren't going that way, if the fellows here are an indication, and I suppose they are extracts of the widest English class. Their only criteria are the physical: they judge, speak, think, enjoy, only in terms of the senses. There is nothing abstract in their lives, no idea for them independent of an external form: and their apex, their sublimation, is the coming together in sex of a man and a woman. And yet you can hold out to me the hope that some day (by dint of trying) I will wake up like them! I believe you no more than I believe your favourable judgement of the book I tried to write. I may be perhaps as like the others as that is like my subject, the subject I tried to capture.

This reads rather too solemn a letter: so let's call it off. Did it ever strike you as a merciful dispensation that we write on sheets, not on rolls?

Will you come to Clouds Hill? I'd like to have you, though it's little worthy of your coming, and I'm afraid Mrs. Shaw (please thank her for her letter and cheque, which I'll explain to her later, when I see her) will find it unclean. I'll send a map showing where it is, to the Hotel. My own movements in Xmas week are restricted, since I'm the clerk who indents for rations for the camp, and they have to come daily, whoever rests. I'll have every afternoon off, and will arrange to be sent your telephone message on the morning of the fine day you'll probably choose for coming.

My noble cycle, the poor beast who allayed my 'shrinking nerves' was taken out secretly by a beast who left her broken, in a ditch: and she is too ruined to mend, even if I could like her again. So I'm not able to go abroad without public leave and a rail-ticket, now. Yours ever T.E.S.

It isn't true, either, that I'm public here: ninety-nine days out of the hundred I'm an ordinary soldier, accepted by all the others. You only see or hear of the exception. I live the rest.

236: TO COLONEL A. P. WAVELL

27. 12. 23. *Clouds Hill Moreton Dorset*

[4 5 *lines omitted*]This place¹ is like Rowton House without cubicles. Xmas night was like sleeping — or lying rather — in a public lavatory with choked drain . . . and it was even worse than the usual lavatory . . . for there seemed to be a heavy sea on, & all the habitués were in need of stewards with little basins. The old army, in my recollection, did at least carry its drink. Don't you agree?

Give my deepest regards to W.H.B.² if ever you see him. Yours ever T.E.S.

I wish Trenchard was a worm, for then I could ease myself by cursing him for kicking me out of the R.A.F. It wasn't my fault . . . or if it was I've atoned for it by now. However T. is one of the really great people, & so I have no vent for my spite anywhere. . . . ototototot!!!!!

237: TO EDWARD GARNETT

1. 1. 24. *Clouds Hill, Moreton, Dorset.*

But what a monstrous idea! My book is a tax, a levy, booty, from the ungodly rich. It is inconceivable that you should subscribe. A sheer waste of money. What do you want with the pictures? I'm keeping for you a copy of the plain text, a gift worth alas only a few shillings, but all that I can afford in my condition. You see I have to give many away, and can't give, can't even make a start of giving, the pictured edition. So I've com-

¹ Bovington Camp. ² General Bartholomew.

promised by stipulating on a number of copies of the plain text.[1]

Yes, it will be revised, but only in petto. No good cuts or noble changes, no re-writing: just punctuation, and insect-blemishes removed.

It's good of you (i) to like *The Terrapin*[2]

(ii) to put Cape on to it.

I've never met the author: and only glanced through the poem in typescript in a taxi. Augustus John possessed it then. It struck me in the face: and is, as you say, sensational enough to sell. Full of echoes though.

Very busy: am quartermaster's storeman and clerk, and pre-occupied much with the 'amazing convolutions of my mind'.

T.E.S.

238 : TO SYDNEY COCKERELL

13. 1. 24   [*Clouds Hill*]

Dear Cockerell, Did I ever thank you for *The Rover*? A very good book; but not better than the other Conrad's. Don't you think a man would strain himself each time to surpass the last mark? There is no strain in this.

About the Tokio professorship[3] . . . not for me I'm afraid. I'm not going to be respectable again. Also I'm not fit either to be respectable, or to preach what I don't practise. Literature is beyond my grasp as a craft, & I don't aspire to it as a science.

Haven't heard of Charlotte Mew:[4] but all the women who ever wrote original stuff could have been strangled at birth, & the history of English literature (& my bookshelves) would be unchanged.

Is it true that Doughty is writing again? Yours   T E S

[1] Lawrence did in fact give away a number of 'incomplete copies', with two or three pictures left out. But the copy he gave Edward Garnett was a complete copy.

[2] *The Flaming Terrapin*, by Roy Campbell; this was published by Cape later in 1924 and was Campbell's first published poem. It was Lawrence, however, who had put Cape on to it. See letter No. 230.

[3] A series of writers have been Professors of English literature at Tokio University; Edmund Blunden, Robert Nichols, Peter Quennell, William Empson.

[4] Author of *The Farmer's Bride* and *The Rambling Sailor*.

239: TO BERNARD SHAW

14.1.24.

My Lord, I couldn't write to you yesterday, though I tried to: and tonight's is only an apology for being still stupid.

Your letter of your efforts with the P.M. . . . but really you should not. If I won't do that sort of thing for myself, other people should not do it for me. It's awfully good of you . . . but awfully bad for me. Please let up on it all. The army is more or less what I ought to have, and in time I'll get to feel at home in it.

And please tell Mrs. Shaw that if ever I write anything new (I try hard not to) I'll send her a copy direct. This will save her wasting money on owls[1] or Doughty's[2] in the future.

A Yank firm (Bone & Liverpool, or something) have pirated my *Arabia Deserta* preface, and are cheerful that the book is selling well in the States. It's nice to feel good enough to be stolen.

May Ramsay MacDonald soon succeed Baldwin. . . .
Yours sincerely   TES.

240 : TO D. G. HOGARTH

21.1.24

A prolonged time without writing: — but there has been (and is) nothing to say. The Xmas spectacle of camp took out of me the zest I had won in Oxford. [*5 lines omitted*]

Arnie is now in the States (Boston, Philadelphia New York, apparently) on his way to England, which he will reach next month. Subscribers add themselves silently to my list: — about 15 now. Whittingham & Griggs are completing the first four chromo-lithos: and Pike (the suggested printer) is preparing me specimen pages. These will be sent you on receipt, about a fortnight hence.

[1] *The Winter Owl*, edited by Robert Graves, contains an abridged version of Chapters LXV, LXVI, and LXVII of *Seven Pillars of Wisdom* which also appears to have been rewritten by another hand.
[2] In order to read Lawrence's introduction to *Arabia Deserta*.

Any progress with John? He is willing & anxious to try again. I only hope he will achieve another drawing as great.

Shaw (the genuine one) was here lately: full of quaintnesses upon the supposed oddity of my position in camp (now absolutely normal, though I haven't been able to make myself like the rest in mind or manner). Also very bracing, though such sureness of success has closed his pores.   E.

Address now: T E Shaw, Clouds Hill, Moreton, Dorset.

241: TO HARLEY GRANVILLE-BARKER

7.2.24.

When your letter came, and said 'a month' I sighed with gladness that there was so much time to work out a reply . . . but the days have dodged me somehow, and I'm all unready still.

You see, while you have been so magnificently persistent with my literary 'builder's yard' I've been reading that polished four-square play of yours.[1] Is that a comic picture? Of an author and a would-be (would have been?), exchanging books, and tasting each other meditatively.

Anyhow that's what I've done, with barren results. Your work is so hard, so intricate, so packed. It is the essence of thought, a variety of mental Bovril. Shaw (the real one) talked of it with me, deploring your profusion of material, your introduction of stuff which would have made eight plays if beaten out thin.

I rather like the pemmican of letters, or rather I used to like it, when my head was at ease to think over the words I gave it through my eyes. I thought then that a man could not work himself too hard, when he opened a new branch to the public. After all the suffrages worth having are the people who will read your play with the eager effort you put into it.

And yet, and yet . . . your leisure is so abundant that perhaps you have been cruel to the larger audience. I don't see you somehow as only a highbrow for highbrows: but haven't you been forgetful of the duties of the many. I get up in the morning, and

[1] *The Secret Life.*

clean boots and make beds and carry coal and light fires ... and then all day long I work till five o'clock ... and when in the evening the choice lies between an easy thing, like *Methuselah*, and a hard thing, like yours: why without my will my hand strays to the left, and I read Shaw. It's not out of sheer laziness: pre-digested food is wholesome to a stomach which is weary.

However a bit too much of this. It is a very great thing, that play of yours. I hate plays, because I'm no theatre-goer, and the unpractised form is knobby and uncouth to my wits: but the characters come through the writing with a shout. Your politicians are really politicians: and though I resent the death which unties a problem I suppose you felt that it would be unhelpful in you to leave a tangle to the crowd for their late supper. The thing is clearly meant to be played, isn't it? Otherwise you would not have sacrificed as much to the stage-technique.

Strowde is the person who interested me most. Your women passed me by, (in revenge perhaps, for I usually pass them, in the flesh): your Serocolds are too usual to be more than ornamental, and I resent a young man's taking rubbish seriously. But why did you make Strowde so weak? There is a luxury in keeping outside, but it is a poor man who will lie asleep in that: and you don't express the fear he must have had of being *pulled* back ... the conviction that he'd have to sell the part of himself which he valued, for the privilege of giving rein to the part of himself which others valued, but which he despised or actually disliked.

Also you have missed out the animal. All your characters are intelligences, most of them very witty intelligences (your dialogue is an amazement to me: some ass said Henry James: but *he* was a porpoise, not a fencing master): but they couldn't be as witty as all that without cracking sometimes, and letting the roar and growling of the beast be heard. Here in camp it's the lesson stamped into me with nailed feet hour after hour: that at bottom we are carnal: that our appetites and tastes and hopes and ideals are beast-qualities, coloured or shaped somewhat fancifully, but material always, things you can cut with a knife: and you have hidden that, out of shame perhaps: out of fear perhaps: or, like Shaw, in revenge.

It seems to me that I have doubly wasted this month, if I've put off sending you a decent answer, only to write piffle at the end of it.

Per contra I've been very grateful for your letter. I've a despairing wish to believe well of that awful book of mine, though it's a nightmare to me, and I can never agree that it's any good. I wanted to ask you to read with a pencil, and to hack out the rubbish as you went: but it seemed too greedy a request. It's pretty shameless to ask a man to read it all.

Subscribers to a thirty-guinea limited edition of a hundred copies are coming in, two or three a week. I'm glad to think that you've got it over already.

My regards to Mrs. Granville-Barker.　　　　　T.E.S.

242: TO ERIC KENNINGTON

10. 2. 24.　　　　　　　　　　*Clouds Hill Moreton Dorset.*

Dear K., I'm unable to improve the libel chances. It stands this way. The book is libellous, as against Some Englishmen, Some Frenchmen, Some Arabs, Some Turks. The danger of proceedings runs in this national order.

I'll do my best to prevent them
  (i) by toning down
  (ii) by informing my victims, before proofs are passed, of what I say about them.
but I don't guarantee the efficacy of either proceeding.

Consequently the wise man must prepare for trouble. As I explained, the trouble can't hit me. A soldier is too poor a being to pay damages, too degraded a being to fear imprisonment.

I intended to tear off the printer's name, and lay claim, if challenged in the first six months (after that there is no real risk) to have printed it myself. I've asked law-men, (not professionally, but in friendly guise) and they tell me that in the circs. no action could well be taken against my printer. He must take my wages, and is not himself, but an extension of me. Pike will make the form of the book a credit to our firm . . . and if there are no libel actions (odds 90 to one there won't be) then he shall have all the credit of the appearance. If there is trouble I get it.

Meynell[1] wouldn't ever come in. He could say simply that Pike had hired of him a press.   E. L.

Many thanks for the Roberts photos. *I think it's a good piece of work*: though at first glance it puzzled me.

Some Nashes attached for judgement. Please tell me what you think of them. One is of 'A wilderness of sandstone peaks'.

243: TO E. M. FORSTER

20. 2. 24

I've been transferred from B. Company: so a man brought your letter over to me two nights ago just after I had gone to bed with a bout of malaria: and a miracle happened: the fever left me and I sat up in bed and read it all! This book is my only one, & I have a longing (which I seldom admit) to hear what men say of it.

In your case it is wonderful. Writers & painters aren't like other men. The meeting them intoxicates me with a strangeness which shows me how very far from being one of them I am. Of your work I only know *Howards End* & *Siren* & *Pharos*:[2] but that's enough to put you among the elect . . . and yet you bother to write to me whole pages about my effort. No one else has done that for me[3], and I'm abnormally grateful. Grateful even to the point of wishing for more — not written of course, but to ask you of some of the difficulties I've met. However you will be spared this probably. The army does not let me off at practical times.

Your division of books into the active and the passive pleased me. The fluid ones are those written by writers: and the static ones are those (the many more) written by imitators like me. The second have no justification of being, except the scarcity of the real thing . . . and the need of books which shall be tools, ancillary. Works of art have their own life, and so aren't best fitted to be railway timetables, or dictionaries, or histories.

My thing was forced from me not as a poem, but as a complete narrative of what actually happened in the Arab Revolt. I didn't

---

[1] Francis Meynell had recently started the Nonesuch Press.
[2] *The Story of the Siren* and *Pharos and Pharillon*.
[3] Edward Garnett alone had been writing about *Seven Pillars of Wisdom* for months.

think of it till all was over, and it was compiled out of memory (squeezing the poor organ with both hands, to force from it even the little lively detail that there is). If I invent one thing I'll spoil its raison d'être: and if there are invented conversations, or conversations reconstructed after five years, where will it be?

Also, you know, I feel profoundly dejected over it all. It reads to me inferior to nearly every book which I have found patience to read . . . and that is many. If it is the best I can do with a pen, then it's better for me to hump a rifle or spade about: and I fear it's the best I can write. It went through four versions in the four years I struggled with it, and I gave it all my nights and days till I was nearly blind and mad. The failure of it was mainly what broke my nerve, and sent me into the R.A.F. . . . where I found six months of full contentment. The Army is a sad substitute. However I'm off the point.

War and Peace is almost the largest book in the world. I've carried it whenever I had the transport, and ever wished it longer. But then Tolstoi was an enormous genius. While I was trying to write I analysed most of you, and found out, so far as it was within my fineness to see, what were your tricks of effect, the little reserves & omissions which gave you power to convey more than the print says. But it is hopeless to grapple with Tolstoi. The man is like yesterday's east wind, which brought tears when you faced it and numbed you meanwhile.

Your goodness in writing to me with such care shows that you think (or makes me think that you think) there's some hope in my writing. Yet the revise I'm going to give *The Seven Pillars* in the next ten months can be one of detail only: for the adventure is dead in me: and I think it is the only thing I'll ever try to write. The Army is a great assoiler . . . and my two years of it has nearly cured me of the desire to work gratuitously. This means 'without self-satisfaction or money': the first I only get out of hot speed on a motor-bike. The second I never get. My own writing has brought me in eleven pounds since 1914. A scruple (absurd in view of the obliquity of the whole movement) prevented my taking pay while I was East: and prevents my taking profits on any part of the record of the adventure. I can make a little translating foreign novels: but it's not much, and painful work. The army is assured bread & butter . . . and that feels better than a gamble outside. Also I feel disinclined to struggle again for a living. If I can't keep alive without much pain then I won't bother to do so at all.

I wonder why I'm writing all this to you. I think perhaps because you are a stranger, and have been interested in my addled egg. It was an extraordinary experience for me, the reading of your letter.

Some of the people who were with me during the war have read the book, & want copies. When I had money I got a lot of drawings done in illustration of it. Not ordinary sorts of things . . . proper portraits by John & Kennington & Lamb & Spencer & Roberts & Co. . . . I got an estimate for printing all these as well as possible, & the complete text (revised again of course) in a decent quarto . . . and they said £3000. So I've agreed to do 100 copies or about that number, if they can find enough of the ungodly rich to subscribe 30 guineas each for a copy. To date they have got nearly twenty (in two months) and the block-making is started. I've stipulated for liberty to produce up to fifty extra pulls of the plain text for the fellows who fought with me. . . These I'll give them free: but only to the men mentioned by name in it.

It will probably lose me my American copyright, and may lead to pirated editions in England: and this I'll be sorry for, since I grudge others profiting where I refuse to sell. However that's all a piece with the folly of the revolt and my leadership and my story of it. If only I'd written a self-respecting straightforward tale the thing would have been over long ago. My great passion & pleasure in living books snared me into the hopelessness of trying to create, & hence these tears.

If you have the spirit at the book's end (I fancy your halt was on the threshold of a chapter in which I tried to paint a full-length of myself, with paints more gummy than any other in the whole canvasses) I hope you will send me not indeed so much, but something, upon your experiences of the last chapters. I let the activity of the book fall into a trough for twenty pages, to give my imaginary reader a rest before piling up the agony of the last advance upon Damascus.

Do anything you please with any of it you please. I feel giddy at the idea of your taking the trouble. More thanks   T E S.

The safest address is T E Shaw — Clouds Hill, Moreton, Dorset.

[On March 1st, Lawrence wrote asking to be allowed back into the R.A.F. The application was considered carefully. Air Vice-Marshal Sir Philip Game minuted on March 4th, that he saw no objection to Lawrence's return and suggested that he should be sent to a good squadron commander, abroad for preference, who should be informed of Lawrence's identity. Others however did not see the matter in the same light and the application was refused.

For its renewal, and the final circumstances of his return to the R.A.F. see notes on pages 471, 475 and 477.]

244: TO SYDNEY COCKERELL

19. 3. 24   *Clouds Hill Moreton Dorset*

Dear Cockerell, Miss Mew[1]: too much emotion for her art, for her intellect, for her will. Such intensity of feeling is a sign of weakness. She is a real poet ... but a little one, for the incoherency, the violence of overwrought nerves does much harm to her powers of expression.

It's good stuff ... *Beside the Bed*: *On the Asylum Road*: *I have been through the Gates*: *On the Road to the Sea*: these are four excellent things ... but only the passion is molten: the form, the thought, the music, these are unresolved, to be guessed at, or worse, to be supplied by the reader if his passion is set burning by sympathy with hers. I'm frigid towards woman so that I can withstand her: so that I want to withstand her.

Moby Dick ... ah, there's a titan of a book. Do you know *Redburn*, & *Pierre*, two of the less common ones? *Whitejacket* very good: *Mardi* dull: two early S.Sea adventures (*Omoo* & *Typee*), fair. One of his finest works is *Clarel*, in verse: but it isn't as fine verse as his War Stuff. That's magnificent. Melville was a great man.

[1] See note to letter No. 238.

I got £20 for my *Piazza Tales* the other day. Someone is working a Melville boom, & I've sold all my early editions profitably.

Doughty: will you suggest that he makes a new contract for *A.D.* with Cape? Direct, not with Duckworth. He should get better terms for what is now a fine property. *A.D.* is selling hot in U.S.A.   T E L

245: TO C. M. DOUGHTY

30. IV. 24.

Dear Mr. Doughty, Acting on what Mr. Cockerell told me, I've asked one of its readers to send you my book on what happened to me in Arabia.

The format of it is repellent, and the small print hurts the eyes: but it wasn't meant to be read. I must apologise for the nature and tone of the book. My experiences in Arabia were horrible, and I put them down as they happened to me. Consequently the book is not fit for general reading. I've never asked anyone to read it . . . and do not expect you to do so. At the same time you are one of the people whose wishes I cannot refuse.

I hope Kent is still proving a fortunate home.   Yours sincerely
                                                    T. E. LAWRENCE

When *The Seven Pillars* are finished with will you post them to Mr. Shaw, Clouds Hill, Moreton, Dorset.

246: TO D. G. HOGARTH

9.v.24

Yes, that was it. I took thought for a night, & then declined. The job[1] is a hazardous one (T. wants a 'literary' history, the C.I.D.[2] a 'technical') attractive, very, to me by reason of its subject. The terms (three years) compare unfavourably with the six

---

[1] Lawrence had been asked to write the official history of the Royal Flying Corps and Royal Air Force in the Great War.
[2] Trenchard and the Committee of Imperial Defence.

which the Army offers: and the responsibility is one which I'd regret as soon as I had shouldered it. Also it's no use, having gone through the grind of climbing down to crowd-level, at once to give it up for three years decent living. It would leave me older, less strung up to make another effort at poor living. If I can complete my seven years in the Army I should be able to slip quietly into a job of some sort at the end. There is a garage near here which might take me on.

I hope you are fit again: much of the illness which you have had lately I put down to the plague of that ungrateful book. You must feel like a reprieved prisoner.

Here at Bovington I seem to sit still: so still that often I fancy the slow passing of time about me can be *heard*. Isn't it rare for a person, who has been as unsparing as myself, to be purged quite suddenly of all desire? Even the longing or regret for the R.A.F. sleeps now, except when I come suddenly at a turn in the road, on its uniform. *That* was another bar to the job: because I'd have had to visit aerodromes, & each time the homesickness would have made itself felt afresh.

Writing to people I have known is becoming difficult for me. Wherefore . . .   T.E.S.

247: TO MRS. THOMAS HARDY

16. vi. 24   *Clouds Hill Moreton*

Dear Mrs. Hardy, E. M. Forster is coming to my cottage on Friday, to stay till Monday or Tuesday. Probably it is out of pity, to cheer me up. He would be shocked to know that I am pitying him, or rather his sojourn among the beetles & the fallen rhododendron-bloom.

Russell, Palmer[1] & I will go up in turn to keep him company: — but we seem slender fare for a real novelist. So I wondered if you and Mr Hardy could do anything. Of course it depends on your engagements — but *if* they are light, & *if* you feel inclined, & *if* it is good enough weather to tempt Mr Hardy abroad, then tea at Clouds Hill on either Saturday or Sunday would be

---

[1] Privates in the Royal Tank Corps.

good for E.M.F. and a great honour & dignity for the house. It could perhaps be worked in with a visit to Oakers' Wood (if one is due): however anyway, there it is as a suggestion.

The country is beautiful just now. Yours sincerely T E SHAW

248: TO E. M. FORSTER

24. VII. 24

Here it is: possibly you need to know Palestine well to enjoy it as much as I did: it seemed to me of the very best: and my conscience has lately assailed me for not returning it to S.S.

By the way: — of consciences — Did Posh (Palmer that is) ever write to you? Probably not. In revenge I'll betray his confidence. When he got your book & note (about 9.30 p.m. one evening) he marched out of the hut, & was absent till reveille next morning. Indeed he was late for reveille, with an unslept-in bed, & only just avoided trouble there-on-account. By local signs I judge he sat in Clouds Hill part of the night. The book & letter are now hidden in his kit. We're quaint little souls, aren't we?

The night-jar came & made music only in your honour. She has now abandoned Clouds Hill . . . or was there a second and more fortunate stone thrown? She would be less heavy, as a necklace, than an albatross.[1]

I've long ago finished the India book.[2] Half-through I laid it aside for a while, saying 'The sensation is finished. India, a continent, is on the canvas complete.' Afterwards a remorse for the interrupted action took me, & I went on. Then the characters asserted themselves, & became so lively that the continent faded (till near the end) & the book became breathlessly exciting. It's a three or four-sided thing, more like sculpture, therefore, than painting. Extraordinarily satisfying, to the reader, in the multiplicity of its effects & cross-lights & bearings. Purple passages are pp. 251 seq. the roof-conversation. Wonderful that. It advances Aziz & Fielding incredibly: pp. 288 seq. the orgiastic

[1] A nightjar had kept Forster awake at Clouds Hill and he had thrown a stone at it.
[2] *A Passage to India,* by E. M. Forster.

work. That's what I mean when I regret the absence of life in my writing. You can shape so spare & trim a thing out of an innumerable heap of impressions and materials.

The scene in the Club: from p. 180 onwards: wicked: but very nobly done. Did you know that was a possible combination? It's a most punishing chapter for anyone who has, like me, the Englishman's reaction to other people's tragedies. Just before it comes the Godbole conversation, miles away from our mind, but just as present to you. And then chap xiv: the landscape of the caves. Oh, it's despairingly well done.

The truth is of course that you are a very great writer, & that it's irredeemably weak of me to envy you, even to imagine my following or working by your methods. But I've always stood on the plain, like an ant-hill, watching the mountain, & wishing to be one, & can't very well now reproach myself with the longing, since it won't stop.

If excellence of materials meant anything, my book would have been as good as yours: but it stinks of me: whereas yours is universal: the bitter terrible hopeless picture a cloud might have painted, of man in India. You surpass the Englishman & surpass the Indian, & are neither: and yet there is nothing inhuman (like Moby Dick) in your picture. One feels all the while the weight of the climate, the shape of the land, the immovable immensity of the crowd behind . . . all that is felt, with the ordinary fine human senses.

A marvellous book. My final hope is that you never do worse than this again.   T.E.S.

If the flea may assert a kindred feeling with the lion . . . then let me suggest how my experience (& abandonment) of work in Arabia repeats your history of a situation-with-no-honest-way-out-of-it. You on the large thinking plane, me on the cluttered plane of action . . . and both lost.

249: TO ROBERT GRAVES

[? 1924]

[*omission*] What's the cause that you, and S.S.[1] and I (from the S.S. to the ridiculous!) can't get away from the War? Here are you riddled with thought like any old table-leg with worms: S.S. yawing about like a ship aback: me in the ranks, finding squalor and maltreatment the only permitted existence: what's the matter with us all? It's like the malarial bugs in the blood, coming out months and years after in recurrent attacks. Have you leisure? I'd like to send you the book I tried to write those years ago. S.S. read it, and grew kind to me, afterwards: which was a good comment: and if your mind is now accustomed to living, perhaps you would read it for me.[2]

My motive is the selfish one, of wanting criticism. The margins are blank to write upon in pencil. The print is eye-destroying, the length of the book appalling: ... its sincerity, I fancy, absolute, except once where I funked the distinct truth, and wrote it obliquely. I was afraid of saying something, even to myself. The thing was not written for anyone to read. Only as I get further from the strain of that moment, confession seems a relief rather than a risk.   T.E.S.

250: TO MRS. THOMAS HARDY

31. VII. 24.   *Clouds Hill*

[38 *lines omitted*] The Greek play[3] was a tragedy here as well as in the Orestes family! The Staff Sergt. knew I wanted to get off promptly from work, & so he put me on to job after job, from 3.30 onward, till I was too late. This was his revenge for my having been clever a day or two before. The business was so sickening that I went away & had a feast of eggs & bacon, & pretended to be happy without spiritual food.

The Staff Sergt has had a bad life since, & is sorry. Says I can get off early any day I like: I don't like ... now. Yours sincerely

T E SHAW

[1] Siegfried Sassoon.

[2] Graves had been shown only a part of the Oxford Text of *Seven Pillars of Wisdom* in 1922.

[3] A performance of the *Oresteia* of Aeschylus by the Balliol Players in Thomas Hardy's garden.

251: TO LADY SANDWICH

18. VIII. 24   *Clouds Hill Moreton Dorset*

Dear Lady Sandwich, Shaw or Lawrence, as you please [5 *words omitted*] I like the shorter, because it's short! However . . .

Your letter is very kind: and your cheque too. I hope the book, when it arrives next year, will not be disgusting to you, or a great disappointment. Bits of it are decently written, but the whole lacks design & unity, & the action & characters in it have no movement in them, beyond my words. In other words, it isn't a real work of art: only a painstaking imitation. I was very ambitious of making a good book when I attempted it, and my failure is correspondingly great. A smaller thing I could have done better. However again . . .

The invitation requires a new paragraph to itself. Precisely because your house & company would be delightful, I can't risk it. My lot here is $\frac{1}{20}$th of an army hut, & the company is too human, & too constantly with me. If I go away even for a night the return becomes poignant — for by nature I hate noise & fear animal spirits, & like warmth & smooth things & music & books and abstract talk, & colour, lots of colour. When I enlisted I knew that these things were forfeited, & my quaint mind now looks on them as things to be shunned. Time seems not to change with you: — whereas with me it has changed wildly, taking away all the material comforts I used to have, & giving me in exchange the sense that if I'm not doing much good, at least my peculiar talents aren't being misapplied somewhere. It's better to rust out, than to go on grinding other men's lives through the mills of your own political ideas. A leader who sees two sides cannot lead — cheaply, at any rate.

I don't know why I should bother you with all this rigmarole. An alternative excuse would be that I'm in khaki, & have no decent clothes, fit to visit you in. I got rid of what I had, to imprison myself here against this very temptation, and can't afford others.

Apologies. I hope this note won't read rudely.

Yours sincerely   T E SHAW

252: TO LIONEL CURTIS

25.VIII.24.   *Clouds Hill Moreton*

O prophet, A raven told me of your troubles in Gayfere St. I was so sorry that I wouldn't add to them with a letter: they tell me that my letters aren't gay things. That's surprising, isn't it? You'd expect Bovington's slough to breed its opposite. However . . .

'Completely recovered' is your last word. I'm very glad: but such suffering leaves a mark on the mind.

Xmas? at Kidlington?[1] Well, you know, very wisely I deny myself holidays from camp: and I'm useful especially at festive seasons, since my habits enable me to take other people's duties while they enjoy. I told you about the others, last year: but perhaps not that I had done rations and coal-yard to set them free for their orgy. They will hope for my help again this time: and Xmas means something to them. My pernickety mind discovers an incompatibility between their joint professions of soldier and christian: is it that I attach a deeper meaning to either term?

Ave: . . .   T.E.S.

I've written to Hartington too. Subscribers roll in for my book, which lately has been praised by H. G. Wells. Will you ever speak to me again?

253: TO R. V. BUXTON

29. VIII. 24   *Clouds Hill Moreton Dorset*

Dear Robin, I don't like the lady's manner: will you please return her cheques (or replace them by a draft from the special account), with a polite note, that it is my hope to prevent her a double disappointment, since both the manner & matter of the book are, in my opinion, too frivolous for her commendation?

Cuthbert Headlam has written asking for a copy. I've replied begging him to consider seriously if his bank balance can't be better employed than acquiring luxury books. He's a nice creature, & must have one if he insists.

[1] Lionel Curtis had a town house in Gayfere Street as well as Hales Croft at Kidlington near Oxford.

The printing is moving. Oh so slowly: but it moves, & such things gather momentum: it's the first page which costs ... about £400 isn't it? However: if necessary we will sell 120 copies. I'm printing 200, so that there will be a powerful margin.

Did I tell you? Doubleday offers to do American edition (necessary for copyright reasons) for 1002 dollars. That's cheap. I'll try, by selling copy there, to make it pay for itself. Eight copies perhaps in all must be printed in U.S.A. Doubleday will probably want two, Congress Library two: & that leaves four for sale. I'd like to fix 'em at 10,000 dollars each, so that the edition would remain, unexhausted, on offer in the firm's catalogue! Yours   T.E.S.

254: TO EDWARD GARNETT

16. IX. 24.

[30 *lines omitted*]

Hudson gone.

Conrad gone.

Hardy very old: G. Moore gaga; D.H.L. ditto; whom have we to welcome year by year?

(Not Aldous Huxley, not a Sitwell, not J. Joyce, not Wyndham Lewis: somebody lovable).

E. M. Forster: very good; but is he quite great? I like him, but a little shamefacedly.

255: TO E. M. FORSTER

29. IX. 24   *Clouds Hill Moreton*

You will have wondered what I was at. So here is an explanation.

'A' Company store-books went wrong: were neglected, revived, neglected. Got into a hopeless tangle. The storeman departed.

The Company Commander went to my employer, the Quartermaster, & asked for the use of me, to make new ledgers & check all material items. He was granted the loan of me, for a month, & I was instructed to get the job straight in that time. This was very short notice, & I've been putting all my nights into it. Haven't been to Clouds Hill since I got the new job, & will not be able to go, till I finish it, in about ten days' time.

Palmer & Russell have been up, seldom and briefly, since they find the place flat for their solitary selves. So the cottage is damp and abandoned in feeling. Not really of course: — but I've taken opportunity to put paint on the stairs, & the front door, & other places, & the smells won't go off till we get the fires going again. Will you give us a fortnight from now; and thereafter, if only your programme admit it, we will rejoice in your coming.

It is miserable to put you off: but I'd not be able to rest, knowing you in an unkept house: and I couldn't get away to see you, & that would have bred jealousy of the others' luck in my mind.

Does the *Passage* still sell like the *Daily Mail*? I have all manner of problems in my proofs, & would have a field day of discussion, if you were here.

A critic[1] told me 'that E.M.F. plays exquisitely on the flute: more exquisitely than any soloist we have today ... but that he longed to hear an orchestra again'. It would make a good subject for a thesis. 'Quote examples of an orchestral nature' etc. etc. I can't think of one. My 'big' books, *Leaves of Grass*, *War & Peace*, *The Brothers Karamazoff*, *Moby Dick*, Rabelais, *Don Quixote*, are all solo performances. Did he mean Anthony Trollope? — (whom I've never yet read, but who sounds a sort of mix-up)

T. E. S.

This is very important.

Who is F. L. Lucas, by whom have been two excellent poems lately in the *New Statesman*: & who wrote two excellent prose sketches in the defunct *Athenaeum*, just before it defuncked? Really excellent, I mean: a sure, rounded, polished, fluent, fluting voice. Really, really, good.

---

[1] Obviously Edward Garnett.

256: TO R. V. BUXTON

6. x. 24   *Clouds Hill, Moreton*

I've written to Compton Mackenzie. Didn't know you knew him. I've told him that the book isn't worth its price, & that if he thinks better of it you'll send back the £15.15.0. It's rather a compliment, his wishing to subscribe. What a gallery of them . . . him, Wells, Shaw, Walpole, Hardy. [15 *lines omitted*]

Kennington has been busy lately, over his monument, & an exhibition just opened at the Leicester Galleries. So I've left him alone for a month. Meanwhile the printing has reached page 55, in its penultimate form. The final proof will be sent to you, in a few days, for you to look over. It's going to be an exceptionally fine edition.

Much fun lately with the copyright people, who ask for copies for the public libraries. I've replied regretting that circumstances prevent my complying with the Copyright Act. They are hopping mad: and pretend that perhaps I've made a mistake, & don't intend to defy the Act. But I do: and will get away with it! It's a great thing to be a private soldier.   T.E.S.

Hope to get up to London for the second week-end in November, & if that means Friday evening will try & find you. Details later.

Cheque is from Edward Garnett Esq 19 Pond Place Chelsea London. S.W.3.

257: TO SYDNEY COCKERELL

15. x. 24   *[Clouds Hill]*

Your comments are very kind: and have gone on to Pike, who made a profit & loss account of them, & struck a balance, which was on our side.

The only sorrow is the picture. Kennington was moved to incongruous mirth, reading my book, & a dozen Bateman-quality drawings came of it. To my mind they are as rare, surprising & refreshing as plums in cake (I've never had plums in cake, but you know the sort of feeling it would be) & lighten up the whole. It's good that someone is decent enough to find laughter in a stodgy mess of mock-heroic egotism.

My prose-style is just a bad one, & Kennington's comment, unconscious comment, touches it to the mid-riff. (What is a mid-riff?) Of course they don't fit the page, or the style of print: why they wouldn't be screamingly funny, if they did. It's Kennington, pricking the vast bladder of my conceit. Hip, hip, hip, you see, & then a long fizz of escaping air before the poor frog could burst!

G.B.S. read the proof: & left not a paragraph without improvement . . . but some nearly died in the operation. Not a trace of anaesthetic! Bracing of him to treat me by his standard . . . but I'm a poor cracked vessel to adventure among these spinning jars. What a great & glorious person he is: correcting my sludge as if it was the real tissue, and never betraying what sludge it was. If ever you meet her please assure Mrs. Shaw what an overwhelming compliment it was.

Hornby has sent back the proof, with the most printer-like comments. Hogarth has touched on two or three matters of taste. So that Pike and myself are attacking the next section valorously. What a mass of muck it is. Yours ever　　　　T.E.S.

258: TO MRS. THOMAS HARDY

Wednesday [*postmarked* 12.11.24]　　　　　　　　*Clouds Hill*

Dear Mrs. Hardy, I've been in London for a long week end. Hence no reply till now.

By all means the Dress Rehearsal. There is a lordly sense about it . . . and I'll come most gladly — and to an ordinary performance too, for Palmer & myself have asked for tickets.

Once I met Barrie. He was very silent, & rather simple. Mrs. Shaw says he's very nice, as a human being. I think him detestable as an artist. She won't say yes or no to that. I haven't told him my view . . . and won't. So we will not fight on the hearthrug.

It's very good of you to ask me. Yours sincerely,　　T E SHAW

[The business of finaneing the Subscribers' edition of *Seven Pillars of Wisdom* was proving onerous. The subscriptions of £30 a copy were not enough to defray the cost, which turned out really terrific. The book could not have been produced in the form Lawrence wished without the help of Colonel R. V. Buxton, of Martins Bank.]

259: TO R. V. BUXTON

25.XI.24   *Clouds Hill Moreton Dorset*

Dear Robin, There are three conveyances, each of a fresh scrap of Chingford. They shall come to you in order, as I find them. One, I fancy is here: one at Oxford. In a few days. . . .

I have been trying to find a lawyer here to draw me a deed to cover the other, the book overdraft . . . and it has suddenly occurred to me that you could probably get it done more easily. Surely a bank keeps a tame solicitor?

The idea in my mind was that I could assign to the Bank, in case of my death or disappearance, the right to publish* an abridgement (as approved by D. G. Hogarth of 20 St. Giles', Oxford, acting as editor) of as much of *The Seven Pillars* as seemed necessary or fit: and to apply the profits of such transaction to meeting any charges they had against either of my accounts . . . any surplus going, of course, to my brother, who is to inherit my debts and assets, if there are any assets ever.

* ? 'to conclude an agreement with any publisher to publish, on such terms as please the Bank'?

Hogarth agrees to play 'Literary executor' (a pompous term to be used by a mouse, but what else is it?) and I believe that the right to publish a version of *The Seven Pillars* is valuable. Hodder & Stoughton once were willing to go to £30000 for it: and Cape jumped at the idea of it for £7000, which I asked in 1922. He (Jonathan Cape) has still got the sheets of a suggested abridgement, which Edward Garnett made.

Lord, what a job I have thrown at you. But if you have a tame lawyer it will not be difficult.

[6 *lines omitted*]

Is this a possible document? It won't be necessary if I go on all right . . . but I might go off, just as easily. A burst front tyre, or weariness, or the other fate I'm always fearing. You know, Robin, I'm hardly sane at times. Yours ever   T.E.S.

260: TO ROBERT BRIDGES

10.XII.24   *Clouds Hill Moreton*

Dear Dr. Bridges, Your letter was a great pleasure: and I'll call in hopes of finding you, when next I'm in the Oxford direction.

The motor-cycle is a glorious one: but I indulge it only when the weather is not misty, and the roads not wet. Consequently it is no good my giving notice of intended approach. Also even in fine weather my advanced age sometimes feels too advanced for a hard ride.

Sassoon's invention of your clavichord[1] was genius: and everybody worth reading in England rejoiced to join him in giving it you. You had given them so much for so long that they felt their debts irksome: that is why they shrank from talking of them regularly.

I hope either Sassoon or Hogarth warned you that I'm in the army again: otherwise my khaki will seem disagreeable to you. Sunday, of course, is my free day. Yours sincerely,   T E SHAW

[On February 6th, 1925, Lawrence wrote to Trenchard beginning: 'February is "supplication month" . . . so for the third time of asking — Have I no chance of re-enlistment in the R.A.F., or transfer?' In the course of this long letter he gave details of his excellent record in the Royal Tank Corps: he had got 93 per cent on his Rolls-Royce Armoured Car course, and in his official character had been described as 'exceptionally intelligent, very reliable, and works well'.

He pointed out also that he was not the only misfit in the services; that he could easily get others to plead his cause, but would prefer not to, and that he did not believe Trenchard would go on refusing him for ever.

[1] Siegfried Sassoon had the idea of presenting Bridges with a Dolmetsch clavichord on his 80th birthday. More than 200 people subscribed.

Though this letter has been preserved, the only trace of action taken which I can find is contained in the following letter. On April 9th, to Edward Garnett, he wrote pessimistically: 'I've been deceived too often to dare hope now.' Shortly after that we find him bringing influence to bear.]

261: TO R. V. BUXTON

26. 3. 25

Dear Robin, I went to Cape & offered him 125000 words (about 43°/₀) of *The Seven Pillars*, with as many of the black & white illustrations as he wants (two, I expect, or three) for publication under another title in England & America in the spring of 1927.

He agreed, provisionally, & is working out a contract for my approval. Upon its signature (? a fortnight, since G. B. Shaw & others must see it before I commit myself) he will pay £1500 to my account, & a further £1500 after six months.

This seemed to me enough, so I've cancelled the sale of my books. I'd rather keep them than anything I've ever had. It pours money. A builder of Chingford offers me £3. 17. 6. a foot for 400 feet of my hill. I can put him off now, I think? The value rises year by year.

The R.A.F. are flirting with the idea of my return to them. I hope so. To be settled in May.

G.B.S. writes, offering to guarantee my overdraft! Yours

T.E.S.

Don't make any further *hard* efforts after subscribers. The Cape money will clear the Bank of my liability: & I'll expect to place the balance of 50 copies or so when the first batch have been sent out. Meanwhile any names which roll up will be welcome, of course.

Brough has brought out a new & most wonderful 'bike, which will do 112 m.p.h. so long as the tyres will stand it. I'm going to blow £200 of Cape's on that.

Yes, I know what you will say: — but I like the lovely things, & it's the money well lost.   T E S

262: TO EDWARD GARNETT

9. IV. 25.

For days I have meant to write: but something hindered.

The 7 *Pillars* goes so slowly.

I like the Verga book.[1] It is defective in form (pointillé almost, in analogy) but bright and very exciting. Dust-covers call it a masterpiece . . . but if so whereabouts? Low in the range, I fancy.

Did you ever read E. M. Forster's *Longest Journey*? I am struck all of a heap by it: though it is as faulty as Verga.

Can't Cape get F. L. Lucas' poems or prose in a collected volume? The review of Flecker enclosed is by him, and that accident has led me to write about him. He is a Cambridge Don: and the *Athenaeum* first and *New Statesman* later have been printing gems by him for eight years. One poem among the poems is as near perfection as a poem can be.

The cutting is sent you for its other side: the remarks upon not writing books by Affable Hawk.[2] It expresses most excellently what I have always suspected in myself.

There is a faint chance, they say, of my return to the R.A.F. in May next. I've been deceived too often to dare hope now till the fulfilment—and then it will be too late to hope, probably: sad, because the hope is usually the only happy part of an achievement.

Cape has perhaps told you that I flirt again with the idea of an abridgement, for profit. Roughly it would be the abridgement which you made: translated into the revised text.   T.E.S.

My abridgement consists in cutting out every fifth word of the old text: when possible. If the fifth won't go out, the sixth probably will.

263: TO EDWARD MARSH

12. IV. 25   *Clouds Hill Moreton Dorset.*

I waited till I'd seen old T. H.[3] again (yesterday): to revive my memories of what he said. The old man never gives judgements

---

[1] *Mastro-Don Gesualdo,* by Giovanni Verga, translated by D. H. Lawrence.
[2] Desmond MacCarthy's pseudonym in *The New Statesman.*
[3] Thomas Hardy.

upon live writers: so don't quote it. He would not talk to me if he thought I made notes.

Unfortunately a Mrs. [*name omitted*] butted in & spoiled my preparation. His memory for recent events is getting patchy: and it is no good springing a question upon him.

He said 'The Fables¹ ... oh yes ... I thought they were excellent reading. Good.' Then he went on to talk of the rat which found oysters upon the sea-shore, & thought they were ships ... and the quote from Rabelais. It was going to be quite worth reporting ... and then this old hen butted in: & when she had stopped, & I asked again, he had forgotten that he had read the fables. The truth is that a film seems to slip over his mind at times now: and the present is then obscured by events of his childhood. He talked next of seeing Scots Greys in a public-house in Dorchester drinking strong ale, whose fumes made him (aet. 6) drunken.

I'll try again in a fortnight or so. I generally see him every other Sunday.

Many thanks for seeing Winston for me. If he moves upon S. Hoare, S. Hoare will run obediently: it is only his propriety which hates seeing me in the ranks. Pity it is Winston's Budget Season. I've been unlucky for two years now.   T.E.S.

264: TO JONATHAN CAPE

21.IV.25.   *Clouds Hill*

Dear Cape, This is for your private eye, not for Savage. It's about that clause in the contract giving you the refusal of any subsequent book. I'm in a slight difficulty there. Any original book: yes. But a very distinguished person's wife once asked me if I would care to edit or 'ghost', her husband's diary, written quite intimately before he became famous, but showing, very wonderfully, the growth of his mind and the slow accumulation of its knowledge. The book would be Macmillan's, in any case.²

I haven't said either yes or no: and will not, for a long time yet.

---

¹ La Fontaine's *Fables*, translated by Edward Marsh.
² Macmillan is Thomas Hardy's publisher.

'No', probably, since I haven't much desire to undertake so difficult a scissors and paste job . . . but its anonymity appeals to me: and if I felt at a loose end, say two years hence, then I might try my hand as an editor.

Please keep this entirely to yourself. The existence of the materials is not known, even to Macmillan's . . . indeed only five people do know of it. Yours sincerely,   T.E.SHAW.

[By early May it became clear to Lawrence that his application to transfer to the R.A.F. had failed once more. The obstacle which had prevented his transfer the previous year remained unmoved. He was not, however, prepared to accept this refusal tamely.]

265: TO JOHN BUCHAN

19.v.25   *Clouds Hill Moreton Dorset*

Dear Buchan, I don't know by what right I made that appeal to you on Sunday.[1] It happened on the spur of the moment. You see, for seven years it's been my ambition to get into the Air Force, (and for six months in 1922 I realised the ambition), and I can't get the longing for it out of my mind for an hour. Consequently I talk of it to most of the people I meet.

They often ask 'Why the R.A.F.?' and I don't know. Only I have tried it, & I liked it as much after trying it as I did before. The difference between Army & Air is that between earth & air: no less. I only came into the army in the hope of earning my restoration to the R.A.F. and now the third year is running on, and I'm as far away as ever. It must be the ranks, for I'm afraid of being loose or independent. The rails, & rules & necessary subordination are so many comforts. Impossible is a long word in human dealings: but it feels to me impossible that I should ever assume responsibility or authority again. No doubt any great crisis would change my mind: but certainly the necessity of living won't. I'd rather be dead than hire out my wits to anyone importantly.

---

[1] Lawrence had met Buchan in the street and had spoken of his longing to return to the R.A.F.

The Air Ministry have offered me jobs: a commission, & the writing of their history. These are refinements of cruelty: for my longing to be in the R.A.F. is a homesickness which attacks me at the most casual sight of their name in the papers, or their uniform in the street: & to spend years with them as officer or historian, knowing that I was debarring myself from ever being one of them, would be intolerable. Here in the Tank Corps I can at least cherish the hope that I may some day justify my return. Please understand (anyone here will confirm it) that the Battalion authorities are perfectly content with me. Nothing in my character or conduct makes me in any way unsuitable to the ranks: and I'm fitter & tougher than most people.

There, it's a shame to bother you with all this rant: but the business is vital to me: & if you can help to straighten it out, the profit to me will far outweigh, in my eyes, any inconvenience to which you put yourself!

I think this last sentence is the best one to end on, Yours sincerely   T E SHAW

266: TO EDWARD GARNETT

13. VI. 25.

You asked me long ago how I was correcting the old text . . . since when I've had nothing convenient to send you. Here at last is a section (Book VI) ready for Pike, to whom please forward it when you have looked at it (if you want to trouble yourself still with the rake's progress of this deplorable work).

This, being the best written section, is less cut about than any yet: and has lost fewer lines: only a bare $15°/_o$: though a good many lines usually come out in the next stage (galley) and in the first page-proof which succeeds the galley. So not all that I have now left will survive to the end. My judgment gets furry, by dint of staring at the familiar pages.

What muck, irredeemable, irremediable, the whole thing is! How on earth can you have once thought it passable? My gloomy view of it deepens each time I have to wade through it. If you want to see how good situations, good characters, good material can be wickedly bungled, refer to any page, passim. There isn't a scribbler in Fleet Street who wouldn't have got more fire and colour into every paragraph.

Trenchard withdrew his objection to my rejoining the Air Force. I got seventh-heaven for two weeks: but then Sam Hoare came back from Mespot and refused to entertain the idea. That, and the closer acquaintance with *The Seven Pillars* (which I now know better than anyone ever will) have together convinced me that I'm no bloody good on earth. So I'm going to quit: but in my usual comic fashion I'm going to finish the reprint and square up with Cape before I hop it! There is nothing like deliberation, order and regularity in these things.

I shall bequeath you my notes on life in the recruits camp of the R.A.F. They will disappoint you. Yours   T.E.S.

Post Office closed. So the stamps are put on at a venture.

[Edward Garnett was naturally much alarmed by this letter with its threat of suicide and wrote at once to Bernard Shaw who replied:

> I saw the Prime Minister about it during his former term of office . . . I have now sent on your letter to Downing Street with a card to say that some decision should be made, as there is a possibility of an appalling scandal, especially after Lowell Thomas's book. G.B.S.

John Buchan had also appealed to Mr. Baldwin on Lawrence's behalf and the Prime Minister humanely decided to intervene. The evidence for this is contained in letters to John Buchan. On December 26th, 1928, Lawrence wrote: 'I wanted you to know I'm making the best use I can of the gift you led Mr. Baldwin into giving me in 1925,' and on December 20th, 1934, Lawrence puts the whole matter in its plainest form.]

267: TO R. V. BUXTON

20. VI. 25

[9 *lines omitted*] Will you show Salmond the Carline picture, 'The destruction of the retreating Turkish Army by air attack'? He might like to see it.

I don't understand his saying that I may get back to the air. Will you ask him about it? I gathered that I was finally turned down, & have been making all my plans on that basis. Till I hear from you I'll hold up the American book-contract, since I can (if I'm continuing to hope) arrange another £4000 from that source. Otherwise I've got enough, in the further £2350 coming, to frank me over the book-bills, & over the time in which I mop the mess finally up. [*omission*]

268: TO JOHN BUCHAN

5. VII. 25   *Clouds Hill Moreton Dorset*

Dear Buchan, The oracle responded nobly. I was sent for by Trenchard on Wednesday last (horribly inconvenient, for my revolver course did not finish till Saturday, yesterday) and was told that I was acceptable as a recruit.

The immediate effect of this news was to put me lazily and smoothly asleep: and asleep I've been ever since. It's like a sudden port, after a voyage all out of reckoning.

I owe you the very deepest thanks. I've been hoping for this for so many years, and had my hopes turned down so regularly, that my patience was completely exhausted: and I'd begun wondering if it had ever been worth waiting and hoping for. Odd, that the Air Force should seem to me (after trial too!) as the only way of getting across middle age. I wish I could make you some sort of return.

Formalities will take some weeks: but I should change skins in September at latest.

Please inform your family that the bike (Boanerges is his name) did 108 miles an hour with me on Wednesday afternoon. I think the news of my transfer had gone to its heads: (cylinder heads, of course).

More thanks, Yours ever   T E SHAW

[Approval of Lawrence's transfer from the Royal Tank Corps to the R.A.F. was signed by the Chief of the Air Staff on July 16th, 1925, and Lawrence was instructed to put in an application for transfer through his Commanding Officer.]

269: TO EDWARD GARNETT

17. VII. 25. *Clouds Hill, Moreton, Dorset.*

[*7 lines omitted*] You know, I expect, that they have at last revised their decision, and I am to be transferred shortly. My sense is of something ineffable; like ship *Argo* when Jason at last drew her up upon the beach; surely nothing but time and physical decay will uproot me now.

The first effect has been ten days' holiday off letters and proofs. I feel still longing for more rest, and would postpone all outward life if I could ... but to leave the reprint unfinished would not lead to ultimate peace. People like Cape and the subscribers have put money into me, and I feel rather scrupulous towards them. So I suppose the old thing must go forward to its end, though it no longer matters. I've got the only thing I care about — or cared about: for in getting it the care is over.

Uxbridge, I suppose, next month or in September. T.E.S.

270: TO EDWARD GARNETT

27. VII. 25.

Here is the contracted Book IX, for which you asked. They take long to do: and besides them I've to read and correct proofs of three or four earlier books. We have in hand, at the moment, the whole text from page 80 upwards to this point. Alas, it is too long!

You will observe with pleasure that *none* of your suggested avoidances of the stodgy patches of this section have been adopted. Not that they were not great improvements, the right thing to do ... but what's the good of attempting to catch one or two particular fleas in a crowded hen-house? The book is a blemish, itself.

However, I've done a little, in this draft, to improve it. One special lump of stodge has been cut off from the bulk, and isolated. So a once-bit reader can shy off it ever after. The other chapter, that about myself, has lost a quarter of its bulk. It too, being concentrated, can be skipped. Whereas had I embodied its matter in incident, as you suggest, the poor worms would have had to read it all.

Judgments upon this chapter vary. Gertrude Bell, a woman of enormous heart and whirling head, of the book said, 'Approved: all but the libellous untruthful description of yourself.' Very nice of Gertrude. Alan Dawnay, a very cultivated garden, said, 'Whenever anybody is puzzled about you, I lend them your chapter upon yourself. It is crystal-clear, so that afterwards they always understand.' Very nice of Alan D.

271 : TO E. PALMER[1]

25.VIII.25.   *R.A.F. Cadets' College, Cranwell, Lincs.*

When I entered the R.A.F. station at West Drayton (a derelict misery-stricken unfinished factory-place) from its upper windows came 'The Lass of Richmond Hill', violently sung. At once I remembered Clouds Hill, and you, and H.H.B.[2] and I hung my kit-bag on a willow-tree and wept.

They set me sums: which I solved as fast as they brought them. A flight-sergeant came along, 'Hullo Ross!' ... and a dynamo-switch-board-attendant behind him said 'Garn ... that ain't Ross. I was at Bovington when he came up, and he's Colonel Lawrence.' After that things got very complicated. Before lights out I was in charge of the recruits' hut.

Wednesday so passed. Thursday is a blank in my memory. On Friday early they sent me to a doctor. He said 'Have you ever had... ... .?' 'No Sir' 'Have you ever had ... ...?' 'No' (less confidently).

'Have you ever — broken any bones?' This was my chance: I poured over him a heap of fractured fibulae, radii, metatarsals, phalanges, costes, clavicles, scapulae, till he yelled to me to stop. So I stopped, and he made clumsy efforts to write them all down.

Anyway it was all over by noon on Friday. At two o'clock they put me in a tender, and sent me to Uxbridge in charge of a corporal, who was charged to get a receipt for my body. Everyone at Uxbridge was willing to take delivery: but none would sign for

---

[1] Private, Royal Tank Corps; nicknamed Posh.   [2] Sergeant Banbury.

me. At last I was dragged into the Headquarters' Adjutant, the last hope. (All the world else being at the Wembley Tattoo). He glared 'What are you'? I very stilly replied 'Yesterday I was a Pte in the R.T.C.' He snorted 'Today?' 'I think I'm an A.C. twice in the R.A.F.' Snort second. 'Will you be in the Navy to-morrow?' 'Perhaps,' said I. 'I can't sign for you. I don't want you'. 'I don't want anyone to sign for me.' 'Damned silly . . . who the hell are you?'

At this point my feeble patience broke. 'If your name was Buggins, and I called you Bill . . .' Then he yelled with joy, recognising my names for him (as I might call you Posh when you are very old and rich and important) and gave me tea.

Friday night, 6 p.m. I am handed into the recruits' hut. Messenger arrives. A.C.11 Shaw to report to Flight Office at once. 'Sergeant take this man to the Q.M. Stores, kit him at once, and put him into the first train for Cranwell. The Air Ministry have ordered his immediate posting.' Help: poor me: 8 p.m.: two kit bags, a set of equipment, great coat, bayonet, like a plum tree too heavy with fruit. However 'last train gone'. Sergt. and self returned to recruits' hut. I slept: very wet. On Saturday squared tailors and got my stuff altered: polished bayonet: scrubbed equipment.

Sunday blancoed equipment: polished bayonet. Walked round Uxbridge very new in blue. Monday 11 A.M. started for Cran-well. Finished up in a taxi. Reception-hut: hot and cold water laid on to hut: a bath. Heaven: sleep.

Tuesday, today. Reveille 7.30. Hot bath: Heaven: breakfast: H.Q. office: M.O.Adjutant: S.-M. very curious questions. Posted as aircraft hand to B.Flight. Fatigues when the cadets are on holiday: pulling their machines in and out of the sheds, filling up, starting, cleaning etc. when they are here. Sixteen men in flight. Sergt. a speed-demon on a twin N.U.T.[1] Bath-furnace out of order. Cold: wet: not heaven.

Kit inspection once a month: hut inspection once a month: marching order parade once a month: no guards: church parade twice a month. Few other duties. Can do, I think. No P.T. Feel odd and strange: exhilarated: crazy sometimes. Is it going

[1] Motor bicycle.

HH

to meals does that? Haven't spent a shilling a day lately. Will you tell Clouds Hill that all is well so far? People who come to Cranwell often stay there for five years. I will go over to Nottingham on Saturday week, and try to see Brough, who has a 1926 S.S.110 waiting for me.[1] After that I'll get a room in some near village, and begin work. Meanwhile — got to scrub that equipment again.   T.E.S.

R.A.F. issue three towels: Also one pair plain light boots, and one pair marching boots. Slippers of normal Bovington type. No other changes to note. If there is a bunch of letters please insert in a fresh large envelope, and address as above. Willis has envelopes.

272: TO MRS. THOMAS HARDY

26. VIII. 25   *R.A.F. Cadets' College, Cranwell, Lincs.*

Dear Mrs. Hardy, You see, it has happened! Quite suddenly at the end: so that I was spared a visit of farewell. It is best to go off abruptly, if at all.

I never expected the move to be so drastic. Cranwell is not really near anywhere (nor is it anything in itself): and the disorder of falling into a new station is yet upon me. The R.A.F. is a home to me: but it is puzzling to find the home all full of strangers who look upon me as strange. My known past always rouses curiosity in a new station. Probably in a few days things will be comfortable.

Alas for Clouds Hill, & the Heath, & the people I had learned in the two years of Dorset!

Please remember me to Mr. Hardy, who is no doubt wholly taken up now in *Tess*. You have a good actress.[2] I hope it will seem fitting both to you & the public. It is hard to please two masters.

You said to me that I might see that work of yours again, some time. Please don't forget that: though I can't seem either to read or to write in this noise! Yours sincerely   T E SHAW

[1] Motor bicycle.   [2] A dramatised version with Gwen Ffrangcon-Davies as Tess.

273: TO JOHN BUCHAN

27.VIII.25   *Cranwell, Lincs.*

Dear Buchan, Do not distress yourself to answer this. It's a letter of realised thanks, for the great difficulty is over. I feel like a person home at last — to find everyone else grown up, or changed, and the house open to all manner of other people beside myself. A new camp is always such a plunge into unknown.

This is a very comfortable, peaceful, cleanly camp, & will be glorious when I have settled into it. Indeed it is then I should have written to you, & not now, the first day of work, when I am tired. But you aren't in need of beautiful letters!

My thanks pile higher & higher. Yours sincerely,   T E SHAW

274: TO E. PALMER

7.IX.25.   *Cranwell*

How difficult writing is. I have been facing the need of it for some days.

Haven't written to E.M.F. either. He asked for as long notice as you could give him of your visit to London. Tell me too: so if there is a chance. . . .

Seen Dick twice. There is a great gap between the Boys' Camp and ours (a metaphorical gap). Hard to cross.

The kitchen table I bought from Knowles last year.

I have some books to go to you: to-night's parcel will only be a beret, conveying the remains of my Tank Corps period: also 3 keys.

(i) Skeleton, presumably for Jeffrey.[1] Anyone you please.

(ii) Clouds Hill . . . for the babes in it.

(iii) Kit bag: for the brown locked bag in the bathroom. Will you dig out of this

my *black* helmet (motorcycling). There is a brown one: but I want the black one with a fur edging to the forehead.

I also want the black toe-capped leggings, which I left in the bath room. A nearly new pair, like those I used to wear.

[1] Corporal Jeffrey, Royal Tank Corps, nicknamed 'Bones', 'Skeleton', 'Anatomy', on account of his thinness.

I also want a pair of army boots, 56 which I remember flinging at you as I left.

I also want (from the canteen) a housewife: long pattern, stamped 338171. Can you arrange this?[1]

Does Willis wear sixes in boots? I want someone with feet that size to break in a pair of boots for me, till the soles are nearly done: and then to have them soled with rubber by Tangay. This is a reasonable trouble for you: but time does not press me: so wait till the staff is working in full strength again and then think of it.

The cadets are back now, and term has started. This has increased our work to a respectable point. Our six machines have been out all the morning. I have been, in a sense, lucky. The flight's clerk (an aircraft hand, unskilled, like me) has just been posted. So I am book-keeper, and runner for our little group: a 'Willis', so to speak.

We are 'B' flight. A sergt: a corporal, and fifteen men. Of them five are fitters, five are riggers, five are A.C.H's. We have a hangar of our own: and six machines. To these are four officers, who teach the actual flying to the fifteen cadets who are 'on' Bristols and D.H.9 A's this term.

There are no bugles in camp, and no reveille. I get up at 6.40, go over to a near hut for a hot bath and shave (hot water out of action in our lines, till November): breakfast 7.30 to 8. You walk in at your own time. 8.10 a parade, colour-hoisting. All of us together on the square while the cadets (with rifles) present arms. This takes 20 minutes. 8.30 down to the hangar: till 12.30, when we return to the hut. Dinner 12.45. Work again at 2 P.M. till 4.15 or 4.30. Canteen practically no food. No shops within 1½ miles. So we all go to meals, which are much like Bovington, but more systematic, and so quiet. I find them good enough.

On Sat. and Sunday lights out 11 P.M. Alternate week-end passes. A.D. Sat. -M.N. Sunday.[2] No duty-hour passes. Church Parade every Sunday in camp. I went yesterday. Belt and bayonet. Skin inspection weekly, in the hut at 1.15 p.m. Breeches and puttees only for police-duty (once in three months, 24-hour)

---

[1] Lawrence's new number in the R.A.F.
[2] After duty Saturday till midnight Sunday.

and church, or Jankers.[1] Great plenty of these last. The Squadron Leader is hot on punishment.

Equipment inspected once a month in the hut, and once a month on parade (full pack). $\frac{1}{2}$ hours drill every Saturday. Monthly kit inspection.

I miss very much

(a) The quietude of the office for working in

(b) Music

(c) Colour. Lincolnshire is only green.

and I wish there was someone like yourself in camp. The fellows in my hut are all right: but none of them tuned exactly to my pitch.

Yet, it's the R.A.F. and the fact fills me with a perverse, brittle, and nevertheless complete satisfaction. Odd that a man should be so ungrateful, for the R.T.C. was very good to me, and I've jilted her without a regret.   TES

I'm due for a week-end this week. If it is very fine I shall try and reach Bovington. Sleep in Coy stores or some hut: but don't put yourself about, expecting me, for I'm a doubtful starter.

Many thanks for letters and parcels. I hope they are not troubling you. Remember always there is no urgency therewith.

                                                                    TES

275: TO THE HON. FRANCIS RODD

3.11.25.   *Cranwell, Lincs.*

Yes, I'm here now. A queer change from the richness and beauty and colour of Dorset. Lincolnshire is like a picture of a dead earth in green and grey. You feel the curve of the great ball in the wideness of all the local views.

The camp is good. Also the fellows: also the life. Mark me down for a further spell of quite happy existence. That also is an odd change, for I had made up my mind, in Bovington, to come to a natural end about Xmas, when the reprint of my book would have been finished. Here I am too content to work so hard, so it will not be ready much before March.

You don't really want one, you know. Thirty guineas is an

---

[1] Punishment.

absurd price. Wash out the idea. In return I'll put Haslam down for one. Rich men are fair game. He will have to send a cheque for £15. 15. 0. marked 7 *Pillars* Account: payable to T. E. Lawrence: to Manager, Bank of Liverpool and Martins, 68, Lombard Street, E.C.3.

I've got too many subscribers, so am very sticky over these last copies.

I'd like to turn up at your place, but I come to London so rarely. Lincolnshire is very far away. Yours,   T.E.S.

276: TO E. PALMER[1]

10. XII. 25

News for you. Clouds Hill is to be evacuated in the early spring. April or May perhaps. You will be warned in ample time, and Robinson may help you in the taking-over board. There will still be a gramophone and some records there.

Our hut now has a little musical box: and E.M.F. advised me to the ownership of a new German firm's records (complete) of the Kreutzer and Spring Sonatas. They are magnificent. You will laugh with satisfaction to hear that nobody in B. Flight likes them . . . barring of course the last-joined A.C.11. However, his taste is the only one which concerns me. When I hear that you are my tenant they will be sent you for preserving.

I went down to Cambridge last Sunday, and there E.M.F. sat, large as life, but sad-looking, wasted almost, in another man's rooms in King's, the splendiferous college with the extra-splendiferous (and rather horrible) chapel. We talked about you and Middleton, and the world generally. M. writes more letters to him than you do. Then M. always was talkative.

I didn't dare ask about the Scarlatti piano scrap. Have you given it him? I don't want it sent by post, for it might break, and the Brunswick people will not be able to make any more, having lost the matrix. Do let him have it before Xmas, with our best regards. How is your new C.O.? Has B.B. gone, and is the R.Q. troubled? Any news of Jeffrey?[2] He sent me a letter, which

---

[1] Private Royal Tank Corps; nicknamed Posh.   [2] Corporal, Royal Tank Corps.

was as cold and correct as a fishes' kisses. (? a fish's kiss, a fish-kiss: fishes-kisses? . . .) Your Xmas plans? I had a great idea of some time in London, and was given the keys of a flat in Brook Street, off Berkeley Square. Very posh.[1] Unfortunately no leave was offered me. So I'm at Cranwell instead, general fatigues. . . . Crashed off the Brough last monday: knee: ankle; elbow: being repaired. Tunic and breeches being replaced. Front mudguard, name-plate, handlebars, footrest, renewed. Skid on ice at 55 m.p.h. Dark: wet: most miserable. Hobble like a cripple now.   s.

Your posting? a false alarm? presumably.

I've asked A.W.L. to plant trees round the hill-top . . . calling on you for Edkin's help if necessary, unless his own market gardener at Bournemouth plays up.

My respectful salutations to L/C Willis.

277: TO LIONEL CURTIS

14.XII.25.   [Cranwell]

I am aweary, aweary,
I would that I were dead.[2]

This completes the quotation referred to. It freezes: it snows: it blows. I'm cold as cold. The running rivers of my brain are all a-frozen. Don't expect coherence till a thaw sets in.

The sweater: the Canadian sweater? I'm almost sure it's there. I can feel it, by hooking a finger between the third and fourth buttons (next above the belt) of my tunic. But this is sense-evidence only. To make sure, I should have to unbutton my tunic, and look: and the wind is howling so terribly about this hangar that I don't dare.

You said something, when you sent the royal thing, about motorcycling, and Canada: but it must have been made for work in the Flights at Cranwell. They offer me huge prices here, for it: packets and packets of woodbines: spare pairs of boots, a 'civie

---

[1] See letter No. 282.   [2] Tennyson, *Mariana*.

suit' . . . I refuse them all, frozenly waving one frozen hand, in
icy refusal. Of course I should have written and told you: but
. . . but . . . but. . . .

It's cold.

Your envelope is perfectly addressed.   T.E.S.

278: TO SYDNEY COCKERELL

29. XII. 25   *Cranwell*

There, Christmas is safely over, without my running down to
Cambridge. The road is a tempting one, which explains my
thinking of it; but the snow & ice made riding impossible. I hate
going to people's houses on Christmas day, because it's a family
festival, if a festival at all, and merely a false sentiment for single
people. In camp they make it an excuse for eating a lot, &
drinking too much, the usual police regulations being lifted, so
that drunkenness goes unpunished. Yet at Cranwell this year I
have been very fortunate. The rest of 'B' flight went on leave, so
that I have the hut to myself. Sixteen beds at choice. Sometimes
I feel like the last survivor of a sinking doss-house. Still it is very
pleasant to have a solitary bedroom, & quiet, & lack of talk.
I even lent away the gramophone, so that there should be no
disturbance, & passed my spare time reading T. S. Eliot's
collected poems (he is the most important poet alive) and correcting the proofs of an old-fashioned book you can guess the name
of. It's odd, you know, to be reading these poems, so full of the
future, so far ahead of our time; and then to turn back to my book,
whose prose stinks of coffins and ancestors & armorial hatch-
ments. Yet people have the nerve to tell me it's a good book!
It would have been, if written a hundred years ago: but to bring
it out after *Ulysses* is an insult to modern letters — an insult I
never meant of course, but ignorance is no defence in the army!

It was very good of you to ask me down: and I would have
looked in at tea-time if the road conditions had been possible.
I have no fear of mud or rain: but ice-ruts, with a blizzard continuing on top — No, that's not motorbiking weather. Lincolnshire is a very wintry country: the weather is still awful.

Some time next year I'll try to turn up again for a moment.
Yours   T.E.S.

I didn't tell you about Lucas, did I? E. M. Forster had him in
a room at King's for me to look at. The man is magnificent, a
mental athlete. If he is ever sent down or divorced he will write
glorious books. Well worth your knowing.   .S.

279: TO ALEC DIXON[1]

29.XII.25.

The weather barometer points to 'stormy'. My private indicator
is set at 'calm'. Cranwell is the coldest place on earth, and the
windiest: but all the wind is actual. In the metaphorical sense it is
one great rest. As soon as I reached here I told everybody whom
I used to be. It gave me an uncomfortable month. The back of
every chair in the canteen used to sprout a face whenever I
entered: and the airmen generally held their breaths waiting for
a sign. A month that was. After it their strained lungs expired
and inspired air in gulps, and then settled down to normal rate.
When a new man comes to the station he is brought to see me:
otherwise everything is the same as ever it was. God be praised.
The R.A.F. is very good. My discharge date is August 1932.
When I wake up suddenly at night it feels close, and frightens me:
but six years is yet a long time. God be praised as I said before.
      Savage has told me of you and Picton.[2] Well, I go on hoping.
My own ignorance of authorship is so profound, so immense, so
absolute, that I dare not give a verdict in either of your cases.
Authors make themselves by going on writing. Did you ever
read *Martin Eden*, by Jack London? No, it's not like the rest of
his work.
      The Mesopotamian rebellion of 1920? Didn't Miss Gertrude
Bell put together the only account of it in her annual report?
It used to be a sort of blue-book thing, published at Bagdad.
Try a big Public Library: or the British Museum. There was

----

[1] Then Corporal, Royal Tank Corps.
[2] Dixon, author of *Singapore Patrol*, was at this time beginning to publish his work.
His friend Picton, also in the Tank Corps, is an artist in black and white.

also a woman (Buchanan?) who wrote a blank book about herself in Arab hands. They were gentle with her but killed her husband.

Leachman was a thin jumpy nervous long fellow, with a plucked face and neck. He was full of courage, and hard as French nails. He had an abiding contempt for everything native (an attitude picked up in India). Now this contempt may be a conviction, an opinion, a point of view. It is inevitable perhaps, and therefore neither to be praised nor blamed. Leachman allowed it to be a rule of conduct. This made him inconsiderate, harsh, overbearing towards his servants and subjects: and there was, I stake my oath, no justification for the airs he took. Leachman was an ordinary mind, but a character of no ordinary hardness. I do not say a great character, for I think it made its impression more by its tough skin and unyielding texture than by any great spread or degree. I should call him a man too little sensitive to be aware of other points of view than his own: too little fine to see degrees of greatness, degrees of rightness in others.

He was blunt and outspoken to a degree. Such is a good point in a preacher, a bad point in a diplomat. It makes a bullying judge, too. I think he was first and foremost a bully: but not a fleshy bully. He had no meat or bulk on him: a sinewy, wasted man, very yellow and dissatisfied in face. He was jealous of other people's being praised.

For his few days with us in Hejaz we were not prepared. 'Leachman', it was a great name and repute in Mesopotamia (a land of fourth-raters) and we thought to find a colleague in him. After less than a week we had to return him on board ship, not for anything he said, though he spoke sourly always, but because he used to chase his servant so unmercifully that our camp took scandal at it. The servant was a worm, a long worm, who never turned or showed a spark of spirit. Any decent servant would have shot him.

Leachman lasted a long time after that: but one day he spat in a sheikh's face at a time when the veil of terror under which we had worked in Mespot had worn thin. The chief upped and shot him in the back, as he was running out of the tent. Both insult and reprisal were almost unprecedented in the history of the desert. Then Leachman wasn't quite what you call a decent fellow, and the sheikh (whom I met a year later) was febrile. As L. died tragically we must hide his fault. Don't make him a hero in your book. He was too shrill, too hot-tempered, too little generous. Yours,   T.E.S.

News of me, when you want it, from Posh.

[Hogarth asked Lawrence for biographical details for use in an article on him in *The Encyclopaedia Britannica*. I have italicized words written in red ink.]

280: TO D. G. HOGARTH

14.1.26

Some illegible name has written me for a gratis copy of my book, the owner of it having been with me in Arabia. United Services Club. Mentions you. Is it Dowsett, of the Armoured Cars?

Encyc. Brit. Yes by all means. Let me try my hand . . . (*The red ink is not for publication*).

'L's family, though (*Leicestershire*) not Irish in origin, had been settled for some while (*Queen Elizabeth*) near Dublin (60 *miles N.W.*) His only recent ancestor (*since Sir W. Raleigh*) with oriental interests appears to have been that (*rogue*) Vansittart who worked in India beside Clive & Warren Hastings, but not always in harmony with them.'

Does that ring with the right loftiness of the *D.N.B.*?

At it again. . . .

'L. the second of five brothers, was educated privately (*yes*), at the City of Oxford School (*very little, very reluctantly, very badly*), and at Jesus College, Oxford (*not at all*). After passing the first examinations for the Honour School of Modern History he was elected to a Demyship of Magdalen College Oxford, which he held (*in absence*) till 1919. In 1919 he was elected to a research fellowship at All Souls College.' (*which he held for three years*)

'L. was interested in the history of the Crusades, & explored Syria from 1910 onwards studying their records on the ground. At this time he picked up some colloquial Arabic, which supported his request to be attached (*D.G.H. did this for him*) to the British Museum Expedition about to excavate Carchemish, on the upper Euphrates. He worked for the British Museum for some years, and for the P.E.F.[1] for some weeks in 1914. On the outbreak of war he was appointed (*by D.G.H.*) to the Geographical Section of the General Staff, in the W.O.'

After the War.

'L was attached (*with regret*) to the British Delegation during the Peace Conference. Afterwards he resided for a (*constipated*) year in All Souls. In 1921 he was made Adviser to the Colonial Secretary (Mr. Winston Churchill) upon Arab affairs, & as such (*silently*) attended the Cairo Conference, & passed some (*uncomfortable*) later months in Palestine. In 1922 he resigned this appointment to enlist in the R.A.F. in which (*after some interim misfortunes*) he was still serving in 1926.'

I'm sorry. It's the *Encyc.* not the *D.N.B.* and they probably want only four lines. Don't over-stress the war period. As it fades into distance, the war becomes a small affair.   T.E.S.

281: TO J. B. ACRES[2]

15.1.26

Dear Acres, Your letter upon Dostoevsky was most excellent. I've always believed him the greatest of the Russians: though he never achieved an epic like *War and Peace*. He never aimed at the epic manner. When I'm forced to describe *The [Brothers] Karamazov* in a word I say 'A fifth gospel'. It is that intense preoccupation with supra-moral goodness, Christ-like-ness, which marks him so strongly. An epileptic and ex-convict, he drew always from his own experience and feelings. That's why his books are full of neuroses: and his characters so often criminal. There is a sameness too: for D. lived over-much within himself. Not many people are happy enough to strike the balance between inside and outside, and achieve a harmony.

André Gide's book on Dostoevsky was not good. He tried

---

[1] Palestine Exploration Fund.
[2] Of the Oxford University Air Squadron. He had been at Cranwell.

to make him into a Protestant (Gide is a French Protestant) and didn't get to grips with his real powers and depths. Few Frenchmen could. They are too dapper to feel as untidily and recklessly as the Russians. Here ended Friday's letter. A wire intervenes. A week-end.

I must send you more of D. but take a rest between whiles. Have you read *Lost Souls*? (Gogol).[1] I think you spoke of it to me once. This was written on Monday. I give up trying to write.

There are two or three books here waiting for fine weather, brown paper, and string, before venturing to Oxford. Nothing earth-shaking or portentous, like *The Karamazovs*: but man cannot live entirely on either dynamite or beef.

Not this week-end at Oxford. I'm for Welwyn, on business, if the roads clear. Zero here on Sat. Night. My mind is frozen. Good luck.   T.E.S.

282: TO THE HON. FRANCIS RODD

28.1.26

Dear F.R., The 23rd, so Haslam said, was your day of return.[2] I left my keys with him: and he was going to leave them with his housekeeper, if he went to Mexico. All this going is terrible.

I hope you are back, & over the first emptiness of return. I've got to thank you for four exceedingly good nights in London. Four, you will say, is too few to justify my holding those keys all the weeks: but consider the quality of those nights. The place so quiet, so absolutely mine, and the door locked downstairs, so that it was really mine. Why there isn't a lock in my power at Cranwell, not even on the shit-house door! The happiness & security of those nights were very keen.

I didn't read many books: but I worked the bath-machine over-time. The best of thanks possible.

Yours ever   T.E.S.

---

[1] *Dead Souls*, by Nikolay Gogol.
[2] Rodd had lent Lawrence his flat in London, during his absence abroad.

283: TO S. L. NEWCOMBE[1]

10. 3. 26.

My Lord Duke, It is time for you to change your name once more. In 1920 Lawrence was current. In 1921 our names became Ross. In 1923 we changed to Shaw. What shall we become next year?

Hurry up and learn to read. I have written a book: a long book. One copy is to go to your father, since it says rude things about his face and character. One copy is to go to you: so that you shall know what your father is like. Your mother is not to have a copy. She knows more than that already. It is time for me to stop writing. Your worm   SHAW

This letter is intended for S. L. Newcombe, Esq. though I don't believe he can yet read writing.[2]

284: TO EDWARD GARNETT

Tuesday 6. 4. 26

Your letter[3] has interested me much: though you vitiate your thinking by the assumption that books are meant to be read. They are to be written only.

The abridgement is better than the complete text. Half a calamity is better than a whole one. By excising heights and depths I have made a balanced thing: yet I share your difficulty of seeing the shorter version's real shape across the gaps.

Specific points.

(i) The ending. I was overpersuaded to stop on page 644. The natural place is after 'sun', on line 35 of page 635. It fulfils your demands for balance and reflection and sordidness among the triumphs. Pages 632 and 633 are the philosophic climax of the narrative.

If you will consider anew, and approve this new FINIS, will

---

[1] Son of Colonel S. F. Newcombe then aged six. See Letter No. 120.

[2] This sentence is in ordinary script: the rest in block capitals.

[3] Edward Garnett's letter was a criticism of Lawrence's abridgement, afterwards published as *Revolt in the Desert*.

Tuesday 6-4-26

Your letter has interested me much: though you initiate your thinking by the assumption that books are meant to be read. They are to be written only.

The abridgement is better than the completed text. Half a calamity is better than a whole one. By excising heights + depths I have made a balanced thing: yet I share your difficulty of seeing the shorter version's real shape across the gaps.

Specific points:

(i) The ending. I was overpersuaded to stop on page 644. The natural place is after "Sun", on line 35 of page 635. It fulfils your demands for balance + reflection and sordidness among the triumphs. Pages 632 and 633 are the philosophic climax of the narrative.

If you will consider anew, + approve this new FINIS, will you then please so amend your text, and also cross out "a" before "pearl" in the last line of the revised version.

Your statement that the hospital passage would be a wipe in the eye for 19 readers out of 20 puts it out of court, as I put it. This abridgement is to be fit for girl guides.

[ii] To include the death of Farraj meant the restoration of many pages, to explain it. The "private delectation" of 115 people is better than the public delectation of 10,000. My men are not to walk the common street.

Me to write again? God forbid. I do not bear another mis-shaped child. Cast fini. If only I'd has the courage to destroy this one in time.

yours
TES.

Left handwriting constrains to brevity

WRITTEN WITH HIS LEFT HAND

you then please so amend your text, and also cross out 'a' before 'pearl' in the last line of the revised version.

Your statement that the hospital passage would be a wipe in the eye for 19 readers out of 20 puts it out of court, as I put it. This abridgement is to be fit for girl guides.

(ii) To include the death of Farraj[1] meant the restoration of many pages, to explain it. The 'private delectation' of 115 people is better than the public delectation of 10,000. My men are not to walk the common street.

Me to write again? God forbid. I do not bear another misshaped child. C'est fini. If only I'd had the courage to destroy this one in time. Yours ever, T.E.S.

Left handwriting constrains to brevity.

[The following account of how Lawrence broke his right arm was written by Sergeant Pugh of the same Flight at Cranwell as Lawrence:[2]

> Out riding one summer evening, he came across a smash-up between a car (driven by an oldish man) and a pedestrian. When the pedestrian had been safely disposed of, S.[3] was asked to swing the car for the old boy. Nervousness and excitement caused him to leave the ignition fully advanced and on S. swinging, the starting handle flew back and broke S's right arm. Without so much as a sign to show what had taken place S. asked if he would mind retarding the offending lever, and swung the car with his left hand. After the car was at a safe distance S. got a man to 'kick over' his Brough, and with his right arm dangling and changing gear with his foot, S. got his bus home and parked without a word to a soul of the pain he was suffering. Through some unknown reason the M.O. was away for over an hour before his arm could be 'done'. That is a man — S., I mean.]

[1] Chapter XCIII of *Seven Pillars of Wisdom*. In a note on part of the typescript of *Lawrence and the Arabs* by Robert Graves, submitted to him and returned to Graves on August 3rd, 1927, Lawrence wrote:

'It seems to me nearly unbearable that you should publish the story of the death of Farraj. No doubt it is my fault for putting it in print, in the first case. I suggest it be cut right out. The narrative was so arranged as not to depend on it. Garnett included it in his abridgement, which is a main reason why his abridgement was superseded by my own.'

[2] Here printed from the original manuscript. It differs from the version printed in *Lawrence and The Arabs*, which incorporated material provided by Lawrence. [3] Shaw.

285: TO E. M. FORSTER

26. 4. 26

I broke my right arm & wrist trying to start someone's car. It has been a source of discomfort since, & is not perfectly cured. In fact it's twisted a bit. No matter: but it takes away my last hope of being admitted some day to a beauty chorus.

At last, after weeks, I have found Lucas' letter, somewhat crumpled, for I carried it about with me for a while. His sentence about 'a supernatural background' startled me. Perhaps he meant unworldly: or unearthly. Surely not supernatural? I do not believe in that. There is no more rational being than myself alive. It's excess of reason which makes me seem mad to people. Otherwise I've now digested the letter, & can read it coldly, unblushingly. Odd that my confidence in my critical sense should let me condemn as rotten what so many excellent artists praise. I may see Lucas on May 9: & will then try to pin him down to particularities.

Your letter after Lincoln stares me reproachfully in the face. What can I say or do? I have a shell on me like a crab's: so I can't show what I think. It's my opinion that you will yet write (or have written & not yet shown) something very big: bigger than the *Passage*, which deliberately was bigger than any of the previous novels. Greatness lies in the eye that contemplates not in the subject: & your eye has grown very slowly. All the more lasting, thereby. Of course it's a bore being famous. You have cracked the crib, & the swag isn't any longer up to your standard. Consequently you feel empty, for the while: as if the profession was exhausted. But it isn't. Just wait a bit. Ten more years if necessary. You aren't wasting your time: everybody likes seeing you. Your present emotions span themselves into articles for the *Labour Leader*. Very well. There are sparks & flames: affairs of degree. Yours are the most sporting & fiery sparks. They are so good that someone will some day collect a shower of them. You needn't do that. Let the *Passage* represent you for the moment.

Do you remember little Smith, the bearded bookseller of Lincoln? He asked who you were. I told him, feeling pretty pleased with myself. He ordered a dozen assorted E.M.F's. (5/- brand) on the strength of your visit. Sold them. Ordered 20. Is selling them. I told him *The Omnibus*[1] was a book. He ordered two. A Yank came in: guessed he wanted something to read. Saw *The Omnibus*. Said 'That's the best set of short stories ever printed' ... and took the two.

I don't endorse the Y's opinion. v.g. yes ... but the best? No, I don't agree. However my critical judgement, though dogmatic & dictatorial, is (according to Lucas) bad. Hoots. I congratulate you, anyway.

This letter must stop. Pen-holding is a small scale business, & makes my wrist ache: and there are many letters to write.

Writing is a mean snivelling business. It fails to convey anything bigger than its own scrawling miserable pot-hooks. Hoots.

T.E.

286: TO J. G. WILSON[2]

25.5.26 [*Cranwell*]

Dear Wilson, The Windsor copy will be duly sent: but I'm an old-fashioned person, to whom it seems improper that Kings should buy and sell among their subjects. You told me that the advance cheque was Fortescue[3]: and I mean to return it gently to him with the book when it is ready. F. is decent, and will not tell his owner: for I should prefer Him to think He is paying for it, since that is His notion of propriety.

Whittingham and Griggs, the printers of the colour plates, had promised August as their finishing date, before the strike.[4] Now, I suppose, one cannot say. After them there is only the binding. Text is ready, index in hand, map begun. I begin to see light through the back cover, at last. Yours T.E.S.

Me for India in November: so it must end before that.

---

[1] *The Celestial Omnibus*, by E. M. Forster.
[2] Of J. & E. Bumpus: the booksellers.
[3] Sir John Fortescue, Librarian to H.M. King George V at Windsor Castle.
[4] The General Strike.

287: TO MRS. THOMAS HARDY

21.6.26   *Cranwell*

Dear Mrs. Hardy, I'm very sorry about that MS.[1] Always I feared that something of the sort might happen to it. Of course Mr. Hardy can't see it as outsiders will. His life matters so much to him, & he is 80: and he resents other people fussing over something of his own which he cannot himself keep. Especially as he has been reticent always. However you still have the other copies, and they are good. The early, formative, life is so beautifully done. The middle-age is not so important, for the novels cover that. I would have liked a documented, intimate study of his old age, since its reality would be worth a great deal to everyone old, or growing old. Only you could hardly detach yourself cruelly enough to write. that.

There: it doesn't matter. You have done a most excellent thing.

The Greek Play[2] will escape me. We are very busily flying just now, & I am not feeling energetic, when we do get a day off. The inclination is to lie in the grass & watch its greenness turning slowly into yellow. Lincolnshire has a severe winter, & a severe summer: a county of extremes & suddennesses.

The R.A.F. are sending me to India this autumn: in November probably. Did I tell you? I am not sorry to miss the campaign of publicity in which Cape will try to sell my abridged book next spring: but sorry to be abroad for so long. England is the only place fit to live in.

I've told the Bank to transfer the Lemperly copy to you: and despite your 'maid of all work' I've no doubt that the extra expense will not be crushing to you. For myself I haven't given any libraries any copies, though British Museum & Bodleian wanted them. Somehow they feel dehumanised, those places. Do with the extra book just what you please. I wish it was finished. The colour printer is held up for lack of power to move his presses. It may be August or September before he is finished. Everything else is printed & ready, and I'll send the

---

[1] Hardy had destroyed part of Mrs. Hardy's memoir of him.

[2] A performance of the Hippolytus of Euripides by the Balliol Players in Thomas Hardy's garden.

copies out before I go abroad, whether all the possible pictures are finished or not.

The booksellers confirm to me that it is a good investment. They will pay £50 now for a copy, and it will rise yet further after publication. Why not sell Copy No. 11 and share the profit with the maid: — of whom I have the pleasantest recollection. Your house, your dog, your servants, are all of them individualities!

What a sprawling silly letter. There are engines roaring through the corrugated iron partition, & people questioning me upon flight business every moment. There goes a rocket. Rain coming, I suppose.   T E S.

288: TO GEORGE BROUGH

27. 9. 26   *Cranwell*

Dear Mr. Brough, I'm very much in your debt for four years solid pleasure. Would the enclosed be any use to you? I don't want to sign it Ross, since that only makes the newspapers sit up & take notice: whereas they have already made beasts of themselves over the 'Lawrence' name, & can keep it, so far as I'm concerned.

I don't mind your showing it to people (or sticking it up on your stand, if that is a practice at Olympia) but I'd rather you did not print it in a newspaper till after December 15, when I'll have gone abroad. This is supposing it's of use, as a chit. What I really meant it for is best thanks, for a hundred thousand very jolly miles. Yours ever   J. H. ROSS.[1]

[The enclosed letter is printed below.]

289: TO GEORGE BROUGH

27. 9. 26

Dear Mr. Brough, Yesterday I completed 100000 miles, since 1922, on five successive Brough Superiors, and I'm going abroad

---

[1] Lawrence no doubt signed as Ross so as to prevent any chance of the name T. E. Shaw appearing in the testimonial. But he continued to use the name Ross occasionally long after he had changed to Shaw by deed poll.

very soon, so that I think I must make an end, and thank you for the road-pleasure I have got out of them. In 1922 I found George I (your old Mark I) the best thing I'd ridden, but George V (the 1922 SS 100) is incomparably better. In 1925 and 1926 (George IV & V) I have not had an involuntary stop, & so have not been able to test your spares service, on which I drew so heavily in 1922 and 1923. Your present machines are as fast and reliable as express trains, and the greatest fun in the world to drive: — and I say this after twenty years experience of cycles and cars.

They are very expensive to buy, but light in upkeep (50-65 m.p.g. of petrol, 4000 m.p.g. oil, 5000-6000 miles per outer cover, in my case) and in the four years I have made only one insurance claim (for less than £5) which is a testimony to the safety of your controls & designs. The S.S. 100 holds the road extraordinarily. It's my great game on a really pot-holed road to open up to 70 m.p.h. or so and feel the machine gallop: and though only a touring machine it will do 90 m.p.h. at full throttle.

I'm not a speed merchant, but ride fairly far in the day (occasionally 700 miles, often 500) and at a fair average, for the machine's speed in the open lets one crawl through the towns, & still average 40-42 miles in the hour. The riding position & the slow powerful turn-over of the engine at speeds of 50 odd give one a very restful feeling.

There, it is no good telling you all you knew before I did: they are the jolliest things on wheels. Yours very sincerely

T E LAWRENCE.

[In the letter of June 21st to Mrs. Hardy, Lawrence had announced that the R.A.F. authorities were sending him to India in the autumn, and that he was glad he was going to be out of the country when *Revolt in the Desert* was published. The R.A.F. authorities in India do not appear to have been informed of his impending arrival until November 23rd.]

290: TO DICK KNOWLES

3.XII.26   *[Uxbridge Depot]*

Dear Dick, I'm sitting in a very poor hut at Uxbridge ... I spent the whole of my leave, seeing no one, and going to no concerts: not one single scrap of public music all that while: though by the goodness of my dentist[1] I twice heard Harold Samuel play in his house.

I managed to squeeze out ½ an hour in Clouds Hill: and ½ an hour at the Hardys. I had meant to come to you last Sunday, and started about 7.30 A.M. but Islington streets were greasy (I had to see G.B.S. on the way) & I got into a trough in the wood paving, and fell heavily, doing in the off footrest, kickstart, brake levers, ½ handlebar, & oil pump. Also my experienced knee-cap learnt another little trick. Alb Bennett took the wreck for £100. I limp rather picturesquely. . . . Yours   T.E.S.

[On 14th December John Buchan forwarded to the Prime Minister a copy of *Seven Pillars of Wisdom* and quoted from a letter of Lawrence's, which he had received with it.]

291: TO JOHN BUCHAN

[December 1926]

[*omission*] This copy is one of those which I am giving to the fellows who did the Arab revolt with me. They are incomplete in the sense that many plates are missing. I want you to ask Mr. Baldwin if he would care to accept it. He did me the best turn I have ever had done to me, and I think gratefully of him as often as I have leisure to think about my contentment. It is no great return (incomplete copies have no future in the second-hand market) but I am hardly in the position to make any great return, and if he likes books, as I am told, he may prefer a broken copy to none at all. The thing is, anyhow, a rarity.

[The voyage out to India in the troopship *Derbyshire* was, as far as Suez, an unpleasant ordeal. It is described in some pages

---

[1] W. Warwick James. See his contribution on Lawrence's interest in music in *T. E. Lawrence by his Friends.*

of pencil manuscript found at Clouds Hill after Lawrence's death which appear to be notes for a final section of *The Mint*, to be called *Leaves In The Wind*. I have divided the four notes so that each appears chronologically according to the date of its subject. For I cannot tell when exactly they were written, though on the analogy of *The Mint* I believe them to have been noted shortly after the events they describe. Both in subject and style these notes belong to *The Mint*, of which they will give some idea to the general reader.]

292: FROM 'LEAVES IN THE WIND'

Final section *Leaves in the Wind*, snatches of life and letters, misarranged, from 2 lines to pages. M.Q.[1] sentry — the shabby haversack that denoted my office. The wash of the water, the *Derbyshire* swaying in a long slow swell, going over so far, swinging back: ever and again going further, with a muffled musical clash of crockery far away in her depths, oscillating back again — now and then an upward heave, and the slow sinking back. My eyes began to swim, and to see gassy clouds in the corridor, between the blobs of the dim safety lamps. They twinkled so electric blue. Wave upon wave of the smell of stabled humanity: the furtive creeping by rushes along the alleyway of the women to their latrine, fending themselves from wall to wall with the right arm, while the left held the loosened dress across their body. Belches of gas come back up my throat — hullo, I'll be sick if I stay here for ever — yet I promised the guard commander that I'd do two tricks: my poor little ex-apprentice relief got so bad down here after fifteen minutes that they had to help him up to the air. *Swish swish* the water goes against the walls of the ship — sounds nearer. Where on earth is that splashing. I tittup along the alley and peep into the lavatory space, at a moment when no woman is there. It's awash with a foul drainage. Tactless posting a sentry over the wives' defaecations, I think. Tactless and useless all our duties aboard. Hullo here's the O.O.[2] visiting. May as well tell him. The grimy-folded face, the hard jaw, toil-hardened hands, bowed and ungainly figure. An ex-naval war-

---

[1] Married Quarters.   [2] Orderly Officer.

rant, I'll bet. No gentleman. He strides boldly to the latrine: 'Excuse me' unshyly to two shrinking women. 'God', he jerked out, 'flooded with shit — where's the trap?' He pulled off his tunic and threw it at me to hold, and with a plumber's quick glance strode over to the far side, bent down, and ripped out a grating. Gazed for a moment, while the ordure rippled over his boots. Up his right sleeve, baring a forearm hairy as a mastiff's grey leg, knotted with veins, and a gnarled hand: thrust it deep in, groped, pulled out a moist white bundle. 'Open that port' and out it splashed into the night. 'You'd think they'd have had some other place for their sanitary towels. Bloody awful show, not having anything fixed up.' He shook his sleeve down as it was over his slowly-drying arm, and huddled on his tunic, while the released liquid gurgled contentedly down its re-opened drain.

293: TO MRS. THOMAS HARDY

11. I. 27　　　　　　　　　　　　　　　　　　　　*Karachi*

Dear Mrs Hardy, Forster gave me your message about T.H. and our parting at Max Gate. It was my doing. The afternoon was raw and miserable, like the day, and when T.H. turned back into the house to get a shawl (as I guessed) instantly I ran the bicycle out into the road and away, so that no possible reproach might lie against me for having helped him into the danger of a chill.

The knowing you & having the freedom of Max Gate has been a delightful privilege of mine for nearly four years. I cannot tell you how grateful I am to you both: and how much I look forward to finding you there when I come back. Eighty-six is nothing of an age, so long as its bearer is not content with it; in fact it is still fourteen years short of a decent score in cricket.

I hope poor Wessex[1] has a peaceful parting. The killing of animals just because they are ill or old is not a medicine we apply to our own species.

Karachi feels inordinately far away from every interest I ever had. However it will pass. Yours sincerely　　　　T E SHAW

[1] The Hardys' dog.

294: TO S. L. NEWCOMBE[1]

11. 1. 27   [*Karachi*]

Dear Monster, This letter is to say that I ate four of your toffee chunks on Xmas day. They were the last four in the tin. I kept the tin hidden in my kit-bag, and so none of the other airmen had any. They were very good. It was a most excellent present. Afterwards I brought out the empty tin, and we made it the sugar magazine for our Mess. It was two sorts of a Mess. Mess 68, they called it. They are still using the tin, though I am not now on the ship, but in Karachi. Address

338171 AC2 Shaw, Room 2 E.R.S.[2] R.A.F. Depot, Drigh Road, Karachi, India.

A long difficult address: but not a bad place to live in. No trees. Sand and desert, & great store houses full of airmen. We get up in the dark, & work all the morning. I am a sort of messenger, runner they call me, but I do not run: just I waddle like a blue duck. Sometimes I do clerks' work. The officer said 'Can you write?' I replied 'Fluently'. He said 'No, No; is your handwriting good?' I will not tell you what I said then.

About that photograph you asked of me. It is not forgotten, but instead of having one taken out here I am trying to get one from England for you. There are some quite good ones. If there are none left in England I will have one made out here, but it will not be so excellent, as my nose is peeling. Also I am too red. Red comes out black in photographs, & you will not want a photograph of a quite black airman.

Go on being monstrous. Get monstrously long, while I get monstrously thick. Then everybody who sees us together will have fits. Poof.   M.....r

295: TO EDWARD MARSH

2. 2. 27   *Karachi*

Dear E.M., Some address! I hope you got the camel-ride in good order from Kennington. He told me you had rung him up,

---

[1] Then almost seven.

[2] Engine Repair Shops. While at Karachi Lawrence reorganized the procedure of engine overhaul. See letters Nos. 302 and 486.

& that it was arranged. Since the first time I saw it, I've felt that it was a very fine thing, and it was a disappointment when Aitken[1] refused it, on Bone's advice.

The purpose of this letter is for you to file it till the critical moment, and then remind Winston that he's promised me a copy of his Vol III,[2] shortly to be published. Rumour says that there is no duty on books sent by book-post. Sounds ungracious, as a hint, but some weeks they only give us five rupees, & India is more expensive for troops than home service.

Karachi is not too dismal, but Indians are a bit of a come-down after the other races I've had to meet. There's a suppressed meanness about them which makes me regret our likeness in shape.

The voyage out on a trooper (H.M.T. *Derbyshire*) was some-thing vigorous in the way of experience. Your improper depart-ment has ruled that at sea three airmen can be packed into the air-space of two sailors. Kindly meant, no doubt, to keep us warm and comfortable. But in the Red Sea and the Gulf we grew sick of each other's smell.

Try not to forget that book. Half our day is leisure, and I am not very good at entertaining myself. Yours ever   T E S.

296: TO DICK KNOWLES

8.2.27.   *R.A.F. Depot, Drigh Road, Karachi*

Dear Dick, Here we are again. The usual furlong and a half of address. A dry hole, on the edge of the Sind desert, which desert is a waste of sand and sandstone, with a plentiful stubble of cactus on its flat parts, and of tamarisk in its valleys. Over it blow hot and cold winds, very heavily laden with dust. We eat dust and breathe dust and think dust and hate dust on the days when dust-storms blow. At present, in the nominal winter, that is not often enough to be less than remarkable. In summer, they tell us genially, a little breeze rises every midday, blows a dust-gale every afternoon, and dies into a mere dust-soup at sunset.

---

[1] Director of the Tate Gallery.   [2] Of *The World Crisis*.

I'll write again in the hot weather, and enclose you a few grains of the local air as a sample, confirming or denying rumour.

Life in the Depot? 'Cushy'. Work at 7.30 A.M. (parade in overalls). Knock off at 1 P.M. Every day is a half-day, except Thursday and Sunday, which are whole holidays. Church every other Sunday. Drill Parades bi-weekly when a big noise draws near — Sir Sam: the A.O.C.: the G.O.C. (insult to injury[1]!): the King's Birthday: Armistice Day: and a local festivity, 'Proclamation Day'. Weekly or fortnightly when the horizon is clear. No P.T. Guards every two months. (I had six on the wretched boat coming out). No bugles in camp. Also no hot water, till I won a blow-lamp and a dope can, and began to boil myself every three days. Food excellent. Canteen vile. Karachi (place of limited amusement) seven miles off. No occupation for spare hours, and the spare hours make up 15/16 of life, apparently. No roads, fortunately, so I do not wish for a Brough. No wads, so I'm able to do without money. No pay either, to speak of. They keep you short, on 5 rupees a week, till the pay-sheets come out in five months time. By putting two weeks pay together I can get three gramophone records. So the Funeral March, and the Largo of Bach's Concerto for 2 violins in D, and Boccherini's Sonata in A are astonishing Room 2, which cherishes very fondly a preference for Rose Marie. There is a song going on now about 'I wish I'd never met you'. It isn't true, of the company to which I write. I do wish, hourly, that our great Imperial heritage of the East would go the way of my private property... however it's no use starting on that sadness, since my coming out here is my own (and unrepented) fault entirely. Often in the evening I go out to the music of the camel bells upon Drigh Road, and hang my topee on a cactus branch, and sit down under it, and weep, remembering Cranwell and the Great North Road. The camel-bells sound just like a water-tap dripping, drop, drop, drop, into a deep cistern. When they condescend to cease (which is when one or other camel in the string, feeling a natural urge in him, straddles his hind legs and drags or bumps his fellow-camels to a standstill) the quietude of the night smooths itself out like heaven. And the noblest star of all the heavens is one bright red

---

[1] At airmen having to parade for a soldier. See letter 298.

one, whose 60 c.p. incandescent(?) bulb glows on the topmost pinnacle of the Canteen. Of course, as Posh would point out, you can't see it as far as you can the stars in Orion. All things appear to depend on the point of view. Hoots.   T.E.S.

297: TO ERIC KENNINGTON

15. ii. 27.   [*Karachi*]

Dear K., Your photograph has just turned up.[1] It's amazing: and very curious. Of course the plaster gives double pitch to both high lights and shadows: and the top-light is very hard: and these two accidents conspire to reinforce your simplification of the structure of my head and face. Consequently emphasis is piled on emphasis, till the whole almost shouts. The Wood bust[2] becomes a strained joke. Yours is magnificent; there is no other word for it. It represents not me, but my top-moments, those few seconds in which I succeed in thinking myself right out of things. That accounts, so far as the subject contributes any merit to the achievement, partly for the monumentality of the first impression. You have simplified out, and simplified out, and concentrated on what you liked of the material to your hands, and produced — well I liken it to a cross between that Giottesque Dante, and the Gattamelata — Colleone. Only I hope people won't think I look like Table Mountain when I'm darning socks. It's all very well being a public monument after you're dead.

Before I left you I felt that, barring accidents, you were on the way to doing something big. But Lord, you've pulled it together and pulled it up and out and forward more than I thought possible. The face and neck are treated with a dry precision and strength and confidence very unusual in recent sculpture: in any portrait sculpture. I trace a little hesitation in your handling of the lips. But there is a smile on them, which clashes with the 'Entry into Valhalla' motive of the jaw and eyes. They have just started up the hut gramophone on the Trauermarsch, our very best record,

[1] Of Kennington's bust of Lawrence – used as a frontispiece to the edition of *Seven Pillars of Wisdom* published after Lawrence's death. A bronze cast is in St. Paul's Cathedral.
[2] The bust by Derwent Wood.

and I am tempted to draw parallels between Wagner — Siegfried and yourself. But that is an accident of Room 2's taste in music. They had only jazz till I came in with some Wagner fragments and a little Bach. Now the air is a perfect Xmas-pudding of cross-vibrations. Two of them are trying to dance to the Funeral stuff, and the dog has begun to howl. How in God's name can I write coherently about sculpture in this turmoil? Sheriff has just come behind my bed, and yelled into my ear 'Excuse me, but what is an iconoclast?'

I've now safely delivered a short speech on Byzantine religious controversies of the fifth century. Back to the head! The balance and proportion of head, neck and supports are apparently exact. I'd have liked more difference in surface treatment between hair, flesh and clothing — especially the last two. The shoulders are very good, in their conventionality: but the neck of the tunic has a little too much work in it. I'd have cut out the button and slapped the whole of it over with a very wet hand-edge or knife-blade, to give it a dragged or dashed surface. About the hair I can't make up my petty mind. Admitted the effect is a knock-out ... but should hair, a flimsy accident, administer a knock-out as severe as that of the bony structure of the skull itself? The short hair is admirable: the longer hair almost too good, I fancy. But it is precisely at this point that the plaster contributes most to the confusion of my judgement. There is a terrific shadow under the top-lock of hair, and a blinding frontal bone, and a sooted eye. After that the light is kind, over the cheeks and jaw. By the way the structure of the forehead seems to be one of the very best things in the whole and it is very difficult to divide the head up into details. It hangs tightly together as a most convincing portrait of a person very sure of himself who had convinced the artist that he really was sure of himself.

I'd like to bet that you were playing up to my supposed feeling for sculpture, as much as I was taking for granted your interest in psychology. Yet I can't remember much about the sittings except that I went off into a day-dream whenever we were left alone: and that I was usually dog-tired before I ever came. It was such a pity that I had to leave your sittings to the bitter end of my last month and it was no end of a bitter month! Chalk that on to the tail of the score of *The Seven Pillars*. The tail of the score! I'm an optimist, if I think that the worry and shame of that book aren't only just beginning.

Your picture-show must be going forward fast, to judge by a telegraphed paragraph headlined in the papers here a day or two ago, in which G.B.S. suggests my being offered Bachelor quarters in Blenheim, and other sad things. It's a pity people don't generally realise that I can make the most lovely bubble and squeak of a life for myself, without their contributing any ingredient at all. However. The cat's away.   T.E.S.

Intentionally C. is not mentioned in this letter. I hope she is over it, well.

Did you get 4 well-bound copies of *The Seven Pillars?*

298: TO S. L. NEWCOMBE[1]

24. ii. 27   [*Karachi*]

Monster, Look how your envelope wandered over the whole wide East! But it caught me up at last, like the Hound of Heaven. Your picture is that of a ferocious imp. Rifle and equipment! I'll try & send you a photograph of me like that. I look blood-thirsty too, then. You should hear (or rather you shouldn't hear) what airmen mutter beneath & above their breaths when the officers tell us to come out and play with them publicly! It's a dreadful insult for an airman to be disguised as a soldier. Even for a moment. And we look such jokes. You see I haven't managed to get a real photo of myself. There is a camera in our room, but its owner isn't very good at using it, yet. However he is getting better. And meanwhile here is what is called a bust of me. A bust is a thing appropriate in my case. I have deserved, provoked, encouraged, more than one bust in my day. This one was done by an artist called Eric Kennington, in England last December. So it is quite the latest. In gilt brass. That also is appropriate, as a metal. You will have to learn that word APPRO-PRIATE. It keeps on bobbing up today.

Love & brickbats to yourself. My regards to your mother. Tell your father I salute him with both hands.   T.E.S.

[1] Aged seven.

299: TO EDWARD GARNETT

1. iii. 27. [*Postmarked Drigh Road* 3.*Mar*.27]   [*Karachi*]

The book is your own fault.[1] I said you might have a text, lacking illustrations, as a gift. You were scornful of this: and sent me a subscription. So all I could do was to ask Pike, my printer, to send you as well-bound a copy as he could. I hope it was a good one. I deplore the waste of money on a book by a judge who knows so very much what books should be. But you are given, by inscrutable fashion, a chance to redeem an extravagance. Sell the thing, *now*, while it stands at a premium. The son for whom you told me you wanted it, as an heirloom, will much prefer £100 or so.

Your gift of the Allenby pastel is an irresistible thing:[2] but rather overwhelming. It leaves me hopelessly in your debt. Hopelessly, for I see no way in my life and power of ever pleasing you again. My we regard it as yours, while you have walls and I have no walls? Brick by brick I have sold or given away or lost everything I possessed. The course cannot proceed much further, or I will be naked in the world. It's only by rationing my letters to not more than 15 a week (and 15 is nothing of a proportion to those I receive) that I can keep myself in postage stamps. I'm most grateful, for as a portrait of Allenby the drawing is unusually rich, and Allenby is an admiration of mine. The losing all that little private gallery was rather a wrench. I still have a jolly collection of books, and that is all: and the books I haven't handled for six years. They are in St. John's Wood now, I believe, well cared for by a man I met at Oxford, and have liked since.[3]

Edward Thomas wrote very fine poems, and some almost perfect prose. He must have been a beautiful person. I'm glad you are helping to bring him out a little. How much of that you have done! I was sorry not to use your text for the *Revolt in the Desert* abridgement. I wrote twice to Cape, and asked for the loan of it: but he was presumably afraid that I meant to destroy

---

[1] Edward Garnett subscribed for *Seven Pillars of Wisdom* and Lawrence presented him with a copy as well.

[2] By Eric Kennington, now in the National Portrait Gallery. See letters Nos. 496, 498 and 499.

[3] V. W. Richards.

it, and so do him out of his power to produce an abridgement of his own if I made default. At any rate he would not let me have it: and I could not very well go on protesting to him that if I asked for the loan of a thing he might understand that I meant a loan.

In the end I waited till the last three days, and then ran through a scratch abridgement of my own, not looking for the best things to leave in, but for the best bits to cut out. It will be all the same 100 years hence: or very shortly after my death, a nearer occasion. I suppose the complete text will then be reprinted.

This place, Karachi, is a colourless unrelieved desert, without any of the beauty of clean emptiness, for it is all spotted over with odd military and air force magazines or barracks. If my mind takes to itself the likeness and tone of its natural surroundings, then indeed I shall have achieved Nirvana.

Before that last stage I'd like to have copied out and sent you an intelligent transcript of my R.A.F. Uxbridge notes. If the energy comes to me this year or next I'll do you this final disservice — and convince you that there were not the roots of writing in me. The 'fear of showing my feelings' is my real self.

More thanks. Why do you show so disproportionate a generosity?   T.E.S.

300: TO W. A. KNOWLES[1]

31.3.27   [*Karachi*]

[*omission*] That oily creature talking about a wreath! The cheek of it. Thank heaven I never told him any of my work-day names. Otherwise he would have been still bothering me: whereas now you have probably choked him off. A broken arm for doing a man a good turn in starting his Crossley car: a persecution for trying to help an ex-fighting man to a job. These are the wages of good Samaritans to-day. Yours ever   T.E.S.

[1] Sergeant Knowles, of the Royal Tank Corps, Lawrence's neighbour at Clouds Hill and the father of Dick, Bill and Pat.

301: TO D. G. HOGARTH

7.4.27   [*Karachi*]

Azrak, Jefer, Disi, W.Itm, and all sorts of places: from some old
papers which I have been destroying. I don't know whose they
are. Some armoured car or aeroplane fellow's: perhaps Junor's,
for they include a burned view of his aeroplane, & of its crash,
and a photo of Murphy's wrecked Turk machine.[1] Stick 'em in
the cupboard with the other Arabian stuff. You will remember
that some day, if we both come together, we are going to Grainger-
ise a copy of *The Seven Pillars* (which I begin to suspect will
remain the longest work upon the Arab Revolt) with prints of
all the pertinent photographs of the expeditions.

Mrs. Shaw sent me some reviews of *Revolt in the Desert*,
including your verdict, for which best thanks. I'm glad you
have said so much about it, now & last year. I only hope people
won't boom *Revolt* into a best seller. It isn't so very good, though
I'm confident that it's good enough to pay off my debt to the bank.

I hope the Trustees will consult me before selling the film
rights, if offers come to them. Films can be so very bad.

Do you ever see Philby? If so, tell him it was very good of him
to cry me up in the *Observer*. I feel guilty always in his eyes:
guilty of being an unscientific traveller. That's why I never
offered to lend him *The Seven Pillars*. Please also assure him that
no *subscriber* was asked to accept any condition, explicit or implicit, with his copy: though I did diddle old Shorter[2] into
refusing one, by asking for a pledge that he shouldn't write any
of *his* muck about it! Did I ever show you that Shorter correspondence? It was priceless. I don't think I ever was ruder, or
successfully ruder, in all my life! He asked for it, so soul-
satisfyingly.

My books in Arabia were the *Morte*: Aristophanes (I read all
the *Peace*, very gratefully, & without much technical trouble)
and *The Oxford Book of English Verse*. Not so fastidious after all!

Your last paragraph puzzled me. In *The Seven Pillars*, the
last section, the advance on Damascus, reads very weak ... as
though I was exhausted, as perhaps I was, with all the preceding

---

[1] Lawrence enclosed photographs with this letter for Hogarth to preserve.
[2] Clement K. Shorter, editor of *The Sphere*.

chapters. I tried twice to punch it up, a bit, into life, & eventually abandoned it as hopeless: and I put it all, disproportionately, into *Revolt in the Desert*, to give it a chance by itself, with all the best bits of the early sections cut out. The better writing is in the Arabia,[1] Yarmuk raid, & winter war sections: and the very best of all perhaps, is Book I, the first ride up to Feisal: in which good bricks are made without straw.

However it doesn't matter. It is all over & done with.   T.E.S.

302: TO H. H. BANBURY[2]

20. 4. 27.   [*Karachi*]

Dear H.H.B., Yes, I was sent the Woolf review: and laughed. Here are the judgements of the great upon my style.

'So imitative of Doughty as to be near parody.' Woolf in the *Nation*.

'Has none of Doughty's biblical or Elizabethan anachronisms.' John Buchan in *Sat. Review*.

'Gnarled texture twisted with queer adjectives and adverbs.' Woolf.

'Effortless, artless-seeming, adequate prose.' Gerald Bullett.

'Obscure to the point of affectation.' *Tatler*.

'Writing as easy, confident and unselfconscious as a duck's swimming.' *Lit. Digest*.

'Style has a straightforward fierceness, an intrepid directness.' Ellis Roberts.

'The style is like music.' C. F. G. Masterman.

'A scholar's style, simple, direct, free from ornament.' H. W. Nevinson. (*Manch. Guard.*)

'Style here and there affectedly abrupt and strenuous, but mostly without affectation.' Edw. Shanks.

'A cool distinguished prose.' Eric Sutton in *Outlook*.

'Positively breezy.' G. B. Shaw in *Spectator*.

There y'are! Take your pick! I wash my hands of the affair: though I protest that I am not peevish, as Woolf says.

Karachi it still is. Now they have found me a job, in work-

---

[1] That is in the Hejaz before reaching Trans-Jordan and Syria.
[2] Regimental Sergeant Major, Royal Tank Corps.

shops. I follow the overhauling of each engine, as its particles float about the benches, and write a history of its new parts and processes. Tricky, and not either quick or easy to do. Especially for a non-technical man, very vague as to the function of a cam-shaft or inclined drive. I will be in Karachi, (unless the press blow me out) till the boat calls me home, in 1929 or 1931.

Birdwood and Salmond[1] came to us a week ago. Our Stores Accounting Section is a casualty — and deserves it. [2 *lines omitted*]

The Seven Pillars is a quotation from *Proverbs* — 'Wisdom hath set up her seven Pillars'[2] — meaning a complete edifice of knowledge. It was the title of a book I wrote before 1914 and destroyed when I joined up: and I put it on to my war diary be-cause I couldn't think of anything short and fit. The figure 'seven' implies completeness in the Semitic languages. [20 *lines omitted*]

Yes, lice had no blood-feuds or clan prejudices in Arabia. I'm glad you read Doughty just before *Revolt*. How did they compare? I think (despite Woolf) that there is very little of D. in my style, and less in my matter. But D. was keen only on death and life, and I was keen on psychology and politics. So we quarter different fields.

I have not met anything very new and good — except Win-ston's book, which is a superb demonstration of power.

You talk of Candler's critique. But didn't you read *The Seven Pillars* at Bovington? I thought Posh persuaded you to borrow it? It is better than *Revolt*.

Revolt is selling like apples. Something over 40,000 copies in the first three weeks, they say! That pays off my debts, just about. A service fund gets the surplus, if any! Good luck to it. There should be something coming from U.S.A.   T.E.S.

303: TO D. G. HOGARTH

21.4.27   [*Karachi*]

[23 *lines omitted*] Your Doughty discoveries are interesting.[3] Where did he learn his geology, & his survey work? His map

---

[1] The G.O.C. and A.O.C. in India. See letter No. 296.

[2] Compare *Proverbs* IX. i. See letter No. 219.

[3] Hogarth was collecting material for *The Life of Charles M. Doughty*, who had died on 17th January, 1926.

was surprisingly good, all things considered: and he laid a sort of foundation of our knowledge of the Arabian watersheds. There was much more of the scientist in the old man's intention, when he went down with the Haj (of his *secondary* intention, anyhow) than of the poet.

I sent you one letter of his which turned up amongst some Clouds Hill papers here. I do not know where my other Doughty letters can be. There is only Barton St. and Clouds Hill, & I turned all the papers out of Clouds Hill before I left it. The cottage is going to be let. [22 *lines omitted*]

304: TO MRS. THOMAS HARDY

5. v. 27   *Karachi*

Dear Mrs Hardy, I should have answered your letter three months back: but you know how it is: especially in this place, which is just a hot-storage for me, for the years which must pass before I may return to England. Somehow letter-writing rubs in the sense of being away.

The death of Wessex is a loss to me. He was so firm and decisive a being: one who always knew his own mind, and never hesitated to change it, if he thought fit. So doing he showed a very healthy disregard of the feelings of merely temporary visitors. Few dogs appeal to me: but Wessex gained my very definite respect. And the poor old beast (after I felt so towards him) changed his tone, & became very kind. Max Gate will not seem quite right now. He must be a very great loss to you and T.H. I'm so sorry: I hope you and T.H. are otherwise well.

I'm grateful for your kindly judgement of *The Seven Pillars*. It is inevitable that people should call it less good than the 'Oxford' text, in which I first lent it you: but their judgement leaves me cold. Only I have read the two so closely as really to see the differences: and my taste in every case approved the changes. *The Seven Pillars* is 85% of the Oxford text: and the little cut out was all redundant stuff: mostly superfluous adjectives.

The giving away of your second copy will not be easy! Probably you have done it by now. By good fortune its sale-room

value has risen sharply, so that I have not to be sorry for the subscribers who bought it as a speculation.

The Cape abridgement is selling like ripe apples, they tell me.
I hate that little book.

My restlessness, on first seeing Karachi, has faded. I keep
myself strictly to camp, and make my time pass easily enough
with books, reading and re-reading the old things I have read
and liked, but not treated ceremoniously enough, in my youth.
Yours ever   T E SHAW.

305: TO WILLIAM ROTHENSTEIN

12. V. 27.   *Karachi*

Dear Rothenstein, Hot foot by the next mail appeared *The
Enemy*! Wyndham Lewis has done it very well: much better
than *The Lion into Fox*,[1] which was a falling short after *The Art
of Being Ruled*. [4 *lines omitted*]

But on people like Pound, and Gertrude Stein, and Joyce he's
extraordinarily interesting. I wish he would let himself go
properly over the whole area of modern letters, and tell us where
he places D. H. Lawrence, and Forster, and Graves and Sassoon
and all the rest of the people who write. There is so much being
written, and so few guides to help occasional visitors to books
through the masses of them.

However perhaps he will carry it on. If *The Enemy* is successful it may encourage him to branch out into criticism. I take it
his creative side, which produced *Tarr* so long ago, has dropped
off withered.

It was very good of you to send it out. Don't you think the
cover-design, the Tartar horseman, very beautiful? Yours, T.E.S.

306: TO ERIC KENNINGTON

19. V. 27.   [*Karachi*]

Dear K., Somebody, Celandine probably, sent me the *Ulysses* I
craved for. These long dreary slow-marching books are invaluable

        [1] *The Lion and the Fox*, by Wyndham Lewis.

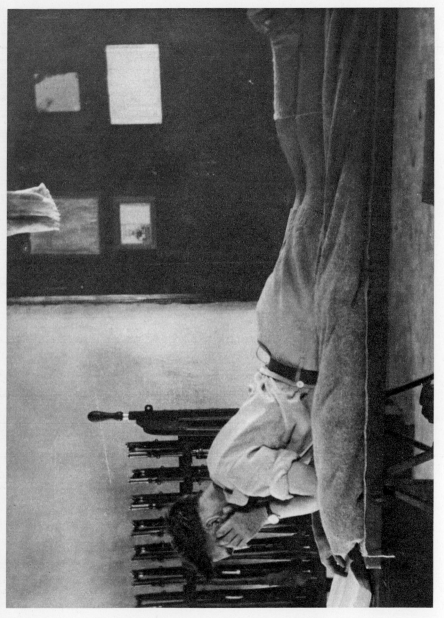

KARACHI 1927

friends in Drigh Road. Arnold Bennett, whose critical judgements I took as gospels, till he bracketed me last week with
D.H.L. as a stylist (a *stylist* ye giddy gods! The greatest lack in
all my writing is a style: to replace the echoes of Oxford and
academic respectability of my prose) said the perfect word about
Ulysses, when he swore that Joyce had made novel-reading a form
of penal servitude. But penal servitude is in character at Drigh
Road.

I hope you continue steadily. They say that Porto Fino and
T.E.L. represented you in Paris. A little like steak and onion: I
hope Porto Fino will not be sold. Its sea and sky were lovely in
your big room.

Rothenstein, provoked kindly by you, wrote to me. I answered
him.

Remember me to Dobson, if ever you are forgiven for carrying
off his (ex-my) *Ulysses*. Tell him I am reading it steadily. Everything is steady in the world now, except Arnold Bennett, who
totters. Yours   T.E.S.

D.H.L. of course is a quite prodigious fellow: and it's a sin
against decency and proportion for A.B. to let the unhappy likeness of our names bracket us publicly. If I could have published
Revolt under any other name I'd have left D.H.L. in his sole use.
It's like writing an ode to a pet rabbit and signing it Shakespeare.

307: TO D. G. HOGARTH

19.v.27   [*Karachi*]

Yours of 24/iv/27 last mail.

I'm afraid *The Seven Pillars* was rather a bitter pill for C.M.D.[1]
to swallow. The tone of it must have shocked him. I did not
send it, till he had twice written to me asking for it. I've always
suspected Cockerell or Garnett of putting him up to ask me: the
old man was long insensible to such things, and seldom looked at
any recent writing   It was a pity he ran into mine: but I couldn't
decently refuse him the sight of it, could I? [*45 lines omitted*]

[1] C. M. Doughty.

308: TO JONATHAN CAPE

25.v.27   [*Karachi*]

Dear Cape, I've been sent wild stories of the genesis of *Revolt in the Desert*. If you like, make a 'third person' note in your *Now and Then* booklet saying:—

The abridgement of Mr. T. E. Shaw's *Seven Pillars of Wisdom* which we were able to publish by arrangement with him on March 10 last, under title *Revolt in the Desert* by 'T E Lawrence', was made by him in seven hours at Cranwell in Lincolnshire on March 26 and March 27 1926, with the assistance of two airman friends, A/A Knowles and A/c Miller. It was received by us (in the form of cut-down proofs of *The Seven Pillars*) on March 30, three days later, and reprinted immediately as we received it. There were no author's corrections, nor was this text ever submitted to anyone for advice or criticism. The only subsequent alterations were the division into chapters and the writing in (at the publisher's request) of three paragraphs to justify the inclusion of two much-desired illustrations from the many in *The Seven Pillars*.

The author has promised the subscribers to *Seven Pillars of Wisdom* that no further copies of this shall be published during his lifetime: and he will make no additions to the issued text of *Revolt in the Desert*.

Revolt was sold to us in order that our advance on its royalties might enable the author to commission extra drawings for *The Seven Pillars*: and the author's contract with us gives him the option of terminating our sale of the book when this advance is fully met.

There: short and sweet! Any good? I think so.   T.E.S.

309: TO SYDNEY COCKERELL

27. v. 27   [*Karachi*]

Dear Cockerell, I'm glad you are over your influenza. It is becoming an annual and universal complaint in England. Something will really have to be done about it. Odd I've never been lucky enough to get even a touch of it. When we are ill they let us rest, and the fellows who have experience of hospital here all praise it. It can't be like the service pest-houses in England, can it?

The last four sentences all end with the word it. C.M.D. would have firmly disapproved. I've always wondered what the old man did think of my stuff, which he finally read at Merriecroft, at his own request. I've always fancied that its matter shocked him as much as its manner!

Beazley is a very wonderful fellow, who has written almost the best poems that ever came out of Oxford: but his shell was always hard, & with time he seems to curl himself tighter & tighter into it. If it hadn't been for that accursed Greek art he'd have been a very fine poet.[1]

My gold dagger is always turning up in odd places: once in the *Times*: then at my bank: now in All Souls and the Ashmolean. It belongs to Lionel Curtis, who paid Spinks' price for it! It was made in Mecca,[2] in the third little turning to the left off the main bazaar, by an old Nejdi goldsmith whose name I fancy was Gasein. But I begin to forget that period. There are so many better days, in Dorsetshire and at Cranwell, to dwell upon.

Your figure of 22000 for the sale of *Revolt* astonishes me. At 30000 the accumulated royalties will pay off the last of my debt to the Bank. I will then be worth just nothing! A freedom-giving state, no doubt: but one can't very well travel comfortably on it!

I shall be with you in spirit on the lawn at Max Gate in July. In a week it will be his birthday. I keep on hoping that he will be alive (and not a burden to himself) in 1931 when I'm due back. It is selfish to want old people to go on outliving their health & strength: but somehow T.H. is different. I'd like his head to exist for ever, like the head and arms of G.B.S. They are supreme works of art. Yours ever   T.E.S.

---

[1] J. D. Beazley, the expert on Greek vases.
[2] See letters No. 134 and 210.

310: TO EDWARD GARNETT

10. VI. 27.   [*Postmarked Drigh Road*]

[*50 lines omitted*] Robert Graves is writing something elementary and plain about me, to Doran's commission. Gawd help' em.

I'd call Figgis[1] better than O'Flaherty, though I've only got this one novel of his to go upon: and am judging O'F. by *The Informer*, and *The Black Soul*, neither of them the work of a man standing on his own two feet. However O'F. is alive and F. is dead, so perhaps you are right. It seemed to me that F. really got the weather and the hills and the water of the sea into his pages, dwarfing his peasants, whose puny minds faded out, in the process. Whereas O'F.'s people are bigger than his background.

Mrs. Shaw was not consulted on the Hospital Chapter.[2] I cut it out so that there should not be an emotional climax at the end of *Revolt*. *Revolt*'s top note now comes during the retreat about Deraa and Tafas: just as *The Seven Pillars* top note comes in the earlier chapter of our ride to the Bridges and failures after them. *The Seven Pillars* is altogether higher in key than *Revolt*, and could carry the hospital chapter without its seeming in any way conspicuous. Whereas it would have stuck out of *Revolt* like a raisin in a sponge cake. My sense of proportion made me sacrifice purple bit after purple bit, in selecting the pages to comprise *Revolt*, and I don't see why the hospital instance should seem worse to you than the rest. If you read *Seven Pillars* you'll see that it's entirely different to *Revolt*. *Revolt* parodies *S.P.*

When an Arab did something individual and intelligent during the war I would call him to me, and opening a bag of sovereigns would say, 'Put in your hand', and this was thought the very height of splendour. Yet it was never more than £120: but the exercise of spreading and burying your fingers in the gold made it feel better than a cold-blooded counting out of two or three hundred pounds.

To have your mouth filled must have been beastly. Yours,

                                                    T.E.S.

Do look, some week-end, at your fat book,[3] and tell me if it isn't better, as a design (damn its ornaments) than it was.

---

[1] Darrell Figgis, author of *Children of Earth*. See letter No. 324.
[2] *Seven Pillars of Wisdom*, Chap. CXXI was omitted in *Revolt in the Desert*.
[3] *Seven Pillars of Wisdom* in the Subscribers' edition.

311: TO EDWARD MARSH

10. VI. 27   [*Karachi*]

Dear E. M., It seems it wasn't Freeman, so much as the *London Mercury*, which was inept: for a 'Clennel Wilkinson' goes one worse about me, this last number. 'The happy warrior' who 'enjoyed his little scraps'. A reckless, cheerful, man of action. 'The fact is that everything worth having in the Arabs comes to them from the days of Saladin, who was born a Christian'. 'The fact is' who told the idiot that? The supreme assumption of it! And Saladin was born a Kurd, which I've never heard tell was the same thing as a Christian. Poof! Piffle!

Also he says that I was a physical weakling. I'm not that yet, despite my extreme age. In fact I passed into the Army as a first-class recruit, in 1923. In 1914 I was a pocket Hercules, as muscularly strong as people twice my size, & more enduring than most. I saw all the other British officers' boots off in Arabia: they went to base, or to hospital, while I did two years in the fighting areas, and was nine times wounded, & five times crashed from the air, and had two goes of dysentry, & suffered enough hunger & thirst & heat & cold and exposure, not to mention deliberate maltreatment, to wreck the average constitution. I go so far as to claim that I've been perhaps the toughest traveller who has ever written his true history. 'Mooning about the towns of South Italy'. Gods!

[*4 lines omitted*]

Winston wrote me a gorgeous letter. Called his *Crisis* a pot-boiler! Some pot! and probably some boil, too. I suppose he realises that he's the only high person, since Thucydides & Clarendon, who has put his generation, imaginatively, in his debt. Incidentally neither T. nor C. was impartial! That doesn't matter, as long as you write better than anybody of your rivals.

He alarms me a little bit, for I feel that he wants to go for Russia, and the ex-bear hasn't yet come into the open. It's hard to attack, for its neighbours, except Germany, aren't very good allies for us. We can only get at her, here, through Turkey, or Persia, or Afghanistan, or China, and I fancy the Red Army is probably good enough to turn any one of those into a bit of her-

self, as the Germans did Rumania. Persia certainly: Turkey will
be very strong, soon, and should be our ally, if common interests
make for anything. China I know nothing of, but she is too huge
for anyone to swallow. The most dangerous point is Afghanistan.
Do you know I nearly went there, last week? The British Attaché
at Kabul is entitled to an airman clerk, & the Depot would have
put my name forward, if I'd been a bit nippier on a typewriter.
I'll have to mug up typing,: for from '14 to '18 I served a decent
apprenticeship in semi secret-secret work, & Russia interests me
greatly.[1] The clash is bound to come, I think. In modern Europe
it was first Spain which tried to dominate: then France had two
tries (Winston's ancestor the spoiler of the first. I wonder what
he thinks of him? England's only first-rate military genius, I
fancy ... but a doubtful honour to us in other respects): then
Germany has her go. It works from West to East, doesn't it?
And England has been the main obstacle each time. Usually
there has been about a hundred years between each effort: but
the tempo of life has grown so much faster since the age of
machines opened, that it's quite on the cards Russia may have her
go in our time. It will be a complicated and difficult affair, which
we will win, of course, after we have learnt the necessary modification of tactics. The Dardanelles & the Tanks both show how
much dead weight has to be moved in favour of a new idea. Do
you know, if I'd known as much about the British Government
in 1917, as I do now, I could have got enough of them behind me
to have radically changed the face of Asia? Russia, to these people,
seems the new and growing idea: whereas there is more promise
and capacity in our structure than she will contain in the next
thousand years.

Apologies. I burble. This is Drigh Road and my proper job
is hut orderly. The explanation of this recent shower of letters
upon you was: —

(i)   My delight in *The Crisis*
(ii) My fury at Freeman's blindness & prejudice
(iii) This letter: my apology for being furious with as little a
      thing as Freeman.

[1] This passage shows that the belief of the Labour Party that Lawrence had been
engaged in secret service work in Afghanistan was not stupid, but only incorrect.

It doesn't seem to me that evolution will produce a No. iv.
So you will have peace now. Yours   T.E.S.

312 : TO ERIC KENNINGTON

16. VI. 27.   [*Karachi*]

Dear K., Perhaps I gave the 'Cheshire Cat'[1] to a man called
Richards, who lives at 3 Loudoun Road St John's Wood. He
keeps all my books (not so many as the word 'all' sounds) and has,
I think a picture or two, also. Let's hope so. I liked the C.C. If
one had tickled it, it would have grinned.

You are an odd person. You say in every letter that your work
does not go well: but that your family does. Why, it's the reverse.
Your family is only two: whereas your successful works run into
dozens: perhaps into hundreds. You can draw, and paint and
sculp. Everything you attempt becomes about the best of its
sort. Midas wasn't in it. Presumably he wanted gold. You, perhaps, subconsciously don't. At any rate, if you do, you haven't
perhaps succeeded. It's about the only direction, though, in
which you have not scored heavily: and I prophesy that in time
you will achieve that too. 'Kenningtons' will be good invest-
ments.

Compare us. I've tried to sculp: — failure: to write: — failure.
I've made other people a lot of money: but can't bear to keep any
of it for myself. I've argued myself out of creation: and go on
living because it is the line of least resistance, and go on learning
because the more one learns the less one knows, and some day I
may attain perfect ignorance, that way.

Hoots.

Wilson[2] tells me a *Seven Pillars* fetched £500, for U.S.A. I
hope it will be yours!

The picture of you and C. sitting in Holly Copse and reading
the great thing would have inspired me, had I been a comic
artist, to a sheer masterpiece! However.

Many thanks for *Ulysses*. It is even worse to read than I had
hoped. Months: and such dull stuff. Joyce is a genius, but an

---

[1] A portrait of Lawrence by Kennington, reproduced in *T. E. Lawrence by his Friends*.
[2] J. G. Wilson, the bookseller.

unlucky one. His writing has the architectural merit of Balham. It goes on for ever, and needn't ever vary in spirit. Why not try a bust of Joyce?

Many thanks for the Auda proof. It has gone on to make old Banbury rejoice. What a thing for the 1st Armoured Car Company when they see their Sergt. Major skipping like a young ram!

I wonder how you settled your war memorial. Accepted it, of course: but are you trampling on the committee?

Dobson once sketched a war memorial in clay. A single file or four or five earth-bound naked figures, marching in step, very close together, weighed down by a huge weight they jointly carried. The idea was good: the shape and outline good, from every angle. And simple. Good for D.   T.E.S.

Do you really like naked women? They express so little.

313: TO R. V. BUXTON

23. VI. 27.   [*Karachi*]

Dear Robin, Your marvellous letter[1] sent me up, with a bounce into the Seventh Heaven.

> Quando io udi questa profferta, [degna]
> Di tanto grado, che mai non si estingue
> Del libro[2]

Somehow I'd never, in my giddiest moments, expected that you would. I enclose a letter to Cape, which you may send on to him, if this six weeks delay finds the Trustees still of this most noble mind. [10 *lines omitted*]

However I live in hope that my most excellent board will continue to act in the spirit of Don Quixote, that finest of all Spaniards. It is incredibly glorious. The fact that I'd have done it myself, at the first solvent moment, is the only thing which lessens your glory. It takes from you the credit, not of the act, but of the intention. However, as *The Seven Pillars* says, the intention is nothing ... but, my God, the Deed, the Deed! (Was it John

---

[1] Saying that the Trustees of the *Revolt in the Desert* fund intended to withdraw the book from publication.

[2] Dante, *Paradiso*, Canto XXIII, lines 52-54.

Drinkwater, or *The Seven Pillars?*) Pardon my apparent drunkenness. I'm happy. . . .

It's good news that the Ashmolean has taken the John drawing of D.G.H. That's the first breach in their wall against modernism. Perhaps they will eventually take the Feisal too.

Kennington tells me your bust is the best of the four. He may, I suppose, like Epstein, produce six of them. Hardly more. Sculptors have to do a mort of work on thin casts, & soon grow tired of repetition work.

My little note on the various editions & quantities of *The Seven Pillars* will, quite likely, bring down the price of complete copies. I meant it to. £500 is absurd.

The idiots think there are only 100 copies.

If Cape does withdraw *Revolt* from sale, it may be wise to make known the reasons

   i. That *Revolt* was reluctantly published to meet a liability.

  ii. That the liability was happily met at 30,000 copies.

 iii. That the sale of the book is now stopped by the author, by means of an enabling clause in the original contract, to avoid making a lot of unnecessary profit.

Eliot[1] could write a letter in this sense, & sign it T. E. Shaw, & publish it anywhere he thought fit.

Glory be! You are an absolute trump.   T.E.S.

Dust-storms yesterday & to-day: & I was on stores guard all last night, in the thick of it. This paper feels gritty!

314: TO MARSHAL OF THE R.A.F. SIR HUGH TRENCHARD

[30. VI. 27]   [*Karachi*]

[*50 lines omitted*] Irak has had five years of peace out of us; if it went up in flames tomorrow, yet that five years would win forgiveness on doomsday for Winston and yourself, the sponsors of its scheme. I was a little demon delightedly rubbing his hands in the background. Surely my share in helping settle the Middle East atones for my misdeeds in the war. I think so, anyway. [*2 lines omitted*]

---

[1] The Hon. Edward Eliot, Lawrence's solicitor and a trustee of the *Revolt in the Desert* fund.

315: TO EDWARD GARNETT

7. VII. 27.   [*Karachi*]

That *Minister's Daughter* by Hildur Dixelius is a very very very
excellent book: one of the rarest and ripest things I've met for the
last couple of years. The real stuff. It is going to rest amongst my
permanent collection of books (which are being kept and used
by one Richards, a Welsh metaphysician in St. John's Wood,
against the hypothetical and probably-never-to-come-day when
I'll have a whole room of my permanent own in which to read
permanent books again): but before that I'll have to get it bound
quietly. This present cover is too bounding altogether. Is that
Yank taste? Doran has made my *Revolt* a proper yellow dog, at
his end, despite Cape's example. *Rosa* I did not much like.

Your exploration of Pembrokeshire must have been enjoyable
for you. Its southern part has somehow avoided the remaining
Welsh. Some Fleming colony, I believe they said it was. They
talk a beautiful soft English, and build white cottages with
chimneys as big as abutments. The coast line is also beautiful,
in my recollection. I remember the green of the land running
down nearly into the sea. What was lovely about Galilee, in
Palestine, was that green grass grew, in Genesaret, right into the
very (sweet) water. But cottages aren't for me, now. Didn't I
tell you what I hope for, when I come out of the R.A.F.? Robin
Buxton, my banker, and now Trustee, is going to try and get me
a night job in the city, either as watchman in a Bank, or caretaker
in a group of offices. They pay fairly: it is a quiet employment,
whose only necessary qualification is honesty: and the work is not
hard. I expect, you know, to fall into age quite suddenly, as I
did into middle age on landing here. My eyes are troubling me
so that I can't read much, or see clearly what I write. I'm going
a bit deaf: and they say (I can't see my own head) that my hair is
now thick with white hairs. I take it that quite likely by 1935
I'll require an occupation which is slow, and full of sitting down.
On the other hand, return to England might cheer me up to a
few more years of motor-cycle madness. Who knows?

That Barker Fairley book on Doughty spoiled itself, by trying
to do too much. He maintained that the *form* of *A.D.* and of

Dawn in Britain was subtle, and designed, and balanced, and cumulative. I think it was accident: and a bad accident. Doughty seems wholly to have lacked the strategic eye which plans a campaign, as the sub-commander plans a battle, or the company officer a trench raid, or the soldier a bayonet-thrust. *A.D.* is hampered by its lack of form, less only than *Dawn*, because there was a basis of fact to follow, and life isn't as shapeless as unassisted and undisciplined art. Why, I think *The Seven Pillars*, that untidy general-provider, is better planned than *A.D.*! That's saying nothing much, either. Both are rotten bad: but *A.D.* has the merits of magnificence in its materials, its vision, its attitude, its prose, its poetry, its author. Whereas the poor *S.P.*!

Yet your son seems to like *The S.P.* Why not give him your second copy for a Christmas present? Thanks to the speculative booksellers it's become a decent present.   T.E.S.

Lucifer and Eve? No: I've never thought of them. Bother all women. They seem to upset the people I like.

316: TO D. G. HOGARTH

7.VII.27   [*Karachi*]

Rex Ingram[1] wrote me from Nice. He is all right: has his complete copy. Pike sent him an incomplete as well, which was overdoing it! But he decently returned the surplus.

I'm writing to Eliot[2] about the idea of stopping the English sale of the *Revolt*. He will probably show you, or send you, my letter. The alternative to stopping it is a cheap edition: whereas my comfort lies partly in its high price. With *The Seven Pillars* at £400 my complete story is quite safe: nobody will ever see it. Most of the owners I hear from are insuring it, or sending it to their bank or strong rooms. In fact it is going to vanish from the face of England, and the rare copies that do come into the market will go to the States, where my fancy pride of 20000 dollars for the Doran edition artificially keeps up the price of possessing a copy. All the same £400 is too high. I'd be glad to see it drop to £150 or so.

---

[1] The film producer.   [2] See note to letter No. 313.

There are no Doughty letters at Clouds Hill. I cleared all private papers out of the house there on my last visit. It is now let, for 12/- a week, to two tenants who take a floor of it each, for week-ending. You never saw Clouds Hill, I think? A tiny brick cottage, with old tiled roof, very high pitched. It stands in a thicket of laurel and rhododendron, with oak trees and a huge ilex stretching arms over its roof. Damp? Yes; for the cottage dates from pre-damp-course days, and the trees drip great rain-drops on the roof for hours after each storm. They patter across the tiles like the first notes of the vth Symphony. Only two rooms, the upstairs, of the cottage, are habitable. They have three-foot walls, and nine-foot roofs, all open. A great deal of oak and chestnut on show: but my repairs to the roof had to be in deal, which we creosoted to bring it to an ancient colour. My gold Meccan dagger paid the repair-bill, and left something over for furniture. I wish I were within reach of that cottage now. This place is dismal: no bright sun, and no heat: only a cloud or sand-dimmed paleness of sunlight, and constant salty breezes from the seven-miles distant sea. An Eastbourne, in fact.

I think that war period must have tuned me to fit real heat: for here I am always shivering and catching colds. Of course it may be partly the change from Cranwell, where I worked hard, in the hangar and on my *Seven Pillars*, and rode hard on Boanerges in any spare daylight. Here we have only 5 hours work a day, on 5 days a week: and my spare time exhausts itself in wandering slowly about camp or aerodrome. I haven't been outside the camp yet, and probably won't, for I got a letter from Trenchard lately which gives me hope that I'll be able to come home when *Revolt* has died away, say in the spring of 1930. Robert Graves' book will put people off the legend of me, and if there is not a cheap reprint in 1929 *Revolt* will be old history by then. It might even be possible to get back in '29. The sooner the better from my point of view. I've turned suddenly, as I always thought I would, the corner into middle age: hair going white, the fellows tell me: and my eyesight and hearing both giving me trouble with their insufficiency. The less time I have to expect, the more I want to spend it in England.

Did you ever hear what happened to the R.A.F. War-history,

which Jones was to have finished? I do not think it has appeared, and it must be long overdue.[1]

Why not lend Sir H. Samuel a copy, if you have an incomplete left? I think that would show him the unfitness of the book to be his possession. But if he still wanted it, after that, let him keep it. Only I judge him as too upright a man to take pleasure in obliquity.

The American copy which still survives should be sent to C.E.O. Wood Esq., H.M. Naval Base, Singapore. Wood is the engineer who rode with me to the Tell el Shehab bridge one night, and he has asked for a copy. Will you send him a letter with it, from yourself, saying that 'you understand from me that he wishes for such time as he requires it.' [23 *words omitted*] There is a shortage of the beastly things. After I come home I'll draw from Doran four or five of the sale copies in his safe, and use those to stop the mouths of entitled [but] disappointed claimants. So we will keep a list, still, despite there being no more incompletes left. The completes we'll hold. One is to be a Brough, for me, in 1930, if I'm still inclined to ride after I get back.   T.E.S.

317: TO LIONEL CURTIS

14.VII.27.   [*Karachi*]

My lord and prophet, How can I write to a man who says he is going to Honolulu? I ask you ... It sounds like a name in a song in variety. And you are just back from S. Africa: and they have killed Kevin O'Higgins, so now you will have to rip back to Dublin. Out upon all this coil of affairs, say I. At least, when I travel, I carry the R.A.F. with me. I move from one service bed to another service bed, from one standard barrack to another standard barrack: from one ration meal to another ration meal. Uniformity is my bed fellow. Your life is chaos. Chaos breeds life: whereas by habit and regularity comes death, quickly.

The Coffee Room of All Souls now has or should have a copy of my *Seven Pillars*: so that the supply of pilgrims to Halescroft[2] may be cut off without cruelty.

---

[1] Published as *War in the Air*, by H. A. Jones. See letter No. 246.
[2] Lionel Curtis's house at Kidlington, near Oxford.

Robert Graves is writing a life of me for Doran, who ramped about England asking many of the worst people to do it. Said he wanted something true. Apparently *Revolt in the Desert* isn't finally convincing to all tastes. On the whole better Robert Graves than another. He is a decent fellow, does not know too much about me: will think out some psychologically plausible explanation of my spiritual divagations: and will therefore help to lay at rest the uneasy ghost which seems to have stayed in England when I went abroad.

But don't imagine that *The Seven Pillars* is great literature. It isn't: but it's one of the best dressed imitations of a book you'll ever see. If only I'd been able to carry the Bank with me, to add a couple of thousand more to the overdraft, and had made *The Seven Pillars* by that much better. I could ruin most gloriously any publisher who would give me a free hand.

I doubt whether D.G.H. would take Magdalen now. Ambition doesn't always die out in Middle Age: and he makes full use of his leisure now. Of course, though, he may leave the Ashmolean soon, and then he might accept.

Poor old Egerton. Hard to die in pain after living so long. Nearly all those old dons have gone, now.

Sir Robert Borden may make All Souls wise: but hardly witty. However P.H.K.[1] must have his occasional joke. The terror-to-come is that his advancing front line may give him capacity for very frequent jokes in time. Warn me when his third chin detaches itself from the second.

You are now on your way to Lake Superior, or to some rocky part of Canada in a Canoe. Well, well. I'll be in Karachi till further notice. That may be, I'm given to understand, only till 1930! Joy.   T.E.S.

I have an idea I wrote you a duplicate of this letter last week. I often mean to write letters. If people would only take the intention for the deed life would be easier.

---

[1] Philip Kerr, now Lord Lothian.

318: TO E. M. FORSTER

14. VII. 27   [*Karachi*]

[20 *lines omitted*] I've read all your books, except the *Passage to India*, several times lately. They beat me. All over them are sayings (generally terrible) which I feel are bursting out from your heart, and represent yourself: but when I put together a sheet of these, the portrait they make is not the least like you, as I've sat at tea with you. Tea, of course, is your drink, as water is mine and beer is Chesterton's and Burgundy is Belloc's. How hard critical work is. I wonder if I'll ever be able to write that article I imagined before I left England. It would be something snatched from the shipwreck which is this visit to India.

'To India' but it isn't that. I haven't been outside the camp bounds yet, and haven't seen an Indian house, nor any Indians except the degraded denationalised ones who work as servants in the camp. I mean not to go out while I am here. Most of my time passes in reading and thinking, while I wander or sit upon the huge aerodrome, a flat clean stretch of sand, nearly a mile square. At night I lie down on my back in the middle of it, and speculate on the chances that some of you will perhaps see these same stars a few hours later over England. A gay life. I've bought 8 records of the choral symphony, & find it very wonderful.

Are the dons any better now? Poor dears, having you sitting among them while they babble must be a very purgatory: and very purgative, too.

And your critical lectures? Aren't they to come out?[1] I'm hoping to add them to the novels, as part of the evidence against you. Do realise that it's your duty to give the world a flag as guide to your course (even a rabbit shows the white of its tail in flight): otherwise the great hunters will never win your pelt: and how other can they keep warm in winter, except they dress in writers' skins? The keynote of this age is critical. Yours

                                                                T.E.S.

Also you are slowly maturing your judgement upon my two texts. Do you remember the fellowship candidate given three

[1] Afterwards published as *Aspects of the Novel*.

hours for his essay, who sat for 2 hours 59 mins, in silence in the great hall, then bent down to the firelight and wrote one single sentence: and won!

319: TO EDWARD GARNETT

1. VIII. 27.   [*Karachi*]

The slow months begin to total respectably. When I got here it was 7/1/27: and now I'm past the half year. Did ever free agent so long to be three years older?

This is a reply to your letter of June 27, which ended up with a well-introduced remark about my Uxbridge notes. I write this on the back of one, to show you that the not sending them as they are is only kindness to you. I wrote them pell-mell, as the spirit took me, on one piece of paper or another. Then I cut them into their sections, and shuffled them, as Joyce is supposed to have shuffled *Ulysses*. With the idea of curing you of any delusion you might be persuaded by the chorus of critical England to entertain of me as a person of literary promise or capacity — where was I? — Ah yes: to disillusion you as to my literary ability — where was I? Ah yes: — to show you that I can't write for toffee, I decided to send them you. You would have thought them the raw material of a paper-chase. So I began at Clouds Hill to stick each class in some sort of order on to sheets of paper, meaning to have them stitched for you. But that did not work, for the sections were too intertwined.

So I am copying them seriatim into a notebook, as a Christmas (which Christmas?) gift for you. It is a posh manuscript, in my most copper-plated hand. It will be bound, and gilt-edged. Can I do more? (or less.) Please regard it as an expensive gift. Copying my old notes is like eating my yesterday's vomit. I add nothing but take away repetitions, where vain. I 'did' three Church parades for example: and I believe they can be boiled to two: or even to one, which would be the quint-essence and exemplar of all my church parades.

Enough of this stuff. Do not expect it for ever so long. It is done against the grain. About a third of it is done. Am I

Do not have any anticipations. I will not pull
off another accident.

1. VIII. 27

The slow months begin to total respectably. When I got here it
was 7/1/27: and now I'm past the half year. Did ever
free agent so long to be three years older?

This is a reply to your letter of June 27, which ended up with a well-
introduced remark about my Uxbridge notes. I write this on the back of
one, to show you that the not sending them as they are is only kindness
to you. I wrote them pell-mell, as the spirit took me, on one
piece of paper or another. Then I cut them into their sections, &
shuffled them, as Joyce is supposed to have shuffled Ulysses. With the
idea of curing you of any delusion you might be persuaded by the chorus
of critical England to entertain of me as a person of literary promise
or capacity —— where was I? — ah yes: to disillusion you as to
my literary ability — where was I? — ah yes: — to show
you that I can't write for toffee, I decided to send them you. You
would have thought them the raw material of a paper-chase. So I
began (at Cloud's Hill) to stick each class in some sort of order on to sheets of
paper, meaning to have them stitched for you. But that did
not work, for the sections were too intertwined.

So I am copying them seriatim into a note book, as
a Christmas (which Christmas?) gift for you. It is a posh
manuscript, in my most copper-plated hand. It will be
bound, & gilt-edged. Can I do more? (or less). Please
regard it as an expensive gift. Copying my old notes
is like eating my yesterday's vomit. I add nothing,
but take away repetitions, where vain. I "did" three
church parades for example: and I believe they can be
boiled to two: or even to one, which would be the
quint-essence & exemplar of all my church parades.

Enough of this stuff. Do not expect it for ever so
long. It is done against the grain. About a third of it is
done. Am I making a fool of myself? Would you rather
keep your "illusion"? There are sixty sheets like this. You
understand they are not emotions remembered in tranquillity: but
the actual fighting stuff. Photographic, not artistic. All were in
pencil. It's better than the Seven Pillars, in its class: as like
as butter and cheese: that is, not like at all: but equally rotten
The S.P. showed that I could not ratiocinate: this that I can't observe

LETTER ON BACK OF PASTED-UP PAGE OF *THE MINT*

making a fool of myself? Would you rather keep your illusion? There are sixty sheets like this. You understand they are not emotions remembered in tranquillity: but the actual fighting stuff. Photographic, not artistic. All were in pencil. It's better than *The Seven Pillars*, in its class: as like as butter and cheese: that is, not like at all: but equally rotten. *The S.P.* showed that I could not ratiocinate: this that I can't observe.

Your letter of 27.VI.27.

[3 *lines omitted*] The Smerwick massacre[1] was more Grey than Raleigh. R. was picturesque, and a braggart. People ascribed to him more action and less sensibility than the truth. Did you ever read his poem ?

I rejoice that you are going to read *The Seven Pillars*: and I'll hope to have your critical opinion, when you end it. It matters to me, for I put months, years, of work into it after you said it was worth working at. You will find hardly a sentence of the Oxford text standing. If I'm any good at all at writing, the revised *S.P.* should betray it.

Graves has worked too quickly. His book is only milk and water. Which of us, he or I, is milk?

A happy ending to a book (? *Revolt in the Desert*, if it is a book: I think it is: a dishonest little sweep of a book) is worth 5 more sales in 10. Cape wouldn't have had a best-seller (but oh yes, a great success d'estime) if the hospital chapter had been kept. And if it had not sold I'd be hopelessly in debt, and forced to leave the R.A.F. (which is my condition of contentment) to earn money and become solvent. Do realize that I was hard up against it last year, and could not be artistically scrupulous. Your standards are appallingly high and high-brow.

[4 *lines omitted*]

John Buchan sent me a jolly letter. 'When you do not get inundated with adjectives' (the dear things, I like driving them four in hand: or 40 under my bonnet) 'you are the best living writer of English prose.' He does not mean it, but I take all praise at its face value.

You puzzled me with your 'Major Herbert Read'. You mean

---

[1] Of Italians and Spaniards who landed on the S.W. coast of Ireland in 1580. Lawrence was interested in Raleigh, his collateral ancestor.

Herbert Read, one of T. S. Eliot's school: a very excellent critic? He won't commit himself. But his mind is keen, and highly (too highly) tempered. I hope he will put something helpful on paper. None of the reviews yet have helped me to write better: yet, for all their writers knew, I might have wanted to.

Do not have any anticipations. I will not pull off another accident.

320: TO D. G. HOGARTH

27.VIII.27   [*Karachi*]

I've been through much of Doughty, of late, and checked Fairley's book on him. *Adam Cast Forth* is splendid. Its goodness defies the lack of form which would have ruined a less great work: but otherwise I cannot see more than great effort and great failure in his poetic work. Doughty's imagination was weak: his sense of scale faulty: and he had no sense of design.

Arabia Deserta remains wonderful, because there his weak imagination had only to select from an array of thronging facts; his sense of scale had a whole desert for its province: his sense of design could express itself only in the aimlessness of his wanderings, and not in confusing the record of his wanderings. *Dawn in Britain* is like the trace of Doughty's journeys in N. Western Arabia, with Arabia left out.

So I conclude that the parts of your book[1] which will matter most are i) Any further light his letters throw on the making of him before he settled in Italy to write *A.D.*

ii) Your dissection of his notebooks.
and '2' is infinitely the more important of these efforts. If you can set side by side parts of the notes, & parts of the finished text, and indicate how the notes were made, & how far they *all* went into the text, or if there was abridgement, or selection, & where the padding is . . . then you will be doing a very great thing. *A.D.* is one of the mystery-masterpieces of the world: and people who ever write will always be grateful to you for making plain how it grew. There is no impiety in studying the

---

[1] *The Life of C. M. Doughty*, by D. G. Hogarth.

works. I should have liked to have had a cut at that part of it, myself ... but it was out of the question that I should ever write anything again. [35 *lines omitted*]

Do you think April 1930 was a just date, to suggest to Sir Hugh for my return to England? That cuts off two years I should properly have done out here: but five is most of the fit years I can properly look forward to, at my time of life. And I grudge Drigh Road my possession all those years. Yours   TES.

My final suggestion as to closing down the English edition of *Revolt* (which would involve no publicity, & little harm to the pocket of the trust. The thing will not sell 100 copies next year) was that Eliot should have his way ... but I suggested that the Cape power of a cheap edition after two years (which I left in the contract because, had I been master, there would have been no *Revolt* after two years) be given up in compensation. Otherwise the cheap edition will appear in 1930 ... and that means more exile, for its guilty cause.

[On August 30th, 1927, Lawrence changed his name to Thomas Edward Shaw by Deed Poll. In a letter of May 20th, 1927, his solicitor, Edward Eliot, had informed Lawrence that it was not absolutely necessary either to register the Deed at Court, or advertise it in the *London Gazette*, and on July 14th Eliot had written: 'You may of course decide not to go on with the formality of the registration and the advertisement, and this will certainly be a cheaper and quieter course to pursue.'

The coincidence of Lawrence's taking the name of Shaw and of his friendship with Bernard Shaw led to a rumour being spread that Lawrence was in fact his son! The best comment on this is contained in a letter from a friend to Lawrence: 'I hear a report that you are the son of G.B.S. If so, he should have repeated the effort. (I mean this kindly).']

321: TO E. M. FORSTER

8. IX. 27   *Karachi*

You get my first letter this week: anyway. Nearly I gave you my last letter of last week: but I had dysentry, and the flesh, being weak, suspected that the head was weak also. So I gave it a few days to settle down. All is very well now.

Your booklet (such a little one!) on *The Novel*[1] is superb. No other word fits it, because there's a complete lack of superbity about the manner & matter of it. So that the total effect is superb shows that the novel really belongs to you. It's like sitting at the feet of Adam, while he lectures to a University Extension Society about the growth and development of gardens. As soon as it came I rolled it out flat, and galloped through it: the names of some of the books & people I liked or disliked were in it, all right. Two days later I galloped across it again, seeing more of them: and this week, if my stretching and shrinking eyes will hold themselves to a page for an hour — this week I'm going to begin to digest it. There's a curious difference in tone, between you and Lubbock.[2] One treats the novel rather like the glazed unapproachable pictures in a public gallery. The other talks of novels as though they were things one writes. I expect you will find it one of the best-selling of your works.

However more of this later. I have really been ill, and sick men do not make good judges. Perhaps it isn't so enthralling as my imprisoned senses make it. [12 *lines omitted*]
Your portrait-purchase I find very subtle of you. Now Frederic Manning always spells it 'subtile'. Do you like F.M.? *Scenes & Portraits* is all of him I know: though also he wrote a life of Sir Wm. White: and a picture of life seen through the eye of an organ-grinder's ape. *Scenes & Portraits* was good. That first picture of the court of the king of Uruk, & of Adam & Eve in the water-melon field, sticks in my very inaccurate memory. Also the picture of Macchiavelli: and the long sermon which Paul preached.

By the way you called your novel-book 'a saucerful of last week's grapenuts'. And I called *The Seven Pillars* a 'builder's yard'. We do well in decrying our goods. Only you have the inestimable sauce of wit to make your seriousness tasty. The other day someone (disappointed) sent me a *Revolt in the Desert* to autograph. Before returning it I read some of it. Punk, of course:

---

[1] *Aspects of the Novel*, by E. M. Forster.
[2] *The Craft of Fiction*, by Percy Lubbock.

but better, so far as form & unity and speed and compactness went, than *The Seven Pillars*. Should I have mightily abridged *The Seven Pillars* before issuing it to subscribers? Say to a half? However I trust much to your collation. Robert Graves says he likes the Oxford text better. Its faults make it less chilly than the *S.P.*, to his diaphragm.

I'm sorry your short story isn't publishable. As you said, the other one wouldn't do for general circulation. Not that there was a wrong thing in it: but the wrong people would run about enlarging their mouths over you. It is a pity such creatures must exist. The *Royal Geographical Journal*, and *Journal of the Central Asian Society*, two learned societies, both found *Revolt in the Desert* indecent. It seems almost incredible.

I wanted to read your long novel,[1] & was afraid to. It was like your last keep, I felt: and if I read it I had you: and supposing I hadn't liked it? I'm so funnily made up, sensually. At present you are in all respects right, in my eyes: that's because you reserve so very much, as I do. If you knew all about me (perhaps you do: your subtlety is very great: shall I put it 'if I knew that you knew . . .'?) you'd think very little of me. And I wouldn't like to feel that I was on the way to being able to know about you. However perhaps the unpublished novel isn't all that. You may have kept ever so much out of it. Everywhere else you write far within your strength.

I've been lending your books a good deal, lately, in camp. I can't get them to like *The Omnibus*, nor *The Longest Journey*. *Howards End* is handed on with commendations from one to another. I have not had it on the shelf more than a day or two for the last six weeks. *Passage* goes out, & comes back, the returning airman being usually puzzled and slightly resentful. 'He doesn't clear things up much', they say: not seeing that you have, at least, cleared a mist of reality from their eyes. Yes, I'd like to see Virginia Woolf's effort: and I'll read your new collection of old stories: and if you dedicate anything to me I'll wear the first page of it as an identity disc. So that when I die the chaplains will know what sort of burial service to give the body. I suppose the new stories date from *The Omnibus* &

[1] Unpublished.

Journey[1] period. If so they will be very helpful. There is a chasm, technically, between *The Journey* & the other books. The deaths in *The Journey* all happen in a half-line, off-stage, looking back over your shoulder, as you write. Nothing of the sort anywhere else in your writings.   T.E.S.

322: TO S. L. NEWCOMBE

9.IX.27.   *Karachi*

Dear Monster, Yes: you shall have your R.A.F. badge: not just yet, for our Q.M.[2] Store is stocktaking. (Your father will tell you the limping one-eyed measly beast a Q.M. is: and what a fuss it makes over stocktaking).

I am glad you like Alexandria. The poor thing about it, I found, was that the 'Groppie' in Alexandria had no great tree-filled garden at the back of the shop: so there seemed no place in Alexandria where an officer in uniform could drink his iced coffee in peaceful comfort. Whereas Cairo was just invented and furnished for people such as I used to be. It would not do now, though. I have not enough piastres to satisfy my thirst with coffee. So I drink water, always. That would be all right if an ass didn't keep on putting overdoses of chlorine in it. So little chlorine goes so long a way with me. The other day I got dysentery too, in spite of all their drugs! One to me, I think.

The Air Force are going to let me come home in the spring of 1930. You will be at Oxford then, off & on, won't you? Expect a loud roaring outside the school gates. That will be my motor bike. The school-masters will not let you talk to ordinary men in uniform: but when they hear the roaring of my bike they will say 'That is not an ordinary airman: that is an extraordinary machine'. So it will be all right.

Otherwise nothing happens: nothing will happen till 1930, probably. Perfect peace.

Loud snores to you, Monster, especially at night. Wake the whole place up. Yours   MONSTER

---

[1] *The Longest Journey.*   [2] Quartermaster.

323: TO DICK KNOWLES

15.9.27.   [*Karachi*]

Dear Dick, Worthy Down: well, the country about you has great merits, though it is not so different from Dorsetshire. You will find man-life very scruffy and easy after your A.A. service. Grown-ups work less than boys, and enjoy life more.

Winchester used to be a very pleasant place: but it is full of troops and the diseases they bring with them. Not a place to take your ease in, improperly dressed. From Bovington I used to visit it regularly: but always had to keep my overalls on. Rumour out here is that the R.A.F. in England now swank about in rain-coats. I hope so.

A.C.1. is not a bad beginning. There is great prejudice among the men against ex-boys of rank. The two classes are so different in tone. The men have enlisted: — which means that they were some way hurt or broken in civy life, to the point of taking flight from it. They all talk of longing to get back: but that is because they have been in the service long enough to forget their previous failure. The ex-boys haven't yet measured themselves against civil standards of existence, and contain a large proportion of the fellows who would have made a success of it. So you mustn't expect the sorts to mix naturally, at first.

Night flying (you are the Virginias,[1] I expect) will be dull and deadly cold, after the first experience: but I'm glad you've struck a flying squadron. In my brief experience, the happy family is the squadron or flight, and the misery of discipline (senseless discipline, I mean) is resident in depots and workshops. Also the flying is a great thing, however dull it may seem to you. People who fly are not the same as people who live on land — if they really fly, with their minds and imaginations, and not merely bodily.

More sermons. Karachi seems to be a sententious place. I go about in fear of this writer's freedom taken with my personality — Robert Graves' book on me. He is a good poet, and means most kindly. But heaven preserve me from public-spoken friends. There are to be in the book some pages from Sergt. Pugh. I

---

[1] Vickers Virginia aeroplanes.

read these, in typescript — and yelled with laughter which was, for once, happy. It's a picture of a saint, in overalls! Such a quaint saint, too.[1]

1930: March, April or May: and there will be a loud shivering on the quay-side of Southampton: and calls for a hot bath. That will be heaven. No baths here. I have a tin tub, and a blow lamp, and a two gallon dope-can of water. Cumbersome, but good.

Best of luck,   T.E.S.

Matchlesses[2] are not dear, and *good*. Second hand is better than new, so long as it is last year's model, and not a crash, rebuilt.

324: TO EDWARD GARNETT

22. IX. 27.   [*Karachi*]

Your letter is an exasperated one: and why not, you'll say, exasperation being a mode like another? I only wrote to you saying that I wanted to come home. I do, badly. But I cannot, till *Revolt* is forgotten, and Graves' 'Life' of me has followed it down the road. I fix the provisionally safe date at April 1930. That will give me five years more R.A.F. life: which, in England, is completely to my taste. Before 1935 your tin mines will all be bankrupt again.

The advantage of the night-watchman billet is that it places me in London, where I would choose to live exclusively, if I have to live in only one place. Nobody but a Londoner can really taste all the pleasure of the country. The R.A.F. pays me 3/3 a day: good pocket money: and recently I made nearly ten pounds out of reviewing eleven books.[3] Money for jam, as the airman says. Only I know by bitter experience that whenever a paper pays me it is just going to cease to appear.

Penance, promise, obstinacy, a vow, self-hypnotisation . . . you catalogue my motives. Isn't it possible that I like being in the R.A.F.? Agreed that exile to India is an unmixed misfortune, for a person whose fit years are nearly run out. But I brought the exile deliberately upon myself, by selling *Revolt* to Cape, and so

---

[1] See p. 495.   [2] Motor bicycles.   [3] For *The Spectator*.

I must make the best of it. Yet it needn't prevent my saying, aloud and often, that it is a heavy price to pay for the comfort of liquidating my debts. I tried every other possible means first, and I think I could just have met them, without Cape's help: but it would have meant my leaving the R.A.F. and three lost years in India were a lesser price to pay.

I am very sorry to hear that your brother was drowned. The Dorset coast is very beautiful. If he lived, as I suspect, in that little piece of lost England between Weymouth and Swanage (excluding Lulworth) then he was fortunate, both living and dying. Of course yours being the loss, you could not see it that way: but to sorrow too much at others' deaths is to contradict ourselves. Which of us would give anything for a generous extension of our own [life]? The thought that the job will end somewhere, may end soon, is an abiding comfort to 99% of the people over thirty.

Yes, I have time to meditate, I suppose. I do meditate, largely and expensively. So your copy of my Uxbridge notes makes such slow progress. I am trying not to rewrite: but I have to rearrange extensively, and to cut out repetitions and expand the sentences which are in an esoteric shorthand. It seems to me that it may all be 50,000 words long: but it is soon to say that. There is not much more than a quarter of it in shape: and even that I dare hardly call in shape: for as I dig further into the loose sheets I continually find myself of 1922 returning to earlier subjects, redoing them better, or correcting what had seemed to him hasty. I think the job may be worth its trouble. It seems to me to convey some of the reality of the Depot at Uxbridge. I called it to you an uncomfortable book once. It is. There is no trace of me in it, hardly a ghostly outline of the principal figure. It deals entirely in terms of 'us': and if one of us is mentioned by name, and gives a phrase or an act of his own, it is only to serve as mouthpiece of us. The unit in the notes is the squad. So it is a libel on the happiness of an airman's life e.g. at Cranwell.

'Concentration, slogging away, rewriting'. You get almost a classical instance of that in *The Seven Pillars*. Yet Graves says in his book that the Oxford edition is the better, because it is not so faultless. He means frigid, possibly: but *The S.P.* is, to my mind, redhot with passion, throughout. Never was so shame-lessly emotional a book. So where does faultlessness, a meiosis for some faultiness, come in?

Graves' book is, as you say, certainly not Nestlés: but it is too laudatory. All the better, of course, to turn the public stomach, and make it spew when it thinks of me. So 1930 will be really a safe date.

[3 *lines omitted*] If you want to see the Irish War done by a decent fellow, read Figgis' book. He is splendid on Achill, and on Casement, and Cathal Brugha, and in showing some of the maze of intrigue in which every honest man gave up hope, except Griffiths. Yet Figgis' book is less good, as a study of rebellion, than my *S.P.*, although he was rebelling in English, and had leisure and understandable characters, and the extreme of drama to help him. I am led to think that I've more of the roots of a writer in me than Figgis had: though the height of a *Children of Earth* is beyond my reach. A novel, that is, in which the characters are the wind and the sea and the hills. His humans are negligible.

Herbert Read is very like Eliot,[1] isn't he? Eliot must be a strong fellow: he dominates all a group, and writes hardly anything.

No, I have not changed ground on the hospital chapter. I have been firm from the start that it was totally unsuited, because of its power, its bitterness, its length, its late position, for inclusion in a popular abridgement. I kept my horrors further back, where the blood was hot, and let the book just run down to its conclusion. You will not realize the difference between a real book (*The S.P.* being as truthful as I could make it) and an edition for general consumption, put out just to make money, and to stop the mouths of those who were crying for word from me. To overweight the last pages with matter emotionally more powerful than anything in the body of the book would be to finish up with a bang. Whereas the bang comes in the third act, properly. I cut out all the high emotion. The preface, the murder in the valley, the killing my camel in the camel-charge, the scene at Deraa, the worst of the winter-war, the death of Farraj, the Hospital — all of it. Your amendment was *out of tone* with what I was aiming at. Too good, perhaps: but that's worse than too bad.   T.E.S.

[1] T. S. Eliot.

325: TO J. G. WILSON[1]

4.X.27 [Karachi]

Dear Wilson, You've got Palmer a most excellent price: I never hoped for as much as £400 for his proofs.[2] It will set him up, probably for good, when he leaves the army in a few months' time and tries to start some business. In the old days I knew Colonel Isham, slightly, via Winston. He never gave me any idea that he was rich, or that he collected books. But he wrote to me some weeks back, and asked if I could let him have a *Seven Pillars*. I replied that they were all gone, and weren't worth their market price. There was an Anglo-Saxon proverb that if wilful would to water wilful must drench. [27 *lines omitted*]

Gertrude's[3] *Letters* came to me, and I read them with delight. They are very good, and well display her eagerness and emotion. I do not think that much of importance was edited out of these particular letters. Gertrude was not a good judge of men or situations: and was always the slave of some momentary power: at one time Hogarth, at another Wilson, at another me, at last Sir Percy Cox. She changed her direction each time like a weathercock: because she had no great depth of mind. But depth and strength of emotion — Oh Lord yes. Her life had crisis after crisis of that sort: and they are all missing from the book. Very probably they were missing from her letters home. A wonderful person. Not very like a woman, you know: they make much of her concern in dress: — but the results! She reminded me, in one dress, of a blue jay. Her clothes and colours were always wrong.

No, we have no wireless, and I don't look at papers: so these current questions only come to me after they have settled down into answers. Sir Henry Wilson's *Diaries*, he showed me some of them, reflected his own unwise, hot, political nature. He was a good soldier and a poor politician — always in one extreme or other, but admired by the sober, since his opinions were always extreme-right. A Die-hard Roger-Casement, with a dash of

---

[1] Of J. & E. Bumpus: the booksellers.

[2] A set of proof sheets of the Subscribers' edition of *Seven Pillars of Wisdom* with the cancelled first chapter. See letter No. 326.

[3] Gertrude Bell. See letter No. 30.

Marlborough. I begged him not to exhibit his folly in cold print. He showed himself pitiably blind, here and there — and I suppose they'll have censored those bits out. If you keep a diary don't prophesy in it — or if you do, correct your prophecies ten years later. So you may carry off a reputation for being wise. I liked Wilson: though he played deep games, not too cleanly: and was a monkey.

Apologies for so long a letter. All's well here. Happy the airman that has no history, and a blank crime-sheet. Yours T E S

[For some months Colonel Isham had been offering to help Lawrence find some financially remunerative work, and had written letters showing that he was genuinely worried about the position that Lawrence had got himself into. Isham, having recently bought the extraordinarily interesting and valuable collection of Malahide Boswell family papers, offered Lawrence employment in connection with their editing and publication.]

326: TO RALPH ISHAM

22/11/27   *R.A.F. Depot, Drigh Road, Karachi*

Dear Isham, Your letter is, I think, about the kindest thing I've ever had. I cannot imagine how you get through life, if it's your principle to lend a hand to every breakdown you see on your road. Meanwhile, please believe that there's one very grateful one, here. I'm answering your letter in the Engine Shop office, where I work; but it is not in office hours; and I'm typing it, because this is the only paper the great but niggardly Indian Government issue for the use of the Aircraft Depot, & it will not carry ink. Generally, not having a secretary, I find it an easier matter to write my letters. Also I don't type well!

I cannot take your offer of a job, of course. It would not do to work for any friendly person, in the first place. Then I am not a literary bird; my writing is better than the stuff turned out by the majority of retired Army officers, so many of whom, in England, put off boredom by what Peacock would have called 'The Pleasure of Composition'; but it has not the smallest pretensions to literature — or is it litter — no, it's lit. Even I am

not ashamed to own that I have never yet seen or read a line of
any of Boswell's books. I would have read them, had I met one
in a disengaged moment, for reading is my greatest occupation,
when, mercifully, work has run out for the time. And if you are
good enough to send me your Boswell book, I'll enjoy it: he must
have been a pretty good writer, judging by the way the proper
people speak of him.

You are, so say the English papers, very lucky in the swag you
carried off from Malahide. I hope it is as good as they say. You
talk of having ten years work on it — which is a colossal thing to
face. [16 *lines omitted*]

This Lowell Thomas book[1] comes as a surprise to me; I'd
imagined he had finished with my war reputation. However he
will not sell much of it. Another 'life' of me is to appear this
winter — by Robert Graves, a young poet of my acquaintance,
who had the kindness to ask my permission before he signed his
contract. I suppose his book is fairly accurate; he referred several
parts of it to me, in draft. On the whole I think I prefer lies to
truth, so far as concerns myself. Still, his book will not last long.
At the worst it will be a rage for a few weeks or months, like
Revolt; and then, a year or so later, I can get home. Probably
in April, 1930.

About your queries from L.T.'s book: —

I was in the Royal Tank Corps, between March '23 and
August '25 and was transferred from it back to the R.A.F.
Exchanges from Service to Service are not difficult to arrange.

Of course, as you know, Lowell Thomas was not with me on
any ride or operation in Arabia. I do not know how long he was
in the country, for he arrived while I was up-country, and I had
gone up again before he left. I expect he was there some ten
or fourteen days, in all; of which we were together in Akaba for
perhaps three. [4 *lines omitted*]

I chose Shaw at random. The recruiting Staff Officer in the
War Office said I must take a fresh name. I said 'What's yours?'
He said 'No you don't'. So I seized the Army List, and snapped
it open at the Index, and said 'It'll be the first one-syllabled name
in this'. [5 *lines omitted*]

[1] *With Lawrence in Arabia.*

MM

Please do not let anything I may have carelessly written to you about the R.A.F. give you the wrong impression that I am miserable or uncomfortable in it. It has been a real refuge to me, and I am grateful to the Air people for taking me in. The airmen are not in the least like soldiers, except in their standard of living. I like many of them, and Service life makes up for its roughness in many ways: — for instance one is never lonely — far from it . . . and it is soothing to know that one's bread and margarine is safe for the term of one's engagement, and that the standard of work expected of one is so reasonably low that one can be positively sure of meeting it. If I were working for any ordinary employer I would be always worrying if I were doing as well as he expected, and I desired. Cheap labour is let off easily.

I am glad you are fond of printing. I think it is one of the richest things any man can do. Have you met St. John Hornby one of the Directors of W. H. Smith & Son, the big English booksellers? He is very rich, and lives in Chelsea, in a huge and terrible house; but in the bottom of his garden is an ex-stable, where he and two printers turn out the Ashendene books. I do not like his type (Caslon is my ideal) but his press-work is the finest ever, and his vellum copies the most sumptuous books in the modern world. Nor does his hobby cost him very much: — less than the upkeep of a car, I believe. He sells his work in small editions. You, I expect, will print your own edition, for the few who really care for good books, and will then let someone have stereos from your type for the million, who will want your new Boswells. You are a most fortunate person: but I shall not envy you if 1930 sees me back in England, fit enough, and rich enough to have a motor-bike and ride it hard. That is my post-war pleasure.

I do not know if you are content with your bargain, as regards those proofs of *The Seven Pillars* you bought. The first chapter is the only surviving copy, so far as I know. It was cut out because G.B.S. called it very inferior to the rest. Since then, young Garnett has called it a vital chapter[1]. . . In the rest of the text are quite a number of faulty or variant readings. I gave it, as a bundle of loose sheets, to one of the Tank Corps fellows, who happened

1 See p. 262.

to be my half-section in the Q.M. stores, where we both worked. He is now in low water, and is desperately realising his household gods. He wrote and told me, and I advised Wilson as the selling agent, telling him not to expect too much, since my fame was only an artificially filled bubble, and his copy not the standard thing. Now I rather fancy your benefaction will make his path easy for life. Comic how things are . . . Just spoiled proofs, you know. If you can think of any personal means by which I could make them more nearly worth what you gave for them, you have only to command me. I'm in your debt for your help to Palmer, as much as for the refused offers to myself.

I expect it will take you two or three years to get out the first section of your treasure. I wonder where I will be then? This address will find me till the end of 1929, probably . . . and after that I will lie on the knees of the Air Ministry: who are considerate and human lords.

Again I'd like to repeat my thanks. Yours ever   T E SHAW

327: TO EDWARD GARNETT

1. XII. 27.   [Karachi]

This is going to be mainly about Read's very excellent note;[1] but first you must hear that I got an even better criticism of my style etc. from a son of yours: — possibly your son par excellence. He puts together my writing and Doughty's, with results of great interest to me. He has read D. Whereas most people only write about him. I've answered him at colossal length; it is easy to write to strangers and I have told him insulting things about his own work. So you will have a local war on soon. I take it he is *The Sailor's Return* and *Into Fox* Garnett? He wanted me to write another book. I told him that I did by accident, before I saw how bad *The Seven Pillars* was: and suggested that he pester you for a sight of it, some time next year, after I send it you. It will cure these ideas that I can write.

Now about Read. I'm going to take him page by page, with the book open on the table. He starts off on a defeatist note, about

---

[1] Herbert Read reviewed *Seven Pillars of Wisdom* in *The Bibliophile's Almanack for* 1928.

the brief life of modern books. He may be talking in periods of geology, and be deploring the present neglect of Aurignacian letters; if he is thinking post-Homeric, then I call his sentiments rot. There has never been such interest in books as there is to-day, nor so much writing, nor so much book-publishing nor so much book-buying, nor so much reading of books, or about books. This century holds the record in every particular. A book's life only begins when the newness has passed off its covers, and when the reviewers have stopped talking. He is confusing the news-value of a book with its being read. Go to . . . 'Great books are written in moods of spiritual light and intellectual certainty'.[1]

I would maintain against him that these moods never produced an imaginative work the size of a mouse from any of the people sterile enough to feel certain. My notion of the world's big books are *War and Peace*, *The Brothers Karamazoff*, *Moby Dick*, Rabelais, *Don Quixote*. Of course we treat of prose. There's a fine set of cores of darkness! But of course his idea of a great book may be different. Probably he uses 'romantic' in some special sense, as a word of abuse. I do not know how the coteries transcribe it now-a-days. We used to mean by it books like the *Odyssey*, as compared with the 'classical' works, which were the *Iliad* or *Marmion* sort of thing.

The title of my book was a reminiscence, for my ear, of a destroyed book of mine. But it fits the new *S.P.* better than it fitted the old. Perhaps Read is not fond of Jewish symbolism? I hate bibliophiles, and did my best to throw them off the track with *The S.P.*; so I did not number my copies, or declare how large the edition was (the published guesses are wide of the truth) or have a standard binding, or signatures, or index, or anything posh. It is heavy, so as to be little carried about. Its type is too large for my taste, but the Lanston people[2] hadn't a decent 11 point in 1923. It is grangerised of course. I said why, in my preface to the Illustrations. Why shouldn't I grangerise my own book? I bowdlerised it too.

---

[1] A quotation from Read's review.
[2] The Lanston Monotype Corporation, which now offers an almost infinite variety of type faces.

The Rothenstein drawing was not asked to consort with the Kennington. It is not possible to put a coloured illustration on a page of type. So all my plates were segregated at the back of the book, in an appendix like a picture gallery. They had no connection, except that of needle and thread, with the text. When he says that the Kennington drawings slip off into the infinite space around them, he puts it better than I ever managed to explain my aim to myself. One doesn't bother, usually, to verbalise one's aspirations. Titles were printed where they went best, because they were just titles superposed on colour reproductions of drawings. He would have had me try to turn them into pictures, perhaps. I wanted them to remain outside the book, and be what they were.

Ruthlessly cutting the text to suit his page . . . any evidence of ruthless cutting, or of cutting, either? I am not aware of it. Of course 15% was cut in making this text from the Oxford version; but my aim and standard of cutting was always the betterment of the prose, and those people who have compared the versions generally give me best with the new one. There are plenty of initial letters not in the top left-hand corner of the page, by the way . . . unless he has the heresy of thinking each page is separate, and not, like trousers, inseparable as pairs. In which case we will not argue where the stress comes on a sheet of type-script.

Of course *The S.P.* is not a work of art. Who ever pretended it was? I write better than the majority of retired army officers, I hope; but it is a long way from that statement to literature. Yet *The S.P.*, if not art, is equally not 'scribble'. It is the best I could do — very careful, exact, ambitious; and a hopeless failure partly because my aim was so high. I think it better to have burst oneself overthinking and overtrying, than to do Max Beerbohmish little perfections. So I have pretensions — and haven't. . . .

I do not like his categorical specification of a hero on pp. 38, 39; who in God's name laid this down? Is the hero to be the changeless thing, in the world? And why make Aeneas your archetype? I can't think of any other character in fiction who fits his definition. Not even von Heidenstam's Charles XII,[1] who nears it, in some respects.

[1] In *The Charles Men*, by Verner Von Heidenstam.

Isn't he slightly ridiculous in seeking to measure my day-to-day chronicle by the epic standard? I never called it an epic, or thought of it as an epic, nor did anyone else, to my knowledge. The thing follows an exact diary sequence, and is literally true, throughout. Whence was I to import his lay-figure hero? Leaders of movements have to be intelligent, as was Feisal, to instance my chief character. Read talks as though I had been making a book, and not a flesh-and-blood revolt.

I also disagree with much of his page 40. I have known intimately English, Turk and Arab soldiers, from experience of the ranks of those armies. I have some acquaintance with French, Italians and Belgians. I entirely repudiate his suggestion that one race is better than another. This is the purest jingoism and Morning Postliness. They apply it to the Irish, and so to myself. He will excuse me from believing so meanly about my own kind. There were compensations in Flanders. The breaking point of man remains much the same everywhere, and many Arabs and English broke down on the Arab front. Many of these would have broken down in Flanders. He writes as if 'adventure' were a delightful thing. It hurts, if it is the sort of time we had, as he implies. Also his saying that the press is mostly in the hands of non-combatants strikes me as not a very illuminating circumstance if true. He is one of the few really fighting men I have heard entertain a bitterness against non-coms. We usually envy them. Agreed a thousand times about Doughty. If only the people who run about after my farthing dip would go and read Doughty. But D. is partly to blame for that. These fellows here, with whom I have lived the last five years, are not so sure in their English as to enjoy *Arabia Deserta*. D. uses hard words for which they would need a dictionary, and his Scandinavian syntax puzzles them. He closed his goodness off from the world by not being as honest and simple in manner as he was in mind . . . and so people like Rosita Forbes and Mrs. Hull and me can still write about the desert.

His last six lines are, I'm sure, very near the truth; except that there too he must pursue his quarrel against the word adventure. He seems beset with whims and bogies. Has he in some way a grudge against something in life? In his writing I see a lack of happiness and of carelessness. In me there is so much of the cold-blooded calculator that I can understand him, I think, more or less by myself. The emotionalism of my *S.P.* is what sticks in his gizzard, and what he means when he girds at its romance and adventure . . . as if these forms of activity had some lien with emotion. You told me he was too intellectual: — perhaps, but not in this bit of work. Here he puts on paper his feelings towards the book, in the purest manner of the impressionists, for whom Middleton Murry has lived in vain. So he is much to my taste, for I feel through the appearance of those who would make criticism a science.

One smile to finish up. I was not a graduate, but an undergraduate, during the war, my degree happened later, I think.[1]

If you see Read once more, please tell him that I got more for myself, for my own enlightenment, out of his note than out of most of what has been printed. One Pope-Hennessy was as good. Your letters, and I think those of Garnett ii, piled up better, you being men of the market-place, as well as of the study. It is a great aid to judgment to know the price of fresh butter and the machinery of parliamentary government. Read is broody by comparison.

The shadow of Hogarth's going[2] is still always there whenever I turn round to think. He was really to me the parent I could trust, without qualification, to understand what bothered me. And I had grown to lean on his knowledge of my motives not a little. Also so much of his goodness lay in himself; and has gone into death with him. That makes it feel wasteful. He had not finished.

Well I have for this week.　　　　　　　　　　　　T.E.S.

[The following is a reply to a letter regretting Lawrence's inability to come to the Mohenjo-daro excavations on the Indus, and saying any friend of his would be welcome.]

---

[1] Lawrence took his degree in 1910.

[2] Hogarth had died on November 6th. Lawrence had written two letters to him after his death, before he heard the news.

328: TO ERNEST MACKAY

2.XII.27.   *Karachi*

Dear Mackay, Your letter is threatening to bear fruit: I wonder if you meant it, or if it is to take advantage of a politeness. I showed your letter to one of the nine hundred, a moulder (aluminium, iron, etc.) who when in Mesopotamia spent ten days at Ur, where Woolley gave him a tent and some food, and good conversation. He liked Woolley, therefore; it is not very often troops get treated as reasonable beings; in India such a thing is not dreamed of. However you come from Egypt, which is a comparatively civilized land; so perhaps it is well. Please consult Mrs. Mackay. You would find the moulder (name of Heir, pronounced like the electrical variety[1]) a decent being. He likes music, especially of the semi-light sort: Schubert to Mozart. Beethoven he finds dry.

However, to business again. He said that he would give his future to visit your digs. I told him you had found practically nothing, and nothing that was not dull. He sniffed at me for prejudiced, because I couldn't go myself. He swore you were not far off: — a matter of 15 Rs. by rail, return. He said one Jones, a fitter aero, would hold him company. He said Christmas would be best of course, because we then get five days holiday — from the 24th to the 28th — but that if you were then full, as I hinted, they could get leave for not less than a week early in the new year. He was hot to write to you at once; but I pushed this eagerness to one side, so that you should have a good chance to back out, if you didn't mean it.

If you can do it, the pleasure of the devils will be inordinate. You need not be afraid that they will be devilish in your neighbourhood. Devilishness is of two sorts, physical and moral. These are nice devils. The Air Force sets a new standard of troops; they are squeamishly timid of being thought to resemble the Army. I think you will find them quite interesting and amusing.

If you are forthcoming, as I rather expect, will you say when would be the best time for them to come, what would be the best way to come, and what stuff they should bring with them?

---

[1] The electric hare used in dog-racing.

Blankets and things like that are camp commonplaces. But of course you may be as richly furnished as we were at Carchemish, where the B.M. housed us richly and gave us good hospitality allowances. Troops are, anyway, not exigent.

They would probably like to do something to get the full flavour out of their visit. Old Petrie used to make visitors string beads, or wash pots, according as they were males or females. I do not know on what scale you work, or what goods you have found. Heir is a decent photographer. Jones I know less about. He is very quiet: reads a lot, I fancy. Of course I've been five years and more in these circles; now they are, to an impartial mind, much the same as any standards anywhere.

Airmen mustn't fly machines: — that is a privilege of officers, and R.A.F. officers are very unlike R.A.F. airmen. It would not be becoming for me to say which set I preferred; though perhaps it may be deduced from my manner of life. So please don't give Heir directions for finding the best landing ground near the digs. Camels are more in our manner.

I hope I am not causing you to swear, as you read all this. If you have too little company, and too few appreciative visitors, then you will not be peeved. I mean well. [8 *lines omitted*]

329: TO DICK KNOWLES

7.12.27.   [*Karachi*]

Today is the anniversary of our sailing from Southampton. I was very unhappy at tearing up my roots, once more. The first time I left England, in 1905, was a dream of delight: not that it was the first time, of course; but in 1905 I began my own, independent, voluntary travels. France, mainly: then further afield, by slow degrees, until the War cut short that development of me into a sort of Hogarth: a travelled, archaeological sort of man, with geography and a pen as his two standbys. Hogarth was a very wonderful man. You never met him. He was first of all human, and then charitable, and then alive. I owed him everything I had, since I was 17, which is the age at which I suddenly found myself. You may have begun a little earlier, since the being torn out of home is an education in itself.

However, there it is; today is one year of my exile finished.
Only two more. I do not show any outward impatience: but I
shall be very glad when it is all over, and myself at home again.
This travel, or rather this residence in the East, is one perpetual
temptation to me to cut loose again on some further project of
my own: and I do not want to take off. Taxying is quite fast
enough for so wing-crippled a duck. Your first journey abroad,
however, will probably be a delight to you. If you do not carry
in your head any conviction that A is right and B is wrong, then
the contemplation of different ways of doing things, different
ways of thinking things, different values, even different habits,
provides you with year-long meals of great richness. And to
watch the reaction of set characters (such as most of the fellows
in Room 2) against their present strangeness, is a delight. I am
sure that it is those in the glassiest houses that throw the most
stones.

I called myself a wing-crippled duck too soon. Are you yet
an A.C.2? So am I. For the moment we are square. The dice
are weighted against me, for I cannot get higher, owing to my
lack of the needful education certificate. And I do not think I
can face the ordeal of working again at sums to pass it! But it is
very important that for the moment we are level.

Your letter about man-service interested me. Yes, it is very
near the beast. Once I fancied I was very near the angels, and the
coming so abruptly to earth was a jar — and a very wholesome
jar. Angels, I think, we imagine. Beasts, I think, we are. And
I like the beasts for their kindliness and honesty: without really
managing to make myself quite like them. I've lived now five
years in barracks, and can honestly confess that I have never been
really one with my fellows. I have sometimes, for a moment,
imagined myself into a unity with them: and before I could seize
it and settle down into it, like a rabbit into a burrow, I'd be
whisked off to another existence, incontinent. This may be my
solitary misfortune (Graves suggests that I'm a unicorn) or it may
be the common fate of man, and that only myself complains of it.
As though I got a hump on my temper because I had only two
legs, whereas a centipede had more than he could count!

Do you ever feel like a unicorn strayed amongst sheep? I

fancy so, from your letter. If so, you must prepare yourself for not ever becoming quite a part of the earth — or quite unconsciously happy. Do you remember E. M. Forster, at Clouds Hill? He wrote me from Edinburgh 'so I'm at peace, and quite happy. But I do not know why every year it becomes more difficult to write down those last two words.' Another unicorn, is it? Often I think every man is. But meanwhile the beast remains, sometimes supine, but sometimes rampant. You will find it taking charge of you, at some weak second of your will: and after that you will either be very charitable and forgiving to others, or you will hide it and be superior. Do not, any way, condemn yourself harshly. It is the lot of us all.

However this is not a helpful nib to write a long letter with. I lost my own good (or serviceable) pen after the Forster quotation, above, and have since tried this one right way up, and back down. Both beastly.

Graves sent me an advance copy of his book. I'm relieved to find only two things in it which hurt — one, the story of Lord Curzon crying — the Middle East Committee. That is the version Sir Eyre Crowe used to tell, and I do not think it quite fair either to Curzon or to me. The differences between us were fundamental. The other is my interview with the King. Neither his account (called 'mine') nor Lord Stamfordham's very exactly fits my memory. I had never a notion of fighting the British in arms: nor was I quite as priggish as Graves makes out.

However, these tiny spots apart, it is a good book.

[*one line omitted*] T.E.S.

330: TO WILLIAM ROTHENSTEIN

8. 12. 27. *Karachi.*

Dear Rothenstein, Many thanks for the second *Enemy*. He[1] digresses too much, in it; so that there is almost no main argument. If he would send his ideas one by one to the weekly press as they occur to him — then what a critic he would be. The background of a general idea, some vague bogey of a time-spirit, would then give depth and strength to his writing. He cuts Miss Mayo

[1] Wyndham Lewis.

wholly to bits: but then she is easy meat. He goes fairly for Sherwood Anderson, who is more his size. I think he is convincing there: but I do not know all S.A.'s work. Then he goes for D.H. Lawrence, who's [*sic*] boots he is not big enough to wear. He does not seem to have read much Lawrence, so far as I can see. He criticises only some pages of his little *Mornings in Mexico*, which are just the snapshots of a literary artist, in the slack time while waiting for a subject — the same way as a barber snips his empty scissors all the time he is moving the comb, and preparing a new grip on an uncut lock of hair. Just the maintenance of a vital rhythm. I'd like, immensely, to see W. Lewis tackling such a thing as D.H.L.'s *Plumed Serpent*, an immense and significant book. A fundamental criticism of that would be wonderful reading. Only he would have to forget his time-spirit obsession. There will not be a new time-spirit till the implications of Einstein have entered the new generation with its mother's milk — say about 1960 or so. We are Newtonians yet.

Lewis is vastly entertaining on poor Ezra Pound. [*5 lines omitted*]

Yet Lewis is a first rate brain, and a very good artist, surely? His drawings impress me with their power. They are really fine, I fancy. Isn't it odd to like all that a man does, and to dislike, almost vehemently, all that he likes? Or is that a natural consequence of living in his generation. Your work will be exactly dateable to your epoch, in the eyes of the future: as will the work of all your contemporaries. The most academic of them, and the most fiercely revolutionary, will all be 1880-1930 . . . isn't that odd? What are these 50 years of a man's production, if his own time takes such possession of him? I think, mainly, that it means that any search or endeavour after *difference* (as an end in itself) is wasted effort.

Miss Gertrude Bell's *Letters* came to me: they are very good — but so on the surface as to be impalpably unsatisfying. Only twice did I feel that she had got actually down to anything. She was born too gifted, perhaps.

Poor Sir Henry Wilson was a fool,[1] behind all his brilliance and power and knowledge. That vitiated his political efforts, and

---

[1] For a more favourable view of Sir Henry Wilson, see letter No. 380.

made him easy meat for all the politicians. Even I had no difficulty in ringing him round, over Mesopotamia. He was utterly
blinded by prejudices, and so a victim, always. No vision over
his wings or tail, only straight ahead. And he was not honest in
mind or straight in tactics.

The death of Hogarth hit me very hard. Oxford was to me a
beautiful place, and a home, because he lived there, for me to
see for a few minutes whenever I passed. I did not want to delay
there: but I did like to see and hear him just for a moment. And
he takes most of his richness into the grave with him, because he
did not express many sides of himself on paper. A great loss: the
greatest, perhaps, or probably, that I'll ever have to suffer. Yours,
[3 *lines omitted*]   T.E.S.

331: TO LIONEL CURTIS

22/12/27   *Karachi.*

Dear My Lord, Thank you for sending me the *Times* account
of D.G.H. It does its best to give the externality of the man;
but everything for which I haunted him and valued him is missing
from their picture. He was my background, in a curious sense;
the only person to whom I had never to explain the 'why' of what
I was doing. He was strangely understanding, and has taken
this personal quality into death with him. All personality is like
that, except the personality of the very great writers and artists,
who are sometimes able, like Hardy, to write themselves out over
and over again in their books, till they have convinced us that the
veins of what natural ores they contained are exhausted. Whereas
nobody could value Hogarth without knowing him. For the
general public he will remain the waste Johnson would have
been without Boswell. In my own case I feel that I have lost what
I valued at Oxford; for D.G.H. was in a real sense a part of Oxford. Indeed I fancy that for me he was Oxford, entire and un-
qualified. He was a don, unimaginable away from the place,
where yet he lived only a few years of his life. But he had what
one would have wished to make the atmosphere of a common
room — such a common room as would have enticed and gratified

Peacock — and I used always to say 'here's a don and a man combined'. He never struck me as a scholar, but as primarily a
civilised person.

However enough of all this. You will be distressed at my
falling to this typographical degradation. It is part of my duty
here to type so much of the technical reports and correspondence
as has to go out of our office and workshop. If I do it not, then
the professed clerk has to supply my place. This would be well,
only that sometimes he will be ill, (everybody is always having
days off duty in this place) and we are the only two 'office boys'
allowed by establishment. So sometimes I will have his job, and
that is mainly the typing of strengths and parade states. Anyway,
I have contracted to learn my way about this beastly machine,
and as I am very slow to learn anything, it has been already a
long business, and will be a long time yet. I am past the two
finger stage, and the scales and practises, and have now to exercise
my leisure for an hour a day upon the vile bodies of those I know.
I propose to wipe off most of my back correspondence; but it is
weary work. It is horrible to allot the same space to every letter,
regardless of size, and horrible to have to strike each letter
separately. Yet so exact is the register of this old and worn-out
machine that the only chord I can rely upon for an impression
without sticking afterwards is the 'il' group. All the other ties I
attempt jam in the gate.

Yes, I'm glad you are saving so much of the land round Oxford.
I would like, though, to see not open land, but land cunningly
inhabited everywhere. I would buy my estate, to save it from the
speculator, and dot it over with little houses, put each where it
hid itself, if it could not be made an addition to the landscape.
Only I would prohibit that disfigurement of enclosures about each
house, that ugliness of wall or railing. They should all open upon
the common land, and should have liberty to plant or dig it,
indeed, but without protection against a visitor. You could make
men behave themselves like reasoning creatures, if you ceased
threatening them with prosecutions: and you would prevent that
privacy growing up. Indeed I would almost say you would
obliterate class. There is none in the common dormitories of our
barracks. I agree that barracks are ugly things: — but then look

how ugly is the declared purpose of troops' existence in the sphere of things. We cannot help being brutal and licentious, for our intention is unholy, and they must fan in us such passions as serve the brute. But put your dons and scholars on common ground, and allow them, if they improve their neighbourhoods, to improve it for everybody, and not just for themselves . . . and see what a new mind you might make. I would have Cumnor Hurst a suburb, and Boars Hill populous. A foreground to the City in the distance.

Enough drivel. You are retired to write your book about the Empire. Good. Remember that the manner is greater than the (?) matter, so far as modern history is concerned. One of the ominous signs of the time is that the public can no longer read history. The historian is retired into a shell to study the whole truth; which means that he learns to attach insensate importance to documents. The documents are liars. No man ever yet tried to write down the entire truth of any action in which he has been engaged. All narrative is parti pris. And to prefer an ancient written statement to the guiding of your instinct through the maze of related facts, is to encounter either banality or unreadableness. We know too much, and use too little knowledge. Cut away the top-hamper.

More preaching. This place induces softening of the brain. I notice an incredible shabbiness and second-rating in all our effort here. We talk so much of the climate. A gowk in a paper of this week said that the climate of Karachi was like a taste of Hell in summer, and pitied his fate in having to serve and work in the place. Well, this year it has not once been uncomfortably warm. It has never been hot, in the sense that Baghdad and Cairo are hot. There is no sunlight, no direct glare to hurt men's brains. A climate like St. Raphael in summer, perhaps. Yet they burble of hardship, and sleep at midday, and wear sun-helmets, and cut the work hours to half the hours of England, and excuse themselves any laxity or indulgences of temper or disposition, under the plea of the fatal sun. It is laziness, pure or impure, and simple or complicated. We could work exactly as men do in England, and be all the better for it, for we would then not have time to remember and cultivate all these fancies of fever and disease.

Believe me, I am ashamed of my race, here. They deserve to lose ground in the world, for their frivolous ineptitude.

Oh, what a moan. Owt else to tell you? no, I think not. You will see I am back in a shell again, changing my skin, more or less by compulsion of instinct, to make Robert Graves' portrait of me a missing portrait. The leopard changes his spots for stripes, since the stripes are better protection in the local land-scape. Ah me.

This hour will not pass. So be it. I will pass instead. Yet the pity of it is that probably I will post you this sheet of nonsense lines, instead of burning it. Take it as what it is, a typewriting lesson, which shows how difficult it is to spell, and how impossible it is to think, for a novice, at least, direct on to the instrument. Now with a pen I can hold my fancy in leash and write what my mind dictates or approves ... but with this thing....

H. G. Wells must dictate his novels. That is where all the 'Damned dots' come from. They are irresistible.   T.E.S.

332 : TO DICK KNOWLES

30/12/27.   [*Karachi*]

Dear Dick, As a rule I work at this machine for an hour a day, and as I get more intelligible on it I am beginning to write letters to the people to whom I am most in arrears. It is not a very good payment of dues, for either I am careful at framing my sentences — in which case spelling and sense go west: or I am spelling carefully, in which case the sentences mean little or nothing: or the meaning is excellent, but unintelligible below the errors in syntax and spelling. I leave it to you to divide this letter into these three categories. You have no idea how hard it is to do four things at once. Later, when I can hammer blindfold like a clerk (Group IV), my stuff will be itself again.

Life here remains as it was when I wrote to you the first and last times from here. A good place in which to mark time, for the food is good, & there is no attempt to control our deportment in camp, and the work is light (too light, I'm afraid ... the ex-cessive leisure takes much filling) and not uninteresting, for the officers are all full out for work; and I have found a sheltered occupation, which delivers me from working parade, first thing in the morning, and from most of the ceremonials. This is an extraordinary place for Ceremonies. An average of one posh visitor a month seems to come here, or to Karachi, and no performance is complete without the presence of the R.A.F. And India is a country of rifles, so that a parade is a military occasion. At all times of the year hundreds of us are being rafted down to the town in Leyland floats, to line streets or honour a cenotaph, or fire a feu-de-joie. From all these diversions of temper my little job as Key-orderly preserves me. In return I get up at reveille (easy . . .) and unlock the shops by 7 o'clock; and lock them up again in the dinner time, when work nominally ceases for the day. But often there is an afternoon shift, and for them again I open doors; and the rest of the time I have the keys in my control, and can use the shop and office as a playground. It was a comfort at Christmas time, when the camp turned very wet. Normally it is as dry as any camp I have met; but the mess, when it did break out, finally, was correspondingly worse . . . I think it was worse than Bovington in 1923, which has hitherto been my high-level of beastliness. No, upon reflection, it was not so bad as that.

Christmas day itself I spent in the guardroom, doing another man's turn. He thought I was doing him a kindness, he being a buffalo, an animal which likes dampness; I thought he was doing me a kindness; so the exchange was mutually satisfactory. The guard were all T.T., at least on duty, and no person came near us to bother us. So I think I scored. Guards are a beastly ordeal, for me. I get in a shaking funk before the mounting, and find it difficult to give the right salutes with a pop-gun at short notice, without muddling myself up. Sheer wind, of course, for actually I know the movements well. But something always comes to flurry me, when it is a performance with witnesses.

You were no doubt at Clouds Hill. I wish I could have been, for the day, though I make no doubt that the tenant (if any) has cleaned it up muchly. But all that has happened since I left England makes me pat myself on the back of myself, for my wisdom in running away. Cranwell would have stood, grumblingly, one book about me; when Graves added himself to the *Revolt*, they would have spat on me. When Lowell Thomas added himself to Graves, they would have spewed on me. It was hard luck, having the two of them at once; though in the end it will be best, probably. At least, nobody can do another, and the soul of the great British public will be turned with rage at its surfeit of my rareness and virtuosity, and will refuse for years to hear me quoted or mentioned. The BIGGER THE BOOM? THE BIGGER THE SLUMP ... so that is comfortable. I hope you will take the crest of the market for the disposal of your *Seven Pillars*. If you ask me when the crest is or was, then I cannot tell you. Posh got £400 for his proofs ... but they were a unique set. I have been a golden gander to lots of people; and if that spare copy of *The S.P.* at Oxford is not claimed by I come back, then it is going to give me a new bike in 1930, and maintenance money for it for two years. I hope the Matchless is going as it should; it sounded right. Just well run in, and nippy in type. When you are my age you will be sighing for heavier things, which are less acrobatic to ride, and suggest ease to their decaying owners. The point of glory in a Brough was that lazy touring speed, maintained, you felt, without effort on the engine's part, for all day.

I wonder where you go, about Winchester. One of my pet places used to be at Ringwood — or rather near it. The forest is fine about Picket Post; though perhaps this is hardly the time of year. We forget the seasons here, where the climate is always as near fine as can be, and the temperature pretty constant through the year, dropping ten degrees a night in summer, from 90° to 80°, and in winter sometimes falling as low as 60° at midnight. Also this place has no direct sun; the nearness of the sea gives us so much mist and there are such continual dust-storms in the Gulf, that the light comes to us always filtered, indirectly. I go about perversely wishing for a really hot day, one which would show the grumbling crowd how fortunate is the climate they have fallen into.

There used to be a little tea-cottage, the last house on the right as you reached the bridge out of Ringwood, on the Wimborne road. It was well run by an amusing woman — a type of 'new poor'. Do not forget, either, the dairy in Wimborne itself, which supplies the best Devonshire cream, under the pretence (and price) of Dorsetshire. I expect you find Salisbury too particularly military for your tastes to go wandering there. The best of Salisbury is the green grass round the cathedral, and some of the houses in the Close. Though there are good houses, old timber halls, in the town. I like Salisbury. Also I read in the papers that they are at last trying to do something to clean up the skirts of poor desecrated Stonehenge. It has become only its shadow, since the war, what with aerodromes and cottages and fences. Once it stood all by itself on its grey hill, as you came from Amesbury, and was magnificent.

There, I must stop talking. I often think of you, and always as a rather shapeless Sidcotted bundle,[1] peering over the rim, or through the floor of a Virgin[2] in mid air. Probably false: but my imagination makes those big machines wander out into the sky, once a month or so, for a day and a night, over England and Scotland, just droning away for hour after hour aimlessly among the clouds, burning so much petrol and oil, & coming home again for breakfast, and then bed, and afterwards more weeks to clean up for another try. Flying is probably by now only a boredom to you. It is more than a year since I got into the air on any pretext, and I look back upon it as one of the few 'different' things. If I had never flown (like most of the fellows here) I don't think I would dare go into the streets in blue uniform.

You wrote something about first going up. It stressed the lack of sensation, I expect. I felt that: but each flight since has felt stranger. The utter separation of the self from familiar things . . . but of course in your case your cockpit is only part of your job. I should not like to take my stool & table & ink-pot with me into space. Yours   T. E. S.

Our library has started subscribing for *J O' Ls*[3] . . . a result of my lending about those copies you sent me. Good effort.

---

[1] Wearing a Sidcot flying suit.
[2] A Vickers Virginia bombing aeroplane — at that time one of the largest types in the R.A.F.
[3] *John O' London's Weekly.*

333: TO MRS. THOMAS HARDY

15. 1. 28   *Karachi.*

Dear Mrs Hardy, This is a Sunday, and an hour ago I was on
my bed, listening to Beethoven's last quartet: when one of the
fellows came in and said that T.H. is dead. We finished the
quartet, because all at once it felt like him: and now I am faced
with writing something for you to receive three weeks too late.

I was waiting for it, almost. After your letter came at Christmas I wanted to reply: but a paragraph in the papers said that he
was ill. Then I held my breath, knowing the tenuous balance of
his life, which one cold wind would finish. For years he has been
transparent with frailty. You, living with him, grew too used to
it perhaps to notice it. It was only you who kept him alive all these
years: you to whom I, amongst so many others, owed the privilege of having known him.

And now, when I should grieve, for him and for you, almost
it feels like a triumph. That day we reached Damascus, I cried,
against all my control, for the triumphant thing achieved at last,
fitly: and so the passing of T.H. touches me. He had finished
and was so full a man. Each time I left Max Gate, having seen
that, I used to blame myself for intruding upon a presence which
had done with things like me and mine. I would half-determine
not to trouble his peace again. But as you know I always came
back the next chance I had. I think I'd have tried to come even
if you had not been good to me: while you were very good:
and T.H.

So, actually, in his death I find myself thinking more of you.
I am well off, having known him: you have given up so much of
your own life and richness to a service of self-sacrifice. I think it
is good, for the general, that one should do for the others what
you have done for us all: but it is hard for you, who cannot see as
clearly as we can how gloriously you succeeded, and be sure how
worth while it was. T.H. was infinitely bigger than the man who
died three days back — and you were one of the architects. In the
years since *The Dynasts* the Hardy of stress has faded, and T.H.
took his unchallenged — unchallengeable — place. Though as once
I told you, after a year of adulation the pack will run over where

he stood, crying 'There is no T.H. and never was'. A generation will pass before the sky will be perfectly clear of clouds for his shining. However, what's a generation to a sun? He is secure. How little that word meant to him.

This is not the letter I'd like to write. You saw, though, how I looked on him, and guessed, perhaps, how I'd have tried to think of him, if my thinking had had the compass to contain his image.

Oh, you will be miserably troubled now, with jackal things that don't matter: You who have helped so many people, and whom therefore no one can help. I am so sorry.　　　　　T E SHAW.

[The two Aircraftmen, Heir and Jones, had stayed ten days with Mackay at the Mohenjo-daro excavations and had gone away with a *Parsifal* record. See letter No. 328.]

334: TO ERNEST MACKAY

18.1.28　　　　　　　　*R.A.F. Depot, Drigh Road, Karachi*

Dear Mackay, They came back in great form, delighted with themselves, and the objects of general envy and admiration.

I am sorry they stayed so long. It was a tax upon the kindness of Mrs. Mackay and yourself. However you have acquired merit. If the Recording Angel has not made the due entries on your conduct sheets, please call me as witness.

They told me that you still hoped I'd make a chance to run up: but I fear it is out of the question. Unless the R.A.F. order me to move. I intend to stay within the bounds of this camp for the duration of my spell in India. After all, a year has passed. There cannot be more than four to do . . . and there may be only two.

Do you see that Woolley has found some more gold stuffs? Drugs, horrid drugs, in the eyes of archaeologists . . . but how the public gape after these things. Full pages in the *Illustrated*. You have Tutankh to thank for the new status of archaeology. Woe's me, I suppose I'll never dig anything again.

However, put me back in England and you can keep your East!

With best regards, Yours ever　　　　　　　T. E. SHAW

Incidentally they returned me your *Parsifal*, thinking it was mine! We are getting it ready for return . . . trying too, to find something as big & strong to go with it! Yours　　　　T.E.

335: TO H. S. EDE

20.1.28.　　　　　　　　　　　　　　　　　　[*Karachi*]

Dear Ede, Indeed I'm getting steadily worse as a letter-writer: but if you sat in Drigh Road (where at this season there is absolutely no grazing for a camel) your hump too would shrink, and you would be chary of exercise.

Instead I picture you and Aitken[1] sitting on the steps of the staircase by the Sargents, and fishing out portfolios from a brown flood with bent pins and broomsticks. It will be amazingly good for the Tate to have lost all its cellar-collection by an Act of God. I can see 'lost in flood' in Aitken's neat handwriting ticketed against purchase after purchase of the Chantrey bequest. Besides you'll now be able to decorate your dining room again. Good luck to the Tate. It deserves it!

Of course your view of death is right, and all that: but it will not save you from a sense of loss when someone you like goes. I had (and perhaps still have) a hedge full of trees: they are old: and whenever one falls I miss something of what used to be the shapeliness of that hedge. So Hogarth is part, a great part, of the background of my life fallen away. He was my realisation of Oxford, the concrete thing which Oxford stood for in my mind. Now Thomas Hardy has followed him into that very rich company. I am sorry for T.H's going, too, though less so, for T.H. had perfected himself in his work, and went into the grave very poor in spirit. Whereas Hogarth put so much of his force into the acts of living.

[1] Ede and Aitken were both officials at the Tate Gallery, which had suffered from the flooding of the Thames.

My Christmas passed quietly, in the guardroom, where I was one of the four on guard. The camp was drunk, as a body: so the guardroom was a good place. I often go there on a holiday, swapping turns with some convivial fellow.

No, I've not been to Kashmir. As a matter of fact I have reasons for staying put: reasons which have kept me within the boundary of our camp since I have been here. So I have not even seen Karachi — which is very far from Kashmir.

My next port of call will be, I hope, Southampton in 1930 or 1932. It seems only a little way off now. The first four years, so the R.A.F. says, are the worst. Yours ever,   T.E.S.

336: TO SIR HERBERT BAKER

20.1.28.   *Drigh Road [Karachi]*

Dear H.B., I don't write, for I have nothing to say: and many people write me business letters, demanding answers: which use up all my spare cash on two-anna stamps. How could there be anything to say from Drigh Road?

The Viceroy came: we worked for weeks beforehand, collecting dust to throw in his eyes. There was a daily punishment list as long as my arm, in his honour.* When the day came I dodged off on a side duty: so set no eyes on him, nor he on me. Ditto the King of Afghanistan. These big men are too big to catch an insect.

Drigh Road will hold me, inshallah, till the end of my term in India. Not yet have I crossed the bounds of camp. I moon about inside and think of nothing, or of Hogarth and Hardy, who have died.

I'm glad the South African buildings are ripening with time.[1] All the world speaks well of them: — which must make you quake sometimes in the night watches. I'd like to see them.

The Bank won't look well while it's half up and half down. I

* I was fortunate. Sheet still clean.

[1] Sir Herbert Baker was the architect of Government Buildings and Parliament House at Pretoria and part of New Delhi and was at this time designing the extension of the Bank of England.

hope you'll scrape the old wall, somehow, to make the whole less of a magpie when it's finished. I'll be back to see it nearly done: and have promised myself the Bank as the goal of my first walk in London. You cannot imagine how I'm looking forward to getting home. But it's too far ahead yet for me to afford to say so often. A weakening entertainment, that thought of getting home.

Cameron[1] paints very quietly, and very pastorally, and rather affectionately, I think. He may be a good team-leader for your decorators. Kennington has rather forsworn painting for sculpture, and is abroad somewhere — or was, months ago. I'm glad you've booked Anrep.[2]

I should sell *The S.P.* if I were you. No book is worth £600 to anyone of moderate income. I feel inclined to sell one, and print a thin-paper edition of four copies, for my private amusement. A pocket edition. Why not? or rather why? Nothing doing, really. There are always good reasons for not doing.

'Trevelyan got a new idea of Christianity', did he! Not a good idea, probably. You know I meant once to write a book on the background of Christ ... Galilee and Syria, social, intellectual and artistic, of 40 B.C. It would make an interesting book. As good as Renan's *Life of Jesus* should have been, if only he had had the wit to leave out the central figure.

I encouraged Graves, to give my reputation the coup de grace. A premature 'life' will do more to disgust the select and superior people (the R.A.F. call them the 'toffee-nosed') than anything. Observe the reaction on yourself.† Admirable! I can only get peace, now, by being digested and tipped out on the rubbish heap. The 'lying quiet' game I've played out, and lost over. Mrs. Bernard Shaw sends me many reviews of Graves' book, and the general tone of them is that they are fed up with my subject.

I wonder why Curtis wants to encase the dagger. Arabia does not produce any wood except palm-wood, which resembles boiled beef in texture: except of course acacia: and in gardens fruit trees:

† Laurentian, that sudden insult. I thought I'd sloughed off those manners with the names.

---

[1] D. Y. Cameron.   [2] Boris Anrep, the artist in mosaic.

and hard thorns, which you reject. They build with Indian teak, at Mecca and Jiddah.

The fellows who come down from New Delhi, where there is a small, fortunate, unit tell me it's a posh place. Not very satisfying, critically, perhaps, but at least the right spirit.

An advantage of this filthy paper which India gives us is that it breaks brittly into brown flaky dust after a short exposure to light. So my 'life and letters' will not include this effort. Adds a new terror to letter-writing, that sort of threat.   T.E.S.

337: TO T. B. MARSON

20.1.28.   [*Drigh Road, Karachi*]

Dear Marson, You must have pushed the unfortunate Boom[1] up to writing to me. It's a joy to get 'em: but please don't. He has so many better things to do. One of my best memories is of him pushing up those big glasses, and saying plaintively 'Marson, may I go?' . . . Now you are out of office you are to be merciful to him. He's so great and clean and splendid a person that he deserves all the best service in the world. It will be a relief to me to hear that he has finally left the Air Ministry. To go on risking himself, after all he's done, seems too wild. He has deserved harbour, after that voyage, with that crew and owners.[2]

Tell him, if ever you see him, that it's time for him to rest. The Air Force is what he'd like it to be, and he's created it after his own image. He must now let the child alone, to take its first steps, and fall down, and hurt itself, and find its own way up again, and carry on. All decent birds hop it when their infants have done their first solo. I know it hurts them: I haven't been a parent, but I cut myself off the Arab Movement, though I wake up night after night dreaming I could help 'em again. I could, but that late help is hurtful to the young.

This applies, a little, to the chicken, or game-cock, of yours.

---

[1] Lord Trenchard. Marson was Trenchard's secretary at the Air Ministry.

[2] The metaphor of the ship, and of the fledglings, was often repeated In a letter of November 3rd, 1933 (not included here) he wrote to David Garnett of Feisal's death: 'I think of his death almost with relief – as one would see enter the harbour a goodlooking but not seaworthy ship, with the barometer falling He is out of it intact.'

He's on the knees of the Gods, now: like Irak: and you and I aren't gods. Even, sometimes, I think that perhaps H.M.T.[1] isn't ... that is in my chilly moments, when all the world seems a failure with which it's a sorry sorrow to be connected. However I know the R.A.F. is 'it', always, or nearly always. (One has to be just going on or coming off guard, even in that, you know, sometimes, except at Cranwell, which was a home from home, for the irks[2].)

[*Two words omitted*] here met me for the first time, the other day, and trod heavily on my harmless, if unattractive face. I think he must have been reading Robert Graves, and felt that I was a worm. Fortunately Salmond happened along next day, and told him I was all right. So my sheet remains clean. I have a terror about that sheet: if I get a mark on it someone will hoof me out into the street again: and I am too old to go wandering any more.

Incidentally don't take that remark about oldness as a moan. For my rackety life and generally damaged condition, I enjoy the most astonishing health, and it surprises myself when I think about it. In India I'm better than in England. Perhaps my lubricating oil is a bit heavy, and it takes a wisp of sunlight to get it circulating freely. Anyway I see myself signing on to convert my 5 reserve into 5 active, next winter.

I hope you will forget Scotland in the calmness of Gloucestershire. There is some very lovely country there. I could hope that you'd drive a dog-cart: only, of course, it'll be a motor instead. But dog-carts go with the exile's notions of England. I suppose money is the main difficulty. I've only been three times broke, by Thursday, since they put us on full pay, here. Then I don't drink or smoke, and never go outside the camp bounds: and haven't been in the canteen since last February: — believe me, St. Anthony isn't in it with me now. There is that sheet to be considered. It was different at Cranwell, where I know that Biffy[3] trusted me. So the old cat could pretend to be a kitten.

I enclose you my last letter: 'cause I can't tear 'em up: and it would put me into the guard-room to be found with it ... You can destroy it for me. The yarn about Feisal isn't true:

[1] Trenchard.   [2] Aircraftmen.
[3] Air Vice-Marshal Amyas Borton, a friend in the Arabian campaign.

he never asked me for one.¹ As for Cave-Browne-Cave: — of course I'd have given an acre or so of my very part-worn skin to hop round the earth with him. Only they haven't any aircraft hands aboard, and here I'm doing a useful job: so I couldn't very well wish for it. There are things barred to even the most distinguished A.C.1 s. (I was promoted that last October!) Can I call myself distinguished, as an A.C.1.? Yes. I think so, fairly. You know I think my reputation is all punk: but it's indubitable that I have one: even I'm in *Who's Who*!

Sorry for writing you such bosh: but I get sort of wound up sometimes. Y——   T.E.SHAW.

[The following passage is from *Leaves in the Wind*, the pencil manuscript notes which I believe were intended for a continuation of *The Mint*. No date is given but the camp must have been Karachi.]

338: FROM 'LEAVES IN THE WIND'

'But it wasn't a grin on my face, Sir. I was half-smiling, in recognition that we are playing a game by its rules. You know, as I know, that this military pretence is only play on our part, and on the parts of all the other thousand men in the camp. Just one chap, perhaps, believes in it, and they make him Sergeant Major. The rest of us pretend to be soldiers, while really we're keen only on our job, and to get on with it. I smiled to encourage myself against the inroad of discipline which was coming to waste my time — and now yours too, I'm sorry to say.'

'Case dismissed. Fall out the escort and witnesses, Sergeant Major. I have something to say to Shaw' — and he warned me to keep my mind off my soldiering. 'Do it, and don't think about yourself so much.' I assured him that I kept my thoughts always to myself, except when provoked beyond reason, as by the processes of military justice, which found a man guilty of being charged with an offence, before he was even brought up for trial and sentence before the authority which had directed his prosecution. 'It riles me unbearably to lose my scalp to a lot of fellows

¹ A copy of *Seven Pillars of Wisdom*.

round whom I can make rings. We are no better than poachers up before a country Bench.' He demurred. I, for example, had just been let off. 'Yes,' I countered, 'The first man off for months — and not because I defended myself, but because I shook you by challenging the system.' He laughed and sent me out.

[The following letter to the Editor of the *Daily Express* was accompanied by a cutting from that newspaper, annotated at the side by Lawrence. Words underlined are here italicized.]

339: TO R. D. BLUMENFELD

2.2.28   *Karachi*

AIRCRAFTSMAN SHAW.

There is a glamour attached to the name of Colonel T. E. Lawrence, 'the uncrowned King of Arabia', which many ambitious men must envy.

Let 'em have it.

There was glamour long before he became Aircraftsman Shaw, and it has been multiplied a thousand-fold since his disappearance from the world of his intellectual equals.

Only 1000 fold? Dear me. Rotten effort.
If I have a world of intellectual equals? What a gang we'd look.

NO SIDE.

A CORRESPONDENT sends me some interesting details concerning the existence of this boyish looking blue eyed dreamer. He has been at the air depot near Karachi for the last twelve months and *seems perfectly happy*. The other men like him because he has no 'side' and do not resent his refusal to accompany them on occasional jaunts to Karachi.

!

I don't think.

A 'profound meditation,' that.
If I had any side, they would knock off what they call my 'block'. Sides are very expensive and dangerous parts, for light-weights.

LURE OF THE DESERT.

KARACHI he never visits. Instead, he goes, when off duty, to the edge of the desert with a pocket full of cigarettes purchased out of his daily pay of a few shillings.

There he chats with the villagers, and joins in their profound Eastern meditations.

'edge of the desert'. Man we're in the middle of it, anyway! Only unluckily I have never smoked!

3 shillings is a few, perhaps: too few, if so.

Knowing not one word of any Indian language; but I suppose they talk English: if there is a village. I haven't seen one.

Punk, that is. Villagers in all countries have their thoughts centering on those parts of their bodies which lie, as the Arabs say, between the navel and the knee. Food and sex: and I don't meditate, not even profoundly, about either.

Dear Blumenfeld, Tell your bright young thing that it's a rotten effort. I could do better than that in my sleep. I hope he'll be content, however, to forget it. I'll promise, in return, not to write fancies about him.

India, or Karachi at any rate, is a dust-heap. For Karachi read 'Drigh Road' seven miles outside the town, where our aerodrome lies. I have not been outside the camp since I got here, so the dimensions of the dust heap, to which (by which, and at which) I swear, are one mile by one mile and a quarter. If it's a fair sample of India, then so much the better is England.

The climate is astonishing. Never hot enough for a sun-helmet, never cool enough for an overcoat. If it is ever brought near England by an air service, the poor old Riviera will pack up. Twelve months of an Italianate spring!

Not being very fond of Italy I'll relish my life sentence to England, when the good gods give it me in 1931. Indeed, it will be very good. I don't care if it snows and rains and floods and freezes.

If anybody else writes a book about me I'll kill him, painlessly and naturally, but very quickly. Nor will I ever write another book about myself. That *Revolt* made £17,000 by the way, for the royalty owner, who wasn't me! Good going. It's dead now.

Please remind your wolves, on the 1st of each year, that 'Colonel Lawrence' is on the *Daily Express* Black List, and never to be mentioned: and then you may believe me Your very sincere

T. E. SHAW.

340: TO SYDNEY COCKERELL

2. 2. 28   [*Karachi*]

Dear Cockerell, I've sat staring at your letter for a week: the rest of the Hardy story was so plain there to see. I feel very much for Mrs. Hardy who remains like a plant which has grown up in a pot, from which the pot is suddenly stripped. She will find it hard to begin life again, the third time. For T.H. none of us can have great regrets. His life was a triumph, just because it was prolonged for that last, unexpected, twenty years. It must be restfuller, too, to be certainly dead, than to be precariously alive.

Remains the problem of the D.G.H. Doughty book.[1] It is that which out-faces me. I can live, easily, as an airman (but *easily* only as that). I could die, I hope, willingly, as T.H. would die: but when it comes to writing, writing responsibly, then I dither.

It is out of the question that I should write the Hogarth-Doughty tribute you picture to yourself. My writing is bad: and I'll do no more of it. Agreed that however bad it was the public would buy it, if signed: look at the publicity I've had. But I'd rather starve than feed myself that way: and I think it would be better for the widows to starve than be fed that way. Moral prostitution; no else.

What I had feared was that circumstances might point me out as the one person to oversee and smoothen D.G.H's draft chapters: and that if I did much to them I might put a page or two on the back saying what D.G.H. was, and how sorry a botch

---

[1] Hogarth's life of Doughty had been left unfinished. It was completed by Hogarth's son.

any successor would have made of his improving: and so I'd taken it up, without experience, hoping that people would easily see my patches in his masonry, & blame any unsightlinesses in the construction on the guilty shoulders. But if Armstrong puts his oar and his name to the book, then my anonymity becomes impossible. It would be unfairly ascribed to him. Three names on a title page are ridiculous. So do, for heaven's sake, call the whole job off. I'm sorry you have found the text so incomplete. I'd been hoping that it would smoothly round off the life of D.G.H: by bringing him back to letters, in the end. Yours

T.E.S.

341 : TO COLONEL A. P. WAVELL

9. 2. 28   [*Karachi*]

Dear Wavell, I am reading your book,[1] and liking it very much. My first vanity, when I got it, was to look up myself in the index! I apologise for this: but so many people have either overdone or underdone the Arab business that it's a real pleasure to see a fair statement of the case; so I take back my apology. You have thrown several of your rare flowers at my person: this wasn't necessary, you know! The author has only too good an opinion, already, of his rotten prose. I haven't, of course, yet got very far. Indeed I've only turned it over and read the tit-bits: they have left me with a sharp appetite for it all: and as leisure serves me I'm going right through, checking each move with the map. I fancy there will be more lessons in the Palestine Campaigns than in the French ones. I hope you have kept the enemy always in the picture. War-books so often leave them out: and neither Liman nor Kress is very palatable.[2] No, India is not good. We are seven miles from Karachi. I have passed a lot of self-denying ordinances, one of which keeps me within camp-bounds, another forbids me the canteen, a third prevents my ever sitting down on another bed than my own. Imagine me as a plaster saint: but

---

[1] *The Palestine Campaigns.*
[2] Liman von Sanders and Kress von Kressenstein, German generals with the Turkish army.

even that wasn't enough. [44 *words omitted*] Salmond, knowing
that, stepped in and saved me. So all is well, & my conduct sheet
still white. If I'm lucky it will be England in 1930. The only
decent thing about India is the climate here: never cold enough
for an overcoat, or hot enough for a sun-helmet. A marvellous
relief after Arabia and Egypt.

I'm glad you have the mechanical side to play with. It will
completely change the face of future tactics, I think and hope.
The abolition of the rifle, shall we say? A very good riddance.
Give my regards to Barty and Clayton,[1] if you meet them some
while.

That fat-head [*name omitted*] is going to write a book against
Gertrude & me. Cat & puppy, it was. Will he call us soul-
affinities! Fat-head again to him.

Very many thanks indeed for the book. I'll try to write to
you again, when I've done it justice, so far as reading-time goes.

T.E.SHAW.

342: TO D. G. PEARMAN[2]

[Karachi]

Dear Pearman, This not a statement. There is nothing I
wish to say. The consequences of what we did are going forward: and we have only the duty of spectator. Too much is
being said.

However, if you are committed to saying more, then I hope
you'll stress the *local* nature of the Arab Revolt. The Arabic-
speaking peoples are as diverse as the English-speaking and
equally distinct. From Morocco to Mesopotamia is as far,
spiritually, as from San Francisco to Aberdeen. Further there's a
world between the Beduin at Azrak, and the peasant at Amman:
— though the journey is only fifty miles. Only a criminal would
wish to make them all alike.

Our aim was to free from Turkey, and make self-governing,
not the Beduin, who have a secure, unenvied freedom: but the

---

[1] Generals Bartholomew and Clayton.

[2] An officer who served with the Headquarters of Colonel Buxton's Camel Corps and has
published two sets of lantern slides of the Arab Revolt with Newton & Co., London.

settled peoples of Syria and Irak. To avoid upsetting places like Egypt and Algiers, the Arab Movement had to be kept within these dykes. In the Middle East religion has completely yielded to nationalism as the motive in politics. So our job was relatively easy.

When people talk of Arab confederations or empires, they talk fantastically. It will be generations, I expect — unless the vital tempo of the East is much accelerated — before any two Arabic states join voluntarily. I agree their only future hope is that they should join but it must be a natural growing-together. Forced unions are pernicious: and politics, in such things, should come after geography & economics. Communications & trade must be improved before provinces can join.

The nearest approach to an Arab Empire at present is Ibn Saud's. It is a figment, built on sand. Nothing static will rise in the desert, which has seen hundreds of such tyrannies as his, all cemented (less liberally, perhaps) with blood. It will pass.

The only places where Arabic governments are being attempted today are Hejaz, Yemen, Irak, and Egypt. Of these Hejaz is better under Ibn Saud than it was under Hussein. Hussein was a legacy of the war. We were in his debt, for armed help, and couldn't (can't) say all our detestation of his misgovernment. I was glad beyond words when he went. Ali, his son, was a decent fellow, who did not deserve his father's legacy of hostility with Ibn Saud. But of course he went out. I do not think that Hejaz can ever become a great place. Interesting though.

Irak is the most hopeful spot. It has done wonders since 1921, when Winston started it: or re-founded it. The war-administration there was not profitable either to us or to the Irakis.

Syria should have been better, just at first, than Irak, for its people were more advanced & more experienced. But the French after turning out Feisal refused a single central government of all but Lebanon: and broke it into four. So tiny a place cannot afford five administrations. Eventually it will find such another solution as Irak: but you can gauge the good fortune of England in having had Winston Churchill as its Colonial Secretary in 1921, by comparing the cost of Irak, since then, with the cost of Syria: and the happiness of Irak with the misery of Syria. French pride is engaged, and they refuse to learn by their mistakes. We turned over a new leaf, after Curzon went.

Do make clear to your lads, whoever they are, that my objects were to save England, & France too, from the follies of the imperialists, who would have us, in 1920, repeat the exploits of Clive or Rhodes. The world has passed by that point. I think, though, there's a great future for the British Empire as a voluntary association: and I'd like it to have Treaty States on a big scale attached to it. We've lots of Treaty States now, from Nepal downwards: let's have Egypt and Irak, at least, to add to them. We are so big a firm that we can offer unique advantages to smaller businesses to associate with us: if we can get out attractive terms of association.

There, is this the sort of bilge you wanted? Do with it anything you think useful. What a far cry between us since Azrak. I'd like another bathe in those pools: flies & all. Yours sy

T. E. SHAW.

343: TO MRS. THOMAS HARDY

16. 2. 28   [*Drigh Road, Karachi*]

Dear Mrs. Hardy, I'm afraid I wrote you a very poor letter, the day I heard that T.H. was gone. But just then the news struck me almost as a triumph. He had kept it up to the very end: and was through with an existence he had not highly valued. It may be rest, afterwards: whereas for you I could only see present sorrow, and a sense of want. So I was sorrier for you than for myself: indeed hardly sorry for my own loss, at all.

Since then of course I've been reading *The Dynasts*, and I can feel that there is a very great thing gone from my reach. T.H. was the most honourable stopping place I've ever found, and I shall miss him more and more. I wonder if you will be like that: or if time will make the being alone easier for you. Yours ever

T E SHAW

Mrs. Shaw, who was at the Abbey, sent me a wonderful account of it. I expect you saw and heard nothing. These bodies of ours are very tiring silly things.

344: TO EDWARD GARNETT

15.3.28.   [*Drigh Road, Karachi*]

Dear Garnett, I have today posted (as yesterday I finished) the R.A.F. notes.[1] They will come to you, round about through the parcel mail, in some ten days; I sent them by an official by-pass, for safety; as there is no copy, and the making this long manuscript has hurt my eyes exceedingly. I never want to write a thing again.

The notes eventually worked out at 70,000 words: the Uxbridge part was 50,000: and I added 20,000 on Cranwell, (built up out of contemporary letters and scraps of writing which I'd hoarded against such a need) to redress the uniform darkness of the Depot picture. Cranwell was a happy place.

Will you let me hear of their safe arrival to your hand? If the first receiver does not put on stamps, and you have to pay, let me know that also. I have no English stamps here, and this is a gift to you: a very overdue gift. Was it 1923 I promised you the things? So very sorry.

This afternoon I am going out into the desert with some paraffin and the original draft, to make sure that no variant survives, to trouble me as those two editions of *The Seven Pillars* do. So before you get it your copy will be unique.

I think they fit their little book very tightly and well. I imagined the final size of them, from the draft, and had de Coverley bind me up the book, in the simplest blue morocco. It is the blue we wear, and you can imagine the tooling is our brass buttons. If I'd thought of it I'd have had six buttons down the front, like me.

Every word has been four times written: the original (bed-made) note: the pencil draft: a typed copy, to give me a clearer view: and then this inked version. So even if you do not like it, you will know that it is not because I have spared the pains to make it worth your acceptance.

I want it offered to Cape, for publication, in extenso, without one word excised or moderated. Can you, as his reader, arrange this? I'd rather no one read it but you (and David G. who feels

[1] *The Mint.*

rather like your second edition, revised and corrected by the author, but less spontaneous): and I want him to refuse it, so as to free me from the clause in his contract of the *Revolt in the Desert*, tying me to offer him another book. I hate being bound by even an imaginary obligation.

There: it's over. Six months hard correction and copying, all additional to my seven-hour R.A.F. day, and all done in barracks. Surely there should be actuality in its phrasing and feeling? Yours ever   T.E.S.

345: TO EDWARD GARNETT

22. 3. 28.   [*Karachi*]

Dear Garnett, An old friend of mine, Fontana, sent me two chapters (one on Moharram, in Constantinople, the other on an earthquake there, while in a Turkish Court House) out of a book of reminiscences he'd written on Turkey of 30-40 years ago. They seemed to me to be really good writing. I believe Cape turned them down. Am I wrong or was he?

Williamson has sent me a book of his, *The Old Stag*: stories. He seems pleased over what I said of *Tarka*.[1] But he has written a great deal. If I'd known he was so practised I wouldn't have dared write him. I haven't yet read *The Old Stag*. I lie about the earth, like a crust of dung, doing pretty nearly nothing.

Last week I sent you two letters, which was excessive: but I realised, too late, that my R.A.F. notes might be called another book by those who hadn't tried to read them. Actually, they're in an emotional and intellectual short-hand: a précis of the stuff that might have been fused into a book by some writer of the scale and calibre of Kipling. Hopeless for my dregs to do anything with them, now. I fear you will be dreadfully disappointed. I hope Garnett III will be. He jumped off, so soon as I told him of them, with the idea that I was becoming a professional writer! That made me laugh, rather crookedly, on the sorrowful side of

---

[1] On January 20th, 1928, Lawrence had written Edward Garnett a letter of nearly 5000 words almost entirely about Henry Williamson's book *Tarka The Otter*, which he criticized line by line.

my mouth. The worst part of the show is that people tell me how very good my failures are. It shows by how low a standard we judge the work of everyday.

The Trenchard letter will explain itself to you.[1] If he asks for the notebook, it will be out of curiosity only. My handwriting will easily defeat him. Probably you're the only person who'll ever read it all.

Besides him, you, and D. Garnett, Mrs. Shaw has seen some of it. I sent her two batches of the third draft, which is very like your text: only a little rougher. My re-working was no more than planing. The notes were like a rough plank: and here in Karachi I smoothed them, very carefully, to make it possible to handle without splinters and things coming away. Every sentence of the original was used: and very little was added: no significant addition, certainly. Just enough lubricant to make the thing work. Metaphor upon metaphor mixed! I wish I could lie down and sleep for ever.   T.E.S.

Why do I hurry to tell you, so repeatedly, that they are only notes? Perhaps to discount to my own always hoping expectation your inevitably unfavourable judgement. I know it's no good: but I don't like people to say so. Until these there might have been a hope for it.

I think I will print cards 'to announce cessation of non-business correspondence': and send them to every address I can remember, at the rate of 20 a week.[2]

346: TO EDWARD GARNETT

14. 4. 28.   [Karachi]

[9 lines omitted] Opinions are not worth much: they are too subjective. There is no absolute, and therefore no criticism. As you say, I tend to go Tolstoyan with years: I now like H. G. Wells better than Norman Douglas: and call Kipling better than

---

[1] Lawrence had sent Edward Garnett, on March 17th, a duplicate of the letter which he posted to Trenchard that day, explaining how he had come to write *The Mint*, and that it would not be published.

[2] See letter No. 564.

Crackanthorpe:[1] just because their carelessness gives me a sense of power. They feel they have gold to throw away. The stylists are too miserly. Agreed I am a bad example of the too-careful type. [32 *lines omitted*]   T.E.S.

347: TO WILLIAM ROTHENSTEIN

14. 4. 28.   [*Karachi*]

Dear Rothenstein, Yes, I was a sudden loser when Hardy went. Not that I could be a friend of his: the difference in size and age and performance between us was too overwhelming: but because I'd seen a good deal of him, and he was so by himself, so characteristic a man, that each contact with him was an experience. I went each time, nervously: and came away gladly, saying 'It's all right'. That's the spirit in which most of us R.A.F. fellows go up into the air. We are always glad to get down again: yet no consideration would keep us (will keep us) from snatching the first chance to fly once more.

I regret Hardy's funeral service. Mrs. Shaw sent me a copy. So little of it suited the old man's nature. He would have smiled, tolerantly, at it all: but I grow indignant for him, knowing that these sleek Deans and Canons were acting a lie behind his name. Hardy was too great to be suffered as an enemy of their faith: so he must be redeemed. Each birthday the Dorchester clergyman would insert a paragraph telling how his choir had carolled to the old man 'his favourite hymn'. He was mild, and let himself be badgered, out of local loyalty. 'Which hymn would you like for to-morrow Mr. Hardy?'. 'Number 123' he'd snap back, wearied of all the nonsense: and that would be his favourite of the year, in next day's *Gazette*.

I wish these black-suited apes could once see the light with which they shine.

I wonder if Max is right in saying that women write good letters: good for their men perhaps: but Byron and Keats and Horace Walpole and Chesterfield are not to be matched by any four women's letter writing I've read. Perhaps he means of un-

---

[1] Hubert Crackanthorpe, short story writer of the nineties.

published letters: the sort that do not get into print. But even
there I think he would be wrong. There are few good letter-
writers, I fancy: as few as there are good sonnetteers: for the same
reason: that the form is too worn to be easy, and there are too
many who try. It's a less crowded profession, is epic poetry: and
that's why there are few bad epics.

I saw Robert Bridges three or four times, while I was at Cranwell and Bovington. A rarely attractive being: always on the
tips of his toes, and so distinct from the crowd. Even that hill-top
garden isn't rare enough for his setting. But I like his music
room. Sassoon was very happily inspired when he gave him that
Dolmetsch clavichord. Will you remember me to him, if you
write again? I liked him, and he was kind to me.

Hogarth *shone* in Oxford, because he was humane, and knew
the length and breadth of human nature, and understood always,
without judging. Oxford seems to me a quite ordinary fire-less
town, now he is gone. He was like a great tree, a main part of
the background of my life: and till he fell I hadn't known how
much he had served to harbour me.

It is interesting that G.B.S. sits again to you. He is beclouded,
like Hardy and Kipling, with works which tend to live more
intensely than their creator. I doubt whether you can now see
him: you know too much. His best chance would be to find
some foreign artist who did not know his face; and to be painted
by him as 'Sir George Bernard'. So perhaps we would know what
he would have been if he had not written. Lately I've been
studying *Heartbreak House*: whose first act strikes me as metallic,
inhuman, supernatural: the most blazing bit of genius in English
literature. I'd have written that first, if I had choice.

Kennington, and John: both hag-ridden by a sense that perhaps their strength was greater than they knew. What an uncertain, disappointed barbarous generation we war-timers have
been. They said the best ones were killed. There's far too much
talent yet alive.

Two pages of nonsense: for your three sheets. I am in your
debt. But deserts do not produce any social grace. Yours,

T. E. SHAW.

348: TO H. H. BANBURY[1]

14. 4. 28.   [*Karachi*]

I'm writing to everybody this week. For months letters have been rolling in: now they are knee deep. Nine in ten have answered themselves by mere lapse of time (the simplicity of it!). The balance are for it, instantly.

Your *Tarka*, the otter book, has not yet come along. Someone borrowed it. Dozens of my books go out, that way. I am, as they put it, easy. Patience. It is a good book.

I hope you will not have too much fighting. It's all right from behind armour-plating: but I bar the open-air stunt.

[*3 lines omitted*]

The last Montague (*Right off the Map*) was technically admirable, but carping in spirit. I thought it did not do him much honour. After *Fiery Particles* and *Disenchantment* he should have been large minded, always.

I haven't an *Arabia Deserta*: but *The Seven Golden Poems* are very famous. We call them *The Moallakat* — the things that were hung up — presumably at Mekka in the great temple before Mohammed came. They are seven in number, and quite peculiar in form. Imr el kais wrote the jolliest of the seven: but Lebid is good, and Antar, and parts of Tarafa. It was Tarafa who likened Death to a blind camel lounging about in the dark.

There is a Lahore edition, in Arabic, interlined with an English translation by a Colonel Johnson, I think it was (twenty years since I saw the book).[2] The English was rather halting, so you had to peer and guess at the beauty of the Arabic lines.

There is a good translation, into English poetry, by Wilfrid Blunt, a great old man who died lately. His wife, Lady Anne, was an Arabic scholar. She made a prose translation: and Wilfrid, who could speak some Arabic, and liked Arabs, put them into very fine verse. I do not know how far it is at present obtainable in England. The Chiswick Press published them then, as a separate book, and later of course they were included in the two-

---

[1] Regimental Sergeant Major, Royal Tank Corps.

[2] This literal translation was published at Bombay. Lawrence had a copy at Oxford after the war, and it was among his books when he died.

volume collected edition of Blunt's poetry. But neither can be said to be an easy book to find.

The Moallakat are pagan: pre-Moslem desert verse; sometimes warlike, sometimes sententious, sometimes prosy, sometimes humourous. There is a queer vividness and sense of life about e.g. Amr el Kais' one. Whether the seven poems were really written by seven poets or not, Heaven alone knows. They are on one model; and feel much the same to me: but are vastly different in spirit.

There is much early Arabic poetry. You get snatches of it, (very brief and occasional) in Gertrude Bell's *Desert and the Sown*, a vivid, appealing book: and Nicholson's big work[1] has a lot more: and Lyall has translated some: but you know how difficult it is to translate mannered foreign verse into English easy-go-here and there. Only a Fitzgerald once greatly succeeded. Though Blunt has done well. The shorter poems sing, with an intensity which is almost a wail and a sob, at their climaxes. Not *The Moallakat*. They are formal performances. Imr and his girl ate a camel by the pools of Jelajil and pelted each other with strips of its fat! As formal a story as the deed was informal.

The seven poems put together wouldn't make fifty pages of medium print. Quite short. If I have a chance I'll get some private press to reprint them. Sometimes they ask me for poems (of my own!) and I reply with good advice if I feel kindly. T.E.S.

[On December 6th, 1927, Colonel Isham had written from New York to say 'Bruce Rogers has been commissioned by a firm of publishers to arrange for a new translation of Homer's *Odyssey* and to design the book for them . . . Can you and will you undertake it? If you will do so, the publishers will pay you a minimum of £800 . . .[2] You will be glad to know it is not your name they want but your translation.'

On March 4th the famous American typographer wrote a very long letter dealing with the proposal in detail and discussing many other matters, to which Lawrence replied in the following letter.]

---

[1] A History of Arabic Literature.   [2] See postscript to letter No. 360.

349: TO BRUCE ROGERS

16/4/28.   *R.A.F., Karachi, India.*

You start off 'Dear Shaw', so I should say Dear Rogers, or
Bruce Rogers; for we always think of you as a diphthong. Only
it sounds like presumption. If I've been a myth to you, you've
been an exemplar and ambition to everyone who's fond of books.
The difference between you and private presses is that many of
your works are fit for ordinary sale; a more difficult achievement
than doing something de luxe. However we mustn't swap compli-
ments all day.

Two or three times, in the ten days since your letter came, I've
tried to write to you. Something about this *Odyssey* effort frightens
me. It's too big: Homer is very very great: and so far away. It
seems only a sort of game, to try and bring him down to the
ordinary speech of my mouth. Yet that is what a translation
ought to mean. I do it, tacitly, every time I read him: but that is
for my own belly. Isn't there a presumption in putting my
version abroad?

True that the work will be seen by every right-eyed person as
typography, pure and simple. Your medium will hide all its sins.
Only I'd like my work to be worthy of the dress: and I feel sure
it cannot be. Some writers have called my *Seven Pillars* good.
Others (fewer, but I can't help thinking them the more choice
judgements) have said that far from being good, it is very very
bad: perverse, dishonest, pretentious. I suspect they are right,
though I did try, with the better side of me, to play fair and clean
in the writing of it. Only we are all such mixtures, that it would
be a miracle of self-suppression to be good all through.

However, granted that *The Seven Pillars* is not wholly con-
temptible, as prose. I can concede that much, I think. Isn't that
relative goodness due to the heat of my engagement in the Arab
business, and the obligation, the absolute obligation upon me,
to put my share, and the other fellows' share in it, into print?
Can I expect to make a decent thing of a translation of the
Odyssey, undertaken because I want money, and would be
flattered by being printed by you, and like Homer? I like Homer
for myself, and will like him less well if I make a task of copying

him out: and I shan't have any great hope that my labour will open him to anyone yet strange to him.

The Palmer version duly arrived. It is very wholesome, and very loving. Do you think I'll do better? I'd suggest you get a lien on Palmer, in case my sample book is notably less worthy of preservation. Preservation I say ... I mean canonization or apotheosis or whatever is the process of being printed by you. It's amazing you are not a millionaire. You must have refused to chase money with your best legs. It doesn't come to the half-hearted about it. At least I've never caught any: and I've lost wonderful chances of making enough to invest and live on, for good. If bread and butter were assured me for the term of my life, without working for it, how eagerly I could give up this dullness of working every day. Yet I really like the Royal Air Force, and am happy in its ranks, when they leave me unmolested — which is oftener, far, than were I earning a living in civil life.

Isham's first letter about it gave me a wrong idea. I thought some plutocrat publisher was backing you, regardless: the price he offered was so fantastic; and so I thought 'Let's spoil the American' ... a word which many hotel-keepers and others in Europe have often today in their hearts.

Isham hasn't yet written again: but I see from your letter that you have nothing cut and dried. I do not want to spoil you; nor would I if you were as rich as Mellon: because you are B.R.

So let's regard the offer as withdrawn; and do you figure out what you think the proposition can fairly stand, as translator's fee, and I'll tell you if I can do it. No time is being lost, for I have to change camp very soon, and the move will be a wasted month. It's unsettling, to move: and I have to look round the new place for a quiet corner to read in. If I have any chance, till your answer comes, I'll spend it playing with the first book. It is difficult to avoid affecting a style of some sort, in doing Homer.

The anonymity is the rub, of course: but I want to do my best to maintain it. Indeed I'd go so far as to refrain from writing it if I saw the thing was ever likely to be brought home to me. Why shouldn't I send the stuff to you, as it is done, and the Publishers have no dealings whatever with me? There will, as you rightly say, be no interest in the book, except as typography[1]: that is as it should be, for it will be superbly printed: and *not* superbly translated. No one is ever likely to ask you who was your scribe.

Or the second idea you had, of finding some very rich man to undertake the whole expense . . . that would solve the publicity question? What he would want is a genuine B.R. book: and he wouldn't care whether you printed Dutch or gibberish, so long as it was as good as possible, on the page.

Anonymity is, in my eyes, worth sacrificing a very large proportion of the translator's fee, to obtain. Will you please, with this in view, talk it over with the very rich man; and if he does not embrace your proposition, ask your publisher friends if they are willing to take the stuff from you, without asking questions, or answering them? I can invent a name for copyright purposes, if such is necessary: though I can't imagine anyone wanting to pirate a Homer!

I have not seen your *Persephone*.[2] You must remember that I have now been six years in the ranks, and comparatively bookless all that while. We are oily, when we are not dirty, and no good book should ever come near us. All camp property is common, and so all books are ruined in a few weeks. Therefore I will beg of you not to send me any of yours, however recent: I have quite a number of your pre-1922 works, in a friend's house in London. I have not seen them for years, and will not for years: because I can't have them with me, and so I'd rather not have them, at all, even near me. But if you have any spoils or sheets, I'd like them very much. Before I finished my *Seven Pillars* I'd begun to see some of the first difficulties of printing.

You'll find it hard to gather much Mycenaean ornament:[3] however Minoan is a cousin, and there are other varieties of island Greek, which are at least as Homeric. Homer is more an aspiration than a person. I aspire most fervently in him . . . but we know even less of him than of Shakespeare.

Leading is a very good way of clearing a page — if you can afford the space. I was cramming too long a book into 650 pages

---

[1] Bruce Rogers tells me that he has no recollection of ever saying this.
[2] By John Drinkwater; limited edition designed by Bruce Rogers.
[3] To embellish his edition of the Odyssey.

when I printed mine. Two-volume books are clumsy things.
Why some people condemn leading I can't conceive.

My capital letters were designed by Edward Wadsworth, a
very fine artist, for John Rodker, who prints in England. He did
not use them, so I bought them off him for a copy of my book.
Wadsworth did A–W. I had X Y and Z done by Hughes-Stanton
to complete the alphabet (W[adsworth] was abroad, at the time,
and couldn't carry on) and exhausted my ingenuity to bring in
each letter at least once. Rodker would probably send them you:
or Wadsworth (who is rich) do you another set, if you really liked
them. I thought them uncommonly new and delightful.

The Hewlett pages you typed out for me are fascinating. The
introduction says exactly what I'd like to say to everybody who
reads or writes translations; and the verse pages are wonderful.
I can't do anything like that. Hewlett was really a fine poet: I
have seen a trilogy (classical)[1] and a volume of short pieces
(*Artemesia*?)[2] and an epic of peasant life . . . a sort of Georgic . . .[3]
and they were all the real thing. He was also a good prose writer
and a charming critic. His monthly reviews in the *London
Mercury* were the best-reading criticisms of their time. So his
Iliad is, naturally, the best yet. I can see that, even from the
fragment you send. What a pity he never finished it.

I cannot write blank verse . . . at least, I have never yet written
a line of poetry in my life . . . and I don't feel that Homer is the
thing to begin on. So if you ask me to do anything, remember
that it will be prose. Remember too that Morris said prose made
a squarer page.

Amharic writes itself superbly: but I doubt whether the
Abyssinian classics (rather dull church folk-lore, in my acquaintance with them) would repay the beauties of their letters. Nor are
there wealthy patrons: nor any reading public!

To print a first book of the translation, as a high-priced
pamphlet to finance the whole, might be possible: but wouldn't
that raise talk?

There, I think this has glanced at all the things you wrote to
me about. I want to do it, and am afraid: but can get over that
difficulty by doing the sample book for you. I want to be

---

[1] *The Agonists.*   [2] *Artemision.*   [3] *The Song of the Plow.*

anonymous: and value this above a big fee. I know that my writing without my name isn't worth much. In London I can get it published, just: (not always) and they pay me about 30/- a thousand words, at the best, for it. This fact may put my literary gift in its proper perspective, in your eyes! Yours ever,

T.E.SHAW.

350: TO H. S. EDE

16.4.28.   [*Karachi*]

Dear Ede, I am ink-less for the afternoon, and wasting my time, watching over some Aryan brothers who are working. So to fill the void I am scribbling letter after letter. That is not a good way of doing things.

Aitken has disappointed me.[1] I had confidently expected him to report the loss of 13,364 Turner water-colour studies, and all the withdrawn Chantrey purchases. Never has a Gallery had such a chance since Julius Caesar failed to weed out the Library at Alexandria. To his anonymous assistant we owe the selective perfection of Greek literature. The past (just-past) reputation of English art hovered for a moment, a timid butterfly in Aitken's hand: and escaped. Assure him that Nelson was not scrupulous, either in love or war, though he talked much of duty. Assure him also that the mutilations are the chief beauty of the sculpture in the B.M. Knock the Derwent-wooden nose off my bust some day, in Your Great Hall: and see what a fine thing will remain, after the caretaker has swept up.

I'll look forward to seeing your Brancusi bit, some day. Dobson showed me photographs of his work, and they were just right: but I have never seen any one in the round: and sculpture never seems 'it' unless you can imaginatively put your hands round it, back and front, and feel the solidity in between. You'll observe I talk like a grocer, selling butter. Don't expect a perfectly natural airman to know what planes and plastic values and significant forms are. When a man starts talking to me of impastos I say epicyclic gears at him: and a slow fog of mis-understanding creeps between us.

[1] See letter No. 335.

So many plasticians seem to admit to their notice the outside of machinery, and to exclude its purposefulness, which is to put the skin before the will.

I hope that the Gallery has now re-opened, and restored itself, as the best art entertainment in London. You may feel that it's hopelessly slow and cloggy: but I confess that Frys and Ivor Churchills and Courtaulds[1] do not sum up more than the yesterday of expression, in my backward regard. It makes me smile, sometimes, to think that all the varying pictures produced in 1928 will all date themselves, by some subtlety of likeness to 1928, in the eyes of 2028. Yet today we are hardly on speaking terms.

Of pictures and sculpture I'm not talking, now, but of the writing gangs: the Joyces and the Kiplings, the Steins and Wells, the Forsters and D. H. Lawrences: they will all date within 20 years, by some yet-imperceptible solidarity. There will be a common thread between T. S. Eliot and Alfred Noyes.

Your letter of Feb. 4 was particularly ripe, and fertile. 'Clean and clear, hard and cold and BALD' Yes: I think that's a good ambition: (if bald be taken metaphorically. My hair is particularly thick, most unsmart and unairmanlikely thick, at the moment. A thatch against the sun.) In writing nearly everybody tries for hardness and clearness: but the unconscious drag all the while is to cover up. A negro might make quite uncovered things, if he and his people had never thought of clothes: but for a clothed race to be deliberately naked in art intention is to be ever so unnatural. We should not, in thought, pass the bounds we set ourselves in deed: or our ideas will not ring true. And to live bald and hard and clean: ah; that's beyond a fellow's power, except he be solitary. In the ranks of the R.A.F. we get very near it, for the oppression of discipline makes us unable to pretend amongst ourselves, to be better than just ordered bodies: and our outward sameness of dress means that we wear no clothes at all: but not even here do you get a community of understanding.

You say too that my circle centres bit by bit on myself: and therefore turns faster and is dangerous. People who lived in

---

[1] Roger Fry, the critic, Lord Ivor Churchill and Samuel Courtauld have made famous collections of works of art.

Nitrea, in the old days, to fight down the world, did grow their eyes inward: only inside me is too vacant a place to take much exploring. I live, happily enough, just spending and taking the small coin of our trivial working-days. If a fellow has to live in his flight, and wants to, why, soon the edge of the flight is his horizon. All the world frets and tries: and in the end we level off, thankfully enough. I'm trying to get a little bit of that contentment, while I'm still alive. Yours ever,   T.E.S.

351 : TO MRS. THOMAS HARDY

16. 4. 28   [*Karachi*]

Dear Mrs. Hardy, You should not have bothered to answer my letters: you know that these letters to the person left behind when someone dies are such vain, inadequate things.

One thing in your letter pleases me very much: you say you have failed him at every turn. Of course you did: everybody did. He was T.H. and if you'd met him or sufficed him at every turn you'd have been as good as T. H. which is absurd: though perhaps some people might think it should be put happier than that. But you know my feeling (worth something perhaps, because I've met so many thousands of what are estimated great men) that T.H. was above and beyond all men living, as a person. I used to go to Max Gate afraid, & half-unwillingly, for fear that perhaps it would no longer seem true to me: but always it was. Ordinary people like us can't hope (mustn't presume to hope) that we could ever have been enough for T.H. You did every thing you could: more than any other person did: surely that's not a bad effort? You thought him worth more: I agree: but life doesn't allow us an overdraft of service. We can give just all we've got.

The biography is a very difficult thing. They will trouble you very much about that. Do not let these troubles go in too far. What he told you, on November 28, that he'd done all he meant to do, absolves you from infinite toil. He will defend himself, very very completely, when people listen to him again. As you know, there will be a wave of detraction, and none of the high-brows will defend him, for quite a long time: and then the bright

young critics will rediscover him, & it will be lawful for a person
in the know to speak well of him: and all this nonsense will
enrage me, because I'm small enough to care. Whereas all that's
needful is to forget the fuss for fifty years, and then wake up and
see him no longer a battle-field, but part of the ordinary man's
heritage.

You say something about giving me something that was his.
You'll remember I have an inscribed *Dynasts*, which is suffering
the Indian climate. After all, I am, too; and so must the book.
I don't want to lock up a treasure against a day of enjoyment
which may never come: but if you really have anything else, then
please keep it for me, if you will be so good. It will be to fall
back upon, if some white ant, or flood or accident robs me of this
one which I have. Only I feel that his older friends have so much
more right. I only came at the eleventh hour.

Please do not answer all this: it's just me talking to you, as I
used to do in Max Gate, while we waited for him to come down.
I wish I hadn't gone overseas: I was afraid, that last time, that it
was the last. Yours ever   T E SHAW

352 : TO E. M. FORSTER

16 4 28   [*Karachi*]

Dear E.M.F., Forgive the pencil. I am inkless this afternoon.

Don't cut me off from anything you may write in future,
because you've sent me one supremely good thing.[1] I've liked
everything you've written: some of it very much, some of it less:
but liked it all. I've tried to write, myself, and know that a man
doesn't ever succeed in mating sound and sense and expectation.
We land, always, other than we meant to land. That's presumably the fun as well as the vexation of writing. Your less-
good work is very helpful to me, as an amateur of writing: for
our minds are parallel enough for me to see your intention behind
the expression, (or to flatter myself that I do partly and in some
senses see it . . . oh shades of Henry James in this style of letter!)

[1] An unpublished story.

PP

and just because it may not completely come off, so I may be able to see the works inside it more clearly.

And I don't expect you to be always at your best. Indeed I once said that it was the mark of a little writer to be very particular about his standard. The big men (of the Balzac, Tolstoi, Dostoevski, Dickens stamp) are incredibly careless, here & now. They seem to have said 'well, it doesn't matter. If the readers can't see what I mean, they needn't'. There's a lavish ease about their stuff: and an agony of carefulness about the Henry James & George Moore & Flaubert class. These are two points of view. I like both lots. But don't, please, stand on ceremony with me. The most beautiful parts of all the best Greek statues are their mutilations.

What news of Posh? He is out of the service, I think, now. If you still hear of him, let me hear of his fortunes: even of his misfortunes. He must strike a smooth place, in living, soon: if he is to keep going at all.

Do not take my illnesses seriously. They are only indispositions: and may be partly due to my refusal to see that I'm too old to lead a boy's life much longer. They do not allow, in the Services, for grown ups ... the whole treatment and regimen is designed for the immature: and physically I'm in decay, however half-baked my mind may be.

Here is a suggestion which I make with great diffidence and regret, for what may seem to you presumption. Long ago, at Uxbridge, I made some notes on life in the ranks. They are crude, unsparing, faithful stuff: very metallic and uncomfortable. Once I meant to make a book of them, by leaving them to sink down into my mind, & then reviving my memory by their aid, to distil something adequate to what is a very large subject: the enlisted-man-in-uniform.

Only the disappointment which the Arabia book's feebleness bred in me knocked all writing hopes on the head. So I told Edward Garnett, father of the David you know, that he should have the original notes, as a relic. My relics are hawked about, you see, and have a money value. Clouds Hill was floored and roofed out of the sale of my golden Mecca dagger![1]

[1] Bought by Lionel Curtis and now in the keeping of the Manciple, All Souls, Oxford.

Lately I sent Garnett his notes: not the originals, which I've just burnt, but a fair copy, rearranging, pointing, linking, dividing the notes. I've taken away, not one adjective, nor one word, nor one idea: but have lengthened by as much again what was almost a literary shorthand, into what I think is a palatable mess. Palatable? well, hardly: it's presumably oatmeal porridge sort-of-stuff: but a man might get through it, if he added the milk of time and the sugar of patience to its body.

David Garnett would probably lend it to you: but O Lord, it's no hospitality to offer to an esteemed friend. Don't choke yourself: don't try to, if porridge and dry bread & dough make you ill in advance. Really to see it is no privilege, & to read it probably pain: but if you send me your imperfections (as I devoutly hope, for they seem to me more meaningful than other people's perfections) I should at least acknowledge to you the existence of writings of mine later & wiser than *The Seven Pillars*.

I want the existence of these notes kept dark; otherwise asses will want to print them, or read them. Mrs. Shaw: the two Garnetts: Trenchard (my sponsor in the R.A.F.) if he wishes to see them: you. I think that is all I care about. It would have been Hogarth too: but he has gone. He was like a parent who had never stopped growing.   T E S.

353: TO EDWARD GARNETT

23. 4. 28.   [*Karachi*]

Your telegram came this morning, most happily. I was on guard all yesterday and so felt pretty much in the dumps. It is a hateful, painful waste of time: everybody comes off guard thoroughly miserable: and all the day after feels wet. Besides, I'd had to make up my mind to get shifted from this place, as a precautionary measure. If I stay, there's a risk of trouble. So I've asked to be sent up country. It may be worse, or it may be better. I lose a lot of books, and music (only gramophone music, but the potted stuff is very well, for people away abroad), and the little conveniences I've arranged myself in the last fifteen months; and begin again. I'm stared at, a good deal, my first month in a new camp.

However the telegram was cheerful. It had my 'Ross' number on it, which excited the Orderly Room: for it was delivered as an official message. I don't know how you sent it. They presumed it was in code, and had a good try at it with their code books: then delivered it to me in despair, wondering if it was mine. I read it in a minute, and was delighted to know that the thing had brought up safely. It took so long to copy out, that I'd have grudged the Post Office its acquisition.

Also I'm delighted that the recipient likes his present. I am very deeply in your debt for advice, and experiences among books, & kindnesses: and I've been wanting for ever so long to make some return. Only being so nearly a pauper, by my own wish and will, I can't easily gratify a particular person. It is like making bricks out of thin air. So it was really kind of you to telegraph.

Do not let your enthusiasm for new notes in writing run away over *The Mint*. It is a new note, I fancy: I've never read any other book of exactly the same character. It is fragmentary, and has the dry baldness of notes: none the worse for that, for *The Seven Pillars* was prolix: and this *Mint* is not long-winded: or not often long-winded. Doubtless it would come down $20°/_0$ with advantage; but in so short a book (is it 80,000 words?) the dozen pages more or less hardly matter: also it isn't a book. It's a note for your private eye: a swollen letter.

It is well-written, I fancy, as prose. The labour of *The Seven Pillars* taught me a good deal about writing: and I have worked very hard at other people's books and methods. So by now I must have acquired the rudiments at least of technique. I'd put *The Mint* a little higher than that: and say that its style well fitted its subject: our dull clothed selves; our humdrum, slightly oppressed, lives; our tight uniforms: the constriction, the limits, the artificial conduct, of our bodies and minds and spirits, in the great machine which the R.A.F. is becoming. I had to hold myself down, on each page, with both hands.

A painted or sentimental style, such as I used in *The Seven Pillars*, would have been out of place in *The Mint*, except in the landscape passages, where I have used it. But I doubt whether any un-versed reader would be able to connect the two books by any tricks of authorship.

The form of the book took a lot of settling. I worked pretty hard at the arrangement of the sections, and their order. Mainly, of course, it follows the course of our training, which was a course: but where I wanted monotony or emphasis, I ran two or three experiences together, and where I wanted variety I joggled 'em up and down. I got all the material out into a skeleton order, and placed it, so near as I could: then I fixed in my own mind the main curves of idea which seemed to arise out of the notes: and re-wrote them with this intention in the back of my mind. So I fancy there are probably hundreds of tiny touches (perhaps only an adjective or a comma) of a tendencious nature, which help to guide your intelligence to the ends I had in view. Only here again I was hampered, as in *The Seven Pillars*, by having true experiences to write about. I took liberties with names, and reduced the named characters of the squad from 50 odd to about 15: else there'd have been too many fellows in the book, and they'd have confused the picture. Otherwise it is exactly true.

Force — oh yes, I expect parts of it are forcible. That's the worst of feeling things as strongly as I do. Only I hope that some of my contentment and satisfaction in the R.A.F. appears, as well as the abuses I saw. So often we tend to take the sweets for granted. That's why I'm hoping that Trenchard won't ask to see it. He sees the R.A.F. from the top, and I see it from the bottom: and each of us, no doubt, thinks he sees straight enough: but I swear I'm as keen on it as he is: and I do all I can, down here, to make it run smoothly. It's only the little unimportant things in the R.A.F. that make airmen's lives sometimes a misery. I itch to tell him of them, and have 'em swept away. He is like a tank when he gets going.

However, it's no use going into all that. You like the booklet: which I made up to please you. Don't let the snare of ownership stifle your judgment. It is not a classic: but the précis of an (unwritten, and never to be written) book: and as it is not to be published, itself, you and I will never be able to check our judgments by public opinion. So: — regard it as a notebook of mine, given to you because you liked my *Seven Pillars*, and because I had no further room nor reason for it. I won't tell you it's rubbish: for I wouldn't have given you what I believed to be rubbish, but it's pretty second-rate, like me and my works: it's the end of my attempts to write, anyhow: but please believe that this inner conviction of the thing's not being good enough only increases the momentary pleasure which I obtain from having you praise it. I'd so like something of my creating to be very good: and I bask for the moment in the illusion of your praise. Very many thanks therefor.   T.E.S.

[On April 10th Trenchard wrote Lawrence a letter showing his regret at the R.A.F. being involved in trying to stop the raiding of Iraq by Ibn Saud's partisans, since people who spent their lives raiding in a traditional manner could not be expected to understand our point of view, and our methods of bombing from the air seemed brutal to them. A more chivalrous and humane letter cannot be imagined.]

354: TO MARSHAL OF THE R.A.F. SIR HUGH TRENCHARD

May 1. 1928.   *Karachi*

THE R.A.F.

[*50 lines omitted*] Please make no mistake here. I've enlisted twice in the British Army, and twice in the Air Force. I've seen from the inside the Turkish and Arab armies, and something of the Navy. The R.A.F. is streets finer, in morale and brains and eagerness, than the lot of them. In ten years it's become the best Service. Agreed it is not perfect. It never will be. We grumble — over trifles, mainly customs of dress which you've inherited from the older services. [*60 lines omitted*]

THE WAHABI BUSINESS

I'm sorry for the Beduin, high-spirited, ignorant animals, led astray by fanatics. Religious theories are the devil, when they are ridden too hard, and begin to dictate conduct.

An accommodation between Ibn Saud and Feisal could be arranged, but would not cure your trouble, at the moment. I don't think they are the main people, or the parties with the initiative. Ibn Saud was a fine company-commander, who's a

bit out of his depth with a battalion. He's trying to bestride
two worlds, the desert and the towns. It has never been done so
far, except episodically. Feisal wanted to attempt it, in 1918: and
I broke him away, then, from the nomads, roughly. I don't
believe you can yet unite, or federate, or crush into one tyranny
even, any two Arabic-speaking districts; *yet*. Ibn Saud can only
recover the Mteir and Ateiba by forgetting the towns, or by
using the towns to crush them. By the first course he loses his
revenue. He's too indebted to the tribes, and I hope too decent
a fellow, to do the second. If you squeeze him he may try to do
it; and will then, I think, break himself — to your loss, for he is
our one real asset in his kingdom.

The fellow you need to influence is Feisal el Dueish, or whoever is the driving force behind the raiders. If I were at Ur, my
instinct would be to walk without notice into his headquarters.
He'd not likely kill an unarmed, solitary man (Arabs are very
curious-minded) and in two days guesting I could give him
horizons beyond the Brethren. He would make a wonderful
border-warden, if he once got out of the ruck. Men of decision
are rare in the Desert and in London.

I beg of you not to order your Political Officer to execute this
suggestion straight away: or Feisal may execute your P.Os.
Such performances require a manner to carry them off. I've
done it four times, or is it five? A windy business. It's only my
primary instinct. To change it into a plan would require local
knowledge, of the situation's details, and the local casualties, and
temper. In the East, if you have your ear right close to the
ground, you hear everything that's happening, and a great deal
more. The selective ear tunes out the false news, and that's the
difference between good politics and bad. [6 *lines omitted*]

Of course there's no danger in the Shamiya situation: it's a
nuisance only. It should not be expensive, unless you try to
meet like with like. Beduin on camels will make a meal of any
civilised camel-corps: or of infantry in the open: or of cavalry
anyhow. Nor does a static defence of a line avail. You need an
elastic defence, in depth of at least 100 miles. Explored tracks for
cars, threading this belt, approved landing-grounds, sited pill-
boxes of blockhouses, occupied occasionally and then fed and

linked by armoured cars, and supervised from the air. Care will open almost the whole desert to motor traffic, and petrol is the tactical key to the situation. I could defend all E. Transjordan with a fist-full of armoured cars, and trained crews. [70 *lines omitted*]

355: TO HIS BROTHER, A. W. LAWRENCE

2.5.28.   [*Drigh Road, Karachi*]

Dear A., I am leaving Karachi soon, for some squadron up-country: and shall not regret going, on the whole. Will let you have my new address, when I have it.

They are nibbling again at the *Odyssey* idea. Hope it comes off.

Do you remember my telling you that you were my heir? There'll be about four pounds to inherit in cash, and £18 in the Bank, and some books, and Clouds Hill (perhaps). Not Pole Hill, which goes to Richards.

Also my copyrights which now no longer include *Revolt in the Desert*: but you will be O.C. *The Seven Pillars*, and the greater controls the less: so that should make up for the disappointment of the preceding paragraph.

I'm not consciously dying yet: I'm detailing these past facts to add a present fact to it. I have written out a clean copy of some notes I made in 1923 at Uxbridge, on a recruit's life in the R.A.F. of the time. They total some 80,000 words, and there-fore amount, pretty well, to another book. Edward Garnett, of 19 Pond Place, Chelsea, is the owner of the manuscript, at present the sole copy. If he has it typed, which he may do, for security's sake, I'll have a copy sent to you. Garnett's son David will presumably inherit from his father, eventually.

The copyright of this MS. of course remains mine, for life: and passes to my heirs, for the statutory period, which I believe is 40 years after death.[1] I will not publish these notes (whose present name is *The Mint*) in my day. And I hope that you will not (without the permission of the Chief of Staff of the R.A.F. for the time being) publish them, if the option is yours, before 1950. They are very obscene.

---

[1] A mistake as to the law of copyright.

Regard these things as possible windfalls for your child. They will not profit you much. What else? You know that John Snow, of Mallam's, the Solicitors, in St. Giles, Oxford, has my will: and that Eliot and Robin Buxton (R.B. c/o Martins Bank, 68, Lombard Street and the Hon. E. Eliot, c/o Kennedy, Ponsonby and Ryde, of Guildhall Chambers, Bishopgate St.) are trustees and owners of *Revolt in the Desert*: and that Eliot has my Power of Attorney, to look after *The Seven Pillars*: and that Richards (V.W.) of 3, Loudoun Road, St. John's Wood, N.W.8., has my books and can explain the situation of Pole Hill.

There, I think all those things are clear. As I say, I'm not conscious of dying: but while I'm informing you of the existence of *The Mint* I'd better put you again informed of the other arrangements. Handy-like, to have it in a nut-shell.   T.E.S

356: TO EDWARD GARNETT

2.5.28.   [*Karachi*]

Dear Garnett, Trenchard seems to have feared that I meant to publish the book, or that you could. I have written and wired to him that you can't, and I won't. So I hope that will make it well. I like Trenchard, to an unlimited degree, and admire him: and wouldn't hurt him for anything. All service men think printing ink is a sort of devil or dragon, threatening them. Trenchard will also be terrified of yourself, as a pen-man. Are not pens mightier than swords? R.A.F. officers carry a little silver-gilt sword, but only in full dress. They fly quite unarmed.

I have told him that in my life-time nothing of *The Mint* will be published: and that I have asked my brother (who is my heir) to with-hold it till at least 1950. That should see us all off the stage.

Eddy Marsh's letter[1] made me laugh. He was called in naturally by Trenchard, for Eddy has a great political reputation as a literary leader. They feel that he, if anyone, can tame the rages of these incalculable creatures and make them safe. Marsh you know of course . . . I've found him sincere always; and he

---

[1] Marsh had written to Garnett on behalf of Trenchard, to arrange a meeting between them.

serves Winston with all his might. Also he is uncommonly kind-hearted, and unofficial, after nearly 30 years in the Civil Service. So he is made of tough stuff, somewhere: though I agree his appearance and manners disguise his material.

Trenchard you will heartily enjoy. He can't write: he can't speak: but he is a very great man. Incidentally he is the R.A.F.

Your bronchitis must have been bad. I know you've had it before, by your own telling: but I didn't know that it kept people a fortnight in bed. My idea of it was a sort of cold in the head, with a stifled voice and inactivity, as its effects. Apparently it is worse. Once it's better is it done with? or is it only a symptom of chest-trouble? I mean, are you better now? or do you have to take care always? It is alarming how ill lots of people I know have been. Hogarth gone, and Hardy: G.B.S. and Mrs. Shaw both ill. Mrs. Wells gone: and lots of the non-public figures, who are my special pleasure. Eighteen months, it is, since I came away. At this rate England in 1930 will be a very strange country to me.

I sent you a wire, asking you to lend the M.S. of *The Mint* only. In your letter you say you will have 'typescripts' made. This I regret. I'd prefer it to be only in the single copy. Safer so, against dissemination. Also my handwriting is more difficult, in its first 50 pages, than usual: and so the M.S. protects itself against the idly curious. Do not send me a copy of the type-script, any way. Post one, if there is a spare, to my brother (8, Talbot Road, N.W. 6., I think he is. A. W. Lawrence he calls himself) its owner some day, if he goes on living and I don't. Lock the other away in some safe. Please do not let people talk of it, as a book. I shall declare that there isn't one, if anybody publishes a story about it: which might embarrass the tale-teller. Just read it, and like it, if you can, and then shove it in your book-shelf, and forget it. Garnett III will realise on it, a decent but not-Lewis-Carollish increment, some day.

I've suggested to Faber (of F. & Gwyer) that he looks at the Fontana script. F. is an old man, very queer: a natural scholar: he hasn't much of the pride of authorship: wants his name kept out of it: and is modestly prepared to re-write and adapt. It struck me (the two chapters I read were of an earthquake in a wooden court-house, and of the Moharram blood-ceremony in

Constantinople) as quite extra distinguished. As for selling: —
if *Revolt* sold, and *Horn*, and the *Sheikh*,[1] what won't!

I'm so glad the *Poor Man's House* has got into the Travellers
Library: Cape must add *Alongshore*, and *The Holy Mountain*,[2] and
some Crane (*Jenny* is right out of print, and unprocurable[3]). The
airmen here have adopted the Travellers Library as a hobby.
Many of them buy one a week, just for fun. It is an uncommonly
good series. I recommend a novel of Henry Baerlein, about the
Children's Crusade: don't know its name.[4] Very good stuff.
And why not do *Marie Grubbe*?[5] Or must they all be English.

My Heart and My Flesh. Admirable, but too anxious: too dry:
a little Steinish. Not as wholesomely flesh-like as *The Time of
Man*.[6]   T.E.S.

Did I tell you I leave Karachi very soon for some squadron
up-country? I'll send you an address when I next have one.

357: TO BERNARD SHAW

7.5.28   *Karachi*

Dear G.B.S., Your letter was a great delight to me, but you
have read too much of yourself into me. So parts of what you
say do not seem to me to fit *The Mint's* circumstances, or my
situation.

You say 'record of fact' or 'work of art' ... Neither, I fancy.
When I had writing ambitions, they were to combine these two
things. *The Seven Pillars* was an effort to make history an
imaginative thing. It was my second try at dramatizing reality.
The Mint is my notebook of preparation for another try. After
1923, when I re-read *The Seven Pillars* in cold print, and saw
that it did not begin to be what I'd intended and hoped: — then I
gave up the notion of writing a book about the R.A.F.: or of

---

[1] *Trader Horn*, by Aloysius Horn; and *The Sheik*, by E. M. Hull.
[2] These three books are by Stephen Reynolds.
[3] A slip of memory; *Maggie*, by Stephen Crane, is meant. See p. 708.
[4] *On the Forgotten Road*, by Henry Baerlein.
[5] *Marie Grubbe*, by J. P. Jacobsen.
[6] *My Heart and My Flesh* and *The Time of Man*, by Elizabeth Madox Roberts.

writing any sort of book about anything. Don't imagine that because *The S.P.* may be better (in another direction) than my private judgment of it, I thereby become a writer.

'*What to do with it?*' Why, nothing. Garnett asked me for the notes, as a personal souvenir: but for that they would have been burned years ago. Now they are copied out clean and given to him. Surely the job is finished? I can't conceive of their being of any value to humanity. The experience they recount is open to anyone who likes to enlist. If Garnett loses them by lending them to someone prudish, not one of my hairs will turn. Writing books seems inevitable, somehow: but publishing them is an indulgence.

So neither your '*place on record*' or '*save from destruction*' seems to me worth the expenditure of anyone's time or money. You suggest printing 20 copies for record. Cui bono? Harm to myself, for twenty copies will be talked about. Harm to the R.A.F., for fools would not see the solid kindness behind the troubles they inflicted on us: and the R.A.F. is my home, of which I am very fond. I am like Charles II, too old to go wandering again. *The Mint* is not an episode in history, like *The Seven Pillars*, which had to be put on record. My enlistment was a personal experience, only. Libraries like the W.O. (to which you suggest a copy might go) are open only to the officer-class, whose supremacy is based on their not knowing or caring what the men think and feel.

'*Revise*', you suggest, for general publication? I do not think it interesting enough for anyone's revision. Nor do I intend to publish another book: — ever, I was going to say, but ever and never are vain words in a man's mouth. Yet I think I can say that I'll be a different character, before I publish anything else. Look how you are turned inside out daily in every paper, at the pleasure of any worm. God deliver me from the folly of ever returning to that game. You can only keep the press within the bounds by assuming always the offensive ... by chucking to them, as it were, the less intimate details of your equipage. It's a tight-rope game, which only a very cool-headed person dare play. Not for me. You say '*the slightest reticence or self-consciousness would be unpardonable*' ... that from the old fox (pardon the metaphor) who throws a red herring in the pack's face at every twist of the chase! You are all reticences. When I met you I discovered that the public Shaw wasn't even a caricature, much less a likeness, of the private one. Do you think an ordinary fellow could get away with it? Your advice would sink my ship: would sink any ship which had less than your speed and power of manœuvre, and hitting power.

'*If you have contracted to give Cape the refusal of your next book you must fulfil your obligation in the customary sense without ... unusual condition.*' I do not see why. Cape is told he may publish it, if he prints it textually: my terms (to him and to every other publisher) being a million down in advance of royalties. He refuses. Nobody else takes his place: the book is not published. I am free to accept (for instance) an offer I have from an American printer to translate (anonymously) some Homer into English for him, at a high fee. That surely isn't poppycock? I warned Cape, when he put in that clause, that I would, if I was strong enough, not publish another book. I do not think it even sharp practice. I am not proposing to change publishers: merely to exist, in future, without a publisher.

That is the end of your page 5 and the business half of your letter. Don't you agree that my position is at least a possible one? You might as legitimately take hold of a bunch of letters that I had written, week by week, to someone and say that they should be either,

    (a) printed, uncensored, for record
         or
    (b) revised into an autobiography of general interest.

The Mint is a private diary, interesting the world only in so far as the world might desire to dissect my personality. And, like my betters, I disapprove of vivisection. Things so discovered aren't worth the *cost* of finding.

Your literary criticisms are much more exciting. You put your finger on two of the three or four inventions in the book: first the purple night-scape in the story of the dead infant. What Corporal Williams said was: 'Christ, it was as black as hell.' I found that in my notes, and copied it. When I read it, stark on paper, here in Karachi, the whole story felt true. So I pulled out his too-likely phrase, and piled black Pelion on Ossa, to shake the scene out of fact into Dunsanity. Overdid it, of course, as usual. Now I'll write and tell Garnett to cross out the purple lines, and restore the bald reality.

The other passage, about Queen Alexandra,[1] shows that I've wholly missed my target with you. As I worked on it I was trying to feel intensely sorry for the poor old creature who had been artfully kept alive too long. I was trying to make myself (and anyone else who read it) shake at the horrible onset of age. And you find a touch of the grinning street-arab. Mrs. Shaw found it cruel. I was saying to myself '*You*'ll be like that, too, unless you die sooner than the Queen . . .' but it wasn't just personal. There were all the hundreds of younger fellows round me in the church, and I was smelling instead the decay of Marlborough House. It only shows how aims miscarry. I didn't want to take it out of the parson even.

That's the sort of thing that pulls me up with a jerk when I let the comment of other people influence me to think myself a writer. Perhaps I have a punch in each hand: I know I feel things passionately; but you wouldn't call a punch-owner a boxer, if his aim in the ring was such that he knocked out the referee, and downed the four posts. And if you'd tried to paint a Japanese sunset, and the best critics of art in England gasped and said 'Sheer genius, that portrait of Mr Lloyd George': what would you judge yourself then? I'm like a hen who lays a clutch of Mills' bombs in a flurry of ambition to play tennis.

As for Graves' book . . . I think it makes me *do* far less, and seem to *be* something far greater, than the truth. As pieces of virtuosity, my settlement of 1921 (the harder thing) and my campaign were subtle and successful. He misses the subtlety, and does not attempt to set out the success: nor does he give me credit enough for my realism. I've always accepted the half-loaf as better than nothing: — for the other people, my clients.

This doesn't sound a grateful letter. You have sent me seven pages. That is a great honour, and pleasure: and I'd like just to say so, and have done with it: but somehow you provoke

[1] See Lawrence's footnote on p. 609.

argument. There is a waywardness in me, which would like to make me prove myself not a Shavian character, nor fully captured by your pen. If you were here in the flesh (or, better, me there) you would persuade me that you had really set out my motives and course. As it is, we are 18 months and 5,000 miles apart. Yet it is very good of you. Yours   T.E.S.

358: TO R. V. BUXTON

10.5.28.   [*Karachi*]

Karachi has been bad, lately: and I have asked Sir Geoffrey Salmond to take me away to some squadron up-country. It's not our Section Officers who are concerned. I like the puzzled honesty of F/LT Angell, my immediate C.O., and he is very decent to me. But higher up they panic, apparently, over my mere existence in their camp.

Moving is no fun. For nearly a month the new camp gapes at me, expecting me to belie my ordinary shape by doing something extraordinary: and I grow red all over, and my spine trickles damply. I know it is silly: but people's eye-sight tickles one's skin nearly as perceptibly as their fingers or their breath would tickle. And scrutiny at such defencelessly close-quarters as our barrack-life imposes, hurts a good deal.

Also the beginning again from the bottom to make oneself a nest in people's estimation is tiring. And I have to leave behind my books, and the electric bath-heater which I've been able to rig up out of local material and ingenuity. It was a good bath-heater: gave me 14 gallons of bath-hot water in a half-hour, for the cost of a unit of electric current, and the R.A.F. (not knowing) pays for the current. I have had two baths every day this financial year. Hot water is very near Heaven. You know Karachi is a chilly place. [*90 lines omitted*]

359: TO EDWARD GARNETT

17.5.28 [*Karachi*]

Now your long letter has come to me; after I'd copied the other side of this sheet for your eye. I wanted you to like *The Mint*: and I'm ever so glad you do. Please do not let the proprietary feeling warp your judgment. It is well written, in its way, and well-observed, too, so far as it goes. Being a small thing, of limited scope and range and aspect, my deficiences of talent are betrayed less than, for example, in *The Seven Pillars*. In *The S.P.* I tried to draw a movement, and a country, and a race at war. The result was rather a flop. In *The Mint* I just picture the experience of a handful of my own countrymen during some months. Of course it was more successful.

Your praise goes further however than this: and I cannot follow you into it. *The Mint* is only notes: ever so much that should have been there is forgotten. They worked us too hard at Uxbridge (where I was weary after 1½ years with Winston, with the 3rd version of *The S.P.* to write, meanwhile) for me to have proper leisure to see with untroubled eyes: and the re-writing here, done carefully and arduously over six months, every day, and all my spare hours from 2 p.m. till bed-time at 10 o'clock: — even that was not untroubled. So do not imagine that you have, in *The Mint*, my full strength, as it was lavished on *The S.P.* You have me six or seven years older: that is it.

One thing which you say I must challenge: that I put much of myself into it. It is not true. *The S.P.* is unbearable to me, because of the motley I made myself there for everyone's seeing. That's why it won't be published, in my living. *The Mint* gives nothing of myself away: personally, I shouldn't mind its appearing to-morrow: but the other fellows wouldn't understand how I'd come to betray them: and Trenchard would not have it. It would hurt him: and I value his regard beyond that of most men. He is very great. His R.A.F. is bigger than my *Mint*: and I'd not dream of doing anything which would imperil the R.A.F. or blacken it: or make him think it was imperilled or blackened, or in danger of it, through me.

So please be discreet in your showing *The Mint* round. That is why I asked you not to circulate a typescript. The MS. is obviously as private as a letter, and people will respect it . . . but a typescript is a chilly inhuman thing.

My terms to Cape, and to every other publisher, are a million down in advance of a royalty of 90%. Make clear to him, when you submit it, that I am not proposing to change my publisher: merely to do without a publisher, in future. He realises that I dislike being bound, even by fictitious ties: so here's a fiction for a fiction!   T.E.S.

Assure Cape that I haven't any more notes or MSS. in my bag: and no projects of writing in my head. That is all over, I think & hope. I leave for Peshawar (20 Squadron, R.A.F.) on Wednesday 23rd May.

[On the back of this letter is written: *Extract from a letter to G.B.S.* Lawrence had copied out his letter to Bernard Shaw (No. 357) from the passage beginning 'Your literary criticisms are much more exciting', to the words 'to play tennis'. Lawrence had added a footnote to the reference to Queen Alexandra, which runs: 'Is copied from a letter to Mrs Shaw at the time, and which she kept, and loaned back to me, last year. Much of the Cranwell part comes out of private letters of the time.' The letter then continues as follows.]

The rest of G.B.S.' letter was practical, and dealt with the future of *The Mint*, and how it could be published, or revised, or privately printed, or what.

I replied that writing books might be an inevitable act of nature: but that publishing them was an indulgence. This *Mint* was a note-book for a book that will never be written. So it has now no raison d'être: except that you asked for it, as a souvenir of me; and therefore it escapes the flames. But as for publication, he might as well grab a bundle of my letters and insist on censoring them into a polite volume. *The Seven Pillars* was given a restricted circulation, because it was historical — the only record of its experience . . . The experience of *The Mint* is open to anyone who enlists: and therefore it has no scarcity value.   T.E.S.

G.B.S. and Mrs. Shaw had your text of *The Mint* shown them before it was posted you. No one else saw it, or any part of it.

[Extract from a letter from David Garnett[1] to Lawrence, May 20th, 1928.

In ordinary life this emotion [the horror of institutional life] is never aroused, this instinct or emotion of a weasel in a steel trap. When I feel it my intelligence falls away, even my cunning is gone, I am tooth and claw as I was at school, or in the doctor's forceps at the moment of my birth. So the shock of the book on me has been very great, reminding me on every page of this emotion, and making me live through it vicariously, which I have felt strongly in the past, but which I had forgotten: the emotion of the weasel in the steel trap, biting the keeper's boots ... *The Seven Pillars* was a triumph, this an agony. ... In *The Mint* you have made me experience the worst horrors imaginable. The Damascus hospital is sweet with the smell of flowers compared with the corroding breath of servitude: the cowardice of being bullied, and waiting for the insulting order ... Evils change, and there is that in *The Mint* which would change the design stamped, though, alas, it would not stop the process of stamping altogether.]

360: TO DAVID GARNETT

14.6.28.   *Miranshah Fort, Waziristan*

You see, I have changed dust-holes. This is all ringed by mountains, and on the edge of Afghanistan. There are only 25 of us. We live behind barbed wire. The life contemplative. The peaks round us are sharp, like bottle-glass, and our Fort is in a pit.

Into which drops your sudden letter about *The Mint*. *The Mint*? Why I wrote it in 1922. It feels incredibly far off. What was it *you* wrote six years back?

There are some gorgeous things in your letter. I got to your sentence 'the air ... a new form of transport'.[2] Ha Ha. Tell Belloc that yachting is only an obsolete way of going somewhere. Candide indeed. He liked (I believe) digging in a garden: which seems to me about the saddest employment on earth. We are not alike! By 'we' I mean you and Candide, too. As for physicists ... 'rot 'em.

---

[1] See letter No. 364.   [2] Compare letters Nos. 425 and 445, after I learned to fly.

A marvellously good thing: — ' *"The Seven Pillars" . . . was a Triumph. This an agony.*' You have it in one word. I should have written *an agony* after the Title:[1] only for the third part, which is not unhappy. Actually the R.A.F. is excellent living: — sometimes. Here, for example, and at Cranwell. I look back on Cranwell's eighteen months as the happiest I've ever spent.

Trenchard (the person most concerned in the R.A.F.) is going to read *The Mint*: or is going to try to: so it will be interesting to see if it has any good result in making life easier for the serving fellows. I fear he will not share your feeling that we suffered too much. [10 *lines omitted*]

The lack of second-remove stuff — intellect you call it — in *The Mint*, as compared with *The Seven Pillars*, is surely fitting: one is a recollection of two years in the life of a people: the other is a few weeks of strained physical effort in a hut-full of recruits. I wasn't looking on, when I wrote it. I was one of them. Brains take longer to work than senses. So *The Mint* is purely sensory or sensual. I doubt that brains in it show themselves anywhere: (I hope they don't) except in the not-showing themselves. You try writing such experiences without a reflexion: and you'll see that your criticism is one of the best commendations the little note-book could have earned. If I'd seven-pillared it, by recollecting it in tranquillity — or rather in changed conditions — I'd have done something very unlike the notebook: and very unlike *The House of the Dead*, too. *The House of the Dead* is fine, strong, wonderful: but D.[2] had not a crisp side or word in him: so it lacks the particularity of reported notes (*Mint*) or the subsequent rationalisation of experience (*Seven Pillars*). That's my memory of Hogarth's translation,[3] read 10 years ago and not since.

Incidentally the original *Seven Pillars* was more like *The Mint*. It was losing the draft of it which caused it to be written at a distance.

When you see me in the flesh you'll probably laugh. My appearance is painfully undistinguished! In 1930, I hope it will be. The getting back to England will be an inordinate pleasure. I get shivery when I think of the streets in Westminster, or the roads in the English country. O, put me back, and see how happy

[1] See letter, No. 361.   [2] Dostoevsky.   [3] Translation by C. J. Hogarth.

I'll be. There's just a film to come out and be forgotten: and then I streak home top-speed. My R.A.F. incarnation should endure till 1935, if I am lucky.

You are right about the absence of flowers in *The Mint*. There is a severe beauty in some buildings, which would only be reduced if creepers were grown over them. I tried — deliberately — for that. You see, as I suppose every writer who reads it will see — how deliberate the construction and arrangement of *The Mint* is. I called its proportions the worst side of *The Seven Pillars*: and was determined that (what S.S.[1] calls the architectonics of) whatever else I wrote should be, at any rate, calculated.

Your liking for the first-afternoon-football-match pleases me. That page was meant like a seat for anyone tired with the idea of effort. So was the whole third book put in like a benediction after a commination service: and the very occasional landscapes and lyric paragraphs, between stresses.

Old Lincoln (the Steep Street is, or was, Ermine Street) delighted me. The Cathedral, as you saw, I did not like. Yet perhaps it's only because it succeeds too well. I do not think it disappoints as much as it chills. We come to it expecting to be cheered: and it tells us that we are no good at all. (Remigius excepted: the Norman arches and the font, and the organ-tones are lovely.)

'The worst horrors imaginable'. Oh no! I've not anywhere, here or in *The Seven Pillars*, really taken the lid off horror. If I told you of our troopship on the way out to India now: — that had the horror of almost final squalidity.[2] I do not think that it is human to go very far into the mechanism of life.

Don't you like Rupert Brooke's sonnets? They are wonderful: especially for a man who was not very good in anything he wrote. Really, people are odd. They are writing apologetically of Rossetti, in the papers, everywhere. He was a magnificent poet. Morris is half-praised. Morris was a giant. Somebody said that Dowson wasn't a great poet; or Flecker. God Almighty! Must everyone be as seven-leagued as Milton and Byron and Hardy? The English world is full of wonderful writing, by live men and dead men. Look at *Mr. Weston's New Wine*.[3]

---

[1] Siegfried Sassoon.   [2] See letter No. 292.   [3] *Mr. Weston's Good Wine*, by T. F. Powys.

I must apologise for that letter which talked about French literature. Your previous note suggested that I might be anti-French, biased against them for political reasons. Whereas I'm always reading the Frenchmen I like: none of them boulevard idols: but wonderful in my eyes.   T.E.S.

Write a fairy story? No. I won't. I propose, in all humility, not to write anything of my own again. Just lately I've been trying to translate a little Greek book, to earn £30 which a Yank has promised me therefor. I have, at different times, done a lot of translating. I think it is the best way of learning to use words. Much harder than choosing one's own ideas, and clothing them. Have you ever translated?

361: TO JONATHAN CAPE

30.6.28.   *Miranshah Fort, Waziristan*

Dear Cape, Garnett has my second book *The Mint*, an agony of the Royal Air Force, which he will offer you for publication, *as it stands*, soon. This is in accordance with the terms of our *Revolt in the Desert* contract. I am not offering it to any other publisher, if you refuse my terms, since I do not, really, want it published at all. So don't get huffed that I'm changing my publisher. I'm not: I'm just proposing to live without one, in future!

By the way I'm asking £1,000,000 down in cash, in advance of royalty, on *The Mint*. I hope you will regard that sum as a compliment to the firm. I wanted to make sure they would refuse it: and I feared that any lesser figure might be within your reach. They say you had five of the six best-selling books of last year. You've made your own firm, out of nothing at all, in just a very few years: and must be very proud of it: for it has a character, as well as a credit balance. Your books are the most workmanlike in London.

I've left Karachi, for good: and have, I hope, settled in this queer little place, a brick and barbed-wire fort on the Afghan border. We are not allowed beyond the wire: so that we have few temptations except boredom and laziness. I'm never bored: and

for the laziness I've just done a sample 400 lines of a prose translation of some Greek poetry, for an American firm, that wants to
produce something de luxe. If they like it, they'll ask me to do
more. My ambition is to earn £200 in the next 19 months, and
then come home and buy a motor-bike!

If the Yanks fail me, I'll pester you and Doubleday for some
job of anonymous translating. I write quite decent English
prose, they say, and it seems a pity to let a talent like that rust.
Yours,   T. E. SHAW

Sharp practice, I think, this *Mint*: but as you lose no money
over it, and I gain none, honours are even: and I may want to
undertake this Greek job.

362: TO H. S. EDE

30.6.28.   *Miranshah*

Well, I've moved from Karachi, and come up to the most remote
R.A.F. Station in India: — and the smallest. We are only 26, all
told, with 5 officers, and we sit with 700 India Scouts (half-
regulars) in a brick and earth fort behind barbed wire complete
with searchlights and machine guns. Round us, a few miles off,
in a ring are low bare porcelain-coloured hills, with chipped edges
and a broken-bottle skyline. Afghanistan is 10 miles off. The
quietness of the place is uncanny — ominous, I was nearly saying:
for the Scouts and ourselves live in different compartments of the
fort, and never meet: and so there's no noise of men: and no
birds or beasts — except a jackal concert for five minutes about
10 p.m. each night, when the searchlights start. The India
sentries flicker the beams across the plain, hoping to make them
flash in the animals' eyes. So sometimes we see them.

We are not allowed beyond the barbed wire by day, or outside
the fort walls by night. So the only temptations of Miranshah
are boredom and idleness. I hope to escape the first and enjoy
the second: for, between ourselves, I did a lot of work at Karachi,
and am dead tired.

Here they employ me mainly in the office. I am the only

MIRANSHAH 1928

airman who can work a typewriter, so I do D.R.OS[1] and correspondence: and act postman, and pay clerk, and bottle-washer in
ordinary. Normally flights do two months here, and get relieved:
but I will try to get left on. It's the station of a dream: as though
one had fallen right over the world, and had lost one's memory of
its troubles. And the quietness is so intense that I rub my ears,
wondering if I am going deaf.

You, meanwhile, broadcast, and lunch with Margot[2] and 'see
life'. Well, in good time. If 1930 is kind to me, it will bring me
back within holiday distance of London, and by coming to see
you I'll shatter the too-favourable image of myself which your
imagination has created. Graves is really too good to me too:
makes me out a wonderful chap: and the fellows in camp sit on
their beds, round mine, and read tit-bits of their books at me, and
say 'Now, who'd have thought that, if he'd known you?' They
regard my legend as a huge joke: if it wasn't *my* legend, I'd do
ditto.

Miss Fry I do not remember. More people, however, know
me than I know.

America? I will not go there: but they are doing a vast lot of
interesting writing there, prose and poetry. Try and see Kreym-
borg, and Cummings, and Vachel Lindsay and Sherwood
Anderson. They must be interesting. Yours ever,   T.E.S.

363: TO BERNARD SHAW

19. 7. 28.   *Miranshah*

[38 *lines omitted*] I agree of course, that hand-setting[3] is to-day
no more than an affectation. You can do beautiful work by hand,
every bit as good as mono, and nearly as good as lino: but the cost
of it falls on flesh and blood. It ranks with boy chimney-sweeps.

No, I am not adjutant, to this camp. Just typist, and i/c files,
and duty rolls. I do what I am told to do, and re-write the drafts
given to me, meekly. The officers would need to be better than

---

[1] Daily Routine Orders.   [2] Lady Oxford and Asquith.
[3] Lawrence was still interested in printing methods, and even after this date contemplated buying a hand press. See p. 844.

they feel themselves to be, for me to safely exceed the normal rank of R.A.F. clerk. Also I'm not much good as a clerk: though I type a bit better than this, in the daylight.

You ask what is my expectation of life, when I'm discharged. I can tell you, without many 'ifs'. If Trenchard is displeased with me over *The Mint* (those notes on the R.A.F. which you saw, and he has seen) he will make me leave the R.A.F. in February, 1930. If he does not bear me any grudge, he will leave me alone here and at some camp in England, till 1935. Or Trenchard may himself leave the Air Force, and I find kinder treatment from his successor. However, in 1930 or in 1935, I will have to go out. My notion, if I have then a secured income of a pound a day, is to settle at Clouds Hill, in my cottage and be quiet.

If I have to earn my bread and butter, I shall try for a job in London. The sort of job will depend on my health. My body has been knocked to pieces, now and then, and often overworked, in the past: so I do not feel sure of lasting very well. I have thought of a night-watchman job, in some City Bank or block of offices. The only qualification for these is Service experience; and honesty is the necessity which bars very many ex-service men from getting them. I can get good references, from people bankers will trust, so I have good hope of getting placed. Better than that, almost; for Sir Herbert Baker, the architect, who is building the new Bank of England, has spoken of me to the Council which runs it, and they have put a minute in their book that my application is to be considered as favourably as possible, if or when I apply.

You see, I have no trade to take up, and am old to learn, and tired of learning things. So I must look for an unskilled job; and I want an indoor job, if possible, in case I am not very fit. And I like London. And I'd like to work by myself. It is not easy to get on terms with people. On night work nobody would meet me, or hear of me, much. I have been thinking hard for the last two or three years of what I should go for, if the R.A.F. came to a sudden end (you see, it is precarious: I depend on the favour of Hoare and Trenchard, and am the sort of fellow on whom people hang tales and believe anything, though I do my honest best to worm along inoffensively) and I have listened or joined myself to the other fellows whenever they have discussed civy jobs: —

and of everything I have heard, this nightwatchman job sounds the most likely for me to be allowed to hold for good. You see, there is more demanded of you than that the safe should be unbroken next morning. You come on duty as the last clerk goes, and the door is locked. You come off duty when the first comer opens the door in the morning. No others ever hear of you, as an individual.

Thanks to Baker speaking to the Bank Committee, with whom he is in weekly touch, my way to the job seems to have been made suddenly easy. His letter telling me only reached me here, so you see it is recent news. I hope you will not tell anyone about it. The Bank Committee will not. The rest of the formalities would be done by their Staff-man. I will not have to see any of the big noises. The Bank of England is rather more than I had hoped for (or wanted) as it is really too good. Also the smaller Banks let their night men sleep in. Of course the new Bank building will have more room in it. A gorgeous place to live in, don't you think? but that is a trifle, anyhow. A single man can live anywhere, if his tastes are quite plain. Mine are getting plain. Up here I have begun to think with pleasure of the idea of eating ... once or twice.

Please do not laugh at this sketch of my intentions. What I have wanted and tried to do has always come off, more or less, except when it was trying to write; and then, despite all the good you have said of my books, I am assured of failure. Not complete failure, perhaps. I explain your and my different judgments of my writing by my knowledge of the standard at which I was aiming, and your astonishment that a 'man of action' should be able to do it at all. A relative failure, let's call it. My aim may have been too high for anybody; it was too high for me. But I think one says just 'too high', not 'immodestly high'. I do not think aims are things modest or immodest; just possible and impossible. It is more than ten o'clock, which is after half the night for us, so I must stop tapping away on these keys. It's awfully hard to make up a sensible letter on a typewriter, or so I find: so please forgive the crudities there are. And forgive also the bother [*name omitted*] gives you, if he does. I find I can't refuse anyone the chance of making the money, out of me, which I will not make for myself. The stuff is boring. I'd give it, like a Dukedom, to anyone who'd accept it. Yours ever   T.E. SHAW

I haven't answered your last line 'What is your game *really*?' Do you never do things because you know you must? Without wishing or daring to ask too deeply of yourself why you must? I just can't help it. You see, I'm all smash, inside: and I don't want to look prosperous or be prosperous, while I know that. And on the easy level of the other fellows in the R.A.F. I feel safe: and often I forget that I've ever been different. As time passes that war and post-war time grows less and less probable, in my judgment. If I'd been as accomplished as they say, surely I wouldn't be in the ranks now? Only please don't think it is a game, just because I laugh at myself and everybody else. That's Irish, or an attempt to keep sane. It would be so easy and so restful just to let sanity go and drop into the dark: but that can't happen while I work and meet simple-hearted people all day long. However, if you don't see it, I can't explain it. You could write a good play, over a room-full of Sydney Webbs and Cockerells asking me 'why'.   T.E.S.

364: TO E. M. FORSTER

6/8/28.   *Miranshah*

Dear E.M.F., Your wonderful letter about *The Mint* has given me about eight readings of unalloyed pleasure, so far. It is a gift that, of mine, of being able to read so loosely that I can go on reading a thing for time after time, and enjoy it always. Now I am going to read it again, time 9.

No, it is properer to write and thank you for it. It is just like the letter of one writer to another. Marvellous, that you and I should be on such apparent terms. I looked up to you for years as a distant but impeccable star. Now you are no further from me than the thickness of this sheet of notepaper, and my re-luctance to cover it with black marks . . . and not impeccable, since I have found your critical judgement partial to my imper-fections. However perhaps I am your blind spot.

Do not swoon with the eccentricity of this typing. I am doing

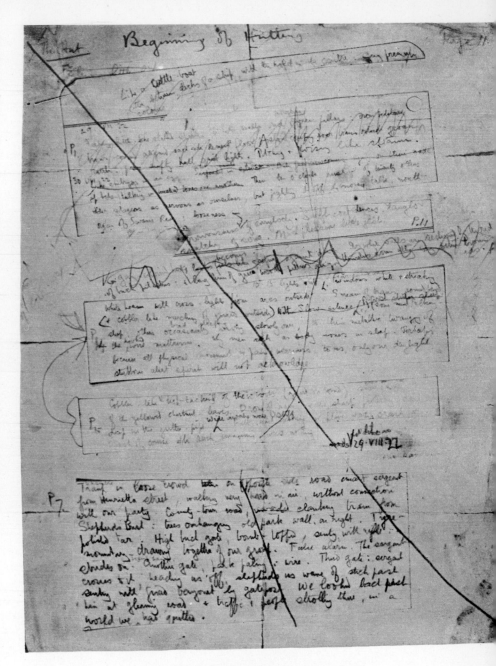

PASTED-UP PAGE OF *THE MINT*

it in the dark, and there is not a bell to ring at the end of lines. I only turn over when it stops at the far side. And I cannot feel with my finger-tips exactly where I am striking the keys.

The (Hitherto) youngest Garnett[1] wrote me a most queer letter* about *The Mint* (forgive my egoism in talking about it all the time. To write an unpublished book is to hear nothing, except from you & the Garnetts and the Shaws, what sort of a book it is ... and one does wonder, you know). He said that it was a study in pain, and that it had hurt him; I did not think it very horrible anywhere. Now there were things I did write about the Tank Corps which were horrible ... but *The Mint* is not abysmally cruel or crude. Surely not. You get on the side I'd like to stand, when you deduce from it that cruelty is not universal nor basic in humankind. I am sure it is not.

You put the first & second parts before the third, as writing. I am interested by that word. Every night in Uxbridge I used to sit in bed, with my knees drawn up under the blankets, and write on a pad the things of the day. I tried to put it all down, thinking that memory & time would sort them out, and enable me to select significant from insignificant. Time passed, five years and more (long enough, surely, for memory to settle down?) and at Karachi I took up the notes to make a book of them ... and instead of selecting, I fitted into the book, somewhere & somehow, every single sentence I had written at Uxbridge.

Now tell me. Did my mind select at the time ... or is there no truth that art is selection ... or does my book lack selection. Is the whole affair there, and the trees cluttered up by redundant twigs & blossoms?

I wrote it tightly, because our clothes are so tight, and our lives so tight in the service. There is no freedom of conduct at all. Wasn't I right? G.B.S. calls it too dry, I believe. I put in little sentences of landscape (the Park, the Grass, the Moon) to relieve the shadow of servitude, sometimes. For service fellows there are no men on earth, except other service fellows ... but

---

* It was a quite absurdly laudatory letter, too: only so queer. More like a woman than a man.

[1] David Garnett: see p. 610.

we do see trees and star-light and animals, sometimes. I wanted to bring out the apartness of us.

You wanted me to put down the way I left the R.A.F., and something about the Tanks. Only I still feel miserable at the time I missed because I was thrown out that first time. I had meant to go on to a Squadron, & write the real Air Force, and make it a book — a BOOK, I mean. It is the biggest subject I have ever seen, and I thought I could get it, as I felt it so keenly. But they broke all that in me, and I have been damaged ever since. I could never again recover the rhythm that I had learned at Uxbridge, resisting Stiffy . . . and so it would not be true to reality if I tried to vamp up some yarn of it all now. The notes go to the last day of Uxbridge, and there stop abruptly.

The Cranwell part is, of course, not a part, but scraps. I had no notes for it . . . any more than I am ever likely to have notes of any more of my R.A.F. life. I'm it, now, and the note season is over. The Cadet College part was vamped up, really, as you say, to take off the bitterness, if bitterness it is, of the Depot pages. The Air Force is not a man-crushing humiliating slavery, all its days. There is sun & decent treatment, and a very real measure of happiness, to those who do not look forward or back. I wanted to say this, not as propaganda, out of fairness, the phrase which pricked up your literary ears, but out of truthfulness. I set out to give a picture of the R.A.F., and my picture might be impressive and clever if I showed only the shadow of it . . . but I was not making a work of art, but a portrait. If it does surprisingly happen to be literature (I do not believe you there: you are partially kind) that will be because of its sincerity, and the Cadet College parts are as sincere as the rest, and an integral part of the R.A.F.

Of course I know and deplore the scrappiness of the last chapters: that is the draw-back of memory, of a memory which knew it was queerly happy then, but shrank from digging too deep into the happiness, for fear of puncturing it. Our contentments are so brittle, in the ranks. If I had thought too hard about Cranwell, perhaps I'd have found misery there too. Yet I assure you that it seems all sunny, in the back view.

Of Cadet College I had notes. Out of letters on Queen Alexandra's Funeral (Garnett praises that. Shaw says it's the

meanness of a guttersnipe laughing at old age. I was so sorry
and sad at the poor old queen), for the hours on guard, for the
parade in the early morning. The Dance, the Hangar, Work
and the rest were written at Karachi. They are reproductions of
scenes which I saw, or things which I felt & did . . . but two years
old, all of them. In other words, they are technically on a par
with the manner of *The Seven Pillars*: whereas the Notes were
photographs, taken day by day, and reproduced complete,
though not at all unchanged. There was not a line of the Uxbridge notes left out; but also not a line unchanged.

The only photographic chapter of *The Seven Pillars* was the
account of the tribal feasts, in Wadi Sirhan, when we stuffed
meat and rice till we were sick. For that I had photographic notes,
which only required rearranging. I wrote *The Mint* at the rate of
about four chapters a week, copying each chapter four or five
times, to get it into final shape. Had I gone on copying, I should
only have been restoring already crossed out variants. My mind
seems to congest, after reworking the stuff several times.

To insist that they are notes is not side-tracking. The Depot
section was meant to be a quite short introduction to the longer
section dealing with the R.A.F. in being, in flying work. Events
killed the longer book: so you have the introduction, set out at
greater length.

'You hadn't, that is to say, communicated your happiness to
me' — nor convinced my rational side of it. The happiness is real:
but sensory, only, I think.

'*The Mint* is not so great a work as *The Seven Pillars*': — but
possibly better, as Garnett thinks. It is so tiny a theme and work;
perhaps I have a cherry-stone talent. *The Seven Pillars* is a sort
of introspection epic, you know: and it would have taken a big
writer to bring it off.

'There seems no reason why you shouldn't write all sorts of
books'. Why, I feel as dry as a squeezed orange. I do not think
it is at all likely that I will ever be moved to write anything again.
The Mint dates from 1922, when I hadn't looked back in cold
blood at *The Seven Pillars*, & seen how they fell short of my
fancied achievement. Too ambitious, the little soul was: and so
he's come a fearful cropper.

There are no women free in Waziristan to explore: so that point does not yet arise. 1930 before I come home. 1935 (if I am lucky) before I get thrown out of the R.A.F. . . . and then I have a promise of a job, as night-watchman in a City Bank. So life is all mapped out safely, for long enough ahead.

It is good to feel a little safe. Often I get sorry over all the chances of money I have thrown away. One does need money, to the bread & butter point, to keep one's behaviour decent.

The Mint mustn't be published till after 1950 . . . when it will be so stale that nobody will much want to publish it. The new point of view, to which you (surprisingly . . . for I did not know there was one) allude, will be old, by then.

More & more thanks. You have given me vast & unalloyed pleasure.   T.E.S.

365: TO E. M. FORSTER

28/8/28   [*Miranshah*]

Dear E.M.F., I am happy in another wonderful letter from you about *The Mint*. I suppose mothers & fathers make secret fools of themselves, over their children, in the way I do over my books. I can see what ungainly, silly things they are: yet I can't help feeling happy & warm, in the hollow place between my ribs & my navel, whenever somebody, even a futile somebody, speaks well of them. And when you, who are one of the shining ones of the English language, say nice things . . . well, you can't imagine how the worm then tries to uplift itself! I am not impugning your imagination, in that remark, but your worminess. Never having been a worm, you can't really *know* a worm's feelings.

Pickard Cambridge, an Oxford philosopher, rushed out to his villa's lawn, in a great thunderstorm, & dug up clod after clod of it, clumsily, with a spade: 'to relieve the worms oppressed by their covering of grass', as he told his wife, who was trying to drag him in, out of the wet.

Of course *The Seven Pillars* is bigger than *The Mint*. I let myself go in *The S.P.* and gave away all the entrails I had in me. It was an orgy of exhibitionism. Never again. Yet for its restraint, & dignity, and form, & craftmanship, *The Mint* may well be better. By that I don't mean that *The Mint* has *no* emotion, or *The Seven Pillars no* balance: only comparatively it's so. E. Garnett, curiously enough, calls *The S.P.* reticent, and *The Mint* a giving away of myself. Why, so far as myself is concerned, I wouldn't hesitate to publish *The Mint* tomorrow!

In truth however, the publication isn't in my hands. Trenchard is not the primary obstacle: though for him I have an admiration almost unlimited. He's a very great man. I think he over-estimates the harm which *The Mint* would do the R.A.F.: but what really holds me back is the horror the fellows with me in the force would feel at my giving them away, at their 'off' moments, with both hands. To be photographed, they put on what they call 'best' clothes, & brush their hair, & wash. To be portrayed, as in my book, unadorned would break their hearts. You must remember that *The Mint* is photographically exact: many of them have their real names! No hut-full could trust itself to live openly together, if there was a risk of their communion becoming public copy, in a few years time.

So *The Mint* shall not be circulated before 1950. By then the characters will not matter. Poor old Stiffy is keeping a hotel in Essex now. He'll be dead, & Trenchard, & perhaps myself: (dead or aged 62, the last item. What a quaint performance *The Mint* will seem to a white-beard of 62!)

I cannot understand quite why E. Garnett chides me so. Surely he over-estimates the importance of publication? Books give pleasure: but think how many good ones there are which you haven't yet read. Why fuss over one more or less? Especially as I don't propose to burn it. It is quite safely preserved, & if our next generation want to read our stuff, then they'll have their chance. Usually it's the next but one which revives us, after much derision.

He calls me a writer, & curses me for not writing. Really, I am not a writer, I think. There's no sort of demon lurking in my brain urging me to put down on paper, or that. Yet, despite this handicap, I'd point out that I have written two books: one of 300,000 words, & one of 80,000 words, in nine years. It seems to me not much less an output than — let's say — yours (though

I don't mean to suggest that my stuff ranks in the same class as what you do). Edgar Wallace writes a lot. But he's even less like *The Mint* than your novels are. *The Seven Pillars* was a most exhausting performance. It is in its fourth edition, in the Subscribers' text. *The Mint* has been written out four or five times. Young Garnett found parts of it careless. I can assure you that parts of it may be incompetent, but not a word is careless or uncalculated. I've done my very best with every line of both books. Overdone it, rather than underdone it. Edgar Wallace does not take half my pains, I think.

What you say about the emphasis I get on simple words like Moon or chocolate biscuits, mayn't it be partly because I do try & feel every article or emotion which comes into the book? I tie myself into knots trying to re-act everything, as I write it out. It's like writing in front of a looking-glass, and never looking at the paper, but always at the imaginary scene. That, and a trick of arranging words, so that the one I care for most is either repeated, or syllable-echoed, or put in a startling position.

You'll laugh at all these tricks & dodges of the amateur, trying to get the effects of an artist, by synthesis. Yet your praises show me that I've sometimes pulled it off.

As for showing *The Mint* round: that is rather the Garnetts' privilege, isn't it? I've given them the editio princeps, and they can show it, or lock it up. I've begged E.G. not to let its existence get into the literary gossip pages. Because I should then have to tell a lie, and deny that it exists. As a matter of fact I have written a letter to Savage, who acts as agent for *Revolt in the Desert*, and told him to say so, publicly, if anything comes out.

'Waiting for your next — ladies or fairy tales or . . .' The same to you: only for Heaven's sake don't drag yourself unwillingly into print. Nearly every author has written too many books. I like long books: but few books. If you do no more — why I shall re-read (I often do) what you have already done. If you write more, I shall read them too: but I do not value the to-come above the alreadys.

My next — if an American of wealth is attracted by the sample Book 1 I sent him two months back, & offers me good terms for more — will be an English literal translation of the *Odyssey*, to be published without translator's name, in the States. In translating you get all the craftsman's fuss of playing with words, without the artist's responsibility of their design & meaning. I could go on translating for ever: but for an original work there's not an idea in my head.

Such an egotistical letter: but you rather asked for it: and making me try to justify myself forces me to dig in, for motives & reasons. You know, I hope, that in reality I don't think very much of — or about — myself. Yours   T E S.

366: TO E. M. FORSTER

12.XII. 28.   *Miranshah*

We have had an idyllic two and a half months here, under the best & kindest C.O. of my experience. Now he is on the point of going. We hope the new C.O. will be easy on our comfort-loving souls. When Miranshah is good, it is very good. In August & September it was horrible.

The last sentence of your letter wants me to ask you to return the 'Oxford' *Seven Pillars* to Wilson.[1] Why should you, except to rid yourself of an incubus? It is large, and, I fear ugly: and very hard to read: but curious, too: don't forget it's what's called a 'collector's piece'. Some swine would call your Blake a collector's piece: but they are wrong. I wish I could sit under your small (or big) trees and read a song or two songs of innocence, tomorrow.

Probably it's icy cold, and you are sitting near the fire, feeding the cat on buttered toast — if cats eat buttered toast. Cats are wiser than dogs. Yet, I assure you, it is cold here. Our ring of mountains has 4000 feet of snow on it: but we have tons of wood, & I have a fire all to myself in the office, where I do everything but sleep. Life is good.

Did I tell you I'm making the 25th (rotten) translation of the *Odyssey* into English? They offered me £800 to do it all,* and I fell for the cash, & do not yet regret it, though it is an impossible

   * anonymously!

      [1] J. G. Wilson of J. & E. Bumpus, the booksellers.

job to do well, and a heart-breaking job to botch. However botched it certainly is.

I think the *Odyssey* is mock-heroic: a sort of Selfridge-Epic: more like *Sigurd the Volsung*[1] than *Marmion*. It's awfully well written: clever as seven devils: and very hard to put into clear English. It's Wardour Street, itself, in Greek & all rings false. But gorgeous. I wish I had written the *Odyssey* & not *The Seven Pillars*. I say, *The S.P.* won't be easy to translate!

I read *The Well of Loneliness*:[2] and was just a little bored. Much ado about nothing.

As you say, happiness doesn't 'write' well. I don't know any entirely happy book — unless it's *The Private Papers of Henry Ryecroft*.[3]

Can you give me Posh's address? I must write to the little sinner.

Middleton I did write to, lately. Your   T E SHAW

367: TO JOHN BUCHAN

26.XII.28   *Miranshah Fort, Waziristan*

I have to report progress: the first seven years of my engagement in the service are nearly ended. So I have applied to be allowed to extend for five years more: or rather, to convert into active years the five that I would normally have passed in the reserve. Trenchard agreed to this, as one of his last acts. So I am 'booked' till 1935. I wanted you to know that I'm making the best use I can of the gift you led Mr. Baldwin into giving me in 1925. Will you tell him, if ever you see him at leisure, that I'm still thanking him, whenever I think of it? The R.A.F. still suits me all over, as a home: quaint, that is, for it's probably not everyone's prescription. However, there it is. I feel Trenchard's going, almost as a personal loss.[4] There was a breadth and honesty, and devotion, about him that made one accept his headship as according to the course of nature. I do not think that any other man in the three kingdoms has had his job — and privilege — of making, from the first man upward, a whole new arm. His work

---

[1] By William Morris.   [2] By Radclyffe Hall.   [3] By George Gissing.
[4] Trenchard did not retire from the Air Force till later in 1929.

has been very good. The R.A.F. hasn't yet found the way out between the rocks of discipline and individual technical intelligence — but it goes forward, and is very hopeful. Its salvation lies in its own heads, to work out internally. It is something new, in services: and I find it fascinating to watch its infant years. Some of it I put on paper, as notes on a recruit's life in the (quite misdirected and harmful) Depot at Uxbridge: about 1922 that was. Trenchard read it lately, when I made a gift of the manuscript (not to be published, of course) to Edward Garnett: and he wasn't pleased about it. But of course it is ancient history. If ever you are at a loose end for reading matter, & feel strong enough for a crabbed manuscript, then borrow it off E.G. (you probably know him: critic, and midwife of many good writers) and have a smile at the adventures of a jelly-fish among sergeant-majors. The poor fish laid 80,000 words in his tribulation!

On the whole, though, you had probably better not. For the last weeks I have been reading, inch by inch, your *Montrose*: keeping it in the Wireless Cabin, which lies between our barracks & our offices, and from which I have to collect 'in' signals several times a day. I used to take ten minutes off each time, for *Montrose*, which came as a revelation to me.

I had not suspected, from my desultory reading of the Civil War, that such a man then existed. The *style* of his last words on the gallows! and those profound memoranda on political science. I've tried to think back for other military commanders who could write like that, and I'm bothered if I can think of one: Xenophon was only a Walter Long[1] kind of a sportsman, beside him, & J. Caesar too abstract. Your man stands out, head and shoulders.

He has been unlucky in waiting three hundred years for a real biographer: but he must be warmly happy, now, if anything of his personality can still feel. You unwrap him so skilfully, without ever getting, yourself, in our way. The long careful setting of the scene — first-rate history, incidentally, and tingling with life, as if you'd seen it — & on top of that the swift and beautifully-balanced course of action. Oh, it's a very fine thing.

I'm glad you allow common-sense to interpret the documents. A fetish of the last-school-but-one was to believe every document.

---

[1] Conservative cabinet minister and type of John Bull.

As one who has had the making of original historical records I know how weak & partial and fallible they are. Fortunately you have been a man of affairs, and so are not to be taken in, like a scholar pure.

There is great labour behind the book, which yet reads easily, for your digestion has been able to cope with all the stony facts. Your small characters (often only a word long) brighten the whole thing. Incidentally, you have been honest to see the fineness of Cromwell, under the homespun. Argyll is unforgettable: Huntly, too: and Hurry. Alasdair less so. He didn't Colkitto[1] enough to live in my reading. I wonder why? Didn't you want him to clash with Montrose, in prowess? Also you left out Rupert — I mean, you mention him, well enough, but you do not make him walk & talk, whereas you bring to life Elizabeth & the Palatine circle. I suppose you were concentrating your high lights. Charles, the king, is finely drawn, as a shadow on the wall of his contemporaries. I suppose you know the fineness of your writing? The way you line in the execution of the King is marvellous. Montrose would have envied you those two or three sentences, & the full-stop and paragraph, after them. [18 *lines omitted*]

As I read, I have a habit of keeping a sheet of paper in my page, and if the book is worth it, writing down the goods and bads which strike me. Montrose's sheet was very full, of bits which had given me pleasure: but it's no use my handing these on to their maker.

How strangely like the dying verses of Montrose are to Raleigh's 'Blood shall be my body's balmer' (I quote from memory, but I expect you know the poem).

Too long, this letter. But I couldn't help telling you of the rare pleasure your book has given me. Its dignity, its exceeding gracefulness, its care for exactness, and the punctilio of your manners, fit its subject and period like a glove. You've put a very great man on a pedestal. I like it streets better than anything else of yours. Yours sincerely   T E SHAW.

---

[1] Colkitto, Sir Alasdair Macdonald's nickname, means, in Gaelic, to fight with both hands at once, i.e. with claymore and dirk.

FLYING BOATS

INTRODUCTION TO PART FIVE

L AWRENCE had regretted going to India directly after it had been decided that he should be sent there, but he had accepted it because he wanted to be out of the way during the publicity attending the appearance of the Subscribers' edition of *Seven Pillars of Wisdom*, of *Revolt in the Desert* and of Graves's book. On the borders of Waziristan he believed that he was safely out of the way, and translating Homer, reading John Buchan's *Montrose*, and taking a large share in running the small camp, he was leading an extremely hard-worked and happy life.

He was once more to be the victim of his own legend. As early as July 23rd, 1928, an enterprising journalist had been trying to fasten a story on to his return to the East. The Press Department at the Air Ministry reported to the Chief of the Air Staff on that date:

'The *New York World* has had the following jam sub-mitted to it about the alleged activities of Colonel Lawrence'.

Under the heading:

COLONEL LAWRENCE'S MYSTERIOUS MISSION
NEW AIR FORCE CORPORAL'S LONG TREK THROUGH
NEAR EAST

the article gave a lurid account of how Lawrence, last heard of in Peshawar, disappeared disguised as an Arab Sheikh and after travelling through Persia, had made a new agreement with Riza Khan during the absence of the Soviet diplomats. From Persia he had gone to Arabia 'where Ibn Saud had become a nuisance'. He there had detached the Yemen from Italy and had settled a critical situation at Aden. 'Ibn Saud will be dealt with soon. The whole of British policy is dependent upon the guidance of this stormy petrel of Arabia.'

The *New York World* honourably preferred truth to sensation and the article was not published. But towards the end of the year the westernizing King of Afghanistan, Amanullah, had brought his unpopularity to a point where the conservative majority of his subjects rebelled, and the 'uncrowned King of Arabia at the head of the British Secret Service' on the borders of Afghanistan provided excellent copy for journalists all over the world, and a focus for the suspicions of English socialists and anti-Imperialists. Members of the English Labour Party became honestly convinced that the rebellion was due to the machinations of the Government of India and that Lawrence had been instrumental in bringing it about.

On December 5th, 1928, a paragraph had appeared in the *Daily News* stating that Lawrence was busy learning Pushtu. 'It is inferred he intends to move into Afghanistan.' It seems conceivable that this report may have arisen from a fellow airman's looking into Lawrence's Greek Lexicon.

The *Daily Herald*, which warmly championed Amanullah's reforms, took the question of Lawrence's activities up hotly.

[*Daily Herald, January 5th*, 1929]

LAWRENCE OF ARABIA
ARREST 'ORDERED' BY AFGHAN AUTHORITIES
STARTLING REPORT

A sensational message reached London last night from Allahabad, stating that the Afghan authorities have ordered the arrest of Colonel Lawrence, known widely as Lawrence of Arabia, on the ground that he is believed to be assisting the rebels to cross the frontier. They describe Colonel Lawrence, says the B.U.P., as the arch-spy of the world.

Photographs, supposed to be of Colonel Lawrence, have been secretly procured from India, and distributed among the Afghan commanders, it is stated.

If this be true — though in well informed London circles it is received with reserve — Lawrence of Arabia is maintaining his reputation as one of the most startling persons in the world.

For some time his movements, as chronicled, have been mysterious, and a few months ago it was stated that he was in Afghanistan on a secret mission, though earlier in the same week it had been reported that he was in Amritsar, posing as a Mohammedan saint.

[*Daily Herald, January 7th,* 1929.]

LAWRENCE OF ARABIA
AFGHAN ARREST 'ORDER' UNCONFIRMED

No confirmation was available yesterday at the Afghan Legation in London of the reported order for the arrest of Colonel Lawrence of Arabia, on the alleged ground that he had assisted Afghan rebels to cross the frontier.

According to a B.U.P. Moscow wire, the official Kabul newspaper, *Amany Afghan,* referring to the story reported in an Indian newspaper that Colonel Lawrence organised and headed the Afghan revolt, considers that the role played by Colonel Lawrence has been exaggerated, declaring: 'We do not believe in Colonel Lawrence's power and skill. He is only an Englishman.'

A strong denial that he is Colonel Lawrence, or that he is in any way connected with any State or Government, has been issued by Syed Pir Karam Shah, the Mohammedan, who was mobbed by an infuriated crowd at Lahore on the occasion of the funeral procession of Lala Lajpat Rai.

Karam Shah was seriously injured by the mob, which was fully convinced that he was 'Lawrence of Arabia' in disguise, and statements to that effect are still appearing in the vernacular Press.

In the circumstances, the decision of the Government of India to have Lawrence sent home immediately was natural and inevitable. Labour Members of Parliament would certainly not believe that Lawrence had been reorganizing the routine of engine overhaul at Karachi, even if they had been told so, or that he was using his leisure at Miranshah to translate Homer. Lawrence was therefore, to his great indignation, flown from Miranshah to Lahore on January 8th, 1929, and thence to Karachi on the 9th, where he was met by a senior officer of the R.A.F. who explained the matter. He left Bombay on January 12th on board S.S. *Rajputana,* with instructions to proceed to Tilbury and to report to the Air Ministry on arrival, unless he received orders to the contrary. Lawrence had to leave behind most of his possessions, including his gramophone and records, and was very indignant. But the pathetic figure of Karam Shah invites even greater sympathy.

The uproar about Lawrence's activities was however only beginning, and it is now easy to see that the efforts of the Air

Ministry to avoid any publicity on his return were a blunder which only served to multiply the suspicions that the Government was hiding something.

The following message had been conveyed to Lawrence on board the *Rajputana* on January 17th.

> On your arrival the press will I am afraid meet you and as much as possible will try to interview you, and photograph you. Endeavour as much as possible to avoid being interviewed.

With the Press campaign, alarm at the Air Ministry increased, and instructions were given that an officer in mufti should meet Lawrence at Plymouth and get him away unbeknown to anyone, with instructions to go on leave straight away, until he was sent for.

These measures might almost have been designed to defeat the objects of the Government of India in sending him home, and resulted in a natural endeavour on the part of newspaper men and politicians to arrive at the truth about what Lawrence had really been doing.

On February 4th, the *Daily News* had a column headed:

GREAT MYSTERY OF COLONEL LAWRENCE

SIMPLE AIRCRAFTSMAN OR WHAT?

TIME THE TRUTH WAS KNOWN

THE ARCH-SPY

A leader of the same date said that he should not be allowed to masquerade in the R.A.F.

The *Daily News* was informed that Lawrence had been posted to Cattewater on ordinary service duty, and the Press generally informed that since he had joined the R.A.F. he had performed the duties of an Aircraft Hand and nothing else.

But this concealment and mystery were clearly unsatisfactory and questions were asked in Parliament, concentrating upon Lawrence's using the name of Shaw, the change of name by deed-poll having been concealed from the public.

Hansard. January 30th, 1929

MR. THURTLE asked the Secretary of State for Air whether it was known at the time Aircraftsman Shaw, whose real name is Colonel Lawrence, enlisted in the Royal Air Force that he was enlisting in a false name; and if so, why this was permitted?

SIR SAMUEL HOARE. Colonel Lawrence's identity was known when he transferred from the Army to the Air Force under the name of Shaw; he preferred to be known by that name, and no objection was seen to his being accepted for service under it.

Hansard. February 6th, 1929

MR. THURTLE asked the Secretary of State for Air if it is customary for the Air Force to accept recruits for service under assumed names when it is known that such names are assumed?

SIR SAMUEL HOARE. There can hardly be said to be anything 'customary' in a matter of this kind, but it is well recognised that men do enlist under assumed names, for a variety of reasons, and definite provision is made in the regulations that a man who has done so may subsequently have his true name recorded by making a statutory declaration in the prescribed form.

MR. THURTLE. Will the right hon. Gentleman answer my question as to whether the Air Force accept a recruit when they know that he is using an assumed name?

SIR SAMUEL HOARE. The answer is, 'Yes, they do'.

Mr. Thurtle had given notice that he was going to ask further questions, and Lawrence felt sure that he would once again be turned out of the Air Force unless Parliament could be muzzled. He therefore decided to beard his persecutors, and one afternoon walked into the House of Commons and asked to see Mr. Thurtle and Mr. Maxton.

This visit, which led to a close friendship with Mr. Thurtle, entirely put a stop to the mistaken persecution, but it called forth a reprimand from the Air Ministry, and Lawrence was made to promise not to take any such step in future without leave. The whole affair, conducted by the Air Ministry largely in secret cipher telegrams, which had to be specially locked away or hastily burned, had been handled in quite the wrong way. Publicity of the fullest possible description ought to have been welcomed from the first, since it was the truth and the truth only which could allay suspicions. It is easy to be wise after the event.

But though it may seem that the circumstances of Lawrence's return, and the publicity which followed it, were such as to increase his persecution mania and foster his eccentricity, they counted for little in the long run. For some weeks he was anxious, angry, and sore; for some months he suffered intensely from the cold of the English winter. But though neither he nor anyone else realized it, Lawrence's return soon brought him renewed health, happiness in himself and in his work, and six years of comparative peace, during the last of which he was wrapped up in doing an important job.

All this was being brought to him by the officer who came alongside the *Rajputana* at Plymouth, and got him away without the reporters seeing him, and to whose squadron of Flying Boats at Cattewater Lawrence was now posted. Wing Commander Sydney Smith became not only Lawrence's Commanding Officer, but also a close personal friend who valued him as he deserved, and knew how to get the best work out of him in the interests of the Air Force. Lawrence became his Wing Commander's clerk: as such he had much to do with the arrangements to be made the following summer for the Schneider Cup race.

Incidentally while he was at Mount Batten (as Cattewater was renamed) he got a certain amount of flying on a Moth seaplane shared by Major A. A. Nathan and Wing Commander Sydney Smith, who tells me:

Shaw looked after the Moth in his spare time. During the weekends he flew a lot with Nathan as his passenger, and I remember they made several flights to the Channel Islands, and also to the Scilly Isles. In fact they explored most of the inland waterways of the South-West coast of England.

The registration number of this machine was G-EBYV, and it was one of the very few private Moth seaplanes in England at the time. The floats were detachable and could be changed over to wheels in about two hours. Major Nathan had some trouble about its airworthiness certificate and Lawrence used to tell a long comic story about a correspondence which he conducted with the Air Ministry on the subject, under Major Nathan's name, taking advantage of the fact that the regulations were different for land planes and for sea planes. By means of this he postponed the expense of an A.I.D.[1] inspection for several months. I have been unable to get this correspondence unearthed.

I include on page 639, since I cannot date it at all precisely, a section of the roughest pencil notes on the manuscript pages *Leaves in the Wind* which I believe were notes for a book covering later experiences in the R.A.F.

While Lawrence, was at Plymouth, Major Colin Cooper gave him his Biscayne Baby speedboat — one of six made by the Purdy Boat Company,[2] 'the six best things that the United States have made'. The possession of this speed boat added to the dissatisfaction which Lawrence and his superior officers felt with the slow naval types of boat provided to serve as tenders to flying boats. In the event of a crash something really fast was essential to save life. Lawrence accordingly started a campaign to impress the Air Ministry with the need of a new type of boat to act as tenders, and in many other ways in conjunction with flying boats. This brought him into touch with Flight Lieutenant Beauforte-Greenwood and Lawrence soon got the chance to become one of the team of men working to produce an all-weather marine speedboat of revolutionary design.[3]

He had found something really worth doing in the R.A.F. and he did it with all his might. He enjoyed almost perfect freedom from petty restrictions, and for a great part of the time was working with men who were proud to have him among them. 'Discipline itself is not necessary', he wrote at this time, because it had been replaced by devotion to the job that they were doing on the part of all ranks concerned. It was the work of a team and they did it so well that the other services had to take notice.

[1] Air Inspection Department.   [2] See Letter No. 418.   [3] See Letter No. 438.

Indeed the permanent effects of Lawrence's later years in the R.A.F. may be most noticeable in shipbuilding practice and in the Navy, and his influence on these has not yet reached its fullest extent.

He left the R.A.F. at the end of February 1935 and had trouble with reporters who for a time kept him away from Clouds Hill. He was once again planning to start a hand printing press — the dream which was never realized. But I have reason to believe that, had he escaped the fatal accident of May 13th, he would later have felt called on to take an active part in reorganizing the national defences.

Not the conquest of the air, but our entry thither.
We come.
Our soiled overalls were the livery of that sunrise. The soilings of
our bodies in its service were prismatic with its light. Moody or
broody. From ground to air. First we are not earthbound.

In speed we hurl ourselves beyond the body.
Our bodies cannot scale the heavens except in a fume of petrol.
The concentration of our bodies in entering a loop. Bones, blood
flesh all pressed inward together.
Not the conquest of the air. Be plain, guts.
In speed we hurl ourselves beyond the body.

We enter it. We come.
Our bodies cannot scale heaven except in a fume of burnt petrol.
As lords that are expected. Yet there is a silent joy in our arrival.
Years and years.
Long arpeggios of chafing wires.
The concentration of one's body in entering a loop.

368: TO H. G. HAYTER[1]

22. 1. 29.   [*S.S. Rajputana*]

Dear Hayter, It feels months since I was in Miranshah — and
is just a fortnight. Everything is very strange.

The telegram from you & Daphne arrived on board just as
the ship sailed. It was very kindly of you. I hope it will indeed
be better, now: but at Port Said, last stop, they picketed the quay-
side to prevent my going ashore. I'd like to say something with
a B in it about the India Government. In London I'll find out
what really passed, concerning me, and try to ensure that they
do not serve anyone else so.

I forgot two books, as I left: if they are still there, & it is easy

[1] Aircraftman at Miranshah.

for you, please send them also to T E Shaw, at 14 Barton Street. They are volumes I & II of William Morris' book *The Well at the World's End*. Fine things, and I am fond of them: but no matter if they are out.

Major Peirrot, who used to be Political Agent at Miranshah, is on the ship, going to England: and I will get him, or one of the other passengers, to take this up from Marseilles to post in England. I go round with the ship, of course: and do not get to London till February 1. There is no news yet of my posting: but I believe it may be Cattewater, where the ship stops for an hour or two, on her way up Channel. Corporal Easton will be jealous of me. I will be quite content and happy if I do not get the sack out of all this.

The only blessing has been the dodging a return by trooper. This is a 16000 ton ship, & we have had a smooth journey. Second-class is comfortable. I have a cabin to myself, as the ship is nearly empty: and pass the whole day in it, working at that Greek book. Since we left Bombay I have done three sections of it — just as much as I did at Miranshah, all the while I was there. So you see things have moved. They are not finished, these sections: they will need fair-copying and typing out in London, during my month's leave: but they represent a good two months of Miranshah production, done in two weeks. Voyages are binding things, & I'm lucky to have had this job to keep me busy.

At Karachi an irk[1] lent me a civvy suit: so I sort of pass muster in the crowd. They stare at me too much for comfort. However, there it is. I shall be stared at, goodness knows, a lot more in England.

You will have heard from Mr. Olson that I wasn't allowed to go to Delhi. So I could do nothing, with the A. V. M.,[2] of what I'd hoped. How is my successor? Does he curse me, all the day, for leaving everything loose? To go off at a night's notice, like that, wasn't fair on me.

I will send you a line after I've reported at the Air Ministry (yes, that's my orders: bad ones, I fear) to say what next: or when the death sentence will be carried out.

Again many thanks for that telegram. Yours   T E SHAW.

---

[1] An aircraftman.   [2] Air Vice-Marshal.

369: TO E. M. FORSTER

5/2/29   14 *Barton Street, Westminster, London, S.W.*1.

Dear E.M.F., I am being hunted, and do not like it. When the cry dies down I'll come out of my hole and see people — unless of course the cry doesn't die down, and the catchers get my skin. I have a terrible fear of getting the sack from the R.A.F. and can't rest or sit still.

Some anonymous person or persons bought and sent me a very large and new and apolaustic Brough:[1] so if my life is saved out of the hands of the hunters, it will be a merry one: yet there's a fly in the jam. So large a present (valued at three years of my pay) pauperises me a bit, in my own sight, for accepting it. Yours

T E S.

Of course, all Clouds Hill is yours, to take away. Are you ever in London?

370: TO ERNEST THURTLE

9/2/29   14 *Barton Street, Westminster, London, S.W.*1.

Dear Mr Thurtle, I doubt whether you properly observed the street's name or the number of the house, the other night. Will you hand it on, please, to whoever will return my books — and please remind them to be uncommonly discreet over *The Mint*, the R.A.F. book; for I have been told by the Powers that my visit to the House was not approved: told very distinctly, I'm afraid.

It was very pleasant for me that you were so reasonable, that night. You will realise that I can't spend an hour with everybody, explaining that there is no mystery: and I'm delighted to have had the chance, by lending you those two books, to give myself away to you completely. If Mr Maxton will read some of them, he'll never be nervous about me, either, again. Yours sincerely

T E SHAW

---

[1] Mr. and Mrs. Bernard Shaw.

371 : TO ERNEST THURTLE

28/2/29   14 *Barton Street, Westminster, London, S.W.*1.

Dear Mr Thurtle, It is nice of you to suggest our meeting again: but my time is very short. There is only Monday, Tuesday, and Wednesday left. Those are duty days, & you'll be in Westminster: so it would presumably be Soho, & not your plutocratic home! However probably you are tied up for all the time. I am free each night.

The getting back to camp feels to me the most desirable thing. I am longing to be in harness: and hope that you will not be able to abolish the three Services before 1935.

'Persecution' was a word I used in jest. Really, I could see that you were asking your questions to find out the truth: and I was glad of the chance of showing you the truth about me, so far as I could. You'll have seen that those books were not meant to throw dust in their readers' eyes: and it pleases me very much to have had you see them: Yet it would not please me to have everybody see them. My affairs don't seem worth that general interest.

Au revoir, some time: if it isn't on one of these next three evenings! Yours sincerely,   T E SHAW

372 : TO R. D. BLUMENFELD[1]

28/2/29   14 *Barton Street, Westminster, London, S.W.*1.

Dear Blumenfeld, I got ticked off by the Air Ministry, and told that I'd get the sack if I saw any more newspaper people— So since this I've been sort of paralysed. Thank heaven the subject of me has blown over for the present. I wonder what the next spasm will be about.

It was very good of you to see [*name omitted*]. A poor thing, I think. The fighting services haven't done very well, in political chiefs. However this remark is insubordinate, too. So I'd better shut up. They are sending me to Plymouth in a few days. I think the getting into camp again will be lovely.

More thanks. Yours,   T. E. SHAW.

[1] Then Editor of the *Daily Express.*

373: TO EDWARD GARNETT

14.3.29.   *Cattewater, Plymouth*

There, the address is easier than the usual Air Force address. I like the look and feel of the little place, too; but the cold is killing: just that.

I could not deliver *Lady Chatterley* to you, though I tried twice: and I didn't post it, not feeling sure of the little mountebank.[1] You may be evil-seen by him.

So eventually I dumped it on Garnett III,[2] who has promised to return it you. I liked spots of it: but the whole hadn't very much meaning for me. Of course it is outside my particular experience — thank the Lord.

As for *The Mint**: that too I dumped on G. III (why use him as an angel, I wonder?) who knows F. L. Lucas and thinks him a good critic. Incidentally he has written some v.g. poems, lately published by the Woolfs.[3]

Maurice Baring asked if he might see *The Mint*. I agreed vaguely. The word can be carried away on the breath of the wind, as Homer would say, if you do not wish to hear it! I am neither for it nor against it. Yours   T.E.S.

* which Dawnay dumped on me on Sunday last — no, Sunday week!

[The following letter is an answer to an invitation from Edward Marsh, a member of the Hawthornden Prize Committee, to present the prize to Siegfried Sassoon for *Memoirs of a Fox-hunting Man*.]

374: TO EDWARD MARSH

19.3.29   *Cattewater, Plymouth*

Dear E.M., I can't do that. It would be to arrogate to myself a claim to literary judgement, on the strength of one book produced

---

[1] Sir William Joynson-Hicks, afterwards Lord Brentford, who, as Home Secretary, made many ill-judged efforts to suppress works of art, including books and pictures by D. H. Lawrence.

[2] Lawrence referred to David Garnett sometimes as Garnett two, sometimes as Garnett three, depending on whether he counted in his grandfather or not.

[3] *Time and Memory*, published by the Hogarth Press, 1929. See letter No. 382.

under stress of external circumstances. A castaway on a desert island might similarly build himself a raft — without being a shipwright in after life. Writers are people who go on spinning their experiences into books, for sheer love of it, or inability to refrain. It's for this feeling that I wasn't really of the craft that I've stopped reviewing.

I hope S.S. will understand. I enjoy his work, because it touches nearer to my own train of mind than the work of anyone else publishing. Every verse of his makes me say 'I wish to God I'd said that': and his fox-hunting gave me a shock of astonishment that he was so different and so good to know. If I was trying to export the ideal Englishman to an international exhibition, I think I'd like to choose S.S. for chief exhibit. Only I wouldn't dare, really, to give him a prize. Some day, perhaps, if I wrote more, I might qualify for one at his hands. Only I have nothing to write, now.

If that happy day arrives I shall cut the ceremony: which would be rather a spavined ceremony, perhaps, without a prize-winner. I hope S.S. will turn up, this year. It is a very good thing you are honouring him. There have been some good Hawthornden books: but none better than these two. Yet what a horrible ordeal for him to sit there, eating, while people get up and say so![1]

Cattewater has been very cold, so far, but is a friendly-feeling and tiny camp, with sea on three sides, and barbed wire across the root of the peninsula. I think it is going to be all right. The sea is only 30 yards from my window!

I should thank you for the honour of your invitation: and shall feel that way about it so soon as it is safely refused. Yours T.E.S.

375: TO H. S. EDE

20.3.29   *Cattewater, Plymouth*

Dear Ede, Here we are. Cattewater proves to be about 100 airmen, pressed pretty tightly on a rock, half awash in the Sound:

[1] One is not given a meal in addition to the Hawthornden Prize.

a peninsula really, like a fossil lizard swimming from Mount Batten golf links across the harbour towards Plymouth town. The sea is 30 yards from our hut one way, and 70 yards the other. The Camp officers are peaceful, it seems, and the airmen reasonably happy. That is good hearing, for me, as I have to share their good fortune.

About your Gaudier book. It's really very good. Gaudier is quite clear, and so is she.[1] They both come, very intensely, *through* what you have written. That means you have done it well, in the large sense. In the smaller sense, syntax and the power of paragraphing, you have not done so surely. I could pick holes in any page; but the little things can be learnt, and are learnt, by going on writing: whereas the big thing, which is right in this case, comes right by instinct. So you are fortunate, and will probably write another book, after this one, and it'll be better than this. Do not leave Garnett to correct anything you can achieve yourself, by taking pains. Your own work is better, the more thoroughly you do it, for nobody else will really care as much for this book as you do. That's the way, always. Yours

T. E. S.

376: TO F. L. LUCAS

26.3.29   *Cattewater, Plymouth*

I don't want to write tonight, but I must. I'm on Fire Pickets all this week (i.e. distracted & oppressed) and can't settle down to read or write. However if I don't write you'll wonder what's the matter.

Your letter about *The Mint* delights me because it is really useful. Detailed criticism is the only useful kind. Ever so many thanks. Now I'll run through it & see if there are notes to reply. [18 *lines omitted*]

Others besides yourself have been troubled by the gap between

---

[1] The strange relationship of the young French sculptor of genius, Henry Gaudier, with the almost equally remarkable Polish woman, Sophie Brzeska, was the subject of H. S. Ede's *Savage Messiah*.

Depot and Cadet College. I was very unhappy at Farnborough, & decided not to put it on record. [10 *words omitted*]. After it I had 2½ years Tank Corps, which is a different subject, & would I think only confuse the R.A.F. picture. From the Tanks I returned for three days to Uxbridge, the R.A.F. Depot, & *went thence to Cranwell*, as I describe. That gave me the chance to carry the story straight through. Do you think I ought to expand the 'explanation' into greater length, & detail the Farnborough & Tank Corps digressions? I have some raw notes: but they are pretty grim reading.

My bowels have twice or thrice destroyed my poise of stoical indifference, which is proper to a man of action! A bit of a handicap, is funk: to people of the V.C. class, in which reputation would put me! Of course I know, in myself, that I'm not a brave person: and am not sorry. Most brave people aren't attractive.

In 'Last Post' the all clear signal I handed down the hut was that Corporal Abbinett was again in bed! Sorry. Too much compression there, apparently.

I do think that conscious, deliberate exercise is an evil thing: but I didn't class 'prostitution' as important. There are so many prostitutes that one can't take them tragically. [7 *lines omitted*]

I would like to say much more about Trenchard some day. A very noble and unusual person.

We do regard flying as a sort of ritual: more an art than a science, it is. Unreasonable to expect other people to feel like that, of course: but it is not an unpresentable Crusade: compared with the Lord's Sepulchre.

You don't like my saying that the old Depot is reformed away: and wish for a moral. But I tried not to moralise or condemn more than the instruments through whom the system worked. As a victim I have hardly the right to condemn.

I am glad you feel the difference between Cadet College & Depot. E.M.F. said that Cadet College didn't 'come through' as a happy place. I re-read the MS, before it went to you, & was inclined to disagree with him.

It seemed to me to contain better 'bits' than the first two parts. No doubt they are too 'bitty': a whole Cadet College would be longer than Depot.

Speed is a wonderful thing. I wrote a string of articles about bike rides: but the *Motor Cycle* paper would not take them — so this is the sole survivor. Last Saturday I had a good run up to London (235 miles) & returned on Sunday. Averaged over 40: and touched 94 at times. A nobly running bike.

Of course one is always apart & intact: but to see another airman in the street is (for me) like one ship sighting another at sea. The sea becomes not lonely, all at once.

Yes, I would like the dedication of your novel:[1] everybody would. You are a very good writer. Your poems (of which I'll write to you when I feel less unworthy of them) prove it. They are a delight. Yours   T E S

377: TO W. M. M. HURLEY[2]

1.4.29.   *Cattewater, Plymouth*

[*24 lines omitted*] Cattewater is a quietly decent station, rather new: but it feels promising. I've begun unluckily by clicking Fire Picquet over the Easter holiday — There isn't anyone in the R.A.F. who does as much holiday duty as I do. That is the firm conviction of at least half the airmen enlisted!

It is quaint your being at Amman. Difficult flying; the hardest, I think, there is. That Jordan valley is a terror in summer and the Palestine 'dromes are not too good.

Peake is a very good fellow. He has stuck splendidly to three or four thankless jobs, and made a deal out of them. A hot, impatient, soul, too.[3]

I enclose you some sample pages of Joyce's latest (not yet ready for publication in book form) and remarks by A.E. on Joyce and his poetry. There is this colony of dispossessed English and American and Irish writers living rather intensely in one another's cheap lodgings in Paris and writing desperately hard. I fancy, for myself, that they are rather out of touch with reality; by reality I mean shops like Selfridges, and motor busses, and the *Daily Express*. At least there is a hot-house flavour about their

---

[1] Lucas dedicated *Cecile* to Lawrence. See letter No. 415.
[2] Flight Lieutenant, R.A.F.   [3] See letter No. 147.

work, which makes me wonder if it's a wholesome day-to-day food. Remarkable, certainly, but a bit funny. However people who do not practise writing aren't really qualified to judge of it. Yours sincerely,   T. E. SHAW.

378: TO ERNEST THURTLE

1.4.29.   *Cattewater, Plymouth*

Dear Thurtle, (This sounds very familiar) I have read your little bomb. It would modify all subsequent wars. I do not see it coming off: but I think the death penalty will cease pretty soon. The debates on it in the House make my blood boil. I wish I could talk to some of the old stagers for a few minutes, about funk & courage. They are the same quality, you know. A man who can run away is a potential V.C.

A possible modification of the enlistment regulations *might* be brought in by some progressive government: to allow service men to give notice (a month, 3 months, six months: even a year: plus such money penalty as seems equitable) & leave the service in peace time. At present to buy yourself out is difficult. The application is usually refused. Anyway the permission is an act of grace: whereas it should be a right. I think the knowledge that their men could leave the service would effect a revolution in the attitude of officers & N.C.Os towards us. It would modify discipline profoundly, for the good, by making it voluntary: something we could help, if we wished. We would become responsible, then, for our behaviour. At present we are like parcels in the post. It is the peace-army & navy & air force which is the concern of parliament. War is a madness, for which no legislation will suffice. If you damage the efficiency of war, by act of Parliament, then when the madness comes Parliament will first of all repeal its damaging acts. Wars, in England, well up from below: from the ignorant: till they carry away the (reluctant) Cabinet.

Graves' book isn't apocrypha [8 *words omitted*]. I eat anything except oysters & parsnips. I live in barracks (i.e. we dog-fight promiscuously). What is handshaking? The reason I had no overcoat was financial. It seemed a wicked waste of 3 or 4 pounds, for a mere month.* When I felt cold I changed into uniform. G.B.S. lent me his second overcoat: but it was too gigantic a cloak for my normal wear. If it rained: yes: or late at night. Our evening was not too chilly. I'm very susceptible to cold: in England I'm always getting into hot baths, whenever they are available: because then only I am warm enough. Yet I never get what they call 'a chill'. Odd: because usually I get all the infections going!

Please don't get the public feeling that I'm different from the crowd. By experience in many camps I have assured myself (so certainly that all the print in the world won't shake my conviction) that I'm a very normal sort of Anglo-Irishman.

Women? I like some women. I don't like their sex: any more than I like the monstrous regiment of men. Some men. There is no difference that I can feel between a woman & a man. They look different, granted: but if you work with them there doesn't seem any difference at all. I can't understand all the fuss about sex. It's as obvious as red hair: and as little fundamental, I fancy. I will try & call at Temple Fortune Hill, & pay my respects: but I will make no promise. London's centre holds so many pleasures for one who has wasted 20 years abroad: and I'm selfish enough to go walking by myself usually. A sense of social duty does sometimes overcome me, & while it lasts I pay calls, & try to recall my manners. Only so often (especially in new houses) I feel like a Zoo beast without bars to defend me. There are all these absurd stories, with, in my fancy, people watching to confirm them, or make new ones. I know that is absurd: but you can write it down as a nervous affliction. The wearing a false reputation is as itchy a job as a false beard. Mine drives me crazy.

Yes, I get a huge correspondence: and the answering the justifiable percentage (20°/$_0$) makes an inroad on my time. Also there is a Yankee dealer who pays £20 for my letters. Would you write, *ever*, if that happened to you?

---

* I daren't spend my little reserve of cash. Any moment press chatter may extrude me from the R.A.F. & I've got to live while trying to find a rumour-proof job.

If ever you come to the far west, by all means let me know, & if I can we'll meet somewhere: but my bike has no pillion: so you are safe not to break the speed law on my tail. Airmen are not allowed to carry pillion riders, or ride pillion. Another injustice! Poor troops. Yet I wouldn't change with any civilian. Yours

T E SHAW.

Cattewater is shaping well. I shall like it, in the warm weather (if any).

379: TO H. A. FORD[1]

18.iv.29.   *Cattewater, Plymouth*

Dear Flight, Here we are: and as for choking off the Press — he will be my friend for life who finds how to do that. I do nothing — and they talk. I do something — and they talk. Now I am trying to accustom myself to the truth that probably I'll be talked over for the rest of my life: and after my life, too. There will be a volume of 'letters' after I die & probably some witty fellow will write another life of me. In fact there is a Frenchman trying to write a 'critical study' of me, now. They make me retch — and that's neither comfortable nor wholesome. I have thought of everything, I think: to join a newspaper (they do not eat each other, the dogs) — but what a remedy for the disease: to emigrate — but those colonies are as raw as wood alcohol: to commit some disgraceful crime & be put away: — but I have some people whose respect I struggle to keep. I don't know.

Meanwhile here we are. Cattewater treats me very kindly, & I have work enough to keep me pre-occupied: and in the evening a musical box to discourse Beethoven & Elgar; Oh, a super-box, like a W/T[2] set inside, with an exquisite smoothness and fullness of tone. I assure you, it is good.

I read your 9th Symphony score very often, trying to keep pace with the records. Music, alas, is very difficult. So are all the decencies of life.

In August I may be in Malvern. They are doing G.B.S.' new

---

[1] Flight Sergeant, R.A.F.   [2] Wireless Telegraph.

play[1] there on Aug 19th.21.27. & 31. and *Heartbreak House*, a marvellous work of art, on 23. & 28. and I'd like to hear them. It is not sure, for the Schneider Cup may make me very busy about that time. But if possible I'll be there. Any chance of you? It is near Shrewsbury: perhaps I might come over one night?

Yours   T.E.SHAW

That snobbery 'He does not associate with the other airmen, except a few of the more intellectual' — God, it's poisonous. If I could get that reporter by the neck he would want a new one in 5 minutes.

380: TO H. H. BANBURY[2]

18. 4. 29.   [*Cattewater*]

Dear H.H.B., Yes: seaplanes involve motor-boats, and so we grow 'webbed' toes. This camp stands in the sea. I think it will be lovely, if the sea gets hot and the sun too. Meanwhile I am still mainly conscious of the cold.

I have heard Carden Lloyds working. They crawl up and down Clouds Hill, to the temporary damage of its peace. However, what's temporary?

Yes, Lydd is on the sea-edge of beautiful country. You should be able to find plenty of appetite for driving round it. There is something about S.England which makes me, in every valley, on every ridge, say 'Oh, I want to have a room here, and sit in it looking and looking!' If my name was Rockerfeller, I'd have 3428 cottages, and spend my time flitting from one to the other (a different name in each) round every ten years spell of my unendurably long and slow life.

Three Persons[3] wasn't as good as it seemed at first. The Wilson article left out of him his greatness — an extraordinary fellow he was. House was respectable and serious. Upon me he was irritating. He patronised me, I thought, damn him. What does he know about prose that he dares praise mine? [2 *lines omitted*]

---

[1] *The Apple Cart*.   [2] Regimental Sergeant Major, Royal Tank Corps.
[3] *Three Persons*, by Sir Andrew Macphail, 1929, dealt with Colonel House, Sir Henry Wilson, and T. E. Lawrence.

[Sir Edward Marsh informs me that, having heard a rumour that Lawrence had read D. H. Lawrence's *Lady Chatterley's Lover* three times in borrowed copies, he sent him his own copy as a present as 'his need was greater', and that in consequence Lawrence lent him *The Mint* to read. The following letter is remarkable, and Lawrence's letters to Lionel Curtis (Nos. 205 to 209) about the privates in the Tank Corps do not bear out his claim that he had 'met only a handful of people who really cared a biscuit' for 'the sex business'. The most interesting thing is that after his several readings of a book which went so much against the grain, Lawrence was able to make the best criticism I have read of *Lady Chatterley*: one which shows complete sympathy and understanding of its author. See letter No. 411.]

381 : TO EDWARD MARSH

18.iv.29   *Cattewater, Plymouth*

Dear E.M., What a cursed shame, to write to you the 25th letter of tonight! Tomorrow at dawn I'm due to fly to Calshot, for a day or two or three in the forthcoming Schneider Cup zone: and I saw the vast pile of letters in my locker and said 'those shall be answered before I go': and they are all finished. Yours wasn't a letter but something very magnificent: *Lady Chatterley*. I'm re-reading it with a slow deliberate carelessness: going to fancy that I've never read a D.H.L. before, and that it's up to me to appraise this new man and manner. D.H.L. has always been so rich and ripe a writer to me, before, that I'm deeply puzzled and hurt by this *Lady Chatterley* of his. Surely the sex business isn't worth all this damned fuss? I've met only a handful of people who really cared a biscuit for it.

This isn't a letter: it's only a receipt.

By the way, are you all right (speaking terms, I mean) with Maurice Baring? Because I sent him my R.A.F. ms two or three days ago, and it might interest you to borrow it off him when he's finished it. M.B. is an amateur of the R.A.F., like me: but he doesn't know the other ranks in it, and won't like their dirt and brutality. In some ways it's a horrible little book. Like over-brewed tea.

Ever so many thanks for the book.   TES.

382: TO ERNEST THURTLE

26. IV. 29   *Cattewater, Plymouth*

Dear Thurtle, I hope you successfully pass the test[1] next month, & go back again for seven years. If your people win, do try & carry them with you about the death penalty. I feel it a blot and reflection upon your fellow-humans who have been brought to enlist in the Services.

Yesterday I met Lady Astor, who said nice things about you. She's sickening, too, with election fever. I hope she gets in. A rare creature: very swift and yet kind.

I will call, if I can: but I'll promise not to keep on calling! My feet are happy when they tramp up down London: and to go into a house breaks the rhythm, & is a deprivation. A little of it is good, as variety: but if I did all I should, there would be no street-time left.

I've been in London (for a night) twice, since March 7. Not bad. Last run took 4 hrs 44 minutes to do — and about two days to recover from!

If the public would let me choose the next House of Commons, it would be a decent & friendly little gathering. One despairs rather, though, over this electing business. Hot blood isn't a good counsellor.

I must put in a last word about my abnormality. Anyone who had gone up so fast as I went (remember that I was almost entirely self-made: my father had five sons, and only £300 a year) and had seen so much of the inside of the top of the world might well lose his aspirations, and get weary of the ordinary motives of action, which had moved him till he reached the top. I wasn't a King or Prime Minister, but I made 'em, or played with them, and after that there wasn't much more, in that direction, for me to do. So abnormal an experience ought to have queered me for good — unless my skin was as thick as a door-mat. What feels abnormal is my retirement from the active life at 35 — instead of 75. So much the luckier, surely.

Here's a good little poem of F. L. Lucas, a Cambridge don

---

[1] The General Election of May 1929.

and very subtle fellow, to cap my not very imaginative explanation. Yours   T E SHAW

> They laid Protesilaus to his sleep
>   Beside the Hellespont: there long ago,
> Out of his dust where now the peasants reap,
>   Twin elm-trees used to grow,
>
> Set by the nymphs, and taller in their pride
>   Than all the trees of Hellas. Day by day
> Their boughs climbed upward till their tops espied
>   The fields where once Troy lay —
>
> And straightway withered.[1]

383: TO A. E. CHAMBERS[2]

27.IV.29   *Cattewater, Plymouth*

Dear Jock, So there you are. One said dead, one deserted, one signed on: and all the while you sort letters in the Post Office. Such a nice job, sorter. If you send the Glasgow letters to Costa Rica nobody can trace it to you: and the *Daily Mail* makes a snappy paragraph & *Punch* ditto.

I am now at Cattewater, & very seldom stir out of camp: so we can't hope to meet till my leave comes, if come it does. I hoard that month, against the dread day that a film about me may be released. *If* it comes I take the month, & hide somewhere.

Clouds Hill is still there. I saw it for an hour in February. It is lovely as ever: only chimney-pots are added as a monument of the new tenants' taste. Jock, the old tenants were 'some' people. You & me, & Guy, of the R.A.F. and the brothers Salmond, (Marshals of sorts) Hardy, Graves, Siegfried Sassoon, poets: Forster, Tomlinson, Garnett, prose-writers. Spencer & John, artists. It was a good place while it lasted. I wish there was a Clouds Hill in every camp, assigned for the use of aircraft hands.

One Serg-Pilot Thomson asked lovingly after you lately. I told him you were dead. He said it was unlikely. More probably you were making someone carry a bag of your books.

---

[1] The complete poem consists of ten stanzas, and was published in *Time and Memory*. See letter No. 373.

[2] Chambers had been an Aircraft Hand at Farnborough with Lawrence.

The books have not increased much, in the last five years. Sometimes I send three or four to join the others in Richards' hands: sometimes I part with a few. Richards himself has now gone to S. Wales, & his brother, Dr. E. M. Richards of 3 Loudoun Road, St. John's Wood (not so far from Dollis Hill: Oval tube & then walk it, probably) has them in his house. If you had this letter, & found him in, he would let you take a bag-full of them away, & exchange at leisure.

Jock, I'm very weary of being stared at and discussed and praised. What can one do to be forgotten? After I'm dead they'll rattle my bones about, in their curiosity. Au revoir   T.E.S.

I've put W.C.Chambers, because those obviously aren't your initials. We always called you Jock for short. What's C.E. in the address?

384: TO DAVID GARNETT

4.5.29.   *R.A.F., Cattewater, Plymouth*

Now there are three things to write to you about. *No Love*,[1] Shakespeare and [*name omitted*]. In that order, I think.

What took me at once in *No Love* was the reality of the people: more especially of the minor people. The Admiral was best of all. It was a most vivid study of several admirals I have known. The scene in the bakery, where he comes in and reads a poem, for which faculty nothing in anything you had said had prepared us, is altogether admirable. It struck me like a ballet. There was something so deliberate in its orchestration and arrangement, and the balance of art and life most beautifully kept. You realise, probably, that you stand wholly outside the realist movement. Your work is symbolist, through and through. Everything of yours which comes off does so by virtue of some significance carried in the acts or words: a significance not stated anywhere, nor possible to state, nor implicit nor concerned with anything the people you create may be doing or saying. It just happens, every now and then, that one halts and says to oneself 'This is

---

[1] *No Love*, by David Garnett. Compare letter No. 394.

tremendously important: this *matters*'. How or why God knows. You have no notion, I expect, that anything is wrong. However it happens.

Excuse the typing. A new typewriter, to me; and me set to use it a bit, to get my hand in. I'm just dreaming along on it by touch.

Back to *No Love*. Roger is better than Benedick: at least I think so. Do not ask me to qualify every phrase in this letter by 'I think so'. I do. Simon was very real as a boy (incidentally your children are all good) but he was faint towards the end. Did you get exasperated with the bunch of them? I did, rather. They seemed to lose their way in life, and to stray a bit aimlessly. Of course that is real too: but an author's characters should be better than life, or it's hardly worth our mind's while to invent them. If all we did was to invent people who were passably real, it would be easier and more realistic yet to go and procreate real children on any woman. Notice that 'we': I talk of myself as an author!

Wherefore I did grow angry with Simon, and Cynthia (she is a bit of a ghost all the time) and Benedick, after the elders were dead. You see, the elders were the better drawn, and the riper people. Your young ones never got grown up at all: only the shine of youth seemed to rub off.

Last book of yours I read left me with an abiding sense of a low country: fennish or next door to fens: water and willows or poplars, and an air that was moist. In this book there is no landscape at all: or only one old tree arching over the sleeping kids on the shore. Otherwise a void in which these astonishingly real people gyrate and hover. London does not appear, nor the bombardment, convincingly. The people, Benedick and Cynthia, are alive in it. They wake up astonishingly, during that London leave. It is their final kick before they die on you: but London remains only a back-curtain. I suspect you meant this too. One is always pulling up at some astounding simple line or move on your part, and saying 'Is this the simplicity of a child or of someone so grown up that he can be childish?' There is a feeling as of superb skill and deliberation about the progress of your novel. This limpidity is too good to be true. It is not Defoe, but Swift or Kenneth Grahame. Apologies for likening you to K.G. Nor do I mean to liken you, here, to any model. Your first three books were resonant with echoes of other men's styles and work. Not this. It is independent.

However, as I say, I'm sorry that you denied yourself land-scape. It is nice stuff. You do it well, too. Perhaps you do not know that side of the Hayling-Portsmouth area well enough to let yourself go? Another time I hope you will put your people in a non-geographical place, and let yourself go, descriptively. If you can get walking and talking people, you have got one third of what the novelist wants. The other third is something keener seen than the earth of our eyes, to set them in: and the last third is something for them to say better and richer and riper than the stuff we can say ourselves. You have put each of the ingredients into one or other of your books. Now I want you to stir them together into one pudding.

So much for *No Love*. Forgive the crudity of my criticism. I have no theory or notion of art: but I do like to read novels. And there are so many almost good enough: and so few that are quite good enough to be better, like yours. You are growing all the time. Yet I wish that you had not written *Lady into Fox*. Every-body will urge you all the rest of your life to make them more toys of the spirit.

We turn over to the Nonesuch *Shakespeare*. There you[1] have created a most marvellous pleasure. I have handled it ever so many times, and read *The Tempest* right through. It satisfies. I do not feel that I shall ever need to think again of an ideal Shake-speare. It is final, like the Kelmscott *Chaucer*, or the Ashendene *Virgil*. And it is a book which charms one to read slowly, an art which is almost gone from us in these times. Every jewelled word which Shakespeare uses stands out glowing. A really great edition. The tact and grace of your editor have been sur-passing.

I think I like the size and shape and binding almost as much as the text. The paper too is just right. Altogether a triumph. It is overwhelmingly good of you to have given it to me. One of the best things is that it can be done again. Nobody will ever

---

[1] David Garnett was a director of The Nonesuch Press.

dare to produce the old type of edition now, while your text stands there to reproach them. It means a permanent improvement in Shakespeares.

Now for the woman. Ouf. [*50 lines omitted*]

385: TO ROBERT GRAVES

5.5.29   *Cattewater, Plymouth*

Dear R.G., Forgive the typing. It is a new machine, on which I am to be efficient tomorrow: this is Sunday, and I'm taking my rawness off on it, by typing a dozen private letters, before tackling any R.A.F. stuff. [*omission*] Honestly, R.G., hasn't the scale of your judgement been out, lately? It is not my business, and I cherish my own freedom to do as I like too much to dream of interfering: but you have been so drastic in your condemnations of ordinary people, of late, that I've been afraid to stay near you. You see, I know by the best of all proof (contiguity with ordinary men in barracks) how ordinary I am; and because ordinariness is not wholly a flattering feeling, I have been led to look for my own likes in ordinary people: and from that I have grown to see the ordinariness in nearly everyone. But whereas that makes you rage and condemn, it makes me feel akin and friendly. I like your stuff, because so often you seem to me to say clearly something that all our generation is trying to say. There is no monopoly of feeling: lots of people are feeling like you: but only an occasional man can say it decently. It is a great thing to have the power of words: but it does not make one man different from another in kind, as something that L.R.[1] said when we last met half-implied.

God Almighty, what a sermon when you are down with an abscess (that is rotten, but cures itself) and unhappy and do not want to ramble about inside the meaning of life. It is raining here, has been raining dismally since last night. I have done a Church parade, and the Hut is full of wireless and gramophone music (by the way, I never thanked you for the new Sophy,[2] which added a new horror to life for weeks. Sophy is always a battleground, like all things vitally vigorous. The Hut is divided into

---

[1] Laura Riding.   [2] Sophie Tucker.

pro-Sophy and anti-Sophy, and squabbled as nearly as Huts can squabble) and I have come back into the Office to hammer out this stuff for you. I should be doing Camp Standing Orders, Order no. 15 (Fire Orders), but it is too cold for my fingers to type sensibly: also I've been thinking about you since yesterday when the letter came. There is a horrible little trawler outside, that keeps on edging nearer and nearer to the rocks on the South side of the Camp. I suppose it's the wind, dragging her anchor. They are getting steam on her, to save the expense of a tug. If she does not get her steam going in the next hour or two, the little beast will go ashore in front of the cookhouse, and then the duty boat (for one of whose crew I'm a stand-by this afternoon) will have to go out and do the life-saving stunt. It is humiliating to save someone's life at no risk to one's own. Also it is as cold as charity. Since I came back from India, I have been always cold. I wish England could be towed some thousand miles to the South. [16 *lines omitted*]

386: TO H. G. HAYTER[1]

26. VI. 29   *Cattewater, Plymouth*

Dear Hayter, I am a miserable slut not to have written to you before. Alas, I'm so weary of being yet a crawler on the surface of the earth that I would rather sleep than eat or think or work or read or write. Too lazy even to put a record on the gramophone.

You did very well to let F/Lt Smetham have those records: and he stumped up decently for them. I hope that 28 Sqdn. have settled in peacefully and are decent souls. How's Corpl. Easton? Tell him to come home. England is better than Miranshah.

I've got my A M W O's[2] published, about bayonets to church and overcoat top buttons. Now I want bayonets declared obsolete and kit inspections made annual. After that we must wash out sticks. O Lord: and I am so tired, and want so much to lie down and sleep or die. Die's best: because there is no reveille.

Tell Corpl. Easton that his wife is looking ever so much better. She and I sat in committee on his last letters. I think all's for the

---

[1] Aircraftman at Miranshah.   [2] Air Ministry Weekly Orders.

best: except the change of Government, which puts Nancy's nose out of joint. Who's Nancy?[1] Why, ask the Corporal.

Sgt. Cowton I met in London ten days back. We had an 8 o'clock breakfast at Lyons in the Strand on Sunday: when you were in bed and your hound on top of you. Pegsy-Wegs Erben, a photographer from Miranshah, turned up here yesterday, disguised as a Corporal. So you can hope. Cattewater is very good: but I am too tired for a MacDonald. If it was Miranshah I would dodge under a net and forget my sins and the world's weariness.

Oh, the books. I got bundle upon bundle of them, & Sgt. Cowton has others. Every possible thanks be given to you. My new bike is a peach. 4000 miles, only, on it: but all good. Alas, how tired I am of bikes & books & music and food and drink & words and work.   T.E.S.

387: TO ERNEST THURTLE

26. vi. 29   *Cattewater, Plymouth*

Dear Thurtle, (Yet it doesn't sound right: M.P.s are Misters surely, being our Masters)

I did not write after the election: there are so many M.P.s that one can't write to all. I'd hoped too for some crumbs of office to come the way of the more vigorous Labour people: and am disappointed. Ramsay seems to be infected also by the safety play of his enemies. The country is prepared (longing, in fact) for someone to take just a tiny risk, for once.

Now the session has started, and I hope it will be educative. Unless the change of Government means a change of policy we'd better wash the Commons out and concentrate on the Civil Service.

I am hoping especially that you will let Trotsky[2] into England: that you will make peace at once with Russia and the States: and that you will abolish the death penalty for cowardice in war. I have run too far and too fast (but never fast enough to please me at the time) under fire, to throw a stone at the fearfullest creature. You see, if I did, I might hit myself in the eye![3]

[1] Lady Astor.   [2] Trotsky had asked permission to visit England.
[3] See letters Nos. 408 and 409.

Cattewater is a good station, and we are happy-ish.

Remember me, some day if you see them, to Maxton and Malone. After the Schneider Cup race, after September, I hope to get leave and will then try to look you up.

Do you know Montague, the U.S. of S.[1] for Air? Sassoon was very good & painstaking. I hope M. will shape well, in his place. Yours   T E SHAW

388: TO F. N. DOUBLEDAY

28. VI. 29.   *Cattewater, Plymouth*

Effendim, I have done ten days solid duty in camp, and am again free to go out: only instead of that I write you a line, to recall that very golden day we had. Do you know, It was all exquisite? Kingswood, Kipling, Knole, Ashdown Forest, the lunch. Years since I drove, lordly, in a pleasure car: the R.A.F. has its transport, of course, but that is hardly driving. The leisure of our progress along the roads, and the warmth and good talk inside the car, all left a happy feeling. It was a great, exceptional day: and as it gets more distant I perceive my debt to you an increasing one. You is plural. Mrs. Doubleday at last loses the distinction of a postscript. She made half the pleasure of that trip. I hope that you and she also still enjoy it. Of course it isn't so rare a pleasure, for you. You (and she) would have to join the Air Force to squeeze all the flavour out of luxury. Only when one person is as happy as I was, the other two must have felt some sunshine.

The R.A.F. here appears to value my services. At least I work all day at its jobs. Just I have half an hour in the morning, before breakfast, which I keep for my own reading. I make the half-hour, by getting up before reveille. One can't *read* in odd half-hours: reading is to soak oneself hour after hour all day in a single real book, until the book is realler than one's chair or world: but I've done most of *The Brook Kerith* in these half-hours: and tasted the Heinemann life[2] (only half-kind to him, that book is. It feels as though the poor little man hadn't been properly understood)

---

[1] Under Secretary of State.
[2] *William Heinemann, a memoir,* by Frederic Whyte.

and read all Enid Bagnold's *Happy Foreigner*. That last is surprisingly distinguished. I give her full marks for a good book.

Frere-Reeves[1] wrote to me, two excellent letters, about good printing. I shall go to see him when, or if, I get leave in October. I have a design of sliding down some odd day (Dear, it *will* be an odd day!) if he permits it, and I achieve it, with Bernard Shaw and Mrs. Shaw to look at Kingswood.[2] You would like Mrs. Shaw. She is quaint and comfortable, and fresh, and kind. G.B.S. is exciting, per contra. Together they are like bacon and eggs, and [a] harmony in blue and silver. I fear I talk nonsense.

Do go on writing your memoirs. Put in that story about the roses pinned to the pickets. Dictate quite a lot, for then that dry sparkle will cling to the words. Pens are stiff things to hold, and they make our words too mannered.

Not to spoil the pleasure ship with work I put a business request on a spare sheet. Remember me very much to Mrs. Doubleday. Tell her to start imagining another excursion for next time. If its only $\frac{1}{10}$ as good as that it'll be good enough. Yours,   T. E. SHAW.

I've had twinges of conscience since, that perhaps I tempted you to overdo things that day. I am so indecently fit and durable. I hope you were not ill or tired, even.

389: TO MARSHAL OF THE R.A.F. SIR HUGH TRENCHARD

12/vii/29.   *Cattewater, Plymouth*

Dear Sir Hugh, This is immensely important, quite different from last time. I have been saving it up for you for years: — not that you are the right person to go to, at all: but you are more likely to display imagination upon the matter than any other person of greatness in the Air Ministry.

These Airships:[3] one or two of them are to have trial trips soon. Some say to the States, others say to Karachi. I have seen the

---

[1] Partner in William Heinemann, Ltd.

[2] Printing works belonging to Messrs. Heinemann at Kingswood, Surrey. Doubleday had, at that time, a large interest in Messrs. Heinemann.

[3] The R.100 and R.101 (ill-fated as is usual with airships) were approaching completion. Lord Thomson, Labour Secretary of State for Air, was greatly interested in them.

shed at Karachi, and the Mast at Ismailia, and think it likely that sooner or later one of them will go that way.

Well, by going just a few miles out of their course to the south-ward they can pass over the Ruba el Khali, the so-called 'Empty Quarter' of Arabia. This is a huge area of many hundred thou-sand square miles. No European has ever crossed it, nor any Arab any of us has actually questioned. All the Geographers refer to it annually as the great unsolved question of Geography.

Now, I want the trial trip of the airships to settle the Ruba el Khali. On every later trip they will be running to schedule, unless some American millionaire hires them for a million a second to go over the desert for him. On the first trip they will be inhabited mainly by their crew, and it will be easy to deflect them. To go over the empty quarter will also be an enormous advertisement for them: it will mark an era in exploration. It will finish our knowledge of the earth. Nothing but an airship can do it,[1] and I want it to be one of ours which gets the plum.

If you consult the map you will see that it is a very slight diversion from their course between Karachi and Ismailia. I would like it to be an unheralded diversion. Not a newspaper stunt exhausted by superlatives before it begins. Take the geographical world by surprise.

The Navigator of the airship will be getting his W/T[2] bearings & time signals all the way, and will plot his course exactly. I do not think there will be anything much to see — sand, sand, & hills, perhaps — but the comfort of having finished, in twelve hours, what man has been projecting for 50 years. . . .

Do think it out, properly, and say yes. I do not ask to be let go, myself. I'd love it, of course: but the important thing is to get it done, without talk: and I think you have enough weight with the Civil side and with Burney's company[3] to get it done.*

Yours,   T.E.SHAW.

Cattewater is still v.G.

* Push me on to them, as advocate, if they are constipated.

[1] See letter No. 435 for Lawrence's enthusiasm when Bertram Thomas crossed by camel. St. John Philby has since then crossed the Empty Quarter in the other direction.
[2] Wireless Telegraph.
[3] Sir Dennistoun Burney was responsible for the design and construction of the R.100. The Airships were controlled by the Civil Aviation Department of the Air Ministry.

390: TO B. H. LIDDELL HART

14.VII.29   *Corfe*

I'm here, temporarily settling some problems concerning my
Dorsetshire cottage. Going back this afternoon. I hope this
letter will arrive in time. Your wire was sent on to me.

1. Directly, the C.A.S. might abolish, by a word, bayonets and
walking-out canes. Bayonets because they are costly (16/- each),
take long to maintain (about 1 hr. per month, except where a
buffing-wheel is available), ugly, and useless. I'd call them dangerous, for there was an idiot Squadron Leader who used to practice
open-order attack, in France: waving a sword himself. A fool
like that might easily throw away a squadron. Aircraft are a long-
distance weapon, and bayonets are out of place in them.

2. The walking-out cane I can leave to common sense. You
saw mine: and saw that it's a silly bodkin of a thing, no use as
stick or weapon, and no ornament. It was designed, I believe, to
keep troops hands out of their pockets: but R.A.F. tunics and
breeches have inaccessible pockets, in which no man can keep his
hands. Whereas hands and stick both go into our overcoat
pockets.

The C.A.S. (Trenchard) has already done two or three of the
reforms I urged on him, and repeated to you. So the job is
lightened.

3. Kit inspection is another bore. It's supposed to be held
monthly, and troops have to show all their kit. This is ridiculous.
Our working dress is inspected daily, our walking-out dress
weekly, in the normal course of duty. All that is required
(besides these two suits, in case of active service which is the
justification of kit inspection) is spare socks, spare shirts, pants.
Instead of laying everything, which confuses the eye of the
Inspecting Officer, and involves everything being very tightly
folded, to be got on the bed, troops should (once a quarter) leave
out on their beds their spare underclothing, and go off to work.
And the inspection should be done by the Flight Officer and his
N.C.O., at leisure. It shouldn't be a parade, or a beauty-show:
but an inspection to make sure that our normally-invisible kit
was serviceable and complete. There is no need for us standing

by. That makes us hot and ashamed, and the decent officers feel like nosy-Parkers, and avoid looking at us.

4. The last thing is a very small point. In the navy, an officer or N.C.O. entering the men's mess takes his hat off, whether on duty or not. The airmen would like this to become the general rule in the R.A.F. It is in some stations, where the C.O. is ex-navy.

There were many other things I'd like to talk about: marriage-establishment rosters, overseas-rosters, posting of airmen in England to the stations most convenient to them (a Scotchman in Plymouth: home fare — £5: an Englishman in Leuchars: ditto). Pillion-riding on motor cycles (airmen are the only people in England forbidden it: not soldiers, not sailors. It's rather an insult to what we fondly hope is the most dangerous service). The week-end pass (I'd make after duty Saturday till Reveille Monday free for all men not warned for duty. Every station keeps a duty crew). I'd make an Air Ministry regulation about plain clothes. At present one C.O. allows them, and another restricts them. Chaos and irritation. It is a very valued privilege, I'm sorry to say. Church parade. This is the most annoying parade of the week. Couldn't it be made voluntary? I think I could get the consent of the two archbishops to that, if the Air Ministry is shy of the C. of E.

391 : TO LADY ASTOR

22/7/29.   *Cattewater, Plymouth*

Dear Lady Astor, I do not know when, or with whom, I have ever maintained for so long so hot a correspondence. Clearly we are soul-mates.

Incidentally an American dealer pays £20 for interesting letters from me: so heaven knows the prices which infatuate collectors will give for yours. Are we worth it? I mean, aren't we rather wasting our sweetnesses on the already sweet?

I enclose the telegram, as it came to me. I had been in London, on R.A.F. business, and found it waiting my return. I said 'Goddes, who is it?' for necessity causes me to write about 50 letters a week, and some of them might have brought down terrible people to Cattewater. However, no one came. Peace.

Auf wiedersehen (Dirty dogs, they *have* stopped off poor Trotsky[1]: penalties of success!)   T.E.S.

392 : TO MARSHAL OF THE R.A.F. SIR HUGH TRENCHARD

29.VII.29.   [*Cattewater*]

Dear Sir Hugh, I knew you'd consider the Empty Desert idea: I hope it will be in your time. Philip Sassoon would have helped it, with his imagination. I don't know your present team.

I spoke about it to G.B.S. and said if he met Lord T.[2] would he urge it on him? Unfortunately he wrote to him, instead. Writing isn't so supple an appeal. Also he seems to have mentioned me, which of course disquiets the civilians. I wanted the job considered on scientific grounds. It is the last piece of exploration on earth. Doing it completes our knowledge of the globe. It can only be done safely, cheaply and quickly by an airship. I want the doing it to be an Air Ministry deed, without press warning or pressure, beforehand. Let us* get the credit: and for the Lord's sake do it quietly. If I am of the crew, I'll get the credit: the press loves that sort of cheap personal touch. It would be much better if your maps staff officer went, and your best navigator, and a draughtsman and an intelligence man, to write something plainly official. Yours sincerely,

                                          T.E.SHAW

* Us is the R.A.F., in case you don't know!

393 : TO LORD LLOYD[3]

29.VII.29.   *Cattewater, Plymouth*

This disgusts me[4]: first me, then you, G.L., what in God's name is the matter with our blasted governors? Thank the Lord the

[1] Trotsky was refused asylum in England by the Labour Government.

[2] Lord Thomson, Secretary of State for Air.

[3] Lawrence's close friendship with Lord Lloyd dated from the time when they worked together in the Arab Bureau. They were also together in operations against the Hejaz railway. See *Seven Pillars of Wisdom,* Chap. LXXII and Chap. LXIII.

[4] Lord Lloyd had resigned the High Commissionership of Egypt.

worst lot are out.[1] Winston I liked, and Philip Sassoon: but if all the rest were drowning across the way in a ditch I wouldn't take the trouble to go over and push 'em under.

It's a magnificent bang, you've come out with: go to the National Portrait Gallery and look at the head of Warren Hastings, and learn how to grow old: but I've been sick at fearing how you would hate the ending of things. *You* haven't an Air Force to fall back on: only the mouldy House of Lords.

Let us meet sometime. I'm not a corpse, quite: but it's horrible being out.   T.E.S.

394: TO H. S. EDE

29.vii.29.   [*Cattewater*]

[20 *lines omitted*] Another and another letter from you turns up, unanswered, I'm afraid I'm a beast. One holds an admirable summation and demolition of the thesis of *No Love*: I am entirely with you. Such titillations of the spirit are prostitution, and nasty Maddox St. prostitution at that. Better be like a healthy bull and cow in a field.[2] [12 *lines omitted*]

The Meynells. I have not met them. Do not worry about David Garnett's criticism.[3] The man is over-educated, too good a craftsman, and so short-sighted. People chasing anything big have no use for rules. Your Gaudier is the goods.   T.E.S.

395: TO SYDNEY COCKERELL

29. VII. 29   [*Cattewater*]

Dear C., Statues are so difficult, unless someone quite first-rate does them. Epstein is the obvious choice, only he is not, I expect, a Hardy lover, and when he improvises he is not enchanting. Night on the Underground House is lovely: and

---

[1] The Labour Party having won the General Election in May.

[2] Compare letter No. 384.

[3] Of the manuscript of H. S. Ede's *Savage Messiah*, a life of Henri Gaudier-Brzeska, which had been offered for publication to the Nonesuch Press.

Day rather forced. The Hudson Memorial is a gem: and the Medical building quite meaningless.

Dobson is a good sculptor, and might do something as beautiful as his Welsh War Memorial design: but he would hardly work to order. Kennington would do a fine design, but he never met Hardy. Gill — would Gill be good, do you think? It is embarassing to have four good English sculptors: embarrassing & unusual!

Dorchester of course wants to possess T.H. Too late, poor things. He has assumed half Wessex for his own.

I hope to see the 2nd *Applecart*: 27th Aug.[1] I think it is. A very difficult date for me, as I am one of the groundsmen for the Schneider Cup.[2] Yours   T.E.S.

396: TO ERNEST THURTLE

29. vii. 29.   [*Cattewater*]

I nearly rang up your house last Wednesday, when I was in London on duty, and invited myself to tea. Only after all it seemed nicer* to go out along the Embankment. I hadn't been in London for a while, and so wanted to see it. They have smashed Lambeth Bridge, & will now destroy Charing Cross. If it was Westminster, now, I should not grieve. Westminster is too wide, and rather tinny. I like it only for the Wordsworth ['sonnett' 'sonett' *crossed out*] sonnet.[3]

I tried to sum up the loss I felt when the Tories went out, and found that I was sorry Philip Sassoon had lost the Air Ministry. Also I feared that Tom Jones[4] would regret losing Baldwin.

* This reads frightfully rude. It was a hot day, my uniform felt as tight as an alderman's skin, my boots as heavy as lead, my legs like balusters. The embankment was really nicer than the tube to Golder's Green.

1 See letter No. 379.
2 Lawrence had written to Robert Graves in May about his leave: 'The annual I cannot have till after the Schneider Cup race on the seventh of September. I am doing the clerking and correspondence for our C.O. who is the big noise on that.'
3 This letter and the preceding one are good examples of Lawrence's erratic spelling.
4 Then Secretary to the Cabinet.

Perhaps he will not. I am glad you partly like Montague.[1] Lord Thomson does not hold my respect, not that I know him, but he wrote a bad book, and took a peerage.

You are amusing about Trotsky: but he's so much one of the big figures of the world that I'd like England to have the honour of housing him. I confess I am not afraid of him or his work. If the country isn't contented enough to refuse revolution, then I'm a very poor judge of a situation.

Don't fly off with the idea that I laud this contentment: I think the planet is in a damnable condition, which no change of party, or social reform, will do more than palliate insignificantly. What is wanted is a new master species — birth control for us, to end the human race in 50 years — and then a clear field for some cleaner mammal. I suppose it must be a mammal?

Your attempt to abolish Church Parade was good. To achieve it you must proceed administratively. The House publicity renders such reforms impossible. Lobby the Archbishop of Canterbury. Persuade him to suggest it to the P.M. See that the change is put on grounds of true religion. Persuade the P.M. to whisper it to the S. of S. for War. Then ask your question . . . and the S. of S. with a pleased smirk says 'The matter has been the subject of ripe consideration in my department, and I am glad to say that the Chaplain General has worked out a scheme (for putting into force immediately) which will meet the changed conditions of our time, in the matter of religious observance.' Always get it settled before you speak to more than two ears at once.

You, too, have seen how close my reputation sticks. Will you believe that the Foreign Office asked, that day I was in London, if they were sure I was not now in Kurdistan, where tribesmen are fighting the Persian troops? The imbecility of official minds.

T.E.S.

Democratise the Services? O Lord, that doesn't matter. Make them decent for all classes, please, by delivering us of superstitions & callousnesses.

---

[1] Frederick Montague, Labour Under Secretary of State for Air, 1929-31.

397: TO WILLIAM YALE[1]

22.x.29   14 *Barton St., Westminster*

Dear Yale, Robert Graves passed me your letter, and I have delayed answering it, while I tried to borrow for myself a copy of my *Seven Pillars*, to see what I said 10 years ago. However I've not found one, and my leave expires on Thursday, so I must write from memory of what happened in Damascus. [*37 lines omitted in which Lawrence gives particulars of his action with regard to the Damascus Hospital described in Chapters CXXI and CXXII of 'Seven Pillars of Wisdom'*] I left on October 4th, I think, for England.

About the Lebanon & Beyrout. I had secured a promise, from Feisal and his staff, that they would leave it alone, for the European allies to occupy. This promise was made me in Wejh, as Graves seems to have stated. (I have no copy of Graves' book, either!) Upon the taking of Damascus, Feisal & myself lost control. The Syrians (Ali Riza[2] & the Bekri brothers) took charge, and galloped (metaphorically) straight for the coast. My intention had been to occupy from the gap of Tripoli northward to Alexandretta, and I had told Feisal that in the welter which would follow victory he would stand a very decent chance of getting this area eventually allotted to the Syrian kingdom upon terms. I still think that it was a possibility, and that the precipitate occupation of Beyrout and Lebanon wholly threw away the local people's chances. Shukri was sent to Beyrout by Ali Riza. I was much too engaged in struggling with difficulties of Damascus to attempt to cope with Ali Riza. Anyway, all my thought was of going home, where I meant to get transferred to the French front. The eastern business was badly on my nerves.

There was nothing either Sherifian or mine, therefore, in the occupation of Beyrout. I was opposed to it, on grounds of interest, and Feisal had ordered his people to have nothing to do with litoral Syria south of the Tripoli gap. You can support this statement, perhaps, if you will see that no one of the Sherifs, or of the Arab army, or of us, went there. It was entirely a Damascus move: as was the fatuous proclamation of King Hussein in Damascus. These things were as much anti-Feisal as any-

---

[1] Professor of History, University of New Hampshire. See pp. 282 to 294.
[2] See p. 226.

thing. The Damascenes hoped to avoid the near activities of Feisal by appealing to the distant Hussein, who hated Feisal. I had no intention of proclaiming or creating any king in Damascus. Feisal governed it as an army commander of Allenby's, an unassailable position. King Hussein was a nuisance to me, only. If Shukri told you I had urged him to Beyrout, it was probably that he was getting frightened at the magnitude of his error, and wanted to make-believe that he had authority.

Your remark that 'British political officers were working to create a situation in Syria which would make impossible ... the Sykes-Picot treaty' amazes me. The S-P treaty was the Arab sheet-anchor. The French saw that, and worked frantically for the alternative of the mandate. By a disgraceful bargain the British supported them, to gain Mesopotamia. Under the S-P treaty the French only got the coast: and the Arabs (native administration) were to have Aleppo, Hama, Homs, Damascus, & Trans-Jordan. By the mandate swindle England & France got the lot. The S-P treaty was absurd, in its boundaries, but it did recognize the claims of Syrians to self-government, and it was ten thousand times better than the eventual settlement*

In justice to England I must add that financial pressure, the Mesopotamian rebellion of 1920, and perhaps conscience aroused by my agitation in London, did finally persuade England to abrogate, de facto, her mandates in Irak and Trans-Jordan, though she still holds them, de jure, to exclude third parties. It is my deliberate opinion that the Winston Churchill settlement of 1921-1922 (in which I shared) honourably fulfils the whole of the promises we made to the Arabs, in so far as the so-called British spheres are concerned. If we had done this in 1919 we could have been proud of ourselves. The French had made no promises, and they refuse to adopt our liberal policy. That is a pity, but past our curing.

This letter has grown too absurdly long. As if anybody now

* This should be qualified. There was a secret Paris settlement, a working arrangement between Clemenceau & Feisal, which had germs of hope: Millerand tore it up, & launched Gouraud on Damascus with his army!

cares what I did, or you did, or England or France or the Arabs did, ten years ago. Leave it for 50 years. If Irak continues to put up a decent show, across three generations, then the Arab Revolt was worth while. In our lifetimes we cannot reap either credit or disgrace: and after I'm dead my bones will not care. Winston's settlement so pleased me that I withdrew wholly from politics, with clean hands, I think, and enlisted in the Air Force, where I have the happiness to be, still. It is not glorious, but very free of cares, healthy, and interesting. I have not been to the Middle East, or read a book or article about it, or written or received a letter thither or thence, since 1922 when I joined the R. A. F.

You say you want to read *The Seven Pillars*. It is a rotten book, a dull book, hysterical, egotistical and long. It is also (God be praised) rare. As I said, I can't borrow a copy, here, for my own reference in writing you. I believe some copies did go to U.S.A.; but they say it's a large country. Mrs Lamont had one. Doubleday the elder had one: also Kermit Roosevelt. Speculators pushed its price into hundreds of pounds, & all wise people promptly unloaded: so I hope they have parted: for the thing has slumped. That's the English edition. There is also a U.S.A. edition, not complete. A copy of this is available, I fancy, in Congress Library at Washington: but how Washington lies from New Hampshire I don't know! Believe me, if you don't see it you miss nothing.

Oh! peace negociations! Feisal and Jemal were carrying on quite serious peace negociations all 1918. I saw both sides' letters unbeknownst: I should have been morally indignant with Feisal, only England was secretly negociating with Talaat, also to my unofficial knowledge, all 1918 too. All is fair in love, war, and alliances. Poof! Me for the Air Force! Yours sincerely

                                                    T. E. SHAW

[More difficulties were in store for Lawrence. Wing Commander Sydney Smith, Lawrence's C.O., was a member of the Committees responsible for the arrangements for the Schneider Trophy race held in September 1929, and Lawrence, acting as his clerk, was closely concerned in carrying them out.

This brought Lawrence into prominence. He was seen chatting to many distinguished persons on familiar terms, and the spectacle of an aircrafthand so employed exasperated and scandalized the sense of fitness of the Labour Secretary of State for Air, Lord Thomson. See letters Nos. 401 and 410.

Liddell Hart gives the following particulars:

The evening after my return [in late September] T.E. dropped in to see me and told me that he was under sentence of expulsion from the Air Force — by the original arrangement, his contract of service could be terminated at any time by either party. He had come up to London to make a personal protest against the decision, and I gathered from him that certain friends were interceding on his behalf. Next day I did what I could to help. A day or two later I heard from T.E. that he had been reprieved — I cannot remember whether I learnt of this by telephone, letter, or visit. But I did not hear full details until a month later when he came in to see me after I had returned from my holiday. This time I found time to make notes of some of the points he mentioned, and had a particular reason for doing so.

L. had interview with Trenchard, not on Thursday, September 27th, as arranged, but on Monday, September 30th ... T. told him he was reprieved on condition that henceforth he did an ordinary A.C.'s job solely; never went out of the country, even to Ireland; never visited or spoke to any "great men" — e.g. Winston, Austen, Birkenhead, Sassoon, Lady Astor (i.e. all politicals). G.B.S. not banned — and when he told G.B.S. the latter rather annoyed at not being counted.

L. feels that R.A.F. is foolish not to get more than daily 3/- worth out of him. Had, however, only done ordinary A.C's job until Schneider Cup. Real cause of trouble was that he was seen talking to Balbo at Schneider meeting. The R.A.F. put a working party on to their own slipway to clean it and left Italian one slippery with green scum. And L. got Italian slipway cleaned at Balbo's request.]

398: TO W. H. BROOK

30.XII.29   *Mount Batten, Plymouth*

Dear Brook* Stokes[1] that was. It is rather fun hearing from you. I forget what I wrote exactly in *Revolt*: I hope it wasn't rude. Some people said I was rude to everyone. You didn't deserve it, if so, for you and Yells did a very good job of work there with us. Probably there is a lot more of rude remarks about you in the bigger book, *Seven Pillars of Wisdom*: but that, thank God, you'll probably never see. I haven't copies of either the little book or the big book. That's what I think about them. . . .

The poor kid — am I to god-father him? Fathering I've dodged so far: god-fathering is possibly easier, as one doesn't have any financial responsibilities. Don't tell the child he's named after me, because then he would have to change to Shaw, and again to something-else later on, like me! Of course I shall be very pleased: but you say the little misery is only a few weeks old. Perhaps he will turn out a violent pacifist (unlike his father) and curse us both as a couple of blood-stained old dodderers, when he is old enough to curse. They talk, I believe, at about two (parrots not before five) and walk at much the same age. Infant camels, as you have probably told Mrs. Brook, can walk three hours after birth. One up on them.

You do not say what you are doing now. I assume that it's not what you did in Arabia: though parts of Brecon would lend themselves well to irregular war. I've come down in the world — enlisted about eight years ago (when the politics of the Middle East got smooth, and let me go) and propose to stay on enlisted till my beard is long and white. It is a life which pleases me — few cares, some friends, a little work, much laughing.

I must stop: you'll be getting bored. If ever the summer arrives next year, and the roads get hard & dry, then I'll try & roll up on a motor-bike and teach the young idea road-sense. Let's see, he'll be about one then: not old enough to hold a licence, but coming on. Yours   T E SHAW.

* Please note (for imitation) the entire absence of ceremony!

[1] Brook was the Stokes gunner of *Seven Pillars of Wisdom*, chapter LXVI.

8.1.30   *Mount Batten, Plymouth*

'10 St James Square will always find us'. Good. I have been meaning to write to you for months. 'You' is good. Which? Don't ask me.

F/Lt Smetham sent me from Kohat in India two photographs of myself: one life size (about): the other more of a white man's burden. These, he said, were for you and All Souls. Fortunately I played buffer state between him and an outraged Oxford Society: (*photograph* in the College! Lord!!!) and stuffed them into a bag in Barton Street. Not but what they were beautiful photographs:[1] T.E.S. against a Waziri desert, softly lit, nursing his excessive chin with one bent arm.

An American lady, Mrs. [*name omitted*] of Euclid Avenue Ohio, wrote to me last week (via the War Department, London) 'You are my ideal of a real he-man'. The letter had been opened in Air Ministry. I hope they take it to heart. That's the dope they want in the R.A.F.

In October, on a beautiful sunny afternoon, I burgled your house. Ralph was kind to me, and let me out. We found a title deed to some land of mine in Epping Forest, and sent it to the Chingford Urban District Council, whom the Forest Commissioners are bullying into buying it. The house was a wilderness of bricks: and not itself therefore. I suggested to R. that perhaps Mr. Curtis was building an Empire: but he said it was an enlarged study. That is like the Admiralty, whose staff grows as the Navy shrinks.

In a few days you go to the U.S.A. Excellent. Do not hesitate to go from them, too. If you see Ivy Lee, will you give him my regards? He sends me papers sometimes: and I cannot retaliate. Now if I were you, I'd dash him an interleaved few chapters about the Jewish Constitution and settle him for good.

I spend innocent days R.A.F.ing: and all night study to turn Homer into English. Why? Why for money, of course. I am broke at present.

Will you (Sing.Fem.) ask You (Sing.Masc.) to get the Rocke-

[1] One is reproduced opposite p. 614.

feller Institute to dash me a million dollars (less would be infra dignitatem, as O'Casey says: do try and see *The Silver Tassie*, his play, in New York. It is astounding) upon some pretext or other. Homer is so slow a way of earning money.

No news. Since Nov. I have not been out of camp, except once a month, to get my hair cut. It blows: rains: hails: and we are all healthy and happy. May you be so too.   T.E.S.

400: TO W. H. BROOK

8.1.30   *Mount Batten, Plymouth*

Dear Brook, Don't believe more than ⅛ of any yarn you hear of me: or 1/16 if it is printed. I never do. They say I don't answer letters because I don't write letters without some good reason, or more than ten letters a week. Hang it all, a fellow must sleep sometime! And letter writing is what the R.A.F. call a 'bind'.

Good for the proxy for the Christening! I hope the kid yells blue murder all the time. I should, if a padre picked me up & poured *cold* water on my face.

As for coming — yes, a Brough does eat up the miles; but I seldom go out of camp, for one reason and another, often financial! Brecon is not near Plymouth — not a Wednesday afternoon run: and I don't ever week end — so I shall not hope to turn up till I get my month's annual, in the late summer, perhaps. I will write you again before that.

As for Arabia — that was twelve years ago, & I've got old & wise, and have forgotten it all. What a lovely place Rumm was! I believe nobody has been there since 1918. Yours   T E SHAW

401: TO H. G. HAYTER

8. 1. 30   *Mount Batten, Plymouth*

Dear Hayter, Alas, our kidney and bean at Lyons will have to wait. I am up to the neck in Greek, again, the next section of that stuff I used to wire into at Miranshah. They gave me a hundred for what I did out there: on that I made merry all last summer (with that & the Schneider Cup, to which I was clurk) and now I'm broke, and chasing hard at the second hundred. Till it comes I can't do London — not much before May, I think.

Life here goes smoothly. In November I had a tiff with Lord T.[1] our present boss. He tried to sling me out: I double-crossed him. So am airmanning on. Our C.O. here is a treat. Grub is better than Miranshah grub: Plymouth is a rotten hole; the sea is lovely, in summer, & hell in winter: and it's work work work. I wish Greek had never been invented.

An Italian bad-hat[2] dashed me one of those electric gramophones: and it sits in our hut. Everybody else plays it very well. Greek Greek Greek for me. All the same that portable was good at Miranshah. I hope yours is doing its stuff.

I ought to write to Corpl. Easton: indeed I ought: to how many people should I write? about 13426897438, I think. To how many will I write — perhaps 6 or 7. Alas. I am a miserable sinner.

Let me know about Heyford later. I was nearly sent there: and would like to know
1) Guards or Fire Pickets?
2) Drill Parades?
3) Equipment (I haven't drawn my blue yet!)? When worn?
4) Bullshit generally?
5) Week-ends?
Just in case. Yours   T E SHAW

Will pink envelopes float up Heyford way? Or are you married, and a monthly postcard?

402: TO LORD LLOYD

13.1.30   *Mount Batten*

Dear G.L., I've thought it over[3] during a bad week-end of gale, in which we nearly swamped ourselves rescuing a derelict: and I have decided against.

---

[1] Lord Thomson.
[2] No doubt one of the party which had come over for the Schneider Cup, if there *are* Italian bad-hats.
[3] Lord Lloyd had invited Lawrence to fulfil a plan which they had made during the war to ride by camel in peace time across the Nejd and down to Oman.

Lord Thomson would make great difficulties, but that is not the real reason. Actually it is the weakness of the spirit which I fear. If I went back there I might be drawn into things again: and it is better that I keep clear.

It was very good of you to ask me, and I would have loved it. Only Arabia and book-writing are two of the things which I must not do, obviously. I hope you go, and like it. Ibn Saud has my respects as a King: [3 *words omitted*]. He will be better — but weaker — now he tries to rule without the Akhwan.[1]

It will be a wonderful trip. Commend me to them both: I.S.[2] and Feisal. They are doing a fine thing, between them.   T.E.S.

403: TO LADY ASTOR

19. 1. 30   *Mount Batten*

Dear Lady Astor, What an undisciplined person you are! I was given positive orders to cease from meeting you, so far as that lay in my power: so I can't come and see you. It would not be fair to the terms on which I have been in the R.A.F. for the last eight years, and on which I hope to serve for five years more.

I haven't got a heart: only the former site of one, with a monument there to say that it has been removed and the area it occupied turned into a public garden, in pursuance of the slum-clearance scheme.

I know, respect and like Tom Jones.

I am duty crew here (one week's engrossment in motor boats on the Sound & Cattewater) so cannot be spared for the Naval Conference. 'Sink the Lot' would be my advice, only alas I have not been asked it!

I was 'taken' to Flete: the Wing Commander promised in my name, & asked me so warmly that I couldn't (lacking a heart) say 'No'. It shall not happen again.

I sit very tightly in Camp, working hard to make myself petrol money for next summer's activities. Next summer, I hope to motor-bike, & speed-boat and fly a bit: the last if I can get Sir

[1] The Puritanical Wahabi Brotherhood.   [2] Ibn Saud.

John Salmond (now my lord & master) to relax Trenchard's order against my flying.

I should like to hear Lord Thomson's opinion of my abilities! My opinion of his character hasn't been asked for, but I'm quite willing to hand it on through your 'curious but direct' way if you think it would be wholesome. It is not very kindly.

Alas, I am out of date. I cannot conceive why Lionel should want Geoffrey Dawson[1] to see Malcolm MacDonald: or why any of them, backwards or forwards, should want to see another. However cats may look at kings. Only I mustn't look at you. That proves that you aren't a king, & me not a cat. That proves that you aren't a cat & me not a king. I wish I felt as safe, for you, as I do for myself.

You are *distinctly unsatisfactory* about [*name omitted*]: please allow Mrs Shaw, who is as wise as 10 000 of you & me, to look at her and say the right word. I do not trust the judgement of anyone in either the House of Commons or the House of Lords. Yours ever   T E SHAW

Japanese sunset effect obtainable by underlining the 'I' in letters for your enjoyment and necessary inaction, please. You will notice that I win by three to one.[2]

404: TO W. A. KNOWLES[3]

10/2/30   *Mount Batten, Plymouth*

It is very good of you to keep the place warmed occasionally. More books go to you almost at once. You'll find some of the packets have quite decent things amongst them — though generally they are what the troops call my 'binders'.

I wish I had the cottage near this camp. For the last four days we have endured an agony of cold.

---

[1] Editor of *The Times*.

[2] The nominative capital I in the original is in every case underlined.

[3] Sergeant Knowles was Lawrence's neighbour at Clouds Hill and the father of Pat and Dick and Bill.

Is Pat still there? My regards, if within reach. Poor E. M. Forster has lost nine of his trees (he has a plot of ground, too, in Surrey) and is miserable about it. I gloated back at him that all my old wrecks still stood firm. But is it firm? This N. wind will try them, bitterly.

There are lots more books likely to follow. Let me know when the shelving gets full: and then try & find me a chippy to run shelves like the present, but in oak, the full depth and height of the chimney-breast, on each side. That will hold 500 books. Years yet.

Chingford, my other patch of ground, is not yet sold. So I am temporarily financially embarrassed. Good for me. I stay in camp and translate Greek, instead of gadding about the earth. Yours   T.E.S.

Pull Bill's leg for me, please.

405: TO DAVID GARNETT

14.2.30   [Mount Batten]

I once knew Rawlinson's *Herodotus* well. It is — respectable, I think. Not as good as Herodotus, one of the best of men, deserves: but what he got. Yet I think there is (in Christchurch Library, perhaps) extant a MS version of Herodotus in English by Francis Hickes,[1] who did Lucian's *Vera Historia* into an excellent prose: not Elizabethan: plainer than that: definitely Stuart. If Hickes did do it, then he might be worth your while editing well.

Rawlinson's notes, of course, will not now do. They are pre-Ramsay, as regards Asia Minor, and pre-everything, in Egypt. There is your difficulty. You will not find an archaeologist today broad enough to straddle the Middle East. Hogarth was the last archaeologist to marry humanity and science in that fashion. How nobly he would have done Herodotus!

---

[1] I was unable to find any trace of this in Christ Church library. Francis Hickes completed Jasper Mayne's translation of Lucian's *Dialogues* (1638) and *True History* (1663).

Garstang is the Asia-Minor name, after Ramsay, who is rather beyond your reach. [1 *line omitted*] Woolley next comes to my mind. A good fellow, witty, sociable, experienced; an admirable digger, who from two broken bricks will deduce a palace. Only your *Herodotus* would be too complete under Woolley's hands. [2 *lines omitted*]

Honestly, I do not know. I rather think I should not employ a specialist, but rather a gatherer-together of knowledge: and I am out of date, with them, and know too few to pick a best. I have been impressed with the verve and ruthlessness of my own brother — a younger brother — who calls himself A. W. Lawrence, and has published two books on Greek sculpture via Cape.[1] He has dug in Mesopotamia, and travelled over the earth, and owns a good pen. I wonder if he would do you, and if you would please him? His address is c/o The British School of Archaeology, Athens. If he wouldn't do it himself (the young man only does what he pleases, rather haughtily) he would at least tell you who was the boniest and most wilful of the younger men. Do your best to get someone really good. Herodotus is a marvellous fellow. I incline to credit everything he saw, and to give him credit for intelligence and judgement in sifting the stories that he heard. Also he is pre-eminently human. A first-rate *Herodotus* would be a most useful book: only I'm worried to think of Rawlinson as the vehicle. Good of course, very good, as scholarship goes: but Rawlinson was too sober. And the notes aren't easy, for, as I say, Herodotus straddles Greece and Asia Minor and Persia and Syria and Egypt: and modern archaeologists get famous by digging only one thing. Alas for Hogarth's dying: I think you might do worse than try my brother, at least for an opinion.[2]

I'd like to see your flying thing. Flying is, as you know, one of my madnesses. [*name omitted*[3]] No, I do not remember him. Too many people remember me at Uxbridge! Actually I was not identified then with my past, so no one noticed me.

---

[1] *Later Greek Sculpture* and *Classical Sculpture*.

[2] A. W. Lawrence edited the edition of *Herodotus* published by the Nonesuch Press, on which I had sought advice.

[3] A ground engineer who had told me he had known Lawrence at Uxbridge.

406: TO FREDERIC MANNING

Dear Manning, No, it wasn't Rothenstein: and I cannot get up to London this week. Now-a-days I'm lucky to fetch London once in three months, and it is only a month since I was there. As for the authorship of the book[1] — the preface gives it away. It is pure *Scenes & Portraits*. How long, I wonder, before everybody knows? You need not worry at their knowing. It is a book everyone would have been proud and happy to have written.

Of course I'm ridiculously partial to it, for since 1922 my home has been in the ranks, and Bourne[2] says and thinks lots of the things I wanted to have said. But don't imagine that I'm anything like so much of a lad as he was. The R.A.F. is as gentle as a girls' school, and none of us drink.

I have read too many war books. They are like drams, and I cannot leave them alone, though I think I really hate them. Yours, however, and Cummings' *Enormous Room* and *War Birds*[3] seem to me worth while. *War Birds* is not literature but a raw sharp life. You and Cummings have produced love-poems of a sort, and yours is the most wonderful, because there is no strain anywhere in the writing. Just sometimes you seem to mix up the 'one's' and 'his's': but for that, it is classically perfect stuff. The picture about ⅔ through of the fellows sliding down the bank and falling in preparatory to going up for the attack, with the C.O.'s voice and the mist — that is the best of writing.

I have read *Her Privates We* twice, and *The Middle Parts of Fortune*[4] once, and am now deliberately leaving them alone for a while, before reading them again. The airmen are reading the *Privates*, avidly: and E. M. Forster (who sent me a paean about the *Privates*) has *The Middle Parts*. Everyone to whom I write is loudly delighted with the *Privates*. I hope the sales will do you good.

Peter Davies is trying to use my dregs of reputation as one

---

[1] *Her Privates We*, by Frederic Manning, published anonymously by Peter Davies.
[2] The hero of *Her Privates We*.
[3] By Elliott Springs, See letter No. 452.
[4] A larger and unexpurgated version of *Her Privates We*, published in a limited edition.

more lever in the sales. Do not let that worry you. Adventitious sales and adventitious advertisements are very soon forgotten: the cash will remain with you, and your book be famous for as long as the war is cared for — and perhaps longer, for there is more than soldiering in it. You have been exactly fair to every-one, of all ranks: and all your people are alive.

This is not a very sensible letter. I am very tired, and this weather gets me down: only I owed it to you to thank you for the best book I have read for a very long time. I shall hope to meet you some day and say more — and bore you by saying it — for what is so dead as a book one has written? Yours T. E. SHAW

407: TO CAPTAIN SNAGGE

4.3.30.   *Mount Batten, Plymouth*

Dear Snagge, Your letter showed, fortunately, that you are prepared for my not coming.[1] Plymouth is too far, and I am busy putting a Greek book into English (for hard cash!), so never go out at all, not even to the town outside our gates. I call it dissipa-tion to get to London three times in the year: and manage that much by favour of the C.O. here, who gives me a giant week-end very rarely.

I'd have liked to have seen Jaafar Pasha (is it Pasha now? 'Sheikh Jaafar', King Hussein called him. Time has its revenges) again. All my memories of the war, whenever he is in the picture, are pleasant ones. You know, he made even Tafileh in winter-time a joke. When the papers told of his coming to Weymouth, lately, I looked up the times and distances, wondering if my motor-bike would get me there and back in the half-day: I might have tried it, if it had been summer time, for Saturday is always a half-day.

Will you give him my best regards? I imagine, somehow, that he is going back to Bagdad soon: in that case I'd like him to

---

[1] Admiral Snagge explains: 'This letter was in reply to an invitation I sent to Lawrence to attend a luncheon party which I gave in honour of Jaafar Pasha, then Minister for Irak in London, who had been handed over to me as a close Prisoner-of-War on board H.M.S. *Humber* during the Senussi Operations, and whom I had known subse-quently when he became the General commanding the Arab-Beduin Army at Akaba.'

remember me to Nuri and the others: and especially to tell the King that I watch the history of Irak with great pride. It is a lasting pleasure to me that so much construction should have come out of all the destruction and effort of the war. It was in places like Jerdun and Deraa that the new Irak was founded. Jaafar is very lucky in being able to help in the two shows. I hope Young is playing up well.

There are two other things I would like off Jaafar, if he will be so good — a word to say what the two enclosed letters are. One I can see is from Auda ibn Zaal: and the other I think must be from poor little Sherif Nasir ibn Radhi, of Medina. Only I had heard that he was dead. I cannot read Arabic, and cannot make out what it all is.

Tell him, please, that I am so sorry not to have seen him all these years. The photographs in the paper show that his shadow has grown less; but if he sees Joyce he will see that *his* shadow has grown greater.

I'm much as before, except for my beautiful long white hair. If Joyce turns up too, why then give him my regards also. Explain how the R.A.F. holds its slaves in remote places, so that they cannot see their friends.

It was nice of you to ask me. Yours ever,   T. E. SHAW.

408: TO ERNEST THURTLE

8/3/30   *Mount Batten, Plymouth*

Dear Thurtle, More power to your elbow. The cowardice charge is a blot on us.

About helping you — as a serving airman I must not make reflections upon military matters. *Before I joined* I could & did say what I pleased. I cannot prevent your quoting what I then said: so your best tactics are to say 'As Colonel L. said some years ago' or something of the sort: do not ask my permission, because I cannot give it; and yet I would love to be taken advantage of, in this cause! 'Lawrence' is better publicity than 'Shaw'. It's quite a good quotation; rings true & likely: them's my sentiments exactly.

Sir Ian Hamilton might lend you a hand. He is an un-official general. I cannot think of anybody else likely to be useful. To have circulated a petition at that V.C. dinner some months ago, & got them all to have signed it, would have been the right thing.

'Courage & chivalry' attached to me! Do remember how lately I was burned in effigy on Tower Hill:[1] you must be careful, or they will burn you too. Now if the Die-hards had burned me I should only have laughed.

This is written in a hurry, between duties, so excuse its scrappiness. I'll write to you again soon. Life is smooth, & not bad. Yours   T E SHAW.

409: TO ERNEST THURTLE

13/iii/30

Dear Thurtle, The way I have it is

'I have run too far and too fast under fire (though never fast enough to suit me at the time) to dare throw a stone at the fearfullest creature. You see, I might hit myself in the eye.'[2]

And I should introduce it neatly by saying Col. L. *on his return from Arabia* said (neat introduction of the word 'Arabia' to distinguish which Colonel L, without the pseudo-title of L. of A.)

My position should be the same as Ian Hamilton's: but I've had the luck of an interim in civil life. Yours   T E SHAW

410: TO JOHN BUCHAN

21/3/30   *Mount Batten, Plymouth*

Dear J.B., This is disastrous. A day or two ago I got a letter from St Andrews, asking if I'd take a Doctor of Laws in May next. I naturally concluded it was a student leg-pull, and sent it cheerfully back to the address given, saying that it was no go. How could I be expected to imagine it was serious?

[1] At a Socialist meeting, when Lawrence was the Arch-Spy of Imperialism.
[2] See letter No. 387.

Now it seems you were at the bottom of it, and they meant it. It feels an incredible thing to have happened. I thought that honorary degrees were only given to more or less important people. St Andrews is a charming little spot, and I loved its University: I'd have liked to have wrapped it up in a clean napkin, like a Stilton, and kept it on my side-table for an ornament. It seemed to me almost the ideal spot for taking learning to one's mistress.

How am I to get out of it now? It would mean endless trouble.

1) Leave for the occasion.

2) Plain clothes? — only airmen are now forbidden plain clothes.

3) A lot of money . . . calculated on my pay of 27/- a week.

4) A lot of publicity. Lord Thomson put all sorts of silly restrictions on me last September: to stop flying, & drop Winston & Philip Sassoon & Lady Astor and Austen & Birkenhead: he would undoubtedly sack me if I appeared in public at St Andrews.

Of course I can see that these things can be got round — but only by influence, which leaves always a soreness behind its application. The Labourites think I'm an imperial spy, & the Die-hards thought I was a bolshie, and Lord T. says I'm a self-advertising mountebank. So it would be better for me if the matter could quietly drop. The mere being taken into consideration for an honorary degree is the honour of it. They've conferred that on me: won't they drop the actual degree, as it would do me harm? You can wangle that as you have (undoubtedly) wangled the other! Try . . . please.

It was exceedingly nice of you. I don't think I have ever been so surprised in my life.

Plymouth remains excellent. We live most excellently and amusedly, and the whole station is happy. This R.A.F. is a good solution of most difficulties. That is why I cling to it so closely, and do not want to imperil myself. Yours   T E SHAW

[3 *lines omitted*]

411: TO HENRY WILLIAMSON

25.3.30

What D. H. Lawrence means by *Lady Chatterley's Lover* is that the idea of sex, & the whole strong vital instinct, being considered indecent causes men to lose what might be their vital strength and pride of life — their integrity. Conversely, the idea of 'genitals being beauty' in the Blakian sense would free humanity from its lowering and disintegrating immortality of deed and thought.

Lawrence wilted & was made writhen by the 'miners-chapel-dirty little boy, you' environment: he was ruined by it: and in most of his work he is striving to straighten himself, and to become beautiful. Ironically, or paradoxically, in a humanity where 'genitals are beauty' there would be a minimum of 'sex' and a maximum of beauty, or Art. This is what Lawrence means, surely.

412: TO R. V. BUXTON

[1930]   *Mount Batten, Plymouth*

Dear Robin, Yesterday a tall thin creature walked up to me in the Camp: grinned at me: afterwards I saw that it was my young brother, a queer creature, who is 30 and has a wife and one child. I thought he was in Spain, and said 'What on earth brings you here?' 'House-hunting' he replied: as if there were any houses at Plymouth. Absurd.

It seems they really do want a house. It must, they say, have one large room, to serve as a study (he writes real books, not trash): nothing else matters, I gather. Should be within economical distance of London or Oxford, for the library's sake. Which is why they went to Bodmin to-day, I suppose, to look at a reformed farm-house.

Suddenly I have remembered your cottage-farm: you said you had no tenant. Is that so? Do you want a queer vague definite creature living there? Would it fit an oddment, a spare part, a child-of-the-old-age of my two extraordinary parents?

We got madder as the tale increased. I was only the second son, he the fifth. It ended then, God be praised.[1]

I picture you in pink, very mud-splashed and weary, late for your bath, & spoiling the dinner by keeping; all for inability to tear yourself away from my masterly depiction of life in the R.A.F. Only it isn't like that at all.

Lately a letter came to me from St. Andrews University (a miniature & charming place in Scotland) offering me an honorary degree as Doctor Of Laws. 'Ha Ha' said I 'some undergrad is pulling my leg.' I replied accordingly, and have had dignified remonstrances from John Buchan & Barrie: it seems Baldwin particularly put my name. Worst of all, in honest praise of St. Andrews I said that if it were mine I'd wrap a clean napkin round it & keep it on the side-table to gloat at, like a Stilton. Apparently they dislike Stilton. Barbares! Hoots mon: aweel.

T.E.S.

413: TO FREDERIC MANNING

2.v.30

[15 *lines omitted*] The *Epicurus*[2] is being read by me, very gradually. Only I began with Epicurus himself and will read the introduction last. It seems fairer to the old man to see him with my own eyes before you tell me of him. Not so? [7 *lines omitted*]

Your letter about A.E. was pleasing. Thanks to Mrs. Bernard Shaw I had been for nearly two years a reader of his *Irish Statesman*, a little paper he has been doing in Dublin. Of course A.E. is a wonderful poet, and great man. You'll have noted that even George Moore cannot say anything caddish about him; but his paper was something special. He wrote everything in it which mattered, and his stuff glimmered like a candle-light against a background of intense darkness. I got the fancy, when the *Statesman* stopped, that Ireland had gone out. He seemed the only civil intelligence there!

---

[1] When A. W. Lawrence married, Lawrence wrote to him: 'If there is no insanity in the family there will soon be!'

[2] A new edition of Epicurus's *Morals* to which Manning had written an introduction.

It may have been because his Protestantism isolated him in a clerical country: but all I can say is that A.E. seemed to be very different from the rest of his world. He is also a most sane, moderate, wise and original critic, who criticises as a workman, not as a scientist. That is refreshing. I'm told that he is old now, and tired. Anyway I know he is remarkable. We had better not meet, for my talking, that he wished to hear, isn't any good. I'm not Irish enough for that! Yours,   T.E.S.

414: TO ERNEST THURTLE

2. V. 30

I have not been very good lately, perhaps. When your letter came I said Nunc dimittis ... and the servant through whose faithfulness this great work had come about didn't seem to matter. He had done his duty: that was all.

Then the Lords gave me a fright. Lord Allenby too,[1] whom I like and admire. Surely if I had been in London, able to see him, he would at least have kept silence— if not supported you.

Yet ... doesn't it make you surer you were right, to see all the General Staff opposing you?

In the end you downed the Lords, as you had downed the Government. I feel it is a blessed victory. The old state of law hurt me. It was such a damnable judgement upon our own flesh & blood.

There are 1000 other Service reforms which should be carried through, to make them abreast — in morality & decency — of normal public life and opinion. Perhaps you may do more, in your time: but this effort will have made you very marked, for the moment. Perhaps you should break out in a new path for the next few months, to re-habilitate yourself.

I haven't really said thank you for all you did: because I feel that it was only your duty really. People who care anything at all about their countries don't like to see them fouling themselves.

Curse the Brass Hats: poor reptiles. They always swear that these things are necessary to discipline. A word in your ear —

---

[1] Who had opposed the abolition of the death penalty in the army.

XX

discipline itself is not necessary. We fight better without it.
Yet being Englishmen we are born with it, and can no more
lose it than our finger nails.

Go on pulling the right strings. It gave me, after yourself,
perhaps the next purest joy in England. Yours   T E SHAW

415: TO F. L. LUCAS

3-v-30.

I have now read *Cecile*, for a first time. After I have read it again
I will feel more sure of what I think about it. That is the worst
of my slug-like mind. It delays its impressions far beyond most
men's.

However I am pretty sure about some things — and the first
is your advance as a novelist. That first book was very good:
it had higher lights than this: but there is no comparison in
sustained weight and momentum. This book hangs solidly
together and goes forward, all in a piece.

Also your range widens. There are excellent main characters:
or not perhaps excellent, but credible and vivid and diverse and
likely. Yet it is in minor pages that your skill shows itself best,
amongst the people brought in just for a moment, to adorn an
angle and deflect your current. That picture of the King, &
Vergennes & Gaston, near the end. That is magnificent. You
got, there, as near to the reality of a royal audience as anyone
could.

Landscape & atmosphere, sun & light and wind & cloud &
rain, one takes for granted from you. After all, they have been
perfectly done in your poetry. Sometimes I felt them a few lines
too long. The novel is (more than you perhaps realised) a novel
of action, and one grudges a little anything that delays its speed.
I do not think this is a criticism. I would not take anything out.
The landscapes, the arguments, the politics-and-meaning-of-the-
universe-discussions, are so many whets to sharpen us in search
of the next move of your people.

I fancy this is not wholly what you intended. You were trying
to write a study of the inter-actions of marriage and companion-

ship upon a group of characters: and you were more keen on their psychology than upon their doings. Well, each man to his taste. I was more interested in what these various people did — in the expressions of their moods in action, than in the moods themselves. That happens to be my make-up.

I can see, too, that in writing *Cecile* you were, in a sense, clearing up your own history. So far, good. I think there is a very rational balance and proportion — sanity almost — in all but Gabriel who hardly comes off. Yet I have a brother who is a saint, and so I know how baffling saints are.

The talk is one of the best things in your advance. You can now handle conversation, & keep the threads distinct. That is uncommon. I think you will write more novels. This deliberate & successful expression of yourself through the mouths of a battalion is significant. Yet I'd give all the novels in the world for 1/1000 th of its poetry. What is it that makes a tiny poem seem infinite, and a great novel too short?

The dedication makes me feel quite warm all over. It was ever so good of you: for I'm a bit of a renegade in letters. Probably if I went on trying I could achieve more second-rate work: and do not think it worth while. My jobs in the R.A.F. seem more useful. Yours   T.E.S.

416: TO FREDERIC MANNING

15.v.30   *Mount Batten, Plymouth*

Dear Manning, That would have been a pleasant letter to get, for the tallest author alive: and therefore many times pleasanter for me, who think myself no great shakes at writing, from one whose writing I so vainly admire. Your prose has a very definite and deliberate manner, which appeals to me, as most 'airs' do. Your poems have helped you to that concision and force. The best of poetry is all the clauses it leaves out, and that is why poets so often write such tough and nervy prose — or so I fancy.

Your remarks hit off very closely the obstacles that attended the delivery of *The Seven Pillars*. I was a rather clumsy novice at writing, facing what I felt to be a huge subject with hanging over me the political uncertainty of the future of the Arab movement.

We had promised them so much, and at the end wanted to give them so little. So for two years there was a dog fight, up and down the dirty passages of Downing St.,[1] and then all came out right — only the book was finished. It might have been happier, had I foreseen the clean ending. I wrote it in some stress and misery of mind.

The second complicity was my own moral standing. I had been so much of a free agent, repeatedly deciding what I (and the others) should do: and I wasn't sure if my opportunity (or reality, as I called it) was really justified. Not morally justifiable. I could see it wasn't: but justified by the standard of Lombard St. and Pall Mall. By putting all the troubles and dilemmas on paper, I hoped to work out my path again, and satisfy myself how wrong, or how right, I had been.

So the book is the self-argument of a man who couldn't then see straight: and who now thinks that perhaps it did not matter: that seeing straight is only an illusion. We do these things in sheer vapidity of mind, not deliberately, not consciously even. To make out that we were reasoned cool minds, ruling our courses and contemporaries, is a vanity. Things happen, and we do our best to keep in the saddle.

After the Arab business I rather foreswore saddles. The R.A.F. is a socket in which I fit safely: after many tribulations, as you will discover if P.D.[2] lets you read my *Mint* which describes how the Air Force rounds off its pegs to fit into their holes. Now-a-days my mind does not concern itself greatly with abstractions. Hence the red face and round belly and comfortable port. I think I am happier than most people.

What you say about the descriptive stuff slowing down the narrative pleases me, rather. I had suspected it. Descriptions shouldn't be more than a line or two. Only I was not really out to make a masterpiece (— or was I? I think I wanted to, and felt that I could not, and had not) and the sense of the country and atmosphere and climate and furniture of Arabia hung so tightly about me that I put too much of them into the story, in hopes that they would make it life-like. I wake up now, often, in

---

[1] Lawrence used this phrase in other forms, one of which is quoted on pp. 263-4.
[2] Peter Davies.

Arabia: the place has stayed with me much more than the men and the deeds. Whenever a landscape or colour in England gets into me deeply, more often than not it is because something of it recalls Arabia. It was a tremendous country and I cared for it far more than I admired my role as man of action. More acting than action, I fancy, there.

Your seeing Jahveh and the Baalim is of course what I was trying to convey.[1] My two years taught me the inwardness of all Semitic history, from its beginning: and that includes Zeno and other unexpected persons. As for my harnessing to my go-cart the eternal force — well, no: I pushed my go-cart into the eternal stream, and so it went faster than the ones that are pushed cross-stream or up-stream. I did not believe finally in the Arab movement: but thought it necessary, in its time and place. It has justified itself hugely, since the war, too. So, even to a political or statesman, the conflict is measurable and significant. I am still puzzled as to how far the individual counts: a lot, I fancy, if he pushes the right way.

Joyce[2] and his party try to 'present objects to the vision simply by enumerating' not all, indeed, but a careful selection of their qualities. I was at least as selective as Joyce, in intention. Only perhaps I didn't see, precisely enough, what was significant. I'm sorry about 'dolerite' and 'striated' ... but these seemed easy enough, after one had thought of them. I tried not to be technical, unnecessarily.

'Slowing down the dramatic action' Yes: as I hinted, much of the dramatic action was very reluctantly put in. It felt cheap, then, and looks cheap now. I preferred Arabia when I wasn't in it, so to speak!

I'm so glad you didn't tear the letter up: because it has given me a great deal of innocent pleasure ... or is the pleasure that would be vanity, if the recipient believed it earned, innocent? ...

The first draft was not destroyed by me, but stolen from me; left behind in the refreshment room of Reading Station, and taken by some unknown! It was shorter, snappier, and more truthful than the present version, which was done from memory. I do not think it was franker and angrier, for I do not get angry

---

[1] In *Seven Pillars of Wisdom*, Chapter LXIII.   [2] James Joyce.

much, and 1920 (the date of this text, in the main) was a worse
year for me than 1919, the date of the first draft. My compromise
with fate you will see happening gradually in 1922-23, as I
settled into the R.A.F.; if you read *The Mint*. Here is the
chronology:

1914-1918	:	the War.
1919	:	Peace Conference: misery
1920-1921 (Aug)	:	Dog fight in London with the British Government
1922	:	Eighteen months work with Winston Churchill settling the Middle East after my lights.
1922 (Aug)-1930	:	R.A.F.

It is exceedingly good of you to have taken all that trouble.

T.E.S.

417: TO B. H. LIDDELL HART

26.vi.30   *Plymouth*

Alas, I got *The Real War*[1] weeks ago. From before that date till
now I have not opened a book to read it. The weather? Malaise?
A great deal to do? *Odyssey?* I do not know: there are so many
causes.

I was at the Shaws' last week end, and they asked if I was
reading it, saying it was particularly good in its characters of
generals. I expect it is. O for a wet week, to drive me back upon
books again! Only in summer time, by fits and starts, books
seem impossible things.

Arab reactions to air bombing? I think they feel our own
intense irritation and vain rage at an attack to which there can be
no response. There is something cold, chilling, impersonally
fateful, about air bombing. It is not punishment, but a misfortune
from heaven striking the community.

The R.A.F. recognises this, and bombs only after 24 hours
notice given. So the damage falls only on immovables.

[1] A short history of the Great War, by B. H. Liddell Hart.

It is of course infinitely more merciful than police or military action, as hardly anyone is ever killed — and the killed are as likely to be negligible women and children, as the really important men. Only this is too oriental a mood for us to feel very clearly. An Arab would rather offer up his wife than himself, to expiate a civil offence!

418: TO F. N. DOUBLEDAY

2. IX. 30. *Mount Batten, Plymouth*

Effendim, I have been slow in answering your letter, but I was occupied in gathering some money, which I have thrown (or rather, reserved for throwing) into Purdy's lap.[1] In fact I have written to him this week for a spare shaft and gear wheel for my boat-of-boats. It is very good of you to have told him I'm all right. He will trust me about bills. All the more needful, you see, that the trust is not misplaced. Now I have £10 in hand, so all is well. Boat-owners should be millionaires, I fear. You should get a Purdy boat, and have Mrs. Doubleday drive you over the water. On hot days (phew, it has been hot here for a fortnight, a little taste of heaven, which I feel will be sub-tropical) to run at 40 m.p.h. over the rise and fall of a tired sea-swell is the most refreshing feeling in the world.

So good has Plymouth Sound become, in consequence, that I have done little else but enjoy myself for three weeks. Since you left, until this last period, summer was only a wet ruin. *Now* all is well.

New York, so the newspapers say, has had heat-wave upon heat-wave. I hope that is true, and that life at Oyster Bay has been open-windowed, leisurely and iced: while the sweating myrmidons in Garden City behind the scenes have been struggling with giant presses, rolling off dollar books by the half-million. The dollar books will be a benefit to the whole world, if they succeed: and if they fail, you will have dropped money most nobly. After 50 years of success you are entitled to lose money grandly. After all, what fun would there be for Nelson,[2] if you

[1] See p. 637.   [2] F. N. Doubleday's son.

left him no markets to conquer? and with a name like that, Nelson Doubleday, conquering becomes not merely an instinct but a duty.

I say, have you considered acquiring all the rights to Noel Coward? [16 *words omitted*] He writes English like Congreve, and when G.B.S. goes will be the main force in the English theatre. I should nobble him, if nobbleable, on both sides the Atlantic: if I were a publisher: but Lord, what a rotten publisher I should be.

Mrs. Doubleday has the final paragraph: and at once I think of both your healths. I hope she is well: and strong enough to do all she wants for you. Your lack of mobility makes hers so very important and so she is tempted to over-push her strength.

I flew over Kipling's garden last Saturday, and again yesterday, on my way back here from Folkestone. We tilted the Moth up on one wing-tip and spun round and round over his garden. I wonder what he said: and can guess it nearly. That's where you and I have the advantage over Mrs. Doubleday. She couldn't guess, ever, what an angry poet would say! Yours   T. E. S.

419: TO NOEL COWARD

6. ix. 30.   *Mount Batten, Plymouth*

Dear N. C., It is very good to laugh: and I laughed so much, and made so many people laugh over your 'may I call you 338'[1] that I became too busy and happy to acknowledge your letter.

I hope Liverpool went off well. Edinburgh — so the press said, but how they lie — went into fits over your mixed grill. I fancied you were coming thence direct to London, but clearly not. It must be very hard and uphill work winning province after province before attacking the headquarters: and London is likely to be your easiest conquest, too. The bits I saw[2] went so swingingly.

Your praise of my R.A.F. notes pleases me, of course, more

[1] Noel Coward had begun a letter to Lawrence written on August 25th, 1930, 'Dear 338171 (May I call you 338?), I am tremendously grateful to you for letting me read your R.A.F. notes . . .'
[2] Of *Private Lives*.

than it puzzles me. I'm damned if I can see any good in them. Some artifice — yes: some skill — yes: they even come off, here and there: but the general impression on me is dry bones. Your work is like sword-play; as quick as light. Mine a slow painful mosaic of hard words stiffly cemented together. However it is usually opposites that fall in love. At any rate I propose to go on looking forward, keenly, to seeing more of your works and work, and perhaps of yourself, if a kind fate lets me run into you when you are not better engaged.

I'm hoping to get to London some time in October, for a week-end perhaps. Yours   T E SHAW.

420: TO F. N. DOUBLEDAY

10. IX. 30.   *Mount Batten, Plymouth*

Effendim, Clear contrary to tradition and normally impossible for me to send you two letters running. Only they have told me lately that you are really sick, this time. Evans[1] has been the informer upon you. He says you have had four doctors and an operation.

That, if you will pardon me, is better than one doctor and four operations. Either American doctors work in squads: or there have been three disappointed ones. It is a good rule, with doctors, to ask the advice of the most reputed. If he says anything disagreeable, go round the town saying, 'Old so and so is out-of-date.' Then try another, and persevere till you find one who says the thing you feel to be right. Then return round the town and say that everybody is going to this last fellow. He will be so grateful that he will not send in a bill.

Evans, I needn't naturally tell you, is worried. He would be. I wrote back to him cheerfully and said 'Effendim is a hard case. When Effendim wants to hop it he will: till then all the doctors in two hemispheres will only annoy and enrage him. When he is enraged enough they will quit and declare him cured.' The only thing likely to make him hop it is (a) the failure of the dollar book, or (b) the publication by Heinemann of a best seller. (a)

---

[1] Partner in William Heinemann, Ltd.

would show him that Nelson was wrong (nunc dimittis: my firm can err). (b) would show him that Heinemann could do without him. I am glad to say that the latest bulletins report the dollar books as the only thing in the American markets moving upward, while Heinemann's have not yet acquired Ethel M. Dell. Or is E. M. D. past?

Effendi, I am out of date. These young people are too much for me. If you will cede me half a palm tree, or whatever proportion of a palm tree will provide me with 365 cocoa-nuts per annum, in the Bahamas, I will retire from the world and lunch regularly with you and Mrs. Doubleday.

Last Thursday I broke two ribs in my chest (these are worse than stomach-ribs) so I am still sore and miserable about life generally. What you can be feeling like, with a hole six inches across in your stomach I can only guess. However this letter and me are eight days off from you. So there is no harm in posting it, as you will be fractiously convalescent before it brings up.

Please tell Mrs. Doubleday that her last paragraph is filled with the sympathy she deserves. You are the centre of attraction and having a terrific time. Just think of her misery meanwhile. Really Effendi, you shouldn't scare all your friends stiff, like this. We want you to go on for ever. Yours,   T. E. S.

421: TO F. N. DOUBLEDAY

18. IX. 30.   [*On leave in Scotland*]

Effendim, Rotten pen and foul paper, but here on the North East edge of Scotland I've just heard that you are 'out of the wood'. So much to be thankful for, yet no more than is fitting. Understand, that yourself and illness do not go together! I think of you always as part pirate, like Kidd, part buccaneer like Morgan, with moments of legitimacy like Farragut. It is unthinkable to think of an Effendi incapable of bearing arms. So please recover quickly that we may laugh again. Meanwhile come on leave with me for ten days!

Come northward many miles above Aberdeen, and then strike towards the sea across the links, which are sand-tussocked desolations of charred heather and wiry reeds, harbouring grouse to whirr up alarmingly sideways from under-foot, and rabbits so lazy that they will hardly scuttle their snow-white little tail-flags from the path. Add a choir of larks and a thin high wind piping over the dunes or thrumming down the harsh stems of heather.

They are three miles wide, these links, and ever so desolate, till they end abruptly in a rough field whose far side is set on edge with a broken line of cottages. Behind their roofs seems to be pure sky, but when you near them it becomes sea — for the cottages have [been] built round all the crest of the grassy sea-cliff and down it too, cunningly wedging their places into its face wherever there was a flat of land as wide as two rooms. Almost to the beach the cottages fall. Beach, did I say? It is a creek of sand, cemented along one side in a grey quay-wall from which and from the opposing rocks up run the grass-grown cliffs in heart-comforting bastions to the houses fringed against the sky. The creek's a fishing port. You could find room to play a game of tennis in it, perhaps, if the tide went dry. So there are no bigger boats than dinghies and no room for any: nor heart for any with the jaws of greycold reefs champing white seas outside, all day and night.

Imagine whole systems of slate-like slabby rocks, flung flatwise and acres square, thrusting out into the maddened North Sea which heaves and foams over them in deafening surges. The North-Easter, full of rain and so misted that our smarting eyes can peer only two or three hunched yards into it, is lifting the waves bodily into the air and smashing them upon the rocks. There is such sound and movement out there in the haze that our eyes keep staring into its blindness to see the white walls rolling in. The concealed sun makes all white things half-luminous, so that the gulls become silvered whenever they dip suddenly to turn a knife-edged cartwheel in the spray: and the thunder of the seas enforces a deafened silence on all other things, so that we feel as much as see the energy let loose. Each big wave makes the air quiver and sends a shading reverberation across the shore about our bodies.

That is the fighting of the sea against the land: and the sea's casualties have filled the port, around the elbow that the jetty makes. There the water is stifled and heaves sickly under a mat of sea-suds one foot thick. You know the creamed and bubbly foam that blows up a beach when the wind rises and the sea, together? Well, that flocculent stuff is all impounded in our bay, filling it so full that black water and jetty and steps and rocks and beach are all invisible, buried under it like a corpse in a blanket.

'Curse the fellow and his seascape, you are saying.' Am I paid to read his manuscript? Peace, Mrs. Doubleday will take it away and burn it, so soon as you roar in anger.

What are we doing here? Nothing, practically. There are 3 of us — Jimmy who used to work in Canada but came home in 1914 and was a gunner for four years in France: now he jobs horses in Aberdeen: — Jock, the roughest diamond of our Tank Corps hut in 1923; — and me. We have Mrs. Ross' cottage lent to us and reluctantly in turn sweep its floor and fetch the water and coal. For meals thrice a day we spread our coats to the wind and fly to the cliff-top, where the Mrs. Baker-and-Butcher feeds us in her parlour. Then heavy inside, we slide down hill to the cottage again in the cove: for ours is the nearest hovel to the high-tide mark. That is good in fair weather and exciting today. Great flocks of surf beat tattoos on the roof till the tide turned.

But what do we do? Why nothing, as I said. Jimmy has his horses to groom and feed and exercise. Sometimes we do the last for him. Jock fishes: boys bring him mussels and he waves a pole from the quay at the wild wild waves. Once up came a codling from the yeasty deep, the poor orphan taking pity on him. He brought it us in silent manly pride, and we made him clean it. Scrape scrape his knife went, like a man cleaning a flower-pot. We helped him eat it, too.

Most of our food is fish, I remember. There is a local industry, called sperling. Cut open a round fish, flatten it, dry him bone-white for days on a rock of wire netting, smoke him, boil him in milk. Not bad, tasting like dull veal. The local people are lovers of sperling, though, and taste more in them than I do. Then there are baby soles, four-inch things too small for sale in the city with the adult soles. They are fried and delicious. Down with great soles henceforward.

The cottage has 3 rooms. Jock took the middle one with big bed and fire-place. Ours open from it and are cold. So we make his our sitting room, and have pushed the bed into the corner, farthest from the fire where I sit and think all day, while turning over the swimming suits to dry. Also I eat pounds of peppermints (pan-drops they call them: Aberdeen and excellent) or read H. G. Wells' *History* in a dollar edition lately produced, as you may have heard, by a young and pushing publisher in the States. I wish I had a dozen copies to give away: but only one ran the customs gauntlet to do Cassells out of his English rights. Believe me, it's a good book. 8/6d in England and a dollar in the almighty-dear States.

I tried to get Heinemann's elephant book *Novels Today* in Aberdeen but they had it not. Distribution faulty, for Lady Eleanor Smith and Strong are both first-class. The book-shop lady tried to work off on me a thing called *Angel Pavement*, also by Heinemann. She said everybody was buying it. 'Not quite everybody', I protested politely. 'This very man' she said 'wrote *Good Companions*'. 'Dreary artificial sob-stuffed thing' I snorted, having luckily read *Good Companions*. 'You *are* hard to please' she grumbled, offering me *The Boy's Book of Colonel Lawrence* at a reduction, seeing I was in uniform and he now in the R.A.F. I told her I knew the fellow, and he was a wash-out: then I bought a *Daily Express* and escaped the shop. Alas, for I wanted to read *Dewar Rides*[1] again.

Effendi, what folly makes me want to talk rot to you when I hear you are ill? The whole man is a gladiator: who demands tall talk? Why babble when he is (temporarily) hurt? God knows. Ask Mrs. Doubleday to take the nasty thing away again.

Our tea-time now. The winds have stopped, but the waves increase. They are so big that only two roll in to the minute now. I wish you could hear the constancy and fresh repetition of their thunder, and the sharpness and loneliness of the gulls questing through the spume. The poor gulls are hungry from the storm and beset our roof for the food-scraps we throw away. They have the saddest, most cold, disembodied voices in the world.

Evening now. I must go up the shop for oil for the lamp. The

[1] By L. A. G. Strong.

shop is the post office and I'll then send this off, before its length frightens me and makes me burn it.

Au revoir, Effendim, soon, let's hope.   T. E. S.

P.S. for Mrs. D-D — Make it London next summer too! and we *will* get to Kipling this time.

422: TO NOEL COWARD

5. x. 30

Dear N. C., I was at the second night,[1] and wondered to see how perfectly the finished product went. Just once it slipped, when she drew the curtains and the daylight took 20 seconds to come! Yet I'm not sure that the bare works you showed me that afternoon were not better. For one thing, I could not tell always when you were acting and when talking to one another. So I would suggest my coming to another rehearsal, only there seems nothing to prevent these plays of yours running for ever, and so you probably will never write any more.

Gertrude Lawrence is amazing. She acts nearly as well as yourself. I was sorry for the other two. They were out of it.

The play reads astonishingly well. It gets thicker, in print, and has bones and muscles. On the stage you played with it and puffed your fancies up and about like swansdown. And one can't help laughing all the time: whereas over the book one does not do worse than chuckle or smile. For fun I took some pages and tried to strike redundant words out of your phrases. Only there were none. That's what I felt when I told you it was superb prose.

You'll be sick of letters about it, so I'll shut up. Yet I had to tell you how much delight it gave me. Yours   T E SHAW.

---

[1] Of *Private Lives.*

423: TO WILLIAM ROTHENSTEIN

18. x. 30.   *Mount Batten*

Dear W.R., I did get the Cresswell book:[1] long ago: and I am a miserable sinner. Only not without redeeming feature, for the book made me write to Ede about it, and he told Cresswell, who has sent me his *Poems* as well (and I have not yet written to him about them. Another sin. Alas).

The book was queer. Something real to say, and a borrowed voice to say it in. That was queer, because Cresswell is not young enough to be permitted affectations. I felt, however, all through that behind the style a quite honest personality was hiding. He has, I'm told, won a good deal of credit and some abuse for the book. So perhaps he will be encouraged to go further. Anybody who writes a very good first book is doomed.

Have you read *Other Man's Saucer?*[2] My last sentence brought it suddenly to mind. If its characters are imagined, then he's a coming author. If they are his own circle, then he's not. It is as striking, in its way, as *The White Peacock* of 1912,[3] was it? Heinemann published it, this year.

In the other direction I commend Algernon Blackwood's *Dudley and Gilderoy.* Yes, I know that normally he is no good: but this and his Autobiography[4] and *The Centaur* are different. This is much the best. Very distinguished indeed.

Geoffrey Dennis I do not think I know at all. I shall taste him with pleasure. Often I ask people for the names of 'under-30's', fellows whose second book is better than their first, and who are not yet thirty. Only they will so seldom tell me of one. There must be several promising things in the offing; for the war is, thank God, at last over and done with. The poor old war creatures bore everybody so much that we give them too little credit, I fancy. Yet Sassoon's books; Manning's; *War Birds*; *Ermytage and the Curate*;[5] all those stick in my mind: and so will *Salute to Guns*,[6] I fancy, though I read it too lately to say for sure. Sassoon comes out on top of all us war-timers, I think. More vigour, more grace and swiftness of movement, more fire and heat —

---

[1] *The Poet's Progress*, by D'Arcy Cresswell.   [2] By Keith Winter.
[3] D. H. Lawrence's first novel, published 1911.   [4] *Episodes Before Thirty.*
[5] By A. M. Cogswell.   [6] *Salute of Guns*, by Donald Boyd.

that's in his poetry — and more tranquil charm, in his prose. S.S. strikes me as probably a great writer, all in all.

Wasn't it delightful to find Manning coming out so suddenly as a real flesh-and-blood figure. Beautiful as are *Scenes* and *Epicurus*, ever so much more worth while is *Her Privates We*. Yours,

T. E. SHAW.

424: TO ERNEST THURTLE

25/x/30.   *Mount Batten, Plymouth*

Dear E.T., Yes, I know Church End, having had friends in Windsor Road which is not far from you. It is quieter than the main Golders Green part and has some views and greenery within reach: not that you will have time to see them!

Yesterday you were in the headlines as a Junior Lord. Odd, isn't it, how things happen unbeknownst? Ten years ago Lords, senior or junior, were out of your reach and wish; now you take it as a commonplace. I hope it means that you are marked for office upon the next re-shuffle. Shuffle it generally is, by the way. I suggest your specialising upon a fighting service, preferably Air. There are fundamental changes in the status of 'other ranks' due and over-due. One resents the private opinion of the services being twenty years behind public opinion in all matters of common decency. An untrammelled-by-social-prejudice S. of S. could work a little revolution, for great good, in two years.

[2 *lines omitted*] In the R.A.F. there exists a jealous and ineradicable feeling against lighter-than-air ships. We are so pinned to aircraft that we cannot hear a good word of gas-bags. Nor was R. 101 a particularly good gas-bag. Yet her crash was an error of navigational control, I fear, and no direct fault of the ship. That re-filling the water ballast before Beauvais, coupled with a failure to allow for the weather influence upon the altimeters, killed her and the poor crew. It was not Lord T's[1] fault; yet he was a bad Air Minister. We all like Montague so much better.

I get no news of Afghanistan, so the last sentences of your letter remain obscure. But I would have you too contemptuous of the foreign policy of the Government of India to credit it with

---

[1] Lord Thomson was killed in the crash of the R 101.

being either good or bad. It will be just fatuous. I do not think that Amanullah was in the least degree Russia-inclined, anyhow.

I continue in Plymouth, moderately quiet and immoderately happy. If ever you see the artful Maxton, please give him my regards: and we will meet some day, either in Finchley or in London. Not in winter, though! Yours   T E SHAW.

425: TO DAVID GARNETT

19.11.30

I send back your flying notes.[1] They are uncommonly well done, and have pretensions — or at least they achieve effects, and such things seldom come unawares. I think they are the beginnings of a most excellent (and widely sold) handbook on the art of amateur flying. Keep them going till the solo day has come, and after it for any out-of-the-way-yet-communicable flights: and the result will be a joy to everyone who likes the air. They feel so real and direct and modestly true. Very good.

I'm sorry E.G.[2] does not approve your manly skill: for your power of writing in these pages would delight his critical sense. It is nervous and exacting prose. Few pilots are really born — none after 21 years old — but almost every man alive can be made a pilot. I think you will find Moths easier than Bluebirds to land. Cross-country work is the best part of flying. I hate stunting, and everybody hates being stunted.

My life, as you very rightly should have said, does not count, just now. Homer is $\frac{3}{4}$ finished and going hard — not strong, certainly. Otherwise it is just R.A.F.: quietly content. I have nothing of my own to write, and no leave due till April next, and perhaps not then.

I have been owing you a letter for months over Shakespeare III. I hope this great work (it establishes itself each time I read it as the only Shakespeare) is not straining the Nonesuch resources too much in this lean time. Everybody is very hard hit and the luxury book will suffer.

Imitation being a compliment, you would enjoy seeing the

---

[1] These Notes were continued and published as *A Rabbit in the Air*.
[2] Edward Garnett.

YY

Faust produced by the Bremer Press in Munich lately. It is not so well done, but cheaper.

Actually I am still reading Shakespeare ii, having taken the chance of what I hope is the slow production of your edition to read him all through again. Parts are very heavy and very bad: and then the next page will take one's breath. What a queer great man. Dimly I feel that something went so wrong with his life that he lost heart, foreswore London, and abandoned his work. I wonder. It could only be some internal vice, for nothing from outside could hurt such a one.

I should like to come up towards the flat lands again, but cannot. The *Odyssey* must finish before the spring and that means 45 hours a week — on top of my R.A.F. 48 hours: and that makes a full working day all through, without the indulgence of week-ends. Fly down to me, some day, instead! Yours,   T.E.SHAW.

They give the actual feel of being in the cockpit and looking out. So few people are qualified both in foreground and background; that makes them so satisfyingly true.

426: TO W. A. KNOWLES

22.XI.30

Dear Knowles, I've wanted to get up for the last three weeks, but have been prevented.

How goes the garage?[1] Not going to be an eyesore, I hope? Mother told me you had all the concreting done before the weather turned bad, so I suppose that will have set well. Good.

The book-case by the fire is point No 2: and point No 3 (which will not wait) is a moving forest of rhododendron trees coming upon you from Derbyshire (rail to Wool, I think) for planting in the neighbourhood of the cottage. Will you find some plant-wise man & make him put them in at the likeliest places. I understand they are the latest Tibetan and Chinese trees of all sorts of shapes & colours! Yours ever   T E S.

If any varmints are at home, offer them my regards, please!

---
[1] Being built at Clouds Hill.

427: TO ERNEST THURTLE

28. xi. 30.   *Mount Batten, Plymouth*

Dear E.T., I am rather troubled over this Russian business, where some unfortunates are being tried for, amongst other things, treasonably associating with me as British Government Agent in London in 1927![1]

I know they do not much believe any English official word: but I was demonstrably in India all the time from December 1926 to February 1929. Would it be any good getting some private person they trust to tell them so? Or could anything be done? They may hang these poor creatures for all I know, else: and I would like to do something for them, if there is anything. Now Lord Thomson is gone the Air Ministry will not be so tender on my subject. Yours sincerely   T E SHAW.

428: TO ERNEST THURTLE

5th December. 1930

Dear E.T., I am grateful for your trouble taken. I think your suggestion about a question in the House might be good, and can do no harm. The fellow you put up should ask the U/S of S for Air for my movements & stations (with dates) from Jan 1926 to date: or else ask *with reference to the Russian statements* (the press will prick up their ears then) the dates of my departure for & return from India, and the stations I was posted to in India, with information as to what leave, if any, I had during my service in India — because I took no leave, to prevent silly stories of my activity arising.

I agree that a fact or two may make no difference in this trial in Russia: but the trial is being conducted also in the press of many countries, some of them so hostile to Russia that they will seize upon any point to her discredit.

It would be most tactful if you would ask Montague whether he resented this, before having the question popped. Yours

T.E.S.

[1] The Russian Courts elicited confessions proving conversations with Lawrence in England when he was in India.

429: TO EDWARD GARNETT

5/xii/30

Dear E.G., What a good book it is![1] I ungratefully delayed writing while I read in it. How nearly big, as poet, Blunt was. Only his vanity saved him from doing really good things in three or four roles. I think these Gregynog people are printing beautifully. I understand the money is the Davies family, and that Tom Jones is in it, somehow. Hodgson, the pressman, of course was mine.[2] Who runs the press? And who chooses their books? They have taste. I would like them to do Crane's *Jenny*[3] (out of print and hard to get) and Vansittart's *Singing Caravan* which Heinemann printed poorly: and there is room in England for a *really fine* translation of *Niels Lyhne* by Jacobsen. You put me on to two of these. Did I ever put you on to the Vansittart? It is that rarest English thing, light poetry.

I do *Odyssey* all spare days and half the nights: with luck it will be finished before the end of March. What a relief. I am tired of all Homer's namby-pamby men and women.

It is very good of you. I have just had the new *Scenes and Portraits* by Manning, which is inscribed to me. Really, I am coming on. If only I did not so intensely admire these people who seem to like me. What one needs is the love of one's enemies! Yours,   T.E.S.

430: TO R. V. BUXTON

29. XII. 30

Dear Robin, I hope you are hunting strongly.[4] I am not. All my non-R.A.F. hours go on the musted and fish-smelly Odysseus.

My speed-boat busted a gear wheel and a propeller shaft: so

---

[1] *The Celebrated Romance of the Stealing of the Mare*, translated from the Arabic by Lady Anne Blunt and done into verse by Wilfrid Scawen Blunt, reprinted by the Gregynog Press.

[2] Hodgson was Manning Pike's assistant in printing the Subscribers' edition of *Seven Pillars of Wisdom*.

[3] Lawrence had made the same slip before (see p. 603). Cf. D. G. Rossetti's poem.

[4] Buxton is a foxhunter.

I wrote to the makers for a spare, and asked them how I was to repay their kindness, they being near New York. They say that my Bank can arrange it.* Probably it can: though as dollars change from day to day it seems difficult. Something fresh my sending money to the States. Usually we receive it thence. All's fair, I suppose. Any way the boat is good.

I may be in London next month, & will call at the new House — not that you'll be there, but I'd like to see how it feels, in use. I expect everything has settled down. I hope it works as well as it looks. Yours   T.E.S.

* The exact phrase they use is 'You may pay us with a draft drawn on your Bank'. Now, how did they know I had a bank?

431: TO BRUCE ROGERS

31/1/31

Dear B.R., Forgive the typewriter: I write in office hours, and they mistake the yapping of this machine for my work.

Your letter is very re-assuring. Under such conditions the *Odyssey* can harm nobody and nothing. I am only doubtful if it will do anyone any good!

We must do our best to get the whole of the luxury edition placed before the date of publication: then the popular version will matter less.

As soon as the price is fixed I have several of my friends to inform about it. They will wish to subscribe to Walker's direct,[1] which benefits the firm to the extent of the booksellers' commission.

The arrangements you suggest for the U.S.A. edition sound admirable. Not many copies either of a Harvard or a Knopf edition would be brought into England, for there is no demand in England for more versions of the classics. I do not think the point demands any safeguarding.

I return XVIII-XX, with some minor changes and the necessary embodying of the W.[2] corrections. Only I have refused

[1] Emery Walker published Lawrence's translation of the *Odyssey*.
[2] W. was called in as an expert to give an opinion.

to accept his championing of the ancient theory of hollow-bladed axes. The metaphor from ship-building seems as clear as daylight.

You may have thought me cavalier in preferring my own way to W.'s professional suggestions, sometimes: not his verbal suggestions, but his archaeology. Yet, actually, I'm in as strong a position vis-à-vis Homer as most of his translators. For years we were digging up a city of roughly the Odysseus period. I have handled the weapons, armour, utensils of those times, explored their houses, planned their cities. I have hunted wild boars and watched wild lions, sailed the Aegean (and sailed ships), bent bows, lived with pastoral peoples, woven textiles, built boats and killed many men. So I have odd knowledges that qualify me to understand the *Odyssey*, and odd experiences that interpret it to me. Therefore a certain headiness in rejecting help.

I have no more for you yet. My R.A.F. interruption is almost over, pro tem, and I hope to get xxi into shape before another week is passed.

The pleasurable memory of this *Odyssey* business will be our relations. I have found you the most considerate editor and producer imaginable, and it has been very enjoyable to work for you. The money will also be pleasurable, and alas also, too soon, a memory!   T.E.SHAW.

432 : TO BRUCE ROGERS

25/2/31.

Dear B.R., I have yet a confession of delay to make. First, a delay in London, then a visit of some people to Plymouth; then another business trip to London: then a crash of a Flying Boat, followed by its Court of Enquiry and an Inquest: and tomorrow a detachment to near Southampton for ten days to test a new fast motor boat for the R.A.F.

The upshot of all this is no more *Odyssey*. I am still working on Book xxi and it will be the end of April before I finish, if all goes well after this ten days. I am sorry again.

I have your *Bible* sheets always in the workshop office, on public view, and I call them superb. So undemonstratively

superb, too. Till they are familiar one does not see how wholly
good they are. At first glance one just says '*Bible*, of course:
good one, too.'

Yes, I know the Butcher and Lang view of the axes trial. All
other scholars have followed them, more or less. I have found
copper axe-heads with openings in them like that.
Nobody could have shot through one of them at twenty
yards, much less 12: and if he did, the merit would
have lain with the placer of the axes, and not with
the archer. Whereas the text shows that they
were not put up with plumb-line and spirit-level. Only stamped
firmly into a trench scratched by Telemachus into the earth floor
of the hall. And Telemachus had not set out axes before. They
must have been in only a rough line.

If the axes were about 4 feet long, and 6 inches be taken off for
what was put into the ground, then a 5 foot 6 inch man standing
20 yards off could easily shoot through an alley of them: no
difficulty of trajectory would arise: and the spectators sitting at
their tables could see the arrow pass through:

Whereas with your suggestion of shooting through the
ears of 12 axes so, it would require a slow-motion
cinema to prove that his arrow passed so and no higher:
and the trajectory and angle-of-stance would both complicate the
point.

I suspect we make too much of the shooting test. Nobody
seems to have been struck with astonishment at it. Stringing the
bow seems to have been the more difficult job.

'Through' leaves the problem open. I should prefer it, therefore.

Personally, as archaeologist and archer, I like my own notion
of two rows of axes, six-a-side: and nothing else fits all the Greek
and yet remains a possible feat. I admit that possibility is not
what the public prefer. They feed poor Elisha by ravens, rather
than by Arabs, which the text could equally read: only I feel that
the *Odyssey* should, so far as possible, make sense. If you leave
standing my 'alley of bilge-blocks' and the word 'through' as
now amended, then both parties are served: which is a good
compromise.

Homer can't have meant only axe-heads — to shoot through the handle-holes: for then he would not have plainly called the bilge-blocks of oak. Besides bilge-blocks are man-high, nearly: and always in pairs.

There wasn't a platform to shoot from: only off the bench on the floor: and most ancient archers with these short bows shot kneeling. It would not be a standing-man's height. I think a 4-foot axe-handle would be ample: and most battle axes are $4\frac{1}{2}$ to 5 feet tall.

These re-curved bows (I was handling one yesterday) are most cunning things built up of sinew and birch bark and wood and horn. Relaxed they are an oval about 30 inches by 18: strung they are $4\frac{1}{2}$ to 5 feet long. One strings them usually half-sitting, putting the one end between the thighs and pulling on the other horn, while pressing down the centre-grip. When it is bent right out and over the other side one slips the string up the blade and notches it.

As for the pun, by all means soften it. They are out of our fashion. Only put a comma after 'destroy'. The Greek does not use the word destroy nor suggest destruction. I only looked for an English word with the syllable 'troy' in it. Read 'An ill-season took Odysseus in his hollow ship to destroy or des-troy — or desTroy (comma) that cursed place I will not name'; it's not to destroy-the-place: but to a place called destroy: or 'no-troy' perhaps.

Palmer translated *Odyssamenos* (the pun-word) as 'odious'. I think there is no other English word which preserves even the shadow of a pun. The Greek word means grieved, angered, disgusted, peeved. Odious is not very close: it refers to the other men and women, and not to Autolycus; he was fed up with them, not they with him: at least he thought so. I have no doubt the disgust was mutual, myself: and so odious is rather good. But it does stretch things. Palmer says 'since I come hither odious to many men and women ... therefore Odysseus be his name'. I should have said — 'let his name be Odysseus, for their odiousness'. Or better still 'for the odiousness' or 'in odiousness' (this is really pretty good).

In great haste.   T.E.S.

[On February 4th, 1931, an Iris III Flying Boat crashed near Plymouth. Lawrence was one of the rescue party and gave evidence at the inquest on February 18th. The following impression by Lawrence is written in pencil on the sheets of pencil manuscript headed *Leaves in the Wind* which I believe to be the first rough notes for a continuation of *The Mint* covering Lawrence's further experience in the R.A.F. I print it here as it may refer to this crash of an Iris Flying Boat. There were several other crashes, one being in March, 1933.]

433: FROM 'LEAVES IN THE WIND'

Iris crash — sea molten-visioned aluminium. Poor [*name omitted*] drunk with foolish laughter, like captive balloon whose gas wobbles it drunkenly as the strands that tether it to this earth are parting, one by one. Rest drawn, bleak grey-faced, tardily quarrelling amongst themselves. No joy but [*name omitted*] laughingly. We got on to him, he promised betterment. Six of us crushed together in the crushed canister of the hull were bubbling out their lives. Great belches of air spewed up rose now and then, as another compartment of wing or hull gave way.

434: TO LADY ASTOR

[*Postmarked Mar. 2, 1931.*]

Viscountess! Forgive the typing of your slave: he makes his living by his keys. A poor living, as you will see.

I had meant not to write to you before it could be a song of 'nunc dimittis': and that is not yet. I *think* the battle is won. The Coroner was a perfect pet. He asked all the nibbly, difficult, hurtful questions, so innocently and so smoothly that everything came out. The poor officers did nobly (Wing Commander Smith at the head of them, adjuring all of us to tell the truth) and the press followed up, saying nothing mean or spiteful, but scaring the Air Ministry almost to death.

The best results are coming, though slowly. They have set the reforms afoot, and I think they may be trusted to push them through. I am watching very closely and will move another little lever or two when or if it is necessary. There has been no reflection upon me, and no threat to end my happy days. Good.

I need hardly say how grateful I am to you for your help. It is such a pleasure to get a thing done cleanly and naturally, without fuss. Nobody knows that anything has been done, and yet, I fancy, there will not be another case of this sort in our memories.

Now I am deader tired than ever; I type because my eyes are so faded. Tomorrow I get a change from Mount Batten, for I go to Hythe, near Southampton, for ten days instruction in a new fast motor boat being built for the R.A.F. Not very fast, I'm afraid, but faster than the old crocks.

To get away and forget camp for these few days will be a little bit of heaven. Ring me up if you come to Plymouth after March 9th; and let me take you up the Tamar for a picnic-tea.

T.E.S.

If you see Walling any time please tell him he did a very good piece of work.

435: TO EDWARD MARSH

10th March, 1931.   Mount Batten, Plymouth

Dear E.M., This letter, typed more or less ill, is for your owner,[1] please. May your polish and style support its bluntness, in his eyes!

A namesake of his, Bertram Thomas, our Agent at Muscat, has just crossed the Empty Quarter,[2] that great desert of southern Arabia. It remained the only unknown corner of the world, and it is the end of the history of exploration. Thomas did it by camel, at his own expense. Every explorer for generations has dreamed of it. Its difficulty can best be put by my saying that no Arab, so far as we know, has ever crossed it.

---

[1] J. H. Thomas, then Secretary of State for the Colonies. Marsh was his private secretary.
[2] See letters Nos. 389, 392 and 456.

Now something good must be done for this most quiet and decent fellow, in the Birthday Honours, if not sooner. It may be all arranged; but if not I beg you see to it. Do not let the swag be all carried off by the Rositas and Lawrences of the vulgar Press. Here is one of your own men doing a marvel.

Give him a K.[1] will you? Well, it's a mouldy sort of thing, but as a civil servant he cannot refuse. So it would do: but your sense of fitness, which o-emmed Henry J.[2] (now I address E.M. & not J.H.T.) might prefer a C.H., or some other honour of which I know nothing.

Properly he should be India Office; but his success decorates England. K.C.S. eyes or ees would be unfitting. Better a Michael & George.

I trust the imagination of J.H.T. to understand your enthusiasm & mine for what is the finest geographical feat since Shackleton and to persuade his colleagues into action and unanimity. It will be a welcome change for them all.

Will you also say that his *Seven Pillars* is not forgotten? This is not bribery of a Cabinet Minister, but the paying of a forgotten debt. The only available copies are of the U.S.A. edition, and it may be weeks yet before I have the chance to get it brought safely through our Customs. Yours constantly (but not too often!)

T.E.SHAW.

436: TO G. W. M. DUNN

11/3/31.

Dear Dunn, When I got to *Engines*[3] I said 'Hullo, this chap can write' and wondered who it was. Eventually I turned up your letter, to check if it was by yourself. I think this is about the best thing I can tell you about it. Detailed criticism is the only stuff worth having — plain praise being the most useless and boring stuff in the world — but the only people who can give you detailed criticism fit to help you are other craftsmen working

[1] Knighthood.   [2] Henry James, O.M.
[3] The title of a poem by Dunn, then an aircraftman.

themselves upon your job. Not being a poet I cannot venture towards you.

Yet this cannot be a phoenix — the only product of its sort from your brain. Will you entrust me with other things, however surpassed and out-of-date they now feel to you? I should like to read more.

Next time I see Eddy Marsh I will tell him what you want about Brooke's letters. Brooke seems to have been a personality so dazzling that he took away his friends' judgements. At least so I read it, from what they said, and what poems he left behind him. I only saw him once. He looked startling.

I have been intending to write to you for long enough, but one thing and another soon make me put off the letter business. It seems to convey nothing when done.

Irruptions of R.A.F. work into my spare hours have prevented the finishing of that *Odyssey* translation upon which I depend for my spare cash, this summer. So I am tied here indefinitely till it is over. After that some road-burning, I hope. You may be yet within reach.

So please, more poems if permitted.

Use the adjectives which seem to your senses best fitting: it will then depend on the sanity of your senses whether others find them significant or not. Don't forget that a strain of vulgarity, in its best sense, is indispensable in the greatest art. Your precious artist, however real, comes second to the common man.

Heed no advice or criticism except from your peers.   T.E.SHAW

437: TO S. C. ROLLS[1]

8th. April 1931.   *Mount Batten, Plymouth*

Dear Rolls, You will have been calling me every kind of a skug, for not answering — and I have been doing the service test of a new R.A.F. fast motor boat, and no letters were sent on.

It is exceedingly good of you to have written. I've wondered often where you were, and Goslett has made faint efforts to find

---

[1] Rolls, the driver of Lawrence's Rolls-Royce tender 'Blast', has written *Steel Chariots in the Desert*, an account of his experiences, published 1937.

you. Once we thought of having some sort of a meeting in London to feed each other: only everybody is scattered or lost.[1] I hardly see anyone now, except Colonel Alan Dawnay, who looks me up sometimes. It was a long time ago, that was, wasn't it?

In the last two years since I came back from India I've been twice through Northampton and I'll try and see you this summer during my leave. I always look in at Nottingham on the chap who makes my motor-bike, and that's your way. I'm like you—not fond of writing letters.

I'm glad that life hasn't broken you. I'm cheerful but generally shortish on a Thursday. This Air Force life is full of incidents, and it keeps me busy and happy. One cannot expect good pay for happiness.

You are probably married and have eleven children: if so I think it's a bit more than I'd like.

Gosh: you wrote me four pages. I honestly can't: but if ever I get to your place I'll talk for four hours. It will be queer to see you without about three days beard on each of our faces. We were a scruffy sort of crew: but we did quite a lot of damage to our enemies. Yours ever   T.E. SHAW

'Shaw' it is, always now, and no Mr. about it please. That colonel touch is dead and buried.

[The following letter, if read together with letters Nos. 432, 439 and 440, fixes the date from which Lawrence began to specialize in the new type of motor boats which he had been urging on the Air Ministry. He had, as the reader has seen, had experience of speed boats with his American Biscayne Baby.]

438: TO B. H. LIDDELL HART

13 *April* [1931]   *Mount Batten*

I'm a poor correspondent, I fear. Many times I have been on the edge of writing to say that your war-history[2] has become one of my

---

[1] See letter No. 133.   [2] *The Real War*, 1914-18.

constant reference books, for the main war; and that its chapters on the side-shows are so crisply black-and-white as to make exciting stories of them. Only you know all this, and I'd ten thousand times rather tell it you by mouth.

Now arrive these two letters, and by a chance they find me at Mount Batten. My two-year war with Air Ministry over the type of motor boats suited to attend seaplanes is bearing results now, and experimental boats are being offered by contractors. I've become a marine expert, and test the things for them, acquiring incidentally and by degrees quite a knowledge of the S.W. coast of England! A minor consequence is extensive absence from home, and a major (secondary and indirect) consequence is the paralysis of my *Odyssey* translation. It is stuck at Book xxi, and I begin to despair of finishing it. Motor-boat-testing is an all-time job, and leaves one too exhausted to write.

I hope you have a good holiday. Myself, I am craving only for a little home-life, at the moment. You must arrange to include Plymouth some day in your orbit of duties, and come speed-boating with me. It is fun, for a time.

The P.E.N.[1] suggestion is rather astonishing. A million times 'no' and thank them very much. I thought they always guested writers — and they can hardly call me that on the strength of a war memoir written twelve years ago and only privately printed — or are writers and celebrities all running short and the second rank now due for turns? It is a queer invitation: but such things do happen. I must tell you some day of offers I twice got for honorary degrees at Scotch universities. My second reason, above, is operative in Scotland. You did, I fancy, 'guess my reaction' successfully: only don't be too brusque with Ould. I do not know him, but he may be decent.

The Foch book[2] cannot, I fear, be greatly interesting. He was rather a drab creature, surely, with more teeth than brains. It was irony that made him the successful general of the last phase.

---

[1] The P.E.N. Club, an international literary club.   Herman Ould is the secretary.
[2] Liddell Hart was beginning his study of Marshal Foch.

439: TO A PILOT WHO HAD FLOWN WITH LAWRENCE TO EGYPT
IN 1919[1]

17.iv.31   *Mount Batten, Plymouth*

Dear [*name omitted*], Yes, it found me after so long. It feels like years since we flew together. I wonder what you are now? My doings are fairly public, I'm afraid, if not always very authentic. The truth isn't romantic, usually.

After 1922, when by grace of Winston Churchill I was able to see the Middle East smoothly settled, I washed my hands of politics and enlisted. Since then I have been happy whenever left alone.

I read Buckingham's book[2] years ago. It is good, and I would thank you for your offer of it, only that I live in barracks, and my kit does not allow for the storing of books. They inspect it, sometimes, you see. I have no house or rooms of my own.

I'll never forget seeing your 'bus going down towards the Albanian coast, with one prop hardly turning, and groaning to myself 'There's another one gone.'

That flight put the complete wind up me. We have better busses now. Yours sincerely,   T.E.SHAW.

440: TO DICK KNOWLES

19.4.31.   *Mount Batten, Plymouth*

Dear Dick, I've wanted for so long to write to you, only I am no letter-writer. All the good of life goes out when second-handed on paper. So I used to compromise by asking always after you at Clouds Hill: and now the writing to you is made harder by your father's going. It will be such old and weary news to you, by now: and what can anyone say that is of any use in such circumstances? He was so excellent a neighbour, and I had looked forward to our living opposite one another for ever so long. There it is.

Your letter from Bagdad gave a good picture of an airman's tropical activity. I am glad there was the car, and I am glad that

[1] *See* his account on pp. 276-279.
[2] *Travels in Palestine,* by J. S. Buckingham, 1822.

you have found the country possible. If I returned I would find myself an utter stranger: yet it was a good place for looking upon in the Turkish days. Ugly: yes and dirty and shabby and smelly, but very human. As I get older I feel safer and easier in contemplating the animal facts of existence. It is as though the brains in my head were burnt out.

Now for what happens to me at Mount Batten. There is the Brough in stable: used for transport, not for sport. I go to places on it. The Devon roads are vile, and the camp hard to get in and out of by land. In stable also is a little Yankee motor-boat with a 6-cylinder s.v. 100 h.p. engine. It does 46 miles an hour, roars and bumps, splashes and bucks. When I can manage the petrol (usually an afternoon per week) it goes into the water and makes a playground of Plymouth Sound.

In the office there is the Greek text of the *Odyssey* of Homer, and many sheets of pencil, pen or typed draft translation of it into English prose. By its means I buy the petrol and spares for the bike and boat, and my spare hours are a sad and difficult adjustment between the claims of pleasure and finance.

I have forgotten, or left till last, my working hours. I am clerk A.C.11 in workshops and do the technical correspondence. Actually do it. I write the letters, type them, and do not sign them. The poor C.O. takes that responsibility. Often it is a responsibility. Also I am one of the crew of a motor-boat, and work in what running I can when I'm not clerking. An R.A.F. dull stupid heavy motor-boat, of course.

Just now I am wholly M.B.C.,[1] for the R.A.F. is at last trying to get some marine craft of modern design, a need I have been urging on them (per C.O.'s signature) for 18 months. With some humour the Air Ministry detailed me to proceed to Hythe near Southampton, and carry out the type-trials and engine tests. In the boat-trials we got to Penzance, my crew and me! That was my notion of what motor-boats should be fit for. The A.M. had a fit also. The engine test is now on. It's the 100 H.P. engine used in the Invicta car, and the Vickers Tank. We buzz it up and down Southampton Water, the Spit and the Solent, each of us (two on the job) taking the wheel in turn, while the

[1] Motor Boat Crew.

other checks gauges. The weather is wintry, of course, and the speed-boat (it does 34 m.p.h.) dives through the seas like an inefficient submarine. So I am tired and salty-wet and cold.

Enough of this therefore. If ever you think I could be of any use to you in any way, drop me a line and I will do my best to come up to scratch. Yours ever, T.E.S.

441: TO RAYMOND SAVAGE[1]

10.vi.31.   *Plymouth*

Dear Savage, I, too, have thought of trying some day, after my R.A.F. life ends, to write something, and put it through pseudonymously. Only suppose the bally thing succeeded! We should be in the soup, then.

It therefore seemed to me an impracticable plan. I could only publish it if I could find a real name to father it — i.e. some poor wretch who would acknowledge it as his, if it came off, or didn't come off. The second is easy, the first very difficult for him. Frankly, I think it is too hard to hope for.

So your letter has not opened a way to avoid the responsibility of writing, I fear. Thanks all the same. Yours ever, T.E.SHAW.

442: TO ROBIN WHITE[2]

10.vi.31   [*Plymouth*]

I will never be a sailor, I'm afraid: born too late, though my father had yachts and used to take me with him from my fourth year: but my attempted accomplishment is motor-boating, a very different art, and as difficult. Sailing has only wind and water, and the two-party system is simple to work. With power all manner of complications enter and the art becomes exquisite, and subtler. Only it isn't sailing!

Last week we ran down from Southampton here in 7 hrs in one of the new R.A.F. boats: and this morning (it being most rough and horrid) we chased the *Keppel* out beyond Rame Head,

---

[1] Lawrence's literary agent.   [2] Lieutenant, R.N.

 zz

till she took over too much water for 20 m.p.h. and turned back to the Sound. We turned back, willingly, and kept station till within the breakwater: then home: but the poor *Keppel* has to wait out there.

My own boat is in the shed, till I finish these R.A.F. tests. Almost sick of speed boating, I am, now.

What is the *Viscount*? It sounds like an unarmoured ship, and should not be the smallest of its class, or rank, or shouldn't it be the *Viscountess*? 'She' says the incarnate sailor, stroking the gangway of the *Iron Duke*, 'can be a perfect bitch in a cross-sea'. '*He* surely' I suggest, but the incarnate deny it. What can a mere airman say? Yours sincerely,   T E SHAW.

I should, properly, have the honour to be, Sir, your obedient Servant: but the proprieties have been observed with the Lieut at the top. Unless you are a Commander now. I hope so.

443: TO LADY ASTOR

10. VI. 31   *Plymouth*

Dear Peeress, Indeed and I was asleep & abed. How good of the Corporal to tell you! We had a hard 7½ hours run down from Southampton here in our motor-boat, got in before 7 P.M., ate, made down our beds, & slept nobly till Sunday morning.

Now I hope to be at Mount Batten for a month. Ring me up (before 10 P.M. if possible) and we will meet.

No pillion. The new Traffic Act puts pillion-affording beyond modest means, and forces the love-sick to screw nasty iron-spring-things to their back mudguards.

No speed-boat either, now. I have much testing of the R.A.F. boat still to do, and cannot put my own pet in the water till that is all done.

So you will have to make do with my undistinguished person, unaided except by an anglo-irish tongue. Au revoir.   T.E.S.

444: TO NOEL COWARD

10. VI. 31   *Plymouth*

Dear N. C., I have read your play (which? why your war one,[1] of course) twice and want to admire you. It's a fine effort, a really fine effort.

You know better than anyone what sort of a play it is; I fancied it hadn't the roots of a great success. You had something far more important to say than usual, and I fancy that in saying it you let the box-office and the stalls go hang. As argument it is first rate. As imagination magnificent: and it does you great honour as a human being. It's for that reason that I liked it so much. Mrs Humphry Ward (before your time) once asked Matthew Arnold (also before your time) why he was not wholly serious.[2] People won't like you better for being quite so serious as you are in this: but it does you honour, as I said, and gave me a thrill to read it.

Incidentally the press-man-magnate-son scene was horrifying. That would 'act', surely? Only most of the rest was far above playing to any gallery.

I think it was very good of you to have done this so plainly and well. I needn't say that it's written with your usual spare exactness and skill. You deny yourself every unnecessary word.
Yours   T E SHAW.

No answer. It isn't a letter: I'd wanted to say how much I liked the thing, and failed to say anything worth reading: and so just report progress, gratefully.

445: TO DAVID GARNETT

10.6.31.   *Plymouth*

Dear D.G., You will have thought me buried, or burnt: whereas I have only been away for months in Southampton Water, wholly engrossed in tuning and testing new fast motor-boats

---

[1] *Post-Mortem.*
[2] The legend to Max Beerbohm's cartoon in *The Poet's Corner.*

being designed for the R.A.F. No Easter holiday, no Whitsun: and no near holiday yet, I fear.

The Grasshoppers[1] is however imperative need for a letter. In it you have suddenly broken, I think, into sincerity. The flying is real. For the first time, in all that you have written, I feel a *necessity* of utterance, a fusion of matter and manner so complete that the manner is almost absorbed. Only one precious word I saw — 'sighed' for the prop-tip — and what a good word!

You told me about the tale long months ago, and it frightened me that one with no sense of the air should touch it. There are so many bad flying books. Then you went flying, and qualified yourself superbly, and this little masterpiece is it. I'm only sorry that he should have had but the one eye and a big tooth, like Hinchcliffe. Probably that is an accident.[2]

The book has pleased me quite beyond what I had thought possible. It is the first account of real flying by a real writer who can really fly: and it gave me a very great sense of long distance, and of that incommunicable cradle-dandling which is a cockpit in flight. Yours,   T.E.SHAW.

446: TO G. W. M. DUNN

10.6.31.   *Plymouth*

Dear Dunn, Like me, your main life chokes the side issues. The R.A.F. detached me to Hythe on special duty, to test and tune their new-type speed-boats for the Schneider Cup. So two months flew; leaving me weary and quite unrepentant.

Only the *Odyssey* is unfinished, and the unhappy publisher is unhappier, apparently. However, in his contract I put the clause 'service conditions permitting' and so am saved.

It is to be published by subscription only, through Emery Walker, and will be 12 guineas and then some! My brother is, I fancy, doing Herodotus. I hope so. It would be beyond a joke

---

[1] *The Grasshoppers Come*, by David Garnett.
[2] It was a coincidence. There have been other one-eyed pilots besides the famous pilot who was lost on a cross-Atlantic flight.

if the family competed in *Odysseys:* and he would probably out-do me, he being a scholar.

Even so you have not written any more poems, and don't feel like it? Ah well. There is always the R.A.F. to fall back upon. I am ever astonished at the chance given us. For thousands of years nature has held this mastery of the last element in her lap, patiently waiting for our generation, and you and I are of the lucky ones chosen.

By this lyric outburst you will understand that this morning I was hut orderly, and got checked for dull brass door-knobs: though I had really cleaned them: but a foggy sea-coast station does not deserve brass anywhere.

Some day spur yourself to write something. There was hope in your *Engines*. Yours,   T.E.SHAW.

447: TO FLIGHT LIEUTENANT W. E. G. BEAUFORTE-GREENWOOD

18.VI.31   *Mount Batten*

Dear Flight Lieutenant Beauforte-Greenwood, Here is an advance copy of the last notes upon R.A.F. 200. I see that in all I have written you almost a book upon the boat and her engines.[1] It has been interesting and difficult, and therefore I am very grateful to you for giving me the chance of doing it. This is the third good job I have had in the R.A.F.

You have been very kind in appreciating our work, and the letter received from Coastal Area about Corporal Bradbury should do him good in his trade. I feel particularly pleased about the whole affair, because it has meant our getting so good a boat so quickly.

She left yesterday for Calshot, but got only to Portland. I fancy that big-ship sailors are not always happy in little boats. The water conditions were suitable to a fast run, like what we had in Lyme Bay. The first dent in her beauty was made by Wing

---

[1] Lawrence's report deals exhaustively with the hull, engines, steering, fuel-system, controls, electrical equipment, instruments, maintenance and handling under all weather conditions of the type of boat in question. It is a masterpiece of technology, running to some eighty foolscap pages.

Commander Watkins here: but I did not log it, as he was sorry for doing it.

Do you think any arrangement could be made for a Mount Batten crew (Corpl. Stains, a/c Headon, and Corpl. Bradbury if an engineer is wanted) to take over the boat eventually to be allotted to us, when she is ready at the Yard? They would get her through the Schneider period without battle-scars.

I am sorry about the inconclusive trial of the baby target. It seemed to me extraordinarily promising. The splash was like all the Trafalgar Square fountains rolled together, and it towed beautifully. At a guess I'd put the strain down at about 1½ cwt: but the job wants tackling seriously, first to decide if the wire must be 5 cwt or 10 cwt or 15 cwt and then to invent a suitable winch for dealing with quantities of wire with a suitable brake. Our thing took 20 minutes to wind in! The Calshot party wanted to get away, so would not leave 200 here to go on testing. In a week or so, with the Ferry-Perkins 35-footer, we could settle the 5 cwt wire question, and demand a 10 cwt or 15 cwt, if you sent approval. The winch I would drive just with a belt and pulley, and idle wheel, twisting the belt at right-angles, which is quite feasible for light loads. It could be driven off the R.H. engine at 500 revs, while the L.H. steered the boat, and would bring the wire up in two minutes, thus making it possible to turn safely and quickly. The only day we had for testing it opened in driving mist, which turned to heavy rain and wind. The Sound was quite impossible, being full of sheltering ships. So we waited for high tide at 6 p.m. and went up past Saltash, where the lake was only choppy, and visibility about half a mile. There could not have been worse conditions, for man and boat, and the test was thus unfair on everything. If we can go on playing with it, and get the wire right, I shall try some fast towing behind my own boat, and see if the board does 'take-off' at speed. We could ballast it forward, or alter the pennant, if so, to make it fit up to 30 m.p.h.

In any case, whether you leave the target here or not, I hope you will continue to try it. It seemed to me like the best bombing target yet. Yours sincerely   T. E. SHAW.

448: TO JAMES HANLEY

2. VII. 31   *Plymouth*

Dear Hanley, This has been a scramble, for the posts are slow, and I have therefore had it only yesterday and today: and by chance these have been hard days for us (much flying, and moorings to lay, and a good deal of heavy stuff to move) so that I am more asleep with tiredness than alive: yet it must go off tonight, to reach you before Sunday. They work us fairly hard, in the R.A.F. It is not like the peace-time army. We have enough to do, always, in fine weather.

Now about it. I'm not a reviewer, and my notions of a book take time, like muddy water, to settle down and clarify. It is hot writing, like all of yours. It goes rather higher and further, in Fr Hooley's long soliloquy: there is real thought in that, and the torrent of idea flows well and brilliantly. This seems to me bigger than any other of your writing I have yet seen. But it is unfinished, and how plain & poor the Venus of Melos would seem, with her arms! Work that is not ended is so hard to judge: but you should take it as a good sign that I badly want to read more of it — all there is.

You must work very fast: yet your writing is all good, clear & fitting, and when necessary beautiful. Yet all your own. You have been delivered from the cliché: if the 'viols' on page 10 are real. I heard the Dolmetsch crowd once playing what they called viols, and thought them pretty foul. Also your cataracts puzzled me. There were three of them, quite close together, once as a verb, once an adjective and once a noun. I fancy you overdid 'em. Otherwise your writing is just a transparent medium, through which what you want to say slips invisibly and silently into my mind. I like that: it seems to me the essence of style.

I don't find the development of *Sheila Moynihan* as yet fulfils your MS. note above the title. Priests — yes. Innocence — yes: grasping greedy — fathers, rather than mothers, so far. Poor Mrs. M. was baby-racked, and couldn't care, surely? 'Cold-ice-cold and hungry English mistresses' — not yet: not in the first 130 pages! Something cold wouldn't be out of place, after the hotness you have given us.

Your character-drawing is superb, here & in *Boy* and in *The Last Voyage*, and *Drift*, and in the story of the two soldiers worrying their prisoner. You can draw characters as and when you please, with an almost blistering vividness.

Now a couple of notes on your last letter. Conditions go to make Sex — yes: I suppose so. I don't know much about ships: once I spent a month on the lower deck of a Q boat.[1] There was plenty of flesh talked and dreamed about, and to see, too: only what was seen wasn't what was dreamed about, I think. Anyway there wasn't much done about it. And I've lived in barracks now, for nine years: preferring the plain man to the elaborated man. I find them forth-coming, honest, friendly and so comfortable. They do not pretend at all, and with them I have not to pretend. Sex, with them, is something you put on (and take off) with your walking-out dress: on Friday night, certainly: and if you are lucky on Saturday afternoon, and most of Sunday. Work begins on Monday again, and is really important. I think that we are kinder to each other than your fellows: and less ignorant. Of course the R.A.F. is probably far milder than Liverpool or Glasgow. Service fellows don't fight, and enlist mainly for a refuge against the pain of making a living. So probably we do miss the 'larger life' you try to write about.

You need not bother about the Latin Quarter, or about schools & cliques. They will bother more about you: and if you don't pay attention they will fall to praising everything you do. Whereas praise is always waste of time to hear, and harmful, in overdose. After years of it you look for it and credit it, and then are soiled. Take poor G.B.S. who must have been wonderful when he was your age, fifty years ago. Now he is pedestalled, and not so good as you are. Whereas 50 years hence you may be rotten.

Yeats, I think, suffered in his middle years from Lady Gregory and others: but his later poems have been wonderful. Of course he's a great poet, and alive. I think the second quality the better!

I will not throw *Boy* away. I propose to read it more. It is good. I like it better than *Sheila* (while seeing that it is less) for subjective reasons, because I like men, and ships and Alexandria! I will try & find something not pimpish of me in Arab kit,

---

[1] Lawrence's friend, A. E. Chambers, was a naval rating on a Q ship during the war.

for you. It was long ago, and a scabby episode in my life, I think. Politically the thing was so dirty that I grew to hate it all before it came out more-or-less honestly in the end. So when I see pictures of myself in Arab kit I get a little impatient — silly of me, for it was long ago, and did really happen.

Your sanity and general wholesomeness stick up out of your books a mile high: people with dirty patches in them skirt round and round them, alluding but never speaking right out. They are afraid of giving their spots away — and you can map them, just by outlining the blanks. Whereas, God almighty, you leave nothing unsaid or undone, do you? I can't understand how you find brave men to publish you! Yours   T.E. SHAW

449: TO FLIGHT LIEUTENANT W. E. G. BEAUFORTE-GREENWOOD

14. VII.31.   *Mount Batten*

Dear Flight Lieutenant Beauforte-Greenwood, Here is a final report, so far as present arrangements go, on the little surf-board target. It is very good for its proposed job, I think, the only difficulty being spotting, which is best done from the aircraft, the fixed base-line of 600 yards giving to the observer a good chance of guessing his shot's real position.

I had to give up towing it behind 159, as we did only 13 miles an hour with it, full out; and could only get out occasionally, the other two 35-footers being under top-overhaul for Schneider duty. So I hooked it onto the Biscayne Baby and ran it off its keel! The rough days (everybody said the wire would break in bad water) were great fun, the sea being much too bad for a Southampton upon our last occasion. Once I got it up to 35 m.p.h.: but 20-25 is really its fastest decent speed. For a fast target you would have to re-design, with flared bows and a flattened after-moulding, I think, to plane: with scoop-tubes like air intakes thrust through the floor amidships. You could make it weigh only half of this target's weight, I think.

This one slowed my light boat by about 3 miles an hour only, at its worst.

I think any quantity of reconditioned 5 cwt drogue cable is available, and its lightness and strength makes it ideal for this tow, if it is carefully handled. The art is to wind it regularly and so avoid kinks. If that is done, or if all kinks are cut and spliced, the wire will last indefinitely. The main reason for a power-driven drum is to be able to wind up smoothly, under load.

I'm afraid this photo should have been taken from behind the target, to show that its splash is much the same as my boat's. The 600 yards interval makes it look so remote and small. We have put the target back into station stores, now. It is a bit worn at its edges but still quite good. The Flying Boat very much enjoyed bombing at it.

The towing is dead easy: you can turn any way you please, as slow or as fast as you like. I have doubled back like this  within 50 yards of the target, with it proceeding blissfully in the former direction while I dashed by! Yours sincerely

T. E. SHAW

Mount Batten is sad over the C.O's.[1] posting to Manston on promotion. It is a great loss for flying boats and motor boats as he was keen on water work. Also he was a very good C.O. I wonder if Calshot have bust old 200 again!

450: TO C. J. GREENWOOD[2]

17.VII.31.   *Plymouth*

Dear Greenwood, I think Hanley a very good, if not always gay, writer. *Boy* is very remarkable, in the draft I read. I have not seen your revised text. He is profuse, various, and vigorous.

I hope you are not riding for a row with the Home Office. That sort of thing usually gives the author a kink against decency, and makes him bought by all the wrong people, for all the nasty reasons. Hanley is too good to be labelled by them. Of the evils, I far prefer censorship by the publisher to censorship by the police. If you publish *anything* a fellow writes, you only give the police an easy entry. So do outrage your love of liberty so far as to keep Hanley out of the Courts.

---

[1] Wing Commander Sydney Smith.
[2] A partner in Boriswood, Ltd., James Hanley's publishers.

CONVERSATION PIECE *circa* 1931

Of the two sentences you quote, nothing (on the score of fairness) can be said against the first.

The second is not so fair. I told him that nobody but a sane and decent person could write so freely about — well, filth. As you put it, people in search of a sane and wholesome book for their sons and daughters might blindly buy *Boy* — and be indignant. Can't you even it out? [4 *lines omitted*]

Good luck to you! Yours, T.E.SHAW.

451: TO BRUCE ROGERS

20/VIII/31 *Plymouth*

Dear B.R., Thank you for sending xxi. I checked over your changes and W's, and sent it on to Miss Saunders, with a few very minor alterations of my own. You will be able to pass upon these when the proof reaches you. However I had to leave 'go gay' which W. called American slang (you properly dissenting — it is good Queen Anne colloquial), as nothing else in my head fitted the sentence.

Some weeks ago I sent Miss Saunders the text of xxii. When I read Book xxi on its coming from you, I felt it had movement, and suspense: it was like a prelude to catastrophe: and xxii has done its best to be grim and bloody: or at least to be grimmer and bloodier than Homer. In parts the Greek is poor melodrama, and stinks of unreality: and I am hoping that you (and others) may find my version more credible, as tragedy.

Just before my leave ended I finished off xxiii and xxiv and sent them to London last Saturday. They have been confronting me in the rough, as you know, for months: and are very difficult books. After the slaughter of xxii some quiet finish was artistically necessary: and there were all manner of loose strings flapping from the poem. So Homer (*Odyssey*-Homer, should we say?) started out to tidy everything; and hopelessly lost his way. These 'little' artists, to use little as a term of sheltering affection, find a theme so hard to end. His last movement drools on and on like one of Schubert's, everybody (author included) dying to end it, but mellifluously unable.

I've been wrestling with it intermittently for all these months, trying to get shape into it, in my mind: for if I could have seen it in one piece, then shape would have somehow marvellously appeared. And it did improve: though it will remain a failure, always. You can help, in xxiv, by leaving a space where the scene shifts between hell, earth and heaven too suddenly. The author's cunning deserted him or he tried his skill too high. At any rate he failed to darn over his gaps and transitions.

Mind you, these books are authentic stuff. It will not do, as they said in Alexandria, to end the *Odyssey* where he and Penelope get into bed. This is not a comic opera: but I fancy that poor O-Homer threw his hand in at the end, rather as I did, after trying very hard. He has lavished on these two books some of his loveliest intimacies — only the need was for one or two big things, and he couldn't write big.

Eurycleia stumbling upstairs; the entry of Penelope upon Odysseus; her comment upon his death-story; the funeral of Achilles, where Thetis comes; Agamemnon's praise of the Odyssey; Laertes in his garden; the babbling childhood of Odysseus amid the trees; the welcome of Dolius; the wrangle upon valour between O., Telemachus and Laertes — all these are in the best manner, perfect touches which only imperfectly conceal the need for good construction. It is most true and genuine O-Homer. Even another comic lion, another shipwreck, and more birds arrive, worked in unhandily to cover climaxes he couldn't deal with, straightly.

So when you are disappointed with these two books, blame O-Homer as well as me. I have worked on them till I went blind and stupid. All the revision in the world will not save a bad first-draft: for the architecture of the thing comes, or fails to come, in the conception, and revision only affects the detail and ornament, alas!

Well, it is finished, except for W.[1] and yourself. I am like a man lightened of a burden, who yet feels that he has dropped something. 1927 it began. How long ago that life in Karachi ended! Yours,   T.E.S.

---

[1] See letter No. 431.

452: TO ELLIOTT SPRINGS[1]

20 - VIII - 31   *Mount Batten, Plymouth*

Dear Springs, It is difficult to write real letters to legendary persons. I have been trying to feel that you lay within postal range, ever since Frere-Reeves gave me your book and papers: but somehow it does not carry conviction. Surely the author of *War Birds* is dead. That book reads so strangely like reality: everything in it seems to have been and done and happened. It is improper, somehow, for you to continue still.

I used to fancy that you didn't: that *War Birds* was a transcript of a diary by Grider, or MacGrider:[2] for people used to say that they were with him in France, and some called him one name and some the other. Let me hail you as perhaps, in this instance, the best editor since Moses: Shorthouse in *John Inglesant* runs you close, but did not so wholly fuse his stuff into one tone and narrative.

Since I saw Frere-Reeves I have studied *War Birds* frequently, trying to see differences between this and that, trying to pick out those stories which you worked in everywhere to fatten it. But the quest is as hopeless as the disentangling of the *Iliad*.

In putting together *War Birds* you have achieved what I think is the finest 'actual' book upon the war — dividing books into the photographic and the composed. Of all the actualities yours strikes me as the sharpest, reddest and liveliest. You give the actual feel of hangars and R.F.C. officers' messes and leaves. I am sorry that the rank-and-file do not appear. You live too exclusively amongst the officers: but then you did so live, and that makes it all the more true. A book written by an 'other rank' would not mention the officers. Had you been in an American unit things would have been different, but that is the English way.

You know, I hope, that the British Air Force of today is very grateful to you for *War Birds*, and proud of having carried off, through your writing, so many of the spoils of war. I am myself (after nine years of service in the R.A.F.) very much of an airman,

---

[1] Elliott Springs, an American, had joined the R.F.C. as a pilot during the Great War. He is the author of *War Birds*.

[2] It appeared as such. MacGrider was Springs's close friend in the squadron and was killed in action.

and I know how excited a book makes the fellows when they read it. Of course, the old women are shocked: but that is right. They would be, continually, if they lived in even a peace-time Mess.

I feel less comfortable in talking to you about your later books. I have read two of them and some stray stories: and I feel that you are in the strange position of having once given out more of your strength and reality than you can afford. So you are war-damaged, and that stains your peace-efforts. However, you would indeed be a greedy writer if you went on wanting to write masterpieces.

Do you not think that it is rather up to you to annotate (not for publication, I mean, but for record purposes; for history's sake) one copy of *War Birds*, to show as far as possible how it grew in your mind or under your hand? The book is a permanent book and a real and immortal part of our war with Germany, besides being the history of the beginning of military flying. It ranks with great books, by some accident of your having put yourself into every line of it. Nobody but yourself knows how it was built: and it would be famous and fascinating to put on record its parts and origin.

I am deeply in your debt for telling me so much about it. As I say, I care for *War Birds* above any book of the war, as yet: with the possible exception of Manning's *Her Privates We*: and that is reflective, not photographic, so not a rival. Yours sincerely

T E SHAW

453: TO JAMES HANLEY

21. VIII. 31.   Plymouth

Dear Hanley, Lately in London in one day I re-read the new book right through.[1] Its writing is white-hot and terrific, but as a piece of work it has not the force of *Boy*. For one thing, I suppose, you have never been a maid-servant in Liverpool: nor, I think, was the village-fisherman life of the first pages yours. At least I did not feel (except by fits and starts) the strangeness of the Moynihan family on which you laid stress, to carry the book into

---

[1] In manuscript.

rational experiences. Both father & mother were interestingly drawn, & their priest magnificent: but the inevitable element is missing in the tragedy. I think it over-labours the disaster of being seduced: I could bear it with some fortitude, personally! I think it over-states the proportion in which sex inhabits our minds. Sheila meets two priests — one rapes her. She meets two bus-conductors — both have a shot at it. Now, honestly, you overdo the lechery of bus-conductors. A decent, wearied, cynical and rather hasty-tempered class of men. Also the final coincidence, though perhaps the only way of ending a book keyed so high, is rather a coincidence, isn't it?

The quibble that the priest's performance on the cross might be technically difficult you could rebut, because I judge only by report.

Are you laughing now? I doubt it: yet you will find that others besides me will take refuge in laughter against your over-dose of terror. I think the book is keyed too high. It is amazing: ingenious: unusual: and carries itself off. I do not think anybody but yourself could have conceived it, or would have attempted it, or could have gripped me, as I was gripped while I read it: but it is a criticism, surely, that I kept on crying out 'NO, no' to myself even while I read. You held me, but did not carry me away: and the only justification for extravagance is that it should be wholly successful.

I'll tell you the part of the book I shall never forget; what struck me as perhaps the finest scene (bar the man & wife in *The Last Voyage*) of all your writing — and that was the priest & his church-warden fellow over the bottle of whisky, while the priest sophisticated upon his intended rape. It was unearthly and yet entirely real: really three-dimensional. I could feel all round and about the two creatures while they talked. You can make queerness come to life. Will you rave to hear that I said 'Dickens' as I read it, though Dickens is a man I cannot bear to read?

You see, not being a conscious critic, I cannot tell you what I really thought & felt about the book, nor can I explain what it really was that made me think & feel: but I did imagine that your cause, and your effect, were both of them disproportionate (too trivial) for the vast tone of your treatment. A big thing should, I fancy, be quietly treated, for it states itself: and a small thing has to be underlined and picked out. Your tragedy does not feel inevitable, or typical: it is individual, perhaps accidental. I think what you wanted to describe was the unhealthiness of a celibate priesthood, and that the victim was introduced as illustration. I don't know: but I feel that as an imagination the book lacks the complete appearance of life.

How I fumble! It is astonishing, as writing: whole pages of sustained eloquence such as I've never read in you before. What do I now do with the typescript? Yours   T. E. SHAW

454: TO JOHN BUCHAN

22. VIII. 31   *Plymouth*

Dear J.B., Your letter about my not writing a life of Alexander has been reproaching me for so long that I much pluck up courage to answer you and forget it.

I don't think I am ever likely to write anything of my own again. They pay me for translating things, and that's exercise enough with words to allay and more than allay any remaining itch I may have to write. As for saying anything of my own, there is nothing in the box: not an idea or wish or dissatisfaction or resentment. You have in me a contented being, and no literature rises out of contentment.

Half the books I pick up, now a days, seem to have no due raison-d'être: one does not feel that the author would have burst if he had not got it out. And that discourages me, for I would like my work, if any, to feel like that.

So I think I'm better off just as an airman, and am lucky to find interests enough in the service to occupy all my time and remaining energy. 1935 is the end of my term, and after it I shall feel very lost.

I hope you are better than you were when I saw you in London a year or two ago: and I hope you are finding some sort of a game, in politics or business, to play with interest. Most people I meet aren't happy; for lack of absorption, I think. Yours sincerely

T E SHAW.

455: TO LADY ASTOR

12. XI. 31.

Aha, Peeress, I shall not be there. I'fact, with luck I shall dine that night with the Mrs. Shaw, whom you call 'Charlotte': and perhaps with the G.B.S. himself.

So envy me: and pity yourself. If you were not M.P. for Sutton you too could stay in London! [2 *lines omitted*]

456: TO BERTRAM THOMAS

21. XI. 31   *Myrtle Cottage, Hythe, Southampton*

Dear B.T., Will this reach you, or are you in the States? Both perhaps. I am on Southampton Water (nearly all day and part of the night, often) testing a new marine engine for the R.A.F. This note is to report my failure to make any foreword for your *Arabia*.[1] If you, or it, had been a con-rod, how technically I should have balanced you and summed up — whereas all I feel is a great release and relief, at knowing that your book is good enough. Your journey is told as it deserves: no, hardly that perhaps, or it would be the best travel book yet. It is exceedingly well told and will live for generations. You are a fortunate man. The Foreign Office is displeased with you. You are doubly fortunate and distinguished. I am getting envious. Yours sincerely
                                                    T.E.SHAW

457: TO JAMES HANLEY

28. XII. 31

Dear Hanley, I have owed you a letter for months: it has sat much on my conscience. Here is *Haslett*[2] back, anyway. For months I have been in Hythe, near Southampton, testing R.A.F. motor boats & engines. That explains some of the delay, &

[1] In a subsequent letter of December 7th, 1931, Lawrence wrote to Bertram Thomas saying he had written the required introduction to his *Arabia Felix, Across the Empty Quarter of Arabia.*

[2] *Stoker Haslett* by James Hanley.

2A

much of my distraction. When at this job I cease to think about books & writing.

Haslett is good. It lines up with the other short stories of yours, and holds its own with, for example, *The Last Voyage*. It is not so terrible as your higher tides: nor does it take us any further than the rest. I am pinning my hopes on your new novel, as likely to develop your writing beyond the point reached by *Boy* & the rest.

By the way Marshall[1] told me that *Boy* is being reprinted, with the asterisks cut or replaced by words. That is very good. In its cheap form it reads worse (as regards indecency!) than the limited edition. I think it would have gone much better if you had made the cheap edition a new book, rather than a mutilation.

Forster came to Plymouth in October or November, and I let him read all of yours I had by me. He was very struck with the whole achievement: and particularly with the *Passion before Death*. He asked me to send a letter on for him, writing it after he had gone back to London.

I found Forster a very subtle & helpful critic, over my *Seven Pillars*. Hardly anybody else (of the dozens of critics who dealt with that or *Revolt in the Desert*) said anything that wasn't just useless pap. All Forster's notes on books or writing seem to me workmanlike. After all, he writes, & so knows what authors are up against. In himself he is a very witty, pointed, shy, emancipated person. I like him. You should try to run into him in London, on some visit.

I hope your typing is going well. Incidentally, I think I type better than you! I wish I wrote as well.

Hope to return to Plymouth next month. Yours   T E SHAW.

458: TO GEORGE BROUGH

5. 3. 32   *Hythe, Southampton*

Dear Mr Brough, It is the silkiest thing I have ever ridden: partly because of the perfect tune, partly from the high gear: but mostly because of the spring sprocket, I suppose. The gear is not too high. I can get down to 16 m.p.h.: and she pulls fairly

---

[1] K. W. Marshall, then an employee of Boriswood Ltd., publishers of Hanley's *Boy*.

at 30 m.p.h: and at 50 she is a dream. Just popples along so mildly that I can count the revs.

It was very cold but a beautiful ride. The back plug lasted till I got to Welwyn. The second plug is still running. I took two from your stores: so have made the cheque for 10/- extra, which I hope will cover them.

I think this is going to be a very excellent bike. The crowds that gape at her, just now, will stop looking after she gets dirty: and that may be soon, if only the R.A.F. give me spare time enough to use the poor thing.

I am very grateful to you and everybody for the care taken to make her perfect. Yours ever   T E SHAW.

459: TO B. H. LIDDELL HART

25.IV.32   *Myrtle Cottage, Hythe, Southampton*

Indeed I am a sinner: yet not so bad as you judge, for I wrote at length about your *Foch*. That was last year, in my last visit to Plymouth, between two spells in the boat-yard here. The R.A.F. needed to re-equip itself with new motor-boats, and chose me to test and tune the new boats, and to watch over their building.

Foch is too far behind me, now, for that letter to be re-written. The gist of it was that you left me with a better opinion of Foch, the man, than I had had. You demolish him thoroughly as a soldier: as a politician he needed no other evidence than his own to discredit him. But as a human being he came out well and honourably in what you wrote.

I met the old boy only in 1919, when he was only a frantic pair of moustaches.[1] So I was glad to see the better side. [*15 lines omitted*]

460: TO COLONEL S. F. NEWCOMBE

22. VI. 32   *Myrtle Cottage, Hythe, Southampton*

Dear S.F., Mrs. Shaw gave me your address. It is good to hope that you are settled in England again. Very good: also that

[1] Compare letter No. 511.

your imp has got an Eton scholarship first go. Poor kid! I hope he avoids the manner . . . a nice kid, James.[1]

Do you ever near Hythe (the New Forest one) in your wanderings? I base here, and test or tune motor boats for a living. A poor living — 3/9 a day — but interesting, and I get what I want done. Our boats would interest you. One goes to Malta in August, I hope.

Give me warning if we are to meet. I go away often and suddenly, by water; delivering boats to R.A.F. stations, you see.

If ever you write to the imp, give him my regards and congratulations. Remember me to Mrs. N. too. I hope she is very patient with you both. Yours   T.E.S.

Reprove me if you are a Brigadier, now. Also I forget all the following letters, except R.E. which I believe you grow out of, upon seniority. Gen. Wright did, anyway.

[The following letter was written after a bomb had exploded harmlessly underneath the platform of a school in Egypt where Lord Lloyd was speaking. The Bishop of Carlisle was also present.]

461 : TO LORD LLOYD

23.VI.32   *Hythe*

Dear G.L., This is, you know, immensely distinguished. Most kings, some Presidents (the best, like Lincoln, and some of the not-best, like Garfield and Doumer) but very few private persons . . . off-hand I can remember only Rathenau. It is magnificent, and I congratulate you heartily.

Of course it was only a miss, for which those of us who like you are personally grateful — and misses do not live in history, like hits. Some mean and incompetent Egyptian, I should guess. The poor boobs. Explosives aren't really difficult at all, you know. Only this afternoon I was getting results out of a smoke candle with some of Payn's firework detonators . . . little spitty things

---

[1] Stuart Lawrence Newcombe, known as James.

that a volt or so will fire. I can see the practitioner of the future making use of a telephone connection to fire his bomb.

Or do we flatter you, and is the Bishop of Carlisle really a runnable stag? I cannot stomach the notion. Four and sixty Bishops have I met, and not one of them worth powder. No, I think it was you. The lower fourth had a brain-storm perhaps, and hoped to cut short a speech.

Here is the Lady, very moved over your danger. I write her cheerfully, saying you have been in worse places and run greater risks. But what a scoop: O most fortunate of politicians, what a scoop! Yours ever   T E S.

I lose my character, here in Southampton Water, for I run by every yacht, large and small, and scrutinise it for proconsular bodies. They think me very curious.[1]

462: TO WALTER HUDD

3.ix.32   *Union Jack Club*, 91 *Waterloo Road, London*

Dear Mr Hudd, Ayliff[2] told me you knew I had been with G.B.S. to see *Too Good* last Thursday, and that must be my excuse for writing.

As you can imagine, the first seeing was rather an occasion for me. The part you play is obviously a hit at me, and I felt very nervous, until all was over, lest something in it should hurt.

Actually I thoroughly enjoyed it — or rather I should say that I hope to come one night in London and see it again, for enjoyment's sake. That first time my stomach felt a bit hollow all through.

I thought you did the part admirably. You looked decent (I am always as correct as I can be, regimentally speaking) and I only wish nature had let me look half as smart and efficient as

---

[1] Lawrence used to come out in a speedboat from Hythe to meet Lord Lloyd and sail in his cutter in the Solent.

[2] H. K. Ayliff, of the Birmingham Repertory Theatre, produced Bernard Shaw's *Too True to be Good*, in which Walter Hudd played the part of Private Meek.

yourself. Only I get more gaiety out of my position. It's comic really, and I often see that, whereas you looked grim.

I hope you find the part a comfortable one. Acting and plays aren't much in my line — but I thought G.B.S. had really given you some pretty good chances, which you fully took. The house wriggled with delight over some of your quips and business.

If you want a long run in the part I hope you get it: or are long runs long boredoms? Don't answer this: in fact you can't, for I'm off from here tonight: I have written only to thank you for a very rare and peculiar kindness you are doing my reputation, nightly. Yours ever   T E SHAW.

[Early in September 1932 chits began to circulate between departments in the Air Ministry about Lawrence. Articles disclosing the existence of the R.A.F. speed boats, and attributing them entirely to Lawrence, had appeared in the *Sunday Chronicle* and the *News-Chronicle*, and it was decided to return him from Southampton to his unit if there was further publicity. The decision was unfortunate from all points of view. Lawrence took the event philosophically at first. See letters Nos. 470 and 475.

Luckily for Lawrence the idea of treating him as an asset to the R.A.F., or of advertising him as one of its attractions in order to enlist suitable recruits, never seems to have occurred to anybody. He was still hushed up as though he were something that the R.A.F. should be ashamed of.]

463: TO G. F. J. CUMBERLEGE[1]

6.ix.32   *Mount Batten, Plymouth*

Dear Mr. Cumberlege, I am sorry only now to be answering your letter of July 19th. A day or two after your visit to me I was sent to Bridlington to look after some boats, and there I stayed for weeks, working very hard, and right out of the way. No letters were sent on. I was too busy to want them.

So now, returned to Hythe for just two or three days on my way back to Plymouth, my permanent station, I am faced by a

---

[1] Then managing director of the New York branch of the Oxford University Press, which published an unlimited edition of Lawrence's translation of the *Odyssey* in the U.S.A.

huge pile of letters, more than I can possibly read & answer
However yours is a business one, and such take precedence.

I feel the force of your plea that an English edition might help
B.R.'s[1] recovery of the money he has so generously — and fatally
— spent on buying Isham out of the *Odyssey* translation. If I
could agree to an English version that would be the best argument
to move me. But I have already given so much. I have allowed
it to be put about everywhere that the translation is mine. I have
accepted the idea of a cheap edition in the States. I have allowed my
name to be tied to this, more or less directly. All these are hateful
developments. The only reserved point now is a cheap edition in
England. I have promised myself, again and again, that I will
never publish another book as long as I live. I had a sickener
of publication over *The Seven Pillars* which will last me as long
as I have sense to remember it. If anybody needs money, it is
surely myself, earning 3/9 a day with considerable effort and
pains: but I would rather starve than earn another penny by any
publication. I will not take any part of the proceeds of your cheap
edition. You can pay my share — such as it is — to B.R.: but I
absolutely resist any idea of an English edition of the *Odyssey*
version, to be published by Milford[2] or any other publisher, and
I also object to any batch of sheets or bound volumes coming
into this country for re-sale.

I hope that is clear. The more a book sells the worse for
everybody concerned in it: and, as you say, this version might
conceivably sell. So might others of my unpublished books. It
takes years — and many successive failures — to work off such
a publicity boom as I have 'enjoyed'. I will live and die in peace.
Yours sincerely,   T. E. SHAW

464: TO W. B. YEATS

12.X.32   *Mount Batten, Plymouth*

Dear Mr Yeats, Your letter is dated 'Feb 26th' but this I am
sure is Sept. I am a bad answerer, but not that bad. My delay
this time is because I have been away from Camp on annual
leave — and letters do not come on. Otherwise I would have tried

---

[1] Bruce Rogers.   [2] Of the Oxford University Press.

to say at once how much I have appreciated this compliment of nomination[1] by you. I am Irish, and it has been a chance to admit it publicly — but it touches me very deeply that you should think anything I have done or been to justify this honour. I'm afraid the truth — if people could look inside — would destroy the flattering picture of myself that I have put about.

I knew you had seen my *Revolt*, because you referred to it in your foreword to Gogarty's last Cuala selection: but I never expected this. It is very good of you, and touches me particularly, for I have been reading your work for years. You got your compliment in first, so I will not try to butter back: but you must see how valuable to a flash-in-the-pan is praise from one who has almost a lifetime of growing work behind his judgement.

I set eyes on you once, in Oxford, many years ago, and wanted then to call the street to attention (for lack of the power to make the sun blaze out appropriately, instead!) but fortunately did nothing. I hope that you are going further yet, in poetry, for our benefit. That sounds greedy; but you never repeat yourself, and so everything matters.

Thanks again. It's not my fault, wholly, if I am not more Irish: family, political, even money obstacles will hold me in England always. I wish it were not so. Yours sincerely T E SHAW

465: TO SIR EDWARD ELGAR

12. X. 32.   *Mount Batten, Plymouth*

Dear Sir Edward, In the one week I have had letters from you and from W. B. Yeats — and it is a little difficult for an ordinary mortal to say the happy things when public monuments around him come suddenly to speech. I have liked most of your music — or most that I have heard — for many years: and your 2nd Symphony hits me between wind and water. It is exactly the mode that I most desire, and so it moves me more than anything else — of music — that I have heard. But thousands of people share my liking for your music, and with better reason for they

[1] To the Irish Academy of Letters.

know more about it than I do: so this doesn't justify the kindness of the Shaws in bringing me with them that afternoon. The chance of meeting you is just another of the benefits that have accrued to me from knowing G.B.S., who is a great adventure.

There are fleas of all grades; and so I have felt the awkward feeling of having smaller creatures than myself admiring me. I was so sorry to put you to that awkwardness: but it was inevitable. You have had a lifetime of achievement, and I was a flash in the pan. However I'm a very happy flash, and I am continually winning moments of great enjoyment. That Menuhin-Concerto is going to be a pleasure to me for years: and the news of your 3rd Symphony was like a week's sunlight. I do hope you will have enough enthusiasm left to finish it. There are crowds of us waiting to hear it again and again.

Probably it feels quaint to you to hear that the mere setting eyes upon you is a privilege: but by that standard I want to show you how good an afternoon it was for me, in your house. Yours sincerely,   T.E.SHAW.

466: TO C. J. GREENWOOD

12.X.32.   *Mount Batten, Plymouth*

Dear Greenwood, Marshall has just sent me on your letter about my R.A.F. notes. It is very good of you to have taken this trouble. I can't say, of course, what is to become of this MS. The R.A.F. do not want it read, much less published. My notion was to print perhaps a dozen copies, none for sale, only to preserve what I think has a little merit as a picture of the Air Force of ten years ago. 'Services of the Crown' are so seldom created, that this view of the sucking years of the R.A.F. should have some technical interest.

Meanwhile, of course, I cannot say. Peter Davies estimated much the same, some years ago. My difficulty is not the money, but Air-Staff permission.

If anything happens I will tell you. I hope your publishing goes not too hopelessly: that is all any publisher in England today expects. What a season you chose for your start!

Have just read Hanley's *Ebb and Flood*. A very fine effort. He has definitely enlarged his range, in it. There are good books coming from him. I hope his head keeps above water, too. Yours,   T.E.SHAW.

467: TO MRS. ERIC KENNINGTON

18.x.32.   *Mount Batten, Plymouth*

Dear Celandine, In Athens was a gentleman called Hippoclides who became engaged to a rich merchant's daughter: and they arranged him a slap-up and splendid marriage. The feast preceding it was too much for his poor head, though. He stood on his head on the table and did a leg-dance, which was objectionable in Greek dress. 'Hippoclides, Hippocleides' protested the shocked merchant 'You dance your marriage off.' 'Wyworri?' said Hippocleides: and Herodotus tells the tale so beautifully that I put the jape on the architrave.[1] It means that nothing in Clouds Hill is to be a care upon its habitant. While I have it there shall be nothing exquisite or unique in it. Nothing to anchor me.

I'm glad you saw the little place. When all that fuss inside is cleared out it will be a very habitable and restful place. I am fond of it, and hope to live there, after I leave the R.A.F., which at latest is 1935: and will be earlier if I get old suddenly.

E. H. himself,[2] spurred by your news, wrote to me from Holly Copse. Sounded like himself too. I told him that I would inflict myself upon you one of these winter week-ends, after my mother has sailed. So prepare your garage for an oily visitor.

I wonder if you saw old Theodore Powys at Chaldon. He writes too much — or brings out now for publication too many of the books he has written: but they are good. A strange old fellow, sitting above Chaldon in a brick villa like a broken bit of Bournemouth — and hating all the countryside.[3] Yours ever

T.E.SHAW.

[1] *See Herodotus*, VI, 129. The Greek inscription over the doorway of Clouds Hill was carved by Lawrence and one or two friends serving in the R.A.F. and R.T.C.

[2] Kennington's initials are E. H.

[3] A misunderstanding of T. F. Powys' character which was corrected when he knew him better.

No: your tenant was quite respectably dressed, but spoke only broken English. Probably took me for the police on Eric's track. I can now ascertain your absence without dismounting, by inspecting the brass face of Xto[1] on the door.

468: TO RICHARD WARNER[2]

18. x. 32   *Mount Batten, Plymouth*

Dear Warner, I'm glad Bath fits. So few cities have a dignity, and none display it more than Bath. Perhaps very young people may grow impatient over her, but to me every fresh sight of her, as I come down the hill carefully, is delightful.

Lombard Street goes on. A pneumatic riveter in Glyn Mills taps its pervasive music into the glass room-full of directors: or it should be a room-full, only they have proven cowards. There are no Hollands now, no Martins. Only Robin Buxton holds the tables with his ears full of cotton wool. Brokers still dash in and out, but they are all trying to give money back, not to take it away: and he has to be tactful with them. The city is not itself, since you left.

Fylfot. No. One takes these names for granted. Of course the Weekley suggested derivation is bosh. It does not fill feet. Besides, it was ecclesiastical ornament in the late xii Century before English was used by clerks. They must look again. I suggest a foreign word, anglicised in the later Middle Ages: but I am 30 years stale in archaeology and bookless here.

Boanerges nearly back-fired at your phrase questioning his power to climb Sion Hill. He would do it if you spelled it with a Z. So perhaps I and he will roar at your gate one day. Not till the fine weather comes, however. They only give us Sundays off, here, and in winter-time I ride very little, except to visit my Dorset cottage (and future home) to assure myself that all the trees are growing crookeder and crookeder.

[1] Christopher, the Kenningtons' son.
[2] Warner, formerly Chief Cashier at Martins Bank, had, in that capacity, got to know Lawrence, who advised him, on his retirement, to settle in Bath, which he did. He had written to ask the derivation of 'Fylfit Cross'.

That *Too True* play of G.B.S. was, I thought, very good. The counterfeit me was unfortunately much nicer than the original. Yours   T. E. SHAW.

469: TO SIR WILLIAM ROTHENSTEIN

20. X. 32   *Plymouth*

Dear W.R., I cannot 'Sir Wm. you longer. You are too quick on your feet for a knight. Knights are mounted and armoured figures, stately, slow, reluctant. Very heavy-father. I'm sorry: but it's so.

Are we keeping up a brisk correspondence? I have an idea that I wrote to you only three or four days back. It may have been only an inchoate intention or desire, of course. If I didn't, I thought I did.

Yet that very good book of yours[1] calls for letters. You say you would prefer praise of a picture: but the painters have made that very difficult. Letters are a technique-less art: everybody can write a book, good or bad: and everybody criticises books. The plain man criticises them better than the expert. Your T.S. Eliot is the worst of critics. Arnold Bennett almost the best.

But painting. The public have been taught that painting is 'art': a mysterious involved process of values, only to be appraised after years of study and apprenticeship. Every ignorant person approaches pictures along the 'literary' road. A picture tells them something, or fails. Everybody is ignorant of painting except the few that actually paint. So public interest in pictures declines, out of sheer helplessness. Every exhibition is ringed round with notices 'Keep off the grass, unless you are a gardener'. Alas and lack-a-day. How dare I like one of your pictures. I might be looking at its impasto, whereas you were expressing its polyphony or vibrato. God help the poor.

Willa Cather is exquisite, in her range. There are several such U.S.A. women. Did you ever read any Elizabeth Roberts? Cape publishes. She uses a broader pen than Willa Cather. Lewis[2] is a challenging mind: but it is an unhinged mind. He jazzles me. They say that Manning is unhappy.

---

[1] *Men and Memories.*   [2] Wyndham Lewis. See letters Nos. 305 and 330.

It is a sorrowful thing when a Hogarth, Hardy or G.B.S. dies: but it satisfies another facet of my mind. It's all over and they are out of it without failure: we are safe with them. Men run about always on the edge of the precipice, and when they are safely dead we can breathe again: if we have cared for them. I found this last G.B.S. play magnificent. Tempest-like, almost, as a valediction.

As I leave London for the S.W. I pass along Kensington High Street: and if time allows I turn the bike's front wheel up Campden Hill and ring the bell of Airlie Gardens. It costs me no time and no trouble: and one day we will meet, that way.

About the *Odyssey*. I fully agree with you. My version is fustian: but so is Homer, I think. The more I dwelt on the Greek and struggled with it and its story, the more possessed I became with the view that here was something too artful for decency. It tried by surpassing pains and skill to simulate the rule-leaping flood of authentic greatness. All the talent in the world never approaches genius: the two things are incompatible. The *Odyssey* is a creeping work. It's author was Maurice-something, Baring + Hewlett + William [Morris]. He was out to construct an epic, on the *Iliad*'s model: and it all smells forced. The style is booky, too.

So it is hopeless to make a pawky novel of it, as Samuel Butler did. It isn't. A great man could make a great poem or a great novel out of its material (how much better *Sigurd*[1] is than the Siegfried legends in Norse or German) but a translator can only expose the fraud. I am a translator, definitely, in my version: and you can see through it, I hope, easily: as a mawkish fraud.

Bruce Rogers' typography is beautiful, I think. This dove-gray boudoiry page suits the ladylike tale. As for his roundels, the mass of gold and black fills the empty chapter-heading well enough. I am not fond of vase-painting, I must admit; and so the style of them disappoints me: but he enjoyed fitting them together. If you half-shut your eyes and look at them, you will like their balance and tone.

What's really wrong with the *Odyssey* is Homer. Yours, T.E.S.

---

[1] *Sigurd The Volsung*, by William Morris.

470: TO ARTHUR HALL[1]

22.x.32   *Plymouth*

Dear Brum, An article came out in a Sunday paper, and the
Air Ministry sent me back here to duty at once. So motor boats
are all over. I am a little sorry to be rooted out that way: but
Plymouth is a quiet & easy camp.

I flew over your place lately: and dropped on the College a
pair of Group Captain Walser's pyjamas.

Now for about two or three weeks I can't get up to see you,
though I want to do it. I have got flu and am rather bad with it.
Nearly reported sick a fortnight ago. But as soon as I can I will
come. Yours   T.E.S.

471: TO C. J. GREENWOOD

26.x.32.   *Plymouth*

Dear Greenwood, I must reconcile myself, apparently, to
buying your cheap books and having the dear ones given to me!
It is very nice of you, and I am sorry. Publishers ought to live.

The Cunninghame Graham[2] duly arrived. It is a disappointing
book. Anything about the old Don should have been written
with swagger. He is an artist thereat, as you see if only he takes
his hat off to a lady in the street. His pen swaggers too: and he
cannot therefore sustain a book: though he writes the best five
or six pages imaginable, and has a rain-in-the-air-and-on-the-
roof-dripping mournfulness of Scotch music in his time-past
style. A wonderful old man. *Moghreb el Aksa* was his most
ambitious effort at book-writing, and after it he relapsed into
his proper role, of filling albums with snap-shots — the best
verbal snapshots ever taken, I believe. Not much brain, you
know, but a great heart and hat: and what a head of hair!

I shall be glad, very glad, to have the Hanley. The book isn't
artistically necessary, I thought. Hanley was only getting
something phlegm-like off his chest. If I knew his life-history

---

[1] Late Aircraftman, of Birmingham.
[2] *Cunninghame Graham: his Life and Work*, by H. Faulkner West.

probably I would know that. Accordingly for all the terrific power of it, I cannot regard it as a child of his daylight hours. No doubt I am wrong: but there is too much feeling in it for an extravagance, too much extravagance for cold fury. I shall value my copy, permanently.

I am happy that you have your eye on Marshall. There is something in him that makes me want to help. Don't hesitate to let me know if any eventuality arose. Yours ever,　　　T.E.S.

472: TO S. L. NEWCOMBE

7. XI. 32　　　　　　　　　　　　　　　　*Mount Batten, Plymouth*

Horror! It feels queer to imagine you loose in that huge school.[1] Don't your bones rattle up & down its passages? I hope it keeps on behaving itself properly. Schools are queer places. I was very happy when I had finished with them all. Oxford was like heaven, to finish up with. However there are schools of all sorts, and they change from year to year.

I hear that your father has taken a house in London. That saves you the trip to Malta & back every holiday.

My boat has not been in the water this year, for I have been away from Plymouth during the whole of the time, building speed-boats of a large slow heavy type for the R.A.F. Now they are finished, 32 of them, and me back in the station: but not motor-boating for pleasure at the moment. Too much of that, altogether, this year!

As for coming to Eton ... not yet a while, anyway. I have finished my 1932 leave, and can only get Sundays off, one a month ... and London is a long way for a winter's day-riding. I'll try when the longer days come. Yours　　　　　T.E.S.

473: TO G. W. M. DUNN

9.XI.32　　　　　　　　　　　　　　　　　　　　*Plymouth*

Dear Dunn, I've been up and down twice lately on somebody else's legal business ... so have been off my rails.

---

[1] Eton.

601 sounds good for A.C.Hs[1] ... but there is no question
of my moving before April, anyhow; and then only if this place
changes character suddenly. It is homelike at present, and that
makes up for its remoteness. I should like to be near London, but
that cannot be until there is the new C.A.S.

The *Odyssey* was done as well as I could. No pleasure in it
however. I don't know Cotterill's version. There are 27 prose
English translations!

I'll send you my R.A.F. notes some day. They are in typescript and hard to read. I intended to make a book about the
Air Force, and gave it up after an accident.

Meeting people. I have not met G.K.C.[2]: Shaw always calls
him a man of colossal genius. I cannot read his journalism, which
is perhaps a good sign. T. S. Eliot I have not met. His poetry
is good, if rather sparing. His prose is pompous. His criticism
mock-profound. His range of interests very queer and spotty.
Yes, I'd like to meet him; shall we hunt him out, some day?
He is in u.s.a. now. Epstein I've not met. He's a great
sculptor. John is in ruins, but a giant of a man. Exciting, honest,
uncanny. Barrie is too grim and hard. There are claws under his
fur, obviously. Old, of course, and not strong. He is not forthcoming. G.B.S. is not a vast electric discharge. He is more like
a cocktail. Very beneficent and plain to read. Slightly hard of
hearing and short of sight — by which I mean, prone to imagine
the whole from an incomplete part. You are right about Sybil
Thorndike I think. Eddie Marsh is a charming joke, so kind
and nice. Nice is his word. He does not talk very well, but is
very sensitive to feelings. Beverley Nichols writes well and should
be a human person. He strikes me as smaller than his reputation.

Yes, there are lots of people to meet, aren't there. I want to
meet Yeats and Epstein and Eliot some day and how.

Books. I have two Owens and two Hopkins at my cottage:
or I think I have. Both are remarkable. You shall have one of
each as soon as I am free to get there for a weekend. My life
is full of books, and I get heaps of them, every week. There

[1] Squadron 601 of the Auxiliary Air Force at Hendon was good for Aircraft Hands, but
would not have suited Lawrence for personal reasons, although it was Sir Philip Sassoon's
own squadron.

[2] G. K. Chesterton.

must be 2000 in the cottage, all going to waste in the hope that I will live there after 1935 when I leave the R.A.F. *The Scented Garden* I once saw in a printed English text. It wasn't significant. Flecker (whom I knew very well) didn't value it.

I have not heard of Lawrence Hyde. Who is he, and when did he write . . . or does he? And what are the books? Novels? Yours,   T.E.S.

474: TO G. W. M. DUNN

22.XI.32.   *Plymouth*

Dear Dunn, I went to my cottage last Saturday: but it was all upset. There is a local builder doing his best to repair the roof, and all that kind of thing! So I couldn't find the Wilfred Owen: or at least, all I found was his Sassoon edition, and I'd rather give you the Blunden edition which is fuller.

Of the Hopkins, I found two copies: one was the large paper, with portraits: the other this scruffy little edition. However it is not much disfigured with finger-marks or rude notes: and all the text is there. So please accept it as a pis aller.

I should have sent the large paper and kept this, I know: but Hopkins is a fine poet and I value him — *The Deutschland* and the *Epithalamion* are both sustained efforts. Some of his 'to orders' and his devotionals are a bit laborious, I feel: but every now and then he is astonishing. Very 'repressed-sexy',* I feel. Celibacy has its dangers! Yours,   T.E.S.

* homo-?

475: TO F. N. DOUBLEDAY

2.xii.32.   *Mount Batten, Plymouth*

Effendim, So long, so long since I wrote: but to-day there was an earthquake in our life. It poured with rain from dawn — or rather it was pouring before dawn, when we crept miserably out of bed, and it poured on, it pours on, still. So work was

2B

unalloyed beastliness, and we scrounged about the sheds and shops, too cold to talk. There is an immense wind from the south-west shaking every tin wall and window.

Our Commanding Officer is so meek a man — and he has a close office with a fire and an airman to stoke it: but suddenly he got up and swore terribly, like the troops in Flanders. 'This', he said or conveyed 'is a wretched day. We'll wash out work'.

And that is the earthquake, for the like has never happened before with this Commanding Officer: and the minorest consequence of the earthquake is that I write to you. Ever since you left Southampton in that ship I have hoped for a cause of writing. Here it is.

Are you well? Of course there are wells and wells. I hope yours is a quiet little one. My life runs so smoothly that I should distrust great happiness as much as I would dislike great misery. In the ranks a fellow's spiritual ups and downs get modest, like his means and his circumstances.

Motor-boat building is all over. A Sunday newspaper blew upon that, with headlines that said more than the truth (imagine, can you, a headline that said less . . . my mind boggles at it!).

So the Air Ministry chased me quickly out of that job, and out of my lodgings at Hythe: and back I have been in camp at Plymouth for months. There is not much to do at Plymouth, but I have started some lusty and strong-winded hares, which many solemn departments are chasing. It is nice to see one's betters running hard, isn't it?

How is the States: or are the States? If you are a Democrat the election will have pleased you. Page[1] was, so perhaps you are. Frere-Reeves, when I was in London on duty a month ago, gave me a news bulletin. Everything suggests that business is a hard fight in America, just now, and I am sorry for that. Wallenstein fought battles on his back, but those were quick battles, full of killing and cannon shots, which help to pass the time.

Heinemann is all right, I think. They have so much repute now that writers want to gravitate towards them. Frere-Reeves

---

[1] W. H. Page had been a partner of Doubleday's before becoming American Ambassador to the Court of St. James's.

gave me the D. H. Lawrence *Letters*. I read them all, in daily doses extending over a fortnight. A sad reading, rather because D.H. wrote some lovely novels, and all of them came to me as they appeared, and I had a regard for the silly angry creature. And his letters lack generosity so sadly: couldn't he have said one decent thing about some other man of his profession? Also he was too much on the make. However, I should have been very sorry not to have seen and read those letters. So more power to Frere-Reeves.

Give Mrs. Doubleday my regards, please. This letter is really written with a squint, or twi-nibbed pen, one side thinking of you and one of her. May the firm flourish!

No more. Imagine me as very quiet, very calm and quite well-fed. Bovine, in fact: but switching its tail briskly and with an air of pride when it thinks of its only U.S.A. correspondent.

T.E.S.

476: TO MISS L. P. BLACK

7.XII.32   *Plymouth*

Dear Miss Black, I should have written before to acknowledge the chocolates — but the pudding came, to suspend judgment. Also I have to ration letters now, and write only the more urgent ones. My rule is not more than six letters per day. They grow rather a tax upon my pocket and time!

However yesterday the pudding fell. We had been looking at it for a week & more, where it sat in its toupéed bowl on the shelf of our Marine Stores: and we finally decided we couldn't stand any further delay. So we drew a new galvanized iron bucket from Main Stores — on plea that a motor boat needed it — and hung the pudding from its top and set the whole affair on the office stove. Relays of us kept it boiling all the morning and in the afternoon we suspended work and ate it, with clasp knives, out of packing-paper plates. It was excellent. You would have been astonished to see how quickly it went away. That is the best of youth and cold winds and dirty weather. Nobody broke a tooth on the treasures buried in it. They are very grateful.

I see I have passed over the fate of the chocolates. They went down very well!

It was very good of you. We settled to hold our Christmas now, because the winter leave period is just opening and hereafter our numbers will be going down and up, irregularly. Yours sincerely   T E SHAW

My *Odyssey* has been published in the States in a cheap edition (acknowledged authorship) and is said to be selling fairly. It will be amusing if I can collect some dollars off them. Prose justice!

477: TO G. W. M. DUNN

15.XII.32.   *Plymouth*

Dear Dunn, I got to my cottage last Saturday and in turning over the pile of books, lit upon the Blunden 'Owen': so I dragged it down here and duly posted it off to you.

Owen[1] is a very beautiful technician, with great power of saying (not to mention seeing) things. [2 *lines omitted*] Sassoon has told me a lot about him. Owen was a decent fellow, very modest and not tolerant.

I hope it makes up for the Eliot[2] essays. They went to you because they are interesting, I think. I did not read them all, because many of them have already passed my eye in other publications. He writes freely for the *Criterion* and other papers, you know. His *Dante* I have as a small book. It is excellent.

Many of the other essays are not good. He has a confused and knotty mind, and makes more mess of a simple subject than any other conceived human being. I don't know any critic who more darkens the mists and confuses the faults of his authors. After an hour of Eliot I thank God for Arnold Bennett!

Bertrand Russell is foolish I think. Silly. A fat-head: but there was his book stuck in my locker, and it did help to pack out the Eliot parcel. Poor Owen went off lonely, by himself.

[1] Wilfrid Owen, the poet.   [2] T. S. Eliot.

I nearly sent you Figgis' *Children of Earth* — an Irish novel of great scale: but I feared your mind was above novels.

Music? We have none here. Wireless is a very false-toned caricature of music, I think. Gramophone is my stand-by, and a magnificent stand-by, surely. A Ginn gramophone which broods over my cottage and fills it with the sound of strings, when I want. Mostly old stuff: Beethoven quartets and concertos by anybody. Yours, T.E.S.

478: TO LORNA NORRINGTON[1]

23.XII.32 *Plymouth*

Dear Lorna, I have owed you a letter for months & months & months: and at last here goes —

Thank you so much for your Card, and your father for his. Yesterday I wished you were here, for our two Squadrons both sent us their dinghies, asking us to check the timing and tune them. Corporal Bradbury took one & I took the other. It was miles before we thought they were running well enough to give back again! Yesterday was a perfect day, smooth and sunshiny. Now it is blowing a S.W. gale, and we are all sprayed over. So I am glad the dinghies were yesterday. They are lovely little boats. We have done them up lately, with fresh red paint and silencers and hoods, and even a self-bailer, like real proper motor-boats: and they are the envy of all the waterside of Plymouth.

I hope you get some fun sometimes: but there is nothing like the sea on a warm day for the best of times. If ever there is another batch of boats at Hythe, you must get round your Father & come down with him to the tests.

Best Christmas & New Year wishes. Yours sincerely

T E SHAW.

---

[1] Daughter of Flight Lieutenant Norrington, aged 12. Lawrence often took her out in the R.A.F. boats and taught her to handle them.

9.1.33.   *Mount Batten*

Dear E.A., Your letter (I'm glad you are still in England: to save me reproaches for keeping your article too long) is the sort that the most gratified writer alive would yet thank you for: and I don't feel very proud of my writing. So you can imagine how it pleased me. By all means keep the fat book so long as it suits you. That copy is a collection of spoiled sheets, cut and pressed into smallness, and usually it belongs to Mrs. Bernard Shaw — but she is away on a world cruise with G.B.S.

What the muezzin said was, I fancy — and after fifteen years it is probably fancy — 'wa el besharra'[2] ... No English word or phrase even would translate it, so I paraphrased in his spirit rather than his letter. I only wish that 'ya ahl el Sham' had been better rendered than by 'people of Damascus'. The Arabic 'ahl' is a fine word. The worst of being a habitual translator is that one gets in the way of trying to squeeze every sponge dry — and so few authors really *intend* all the contents of their sponges. Words get richer every time they are deliberately used ... but only when deliberately used: and it is hard to be conscious of each single word, and yet not at the same time self-conscious.

I mustn't slip again into the technique of writing. Writing has been my inmost self all my life, and I can never put my full strength into anything else. Yet the same force, I know, put into action upon material things would move them, make me famous and effective. The everlasting effort to write is like trying to fight a feather-bed. In letters there is no room for strength.

Am I morbid? Only with people inclined to it, I fancy. By myself I do not brood at all, having so much to do. That vision of the wholeness of life is not a visitor to me, but always there, like a background to the diggings and the war and the R.A.F. Wherefore I get a sense of the sameness and smallness of everything, including us: and so I would not voluntarily put another into my place. Too much glory or none? Why I think

---

[1] Lawrence had first met both Ernest Altounyan and his father at Aleppo in 1911. Altounyan's poem, *Ornament of Honour*, a lament for Lawrence, is worthy of its subject.

[2] See *Seven Pillars of Wisdom*, Chap. cxx.

the nones, who eat and drink and chase their appetites, are wholesomer. And I like cats and camels, therefore.

This is a silly letter. So was yours. I liked it, too. English people don't write about the verities as a rule, for the good reason that such subjects exceed us, and we look foolish in their shadow.

The two studies of the Euphrates valley are exactly in place in my cottage, and perfect there[1]. I cannot choose between them, or consider sending one back. Call them lost to you, both! I am most glad to have them, for Carchemish was a happy place, and they form a link.

Would you be so interested in me as a writer — not a visioner of life, but just a penman — as to wade through my next-after-the-*Seven-Pillars* book? It has remained in typescript, and is a study of the R.A.F. recruiting depot. Not much glory, but life, in its way. It is short, rather mannered also but better, as writing, than the earlier book, I think. Yours,   T.E.S.

480: TO ROBERT GRAVES

24.1.33.   *Plymouth*

Come off it, R.G.! Your letter forgets my present [state]. It is so long since we met that you are excused knowing that I'm now a fitter, very keen and tolerably skilled on engines, but in no way abstract. I live all of every day with real people, and concern myself only in the concrete. The ancient self-seeking, and self-devouring T.E.L. of Oxford (and T.E.S. of *The Seven Pillars* and *Mint*) is dead. Not regretted either. My last ten years have been the best of my life. I think I shall look back on my 35-45 period as golden.

Enough of myself: but understand that I enjoy books and pictures and sights and sounds more than I ever did: and new books and new sounds, still. Taste with me has not yet stood still, nor retreated into its past. I am alive and capable with most of our daily emergencies.

Now regard yourself. Recall the hundreds of times we have

---

[1] These pictures by Mrs. Altounyan are still on exhibition at Clouds Hill.

met and talked. You cannot know how much I have seen in you, and learned of you — but please take it for written. R.G. has been a main current influencing my life, for nearly 15 years.

Wherefore it is, and always will be, that any line from you matters more than screeds from others. I know you — almost: and I do not know S.S. or any of my other past. I think Frederic Manning, and an Armenian, called Altounyan, and E. M. Forster are the three I most care for, since Hogarth died.

Of course, there are many people here, in the R.A.F., with whom one lives. And they are well enough: but it is the life of the mechanic: concrete, superficial, every-day: unlike that past excitement into which the war plunged me. I know the excitement in me is dead, and happier so: but the three or four big contacts remain as memories at least.

I said 'as memories', for in my new life I am grown hard of hearing. It is disuse of the pineal ear! ... I read the [*name of book omitted*] several times before answering: and now I have read it and your letter again, carefully: and I'm damned if I have the foggiest idea what it and you are driving at. Further, I'm prepared to swear that did the Air Ministry similarly word their instructions issued in A.M. W.O.'s,[1] not a station in the R.A.F. would comprehend.

Be merciful, Lord, and explain it again, but very plainly, in text-book language. A text-book was the last thing I wrote. *A Handbook to 37½ foot motor boats of the* 200 *class*[2] ... and I pride myself that every sentence ·in it is understandable, to a fitter.

Now then, preach—— Yours   T.E.S.

481: TO R. V. BUXTON

9.2.33   *Plymouth*

Dear Robin, A very decent friend of mine [*name omitted*] lost his cash farming and is broke. They were going to bankrupt him, but I said I could manage £200 directly; and that has saved the situation.

---

[1] Air Ministry Weekly Orders.   [2] See letter No. 447.

He says he wants the money paid direct to the Receiver. So I have sent him a cheque for £200, *for him to fill in the 'pay' name*.* Will you please get me an overdraft to meet this, pro tem.? I will arrange to satisfy the account very soon: but must overdraw first.

No news here. Rotten weather, cold first & wet afterwards. Everybody ill and miserable, except me.

Odyssey selling well in U.S.A. Four printings gone, to date. Looks like netting me £300 by next settling day. Good to plunder the Yanks. Yours   T E. SHAW.

* So the cheque will have two writings on it. (J.H.R. signature of course)

482: TO HENRY WILLIAMSON

13.2.33   *Plymouth*

Dear H.W., I've been grinning through the week-end over *The Falcon*,[1] of which a vellum & gold copy reached me from Faber on Saturday.

By the same post arrived a plain copy, sent me from an indignant reviewer, demanding to know why I had fathered this decadent bilge upon an innocent world! It's a queer world, my mistresses!

The Falcon has that jumpy, nervous, stippled technique that you were developing in *The Dream of Women*. It fits a jazzy subject, and conveys an astonishing sense of movement, all through the tale.

I thought old Homer duplicated too often. Tricks in books feel sharper than in real life. There are several astonishing bits of characterisation. The climax was perhaps your only way out of a difficulty ... but about it I'd repeat my 'tricks' remark. All right in life, but too coloured for a tale.

Wrink I didn't recognise: but all your contemporaries (except Priestley, perhaps) will recognise themselves preeningly. I preened. Are my letters real extracts, or have you polished?

[1] *The Gold Falcon*, published anonymously, by Henry Williamson.

To write the day after's not wise. I can't say how I really regard the book. You are a long way from the chiselled and rather static prose of your beginning: and it is always good to go on, and bad to repeat. Only I sometimes wonder where you are going.

They'll all call Manfred a self-portrait: but somehow I remember you as much more solid than that. I wish I could get over to you and see. Will they leave me in Plymouth this summer, or will it be Hythe, again?

Ever so many thanks for the book. It has been a great pleasure for 8 hours reading, and will be re-read before I write to you properly. Yours   T. E. SHAW

483: TO JONATHAN CAPE

15.2.33.   *Mount Batten*

Dear J.C., I have to apologise: you may have seen that we indulged in another Iris Flying Boat crash here. As usual I went out with the rescue boat, and the aftermath has kept me busy. So the Clyde apprentice was neglected for a while.[1] However he began again last week, and if no further luxuries interfere should proceed regularly. A fortnight? I don't know. Possible.

Ref. your last letter: I don't like Arabic titles. Doesn't the publisher usually decide it? The essence of this diary is its Englishness — or perhaps he would say its Scottishness?

Take no action re books, please, till all the revise is with you. In the R.A.F. we guarantee nothing — except the unexpected. Yours ever,   T.E.S.

484: APPLICATION FOR DISCHARGE

6.iii.33

I, No. 338171 A/C Shaw, E., respectfully request that I may be granted an interview with the Commanding Officer, to ask him

[1] Cape had commissioned Lawrence to vet a manuscript which was eventually published under the title *Garroot: the Diary of a Clydeside Apprentice*, by Ian McKinnon. See letters Nos. 487 and 488.

to forward my application to be released from further service in the Royal Air Force as from the sixth of April, 1933.

I am, Sir,

Your obedient servant,

T. E. Shaw A/C.

Approved, L. W. Dilshire   Flt. Lt.

['The discharge of this airman will cause no manning difficulty' ran the first official note, on the 14th. Then the news spread and inquiries began to come along.

'Are you leaving the Air Force, or have you been kicked out?' asked an ex-C.A.S. on the 17th.

'A/C Shaw desires his discharge if there is no prospect of his being used on other than routine station duties', was minuted on March 28th.

The position is made absolutely clear by the two following letters to the Under Secretary of State for Air, here printed out of their chronological position.]

485: TO SIR PHILIP SASSOON

21. iii. 33.   *Mount Batten, Plymouth*

Dear Sir Philip, Plymouth is 200 miles too far away — otherwise I would have seen you somehow and talked over my affairs, which puzzle me. Do you get into places, sometimes, and doubt what road out to choose? I've been like that since October last, and finally decided to cut the knot. There's an instinct to hide at the far end of the burrow when one is sick or troubled, and I have been both, this winter.

Last Saturday I saw Sir Geoffrey Salmond and told him how I stood. He becomes C.A.S. just before I am due to go, and perhaps I ought not to have bothered him — but it is done, anyway.

Hendon wouldn't have done. [3 *lines omitted*]

I wish I could have seen you, before I went; but Sunday seems to pass so quickly in winter. My bike eats the miles, but in darkness it has to slow up. However, soon I will have all leisure:

and then I should manage Lympne again in summer. Lympne, I feel, is probably your masterpiece.[1] Yours sincerely, T. E. SHAW.

486: TO SIR PHILIP SASSOON

30. iii. 33.   *Mount Batten, Plymouth*

Dear Sir Philip, Your letters are so kind that I wish I could have seen you and explained myself properly. It does not feel proper to expose a lot of problems on paper to a busy man.

Ellington was it? (an Air Marshal, in 'P'[2]) sent a letter this week to the C.O. here, asking him to see me and find out if I had a grievance, as the S. of S. was concerned to know why I wished to leave the R.A.F. I expect the S. of S. was yourself?

I replied that I had no grievance, and was only too sorry to be leaving — but that I could no longer be content to do station duty at Mount Batten. My present job is looking after the boats and their engines here, and that is purely routine and not a day's work, even for my hands. I am a reasonably-skilled mechanic, after all these years, but without ambitions to excel in it.

My feeling was that I should do something more, if I was to justify my staying on in the R.A.F. At Karachi, for instance, they let me revise the procedure of engine-overhaul in the Depot. At Batten Sydney Smith gave me the Schneider Cup ground-organisation. Then the D. of E.[3] gave me the R.A.F. fleet to put on new lines, and I did eighteen months on that and got half-way in it.

So I told the C.O., for Ellington, that if there was any special job in which the C.A.S. thought I could be particularly useful, then I was at his service: but if not I would prefer my discharge. That meant, I am sure, that they would discharge me: many people would be glad to see me go, and I am not fond of pushing in where I am not wanted. The only thing that troubles me is that there is much I could yet do. In these eleven years I have learned every square inch of the R.A.F. and it seems a pity to leave so much knowledge unused.

---

[1] Port Lympne is Sir Philip Sassoon's country house in Kent.
[2] Personnel.   [3] Director of Equipment.

However please understand that I look back upon these eleven years with delight. I have been most happy, and owe the R.A.F. a great debt which will always make me its advocate and silent supporter. I will *not* write about it.

I saw Geoffrey Salmond lately, and told him almost what I have said above. 'I will not go on at Batten, doing routine work. I would like to do more boats', or to see the auxiliary airmen (the R.A.F. of the future, I think!) or, best of all, to do a long flying-boat voyage and write a log of it. I have the ambition to compete with you there.[1] We should have a collection like Hakluyt, for the air — however all these things are unimportant.

When I am free I shall make a pilgrimage to your neighbourhood and hope to find you at leisure for talking. It will feel queer to own all my time! April 6 is my last day. Yours sincerely,   T. E. SHAW.

[Three weeks went by before anything was settled: then on April 21st it was 'decided the above-named airman is to be posted to Felixstowe for employment in work which is done there in Marine Craft section . . . he will be attached to contractors' yards. To avoid publicity he should wear plain clothes . . .'

On April 26th a confidential report stated:

'I think he can very advantageously be employed watching Air Ministry's interests at contractors' yards, in compilation of trial reports, and notes on running and maintenance. He has ideas on high-speed craft worth considering. I propose to send him to Messrs. White, Cowes, thereafter to visit the Power Boat Co. where we have several experimental craft under construction.'

After this the discussion about Aircraftman Shaw's employment tailed off into the question of when and where he should wear uniform, what travelling expenses he should be allowed, and what subsistence expenses when employed on detached duties.

'Are you satisfied he can live decently on 30/- a week plus his pay if he has to go to Cowes for a month in the summer?'

These doubts were set at rest — the thirty shillings subsistence

---

[1] Sir Philip Sassoon had written *The Third Route*, an account of a flying-boat cruise to the East.

was approved and Lawrence was free to get on with the job he cared most about. His ideas on high-speed craft would get consideration.]

487: TO JONATHAN CAPE

12/III/33

Dear Cape, Here is Ian [McKinnon], complete from his first page to the last of his story, on his page 52; and to it I have pinned his last few pages, a dissertation upon the manners and customs of Syria.[1] I think he much esteems these notes; but they seem to me neither science nor romance. Perhaps I know Syria too well to be thrilled: perhaps you will look at these last pages and say what you think. If you want them done out into straight text like the story, then send them back and I will do them; but they seem to me less happy and rather an overweight.

I have added one sentence to the end of the story, on my page 62, to save it ending in the air, with the absurd rehash of Munchausen. Why he tacked this yarn on to the tale of a serious and veracious story of his life, God alone knows. I rather like the quirk to end it; but it is queer.

Books in payment. I have earned them, I think. Will you please pack in case and send by rail to any one of the three or four stations in Plymouth? Addressed to A/C Shaw, R.A.F., Mount Batten, Plymouth. And you will greatly delight His Majesty's airmen.

Title and nom-de-plume of author are to be your work. Please ignore the editor, wholly and completely and for ever.

How hard it is to type with cut fingers. Yours ever,   T.E.S.

488: TO JONATHAN CAPE

28.iii.33.   *Plymouth*

Dear Cape, The books arrived and are being devoured by everybody in armfulls. Very many thanks. It was a good idea, well carried out.

[1] See letter No. 483.

I suggest you try Garnett with the 'Syrian notes': if he found pleasure in them, an appendix would be easy. I am quite willing to set them out in form.

I don't like Arabic transcriptions: and the first thing about a title is to have it easily memorised by the public, for shop or library practice. So I would criticise his title and pen-name.

The note:—it isn't often that a rolling stone sets down, quite so plainly, the ways in which it has avoided moss. To my mind, the usefulness of the story is that it exemplifies the plain Scot abroad, and explains something of our ill-repute and formidability amongst stranger peoples. The unscrupulousness, force, ability of his career: this heedless stravaging about the Middle East: the entire lack of sensibility: the unmitigated plainness of his mind and life! There is something peculiarly unlovely about his relations with his fellows: but he has a liking for his horses and his dogs.

That's what I think about the book: and I note that it comes to about a hundred words: but the publisher should remark that the Clyde apprentice makes many errors of fact in his text . . . and that the editor has left them standing, so as not to give him a false air of authority. This is the Briton unadorned!   T.E.S.

Yes, I've had a bad winter: but survive to enjoy the summer-taste of today. I leave the R.A.F. in a few days — without plans, except for rest.

489: TO MRS. THOMAS HARDY

25.IV.33.   *Plymouth*

Dear Mrs. Hardy, Your note came to Clouds Hill, and I warned Mrs. Knowles of your visit. The flowers do not yet come to much. The laurel has been wonderful, this spring: better than ever I have seen it, and very scented: but you are too soon for the rhododendrons. Only two of mine, and your T. H. Eden Philpotts one have bloomed as yet. Yours is quite picking up, now, with about 20 good flowers: but it takes hundreds of plants to make a show on the hill-side, and for that we must wait for the Pontica to come out. They are full of bud, but not yet showing colour.

My mother must have put in dozens of daffodils and things, garden flowers, near the house, for the whole of my little patch of grass has been full of them. I am afraid I thought them very out-of-place. They spoiled the picture. However the rabbits seem to like them, and I have offered Mrs. Knowles the rest. Clouds Hill is no place for tame flowers.

They are still stuck half-way up their river — or were in mid-February, their last letter.[1] The lapse of time makes me fancy they are moving again. Till they get to Mienchu or return to Shanghai, they will not get our letters. She writes always as if they ought to find them wherever they stop! China is too far off.

My own movements are uncertain. I *think* they are sending me to Felixstowe, in Suffolk, which feels a long way off (like China!); but I know nothing definite. Yours sincerely T. E. SHAW.

490: TO SIR PERCY SYKES[2]

22.5.33   *M.A.E.E.*[3] *Felixstowe*

I hope your review, however brief, will recognise the great merit of Palgrave as explorer and writer, You have my encouragement to shorten the passages dealing with myself (who was deliberately not a geographer in Arabia, to the extent of not publishing my compass traces) if thereby you can do Palgrave tardy justice. He was in the Philby-Thomas class as explorer and wrote brilliantly.

491: TO B. H. LIDDELL HART

26.vi.33

Dear L.H., You talk of a summing up to come. Will you (if you agree with my feeling) in it strike a blow for hard work and

---

[1] Lawrence's mother and elder brother were in China.

[2] Brigadier-General Sir Percy Sykes was at that time compiling his *History of Exploration*. A second letter written after its publication said that Sykes had written almost exactly what he himself would have done about Palgrave and thanks him. This has been mislaid.

[3] Marine Aircraft Experimental Establishment.

thinking? I was not an instinctive soldier, automatic with intuitions and happy ideas. When I took a decision, or adopted an alternative, it was after studying every relevant — and many an irrelevant — factor. Geography, tribal structure, religion, social customs, language, appetites, standards — all were at my finger-ends. The enemy I knew almost like my own side. I risked myself among them a hundred times, to *learn*.

The same with tactics. If I used a weapon well, it was because I could handle it. Rifles were easy. I put myself under instruction for Lewis, Vickers, and Hotchkiss (Vickers in my O.T.C. days, and rifles, and pistols). If you look at my article in *The Pickaxe*[1] you will see how much I learned about explosives, from my R.E. teachers, and how far I developed their methods. To use aircraft I learned to fly. To use armoured cars I learned to drive and fight them. I became a gunner at need, and could doctor and judge a camel.

The same with strategy. I have written only a few pages on the art of war — but in these I levy contribution from my predecessors of five languages. You are one of the few living Englishmen who can see the allusions and quotations, the conscious analogies, in all I say and do, militarily.

Do make it clear that generalship, at least in my case, came of understanding, of hard study and brain-work and concentration. Had it come easy to me I should not have done it so well.

If your book could persuade some of our new soldiers to read and mark and learn things outside drill manuals and tactical diagrams, it would do a good work. I feel a fundamental, crippling incuriousness about our officers. Too much body and too little head. The perfect general would know everything in heaven and earth.

So please, if you see me that way and agree with me, do use me as a text to preach for more study of books and history, a greater seriousness in military art. With 2,000 years of examples behind us we have no excuse, when fighting, for not fighting well.

I like your little book — wherever it does not repeat a told tale. It starts at Chap. 11 by the way, and goes on to page 335. That's what you've sent me. Yours   T.E.S.

[1] The journal of the Royal Engineers.

2C

492 : TO REAR-ADMIRAL SNAGGE

5. VII. 33.   *E. Cowes, I of Wight*

If you found a difficulty in addressing me, how insoluble is my problem in replying! So I've burked it.

It seems that you and I are to lunch with Feisal on Friday, at the Hyde Park Hotel, at one o'clock.[1] Your company will (or would) strengthen me for the ordeal: for I have no civil clothes even imaginable for Hyde Park, or its hotels: and airmen (unless in company of unimpeachable correctness) find it hard to gain access to kings.

So may we meet that midday and proceed in company? I trust so. But where will you be? The Admiralty? . . . perhaps. 23 Whitehall Court? Perhaps. Will you send me a line to make a meeting place. A note addressed A/c Shaw, c/o Sir Herbert Baker, 2 Smith Square, S.W.1, will find me on Thursday night or Friday morning. In fact if you have a slave who does your telephoning, a message can be phoned there: by looking up Baker, Sir Herbert, 2 Smith Square (he is a firm, and has offices as well) in the book.

I hope this is manageable! Yours ever   T. E. SHAW.

Now remains the difficulty of an envelope to you. However, perhaps the 'Admiral' will carry all the responsibility!

493 : TO LADY ASTOR

10. *July* 1933   119 *Clarence Road, East Cowes, Isle of Wight*

Dear Peeress, Three things, my memory says, upon which to congratulate you: order of merit:—

(i) Personal. Your tact in ceding at golf to the Prince of Wales. That is admirable, wholly admirable.

(ii) Social. Your good-fortune in having the new National Sporting Club as your neighbour in St. James' Square. When an evening falls dull you can just step in and see a little boxing.

---

[1] The lunch duly took place. It was almost certainly the last meeting between Lawrence and Feisal, who died exactly two months later.

[7 *lines omitted*]

My own affairs march well. But it should have been Epstein and not Strobl.*[1] Yours proletariately   T. E. SHAW

Tailpiece

The Prophet's[2] house was reduced lately to a cinder. I sent condolences and the monster replied:—

'Yes, all my clothes were lost, but are well covered by insurance'. . . what would *you* put for price on the P's clothes? . . . 'I was lucky to be sleeping at All Souls, so Pat' (his wife, only) 'was alone in the house.'

* I refer to your affairs again, of course. Unselfish   T.E.S.

494: TO MRS. LIONEL CURTIS

1.Aug.33.   *13 Birmingham Street, Southampton*[3]

When I write Mrs Lionel Curtis on an envelope, my pen struggles in my fingers to write Mrs Lionel Tertis: but is there a Mrs L. Tertis? Do try to meet her, and go with her to one of those comic receptions where a footman sings out the guests' names. They would go to the tune of John Brown's Body.

You were very good with your telephoning John, to catch him right away. It should be this afternoon. Why did I not warn you that with John[4] an appointment broken is like a grain of sand on the sea-shore — at Sandown, not Southend, of course. Common, I mean, not rare. He is incalculable: but with infinite tact and patience the fish can be landed. And what a fish! I think he will luxuriate in Lionel's head. You and I will be disturbed. We got to know the Prophet in the forties, when he still roared. John will see him silvery in the fifties, lace like and impalpable and fringed. Alas, it will be an unfamiliar prophet: but it will survive. Do you realise that posterity will call me beautiful, on the strength of those two John pencil sketches so artfully pub-

---

[1] Kisfalud Sigismund de Strobl, the Hungarian sculptor, had made a bust of Lady Astor.
[2] Lionel Curtis.
[3] The lodgings Lawrence took in Birmingham Street remained his headquarters until October 1934, when he moved to Bridlington.
[4] Augustus John.

lished by me in my books? I could wish the prophet the same fate, if I were an optimist.

Blickling[1] — of course. I never thought of it. When your croft was burned, I had imagined your relapsing cosily into little Cliveden's modest splendour. But Blickling is far far more grand: and the Marquess has so many other houses [7 *words omitted*] that you do him a kindness to air one or other. Excellent.

Will you send me a line when the operation is over, to say if they are doing well? Yours   T.E.S.

495: TO EDWARD GARNETT

1.VIII.33.   13 *Birmingham St., Southampton*

So long since I wrote. So long since I went to Hilton.[2] 'Mr. Garnett' said the village postman importantly 'is gone to Spain.' 'Mr. Garnett is unfortunate' I replied, for it was a lovely green day under the trees; and the postman deflated.

Now one advantage of writing so seldom is that I have two things to say. The first concerns *The Mint*, whose copyright vests in the R.A.F. Chief of Staff for the time. Geoffrey Salmond, who was unlike any other Chief of Staff, was reading it when he died, and in the confusion of his papers *The Mint* was lost. So there goes one typescript.[3] I amuse myself imagining some scandalised staff officer filing it away in the Ministry.

And my other thing is an airman poet. I do not know if he is good or not. Both, I think, in patches. But he is a mechanic, and clouds and engines enter his verses naturally, as things he feels. I get warm then: but chill off again when he gets magniloquent, or chalice-ridden. He has read too much of Hopkins (G. Manley. H.) and finds sense in his imagery, where I see only formalism. Dunn, his name is. I have asked him to type out some of his poems, and they will come to you for judgement. I know you do not much read poems, but all the better. It will be a change.

My reading this year? In poetry the new de la Mare, which

---

[1] Lord Lothian's seat in Norfolk.   [2] To see David Garnett, then in America.
[3] It was found again, several years later.

is an advance: and Auden (in spots) Spender (ditto) Archibald
Macleish (fluid and good). By the way, did anything ever happen
to one Henderson (?) who published through Cape a long poem
of W. Raleigh sailing amongst the stars?[1]

In prose. *Eimi* by Cummings. Not so good as *The Enormous
Room*, for his style disintegrates and not integrates, this time.
Too pointillé. But the best thing I've ever read on modern
Russia, all the same. Then *The Book of Talbot*, an act of worship
by Violet Clifton. Very whole-hearted. A life of his boyhood,
by a Blasket Islander:[2] too full of unshed tears, but good enough.
Log of the Sea, by Felix Riesenberg. His notebooks, re-written,
by a sea captain who had taken pains to learn writing. *Captain
Bottell* by Hanley. Not quite a success, but nearer it (damn him)
than any book he has hitherto written. Rather a vintage year,
for books.

John Buchan puzzles me. Did you read his latest? He takes
figures of to-day and projects their shadows on to clouds, till they
grow surhuman and grotesque: then describes them! Now I ask
you — it sounds a filthy technique, but the books are like athletes
racing: so clean-lined, speedy, breathless. For our age they mean
nothing: they are sport, only: but will a century hence disinter
them and proclaim him the great romancer of our blind and
undeserving generation? You have only to try and read Walter
Scott, after Buchan, to feel the rolling of the years.

Enough rubbish. My pen will dry before I get the envelope
written.   T.E.S.

496: TO EDWARD GARNETT

10. VIII. 33.   13 *Birmingham St., Southampton*

Dear E.G., I am back from an extended Bank-holiday-with-
work to find your letter waiting. It alarms me rather, for I read
a note of urgency into your wish to arrange yourself. This I hope
is not true. I am not young enough any longer to see Time as
an infinity before me: and God knows that life's goodnesses are

[1] *The New Argonautica*, by W. B. Drayton Henderson.
[2] *Twenty Years A-Growing*, by Maurice O'Sullivan.

too rare to be worth delaying for. But I would like myself and those I care for to pack off all together. Your going too soon would leave another such emptiness as is Hogarth's place always in my mind.

So this begins by wishing you not long life, but longer.

The picture is due now, for my cottage is being *Odyssey*-finished into the perfect place for my living. By the end of summer (surely this is the finest summer in the history of England?) it will be complete and need only its inhabitant who has yet 18 months of R.A.F. service to do.

If you have packers at call (a pastel is very delicate) then Wool Station on the Southern Railway is the spot. Any article that arrives there, addressed to Mr. Shaw, Clouds Hill, is delivered to my door.

If you have no packer, then please send it by hand to No. 2, Smith Square, Westminster, where Sir Herbert Baker affords me a London home. I will find it there when I next come to London, and will take it over and home by hand.

You know I already possess John's picture of Feisal, the sketch:[1] so thanks to your goodness in reserving me the Allenby I shall have my dual mastership preserved in my cottage for all my time. It will be a queer, rich feeling. In the flesh that double allegiance was difficult: but the two quiet heads on the wall will let me do what I please. I shall grow philosophical, at finding that problem solve itself.

I tried to thank you before. You are not rich enough to fairly make me a present of that size (only by splitting will that infinitive suit my taste) but it is a present that never left me any choice. As unlikely would be the drowning man's asking to know the price of straw. It is so good of you: so happy.

I hark back to the first paragraph, and hope you are not feeling like that. You must not stay here just to please us: but I hope you still want to stay a while. Hearts usually last a man out, if he is kind to them. We grow old, Sirs: all of us grow old. Have I done my best, do you think? My prime is past. In it I worked my hardest at digging Hittites (that labour went unrecorded down the stream), at the war (history is written after

---

[1] Now in the Ashmolean Museum. Reproduced in *Seven Pillars of Wisdom*.

100 years), at *The Seven Pillars* (which I feel is partly theatre), at *The Mint*, which was my purest achievement, though still-born. May I rest now? All the heat in me is gone out, and the endurance that was tougher than other men's.

Bother the *New Statesman*, and the *Odyssey*, and all manufactured writing. Only the necessary, the inevitable, the high-pressure stuff is worth having. If the regiment of authors agreed, how easily would readers keep abreast of output! By your standard Buchan is nowhere: or rather he is with all but three or four living names.

Irishmen are disappointing men. They go so far, magnificently, and cease to grow. They bring forth more promise and less fruition than the rest of the English world massed against them. Give me the man whose first book is not marvellous, whose second is better, and whose third is different. Greatness in writing is a tree with many branches. You do not see it till the tree is old.   T.E.S.

497: TO R. G. GOSLETT[1]

31.VIII.33   13 *Birmingham St., Southampton*

Dear R.G., You are an angel. The bath came, beautifully packed, with all its loose parts in another box. It sits in my garage — or garden shed — awaiting the arrival of its boiler-and-burner-and-tank. The erection of the whole unit is to be signalised by an open-to-all bathing festival, lasting one hour. All Clouds Hill will attend, stark naked.

Meanwhile we progress. My ram[2] was publicly opened yesterday by the oldest (and only) inhabitant of Clouds Hill, with picturesque ceremony. It is the smallest ram in the world. Less than three hours after the opening ceremony the pipe (100 yards long) had filled and water began to flow into the cottage cistern. A pint came through in just four minutes. The oldest (and only) inhabitant took off his R.A.F. cap and drank the pint. It tasted of galvanised iron and red lead.

---

[1] Combined Supply and Ordnance Officer at Akaba, now a bath-manufacturer.

[2] The ram is one of the most admirable of the ingenuities of Clouds Hill. The flow of water from the spring pumps a fraction of itself some fifty feet uphill to the cistern while the overflow fills the pool-reservoir below.

In case a pint in four minutes seems to you little for a bath, let me remind you that the ram works all the twenty-four hours. I am planning a swimming pool and fountain in the lawn-to-be. The swimmer in the pool will be a gold-fish, chosen for his beauty and contentment with a solitary life. The fountains will be fountain-pen-fillers, concreted in the margin of the fish-swimming-pool.

Here is a cheque upon my overdraft, and I am deeply grateful to you for getting me so good a bath so cheaply. If ever you get near Dorsetshire, do call and turn on its stainless taps!

Clouds Hill, Moreton, Dorset.

That is it. The real centre of my world. Yours   T.E.

Cheque to you, as the bill is: if wrong please lodge a complaint and another will be sent! No receipt necessary, please. I lose them, only.

498: TO EDWARD GARNETT

15. IX. 33.   13, *Birmingham Street, Southampton*

Dear E.G., It was very good of you to take that trouble about Dunn's poems. I have written to him about it.

Also about the Liddell Hart book.[1] I talked freely to Howard[2] about that yesterday, dashing up to London and back for the purpose. I had only just time left to get to Waterloo and catch the 6.30, after it: so the Allenby is still at Smith Square. I want to get him down to my cottage direct, when I can. Pastels are too delicate to suffer much travelling.

The D.H.L.[3] MS. would be a delightful possession — but are you sure you want to break up your collection? It should be an asset for D.G. when he wants to build a new wing on to Hilton Hall!

I have now collected all my surviving books in my cottage: and am rather saddened at the gaps that declare themselves.*

* all Hudson, most Conrad, some Doughty.

[1] The project which eventuated in the publication of '*T. E. Lawrence*': *In Arabia and After.*

[2] G. Wren Howard, partner in Jonathan Cape Ltd.   [3] D. H. Lawrence.

They have been in London, with friends, for 12 years, and open to borrowers, who seem to have borrowed one-sidedly: for I have now no Cranes, only one S. Reynolds: no early D.H.L.! Fortunately all the poems remain; only the prose has gone; and I like reading — re-reading — poetry better than prose, I feel, as I get older. I have six volumes of D.H.L. poetry: and bit by bit I shall restore the missing prose books. There are about 1,000 books surviving: so that 200 or 300 alone need be replaced. If I have such a shelf-full, my old age will be provided for.

If you do decide to distribute your D.H.L. manuscripts, a poem by him could be inserted in *Look We Have Come Through* or his early volume (according to date of MS. poem) and it would be pleasant to possess: only, as I said, do not let the thought of that sway you towards dispersing your estate.

I wish we could meet. When the days get rough, I shall try to reach London occasionally.   T.E.S.

499: TO EDWARD GARNETT

25. IX. 33.   13, *Birmingham St., Southampton*

The ninth letter of the night: not fair treatment: but I so seldom feel able to write.

The D.H.L. poem, and *Maggie*,[1] journeyed with me to Clouds Hill last night, and took their places amongst my books. It is so good of you to help furnish the place. Opposite the books Allenby stares hard at whoever enters the room. I had not seen the drawing for years. It lasts well. The poor Allenby, himself, not so well. He has lost sinew in these years. So I like the portrait best. Your saving it for me was an inspiration, of which I shall grow gladder as the times grow old.

Aha! I have found a *Red Badge of Courage*,[1] and the *Poor Man's House*, and a *Holy Mountain*.[2] All in Salisbury, and for a song. A bookseller selling off, broken (I fear) by the badness of our time. My profit, anyway. Bit by bit I shall fill the gaps in my

---

[1] Both by Stephen Crane.   [2] Both by Stephen Reynolds.

shelves. Horrible gaps. Patience. Fortunately I am not a fanatic for first editions!

Crane selections . . . what a good book it might be: but how hard to give it *shape*. He varied so much, and was so instant and pressing, when he pressed. That perhaps is why you fancy he dates. Everybody dates, when the pressure loses meaning: but then they get their second wind.

Little Dunn is so pleased to be taken. I hope he is not hoping too much from his readers.

Your *Capajon* volume[1] is an oriental feast of flavours. I dip into it constantly, and always find a pleasure.   T.E.S.

500: TO EDWARD GARNETT

5. X. 33.   13, *Birmingham St., Southampton*

Dear E.G., It is most good of you to have sent that *Prussian Officer*[2]—a very difficult book to get. I now have all the essential D.H.L. — which is good! At the same time I feel a little guilty of greed: you should have sold this duplicate for much silver money, and had a week-end on the profits. (Or perhaps you shouldn't: some scruple makes me unable to sell books by people I like. I profiteered once on Galsworthy firsts — but that was different. He left me cold.)

The curiosity[3] is indeed a curiosity. I wonder what took you into publishing, forty-four years ago? And so small a book. As you say, the two short sketches show power and a sustained line of excitement which is very instructive. From them I turned to the first, long, story: and was left puzzled. The gift of description, the sense of character — and by contrast the xix[th] Cent. Moral. Very strange it is. Whoever wrote it was no negligible person.

The book-plate is nice: but puzzling: for Ford Madox Brown was alive a hundred years ago, and the forerunner of the pre-Raphaelites. It's no use your pretending to be as old as that.

---

[1] A selection of short stories by authors published by Jonathan Cape, chosen by Edward Garnett.   [2] By D. H. Lawrence.

[3] *The Beggar and other Stories*, by Grace Black, published by Edward Garnett.

Perhaps your father knew him, and he knew you as a child and did it for you as a gift? It is a remarkable spanning of the generations. Did you use it as a book-plate? I'm not able to put any mark in my books — unless, sometimes, T.E.S. in pencil on the fly-leaf corner. Whence, I suppose, my losses partly flow. However from the cottage there will be no borrowers and so no losses!

By my energy and your gifts I am now complete on D.H.L., Crane, and Reynolds. This week-end I am at the cottage, and aspire to read *Wounds in the Rain* or something of the sort — and then I'll try and tell you more about my modern idea of Crane. I remember him as a man of astonishment — one who surprised and shocked, by turns of incident and vivid phrases. Rather that, than a sustained artist. But that is an inarticulate memory, the surviving notion after years of neglect. I have always meant, in my leisured age, to re-read all these men who excited me in my youth.   T.E.S.

Little Dunn is so pleased and happy. Asked if he ought to thank you. I have said we will all three meet in London, some time. I think you would be good for him. He is too timid — and too drastic — by fits.

501: TO LORNA NORRINGTON[1]

24.XI.33   13 *Birmingham St., Southampton*

Dear Lorna, I'm rotten at answering letters. Yours has waited days — but other people's have waited weeks — and it has been on my conscience, which carries so much load these days that it is growing corns.

To-day we began running in the first of the big boats, the $37\frac{1}{2}$ foot things that I think you would like to try driving. As it was the first day we went ever so gently, and stopped again and again to do little jobs on her: but I could see that she was likely to be a very good boat. The wind screen and sliding windows are far better than the old ones.

[1] Aged 13.

There are seven more after this one, and they want 20 hours running each. So the job will go on for the next six weeks. I hope you will be able to work in a visit before they finish.

Of course these are not skittish craft, like the dinghies, but solemn and respectable cabin cruisers. Yet they are splendid to drive, in dirty water. They bounce! Yours sincerely

T E SHAW

Please give Mrs. Norrington my regards. Say that cruisers are warm and comfortable boats, very fit for winter driving.

502: TO R. DE LA BERE[1]

26. XI. 33   13 *Birmingham Street, Southampton*

Dear Prof., Yours is the unkindest cut of all! What has happened is briefly this:—

Twelve years ago I wrote some notes on the R.A.F. Depot . . . and in 1925 I added a word on Cranwell and sent it to Trenchard. A 'book' of 80,000 words, only notes: no continuity or development. To Trenchard I faithfully promised that it should not be published.

Various people have read it (Sir John Salmond holds it now): one chapter was sent by me to your *Journal* — an innocuous chapter. An Irishman is lent the script by a friend of his to whom a friend of mine had without telling me lent it . . . sub-loan upon sub-loan. 'Hot stuff' says the Irishman and copies . . . how much of it? God knows . . . but the *Legion Journal* is then sent a précis of the last three chapters by him, and comes out with a mash of it as an article by me.

Thunder from the Commissioner of Police:[2] from the Air Ministry . . . my head astonished but unbowed. The *Legion Journal* apologises next month. The Irishman has left his rooms — no address — and is laughing, probably. I am the poorer by three chapters, a visit to London, seven stamps (no, eight now) and three telegrams.

[1] Professor at Royal Air Force Cadets College, Cranwell.
[2] Trenchard.

So the *R.A.F. College Journal* will *not* reprint it.[1] In its mangled form it does not appeal to its author! Conceit, that is. Probably it is better in petto.

Has Dunn told you he has found a publisher? Good for him. Garnett called the stuff pretty good. I saw D. in his Squadron at Lympne: very amusing. He was like a slightly irascible bantam-cock in a large harem of hens — who looked up or down to him with vast fluttering respect. From the officers I gathered that he keeps *them* in order, too. Only the adjutant escapes criticism, so long as he gives D. dual and plenty of it! Yours

T.E.S.

Philip Sassoon, Evan Charteris and I spent a giddy afternoon in the cellars of the Tate Gallery, choosing pictures for Cranwell. Chambers of horrors, littered with *worse* pictures than those on show! We got to twenty (it must be a large college) and then felt faint. I hope you don't get them all. We nearly sent you one of myself in blue uniform, looking very bad-tempered. You could have labelled it 'Cadet College 1925-1926'!

503: DRAFT OF A LETTER TO WINSTON CHURCHILL

12. XII. 33   *Clouds Hill, Moreton, Dorset*

Dear Winston, Am I the last beneficiary of your *Marlborough* 1 to express his thanks? Probably — alas.

I have spun it out, partly because I work all day on R.A.F. boat-building and reach evening tired: partly because my room in Southampton (the above address is of my cottage, the 'Chartwell'[2] where I want to retire next year) grows colder and colder as the winter deepens. It sends me quickly to bed. But the main reason for my taking so long is because I have wanted to enjoy it for week after week. I finished it only yesterday. I wish I had not. It has been a rich experience.

The skeleton of the book is so good. Its parts balance and the main stream flows. That, I think because it is so distinct, is the

---

[1] It did so, in its mangled form.   [2] Winston Churchill's house in Kent.

chief balance of this book over *The World Crisis*. *Marlborough* has the big scene-painting, the informed pictures of men, the sober comment on political method, the humour, irony and understanding of your normal writing; but beyond that it shows more discipline and strength; and great dignity. It is history, solemn and decorative.

We think of you always as the nephew of the Duke, and expect you to be partial. Hence we discount some of your advocacy; hence you need not take pains to weigh the judgments you express. Let 'em have it! We want to see you supporting the Duke through thick and thin. A very telling irony you use, about his money!

Do you notice how shadowed he and Sarah are, as persons? Their responsibilities and offices overpower them. Only Colley Cibber's few lines show the flesh and blood that enwrapped these intelligences. It was a hard age.

I expect the end of Volume II will put them back in their bodies again. A very public person inevitably has more clothes than skin to wear. In this volume you set the scene, develop the actors and — put them ready to begin. How odd that Marlborough's strength should have so grown while he was waiting and sleeping, shelved and inactive. That gives an idea of his bigness. I never realised that he attained his premier power without trying for it. The lack of personal ambition in Vol. I is unearthly. He is never trying, at all.

It is most wise of you to write with restraint — not restraint of opinion or point of view, but of expression. *Marlborough* essentially disregards the help of fine writing. You gain dignity that way; and the actual style of the book is distinguished. Your prose has many echoes of the period. I suppose you have studied so much of it, and quoted so much, explicitly and implicity.

By the way I query the 'hospitality' of the second paragraph of page 382. It is possible, but a little more subtle than your usual efforts. Subtlety is a very dangerous quality in Englishmen.

A confession to close it. From 1927 onwards you sent me each part of your *Crisis*, as it developed. The first two volumes followed me to India, and were there read avidly, to lie with the generality of my books. All my life I have been laying by the books a man wants to re-read, as provision for the old age which so quickly attacks time-expired soldiers or airmen.

Unhappily the books had to lie in a friend's house. They were exposed to borrowers, and dozens of desirables are missing. Among these are your first two volumes. I have found in the shops of England other copies of the first printing to replace them. If I bring these substitutes up with me, sometime, will you put your name in them? And forgive me if the originals appear in Foyle's windows for sale? They will be stolen, not betrayed by me. I am so sad at having lost them. They are such good books, and essentially bettered by showing that you have touched them. Yours   T. E. SHAW.

504: TO G. WREN HOWARD

17.XII.33.   13, *Birmingham St., Southampton*

Dear Howard, I confess to a lively apprehension of that potential worst-seller of yours.[1] Please be careful in your puffs. One today said that it contained some yet unpublished *notes* of mine. Not true. It may have some unpublished *letters* from me (few of my friends having yet given up their letters to the press) but that is different.

Few people, I fancy, could know there was a 'life' of them on the stocks and not agree to read it first, for probable errors of fact to correct. Had I read Lowell Thomas, how much trouble I would have been saved! My reading Liddell Hart's effort does not imply either approval or collaboration. I regret it and apprehend it, keenly.

I want to be assured about the title, too. He told me *Lawrence* like that. I must protest (and shall protest publicly, if you insist still) that Lawrence, for this generation, is D.H.L., an infinitely greater man than all of us rolled together. Inverted commas are not enough to avoid trespass on him. Please consider this carefully, or you'll get into deep water. *Colonel 'Lawrence'* if

---

[1] '*T. E. Lawrence*': *In Arabia and After*, by Liddell Hart, published by Jonathan Cape Ltd., in which Howard is a partner. See also Letters Nos. 491 and 542.

you want to use that long name: or some clear indication that I'm not trying to arrogate to myself the use of D.H.L.'s name.

Yours ever,   T.E.S.

505: TO W. E. JEFFREY[1]

21.XII.33   *Clouds Hill, Moreton, Dorset*

Anatomy! This will be late for Christmas, but so much the better. I hate writing Christmas letters.

Posh asked lately what had happened to you. 'The little beast's a sergeant' I enviously snarled. 'Some have the luck' he replied. It is strange thinking for an A.C.1. Do you ever meet the R.A.F. in your country? They are good people.

My life is building boats for them, and I live in Southampton for half the year, overseeing the jobs. Not a bad life. I am never on parade except when I inspect myself on getting out of bed each morning. What a happy life it would be if one got up only whenever the sheets wanted changing! I grow so old and fat and white-haired. Each trooper that returns to England I escort up Southampton Water (in one of my experimental boats) and scan for signs of a long thin sergeant in a beret. No luck yet. Come home soon, for in March 1935 I relapse into a lounge suit, and go to live at Clouds Hill.

That cottage is just as you knew it, outside, only more over-grown with trees: but inside there have been changes. I made some money out of a version of Homer's *Odyssey* in the States, and have put in water, and a boiler and a bath: while the larger ground-floor is now shelved and plank-floored and half-full of books. Upstairs no change, except that I have abolished the bed, and just bug down anywhere, in the rare week-ends I spend in the place.

Mrs. Knowles still lives opposite, and helps to care for the place in my absence. I hope to see you enter it, one day. April 1934 you thought, in your last letter. Do warn me in time.

---

[1] Sergeant in the Royal Tank Corps: his thinness led to nicknames such as Skeleton, Anatomy, etc.

I might be still in Southampton, then: though my true station is Felixstowe in Suffolk.

Banbury is at Lulworth: married: one child and a garden. All serene yet!

Best of luck to you; I shall so much enjoy seeing you. Damn all letter-writing. Yours   T E SHAW

506: TO SIR EDWARD ELGAR

22.XII.33   *Clouds Hill, Moreton, Dorset*

Dear Sir Edward, This is from my cottage and we have just been playing your 2nd Symphony. Three of us, a sailor,[1] a Tank Corps soldier, and myself. So there are all the Services present: and we agreed that you must be written to and told (if you are well enough to be bothered) that this Symphony gets further under our skins than anything else in the record library at Clouds Hill. We have the Violin Concerto, too; so that says quite a lot. Generally we play the Symphony last of all, towards the middle of the night, because nothing comes off very well after it. One seems to stop there.

You would laugh at my cottage, which has one room upstairs (gramophone and records) and one room downstairs (books): but there is also a bath, and we sleep anywhere we feel inclined. So it suits me. A one-man house, I think.

The three of us assemble there nearly every week-end I can get to the cottage, and we wanted to say 'thank you' for the Symphony ever so long ago; but we were lazy, first: and then you were desperately ill, and even now we are afraid you are too ill, probably, to be thinking of anything except yourself: but we are hoping that you are really getting stronger and will soon be able to deal with people again.

There is a selfish side to our concern: we want your Symphony III: if it is wiser and wider and deeper than II we shall very sadly dethrone our present friend, and play it last of the evening. Until it comes, we shall always stand in doubt if the best has really yet happened.

[1] A. E. Chambers had been in the Navy.

Imagine yourself girt about by a mob of young pelicans, asking for III: and please be generous to us, again!

Yours sincerely,   T. E. SHAW.

507: TO HIS BROTHER, A. W. LAWRENCE

26.XII.33   13 *Birmingham St., Southampton*

I'm rather alarmed at your expansive plans, as shown in a letter to Mrs. Knowles. She has a key, and will light fire and lay in stores: but that is as far as she can go. There is nowhere to cook, in the cottage, and no pots or pans or crockery. She has her children in her place — and besides I have made it a condition of the lease that nothing is lent from cottage to cottage. So please do not borrow off her or ask her to do more than the essential preparations. She is exceedingly helpful, but I do not wish her imposed on: and I lend the cottage to all sorts of people, whence the necessity for a hard and fast rule.

As regards bedding, there are the two sleeping bags[1] (of 3 and 2 blankets, respectively) and about four loose blankets, one eiderdown and, I think, two sheets. No third pillow. Two or three face towels and a roller towel. No dish cloths — but then, no dishes.

We have had a misfortune in the spring, which is slowly dwindling. This year's deficiency of rain is at last hitting it. So we have shut off the ram, which pumped water to the cottage, and gone back to buckets, carried. All the neighbourhood is watering from our spring! It still gives about 300 gallons daily, enough for the families, but not enough for the ram, which takes 700.

You will find rough lists of the books and records on the upstairs mantleshelf, in a notebook. Plenty of needles, and a cutter for them. The upstairs fire burns the best, as yet. I have a stainless steel hood-front coming for the book-room fire which smokes in some winds.

There is wood in the woodshed (rhododendron best: the oak is rather green) but the garage is still rather a mess with cement &

---

[1] The sleeping bags at Clouds Hill were embroidered *Meum* and *Tuum,* which was fulfilling an old idea dating from his plans when he was an undergraduate. See letter No. 543.

building stores. Owing to the frost Pat Knowles has not been able to finish the storage-tank. No W.C. now.

I'd suggest your feeding your party at the Black Bear in Wool, or the Ship: or the Red Lion of Winfrith. The heath roads to Wareham & Dorchester are now made up and good. There is Bere Regis too! With wheels food becomes easy.

The cottage has now only two chairs. One for the book-room is being made here, but will not be ready for a week.

I was there over Christmas, with Chambers, who was at Farnborough R.A.F. with me. The place was lovely; quiet, warm, and full of things to do. I look forward to settling there in a year's time, for good.

I hope you can stow your party somewhere and find local food for them! I go generally to one of the two or three soldiers' eating-shops in Bovington.

Tell me what you think of the alterations, done or half-done. I'm very sorry about the empty cistern: but I dared not parch all the neighbours. Clouds Hill is the only water between Bovington and Bere Regis today. Pray for rain.   .N.

508: TO LADY ASTOR

31. XII. 33   13 *Birmingham St., Southampton*

Yours, MI PIRESS, was the only Christmas greeting that I sent: and likewise this shall be my only conveyance for the New Year. O si sic omnes! Confess that my Christmas has been quieter than yours. As for warmth, my cottage (where I went, and by good fortune, for late one night an airman arrived 'to spend the holiday with me') depends for its degree of warmth upon the quantity of firewood its occupant cuts. That other airman and myself cut heaps of logs, and roasted and toasted — ourselves.

My cottage is lovely: but the drought has dried up all the other springs on the heath. So every neighbour draws, by bucket and cask and tub, from mine: and to satisfy their thirsts, I must forgo my bath. So it wasn't, probably, as clean a Christmas as yours.

On Christmas day it was mild and grey: so we walked for fourteen miles and dinnered off a tinned chicken. The long walk made it taste good.

And talking of Christmas presents, those of last year, the two heating lamps, have been doing great service all this cold spell in my cottage. I cannot light the bath-heater, because of the lack of water. So they alone have combatted the chill and the damp, *most successfully*. My books are as dry and well-off as ever in their poor lives.

One day last week (Wednesday I think it must have been) I came to London and registered my motor-bike for 1934. Also I asked after Sir Herbert Baker, who is going on well, regaining himself: and then a memory of a half-deciphered sentence in your last letter caused me to ring up St. James' Square. You were reported absent. I felt glad that you had better things to do.

I am sorry about the dark lady, and rather frightened. Where is safety, if I am rumoured to have lost my heart to a lady of sixty, upon once visiting her after lunch to apologise for not lunching? A lady whom I had met for the first time at Lympne in the summer? It is rather hard, I think. Probably it would be wholesome for me to lose my heart — if that monstrous piece of machinery is capable of losing itself: for till now it has never cared for anyone, though much for places and things. Indeed I doubt these words of 'hearts'. People seem to my judgement to lose their heads rather than their hearts. Over the Christmas season two men and four women have sent me fervent messages of love. Love carnal, not love rarefied, you know: and I am uncomfortable towards six more of the people I meet, therefore. It's a form of lunacy, I believe, to fancy that all comers are one's lovers: but what am I to make of it when they write it in black on white? If only one might never come nearer to people than in the street. Miss Garbo sounds a really sympathetic woman! The poor soul. I feel for her.

I would now like to turn to happier things, and be brisk for a last paragraph: but no use. Those two in China have been silent for a month, which means lost letters or uncivil unrest across their line of communications. They were wrong to court martyrdom thus inaccessibly.

As for my boats — do not credit all that you read in the daily papers, or even *the* weekly one.[1] I ran that first boat two seasons ago, indeed, but only till I saw she worked. Mute inglorious airmen took my place and have carried on since. (Not so mute either!)

I enclose a fragment of some daily paper, sent me by Augustus John. It made me laugh.

Ave atque vale   T.E.S.

O'Casey? Shawn? Indeed yes, I have just finished his new play.[2] The second act of *The Silver Tassie* was my greatest theatre experience, and here is a whole play in that manner. It will play better than it reads.

509: TO GEOFFREY KEYNES

10.2.34   13 *Birmingham St., Southampton*

Dear G.K., I return the S.S. proof-pulls.[3] Thank you for the sight of them (and for the return of the *Too True* offprint). These script engravings are very beautiful, very delicate. Slow to read and impossible to glance over in one blink of the eye, the way one usually swallows short poems the first time, to see if they taste good. These have to be read word for word, and one of them, 'Degrees of groping thought', didn't stand up, in my mind, to such syllabic treatment. I like the others, and shall like the book, if I ever get it! Sometimes I feel inclined to curse all rarities: though S.S. has been generosity itself in giving me book after book.

So don't worry about Meynell's opinion. If I were perfectly candid I should describe them as too good an idea for the general!

I think they seem to go a little ahead of *The Heart's Journey* ... at least 'Vigils' does. A very lovely poem, technically done. I am looking forward very much to reading them all.

---

[1] Lord Astor is the proprietor of *The Observer*.

[2] *Within the Gates*.

[3] Of *Vigils*, by Siegfried Sassoon, the original edition of which was engraved on copper by Charles Sigrist with a frontispiece by Stephen Gooden, for Geoffrey Keynes.

If he does, as we hope, 'go on' now, after his marriage, we shall be fortunate. But if the poor man turns happy instead and writes no more — why, he has deserved it, surely. [9 *lines omitted*]

510: TO LADY ASTOR

15. 2. 34

MI PIRESSE, If you see O'Casey again, before this letter grows cold, will you bless him from me? For I have seen his Park play[1] twice, and it has cost me only half-a-crown in all. That is real kindness.

I don't want to see it again, for it is too painful, despite its beauty. How far he has gone since he was in Ireland, on paper! This play is London and human (and inhuman) nature: all of us, in fact: and about as helpless.

And talking of inhumanity, how dare he pile loads like these upon his actors and actresses? He asks the impossible, but gets, I think, more than he deserves. Poor dumb laden beasts.

The poignancy of Act ii, *The Tassie*, is not here: it could not be, for much lay in the contrast of that act's neighbours, in the wonderful lighting and setting; in the experience which came rawly upon those new from the war. This play deals with the life we all have to lead (temporarily) and so we dare not detach ourselves from it and criticise or pass judgement. That's why I do not want to see it again. However I shall read it once more, in the peace of my cottage, which is ever so far away from his park — and equally solid, too, God be praised.

I was right in feeling that this play would be bigger seen and heard, than merely read.

Bless him again. He is a great man, still in movement. May it be long before he grows slow, stops, returns on his tracks! I have learned a great deal from him.   YOUR AIRMAN

When a rare Irishman does go on growing, you see, he surpasses most men. Alas that they are so rare

Making for Southampton again.   T.E.S.

---

[1] *Within the Gates*, the action of which takes place in Hyde Park.

511: TO A. E. CHAMBERS

5·3·34　　　　　　　　　　　　　　13 *B/ham St., S'ton*

Dear Jock, Indeed, yes, Clouds Hill, house and land and tuum[1] and all loose things inside it and outside it is yours when you please. Any month this year. Changes? None indoors, I think, and few outside. The pool is filled to the brim, and the spring down to 300 gallons per day: but it rained last night. Hallelujah!

There is a whole chestnut tree to cut up. Pat finds it too much for his single self. He is busy roofing in the pool: still a skeleton roof. Pool not yet finished: its lining coat of cement lacking. We hurried to fill it, instead, fearing a drought. I do not know about bathing in it. Depends on the size of the spring. Consult Pat before taking the plunge!

I cannot say so far ahead where I will be in April. Here, most probably; but the R.A.F. disposes.

Liddell Hart commits me to calling old Foch 'a frantic pair of moustaches':[2] but I think it was a Clemenceau mot. 'More teeth than brains' was as far as I got. Au revoir　　　　　T.E.S.

512: TO MISS L. P. BLACK

5·3·34　　　　　　　　　　13 *Birmingham St., Southampton*

Dear Miss Black, Two more absences on duty — but yesterday eventually we cracked the pudding. My landlady boiled and boiled it, spurred on by my promise of a share if she did it properly: and finally we all agreed that it had been an extra-ordinarily good pudding. As a matter of fact, it is too soon to talk of it in the past tense. It is passing, certainly; but there will be more on Wednesday when I get back here from London: and I doubt (unless the landlady is greedy) if even that will be its past tense. A huge pudding and excellent. Thank you very much. They do improve with keeping: and are better apart from the rather forced associations of Christmas, don't you think?

Now about my cottage! Please, no furniture. I have had

---

[1] See note to letter No. 507.　　　　[2] Compare letter No. 459.

great satisfaction and some exasperation in building everything that goes into the place. Fenders, chairs, table, couches. It has two rooms and two of everything, accordingly; the whole place is designed for just the single inhabitant! It has neither rugs nor paint nor plaster nor wallpaper. Panelling; book-shelves; bare wood and undyed leather. A queer place, but great fun. No pictures and no ornaments.

However I agree that you ought to be associated with some item of its interior: your kindness over so many years must be perpetuated. And I went there last Thursday and sat and thought. Tea-spoons, it is: and as tea is for visitors there should be four of them, I think. As yet I have no tea-cups or plates, but I have found a pottery near Poole and a month ago I threw a sample cup and saucer, which is drying. When it dries well, I hope to glaze it with galena, a lustrous brown-black which I used with great success before the war for earthenware — and then I shall have a decent tea-service.

So if you agree, will you send me four plainish tea-spoons for four black tea-cups-to-be? It will be a very pleasant service and memory. Not yet memorial, while we both are alive and kicking; but memory, certainly. I hope to visit Torquay this summer and revive it, too! Yours   T E SHAW

513: TO LIONEL CURTIS

19.3.34.   *Union Jack Club*, 91 *Waterloo Road, London, S.E.*1

My Lord Prophet, Your letter and Philip's[1] wire met me on Sunday in Southampton, as I got back from Birmingham. So this morning I wired to him that I was sympathetic but sorry — and tonight (ordered to London suddenly for an inspection tomorrow at Brentford of a searchlight) I failed to find him in his lordly burrow of St. James.

The defence question is full of snags and is being ineptly handled by Lords Rothermere and Beaverbrook. I agree that the balance of expenditure on Navy, Army and R.A.F. is wrong: but I do not want R.A.F. expenditure increased. Our present squadrons could deal very summarily with France. When

---

[1] Philip Kerr, Lord Lothian.

Germany wings herself — ah; that will be another matter, and our signal to reinforce: for the German kites will be new and formidable, not like that sorry French junk.

All we now need is to keep in ourselves the *capacity* to expand the R.A.F. usefully, when the times make it necessary. For this we must have:—

(1) Aerodromes enough, sited in the useful places.

(2) Aircraft firms well equipped, with up-to-date designers, designs, and plant.

(3) Brains enough inside our brass hats to employ 1 and 2.

(1) Easy — but means another 15 aerodromes, each costing £20,000: they take about three years to bring into being.

(2) In hand; excellent; but hampered by

(3) The direction of R.A.F. and Air Ministry. Our air-marshals are rather wooden-headed, and some of the civilian A.I.D.[1] inspectors and technicians who handle design are hopeless. Consequently our military aircraft are like christmas trees all hung with protruding gadgets, our flying boats are a bad joke, our civil aircraft are (almost) the world's slowest; and air tactics and strategy are infantile.

More money should be spent at once on (1) above: and research made into flying boat development (after sacking the present authorities) and wireless-controlled aircraft. Also to develop the art of sound-ranging, and anti-aircraft gunnery. If I had my way, I would constitute a new Flying Boat department of Air Ministry, and have in a dozen good naval men to give it a start.

Upon the Navy I have views also. Our air bombs are not going to sink capital ships; but will render them useless as fighting platforms, and probably uninhabitable. This in only three or four years time. The defence of surface craft against aircraft will be found in manoeuvre:—in being able to turn quicker on the water than the plane can in the air — not difficult, with small ships, as water give you a firmer rudder. So I expect to see the surface ships of navies in future limited to small, high-speed,

[1] Air Inspection Department.

manoeuvrable mosquito craft, none larger than the destroyers of today.

There are controversial points in the above, and to argue them one must consider smoke-screens, the one-pounder pom-pom, trajectories, dive-arcs, [*omission of an Official Secret*]; all sorts of technical things. But I am prepared to maintain my thesis in most company. Do not, however, take this exposition of it as exhaustive or even fair. To deal with imponderables, layer upon layer of imponderables, more resembles faith than argument.

I wish I could have run through your *Round Table* argument and talked it over with you. Accordingly   T.E.S.

Off to Southampton tomorrow p.m. after a meeting in Air Ministry.

514: TO ERNEST ALTOUNYAN

7 *April* 34.

[18 *lines omitted*] Your poem — essentially it is one, a poetic history — is so long, so interwoven, so exhausting, that it demands full attention. Don't be hurt by the word exhausting. I do not mean wearisome but wearying. It is a strenuous exercise to reach much of it. Like boxing, which is a severe art, whereas golf is easy. You are a muscular poet, and few readers will ever grapple with you competently.

This tax upon your readers is physical. It is possible that intellectually you may make an equal demand. Your metaphysic, your physiology, your philosophy may be as articulated and articulate as [the] forcefulness of your writing. My mind slides over what it fails to understand, and is not troubled at having such depths under its keel. So I do not weary my brain as I read your poems. If your subsequent readers do, why then more of them will fall by the wayside. Be merciful to the reading public! It is not a merit to write, like Blake in his prophetic books, for the very few. The very few are not so useful as the very many. To imagine ourselves — because we are freaks — to be therefore rare and admirable creations is to deceive ourselves. Two-headed chickens and Siamese twins are rare — and unfortunate. Generally they are bottled young. [38 *lines omitted*]

515: TO PAYMASTER-CAPTAIN ARCHIBALD COOPER[1]

8. IV. 34   13 *Birmingham St., Southampton*

Dear Captain Cooper, I had intended to ring you up from the Dockyard to say 'Thank you' for the *Aquarius*[2] before I left — but I went off at 7.30 a.m.; so it seemed too unkind. Then I travelled for three days, and over the week-end I could not find a Navy List to get your proper style. So many explanations . . .

I should apologise for having rung up the Office. If everybody who felt urgent about his ship did so, your life would become miserable. But we were a very small ship, easily overlooked, and (if delayed) very unfit to face the monsoon: so as soon as the pilot told us that there were no orders, I dashed to Mount Batten, to ask the Admiral for help.

You will be amused to hear that no less a personage than the chief Pilot came aboard the *Aquarius* a minute after I got back to her, after taking your message. His previous job had been to take the *Rodney*[3] up. We boasted 270 tons — reduced to 112 by some chicane when Dock Dues are payable. However we got to our berth in a few minutes, and there was a Stores Officer to measure us for a new tarpaulin (it came next day — excellent), another to ask about oil and water, and *three* fitting experts to examine the steering. They plugged in electric light, carried up a brow — did everything they could. The steering proved to be a trifle — just a jam in a chain conduit-cover — not worth alarming you about: but thanks to the despatch of all the other jobs the ship got away to time, and has reached Gibraltar — where she wants to mend some sort of a valve, but has no one aboard now to get her priority treatment.

So thank you very much . . . and if you had to involve greater noises in the effort, please thank them for me, too. We saw the C. in C. landing at Mount Edgcumbe as we came in, so I expect he was not a party. I shall try not to trespass on your kindness again — unless it happens again! It was wholly worth it.

Yours sincerely   T E SHAW

---

[1] Then Secretary to Lawrence's friend the Commander in Chief at Plymouth Station.
[2] Lawrence was on board this R.A.F. ship on her maiden voyage from Liverpool.
[3] 33,900 tons.

If the Admiral *did* hear of it, will you please offer my apologies, and say that I was filthy and labouring, all that day, and disappeared early the next? I could not have paid my respects without neglecting my duty.

Please say also that we are building better and better boats (and the C. in C. Portsmouth has wangled one for six months out of Air Ministry, for himself[1]). Better put the last sentence in very small print! But they are good boats.

516: TO LINCOLN KIRSTEIN

12. IV. 34   *Clouds Hill, Moreton, Dorset, England*

Dear Kirstein,[2] Your letter of last December has been troubling me, for you made it hard to answer, and yet I have to answer it. See now, there are, I think, in the world no men very different from ourselves. I walk the streets of an evening, or work in our R.A.F. camps all day, and by measuring myself against the airmen or passers-by I know that I am just an average chap. You write as though there were degrees, or distinctions. I see likenesses, instead.

You get your idea from having read *The Seven Pillars* and *The Mint*,[3] apparently. Few people have read *The Mint*, but many *The Seven Pillars*. If they all got this same disproportioned view of myself I would believe that there was some falsity of scale or attitude in what I had put down. But these others only find the books natural. I did not mean them to transcend myself, to shout. I hope they do not. Probably they happen upon an unguarded angle of yourself, and so seem to you more significant than is their truth. I have found that in myself. Sometimes a book that is not exceptional to others will mean a great deal to me. From which you should deduce not any superabundance in its writer, but a poverty (in that point) within yourself.

How pompous a paragraph I have written: but you scare me,

[1] Admiral Boyle (now Lord Cork and Orrery), who had been in Arabia with Lawrence, had got tired of seeing him streaking past the Admiral's barge in an R.A.F. speedboat.

[2] Author of *Dance* and promoter of the School of American Ballet.

[3] Kirstein had read *The Mint* while staying with David Garnett but had never met Lawrence.

rather, with your over-impression. Please come and see me, if you get to England again; and then you will see I am your own size — and everybody else's. A very big man will be six feet six: a very small one five feet. Human differences are negligible, except in human eyes.

Pompous again. I am glad you like Melville. He is not enough praised by Americans. Nijinski I saw dance once only, across the whole width of a full London theatre. It was more than beauty, but not like a man. I suppose if I had seen him off the stage he would have been normal. If we meet let us talk a little upon why some people are greater than their work, and others less. I puzzle myself often over that. And why did you so much like *The Mint*, which is a close photograph of our life in camp?

Now for Gurdjieff. I had read some of his work (in French) a long while ago; not this which you have sent me, but stuff as real. It was closer-knit, too, as prose and as argument. I liked it — as I like this *Herald of Coming Good* — but find myself a little to one side, facing perhaps the same question, but from another angle. Perhaps I am English or European, whereas Gurdjieff and yourself are not. Yet Katherine Mansfield... but wasn't she a New Zealander? I do not know, but Russia and its books and movements fail to strike me directly. Strange, interesting, moving — but there is no impact, no actuality. I find a common tint or tone or texture in all Russian work, and it all misses me in the end, however I like it for the moment.

'Man of action' you call me, in the last words of your letter 'who has done what he chose to his full extent.' Do, for heaven's sake, travel down to where I am next time you reach England, and put these ideas straight. We are all poor silly things trying to keep our feet in the swirl. Even if we succeed, it is not more than a static performance, nor deserving of applause. So I beg you to see me, and disabuse yourself of an illusion. Or do I take a single letter too seriously? Yours somewhat bewildered

T. E. SHAW

[With the following letter Lawrence enclosed, for the amusement of Leeson, several numbers of an American magazine containing a sensational serial purporting to be a true account of the experiences of a pilot who had flown Lawrence during the war.

Leeson joined X squadron at Rabegh in January 1917, was afterwards at Wedj and went out with Lawrence for a seven days' trip by car, exploring Wadi Hamdh looking for one of the R.F.C. machines which had crashed. They had a difficult trip; the temperature was 118° in the shade and they had to cut their way through dry brushwood. The country was quite waterless. Leeson afterwards was invalided out of Arabia and though Lawrence asked for him to run mechanical transport at Akaba, he was not allowed to return.

Leeson sent the serial on to other pilots who had been with Lawrence in Arabia, Dutton and Siddons, who enjoyed a good laugh over it.

Leeson tells me that he believes the author of it 'did once fly Lawrence to Ma'an or somewhere like that', and was in the R.F.C.]

517: TO B. E. LEESON

13.IV.34.   13, *Birmingham Street, Southampton*

Dear Leeson, I keep on losing your address; but perhaps there is a providence to send this on. Some U.S.A. mutt forwarded me this precious paper. I don't value it as I should; but it seems to me that it ought to touch you in a very tender spot. What this man saw! What he heard! What he knew! Ah, I am ashamed of my bad memory. I had forgotten nearly everything he remembered. Even in *The Seven Pillars* I had been ungrateful to him, selfish, in not acknowledging his aerial co-operation while I blew up that train (but which train was it, I wonder? I have forgotten that too).

However, there it is: and who the God-forsaken liar is, only you may guess — if *you* can, even. Hail and farewell!   T.E.S.

518: TO C. J. GREENWOOD

16.IV.34.   13, *Birmingham Street, Southampton*

Dear Greenwood, I began the Campbell[1] first — last week, because I have been in the North for three weeks and am only just back.

[1] *Broken Record,* by Roy Campbell.

And having begun it, I finished it in three sittings. The first interval
I said 'There are fools and damned fools ... but even that
doesn't include Campbell'. The second interval I changed mood
and said 'There's more in this than folly. It's good in parts.'
And now that it is all over I slip back towards my first mind.
D.H.L. threw away his reason — but it harmed him. It is all
very well *feeling* hard and quick and hot — but feeling cannot be
put on paper convincingly except to the already converted (and
who wants to talk to his disciples) without brains and logic and
argument to back it up. Roy Campbell makes an ass of himself
all through. A pity — because clearly he isn't a real ass — only
synthetic.

It's the fashion now, I suppose, this naivety. Liam O'Flaherty
writes himself down as a simpleton pure; and so did Gertrude
Stein in an awful autobiography. Did you ever read it? She
admitted to having owned a Ford car for *months* without understanding it — seemed rather proud of this — darned fool. A
Ford!!! [23 *lines omitted*]

519: TO S. L. NEWCOMBE[1]

Wednesday [? 17.IV.34]   13 *Birmingham St., Southampton*

Dear Object, You have caught me in a bad week. I don't
think I can get there on Thursday (tomorrow) anyhow. There
is a boat-job fixed for that day. If it fizzles I shall try to snatch
my bike and run over — and it would be latish afternoon ...
fourish or fivish ... but it is so unlikely that I beg of you to go
for a walk instead. Not that there are many walks in Bournemouth, but if you take a bus first, it can be managed.

Failing Thursday (and almost certainly we fail on Thursday)
then there remains Saturday. Saturday is much more probable.
I shall try to get there soon after lunch, about twoish.

Never heard of glandular fever. Probably you wish you
hadn't. I expect I've had it, and never knew it.

[1] Aged 14.

These modern doctors are getting so clever that hardly anybody of their clients is ever well.

Ice cream sounds like a good diet. Could you mix them, or did they give you that plain stuff that doesn't taste, except of frozen snow? Otherwise you could have walked into a Lyons and amazed the girl by going completely through the Sundae list.

Well . . . improbably Thursday . . . probably Saturday: store up a great packet of cheerfulness for me, as I am feeling very fat and ugly. Yours   T.E.S.

520: TO DOUGLAS CARRUTHERS[1]

2 *May* 1934.   13, *Birmingham Street, Southampton*

Dear Carruthers, I got to the Power Boat Yard to-day, after a fortnight in Wolverhampton, and found your letter waiting for me. Alas, for me Arabia is no longer an interest. I cut away from the Middle East sharply in 1922, when I enlisted: and the R.A.F. has since engrossed me. I have been for three years now helping to improve our breeds of boats.

I remember your Guarmani, and also a Dane's book on Hasa, (translated by Leeds, I fancy). Those quite limited war-time editions must by now be unobtainable.

Some society in the States years ago brought out a great block of undigested Musil translation[2]: and the only concrete suggestion I can make, is that perhaps they might collaborate with the R.G.S. by taking half-cost and half the edition. I cannot tell you what society it was — but they wrote offering me the book, and I had to decline it. Barracks don't provide book-shelving enough!

I cannot comment or make notes. My Arab show was so distracted, and so long ago: and such a sickening lot has been written about it. I hate it.

As for cash — please believe me when I tell you that my total income (for many years) has been below Income Tax level. I wish there was any prospect of its ever reaching three figures again. Two pounds a week would do me so well: you will under-

---

[1] See letter No. 154.   [2] Of the work of the traveller in Arab countries.

stand, however, that it wouldn't come to much, in books! Tastes, to-day, severely simple!

Rule me out please. I'm a burnt squib, as far as Arabia goes; but a tolerable fitter, and handy on a motor boat. Yours

T. E. SHAW.

521: TO K. W. MARSHALL

4.v.34.   13, *Birmingham Street, Southampton*

Dear Marshall, It will by now be all over: I hope it was not too rude an experience.[1] As I said, I think you are wise in taking the step: which isn't really, I hope, either a plunge or a responsibility, but just a good arrangement.

Don't be shy about asking me if ever you feel I could be useful. I'm sure that such an event will not be common!

The R.A.F. have kept me wandering about the earth for weeks now: but at last I have regained Southampton Water, where there are five new boats to run in, with 20 hours each.

If they will leave me to that, I shall be pleased for three weeks. Today was noble sunlight, and the boat behaved beautifully.

[*name omitted*] drew himself slowly and firmly upon me that day: and I have met him once and had a letter: to which I replied. Do not worry: I have seen his like, often. [*name omitted*] showed his disgust: but [*name omitted*] isn't really worth it, uncomfortable though his manner makes me. I am sorry, always, for the patently impotent. It must be terrible to be like that, don't you think?

Cheerio: we are healthy, and can be vulgar, I hope, when we feel inclined.

I've been reading R. Graves' book on Roman history.[2] Hard-hearted and bloody: what a strange road R.G. has travelled. [*one line omitted*]

T.E.S.

[Liddell Hart writes: 'In May I was a guest at a dining club where one of the members told me that he had recently met a man who was introduced to him as "Aircraftman Shaw, formerly

---

[1] Marriage.   [2] *I, Claudius.*

2E

Colonel Lawrence". Subsequent incidents had raised doubts in his mind, and as a business transaction was in prospect he had thought it worth while to take this chance of speaking to me about the man. A few questions, and a glance at a letter he had received, showed me that an impersonation was being attempted. I promptly wrote to tell T.E. about it.']

522: TO B. H. LIDDELL HART

17 *May* 1934   13 *Birmingham St., Southampton*

Always I owe you two letters! Hard luck. I'm very sorry about the lunch with Ll.G. It struck me when I read it as a pleasant dream, and I should have liked to come: but then I forgot. [6 *lines omitted*]

Did you see a bad fake of an interview with me in the *Daily Chronicle*? Its local reporter fell into talk with me, promising not to repeat anything — and then spat out a travesty of what I said and he imagined. The Editor disowned him to the Air Ministry, and so averted trouble from my head!

Now about this other bloke . . . If you see the blighter do rub into him that I never have signed myself as Lawrence since 19 twenty something. He is years out of date. In fact he doesn't sound the right sort of man at all. Do you feel that I ought to do something? It is rather hard to catch him by post. However, there is Eliot; the Hon. E. Eliot. He is a very balanced solicitor, who looks after the legal interests of *Revolt in the Desert*. My trouble is that I cannot well risk legal expenses: but Eliot might feel able to assume that a 'T. E. Lawrence' in being today was an infringement of his trust property, for the *Revolt* Trust owns the property in that name. If so, he could ask the bloke to stop his games, and charge his trouble to the fund. I'd pay a small bill, up to 3 or 4 pounds, but couldn't risk the promising of more. Will you send on the suggestion (or perhaps this note) to Eliot and see if he can square his conscience to the idea? I can conceive of its seeming to him as if he might legitimately be drawn in, if the affair developed — and to prevent that he might stall the fellow off now.

Failing Eliot, I can't think of anybody else who would do . . .
unless you tell the *Daily Express* of the existence of a bogus
Colonel L.! That would properly boil it. . . .

[*2 lines omitted*]

This is very kind of you. There must be many impersonators,
I think, judging by the number of letters I get from stranger-
acquaintances, many of them women of whom I appear to have
taken some advantage.[1] Sometimes when they get too urgent I
have got the police to help me out by asking them to make the
correspondence cease. Only this chap hasn't written to me, so I
can't well do that, now . . . can I? [*omission*]

523: TO K. W. MARSHALL

18.v.34.   13, *Birmingham Street, Southampton*

Dear M., I will do which you please — either write a general
note, or answer the particular enquiry of all or any of the people
to whom you name me as a reference. It is for you to say, but I
fancy the second is likely to be the more impressive way with
smaller people. They will like to get a personal letter. Or wouldn't
they? God perhaps knows. Ask Greenwood.

July and Clouds Hill sound a promising combination. A word
of warning. Since last visit the cottage has changed, somewhat.
The bed is thrown out. There are two sleeping bags, six loose
blankets, and a shabby quilt. Many sheets. A large couch in
the book-room, downstairs: enough cushions to pad a man's
length of the floor, upstairs — and a narrow long floor-cushion in
the food-room (ex-bedroom, upstairs). There are no cups or
plates yet: but some are on order. I cannot say how long they
will take to make them. Six knives, six spoons, six forks. A
small kettle: no pots or pans. Enough towels. Not much water,
the drought having halved the spring's yield. An axe: brushwood
everywhere. The village as it was: one push-bike. You are very
welcome. I will try to look in for an afternoon, but cannot
promise. I am so seldom able to set eyes on it. Patience: next
year I settle in. Keys now with the Knowles'.

[1] See letter No. 557.

Sun-bathing easy: and perhaps plunge-bath possible. It depends on the spring. We have built the tank, if only it will fill it. Bother this dry year! However there is the Lulworth sea, as yet too cold: but not dry.

The Sedition Bill will be a marvellous advertisement for anything it opposes. What fools military men are!

Yes, I write about six letters daily. All of 'em to people who don't matter. It's a pleasure to hear from you sometimes, instead. You only write when there is a reason. Business letters are no trouble. Cheerio.   T.E.S.

524: TO E. M. FORSTER

24. v. 34   13 *Birmingham Street, Southampton*

Dear E.M.F., It is Thursday night, and I have just finished your life of G.L.D.,[1] upon which I have been quietly happy for many evenings. In the daytime I run boats up and down the Solent (and shall do, for another month) and in the evening I try always to read a little.

Your book has been quite precious. The restraint, the beautiful tidiness of it, the subtlety, and its commonsense . . . your glorification of quiet and care for the average man . . . all these points lift it far above ordinary biography. It must have been hard to do, but seldom can an artist have so surely and confidently achieved his aim. The very care to avoid the unattainable is wisdom. Full marks to you. I wish I had known G.L.D.

I found pleasure in your wit widespread over the pages. The sentence 'she forgave him' is almost your best: not so quotable as the smoking-room chairs,[2] but of greater style. I looked back at it three or four times as I read further, just for the pleasure of its finality.

Your quotations, where you quote so often, are quite beautifully inlaid into the texture. It is a very self-sacrificing book too. Very very good.

---

[1] *Goldsworthy Lowes Dickinson*, by E. M. Forster.
[2] The reference is to *Howards End*, Chapter xviii: 'It was as if a motor car had spawned.'

I am late in telling you so: but I was away in Wolverhampton when I got the book, and my leisure for reading is now so small. March next, and I leave the R.A.F. for a boundless prospect of leisure at Clouds Hill. Let us try to meet then.　Yours T. E. S.

525: TO W. BRADBURY[1]

8.VI.34.　　　　　　　　　　　　　　　　　　　B. P. B. Co.

Dear B., Your letter to-day. Norrington spoke to Personnel about you some months ago, and it was on the strength of what they agreed that I made that remark to F/S Pitt.

Now that it's come to the point (it is seldom possible to do anything before, in the R.A.F.!) N. is unfortunately away, at Gardeners for a week and then on leave for a week.

So I've given your note to B-G[2] who will see the P[ersonnel] man and try to smooth your path. B.G. will do his best. I would have preferred N. as he is a serving officer and knows his men better. There should be no particular difficulty, however. Please let me know as soon as you know anything.

It's in my mind to try and ease you into my place, when I go in March next.[3] Keep this to yourself and do not bank too much on it. I think it may come off, if my successor is to be a serving airman: but other powers far senior to me are suggesting that the Boat Department will need two Technical Officers (civilians) as overseers when I go.

I feel flattered but not convinced. There is plenty for one whole-time, but certainly not enough for two. The fitting side of it (metal-work and engines) is the leading job, and any bright fitters would soon mug up the allied-trade accessories, such as hulls and lay-outs and equipment generally. However we shall see. I'm rather hoping that Treasury will say the civvies cost too much.

At the moment we are all up to the teeth in 5 more target boats. Three or four are [to] formate[4] from here to Bridlington in

---

[1] Corporal in the R.A.F.
[2] Beauforte-Greenwood, the officer in charge of Marine Craft, Air Ministry.
[3] See letter No. 561.
[4] To proceed in regular geometrical pattern.

ten days time. We may spend the first night in Ramsgate and refuel from Manston. If you hear of us, come down and look at the fleet. Target boats are fearful and wonderful things.

After that come 6 bomb-loading dinghies, difficult and not very satisfactory craft. Meanwhile the new four-cylinder Gardner 60 bhp[1] light Diesel is having its gear box fitted for test in 159 hull. Probably Charlie Butters will instal at Northam and watch over the first trials. We have also a Lion installed in a 50 mph hull awaiting S-P's[2] return from the Baltic to O.K. her for test. It might do more than fifty, too!

As you see, I've bitten off more than I can finish by March. There will be many loose ends for the next man — The Junkers Diesel (500 hp), Monel and Tungum propellers, the new cruiser-pinnaces, an armed 45-footer for the Chinese Customs, fast targets and tugs for the War Office. All these things are afoot. I reckon two years programme all laid out and filled.

Best of luck to your theory test next week. I altogether agree with your verdict upon the course — yet in such an eyewash job as this of mine, the power to sling the gab would be very helpful. If I could drop a farad or an aspect ratio occasionally they would let me walk over their bellies.

As I say, let me know what happens, good or bad, with yourself. And if you do get to Batten, for the love of Mike, get me back the remains of my tool-kit. A new bike coming, and not a spanner except I borrow it from Leonard's bag. Yours   T.E.S.

526: REPORT ON TRIP OF R.A.F. BOAT NO. 200

[9. *June* 1934]

R.A.F. 200 left Southampton Water for Plymouth, her present station, on Saturday, June 6th, at ten minutes to eleven in the morning, carrying a special crew of five R.A.F. personnel, and nearly twice her normal capacity of petrol and stores. Wind S.W., freshening to 20 miles an hour. Tide contrary. Sea choppy.

[1] Brake-Horse-Power.   [2] Scott-Paine, of the British Power Boat Co.

Engines first set at 2300 to Hurst Castle at 11.40 a.m. There the sea became rougher, the wind and tide coming in together and raising a broken swell. Off the Needles the meeting of the cross-seas provided quite a rough twenty minutes, during which the boat was thrown about vigorously and took some heavy splashes of spray aboard. No rolling, and speed only temporarily reduced, as from Swanage onwards advantage was taken of the shelter of the Portland promontory to open her up to 2500, her best cruising speed, and run over the swell. From St. Aldhelm's Head onwards she was a perfectly dry boat, and this opportunity was taken to refuel her main tank from cans of petrol carried on deck, and from a temporary tank taken on board for the special run.

Portland Bill was reached at about two o'clock, and passed close inshore. The long seas at Lyme Bay gave further opportunity of keeping up her cruising speed economically, as the boat ran lightly over them, steadily and dryly. The tide was now ebbing in her favour. Course was set slightly to the N. of Start Point, and the Devon Coast sighted at 4 o'clock, a long and heavy rain storm making visibility very limited. Off Start Point more heavy and broken seas were met, and speed was again reduced for a time, past Prawle to Bolt Head off Salcombe. The wind then dropped off to half its former strength and the boat was opened up to 2300 revolutions and held cleanly on her course to Plymouth at twenty past six p.m. No water remained in her bilges upon arrival, thanks to the self-bailers arranged in each of the boat's compartments. No solid water was shipped during the run, and the main cabin remained perfectly dry and comfortable throughout.

The engines ran faultlessly. A little oil was added to them on the way, to maintain their pressures constant at 40 lbs.; except for this they were not touched or thought of. The water outlet temperature gauges stood constantly at 45° Cent. The oil put in amounted to 1 gallon, as noted. Before the run to Plymouth was started, the boat did two and a half hours of test and trial running in Southampton Water. The trip round took seven and a half hours; so that her total running on the day came to 10 hours. During this she used 90 gallons of petrol, and 30 gallons remained in tanks upon arrival at Plymouth.

The whole run was made at cruising speed, no attempts to save time or take the shortest course being made. The boat was slowed down whenever the sea conditions made it comfortable to do so.

527: TO LIONEL CURTIS

13.VI.34.   13, *Birmingham St, Southampton*

A puzzling awkward book — your *Civitas Dei* which has lain on my table being read, chapter by chapter, in the evenings after work, for months. Awkward because it poses awkward questions and will not lie still. Puzzling because it is like one side of an argument, like talking with you for all of a day and afterwards forgetting all that oneself had said.

It must have been awkward and puzzling to do, also. Its selection of events from the history of the world seems at first sight so arbitrary, so disproportioned. 'At first sight' for as one reads the argument comes to the surface, like a chased whale, and sounds again under a new sea, and again spouts. I suppose it is likely that in no other way can an argument be carried across the faces of the world and of time. An exhaustive, subtle, engrossing and (even for me, a Gallio in polity) persuasive book.

The bright things in the book are the single-sentence aphorisms that star its pages. Your statements-on-abstract-questions are *perfect*. I always admitted it, you know. Years back in our joint history I pointed out to some careless politician your deadliness in argument, seeing that whereas an Englishman easily resolved each particular problem, and seldom troubled his head to see a principle behind his practice, you—an Englishman— always began with the general, and from that deduced the manner of dealing with particulars. *Civitas Dei* is you at your most devastating. I salute a great swordsman.

Incidentally the book displays courage and common sense, as well as wisdom. For these three things the public will spit on it. Great swordsmen don't care. I disbelieve in even the flat of the sword against wart-hogs and bog-rats. One does not wrestle with a chimney sweep, said someone.

I haven't any comment to make on the book: upon each paragraph you and I could spend a happy hour, while Pat's[1] carefully chosen lunch grew cold or was eaten between arguments unheeded and unknown. But I refuse to write you a book in reply — more especially as I think I agree with this one. Touché, I think.

Points: page 8, bottom: 'industrial' excavators: I doubt it. Railways aren't industry: quarries have helped us little.

       page 18. St. Paul's 'years' in Arabia aren't too certain.

       page 20. Sunlight, thunder or pestilence 'are'; better say 'and' for 'or'.

       page 33. Sheikh, I think.

       page 93. Is it Crookes or Crooks?

       page 102. For Tiberius read Hitler, for Tertullian Goering.

       page 111. Blighter who mistranslated that *Odyssey* was called Shaw.

       page 119. In the quotation, four lines from its end, a possible hiatus after men.

       page 129. 8 lines from end. For theatres read amphitheatres, I think, to accord with modern custom.

       page 150. The leaping coronella is rather a rare reptile in the New Forest, I think.

       197. Technically a carpenter is a craftsman and not a mechanic, now and in the past.

       263. Professor Oman would tell you that King John did not *sign* the Great Charter. If he does say so, tell Prof. O. that you said sign to see how many pedants would presume to confess themselves to you.

       265. Bonfire is a good thing. You mean bale-fire: unless you mean just fire.

       268. Don't you anachronise by talking of the Hall and the Abbey as being on opposite sides of the *road*? See suggested reply to Mr Oman, above.

Not a misprint visible to my eye, but I have read it with bleared and sore eyes, after motor-biking and motor-boating. Forgive the lapses of an aged sense. A very very good book. It's what I call making use of history. Ever,   T.E.S.

[1] Mrs. Lionel Curtis.

528: TO B. H. LIDDELL HART

14.vi.34   13 *B'ham St., S'ton*

I was in London for a few hours yesterday: with Eliot[1] and two Bow Street experts we interviewed [*name omitted*], my imposure, and persuaded him that he was not me. To my relief, he agreed at once. Had he stuck to his statements I should have begun to question myself.

I owe you many thanks for putting me on his track. He was a little worm of a man. The game has been going on for some time, and has extended from the Zoo to Ward Lock, the publishers. Comically enough, he has been under observation as a case by the specialists of a mental institution, still under my former name. We arranged for him to write to his various victims, and explain that there had been a personation. I am not flattered at the thought that he got away with it successfully. An obviously feeble creature with the wrinkling face of a chimpanzee.

I did not feel like London, so came back here at once afterwards. We start for Bridlington (four armoured boats) in a few days.

The photographs[2] are, as you say, excellent beyond the wont of such things. Mrs. L.H. is flattered. You and I get off about par. Very good. I am sending one to China as proof of my health!

I cannot think of aught else to tell you — oh yes: I haven't seen that angry review[3] of my *Odyssey*. Do send it; if it's amusing. About time somebody stood up for Homer. I've wanted to do it myself.

529: TO E. M. FORSTER

26.vi.34   13 *Birmingham Street, Southampton*

Dear E.M.F., Got back from a coast-wise crawl in R.A.F. target boats to find two (amongst other) telegrams needing apology: one from you, suggesting a visit to S.S.[4] with you

---

[1] The Hon. Edward Eliot. See letter No. 522.   [2] Snapshots taken at Hythe.
[3] By a professor of Greek at Sydney University.   [4] Siegfried Sassoon.

present (Ah, if I could: company for heroes) and one from S.S. saying 'Come afterwards, if you like'.

Only, where is it? I should write to S.S. and say why I failed (for the best of reasons, surely, absence at sea). All I know is S.S Heytesbury . . . but where is it, as post-towns go. Not far from Wylie, but that helps my bike, not my letter.

I hope you found him assured and glad? I'd like a line, if you can manage to put anything on paper about him.

I hear that heath fires are raging at Clouds Hill, and am sad and afraid for the little place. I've grown to love it, I fear. What fools we become! Yours   T.E.S.

530: TO GEOFFREY KEYNES

6.VIII.34   13 *Birmingham St., Southampton.*

Dear G.K., Did your nervous system prickle with discomfort a few weeks ago, when S.S. and I at Heytesbury dissected your nature? Not that you came badly out of it. What mostly worried S.S. was your being, despite it all, a surgeon. I had your *Machaon*[1] in the back of my mind, but kept silence upon it. A very luminous work, for all its smallness. You see surgery come to its end eventually, extinguished by the growth of knowledge — but that is the common fate of everything human. Science is not a treasure but an organism, expanding itself, halting, dying, but germinating quickly into a new growth. What seems to me noteworthy, today, is the shortness of our generations, the rapid tempo of life. We seem to accelerate in geometrical progressions.

One must not write like that to a scientist. I intended to tell you of my raid upon Heytesbury. All visitors there intrude, as yet, I think. He and she are like children alone in the world.

The huge house, which they are furnishing for a song in memory of the mansion style: the gardens, so lavishly kept up, the quiet sun-impregnated park: the two laughing strangers running about it, making pretence to own it. Yes, Heytesbury was rather like one of the great villas of Roman Britain, after the Legions had gone.

[1] *Machaon, or the future of Surgery,* by Geoffrey Keynes, M.D., F.R.C.S., appeared in *The Lancet,* May 19th, 1934.

S.S. looked abnormally happy. Much of his hesitant diction has been forgotten. He speaks easily, and is full of private jests. He looks so well, too. I was told that he captains the local cricket team, and the village postman (having exhausted the war books) is going on to his poetry.

Whether it will last I cannot say. The barometer cannot always stand so high. It will be time for outsiders to come along, then.

We spread out on the floor all the proofs of your engravings, with the lovely title-page, and gloated over them. It will be a gracious and estimable book.[1] The reduction of the mandibles and flourishes at the ends of poems, or to fill up short lines, has been tactfully done. The pages are clean and legible. However they yet have to be read slowly, almost word for word. Type has grown so instinctive to our eyes that we swallow printed books a line, if not a paragraph, at once. That is all right, for things currently written, like *The Times*; but these chiselled and balancing verses of S.S. deserve to be read almost as minutely as they were made. What an iconic stillness there is about his images, now! He has progressed from flesh-and-blood (in *Counter Attack*) to bronze. As for *The Old Huntsman*, it is difficult for me often to trace the connection between that early man and S.S. now. At Heytesbury he showed me his first published poems, the cricket verses. They seemed an age away. One of the good things about S.S. is that he changes freely and completely.

What a careless rag-bag of a letter. All it need have been was a note on the Gooden title piece. As I have told you, I think it plainly yet precisely lovely.

The price of the book worries me. Two guineas is so much. I have not, as yet, even brought myself to order a copy. S.S. is one of the few poets that keep step with their generation and I would have him generally read. Him and Yeats and Day Lewis — whereas it would not matter if Noyes and Humbert Wolfe cost pounds and pounds.[2] Can you contemplate a plain edition afterwards, which I can send to my friends?

[1] *Vigils*, by Siegfried Sassoon, engraved by Charles Sigrist, with a frontispiece by Stephen Gooden.

[2] The argument I had used against the Subscribers' Edition of *Seven Pillars of Wisdom* in my first letter to Lawrence.

Enough of S.S. I feel always like an intruder in his company. I would like him to do just what he liked. [10 *lines omitted*]

An awful letter — but I have enjoyed the proof title for months, and kept on saying that I must write to you. Hence this over-doing it — too late. Yours   T E S.

531: TO ERIC KENNINGTON

6. viii. 34.   13 *Birmingham St., Southampton*

Oh yes, I take my time; indeed I take time to answer any letter. Why? Well, I think it is mainly laziness. There is my R.A.F. work which has to be done to schedule, willy nilly: so what is not compulsory is told to wait on the mood. And letter-writing, being difficult, is seldom the mood.

For it is very difficult to write a good letter. Mine don't pretend to be good . . . but they do actually try very hard to be good. I write them in great batches, on the days when at length (after months, often) the impulse towards them eventually comes. Each tries to direct itself as directly as it can towards my picture of the person I am writing to: and if it does not seem to me (as I write it) that it makes contact — why then I write no more that night.

Yet, as you would say if I was there to hear you, the letters as they actually depart from me are not worthy of this strained feeling. At the far end they appear ordinary. Yes, that is because I'm not writer enough to put enough of myself into any work. Or better, because there is not enough of myself to share out and go round. There has been, upon occasion. Both *The Seven Pillars* and *The Mint* (but *The Mint* especially) stink of personality. Where has it gone? Don't know. I'm always tired now, and I fritter myself away month after month on pursuits that I know to be petty, and yet must pursue, faute de mieux.

'What the hell's the matter with the chap' you'll be asking. You send me a sensible working-man of a letter, reporting progress — or at least continuity — and I burble back in this unconscionable way. I think it is in part because I am sorry to be dropping out. One of the sorest things in life is to come to realise that one is just not good enough. Better perhaps than some, than many, almost — but I do not care for relatives, for matching myself against my kind. There is an ideal standard somewhere and only that matters: and I cannot find it. Hence this aimlessness.

It is a pity, rather, that I took so many years teaching myself this and that and everything: for now that I'm full enough to weigh a lot, I've nowhere in which I want to use that weight. If I'd cared less about learning and more about doing things, the story would have been different. It's a common way in the world. The fuller the cask, the less active the damned thing seems to be.

Let's come down to earth. You still carve. I still build R.A.F. boats. On March 11th next that office comes to an end. Out I go. Clouds Hill awaits me, as home (address will be Shaw, Clouds Hill, Moreton, Dorset) and I have nearly £2 a week of an income. So I mean to digest all the leisure I can enjoy: and if I find that doing nothing is not worse than this present futile being busy about what doesn't matter — why then, I shall go on doing nothing. But if doing nothing is not good — why then, I shall cast loose again and see where I bring up.

Is C. well? And Xto?[1] Say that I hope to come and see you some day ... please. Yours   T.E.S.

532: TO B. H. LIDDELL HART

18.VIII.34   *Southampton*

I've come up for breath, after a long period under the weather — including two wasted voyages — to find myself probably too late for the boat. Here is this, the Australian jest[2] about my *Odyssey*, to return to you. The delay in that was because I sent it to Bruce Rogers, the printer, whose idea the *O*. was, and whose is half the responsibility, at least.

I find that his withers are as little wrung as mine. The version was definitely made for non-scholars. I doubt whether this fellow is a scholar (he betrays no knowledge of Greek, only of other translations: had he known or used the original, he could have sunk my translation without trace. I slur over the difficult places, always) but he is assuredly a pedant: and pedants are sure

[1] Celandine Kennington and her son Christopher.   [2] See note to letter No. 528.

to dislike it. I'm glad to have seen it, all the same. He gets quite hot, sometimes!

Here is the Viollet-le-Duc[1] catalogue-entry, too. It isn't a book to possess, but one to refer to. I call it a cheap price for what must be, in England, a rarity. I expect it is common in Paris: but then there is the franc exchange.

Also a letter from a woman to return.

As I said, I fear I have missed the boat, for lately a viking ship came from you: so I place you in Norway. Those longships were very finely built, and perfectly seaworthy. In a short sea they must have been wet: but if one hove-to and waited for it to blow out, one would be safe, if not comfortable. I don't think the Vikings were marvellous seamen. They coasted, and came ashore whenever it seemed threatening. Had they had better ships, they would have gone to America long before the Spaniards.[2]

533: TO THE HON. LADY FULLERTON

27. VIII. 34   13, *Birmingham Street, Southampton*

Dear Lady Fullerton, I waited to finish with this proof[3] before writing to you. Please don't regard it as a lent book, it is only an uncorrected proof. Publishers send these out to their readers, who correct them and throw them away. Please dump it in the W.P.B. when it begins to bore you. Of course the actual book will be better, in print and paper, and will have pictures.

I find it a remarkable book. It is old-fashioned in the sense that the traveller does not keep one eye on himself, in the Peter Fleming manner. He is simple and very observant, and natural. I think he has a gift for writing too, despite some bad grammar.

Thanks to your kindness and the Admiral's, what should have been an awkward visit to Plymouth turned into an excellent time. I do hope the result (or one result) will be Naval help in

---

[1] Author of the *Dictionnaire Raisonné*, the first great work on French Medieval Architecture.

[2] As a great reader of the sagas Lawrence must have known that the Vikings reached America.

[3] Of *Desert and Forest*, by L. M. Nesbitt.

proving or disproving the value of these new hulls of ours. I have a feeling that we are on the edge of a great development in ship-building ... not cargo ships, but fighting and express-passenger ships! That would be a very good thing for the Navy, and for this country. It seems the only possible answer to the Air, so far as I can see.

However we musn't get technical. When we all retire we must try and see each other again. And meanwhile my best thanks. Yours sincerely   T. E. SHAW.

534: TO SIEGFRIED SASSOON

6 Sept. 1934   13, *Birmingham Street, Southampton*

Dear S. S., I should have sent the Belloc book[1] so long ago, but the idea settled in the depths of my mind that I owed you two copies of the Bruce Rogers *Letters*[2] (to raise the disposal-value of your *Odysseys* by 8°/₀) and it was a long time before I could get to my cottage and collect the two copies. Don't try to read them. They are sale-room items, only.

The Belloc gave me some fun. I was sorry he had not pulled it together and shaped it into one tight poem before printing it: and as a water-drinker I incline to smile a little at these wine-palates. They deprive themselves of the faculty of judging between waters, by coarsening their throats with fermented drinks — and that is a loss to their tastes. But H.B. writes with such bragging ferocity that I love him. What a man. I wish I felt as strongly about something.

I hope your grass and trees are enjoying some rain — and yourselves too. Getting wet is better than getting sunburnt, usually: that is, when deliberate.

In March I become a lay-resident in Dorset ... and then let us meet (not too arrangedly) somewhere. I'd like you both to see my cottage, because it fits me, as Heytesbury seemed to fit you. Yours ever   T.E.S.

[1] *An Heroic Poem In Praise of Wine*, by Hilaire Belloc.
[2] *Letters from T. E. Shaw to Bruce Rogers.*

535: TO SIR RONALD STORRS

13.IX.34.

Dear R.S., I have been away for a while, during which your p.c. sat on the edge of Southampton Water, peacefully, in blazing sunshine. If all of the years were like this, no man would need to go abroad.

I hope you are comfortably settled in London, without the urge to gad about.

Here are your K.[1] articles, which I return because I know how rare fugitive writings become in time. Once I did three or four columns in the same paper, but I have never seen them since; they gave me the idea that newsprint is a bad medium for writing. The same stuff that would pass muster between covers looks bloodless between ruled lines on a huge page. Journalistic writing is all blood and bones, not for cheapness' sake, but because unnatural emphasis is called for. It's like architectural sculpture which has to be louder than indoor works of art.

So I'd say that these articles of yours read too 'chosen' for press-work; but that in a book they would be charming. You write with an air (as you talk: your conversation is a work of deliberate art, modelled on Harry Cust, and polished to perfection by long practice, great pains and great gifts) and airs need the confinement of walls or end papers or what-nots to flourish. But do airs flourish? I think they intensify, suffuse, intoxicate. Anyhow they are one of the best modes of writing, and I hope you will try to write, not fugitive pieces, but something sustained or connected by the thread of your life. Look, for instance, at Coleridge Kennard. There is a man of poses and artifices — yet his work, when set in an architectural frame, carries itself. If you can only find a line on which to string your stories you will make a very good book.

I've often said to you that the best bit of your writing I ever read was your dictated account of the report of an agent's interview, pre-revolt, with the Sherif of Mecca on his palace roof at night. If you could catch atmosphere and personality, bluntly, like that, it would be a very good book. These K. articles might

---

[1] Articles by Storrs on Kitchener in *The Times*, June 5th and 8th, 1934.

2F

be blunted. You'll have to use the word 'I' instead of the bland 'secretary': get more speed and harder hitting into your sentences. You talk superbly. It's only a matter of writing not more literarily than you talk, but less even. Anglo-Saxon words and the thumping surprises and brevities which you can bring off so well in speaking. Forget the despatch and the F.O. and try for the indiscreet Proconsul![1] Yours   T.E.S.

536: TO LORD CARLOW

14 September [1934]

Dear Carlow, It's an extraordinary place-name[2]; but then, if one knew Gaelic all would be clear. As for fishing — but then, I'm not sporting. Nor do I greatly like eating the creatures.

On the whole, therefore, Southampton is better for me, especially in this heavenly weather. We are adding the best September I can recollect to a year that has been safely dry beyond the average. 1933 splendid. 1934 — splendid. What a 1935 we have earned! You do well to think of a new yacht. If our arrears of rain come, we will all creep into it (two by two) until it comes to rest on Ararat.

Your voyage sounds like a rough one, at least you were not wrecked like Noel Coward on Corsica from his M.L.[3] But then, you are a navigator. Noah again, you see. Noah was a navigator.

My life? Average busy. In the last month it has been Wolverhampton, Kent, Nottingham, London, Plymouth. In between times I have been at Hythe. No more big boats, for this year. There are 5 dinghies to finish, a new Diesel to test in a round-bottomed hull, and a 24 foot boat for the Australian Air Force.

In the winter they propose to move me to Bridlington, in Yorkshire, to oversee the repair of the ten R.A.F. boats that work the bombing range there. That would cover November to February — and February 28 is world's end for me. It will be queer to wake up that morning and know that thence-forward there is no single thing that I must do. I have never owned my

---

[1] Compare letter No. 537, p. 821.   [2] Acharachle.
[3] One of the M.L. class of boats used against submarines in the Great War.

whole 24 hours — never in my life yet — and this liberty will come so abruptly that I shall be puzzled what to do with it. I wish there was any one thing in the world that I wanted to do. Perhaps vacancy will breed a wish.

Yes, when the *Firefly* comes speeding south again, give me a ring at Hythe and let us meet. I shan't have anything to give you, but your company is exhilarating. So do ring that 102 telephone; if you are in some friendly house that will let you borrow their mouth-piece for trunk calls. It lies on my conscience that you so often ring up vainly, Yours ever, T.E.SHAW.

[*2 lines omitted*]

[In the next letter, the paragraphs numbered 1 to 6 were written after the main body of the letter, on blank pages opposite to the passages of which they are extensions. G.=George, refers to Lord Lloyd throughout].

537: TO LORD LLOYD

30.IX. 34 *Southampton*

Dear G.L., I find the following notes tucked into the back of your very-much-enjoyed-and-valued Vol II:[1]

Eloquence of p. 1. Pity G. didn't oftener let himself go in pure writing. He does it with rhythm and selectivity.

And his biblical suggestion for our Middle East interest is subtle and persuasive. The decay in bible reading may lie at the root of some of our present incuriousness.

P.9. He apologises for a subjectivity of narration — would that it were so. He writes with the far-away and rather regretful omniscience of the gods.

He does not make any too clear the very mixed reception by the Cabinet of the Milner report — and the way it was deliberately shelved by Winston etc.

He gives some life to that procession of dummy frock-coats called 'Ministers' in Egypt — Rushdi, Said, Adly, Nessim, Tewfik and the rest. Not one of them ever mattered for a moment. There were only 3 parties, us, the King's, and Zaglul. In politics (as apart from statesmanship) the moderate is a vehicle only, a

---

[1] Of *Egypt since Cromer*, by Lord Lloyd.

negligible quantity, expressing or conveying only the impulses of the minority that knows what it wants — or does not want. I think one of the faults of the High Commissioner system was that he met too many pashas.

1.   My statement, when they offered me the succession to Allenby, was that I'd shut up the Residency, except as offices, take a room in Shepheards, and ride about Cairo and the Delta on my motor-bike: — and yet 'run' the Government of Egypt, from underneath! Out-Eldoning Gorst, if I may put it so. T.E.S.

p. 51. G. slates Curzon — excellently — for his silly letter.

p. 58. Winston tried to get my consent to take Allenby's place, & so to accept his resignation at this moment. I think G. ought to have said what Allenby did in London, subsequently.

p. 76. Did anybody really care a hang about the Election?

p. 79. The High Commissioner couldn't meet Zaghlul, and wouldn't (quite rightly) support the King. No third course was open to him. To coquette with the Moderates was a waste of time. Zaghlul was so big that till he died no other Egyptian could hope to lead.

p. 102. George puts his finger on the weakness of our position in Egypt. We cannot assist our cause by using force, which is our only final resort. If our army and navy are helpless, what can the High Commissioner do? His chapter on Stack's murder is good — barring the relegation of Antonius[1] to the Preface. Our ultimatum erred profoundly in two ways — by putting the half million indemnity in our pocket (we had not morally earned it — except by our mistakes) and by introducing the Gezira irrelevancy. A nation of shopkeepers, even at moments of high tragedy.

p. 113. Goodbye to Allenby. It was a pity that the old soldier ever took on the political job. You are kind to him, here.

2.   Your book is too consistently kind. The Black Panther[2] should spring, often, and kill sometimes. This Dickensian bonhomie can be overdone. Odd that you should be thought a case-hard reactionary!

---

[1] Mr. George Antonius had rendered valuable services during the Egyptian Army crisis which followed the murder of Sir Lee Stack.

[2] Nickname for Lord Lloyd.

It was a pity that G.L. did not write a plain page to tell his unskilled readers the truth about the Egyptian Monarchy. I know and he knows: but the public don't — and should. It explains much of our impotence in Egypt, I think.

p. 122. 'Selected' — not the right word.

p. 123. The Sudan was a detail. I'd have cut this chapter by 90°/₀, and kept to my main line.

p. 140 onwards. Yes, I know. You harp ever so often on the Declaration of 1922. It gets almost like the Head of King Charles. I wonder when it became so much your foreground: not till after your leaving Egypt, I fancy. To select one of our 46 or so Declarations upon Egypt, and elect to fight upon it is tactics: and you are above all a man of principle. I had rather have seen you declare 'My object in accepting Egypt was to save as much from the wreck as I could, by playing for time, by keeping our official mouth shut, by strengthening our position in Egypt, by cold-storing the F.O.' Your professions upon 1922 read like lip-service.

p. 150. You should have been blunter about Jarabub, and how you put it across the Palace: and you take just the right note, I suppose, about Nashaat. At both these points I should have sunk the Proconsul in the Person, and uttered yawps of some vigour.

p. 156. Admirable. I only wish you had had someone like me out there with you. Your dignity, with a merry devil of an assistant on the staff, might have stirred up an agrarian movement that would have side-tracked politics in Egypt for a generation.

p. 164. Good. Your dry humour tells. Your narrative of the crisis in the next few pages is lively, clear, worthy. A very good chapter. Chapter xi also good writing. Excellent thumbnails in the portraits of Ministers. If only you didn't keep yourself so neat, always. The book is too judicial, too sober, too good.

3. At this juncture let me remind you of the eleven hats, (hats for the Court, for the Play, for the walk-round-the-park, for the train, for grouse-shooting, for golf, for the House of Lords, for Cowes, for going to the Pictures) which are to be counted on the marble table to the right of your hall door. They are significant.

p. 188. I should have welcomed, here, an attack upon the absentee landlordism of Egypt, and the ineptitude of the tenants: with an economic digression upon the financing of the cotton crop.

The Army Crisis. Two chapters is a lot for this. My opinion of the Egyptian Army wouldn't take that much to express. I fancy you deal with it so elaborately because you want a hit at poor Baldwin: and to exemplify the deepening rifts between you and Downing Street. It is the beginning of your down-curve. I wonder who the F.O. critic of you was? You ought to have named him, I think, and explored his motives.

4. Nobody lets daylight into the corridors of the F.O. Why not? Why should those clerks be kept in cotton wool? A little fresh air and exercise would colour their pallid faces.

You are very good on the stupidity of the Sarwat and other negotiations with H.M.G. Your picture of our Cabinet is damning. Very good, too, on the death of Zaghlul. Egypt has marked time since, awaiting a new tyrant.

5. Of course Zaghlul was echt-Egyptian: it just shows how the natural leader will be of Nile blood, and not a Turk or Albanian pasha. First Arabi, then Zaghlul.

p. 233. 'I could entertain little hope of a treaty.' In fact, you were getting on quite nicely without one, and saw no need of it.

p. 235. You should have quitted at this point. You and London were walking different, and diverging, roads.

p. 274. Assemblies Bill. A curious history. What did you intend to do if the Ultimatum had not been accepted? I think you were too greedy in your advice. The Egyptian Cabinet gave way, and your success would only have embittered them. We gained the substance.

p. 277. You and Austen probably rubbed your hands over the action of King Fuad — but he's a poor creature. I prefer the Wafd! To be complete the book needed an outspoken pen-portrait of Fuad.

p. 295. Awful storm-in-a-teacup, this question of local taxation. It gives the notion that Whitehall were determined to pick a quarrel with you — or were looking with grave suspicion at your views.

p. 303. 'The Egyptian Government was convinced' . . . yes: but the Labour Government didn't esteem your Egyptian Prime Minister. Their leaning was towards the Wafd. Muhammed Mahmud wasn't, in their eyes, much more of a democrat than yourself. Your ideal of administrative stability and no politics was their notion of hell.

I don't pay much attention to your next pages. No Labour Government could resist the temptation to recall you. It meant so much credit in the *Daily Herald*, at no cost to themselves. You overstate it when you complain that 'grave charges' were brought against yourself. Your recall did you more good than your appointment — and you know it. If Winston had kept his mouth shut, your pinnacle would have been even higher than it is. What has harmed you, politically, has been your breach with Austen and Baldwin. To be sacked by the Labour Government was glorious: to have been at odds with the Tory chiefs is less assuring.

Your selection of the 1922 Declaration for your basis does not convince me. You ignore the Declarations of 1919, 1920 and 1921. You flout the Declarations of 1923 and 1924. If there were few in 1925 and 1926 and 1927 that was your fault: as High Commissioner you very selfishly refused to let the British Government go on declaring itself. They managed a couple as soon as you went; but since then the fashions have changed, and declaring is becoming a lost art. I suspect you of *liking* the 1922 model.

6. You can write pages of moving, sonorous, and yet nervy prose. It is a very good book. Egypt has been fortunate in her historians.

The concluding chapter slowly rises in tone to a really touching height. Nobody can finish it without rather liking you, for the truth is that you are a fundamentally likeable person, quite human, quite modest, and disarmingly unsure of yourself. You only pontificate and snarl and thump the table to convince your own mind. By nature G.L. is a little bit of a poet, [*seven words omitted*] and liberal. He has made himself, is quick-minded, eager in well-doing, and not patient. He suffers stupid people too long, and is too anxious to do the right thing, to the sacrificing of his own wishes. If he were slightly more selfish, and had fewer loyalties, he would be a great individual success in politics. As it is, he will always be the despair of his friends and the chief target of his enemies. One of his queer traits is to like his enemies and to to be liked by them — more than his friends. 'Friends' and 'enemies' used only in respect of politics. No parallel is to be drawn as concerns such private people as his   T.E.S.

Who very much enjoyed the book, and is very proud to be on (occasional) writing terms with him.

Caveat. The original notes were quite short, and had to be translated to be intelligible. But this fairly copies them.   TES

538: TO C. DAY LEWIS

16/11/34   *Ozone Hotel, Bridlington*

It's an impertinence to write to a writer; but I cannot help it. Your book on poetry[1] is only half an argument. So long as you wrote poems I was content with reading them. Over *Dick Willoughby* I laughed. This, as I say, is different. Probably you are hardened against letters from unknowns.

Why does your period stress so much those few thought-ridden poets, Donne, Vaughan, Crashaw — not Herbert, I think? I suspect a little fashion in it, started perhaps by T. S. Eliot[2] with his cranky passion for the knuckle-end of the Church of England: and that's a consequence, probably, of his being an American. A parvenu longing for roots.

When you talk of poetry being as hard to read as to write you must be thinking of the metaphysical poets. They are much harder to read than in the writing, for they weren't very good philosophers, or clear logicians or subtle metaphysicians. They were afraid of plain statement, and feared that their real minds were foolish. Poets of today feel often that their real feelings are

---

[1] *A Hope for Poetry*, by C. Day Lewis.

[2] A curious example of forgetfulness. The revaluation of Donne's poetry, which Leslie Stephen thought could interest nobody, was the work of Rupert Brooke and Geoffrey Keynes, men of Lawrence's generation and period, and of Sir Herbert Grierson of the older one.

foolish. So they splash something about shirt-sleeves or oysters quickly into every sentimental sentence, to prevent us laughing at them before they have laughed at themselves. But you must qualify that saying about poetry being difficult, either to write or to read. Some poetry! *Kubla Khan* took no writing, nor any of W. Morris' early verse, nor Chaucer's tales, nor most of Shakespeare's speeches. *Paradise Lost* is as easy to read as the *Aeneid* or *Don Juan* — yet these must have been hard to write. Dandyism in style revived with l'Isle Adam.

I hesitate also to attach great weight to the war. My age made me just ripe for it, and I went through it with as major consequence a great faculty for wasting time uncomplainingly: perhaps a sense that time and myself and you and things done or to do were not very significant. As a historian by training I shouldn't like to think that accidental participation in this one war of the infinite series past and to come had made me put it bigly in the foreground of any but its victims. Sassoon wasn't tough enough. It broke in him a good lyric writer. I was glad to see your sensible regard for D.H.L. and Owen. As for Hopkins, he would repay a closer study on the pathological side: the Jesuit at war with the sensualist. I think fear of giving himself away led to those inversions and syntactical quirks. A very fine poet!

I'm glad you concentrated on Auden, Spender and yourself. Auden makes me fear that he will not write much more. Spender might, on the other hand, write too much. You have given numbers of us the greatest pleasure — though for me *The Magnetic Mountain* was a qualified pleasure. In this book your suggestion that it may represent an approach to politics rejoiced me. It was not merely explanation but recantation, I thought. Poets are always (and have been always) savagely political: and the real politician, the politician-by-trade, always carts them properly. Poets hope too much, and their politics, like their sciences, usually stink after twenty years. I call our time very rich in poets, quantitatively and qualitatively.

To make your book invaluable you need to give us an exposuremeter by which we could pick out the one lighted window in the houses they build. Your quotations, — from yourself and the others — aren't those I (or anyone) would choose. Do you believe in a yardstick, or any solvent to divide even the very good from the very bad? We imagine such degrees between contemporaries, while we know in our hearts that the Saintsbury of the future will see the affinities between you and Noyes and Doughty and Housman and Herbert Trench and Drinkwater and Humbert Wolfe and Hodgson and Blunden and William Watson, and will wisely explain the common impulse that led to all these similar blooms.

Thank you for an exciting and quite unsatisfying book: but if you want to make us really happy, you will expose yourself to the risk of writing some more poems: and for the ear, not the eye. These cheap typewriters do poets much harm.   T E SHAW

539: TO J. G. WILSON

20.XI.34   *Bridlington*

Dear Wilson, I'm glad you are taking the plunge;[1] and glad it's you and not me, for there'll be a lot of work entailed. The moving of that enormous stock, its re-valuation . . . heavens! If I were wealthy, I would run an account; but alas, after March I come down to 26/- a week. This R.A.F. has been not merely a joy but a living, to me.

Is the new to be Bumpus? And where will it be? And when? Send me a 6 lined letter of news, as soon as you decide to let people know. I expect you will be printing a notice, for all your victims to learn where the new altar stands.

I laughed when I read your very proper sentence about our dear Queen.[2] Clearly it is time the *Chaucer* relapsed into obscurity again — otherwise it will grow too big for my cottage. It's a wretched book, as Morris built it: too heavy to go by post! So will you please send it to Sir Herbert Baker, at No. 2. Smith Square, Westminster — by one of your delivery people, if you use such aids to distribution? I have some stuff to collect and

---

[1] Wilson had decided to move Bumpus's bookshop from 350 to 477 Oxford Street.
[2] H.M. Queen Mary had visited an exhibition of books at Bumpus's bookshop and had remarked upon and examined Lawrence's copy of the Kelmscott *Chaucer*, which he had lent for the occasion.

take away by rail from Baker's house, there, and shall bear off the *Chaucer* amongst it.

I agree with you. It's a marvellous possession, and *very* good to read. I haven't ever finished it, so it will solace my empty hours at Clouds Hill, Moreton, Dorset, which is the address, I hope, of my old age. A very fit address for an ex-airman, too. [8 *lines omitted*]

Hoping to see you one bright day. Yours   T.E.S.

540: TO ARTHUR HALL[1]

20.XI.34   *Ozone Hotel, Bridlington, Yorkshire*

Dear Brum., This note came wandering after me up here, and I send it on.

No news here, except that I need a set of twist bits: or if not a set, as near a set as I can get. I've been to the only tool shop and they say 37/6. This is beyond me. The only other place at Bridlington is Woolworth's. [8 *words omitted*]

So I remembered that you were a perfectly good carpenter, who recently had to search all over Brum for tools when you were helping Lord Nuffield. Tell me — are there any shops in Brum which sell second-hand carpenter's tools . . . and if so, could you give a look-see upon twist bits? I want decent ones, to do the R.A.F job here: and I have the notion that afterwards I may be able to wangle them (if part worn) away to my cottage, to comfort my leisure. There is so much wood work to do in that cottage, and my tool-kit isn't good enough. I need a draw-knife, bradawls, two gimlets, a morticing chisel, mallet, bench-vice, soldering iron, tenon saw. Just that. So do use some of your spare time to see if the Brum pawnshops are full of good goods.

Cheerio: how's the job? Mine here is 8 till 6, with a dinner hour and two 'smokes'. And regular.

Write also about that visit to Brum. Can we get snapped on a Saturday afternoon? Choose a day without football. How's the Villa?[2] . . . ha ha.   TES

---

[1] Late Aircraftman, of Birmingham.   [2] Aston Villa is a Birmingham Football Club.

541 : TO LORNA NORRINGTON[1]

23.XI.34   *Ozone (Ugh!) Hotel, Bridlington, Yorks.*

Dear Lorna, A lovely day — drizzle, S.W. wet wind, chilly. Doesn't the name of the Hotel give you shivers? I'm sure it was meant for the summer visitor; but it is empty now, and I have two warm and comfortable rooms. So that's excellent.

I'm sorry to hear that you were ill after you got back from Hythe. I hope the boating was not to blame: and I'm sorry that my own little boat would not work. You'd have enjoyed a few minutes in her.

Yes, I'm sorry to be leaving the R.A.F. so soon: end of February, it is; and probably I'll be at Bridlington till then, so we won't see each other for a while. My cottage, however, is near Hythe, so if you get down there next summer, you must drop me a line, and offer me a boat-ride if I will come to see you at the Yard! Yours ever   T E SHAW

542 : TO H. W. BAILEY[2]

23.XI.34.   *Ozone Hotel, Bridlington, Yorkshire*

Dear Bailey, Good Lord, No! One doesn't answer this sort of thing.[3] Bray is quite an honest muddle-headed sort of chap, who believed everything he wrote. His publishers are just splashing what little he wrote about me in the hopes that people will take it up and talk about it and so buy the book. It is pure advertisement and unfortunately it advertises me as well as the book, bother them. Next best thing for a public man, after being praised, is to be loudly abused. It pays.

Only, I don't want notice, and the only way to gain quiet is to be quiet. This will not last six months and doesn't matter.

But you see, of course, that there are two sides to the question. I've been absurdly over-praised by Lowell Thomas, Graves and Liddell Hart: praised for all sorts of accidents as if I had intended

---

[1] Aged 14.   [2] Bailey had served under Lawrence in Arabia.

[3] *Shifting Sands*, by Major Bray, contained statements about the part Lawrence had played in the Arab Revolt, and about his motives, which were corrected by Allenby and by Liddell Hart in interviews published in a Sunday newspaper, shortly after the book appeared.

them and praised for leaving undone things that I simply hadn't the power to do. I think we all worked like beavers, and did the best we could — but if we had known everything there was to know and what was to happen in the next 20 years and a few other little things like that, well, we'd have done marvels; nearly as much as Thomas & Co. say we did. Don't worry about it. Shoot only when necessary. [3 *lines omitted*]

[The offer, of which the following letter is a refusal, was of an extremely important position in the City of London and was the biggest compliment that had been paid Lawrence for many years. The best brains in the financial world were asking him to work with them, because they felt complete confidence in his ability in everything he undertook.]

543: TO THE HON. FRANCIS RODD

23.xi.34   *Ozone Hotel, Bridlington, Yorkshire*

Dear F.R., By the accident that a friend of mine was passing my old lodgings in Southampton as my older landlady was handing your letter back to the postman, it reaches me here, only ten days late. I expect to work in Bridlington (on the ten Air Force boats that are refitting for next season) till the end of February when the R.A.F. goes on its way without me.

I shall feel unutterably lost without my blue covering. Twelve years it has been, of engrossing work with a very happy companionship for the off-duty hours. Few war-relics have been so fortunate as I in the aftermath.

I've even saved money and Robin Buxton has invested it for me until it brings in more than 25/- a week. So if you bogeymen[1] (I read the *New English Weekly*!) don't crash the solar system shortly I should be able to live at peace in my cottage, with all the twenty four hours of the day to myself. Forty-six I am, and never yet had a whole week of leisure. What will 'for ever' feel like, and can I use it all?

Please note its address from March onwards — Clouds Hill,

[1] Rodd is a banker, as well as a traveller and the author of *People of the Veil*.

Moreton, Dorset — and visit it, sometime, if you still stravage the roads of England in a great car. The cottage has two rooms; one, upstairs, for music (a gramophone and records) and one downstairs for books. There is a bath, in a demi-cupboard. For food one goes a mile, to Bovington (near the Tank Corps Depot) and at sleep-time I take my great sleeping bag, embroidered MEUM, and spread it on what seems the nicest bit of floor. There is a second bag, embroidered TUUM, for guests.

The cottage looks simple, outside, and does no hurt to its setting which is twenty miles of broken heath and a river valley filled with rhododendrons run wild. I think everything, inside and outside my place, approaches perfection.

Now to business. That enclosed message ought to have been instantly dealt with, by a plain Yes or No. Will you please say No, for me, but not a plain No. Make it a coloured No, for the Elizabethan of [Blank's] naming has given me a moment of very rare pleasure which I shall not tell to anyone, nor forget.[1]

Please explain how by accident it only came to me tonight, when I got back after work, too late to catch the evening mail from this petty seaboard town.

These newspaper praises lead a fellow to write himself down as a proper fraud — and then along comes a real man to stake himself on the contrary opinion. It is heartening and I am more than grateful.

There — please work all that into your 'NO': explain that I have a chance (if only I have the guts to take it) of next year possessing all my time. Yours ever   T E SHAW.

544: TO B. H. LIDDELL HART

28.XI.34   *Ozone Hotel, Bridlington, York.*

I found this today, digging deep into the pile of slowly-rotting letters that await a reply: I fear it is yours, and should have gone back long ago.[2]

---

[1] The sponsor of Lawrence for this position, whose name is omitted, was acting on the Elizabethan belief that a man who was good at one thing would be good at anything else.

[2] Liddell Hart explains: 'An American historian, Professor Earle, had written to me in June, putting some questions bearing on Middle East affairs before and since the war. I had sent his letter on to T.E.'

I've not anything to say about it. The 'trace' of the Hejaz Railway was drawn by Meissner, a German Engineer. The technical staff (foremen and section men) were mostly Greek and Italian.

Mustapha Kemal was a great patriot, and anti-foreign from 1913 onwards. His Nationalism was founded to combat the pro-German tendency of Enver.

The Oil Company had (contrary to rumour) little or no influence in deciding our policy towards Mesopotamia. I can say this with complete assurance. I know foreigners are always smelling rats — but in practice if you tell a F.O. man that 'Oil' wants this or that, his reaction is to go dead contrary to their wishes, in the name of honesty. I can truthfully say that neither Ll.G., nor Curzon, nor Bonar Law, nor Arnold Wilson nor myself paid any heed to the Anglo-Persian or the Imperial Petroleum Co. The British policy in Mesopotamia was decided on purely Imperial lines.[1]

P.S. I think the German Bagdad participation offers were more onerous than advantageous to us.

545 : TO ERNEST ALTOUNYAN

9.XII.34.   *Ozone Hotel, Bridlington*

Dear E. A., Ah me, but I find you difficult. Your verses[2] twist and turn like eels with your thought ever slipping away from me, and with never a stop. It moves and moves, and moves, until I find myself longing for somewhere to sit down and rest. Have you, in your re-reading of it after the heat of creation, noted its restlessness? All of you and it jigging non-stop?

I think you'll have to make pauses, sometimes, for the readers to draw breath. Imagine it a song you had written, with never a blank half bar even, for the singer to refill her lungs. Now that I have more leisure and cool blood to confront the mass of it, I see that the prose headings and divisions and arguments for which I pleaded were not to explain it (it explains itself) but so many

---

[1] See p. 288.   [2] Unpublished.

landings on which to halt a moment. Otherwise you'll kill your readers. Spenser killed them with his *Faery Queen*. I've read that, heaps and heaps of times. I lived on it till 1916 or so. Yet I know that nobody can really grapple with it because it runs on too fast. What a river you were, in those months. Now you must feel like the Kuweik in September.

No letter from you lately. I had hoped to hear what was the cause of your money forebodings. Do felicitate yourself on having a real craft, a hand-craft, behind you.[1] To be a writer and no more is to be misshapen, lop-sided, unstable. Solid poetry cannot be written by a shaky man. If you let yourself fall down easily you condemn *all* your work. I feel great power in these writings: everything except the power to stand still, and that can only come in a revise.

I haven't got on well with them. I don't know what it is, but my eyes are letting me down. In open daylight I can read, perfectly: and my far sight is as good as good. But by night, or in dull daylight, something goes wrong. I have to put pressure on some nerve within my head, and say 'focus yourself on that line: *see* it' before I can read it, and then not for long. This happened to me once before, in 1927 in India, and I ceased reading and it passed off. But now here it is again. As the light goes now by four o'clock (and we work till 5, from 8) this is cutting into my enjoyment of your script. One cannot get the picture of it in spasms between blind times.

Please commend me once more to your father. We used to get such pleasure from his company, twenty years ago. Queer that I should now spend my evenings in yours! And to D.[2] my regards. Poetry, a profession, a wife, some children: no wonder you are distracted sometimes with over-much going out of you. I hope you may soon balance your mind's account, and write me cheerfully.

Don't be hasty over the poems. They probably represent your life's work, and they will keep. We owe no duty, no immediate duty, to our generation — unless we are journalists.   T.E.S.

---

[1] Ernest Altounyan is a surgeon.   [2] Mrs. Altounyan.

546: TO HENRY WILLIAMSON

11.XII.34   *Ozone Hotel, Bridlington, Yorks.*

Dear H.W., I have so much the better of you: for when I want a talk, it is just putting out an arm and taking a book from my shelves. That's as it should be, at least; but just now I live in this house with a jesting name (here to watch the refit of ten R.A.F. boats for next season's work on the bombing range) and for a word with you yesterday I had to go to York and lay out three days' pay on *The Linhay*[1] . . . which I have been dipping into, with satisfaction, all this too rough Sunday. Too rough for a walk from lodgings. No clothes, poor fire for drying.

What a sentence for No 1! Do you find it hard to begin books? Let me take down your hackles by two quotes from the *Linhay* bad sentences. P. 67 'how heat and the floating algae . . . takes' . . . P. 36 'many old bucks are caught in gins which otherwise would eat young rabbits.'

It isn't fair, for I would like to write like you, easily or grudgingly but copiously, able to make a sentence of all you see and do, with a catching intimate easy speech, like a man in slippers. For a mannered writer, you have the best manners in the world.

Don't vex yourself over Walpole or Shanks or Hanks or Banks: or vex yourself only because they discourage your book-buyers. Or do they? The best way to sell a novel was to persuade the Bishop of London to preach against it. I can conceive Hugh Walpole being second-best. I fancy writers get so wrapped up in their own sort of writing, that they find all variations from it bad. At least, they seem to me to make poor critics of contemporary stuff. You write almost disarmingly well. You write better than Richard Jefferies, splendid fellow though he was. Better for me, that is: I feel more heart and see less eye, in you. You look for the unusual, he for the average. Of course he had an awful life. No Alvis, no country contentment, or comfort, anyhow. Few concerns aside from earning, and no war to light his background. We learned a lot in those years, which makes us immemorially older and wiser than the old or the young.

Stop burbling? All right, I'll stop. Let's get back to history.

---

[1] *The Linhay on the Downs*, by Henry Williamson.

2G

I am discharged from the R.A.F. (my life, almost) next March: and cannot make even the ghost of plans for afterwards. There is my cottage in Dorsetshire (Clouds Hill, Moreton, Dorset) on the heath just north of Bovington Camp, between Dorchester and Wareham. I'll have to go there for my savings have not been very successful: I'll have only 25/- a week. So I must sit under my own roof, and do nothing till I want to do something. Is that a programme?

I hope an Alvis may visit me, for if you ever go to England, via S. Dorset is not much further than via the Plain. In my cottage is no food, and no bed. At nightfall there is a flea-bag, and I lay it on the preferred patch of floor in either room. The ground-room is for books, and the stair-room is for music: music being the trade-name for a gramophone and records. There are five acres of rhododendron and fires every evening from their sticks. It sounds to me all right for living, but then so does your valley — yet you often throw yourself angrily away from it. Well, we shall see. But bring your own food. I shall have no cooking. It smells in so small a house. A tiny house. No water near, alas!

As I said, at the beginning, I have the advantage of you, for when I want a word with Henry Williamson, it is only the stretching of an arm to a shelf. If I want him objective, there's *Tarka*: subjective, there's *The Pathway* or *Falcon* or *Dream of Women*. I feel greedy, at having so much of so many people (though not the half I should have had. Books have gone from my hands wholesale while my back was turned. My cottage holds only the rags of a collection) and at liking them so much without making a return. (By the way, did I ever lend you the typescript of my R.A.F. book? Surely I did, poor return though it is.) Sometimes I sit on my chair amidst the books, afraid to open any of them, not having earned it. If only I could write like I read.

Stop burbling again? All right, but this sea rushing and sliding in my ears won't stop. My room is a tower room, over the harbour wall, and the waves roll all day like green swiss rolls over the yellow sand, till they hit the wall and run back like spinning rope. I want to walk out in the wind and the wet, like at Clouds Hill, and can't, for my landlady's sake.

Keep cheerful. And let us meet after my R.A.F. life is ended.
Yours   T.E.S.

547: TO SIEGFRIED SASSOON

17. XII. 34   *Clouds Hill, Moreton, Dorset*

Dear S.S., Written, this is, from Bridlington: but I have been reading your *Vigils*, and I felt I could not write about them from the 'Ozone Hotel'. My cottage is where they should be read.

They have deeply moved me. They are so . . . gentle, I think I want to say. To be read slowly and in sequence. The rather conscious script helps them, by delaying the eye. These poems are like wood-violets and could easily be passed over by a man in a hurry. When I came to the war-poem I checked for a moment, sorry: but soon saw that it was right. Not if you had never written before; but here in its place among your poems it helps, by translating into quietude the fierce moods that held you for *Counter Attack* and the Satires. Every other one of the 22 looks forward. I can feel the solidity of the war-anger and the peace-bitterness under the feet, as it were, of these poems: they are all the better for it, but so far from it: so far above and beyond.

Sometimes, in a lyrical phrase or an adjective of accumulated beauty, I can link them to your earlier work: but only thus, externally, by a common ornament. Yeats has walked along something of the same path. His *Tower* poems are like the ash of poetry. People offended his taste by putting *Innisfree* into all the anthologies, because they liked it not for the poetry but for the green sap running through it. You are not ashamed of 'suddenly burst out singing' but growing shy of it. Just a word or two hint at happiness, and then your blotting paper comes down.

I will try to write you again about them when I have grown into them a little. They aren't like Shakespeare, at all. They are human and very careful and faint and solitary. Each seemed to me to shut one more door of your gigantic house. There are heaps more doors yet; and of course you might one day open one. By their implications I date the first drafts of all of them from before that day at Christchurch, and I feel that you, yourself, have changed colour somewhat since the writing. You have more colour now, I think, and more colours too.

But these are exquisite poems, exquisite. First reading was

like sitting under an autumn tree, and seeing its early leaves falling one by one. I shouldn't like you to go on writing *Vigils*, world without end. They are seasonal fruits, but lovely. You can dare them because of your past fighting: and those of us who have deserved a rest will feel them and be grateful to you.

That last little volume of political poems[1] had frightened me a little, for you seemed to look back. Here you go a full stride forward. Cheers, and long life to your pen. It is doing us good — and proud.   T E S.

I've read this through and see that I've forgotten to say that these things are streets ahead, in power and beauty and calmness, of anything of yours I've ever before seen. You presumably know that: but when, I ask you, are you going to reach your prime? Near fifty and still a growing poet. It's like T.H. isn't it? He grew till seventy. Don't answer this rot!

548: TO JOHN BUCHAN

20. XII. 34   *Royal Air Force, Bridlington, Yorkshire*

Dear J.B., You'll wonder why on earth I write, and what I now want. Answer — only to tell you that my R.A.F. twelve-year engagement is within a few weeks of running out. I have not tried to extend for 24 years, because my age then would make me a ludicrous airman, even if I lived the whole twelve more. But if I could have remained perpetually young, nothing would have pleased me better.

If you meet Mr Baldwin in the near future, will you please tell him that the return to the Air Force secured me by him (on your initiation) has given me the only really contented years of my life? Please say that I've worked (and played) all the time like a trooper: that my spell of service has been spent in doing my best to raise the pride and respect of the ranks, and to make them pleased with their duties: that amongst my jobs have been a re-organisation of aero-engine overhauls in India, the ground-work for the 1929 Schneider Cup, and lately the development of the

---

[1] *The Road to Ruin*, by Siegfried Sassoon.

marine-craft side of the R.A.F. In four or five years we have trebled the speed and yet reduced the prime cost and running cost of *all* the R.A.F. boats: and now the War Office and the Admiralty are borrowing our boats and copying or adapting our designs for their purposes.

I tell you all this not to boast of it, but to show that you and Baldwin, in gratifying what may have seemed to you my indulgence, have not harmed the public service. I have done all I could, always: and could have done far more, if they had given me more rope. The Air Force is pretty good, down below. I think it deserves more imaginative handling than it gets.

However this note (meant to be a paean of gratitude to two admirable men) mustn't descend into politics. I owe the two of you more than my twelve years work (and another twelve on top of it, were I young enough) in the sheer satisfaction it has been. You have me very hopelessly in your debt: and thank you both very much for it. Yours sincerely   T E SHAW

Some day I'm going to ask another favour — that you will read my notes on the making of an airman, about 60,000 words of typescript, that date from 1922. They aren't to be published: but I rather suspect that as writing they are almost good — or at least a sight better than my previous attempts at your art! I would value (and keep very dark) your real opinion.

549: TO S. L. NEWCOMBE[1]

20. XII. 34   *R.A.F., Bridlington, Yorks*

Dear James, (alias Stewart a word I only cry out when about to be sick — alias Monster, plus or minus other things)
Dear James, as I said before Ahem
Dear *James*

Third time lucky. We're off. Merry Christmas. No, I don't really mean that. I follow the Golden Rule. May you have a quiet Christmas with nothing abnormal to eat. Avoid gluttony, above all. Remember your figure, and the figures your parents ought

[1] Aged 14.

to have. If you observe them over-eating clear your throat gently, to attract attention, and say 'A bit high, this bird?' That will put them off it. If they bring in plum puddings and things, remark in a blasé accent . . . the normal speech, I mean, of Eton . . . 'Isn't it jolly, papa, to keep up these old customs? It's like Dickens, isn't it, I mean, what?' That will throw a chill over the whole meal-time — I mean orgy. You owe a duty to your family at Christmas.

Will you please congratulate your male parent on the balance sheet of Turner and Newall.[1] I think it reflects great credit on his colleagues. Will you also ask him where I can buy the beastly stuff they make? It's no good a private person writing to their head office for some asbestos slates, or a sack of magnesite or a roll of foil. I want a shop address, preferably in London, Bourne-mouth, Dorchester or Poole. I want advice about roof-slates, by the way. Neighbour possesses a tin roof. I want it sheathed in something less visually offensive. Recommend . . .? What?

Will you please congratulate your female parent, on whatever in your judgement is her most salient merit of the past twelve months? Be discreet: select some merit likely to have come into my notice, and congratulate her on that in my name. If you have difficulty, owing to richness or penury of choice, please tell her that I think she's looking very well . . . and add a hint about the digestive severities of the festive season.

Don't wish them any particular sort of a celebration of the birth of Christ. I only do one Xmas letter per year, and that's not really a letter. I send Lady Astor a reply-paid wire of 'Merry Xmas' and she wires back 'Same to you.' If I was Hore Belisha I'd standardise it at a special tariff for quantities. Or do I mean Kingsley Wood? Yours ever   T.E.S.

550: TO C. DAY LEWIS

20/12/34   *Royal Air Force, Bridlington, Yorks.*

Dear Day Lewis, It feels odd to write to a book or two: which is, I suppose, what I am doing. You could say 'ancestor worship',

---

[1] Colonel S. F. Newcombe is a member of the firm.

which is admirable, or would be, if ancestor aforesaid was not having to address the present. Let's forget it.

The *Hope for Poetry*[1] isn't a bad book at all: you dislike it because it's your latest. Give it seven years and you will enjoy it as much as I did.

My Latin wasn't ever much good, so that I have never enjoyed Catullus. I suppose that means that I have never justified the time I spent trying to learn the beastly language? There seem to be ten good Greek books to every Latin one.

Your point about the metaphysicals interested me. Perhaps I don't read them because the sciences are closed books to me. I can't feel that knowledge matters at all. There must be theories, apparently: but one can spend the few active years one has so much more enjoyably out of doors on practicalities — like my R.A.F. boat-building. So I try not to want to think.

By 'recantation' I didn't mean a change of politics, but that I hoped you were getting bored with politics. The ideals of a policy are entrancing, heady things: the translating them into terms of compromise with the social structure as it has evolved is pretty second-rate work. I have never met people more honest and devoted than our politicians — but I'd rather be a dustman. A decent nihilism is what I hope for, generally. I think an established land, like ours, can do with 1% monists or nihilists. That leaves room for me. The trouble with Communism is that it accepts too much of today's furniture. I hate furniture.

Your inclination to re-value theme is very significant. I shall enjoy your next book. I feel that *Ulysses* (slightly) and Proust (enormously) depend on social conditions for their public, which means their value.

Ozone Hotel is not a permanent address. I doubt whether I have one. Perhaps 'Clouds Hill, Moreton, Dorset'. But I shall enjoy buying your book, so please don't send it. After all, you don't write so many as all that! yours   T E SHAW

---

[1] See letter No. 538.

551: TO G. WREN HOWARD

31.XII.34   *Ozone Hotel, Bridlington, Yorks*

Dear Howard, Cape, they tell me, is half round the world: well, well. He will find his books there, too, I daresay.

I'm interested in three of your recents: the Yeates *Winged Victory*, first. How good that he did it in time.[1] It is a very good book, and every R.A.F. mess has a copy. I advise everyone to get it, and hear nothing but praise of it. It would sell stoutly in the States, I think.

The Nesbitt *Desert and Forest*, second. That book has a benediction of old-fashioned decency over it. A classic of the XIXth Century, written out of its time. It also I hear highly praised by all my friends.

The third is Cecil Gray's book on Heseltine.[2] Does it go well; and how are the first two doing? Short of saying anything in print about them, I would do anything I could to help their sales. [9 *lines omitted*]

The sting is in the tail — and I, alas, am the stung. My Air Ministry chief wants a copy of Liddell Hart's book about me. Will you please send it to Captain W. E. Beauforte-Greenwood, Room 366, Air Ministry, Kingsway, W.C.2.

That makes two copies I have had from you, for J.C. sent one, by request, to my Mother in China. Will your Office please render me the necessary account?

And may no other blitherer ever write a book about me till I'm dead, for Heaven's sake.

I hope the firm has its head above water, and that you are finding pleasurable things to do. Yours   T.E.SHAW

552: TO A. E. CHAMBERS

26.1.35   *Ozone Hotel, Bridlington, Yorks*

I had hoped the new nerves would have reformed your handwriting into legibility. God alone knows how you got into the

---

[1] V. M. Yeates, the author of *Winged Victory*, had recently died.
[2] *Peter Warlock: A Memoir of Philip Heseltine*, by Cecil Gray.

BRIDLINGTON 1935

Post Office with it ... or did they mean you for the crypto-graphic department?

It looks (line one of text) as if your leave was not till April 22. Springtime, and that is merry heaven in the land. The second date may be 31 April or 11th May: or is May a verb? Lower down, after an illegible passage, you cycle the Watford by-pass daily. That looks as if you were really better, but I shall not believe it till my eyes convince me.

My plans are to leave the R.A.F. early in March, and make my way slowly by road to Clouds Hill. Thenceforward it lies with the Gods what I do.

The cottage will never be *less* than partly yours, whenever you want it, unless some scurvy married couple borrow it from me again. I don't like women in my place, anyhow; but am too perfect the little gent to refuse them. There have been none threatening as yet this year, however.

It may be wholly yours, if I'm away: it is too far ahead yet to guess. I'm going to try to live there by myself. If I can't afford it, that will be one thing. If I'm bored, that will be another. If I'm plumb scared and go dotty, that will be entirely another. At present all I can say is that I'm going to begin living there, and see.

Your coming will be a delightful change, if I'm there. You know the conditions, so I needn't explain them.

The ram is working strongly, and the cisterns and taps are all full of water, my side and Pat's.[1] The big tank has cracked at its north end, and will have to be undercut and buttressed. I shall get this in hand as soon as the weather permits, so as to have my water ready against the summer fire menace. So perhaps we can fill up by April 22. Or has your long convalescence put you out of love for the agonies of chill water? Civilisation begins with heat (artificial).

I hope you got your books. They were piled ready for post at Christmas: Pat still camps his side of the road. He has an idea of marriage in the offing, and a definite girl in view. If she is a housekeeper by nature, he & she could make a good thing of that spot. But I don't know her views, of him or of country life.

There we are: the only certainty in this world is that the cottage

[1] Pat Knowles.

in March, April, May, June, July, August, or September will be glad to receive you — and friends, if desired. What about the owner? Ah, I can't prophesy. But if I know that you are coming, it will attract me to get free and come there too. 'Free' supposing that [no] outside entanglements beguile me away from home, which God forbid. Yours   T E S.

553: TO BRUCE ROGERS

26.1.35   *Ozone Hotel, Bridlington*

Dear B.R., I was down in London and Southampton (with one night in my cottage — all very well — and a sitting to Augustus John who finished a head of me in oils and did a drawing) while your letter and the play[1] came to Bridlington. So I did not read them till last night, and today I have cabled Yes to you. But I shall not expect it to be accepted. It is too thin for our complicated generations. Her doing it is a compliment to us: to you, me and Homer. Where she quotes, there is a limpid remoteness in the words and I feel them to be beautiful.

No remarks . . . what could one say. But kangaroo and bombardment both project rather from the background. I doubt alabastos, too: aryballos or alabastron, surely? As for fairway, of course you are right. I saw that beach in Phaeacia, with the building ships on the right, and the drawn-up ships on the shingle to the left, with the crowds moving down the ridge between them. That was why I said fairway, because the comers had to thread the lines of ships. Elsewhere — anywhere except [where] the ships are on the scene — it should be highway, roadway, pathway, causeway, or just way itself.

As I said, it is too simple. We need not dream of any fees from it. If there were, let us respect our joint property in Homer XXVII.[2] I call it yours and mine, always. The script is going back.

Don't be alarmed at my vigour in replying. I am not keeping up a correspondence. It is only that I had to answer about the play: and while at it, I shall go through your whole letter.

---

[1] A play by Mrs. Helen Kittredge, based on the Nausicaa chapter of the *Odyssey* and using some phrases from Lawrence's translation.

[2] In the Translator's Note Lawrence wrote: 'The 28th English rendering of the *Odyssey* can hardly be a literary event'.

Yes, I had gathered something of the mishaps to the *Conrad*.[1] They say the anchor-cable parted, which should not happen with today's metals. It is very hard luck on Villiers; I hope he is successful with his Insurancers. His salvage experiences have not been happy. I suspect they did most of the damage.

I shall look forward to the promised photograph of the MUG. Likeness — yes, it's desirable in a named ship; but I hope you have kept scale and broad treatment, too. A figurehead should grow clearly out of the vessel's lines. How fortunate that Conrad had that streamlined face . . . or hair on his face, anyhow. What I shall always remember is his lame walk, with the stick to help him, and that sudden upturning of the lined face, with its eager eyes under their membrane of eyelid. They drooped over the eye-socket and the sun shone red through them, as we walked up and down the garden. Put the camera man in a boat under the forefoot, and have a fish's-eye view of the head, please!

The Press sent me the little *Odyssey*. A good-looking book, great value for six shillings, which I suppose is its present cost. I saw it only for a little while, but thought it to be the same plates as the former Oxford Press edition, not re-set, but smaller-looking. Probably they have trimmed the margins. I continue to feel that we did best in putting the Note by the translator at the end instead of the beginning, in our edition. It is a postscript in spirit, critical; not an introduction, an aperitif. I am glad to hear it is selling somewhat; but it will still be too dear for a school book. Should you meet Finlay[2] ever, will you give him my regards and thanks? If you say Victoria Hotel, Damascus, he will smile and remember our meeting in character, him in Khaki, me in skirts; but deadly tired, I was: unable to talk, or at least to think before I talked.

No, there will be no Korda movie of me. The rumours grew thick, so I bearded the lion-maker and persuaded him to leave me alone. It would have been more ballyhoo, and after March I want retirement.

I am glad you find New York not too depressed. I find my

---

[1] The *Conrad*, a sailing frigate, owned by Bruce Rogers's friend, Alan Villiers, had been wrecked.

[2] John Finlay, author of *Pilgrim in Palestine*, now editor of *The New York Times*.

London men of business growing anxious again about England. Probably 1934 was really a boom year for us. Ah well: provided my nest egg is big enough to bring me 25/- a week, existence at Clouds Hill will be possible. Beyond those rhododendrons the world may have its booms and slumps — provided that I eat.

The binding the *Bible* has been a long problem. My eyes look at all English materials, now; but so far I have not seen anything comfortable and light and clean and warpless. It is time we invented a new board.

After the 1st of March my only fixed point is Clouds Hill (Moreton, Dorset) where letters will wait for me. I may keep away for a while, if the Press features my discharge: or if I feel restless at too much freedom. It is going to be strange.

When you come, we must try to see something of Dorset together. I shall be learning it, and your eyes will profit my judgement. They all think it a good county, for keeps. Yours

T.E.SHAW

[The drawing of Lawrence in R.A.F. uniform by Augustus John, mentioned in the foregoing letter, was destined for a purpose explained in the next letter. Lawrence's mind was running once more upon buying a small printing press, and, for his first book, planned to print a few copies (perhaps as many as a hundred) of *The Mint*, or possibly of a rewritten and greatly expanded *Mint* which should contain the record of his later and happier experiences in the R.A.F.

Pat Knowles tells me that the printing press 'was one of the items in a programme we set up and talked about during the Xmas holidays of 1934. We discussed the erection of a building over the firetank; a good place, for the atmosphere would always be damp and good for printing. He intended to get a small hand press but at that time he was not certain about type; after *The Mint* he intended to print "some good but obscure poet". By May of 1935 I had begun to get together materials for the printing shed and we hoped to start on it by September of that year and get the press in full swing by January of 1936.'

Pat Knowles also tells me of a conversation during a weekend early in March 1935, in which Lawrence told him there was a possibility he would not be able to live at Clouds Hill after all, and that the printing of *The Mint* might have to be postponed for years, since he might again be asked to undertake the reorganization of Home Defence, and if so would feel he had no alternative but to take the job, as it was work of such national importance. After Lawrence's death, Winston Churchill, in an appreciation, wrote: 'I hoped to see him quit his retirement and take a commanding part in facing the dangers which now threaten the country.'

554: TO PAT KNOWLES

31.1.35   *Ozone Hotel, Bridlington*

Dear Pat, Only a month more: I cannot persuade myself that it is really all coming to an end. Almost daily I trip myself up in some research or advice concerning boats, something that might take weeks to fruition.

Good news the Ram. Also good about your affairs. [4 *lines omitted*]

I caught the train just after you went (it was a good idea, that pillion ride — though pretty awful pillioning with a suitcase and masterpiece in one's arms!) and dumped the m-p[1] in London on Emery Walker, to be photographed half size and collotyped, 100 copies. That is my frontispiece — 'airman 1934 type' — if ever I put together my notes on the R.A.F.

China is obviously well,[2] and busy too, the house being full of visiting Europeans. It must be wearing on the soul to have everybody who calls a godly person. Not my society, theirs ... They expect to be on their way down to the coast for England, this time next year: and have clearly no other plans.

I have thought of a good idea, which is enclosed in the shape of many largish stamped envelopes. Will you save yourself trouble by dumping into them, at intervals of about ten days, all letters that arrive there for any of my names? I have warned some of those with whom I have to correspond, that my only future address is Clouds Hill ... and so they are likely to send their letters for me more and more there.

---

[1] i.e. the Augustus John masterpiece.
[2] Lawrence's mother and elder brother were in China.

Don't make a task of it, nor attempt regularity. Just send up an envelope when the mood takes you.

Chambers (Jock) has made a life-like noise again, and asks if he can spend his leave (April 22 — May 11) in the cottage. I have said yes, with me or without. [6 *words omitted*]

I am trying tonight to write some letters to Yorkshire fellows, and if I manage them, will enclose them for you to post. If I send them from Bridlington they may make efforts to see me . . . and that is inconvenient. The boats keep me all day, and are dull things for strangers.

Otherwise? Nothing. Let's see . . . enquire re clinker from Dulleston. Fire-logs from Wareham. Digging out the end of the tank for putting on a reinforcement. The last should be done and dry by April, for us to fill against the fire raisers: I am nearly complete with the engine-and-hose-and-pump order. Yours

T.E.S.

555: TO G. WREN HOWARD

31.1.35.   *Ozone Hotel, Bridlington, Yorks*

Dear Howard, My sense of fitness makes me feel that all book people should take their hats off to Walmsley[1] . . . whose *Three Fevers* has proved not a flash in the pan but the hefty beginning of a family. Of course he may count the E.African flying shocker, but I find it less admirable than these coastal sketches, which are charming. I want to prefer him to Stephen Reynolds, for he has not his predecessor's irritating sense of the difference between a complicated man and a worker: but am restrained by the sense of the surprise I feel, each time he brings a book off. It seems to happen ultra vires, or widdershins; it shouldn't be possible to write great books like that . . . or are they just charming books? I don't know, for I like them too well to judge.

Back to the hat-lifting. My R.A.F. cap (which will crown me for only a month more) doesn't lift; yet after it I shall probably never own a hat. So I can't actually honour him: but if he still sticks close to Robin Hood Bay wouldn't it be fitting if I ran up

[1] *Foreigners*, by Leo Walmsley, had just been published.

there late in February with one of these R.A.F. boats we are over-hauling here (I could call the jaunt a trial, and it would take an hour each way, weather being good . . . and if it was dirty weather I couldn't very well suggest such a trip) and blow my Klaxon towards his beach? He is not reverenced in his own county, I find. In Hull and York and elsewhere I have had mild rows with the local booksellers for their not selling him in basketsfull. I should like to show the R.A.F. here how they stand towards him. If it was summer time, I'd take the fleet of ten boats up and serenade him properly: but we don't launch the first till Feb. 20 and I'm due out by March 1. So that's impossible. Perhaps he is away, spending his enormous royalties at Monte Carlo? Anyhow he's a real writer. Cherish him. Yours ever   T.E.S.

556: TO K. W. MARSHALL

1.2.35.   *Bridlington*

Dear Marshall, It is certainly awkward, and prolongs the un-certainty.[1] On the other hand, at the Assizes you come before a professional Judge, with a possibility of cultivated judgement.

I cannot advise, for my experience of English Courts, or Law, is nil. G.B.S. is an insecure guide, too, I should say; and besides Mrs. Shaw is desperately ill. She didn't like *Boy*, however.

My inclination would be to say 'This book was published in 1932 and has been continuously on sale, in England and the Colonies, ever since, passing through four editions. It was never challenged, or described as indecent, till last month at Bury, in Lancashire. Here is a book of all the reviews it has had, in the British Press. You will notice that no reviewer appears to have perceived any moral objection to the subject or the treatment, and I will confess that no such notion had occurred to myself, until the Bury Police action. I then examined the book again, and perceived that the challenged passages could be charged with an offensive significance, by a trained mind.'

'While the case has been sub judice I have suspended the

---

[1] The prosecution of *Boy*, by James Hanley published by Boriswood Ltd., for indecency.

further circulation of the book, but in justice to the author (who has written many novels of very high critical reputation) I am hoping that your decision will permit the edition again to be released. Naturally I am willing to do all in my power to prevent further copies being supplied to booksellers in the Bury neighbourhood.'

But in cold fact, you'll be in the hands of your counsel. I should go to Chatto & Windus and ask them for advice, pointing out that the case is likely to react on the future of *The Furys* — and they will probably tell you who is a likely lawyer to brief. I believe that the actual briefing has to be done by a solicitor.

It is very hard luck. If you can find out who at Bury initiated the prosecution, and send me his name and address, I will try and get him sent from Paris, by post, a regular supply of really indecent literature: something that will show him the difference between pornography and works of art. Yours ever,   T.E.S.

Bitter Water[1] ... the middle section, of life on the Baltic or N. German island, was most admirable reading. A real slice-of-life. I agree with O'Flaherty's introduction, that Hauser may or may not be going to be a writer — but that he is a personality, anyhow.

The sea or ship-in-port-and-at-sea passages were not so good, I thought. They were like Hanley-and-truth; a bit anaemic. But a real good book, which I should have been sorry to miss. Extravagant of you to send it me, all the same. I do hope this trouble is surmounted. Let me know at once, please, when anything happens.   s.

557: TO ARTHUR HALL

1.2.35   *Ozone Hotel, Bridlington*

Dear Brum, Back again, and the photos here. Thank you very much for them. I call them pretty good: we are as regimental as two button sticks. I look like an S.P.[2] who has just caught you in the Bricklayers' Arms. Anyhow there can't be any row hereafter

---

[1] *Bitter Water*, by Heinrich Hauser.
[2] Service Policeman.

if I call you shortarse, can there? I had no idea I was so tall and thin and hard looking.

If you see the damsel who took them, please thank her from me for painting my face so smooth. She has done us both good: for you aren't (in real life) much more of a masterpiece than myself. Ask your wife for her candid opinion of us as beauty chorus.

How did Aston Villa do tomorrow?

I'd hoped to send you some tool-money, but the luck is still dead out. Wait a bit, before you get anything, please. It might be another fortnight before Felixstowe send me my credits. It is not easy to arrange that sort of thing by post, when you don't know the pay bloke you are writing to.

Meanwhile I've been having a dust-up with the Chief Constable of your town. A Mrs. [name omitted] kept on writing me letters, calling me Jim and begging me to go back to her and all would be forgiven. I answered the first one, saying that I wasn't her Jim and didn't know her from Eve: but she went on writing about twice a week, from a place called [name omitted].

So finally after about two years of it, I wrote to your Chief Copper and asked if as a favour he'd send an officer to ask her to abate her nuisance. I asked him to do it gently, because I thought the poor woman was mad.

He replied in a letter (not even marked confidential) addressed to the C.O. Bridlington R.A.F. saying that Mrs. [name omitted] had been interviewed, was 53, eccentric, a widow, two grown-up sons: that she had lived with me throughout the war, while I served in an Anti Aircraft Battery at Birmingham — and that she had no intention of ceasing to write to me.

I sent him back a snorter, saying that I had written to him personally, and he had no right to communicate with my supposed C.O. That in a big station his action would have led to much gossip, very unpleasant to myself: but that fortunately there was no C.O. at Bridlington, and so his letter had come direct to myself!

Since then, complete silence from my abandoned widow *and* from the Chief Copper.

Please give my regards to the Hallets[1] and to Mrs. Hall. All is very well here, and the work well up to time. Yours   T E S.

---

[1] Hall's children.

558: TO LORD CARLOW

4.2.35   *Ozone Hotel, Bridlington, Yorks*

Dear Carlow, All work and no play here. I hope not so your end. If it is really snowing, you should be able to ski universally, and tumble about promiscuously — when it stops of course. Don't sit under one of your avalanches!

Boats are going well. All armour has been returned, modified from Hadfields, and we are keen on keeping our promised finishing date of March; for all boats. Into the water, that is; not necessarily finished test. I might leave here (and the R.A.F., alas) immediately after.

Sometimes one is lucky with a bale of stored and shop-soiled knowledge ... like yesterday, when I was able to take a solemn party over York Minster, and detail its glass and distinguished Nottingham alabaster ... and to-day, when we sketched out an oil-hydraulic lifting gadget for the armoured hatches. But mostly one's learning is a bundle one keeps on carrying aimlessly about. A man who only stocked serviceable knowledge of current items would be fortunate until he got into strange waters. To acquire more and more knowledge becomes a craving, like drink: with the same hopeless end, for one can no more learn everything than drink Rheims dry.

That little Whitby motor-ship was built at Middlesborough only two years ago. The old fellow runs her more as a hobby than a business!

Other news? I have an Aesop's *Fables* for you, a duplicate that came my way: well printed, and amusing. A private book.

There is *not* going to be a film of me. Korda proved most reasonable and decent, upon acquaintance.

John (Augustus) painted a small head of me last month. It is very good. He also drew me (in R.A.F. togs) $\frac{3}{4}$ length in charcoal. Also good. And he gave me the drawing, which is also good: very good indeed, in fact. John is a great man.

My regards to P. Beg her to avoid avalanches, also, please. Yours,   T.E.SHAW.

559: TO ROBERT GRAVES[1]

4.2.35   *Ozone Hotel, Bridlington*

[*one page omitted*] New page, new subject, I saw Alexander Korda last month. I had not taken seriously the rumours that he meant to make a film of me, but they were persistent, so at last I asked for a meeting and explained that I was inflexibly opposed to the whole notion. He was most decent and understanding — it surprised me in a film director — and has agreed to put it off till I die or welcome it. Is it age coming on, or what? But I loathe the notion of being celluloided. My rare visits to cinemas always deepen in me a sense of their superficial falsity . . . vulgarity, I would have said, only I like the vulgarity that means common man, and the badness of films seems to me like an edited and below-the-belt speciousness. Yet the news-theatres, as they call them (little cinemas here and there that present fact, photographed and current fact only), delight me. The camera seems wholly in place as journalism: but when it tries to re-create it boobs and sets my teeth on edge. So there won't be a film of me. Korda is like an oil-company which has drilled often and found two or three gushers, and has prudently invested some of its proceeds in buying options over more sites. Some he may develop and others not. Oil is a transient business.

Money explained, films considered. Let us now pass to the epitaph.

Yes, Hogarth did the morgue-men a first sketch of me in 1920,[2] and they are right to overhaul their stocks. [1 *line omitted*] I won't touch it myself, but if you do, don't give too much importance to what I did in Arabia during the war. I feel that the Middle Eastern settlement put through by Winston Churchill and Young and me in 1921 (which stands in every particular . . . if only the other Peace Treaties did!) should weigh more than fighting. And I feel too that this settlement should weigh less than my life since 1922, for the conquest of the last element, the air, seems to me the only major task of our generation; and I have convinced

---

[1] An edited version of this letter was published in *The Evening Standard* of May 15th, 1935. It is a reply to a letter from Graves saying he had been asked to write an obituary notice of Lawrence. It will be published in full by Graves shortly.

[2] Compare letter No. 280.

myself that progress to-day is made not by the single genius, but by the common effort. To me it is the multitude of rough trans- port drivers, filling all the roads of England every night, who make this the mechanical age. And it is the airmen, the mechanics, who are overcoming the air, not the Mollisons and Orlebars. The genius raids, but the common people occupy and possess. Where- fore I stayed in the ranks and served to the best of my ability, much influencing my fellow airmen towards a pride in themselves and their inarticulate duty. I tried to make them see — with some success.

That for eight years, and now for the last four I have been so curiously fortunate as to share in a little revolution we have made in boat design. People have thought we were at finality there, for since 1850 ships have merely got bigger. When I went into R.A.F. boats in 1929, every type was an Admiralty design. All were round-bottomed, derived from the first hollow tree, with only a fin, called a keel, to delay their rolling about and over. They progressed by pushing their own bulk of water aside. Now (1935) not one type of R.A.F. boat in production is naval ... We have found, chosen, selected or derived our own sorts: they have (power for power) three times the speed of their predecessors, less weight, less cost, more room, more safety, more seaworthiness. As their speed increases, they rise out of the water and run over its face. They cannot roll, nor pitch, having no pendulum nor period, but a subtly modelled planing bottom and sharp edges.

Now I do not claim to have made these boats. They have grown out of the joint experience, skill and imaginations of many men. But I can (secretly) feel that they owe to me their oppor- tunity and their acceptance. The pundits met them with a fierce hostility: all the R.A.F. sailors, and all the Navy, said that they would break, sink, wear out, be unmanageable. To-day we are advising the War Office in refitting the coast defences entirely with boats of our model, and the Admiralty has specified them for the modernised battleships: while the German, Chinese, Spanish and Portuguese Governments have adopted them! In inventing them we have had to make new engines, new auxiliaries, use new timbers, new metals, new materials. It has been five years of intense and co-ordinated progress. Nothing now hinders the application of our design to big ships — except the conservatism of man, of course. Patience. It cannot be stopped now.

All this boasting is not to glorify myself, but to explain; and here enters my last subject for this letter, your strictures upon the changes I have made in myself since the time we felt so much together at Oxford. You're quite right about the change. I was then trying to write; to be perhaps an artist (for *The Seven Pillars* had pretensions towards design, and was written with great pains as prose) or to be at least cerebral. My head was aiming to create intangible things. That's not well put: all creation is tangible. What I was trying to do, I suppose, was to carry a superstructure of ideas upon or above anything I made.

Well, I failed in that. By measuring myself against such people as yourself and Augustus John, I could feel that I was not made out of the same stuff. Artists excite and attract me, seduce me, from what I am. Almost I could be an artist, but there is a core that puts on the brake. If I knew what it was I would tell you, or become one of you. Only I can't.

So I changed direction, right, and went into the R.A.F. after straightening out that Eastern tangle with Winston, a duty that fell to me, I having been partly the cause of the tangle. How well the Middle East has done: it, more than any part of the world, has gained from that war.

However, as I said, I went into the R.A.F. to serve a mechanical purpose, not as leader but as a cog of the machine. The key-word, I think, is machine. I have been mechanical since, and a good mechanic, for my self-training to become an artist has greatly widened my field of view. I leave it to others to say whether I chose well or not: one of the benefits of being part of the machine is that one learns that one doesn't matter!

One thing more. You remember me writing to you when I first went into the R.A.F. that it was the nearest modern equivalent of going into a monastery in the Middle Ages. That was right in more than one sense. Being a mechanic cuts one off from all real communication with women. There are no women in the machines, in any machine. No woman, I believe, can understand a mechanic's happiness in serving his bits and pieces.

All this reads like a paragraph of D.H.L., my step-namesake.

I do not think for a moment that I have got it right, but I hope from it your sense of character will show you the difference between your view of me and mine. Laura[1] saw me too late, after I had changed direction. She is, was, absolutely right to avoid communication with me. There are no faults on either side, but common sense, the recognition of a difficulty too arduous to be worth the effort of surmounting, when there are so many other more rewarding activities within reach. Don't worry or regret or desire me to change the face of nature. We are lucky to have proportion and toleration to pad our bones. Yours   T.E.S.

What a whale of a letter. Five minutes' talk would have been so much more fun!

[The following note is from *Leaves in the Wind*, the manuscript which I believe to be notes for a rewritten *Mint* to cover the whole of Lawrence's R.A.F. experience. It can be safely assigned to 1935. In February 1933 Felixstowe was not Lawrence's station. In December 1934 memoranda had passed in the Air Ministry on the subject:

It has been decided unless anything to the contrary is heard from Shaw normal discharge action should proceed.

It seems clear therefore that no letter on the subject had been received from him that year.]

560: FROM LEAVES IN THE WIND

Feb. 6 wrote to Felix saying. I must not try to sign on again in R.A.F. as in 12 years time I should be too old to be efficient. The wrench this is; I shall feel like a lost dog when I leave — or when it leaves me, rather, for the R.A.F. goes on. The strange attraction in the feel of the clothes, the work, the companionship. A direct touch with men, obtained no other way in my life.

[1] Laura Riding.

561: TO W. BRADBURY[1]

13.2.35.   *Brid.*

Excellent! If you can come up the 19th, I'll be out of this place about the 23rd. Air Ministry warns me that the Press are getting curious about my movements again. Damn the Press!

My book isn't a bit like yours: no spare parts, no part numbers, and no prices! Only a summary of the work done on boats. I haven't done all Mr. James' work for him! But it is accurate enough to show a skilled man what has happened. By all means bring yours up: and the Logs.

We launched the Dinghy: the quietest and sweetest tick-over of any Dinghy yet! It kicked back, when cold. So we put the ignition back a trifle. Then the front rocker ran dry, and there was no oil flowing down the front lead from head to camshaft front bearing. So we pulled down the rocker assembly, and found more bits of Harry M's. string in the rocker-fulcrum pipe! Took 'em out, and all's perfect.

Send the last engine of 217 when you can. We aim to get the Garage empty by February 27, and haven't too much time. Recasting the controls of 190 and 191 will be a slow job.

Felixstowe are pleased with 159 — but they ran down her battery, starting up! They'll learn, like we did.

Interesting about the Lion. More trouble coming, I think.

I'm sorry about your kid. Twelve teeth out isn't good fun for so small a creature. I hope it doesn't do him any harm.

If we launch the last boat on Feb. 27, as I hope, you should have tested it by March 2 or 3 — and then be free for Hythe again. Don't forget you ought to go to Meadows for a visit soon. They are an interesting firm; not many flies on them.

B.G.[2] has applied for you, permanently! It's bound to come through, I think, and soon. Excellent! I'm as pleased as you, for it has all been done by his own suggestion. I've not had to hint a thing. That is the perfection of method![3] Don't say so, though!

Fetch Stan or somebody up with you: then he and you can test, while Boyle finishes in the Garage. Yours,   T.E.S.

---

[1] Corporal R.A.F.   [2] Beauforte-Greenwood.
[3] See letter No. 525.

562: TO W. BRADBURY

15.2.35.   *Ozone Hotel, Bridlington.*

Good: I'm glad you can get up so soon as the 19th. That eases
my situation. I find these last days rather wearing, and will be
glad to end them suddenly.

About lodgings. There are thousands of empty rooms at
Bridlington; but the Ozone is R.A.F. quarters. My chit only
allows me to claim cash where no official accommodation is available. I don't know what your chit allows you, but better make
sure before you claim. You could ring up the Accountant Officer
at Calshot or Gosport and ask in case of doubt. The Ozone is all
right, but of course you'd be more comfortable outside at 30/- a
week, if you are allowed it. I'm off allowance now, and in billets
with the rest of the airmen; twelve of us now, and 30 more due
on the 20th. All to the Ozone, except those married and living
out.

Spare parts: will you try and get some terminals, about 30, to
fit the latest Champion sparking plugs? In fitting the suppressors,
some have been lost already, and there will be more of them lost
as time goes on. The terminals that went down on the R.13's.,
with the engines, might do. I'm not sure about the threads.

Also if possible a new or part-worn Power adjustable spanner,
as asked for by Sergt. Cambden; also a set of Power feeler gauges,
as supplied in tool kits. Also new or part-worn as available. I
think that is all, unless you see some of those lovely worm-driven
water hose clips lying about. They beat [*name omitted*] clips to a
frazzle.

I'll meet you at 6.15 p.m. at Brid. Station on Tuesday. You'll
wear civies, I expect, and carry blue working kit. The section can
lend you overalls and oilskins, probably. Yours,   T.E.S.

P.S. Boyle has some wants. He has asked for them but not yet
received.

About 5 propellers 14 x 13. Three water pump top elbows, for
Armoured Boats, the type that look aft.

Two rev. counters — instruments only.

If you can get these from Read or Mr. Munro, do!

Don't try and carry the propellers yourself.

563: TO PAT KNOWLES

20.2.35   *Bridlington*

Dear Pat, No more to here[1]. I've finished, and shall push off by bike in a day or two for Clouds Hill, travelling by very slow stages, but arriving there in very scruff order some time in early March.

I shall be glad to get away, now.   Yours   T.E.S.

564: TO LORNA NORRINGTON[2]

24.2.35   *Bridlington*

Dear Lorna, I'm sorry to have been so slow in replying, but I've been run nearly off my feet lately, writing letters to tell everybody that I'm going away. I've had a lovely little card printed 'To tell you that in future I shall write **very** few letters' and I'm going to tuck one into each letter that I write for the next six months!

I was thinking of you today, when our dinghy was jumping over the sea at the harbour mouth here. You would have loved it: the little boat was going beautifully. Your father was looking on.

My cottage is waiting for me, and I'm hoping to like it very much. I shall not get there for a couple of weeks, and will then go away again . . . but I hope later on to settle down there a bit.

The address is Clouds Hill, Moreton, Dorset, so far as the Post Office is concerned. Actually I'm not in Moreton parish, but the postman comes on to me from there, with his sidecar. When I'm away he has a box, into which he dumps them!

As I'm only 40 miles from Hythe, it will be quite easy for me to run over there on a bike and see you, when the weather is nice. I shall enjoy a boat-ride, when that time comes.   Yours   T E SHAW

---

[1] Forwarding of letters.   [2] Aged 15.

565: TO JOHN BUCHAN

25. 2. 35   *Bridlington, Yorks.*

Dear J. B.

This ↑ new style[1] portends my discharge from the R.A.F.
Tomorrow you and I will be alike in one respect — as old Colonels:
neither of us, probably, ever using the rank ourselves, but given
it by an ignorant public habitually.

Today I have posted you the typescript (about 60000 words)
of my R.A.F. journal.[2] You said I might, in your last letter; but
I send it apologetically. Typescripts are messy to read. You are a
busy man. The story has more shadow than sunlight in it. Its
language is often grossly obscene, for it is the language of the
troops. And besides I have a fear that in it I have given away
my limitations more bluntly than I would wish.

However, there it is. The fragment is unpublished, and not-
likely-to-be-published. I suspect it is better writing than my
Seven Pillars, and if you could confirm that suspicion, I might be
tempted into trying to write something again. Retirement without
plan is rather a daunting state, and I am a little frightened of being
completely my own master.

If the weather is anyways possible, I shall cycle down in slow
stages from here to Dorset, to my cottage. The road passes near
Elsfield, and I may, if dry and warmish, call at your house as I
pass. You will be in London, or Nice, or Perth . . . no matter.
Ahead of me there isn't any single engagement . . . after 4 p.m.
today! Yours ever   T E SHAW

566: TO AIR CHIEF MARSHAL SIR EDWARD ELLINGTON

25.2.35   *Bridlington, Yorks*

Dear Sir Edward, Not many airmen, fortunately, write to their
Chief of Staff upon discharge; but I was admitted by the first
C.A.S.[3] so hesitantly that perhaps it is in order for me to thank
his successor for the forbearance which has let me complete the
twelve years.

[1] i.e. addressing Buchan by his initials, as usually.   [2] *The Mint.*
[3] Trenchard.

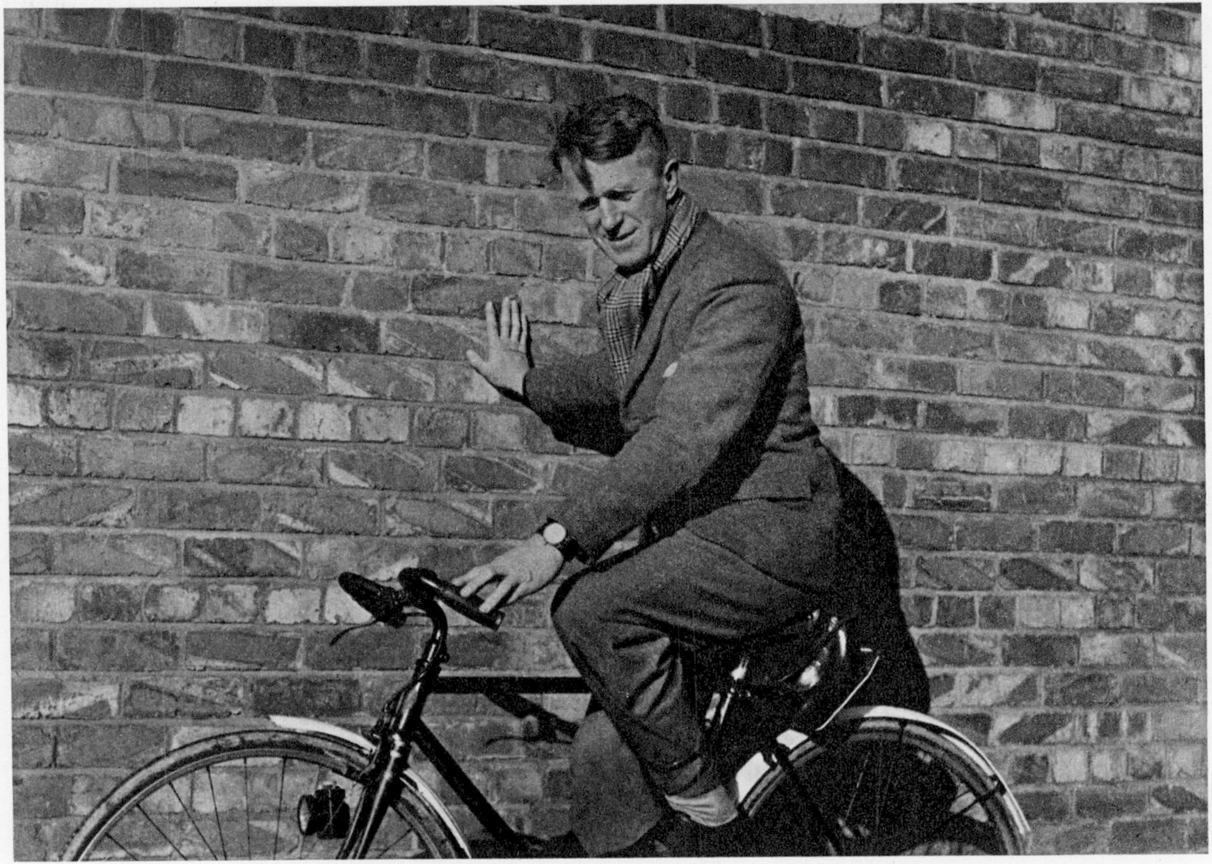

LEAVING THE AIR FORCE 1935

I've been at home in the ranks, and well and happy: consequently I leave with a sense of obligation, though always I have tried in return to do everything that the rules — or my chiefs — would allow.

So if you still keep that old file about me, will you please close it with this note which says how sadly I am going? The R.A.F. has been much more than my profession. Yours sincerely

T E SHAW.

567: TO PETER DAVIES

Thursday, 28 Feb 35

Dear P.D., On Tuesday I took my discharge from the R.A.F. and started southward by road, meaning to call at Bourne and see Manning:[1] but to-day I turned eastward, instead, hearing that he was dead.

It seems queer news, for the books are so much more intense than ever he was, and his dying doesn't, cannot, affect them. Therefore what has died really? Our hopes of having more from him — but that is greed. The writing them was such pain — and pains — to him. Of late I had devoutly wished him to cease trying to write. He had done enough; two wonderful works, full-sized: four lesser things. A man who can produce one decent book is a fortunate man, surely?

Some friends of mine, in dying, have robbed me; Hogarth and Aubrey Herbert are two empty places which no one and nothing can ever fill. Whereas Doughty and Hardy and Manning had earned their release. Yet his going takes away a person of great kindness, exquisite and pathetic. It means one rare thing the less in our setting. You will be very sad.

My losing the R.A.F. numbs me, so that I haven't much feeling to spare for the while. In fact I find myself wishing all the time that my own curtain would fall. It seems as if I had finished, now. Strange to think how Manning, sick, poor, fastidious, worked like a slave for year after year, not on the concrete and palpable boats or engines of my ambition, but on stringing words together to shape his ideas and reasonings. That's what being a born writer

[1] Frederic Manning.

means, I suppose. And to-day it is all over and nobody ever heard of him. If he had been famous in his day he would have liked it, I think; liked it deprecatingly. As for fame-after-death, it's a thing to spit at; the only minds worth winning are the warm ones about us. If we miss those we are failures. I suppose his being not really English,[1] and so generally ill, barred him from his fellows. Only not in *Her Privates We* which is hot-blooded and familiar. It is puzzling. How I wish, for my own sake, that he hadn't slipped away in this fashion; but how like him. He was too shy to let anyone tell him how good he was. Yours ever   T.E.SHAW

568 : TO ERNEST THURTLE

6. iii. 35

Dear E.T., My Dorset 'fastness' is beset, they tell me, by pressmen: so I wander about London in a queer unrest, wondering if my mainspring will ever have a tension in it again.

So I'm not cheerful, actually; but sad at losing my R.A.F. existence. It was good, and I felt useful: also it was noticeably peaceful. I expect there is a good deal to be said for the comfortable shadow of a 'bombing plane'[2] — now a term of abuse, but the only democratic weapon!

Thank you for the book. I look forward to reading it when I get home . . . which is after the ink-slingers go to their homes. Theodore Powys, the brother of Llewellyn, is a rare person.

We must meet some day. In fact, I will again attempt Johnson's Court! Yours   T E SHAW

569 : DRAFT OF LETTER TO THE HON. ESMOND HARMSWORTH

[*March* 1935]   [*Clouds Hill*]

Dear Mr. Harmsworth, I am presuming on a brief acquaintance of many years ago to approach you now (as Chairman of the N.P.A.[3]) on a personal matter.

---

[1] Manning was Australian.

[2] Thurtle had written: 'Let the tanks and the bombing planes rust and rot. Much good will they do us, poor mortals.'

[3] Newspaper Proprietors Association.

You may have heard that about a month ago I was discharged from the R.A.F. upon completion of my engagement for twelve years with the colours.

I take it this discharge marks the end of the active part of my life. I returned to this cottage, which has been mine for many years, with the intention of settling quietly in retirement.

Unfortunately, the quietude has been a complete failure. Reporters and press photographers have visited the place in some numbers, anxious to photograph it and me, or to ascertain my future intentions. This is a very simple district and their enquiries after me have given my country neighbours only too much to talk about. Their eagerness to find me drove me out: and after I had gone it led them to break the tiles of my roof, split the door and trample all over my patch of land in search of me. I have had to ask the local police to patrol the place, in my absence.

I am writing to you to ask if your association can help to relieve me of some of this attention? I quite realize that many of the visitors are freelances: but even these find their market in the biggest newspapers. It would be a great comfort to me if editors could generally deny me further space.

As I said at the beginning of this letter, my retirement is, I hope, for good. I am not under any further obligation to the Government. I am not looking for any employment. I am not writing, or intending to write, any other books: nor am I ever likely to go abroad again.

I have saved just enough money to keep me by myself in modest idleness, and I am very much looking forward to doing nothing. I think I can promise you never again to earn a paragraph, and if you can do anything to help keep me out of sight I shall be most grateful.

This address will find me always and I am ready to furnish (not for publication) any further information anyone of your members may want.

570: TO PAT KNOWLES

19.3.35   *Mr. E. Smith,*[1] 3 *Belvedere Crescent, London, S.E.*1

Dear Pat, I've spent all today with Press Association bosses, and Press Photographing Agencies, making quite a lot of ground. There are good hopes, I fancy, of persuading all of them to leave me alone, and to refuse to buy the stolen products of the free-lancers. I shall know for certain in about three days time; and if successful I shall try to get back to Clouds Hill early next week.

Will you send me current stuff (and any news or needs you have) to this old address, between now and Saturday?

I hope nothing disastrous has overtaken our place. Yours ever   T.E.S.

Romsey on Sunday night; and London by 4 p.m. Monday: 75 miles that second day! Improving![2]

571: TO JOHN BUCHAN

1.4.35   *Clouds Hill, Moreton, Dorset*

Dear J.B., (I cannot call you 'Colonel' any more: after all, I used to be one myself and disliked it. The Golden Rule applies)

Your letter about my R.A.F. notes was one in which anybody would have taken pleasure. I had banked a good deal on your opinion, you being a discreet and exquisite bookman, and that you should say such good things delighted me. Of course the notes are not intended for publication: but I take it from what you say that if ever a subject does arise to excite my writing faculty, I shall be doing no harm in letting rip. At the moment there is no such excitement. All my 12 years in the Air Force I'd hoped to be let go on a long Flying Boat cruise, to keep its log à la Hakluyt. A novel — no, I think not: my writing practice has all been to put down more and more exactly what I have seen

---

[1] Lawrence had rooms under this name, and his landlord, on hearing of Smith's death, described him as: 'Quite the gentleman.'

[2] Riding his push-bike.

or felt: invention would come very hard. A biography — yes, I had wanted to write Casement, Sir Roger; but the obstacle is that the Government refuse all access to those confiscated diaries from which purported extracts were circulated to influential people when he was condemned; and without them there cannot be a life of him written.

Enough of that. I read yesterday in the paper that you have been chosen as next Governor of Canada. A high office, to which I grudge you immensely. It means that for three years you will be spent on public functions, doing them excellently, no doubt, but at the sacrifice of all your private virtue. Also I shall feel that something is missing, round Elsfield way. This is perhaps a queer way of congratulating you on breaking into another preserve of the Lords. Cromwell would approve it; but still I feel sorry. You are too good to become a figure.

It was kind of you to try the National Trust for [*name omitted*]. I have sent him the message, and told him to call on them when he next visits London. The unfortunate man wants badly something other than his present life, obviously. If only he knew what!

My life? Not too good. The Press were besetting this cottage when I reached it. I went to London for a while: they desisted. I returned: they did. The most exigent of them I banged in the eye, and while he sought a doctor I went off again on my wanderings, seeing the Newspaper Society, and the Photographic Agencies, and Esmond Harmsworth (for the Newspaper Proprietors Assn.) with the plea to leave me alone. They agree, more or less, so long as I do nothing that earns a new paragraph: and on that rather unholy compact I am back here again in precarious peace, and liking a life that has no fixed point, no duty and no time to keep.

Don't reply to this rigmarole: print yourself cards like the enclosed:[1] and may you be happy in Canada. Perhaps you may make more out of it than I think: but to me these new countries are bitterly lacking in upholstery. Yours   T E SHAW

---

[1] See letter No. 564.

5-4-35.   *Clouds Hill, Moreton, Dorset*

Dear Greenwood, I must apologise for my seeming remissness: all your letters waited here, while I dodged the pressmen. I have been seeing the bigger noises of the newspaper world, and have promised them never to earn another paragraph, while they effectually leave me alone. An unholy contract which puts me into cold storage — but there seems no alternative.

Now about your case.[1] It seems to me monstrous. To say that every publisher is at the mercy of the discretion of any Police Chief, at any time — why, it makes publication almost an impossibility. This altogether apart from the personal question of penalties assessed upon your firm and yourselves. They seem wholly disproportionate to Boriswood, but would be a fleabite to Macmillan, for example. What evidence had the Judge as to your means?

It does not seem to me that the Authors' Society has much right of entry. Hanley has not been involved (and will not savour being dragged in!) and that rather cuts E.M.F.[2] out of it. It would be a new thing for the body of authors to rush to the defence of a publisher: unless the body of publishers was also active in your defence and should call upon the body of authors to help. What chance is there of concerted protest by the governing body of Publishers? Not much, I gather. The big ones disregard the little ones.

I saw E.M.F. while the case was pending and talked to him about it. He is one of the few writers who might dare lead an attempt at help. Most of them are afraid of the word sodomy. I wonder why?

I thought it would be more effective if I tackled E.M.F. before rather than after judgement. A subtle mind, that one. You are seeing him, you say: he likes Hanley's work (but not *The Furys*) and will help, if he can. I do not know how much he weighs with the Authors' Society. I am so out of things, after all these years.

---

[1] The prosecution of *Boy*, by James Hanley, published by Boriswood Ltd., had secured a conviction for indecency.

[2] E. M. Forster.

I don't want to come up to London again, at the moment: short of cash, full of cottage-duties, very empty in mind, tired-out, and futile-feeling. But I feel, too, that your case is a dangerous one, an inroad on book-security. It ought to be the publishers' move, all the same. I wish Cape was not abroad. He can mobilise the young ones and compel the old stodgers to move. Without him there is no courage in their ranks: and many of them resent your rise.

Let me know how the E.M.F. interview goes, and of any other concrete measures of help. Yours ever,   T.E.S.

573: TO H. S. EDE

5.iv.35   *Clouds Hill, Moreton, Dorset*

Dear Ede, I have not been so long about answering as it has seemed. The Press have still been troublesome, and so I have spent this fine month almost wholly in wandering about the south-country. Very beautiful; all very beautiful. But I have wanted to settle here instead. Ungrateful creature, man!

Now I have persuaded the local police to patrol the place and during daylight hours I keep indoors. It works, so far: but soon I shall have used up my firewood, and then what? Perhaps the pressmen will tire soonest.

About your cheque. I have looked at it for two days, wanting to take it for your sake, but reluctant. You see, it is an experiment I am making . . . have I saved enough to live on in decency, or must I make more? The sooner I can find the answer to that, the better for me. If I take your £30,[1] that will carry me over in unexpected ease for twelve months, and next year I might feel the need of it.

As for the Brough, that is easy.[2] I have licensed it, and yesterday rode into Poole to buy some necessary fittings for the house. It goes like stink and is altogether a marvellous machine. But I should hesitate to call it necessary. A Rolls-Royce goes like . . . scent, shall we say? . . . and is a marvellous machine: but I

---

[1] The cheque was found, after Lawrence's death, in a book at Clouds Hill.
[2] Till then he had been riding his push-bike.

21

am certain that a Rolls is not necessary to my pleasure. I want to find out if the Brough is. If it is, I shall have to save somewhere else, live below estimate, or make more, to be able to afford it. My earning power is potentially considerable: but I hate using it.

You will observe that the whole essay is deliberate, an endeavour to enjoy idleness. That is (by modern standards) not a very moral aim. I do not care. I feel that I have worked throughout a reasonably long working life, given all I can to every cause which harnessed me, and earned a rest. My 'expectation' is less than 20 years, and the last few years of that 20 will be diminishingly pleasant, as infirmities increase. If I am to taste the delights of natural England, as has been my life's wish, I must do it before I grow really old. And I must do it on my own; not at others' expense.

I have no dependants, no sense of public spirit, or of duty to my neighbour. I like to live alone for 80°/₀ of my days, and to be let alone by 80°/₀ of my fellow-men and all my fellow-women below 60 years of age. The golden rule seems to direct me to live peacefully in my cottage.

I hope you will find me here some day: not yet, for all is sixes and sevens, as in a besieged town: but soon. The district is good for walking: and if I cannot put you up or feed you properly, why surely the neighbourhood can. What is Bournemouth for?

Your book.¹ I can't settle to it. These claims are distracting. So I send it back. Economics are like tides. We fail to harness them, yet they ebb and flow. The right thing would be to chart them, but nobody can distinguish their moon. Sorry to be unhelpful.   T.E.S.

574: TO GEORGE BROUGH

5. IV. 35   *Clouds Hill, Moreton, Dorset*

Dear G.B., Your two letters were sent on from Bridlington (I left the R.A.F. a month ago) and waited here for me, while I have been dodging about to avoid my enemies, the Press. This will now be my only and permanent address, I hope.

¹ Maurice Colbourne's *Economic Nationalism.* Ede had asked Lawrence's opinion of the Douglas Credit Scheme.

About your fan. Our propeller experiments were all marine, and they showed how little was known yet, even in that much exercised branch. Air propellers (of the suction type) have been, I am sure, very little studied. Large diameter of course means noise, as do broad tips. Four blades are quieter than three and as efficient. You can push an air-prop pitch up to great steepness, so long as the revs are not extravagant. But frankly I cannot help you. Our props had so different an intention. The water is so solid an element. Have you considered Ethylene glycol for cooling? Or is the engine getting too hot for its oil? In the desert I ran a tiny condenser for our old Fords, and so boiled all day without using a pint of water, and with great thermal advantage. Later they doubled the Leader-tank, increased the pump output, and carried on without boiling. Petrol consumption then increased.

I have wondered of late how the new engine was shaping. You were going to make a new angle of inlet for the mixture. Now you are working on the timing gears! Please tell Mr J.A.P.[1] for me that if I had his sized firm and couldn't get an aircooled twin right in 18 months, I'd eat my test-bench and wash it down with my flow meter!

Meanwhile I've only ridden the ancient-of-days twice this year. It goes like a shell, and seems as good as new. The push-bike is a reality, though. I came down here from Yorkshire on it and have toured much of the S. of England on it in the last three weeks. It is dull hard work when the wind is against: but in lanes, and sheltered places and in calms or before winds, wholly delightful. So quiet: one hears all the country noises. Cheap — very! not tiring, up to 60 or 70 miles a day, which is all that I achieve, with sightseeing: and very clean on a wet road.

The loss of my R.A.F. job halves my income, so that my motor cycling would have been much reduced for the future, even without this 30 m.p.h. limit idea. I had half-thoughts of a touring sidecar, for long jaunts, with the push-bike for leisured local trips, but we shall see. The old bike goes so well that I do not greatly long for its successor. If only I had not given up my stainless tank and panier bags and seen that rolling stand!

[1] Maker of J.A.P. engines.

But for those gadgets my old 'un would still be the best bike in the
S. of England. Good luck with your fan! Yours   T E SHAW

575 : TO FLIGHT LIEUTENANT H. NORRINGTON

20. IV. 35.   *Clouds Hill, Moreton, Dorset*

Dear N., In retirement there are no ranks ... we are all
'have-beens' together: however you will not come to it for some
years. For myself, I prefer work.

The cottage has become quiet, now: except for a beastly tit,
which flutters up and down one window-pane for six hours a day.
First I thought he was a bird-pressman, trying to get a story:
then a narcissist, admiring his figure in the glass. Now I think
he is just mad, and know him to be a nuisance. If he goes on into
next week I shall open the window some day and wring his silly
neck.[1]

My time passes between swearing at him, cutting brushwood,
and inventing odd jobs. No letter-writing any more, except under
extreme need, and no duty. A queer lapse into uselessness, after
that long-drawn series of jobs that made up my life.

Please remember me to Lorna and to Mrs N. I went to Hythe
lately and scrounged a lot more screws. There was a dinghy for
test, tell her!

On Wednesday I hope to meet B.G.[2] there.

Bother that bird: he taps too regularly, and distracts me.
Yours ever   T.E.S.

576: TO IAN DEHEER[3]

20.IV.35   *Clouds Hill, Moreton, Dorset*

Dear Ian, I should have sent this long ago,[4] but in civil life —
or in retirement, anyway — time ceases to have any really sharp
edges. Until I got a note from B.G. this morning, I did not
understand that I had been here more than a few days, or years.

---

[1] The bird continued this practice for some weeks until it was finally shot after Lawrence's accident. It had probably started nesting inside.

[2] Beauforte-Greenwood.   [3] A shipbuilder at Bridlington.   [4] A photograph of himself.

The cottage is quiet now, my activities with the Newspaper Proprietors Association having delivered me at least temporarily from nuisance. My bikes are both well, and myself. The many little jobs incidental to settling into a new place distract me and fill my days. So all is well as could be expected.

Will you be good enough to present the second print to P/O Manning! I have no Air Force list, to find his initials, and I expect you see him very often! I hope Bridlington goes well. It will not be our fault, anyhow, if it does not: for we made the boats pretty good. I hope he is not finding the weather (and Catfoss combined) too interfering. Yours   T E SHAW.

My regards to your father, and to Bill, please.

577: TO MRS. THOMAS HARDY

Easter Monday [22-4-35]   *Clouds Hill*

Dear Mrs. Hardy, I am sorry I missed you the day you came — as also at Max Gate, a week after, when I tried in turn to find you. The *Indiscretion*[1] proved charming. I like the appealing simplicity of the prose . . . like, and yet a very poor relation of, the sweeping sentences that make up *Jude*. I understand why he kept it unprinted, yet it is not a thing to be ashamed of. If only T.H. had found time and will to follow up *Jude* with yet one more work, it would have linked his prose, in power, with his poetry.

You have made a beautiful little book of it. I have enjoyed the reading, and enjoy the possession.

I am worried now about Mother and Bob in China. The troubles are touching their area. They are both longing to come home, now.

Clouds Hill is going to be all right as a living place, I fancy. The last three weeks have been almost unbroken peace. I feel very indisposed to do anything more; and very tired.

Philpotts-Hardy, the rhododendron, is in good flower at the moment, leading his hillside by a month or two towards the

---

[1] *An Indiscretion in the Life of an Heiress*, by Thomas Hardy, which Mrs. Hardy had recently published.

promise of colour. I hope you will be able to see him, some day. Except for Wednesday (when I have to go to Hythe, to my old boat-yard) I shall be here continuously now, I hope . . . though in disorder, as the place is unfinished, and I potter with job after job. But please come, if you are in Dorset soon. Yours ever

T E SHAW

578 : TO SIR WILLIAM ROTHENSTEIN

5. v. 35.   *Clouds Hill, Moreton, Dorset*

Dear W.R., Manning died as I was on my way to Bourne, to visit him. I turned off and rode down here. Your two letters came. Between them I had to go to London and I called at Airlie Gardens: vainly, as usual. I suppose you are still chained to your College. Now Mrs. Hardy has sent me your last note. I am sorry to appear so remiss; but my discharge from the R.A.F. (which had to come) has rather done me in, so that I no longer have the mind or wish to do anything at all. I just sit here in this cottage and wonder about nothing in general. Comfort is a very poor state after busyness.

As for Manning, I cannot say how sad the news made me. He was a lovely person, and it is hateful to see him go out, unfinished. But gone he very definitely is. It makes one feel as though nothing can matter very much.

If I come to London again soon I shall ring your bell once more. Patience will tell, in the end. Only I do not expect to come up yet awhile. Yours ever

T. E. SHAW.

579 : TO ERIC KENNINGTON

6. v. 35.   *Clouds Hill, Moreton, Dorset*

Dear K., All over bonfires, the beautiful Dorset, to-night. Twenty six, I think, so far, from my window. Ah well, poor George![1]

Don't bother about those drawings. Leave it a little while till

---

[1] The Jubilee of King George the Fifth's accession.

I revive my humanities and come up to see you. I plan a raid on Holly Copse, to stay with you for a night or two ... possible? At your discretion, absolutely: but I do not want to interfere with your development as a nurse. What is the illness? I do hope (by your light hearted reference to it) that it's either over or safe.

The tympanum sounds good. I wonder what it is in. Stone goes out of date slowly, I think.

'You wonder what I am doing'? Well, so do I, in truth. Days seem to dawn, suns to shine, evenings to follow, and then I sleep. What I have done, what I am doing, what I am going to do, puzzle me and bewilder me. Have you ever been a leaf and fallen from your tree in autumn and been really puzzled about it? That's the feeling.

The cottage is all right for me ... but how on earth I'll ever be able to put anyone up baffles me. There cannot ever be a bed, a cooking vessel, or a drain in it — and I ask you ... are not such things essential to life ... necessities? Peace to everybody.

T.E.S.

580: TO E. M. FORSTER

7. v. 35

Your arrival will be marked by the setting of a white stone into the new wall. Wool Station: taxi to here: any day after the 14th superb.

Clouds Hill has now two inhabitants: Pat Knowles and me. He lives w. end, and I e. end. We feed in his place and very simply. We will try to make you, if not comfortable, at least endurable for a few days. Splendid. T. E. S.

new address — Clouds Hill, Clyffe, Dorset.
Same hill!

581: TO K. W. MARSHALL

7.v.35.　　　　　　　　　　　　　*Clouds Hill, Moreton, Dorset*

Dear Marshall, I couldn't do just as you suggested: it is very dangerous to come between a carnivore and its prey.[1] But I have made guarded enquiries. My friend knew nothing about the

[1] *Boy*, by James Hanley.

'drive': and after he had sniffed round to find out, he knew there was no drive, so far as his minions were concerned. Nor is there any connection between Bury and London. They regard Lancashire as rather foolish to have done what it did.

[12 *lines omitted*]

I hope Boriswood is unbowed and bloody, under these stresses. It is the right mixture.

Thank them for the new Brown monster.[1] I have not tackled it yet. The noble weather and various causes have kept me out-doors from dawn till dark, and sent me dead-beat to bed immediately it was decent to sleep. But that ceases in ten days.

Commend me to Greenwood, and say that I'm sure my inter-ventions have not harmed him: and hope they may help. But they were very indirectly done. Yours ever   T.E.S.

582: TO LADY ASTOR

8.v. 35

No: wild mares would not at present take me away from Clouds Hill. It is an earthly paradise and I am staying here till I feel qualified for it. Also there is something broken in the works, as I told you: my will, I think. In this mood I would not take on any job at all. So do not commit yourself to advocating me, lest I prove a non-starter.

Am well, well-fed, full of company, laborious and innocent-customed. News from China — NIL. Their area now a centre of disturbance.   TES

583: TO HENRY WILLIAMSON

[*Telegram; postmarked* 13 *May* 35]

Lunch Tuesday wet fine cottage one mile north Bovington Camp
SHAW

[Lawrence rode into Bovington Camp on his Brough motor-cycle and sent off this telegram to Henry Williamson and was

[1] *Daughters of Albion,* by Alec Brown, sent to Lawrence in proof.

riding back to Clouds Hill when he came on two errand boys, riding pedal cycles in a dip in the road. He swerved violently to avoid them, lost control, was thrown over his handlebars and received severe injuries to the brain. His physical vitality was so great that he lay unconscious for nearly five days before he died of congestion of the lungs and heart failure.

The evidence at the inquest revealed a curious contradiction. Corporal Catchpole of the R.A.O.C. who was standing about 100 yards from the road, near Clouds Hill, saw Lawrence on his motor-cycle, travelling at about fifty or sixty miles an hour, pass a black private car, going in the opposite direction, just before he heard the crash. The two boys, whose evidence about times was confused, had no memory of a car passing them.

Mr. Cairns, the brain surgeon, stated that had Lawrence lived he would have lost his memory, been paralysed and unable to speak.

Lawrence was buried at Moreton Church on May 21st.

His bust by Eric Kennington has been placed in the Crypt of St. Paul's Cathedral, and his cottage at Clouds Hill now belongs to the National Trust and is shown to visitors.]

INDEX

INDEX

I HAVE not attempted an exhaustive index, partly owing to pressure of time, but chiefly because there are hundreds, or thousands, of persons, places and books which are mentioned, often only once, but which are never discussed. To take an example, Miss Holmes, principal of the school at Jebail, is mentioned nearly twenty times in passing, but one is never told anything about her. Instead of such bare mentions, I have included subjects of principal importance with sub-headings.

The index should be used in conjunction with the List of Contents and the List of Recipients of Letters, since the addressee of a letter does not appear in the index as such.

The following contractions are here employed; S.P. = *Seven Pillars of Wisdom.* R.D. = *Revolt in the Desert.* L. = Lawrence. G.B.S. = Bernard Shaw.

D. G.